Introduction to
Visual Basic
Using .NET

ISBN 0130418048

90000

9 780130 418043

The Integrated .NET Series from Object Innovations and Prentice Hall PTR

C#

- Introduction to C# Using .NET
  Oberg

- Application Development Using C# and .NET
  Stiefel/Oberg

VISUAL BASIC

- Introduction to Visual Basic Using .NET
  Wyatt/Oberg

- Application Development Using Visual Basic and .NET
  Oberg/Thorsteinson/Wyatt

VISUAL C++

- .NET Architecture and Programming Using Visual C++
  Thorsteinson/Oberg

WEB APPLICATIONS

- Fundamentals of Web Applications Using .NET and XML
  Bell/Feng/Soong/Zhang/Zhu

PERL

- Programming PERL in the .NET Environment
  Menaker/Oberg/Saltzman

INTEGRATED .NET SERIES FROM OBJECT INNOVATIONS AND PRENTICE HALL PTR

Introduction to Visual Basic Using .NET

Dana L. Wyatt

Robert J. Oberg

Prentice Hall PTR, Upper Saddle River, NJ 07458
www.phptr.com

Editorial/Production Supervision: *Mary Sudul*
Acquisitions Editor: *Jill Harry*
Marketing Manager: *Dan DePasquale*
Manufacturing Buyer: *Maura Zaldivar*
Cover Design: *Anthony Gemmellaro*
Cover Design Direction: *Jerry Votta*
Interior Series Design: *Gail Cocker-Bogusz*

Published by Prentice Hall PTR
Prentice-Hall, Inc.
Upper Saddle River, NJ 07458

Prentice Hall books are widely used by corporations and government agencies for training, marketing, and resale.

The publisher offers discounts on this book when ordered in bulk quantities. For more information, contact Corporate Sales Department, phone: 800-382-3419; fax: 201-236-7141; email: corpsales@pren-hall.com
Or write Corporate Sales Department, Prentice Hall PTR, One Lake Street, Upper Saddle River, NJ 07458.

10 9 8 7 6 5 4 3 2 1

ISBN 0-13-041804-8

Pearson Education LTD.
Pearson Education Australia PTY, Limited
Pearson Education Singapore, Pte. Ltd.
Pearson Education North Asia Ltd.
Pearson Education Canada, Ltd.
Pearson Educación de Mexico, S.A. de C.V.
Pearson Education — Japan
Pearson Education Malaysia, Pte. Ltd.

CONTENTS

PREFACE

Microsoft's .NET is a revolutionary advance in programming technology that greatly simplifies application development. In addition to providing support for traditional desktop Windows applications, it provides tremendous support for Web-based services.

Microsoft's popular Visual Basic programming language has been upgraded to take advantage of the new .NET features. Visual Basic.NET, or simply VB.NET, has become a full object-oriented programming language with capabilities comparable to C++, Java, and Microsoft's new language C# (pronounced "C sharp").

This book is a practical introduction to programming in VB.NET and using services provided by .NET. It emphasizes the VB.NET language and is part of The Integrated .NET Series from Object Innovations and Prentice Hall PTR.

An important thrust of this book is to teach VB.NET programming from an object-oriented perspective. This book introduces object-oriented concepts early and includes a case study on object-oriented programming. The book is intended to be fully accessible to programmers who do not already have a background in object-oriented programming. Previous knowledge of Visual Basic is not essential.

The book may also be read by more experienced programmers who desire a simple introduction to VB.NET with many example programs. Although designed for working professionals, the book includes enough detail, careful explanations, and sample programs so that it can be useful as a college textbook.

VB.NET is now a fully object-oriented language. It supports classes, interfaces, interface and implementation inheritance, and polymorphism. It is also highly integrated with the .NET Framework. These features make VB.NET a compelling language for developing object-oriented and component-based systems. This book provides thorough coverage of all these features.

One of the strengths of Visual Basic, and the reason it has enjoyed such widespread use, is the ease with which Windows application can be developed. Microsoft has revamped the way that Windows applications are built under .NET. Windows Forms, used by .NET languages, represents a class library that brings uniformity to the components of a Windows application. The book includes substantial coverage of using Windows Forms in VB.NET.

VB.NET, as a language, is elegant and powerful. However, to fully utilize its capabilities, you must have a good understanding of how it works with the .NET Framework. The book examines several important interactions between

VB.NET and the .NET Framework, and includes an introduction to major .NET classes for collections, files, databases, and threads.

Organization of This Book

This book is organized into five major parts and is structured to make it easy for you to isolate what you most need to know.

Part 1, which everyone should read, begins with an introduction to the .NET Framework. The second chapter provides a short introduction to hands-on programming using VB.NET, so that you can start writing code on .NET right away. The third chapter introduces Visual Studio.NET. It is the latest version of Microsoft's popular Visual Studio development environment and has many features that make application development easier and more pleasant. These chapters will equip you to use Visual Studio throughout the rest of the book.

Part 2 covers the core features of VB.NET. If you know Visual Basic, you will have a definite leg up in learning VB.NET, and you can quickly skim this section, paying attention to the information in the sidebars. Sidebars alert you to either (1) the first time a concept new to VB.NET is introduced, or (2) a significant change to the VB.NET language that experienced VB programmers should note. If you are not familiar with Visual Basic, this section is for you. It will quickly bring you up to speed on the core topics of data types, operators, and control structures.

Part 3 examines the object-oriented features of VB.NET. This language is now fully object-oriented, which is one of the most significant improvements in VB.NET. In this part, we begin by examine how classes are built. Subsequent chapters discuss implementation and interface inheritance. These topics are covered gradually and thoroughly, making this part of the book accessible to readers without previous object-oriented experience.

Part 4 covers Windows programming in VB.NET. Microsoft has adopted a new approach to developing Windows applications that will be readily apparent to previous VB programmers. Systematic coverage is presented on the core topics in Windows Forms, including form design, controls, events, menus, toolbars, and dialogs. The rich variety of useful controls provided by Windows Forms is covered in detail.

Part 5 explores the relationships between VB.NET and the .NET Framework. .NET collection classes are introduced. We also examine the .NET interfaces that classes must implement for fundamental operations such as copying and comparing objects. Delegates, a .NET callback mechanism, are discussed. We also introduce both VB.NET file I/O and database programming using ADO.NET. We look at multiple thread programming and attributes. Attributes are powerful in .NET, enabling the programmer to accomplish tasks declaratively, even while writing very little code. You can implement custom attributes in VB.NET. You can read information about custom attributes, or any other metadata, by a mechanism known as "reflection." The book concludes with an introduction to components and assemblies.

Sample Programs

The only way to really learn a programming language is to read and write many, many programs. This book provides many programs that illustrate features of VB.NET. The programs are clearly labeled in the text, and they can all be found in the software distribution that accompanies this book, available through our associated Web site. Also, a case study illustrates many features of VB.NET working together in combination, as they would in a practical application. We make a special point of demonstrating the object-oriented features of VB.NET. If you are new to OO, reading the case study is a must!

Code
Example

The sample programs are provided in a self-extracting file. When expanded, a directory structure is created, rooted in **C:\OI\IntroVb**. The sample programs are in directories **Chap01**, **Chap02**, and so on. All the samples for a given chapter are in individual folders within the chapter directories. The names of the folders are clearly identified in the text. An icon in the margin alerts you to a code example. The case study is in a directory called **CaseStudy**, at the same level as the chapter directories.

This book is part of The Integrated .NET Series. The sample programs for other books in the series are located in their own directories beneath **\OI**, so all the .NET examples from all books in the series will be located in a common area as you install them.

Web Site

Here's the Web site for the book series:

www.objectinnovations.com/dotnet.htm

A link is provided at that Web site for downloading the sample programs for this book.

Acknowledgments

We would like to thank Mike Meehan for helping this project get off the ground. Jill Harry, our acquisitions editor at Prentice Hall, has provided tremendous support and encouragement and has helped us focus on deadlines. Richard Reese reviewed the manuscript and provided many helpful suggestions. Peter Thorsteinson, our co-author of the intermediate book on VB.NET and the .NET Framework, helped us resolve some issues related to migrating sample programs from other .NET languages to VB.NET. We also want to thank all the other authors in the .NET series, because there is much synergy in a group working on parallel books, even if in the heat of writing we did not always collaborate as closely as we might have. These hardworking people include Eric Bell, Howard Feng, Michael Saltzman, Michael Stiefel, Ed Soong, David Zhang, and Sam Zhu.

Dana's additional thanks: I would like to thank everyone who has provided encouragement, assistance, or the chance for insight over the years. Thanks to the colleagues and students who continually challenge me; you keep me on my toes. Thanks to Bob, for inviting me to work with him on this project. Thanks (again) to Richard, who has a keen eye and great insight, for working with us on this manuscript. Thanks to Natalie, Brittany, and Zachary for being so patient during this process—we can do things again, guys! And most importantly, thank you, Brenda, my friend, for ignoring my grouchiness and supporting and encouraging me, as always, during this project.

Robert's additional thanks: I always have a hard time writing acknowledgements, because there are so many people to thank on such a major project. I usually wind up with a blanket acknowledgement. Thanks to all previously mentioned, and to all the other colleagues, friends, and students—too numerous to mention individually—who have helped me over the years. My wife, Marianne, has provided enormous support and encouragement for all my writing efforts. This project, coming on top of several other .NET books, made it seem like my writing would never end, and so her support is all the more appreciated.

About this Series
Robert J. Oberg, Series Editor

Introduction

The Integrated .NET Book Series from Object Innovations and Prentice Hall PTR is a unique series of introductory and intermediate books on Microsoft's important .NET technology. These books are based on proven industrial-strength course development experience. The authors are expert practitioners, teachers, and writers who combine subject-matter expertise with years of experience in presenting complex programming technologies such as C++, MFC, OLE, and COM/COM+. These books *teach* in a systematic, step-by-step manner and are not merely summaries of the documentation. All the books come with a rich set of programming examples, and a thematic case study is woven through several of the books.

From the beginning, these books have been conceived as an *integrated whole*, and not as independent efforts by a diverse group of authors.. The initial set of books consists of three introductory books on .NET languages and four intermediate books on the .NET Framework. Each book in the series is targeted at a specific part of the important .NET technology, as illustrated by the diagram below.

		C# Learning Pathway	VB.NET Learning Pathway		
.NET Language Introductions	Programming PERL in the .NET Environment	**Introduction to C# Using .NET**	Introduction to Programming Visual Basic Using .NET		
Intermediate .NET Framework Titles		Application Development Using C# and .NET	Application Development Using Visual Basic .NET	.NET Architecture and Programming Using Visual C++	Fundamentals of Web Applications Using .NET and XML

Introductory .NET Language Books

The first set of books teaches several of the important .NET languages. These books cover their language from the ground up and have no prerequisite other than programming experience in some language. Unlike many .NET language books, which are a mixture of the language and topics in the .NET Framework, these books are focused on the languages, with attention to important interactions between the language and the framework. By concentrating on the languages, these books have much more detail and many more practical examples than similar books.

The languages selected are the new language C#, the greatly changed VB.NET, and Perl.NET, the open source language ported to the .NET environment. Visual C++ .NET is covered in a targeted, intermediate book, and JScript.NET is covered in the intermediate level .NET Web-programming book.

Introduction to C# Using .NET

This book provides thorough coverage of the C# language from the ground up. It is organized with a specific section covering the parts of C# common to other C-like languages. This section can be cleanly skipped by programmers with C experience or the equivalent, making for a good reading path for a diverse group of readers. The book gives thorough attention to the object-oriented aspects of C# and thus serves as an excellent book for programmers migrating to C# from Visual Basic or COBOL. Its gradual pace and many examples make the book an excellent candidate as a college textbook for adventurous professors looking to teach C# early in the language's life-cycle.

Introduction to Programming Visual Basic Using .NET

Learn the VB.NET language from the ground up. Like the companion book on C#, this book gives thorough attention to the object-oriented aspects of VB.NET. Thus the book is excellent for VB programmers migrating to the more sophisticated VB.NET, as well as for programmers experienced in languages such as COBOL. This book would also be suitable as a college textbook.

Programming Perl in the .NET Environment

A very important part of the vision behind Microsoft® .NET is that the platform is designed from the ground up to support multiple programming languages from many sources, and not just Microsoft languages. This book, like other books in the series, is rooted in long experience in industrial teaching. It covers the Perl language from the ground up. Although oriented toward the ActiveState Perl.NET compiler, the book also provides excellent coverage of the Perl language suitable for other versions as well.

Intermediate .NET Framework Books

The second set of books is focused on topics in the .NET Framework, rather than on programming languages. Three parallel books cover the .NET Framework using the important languages C#, VB.NET, and Visual C++. The C# and VB.NET books include self-contained introductions to the languages suitable for experienced programmers, allowing them to rapidly come up to speed on these languages without having to plow through the introductory books. The fourth book covers the important topic of web programming in .NET, with substantial coverage of XML, which is so important in the .NET Framework.

The design of the series makes these intermediate books much more suitable to a wider audience than many similar books. The introductory books focus on languages frees up the intermediate books to cover the important topics of the .NET Framework in greater depth. The series design also makes for flexible reading paths. Less experienced readers can read the introductory language books followed by the intermediate framework books, while more experienced readers can go directly to the intermediate framework books.

Application Development Using C# and .NET

This book does not require prior experience in C#. However, the reader should have experience in some object-oriented language such as C++ or Java™. The book could also be read by seasoned Visual Basic programmers who have experience working with objects and components in VB. Seasoned programmers and also a less experienced reader coming from the introductory C# book can skip the first few chapters on C# and proceed directly to a study of the Framework. The book is practical, with many examples and a major case study. The goal is to equip the reader with the knowledge necessary to begin building significant applications using the .NET Framework.

Application Development Using Visual Basic .NET

This book is for the experienced VB programmer who wishes to learn the new VB.NET version of VB quickly and then move on to learning the .NET Framework. It is also suitable for experienced enterprise programmers in other languages who wish to learn the powerful RAD-oriented Visual Basic language in its .NET incarnation and go on to building applications. Like the companion C# book, this book is very practical, with many examples, and includes the same case study implemented in VB.NET.

.NET Architecture and Programming Using Visual C++

This parallel book is for the experienced Visual C++ programmer who wishes to learn the .NET Framework to build high-performing applications. Unlike the C# and VB.NET book, there is no coverage of the C++ language itself, because C++ is too complex to cover in a brief space. This book is specifically for experienced C++ programmers. Like the companion C# and VB.NET books, this book is very practical, with many examples, and includes the same case study implemented in Visual C++.

Fundamentals of Web Applications Using .NET and XML

The final book in the series provides thorough coverage of building Web applications using .NET. Unlike other books about ASP.NET, this book gives attention to the whole process of Web application development. The book incorporates a review tutorial on classical Web programming, making the book accessible to the experienced programmer new to the Web world. The book contains significant coverage on ASP.NET, Web Forms, Web Services, SOAP, and XML.

INTRODUCTION TO .NET AND VB.NET

*P*art One, which everyone should read, begins with an introduction to the .NET Framework. The second chapter provides a short introduction to hands-on programming using VB.NET, so that you can start writing code on .NET right away. The third chapter introduces Visual Studio.NET. It is the latest version of Microsoft's popular Visual Studio development environment and has many features that make application development easier and more pleasant. These chapters will equip you to use Visual Studio throughout the rest of the book.

.NET Framework

Microsoft's popular programming language, Visual Basic, has been a favorite choice of programmers for many years. The ease with which Windows applications may be built, coupled with its wealth of database capabilities, has entrenched it in the hearts of many programmers. In its latest version, Microsoft has revamped Visual Basic, now called Visual Basic.NET (or simply VB.NET), to include full object-oriented capabilities and has provided support to work with the .NET Framework. We examine some of these issues throughout the book as we learn of the powerful services that are provided to the VB.NET programmer by the .NET Framework. In this chapter, we introduce the .NET Framework in sufficient detail so that you can immediately begin programming in VB.NET. For more in-depth information about .NET, you can refer to other books in The Integrated .NET Series from Object Innovations and Prentice Hall PTR. Of particular interest to VB.NET programmers will be Application Development Using Visual Basic and .NET *(Oberg, Thorsteinson, Wyatt), which delves into many important topics that are beyond the scope of this book.*

.NET: What You Need to Know

A beautiful thing about .NET is that, from a programmer's perspective, you scarcely need to know anything about it to start writing programs for the .NET environment. You write a program in a high-level language such as VB.NET, a compiler creates an executable (.EXE) file, and you run that EXE file. We show you exactly how to do that in just a few pages. Naturally, as the scope of what you want to do expands, you will need to know more. But to get started, you need to know very little.

Even very simple programs, if they perform any input or output, will generally require the use of the services found in *library* code. A large library, called the .NET Framework Class Library, comes with .NET, and you can use all of the services of this library in your programs.

What is *really* happening in a .NET program is somewhat elaborate. The EXE file that is created does not contain executable code, but rather *Intermediate Language* code, or IL (sometimes called Microsoft Intermediate Language or MSIL). In the Windows environment, this IL code is packaged up in a standard portable executable (PE) file format, so you will see the familiar EXE extension (or, if you are building a component, the DLL extension). When you run the EXE, a special runtime environment (the Common Language Runtime or CLR) is launched, and the IL instructions are executed by the CLR. Unlike some runtimes, where the IL would be interpreted each time it is executed, the CLR comes with a just-in-time (JIT) compiler that translates the IL to native machine code the first time it is encountered. On subsequent calls, the code segment runs as native code.

Thus, in a nutshell, the process of programming in the .NET environment goes like this:

1. Write your program in a high-level .NET language such as VB.NET.
2. Compile your program into IL.
3. Run your IL program, which launches the CLR to execute your IL, using its JIT to translate your program into native code as it executes.

Installing the .NET SDK

All you need to compile and run the programs in this book is the .NET Framework SDK. This SDK is available on CD, or it can be downloaded for free from the Microsoft .NET Web site at *http://msdn.microsoft.com/net/*. Follow the installation directions for the SDK, and make sure that your computer meets the hardware requirements. (Generally, for the SDK, you need a fast Pentium processor and at least 128M of RAM.) Part of the installation is a Windows Component Update, which will update your system, if necessary, to recent versions of programs such as Internet Explorer. The SDK will install tools such as compilers, documentation, sample programs, and the CLR.

The starting place for the SDK documentation is the .NET Framework SDK Overview (see Figure 1–1).

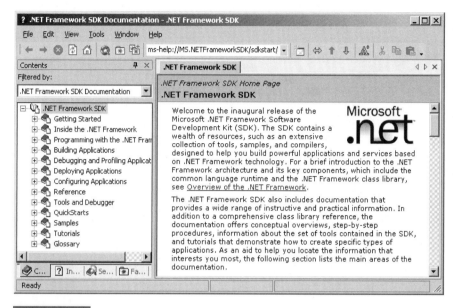

Homepage of .NET Framework SDK.

Installing the Book Software

The example programs found in this book are available on the Web at *http://www.objectinnovations.com/dotnet.htm/*. Download the file **Install_IntroVb.exe** and run this self-extracting file. If you accept the suggested installation directory, the software will be installed in the directory **OI\IntroVb** on your C: drive. There are subdirectories for each chapter of the book. The directory for Chapter 1 is **Chap01.** Sample programs are in named subdirectories of the chapter directory, and we will refer to these sample programs simply by name, such as **Hello.**

Your First VB.NET Program

Code Example

Although we won't actually start to examine the structure of VB.NET programs until Chapter 2, you don't have to wait to compile and run your first VB.NET program. Start at the command prompt, and navigate to the **Hello** directory for this chapter. (If you accepted the default installation, the directory is **C:\OI\IntroVb\Chap01\Hello.**) The source file is **Hello.vb**. To compile this program, enter the following command:

```
>vbc hello.vb
```

The file **Hello.exe** will be created, which you can now run.

```
>hello
Hello World!
```

Setting Environment Variable

In order to run command line tools such as the VB.NET compiler using the name vbc rather than the complete path, certain environment variables must be set. The environment variables can be set using the batch file vsvars32.bat, which can be found in the Common\Tools directory of the Framework SDK.

If you have Visual Studio.NET installed, you can ensure that the environment variables are set up by starting your command prompt session from Start | Programs | Microsoft Visual Studio.NET 7.0 | Microsoft Visual Studio Tools | Microsoft Visual Studio.NET Command Prompt.

Visual Studio.NET

Although the .NET Framework SDK is all you need to compile and run VB.NET programs, the process will be much easier and more pleasant if you use the Visual Studio.NET integrated development environment (IDE). The IDE provides an easy-to-use editor, access to the compiler and debugger, and access to online help. We will discuss Visual Studio.NET in Chapter 3.

Understanding .NET

If you are eager to start learning the VB.NET programming language right away, by all means proceed directly to Chapter 2. The nice thing about a high-level programming language is that, for the most part, you do not need to be concerned with the platform on which the program executes (unless you are making use of services provided by the platform). You can work with the abstractions provided by the language and with functions provided by libraries.

However, you will better appreciate the VB.NET programming language and its potential for creating sophisticated applications if you have a general understanding of .NET. The rest of this chapter is concerned with helping you to achieve such an understanding. We address three broad topics:

- What Is Microsoft .NET?
- .NET Framework
- Common Language Runtime

What Is Microsoft .NET?

In this section, we answer the high-level question "What is .NET?" In brief, .NET represents Microsoft's vision of the future of applications in the Internet age. .NET provides enhanced interoperability features based upon open Internet standards.

The classic Windows desktop has been plagued by robustness issues. .NET represents a great improvement. For developers, .NET offers a new programming platform and superb tools.

XML plays a fundamental role in .NET. Enterprise servers (such as SQL 2000) expose .NET features through XML.

Microsoft .NET is a new platform at a higher level than the operating system. Three years in the making before public announcement, .NET is a major investment by Microsoft. .NET draws on many important ideas, including XML, the concepts underlying Java, and Microsoft's Component Object Model (COM). Microsoft .NET provides the following:

- A robust runtime platform, the CLR
- Multiple language development
- An extensible programming model, the .NET Framework, which provides a large class library of reusable code available from multiple languages
- A networking infrastructure built on top of Internet standards that supports a high level of communication among applications
- A new mechanism of application delivery, the Web service, that supports the concept of an application as a service
- Powerful development tools

Microsoft and the Web

The World Wide Web has been a big challenge to Microsoft. It did not embrace it early. But the Web actually coexists quite well with Microsoft's traditional strength, the PC. Using the PC's browser application, a user can gain access to a whole world of information. The Web relies on standards such as HTML, HTTP, and XML, which are essential for communication among diverse users on a variety of computer systems and devices.

The Windows PC and the Internet, although complex, are quite standardized. However, a Tower of Babel exists with respect to the applications that try to build on top of them: multiple languages, databases, and development environments. The rapid introduction of new technologies has created a gap in the knowledge of workers who must build systems using these technologies. This provides an opening for Microsoft, and some of the most talked about parts of .NET are indeed directed toward the Internet.

.NET provides many features to greatly enhance our ability to program Web applications, but this topic is beyond the scope of this book. For more information, please consult the following two books in The Integrated .NET Series:

- *Application Development Using Visual Basic and .NET* (Oberg, Thorsteinson, Wyatt)
- *Fundamentals of Web Applications Using .NET and XML* (Bell, Feng, Soong, Zhang, Zhu)

Windows on the Desktop

Microsoft began with the desktop, and the company has achieved much. The modern Windows environment has become ubiquitous. Countless applications are available, and most computer users are at least somewhat at home with Windows. There is quite a rich user interface experience, and applications can work together. But there are also significant problems.

PROBLEMS WITH WINDOWS

One of the most troublesome problems is the maintenance of applications on the Windows PC. Applications consist of many files, registry entries, shortcuts, and so on. Different applications can share certain DLLs. Installing a new application can overwrite a DLL that an existing application depends on, possibly breaking the older application (which is known as "DLL hell"). Removing an application is complex and often is imperfectly done. Over time, a PC can become less stable, and the cure eventually becomes reformatting the hard disk and starting from scratch.

There is tremendous economic benefit to using PCs, because standard applications are inexpensive and powerful, the hardware is cheap, and so on. But the savings are reduced by the cost of maintenance.

A ROBUST WINDOWS ENVIRONMENT

.NET has many features that will result in a much more robust Windows operating system. Applications no longer rely on storing extensive configuration data in the registry. In .NET, applications are self-describing, containing *metadata* within the program executable files themselves. Different versions of an application can be deployed *side-by-side*.

Applications run *managed code*. Managed code is not executed directly by the operating system, but rather by the special runtime—the CLR. The CLR can perform checks for type safety, such as for array out-of-bounds and memory overwrites. The CLR performs memory management, including automatic garbage collection, resulting in sharp reduction of memory leaks and similar problems.

Languages such as VB.NET and C# (pronounced "C sharp"), but not C++, can produce managed code that is verifiably secure. Managed code that is not verifiable can run if the security policy allows the code to ignore the verification process.

A New Programming Platform

.NET provides a new programming platform at a higher level than the operating system. This level of abstraction has many advantages:

- Code can be validated to prevent unauthorized actions
- It is much easier to program than the Win32 API or COM
- All or parts of the platform can be implemented on many different kinds of computers (as has been done with Java)
- All the languages use one class library
- Languages can interoperate with each other

We outline the features of this new platform, the *.NET Framework,* in the next section.

.NET Framework Overview

The .NET Framework consists of the CLR, the .NET Framework Class Library, the Common Language Specification (CLS), a number of .NET languages, and Visual Studio.NET. The overall architecture of the .NET Framework is depicted in Figure 1–2.

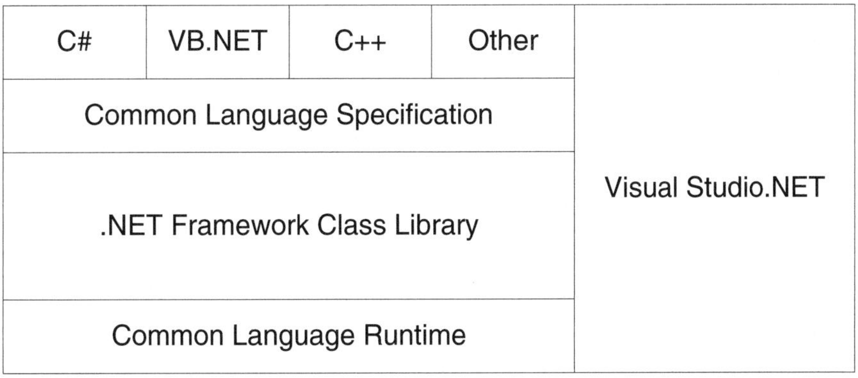

C#	VB.NET	C++	Other	Visual Studio.NET
Common Language Specification				
.NET Framework Class Library				
Common Language Runtime				

FIGURE 1–2 *Overall block diagram of .NET Framework.*

Common Language Runtime

A runtime provides services to executing programs. Traditionally, different programming environments have different runtimes. Examples of runtimes include the standard C library, MFC, the Visual Basic runtime, and the Java Virtual Machine (JVM).

The runtime environment provided by .NET, the CLR, manages the execution of code and provides useful services. The services of the CLR are exposed through programming languages. The syntax for these services varies from language to language, but the underlying execution engine providing the services is the same.

Not all languages expose all the features of the CLR. The language with the best mapping to the CLR is the new language C#. VB.NET, however, does an admirable job of exposing the functionality.

.NET Framework Class Library

The .NET Framework class library is huge, comprising more than 2,500 classes. All this functionality is available to all the .NET languages. The library (see Figure 1–3) consists of four main parts:

1. Base class library (which includes networking, security, diagnostics, I/O, and other types of operating system services)
2. Data and XML classes
3. Windows UI
4. Web services and Web UI

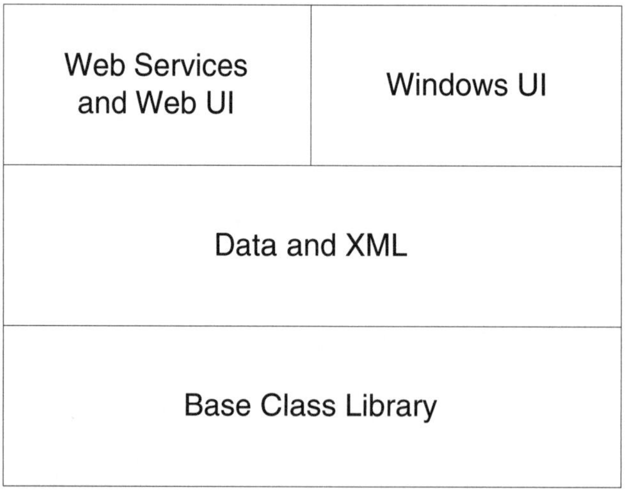

Web Services and Web UI	Windows UI
Data and XML	
Base Class Library	

FIGURE 1–3   *Block diagram of .NET Framework Class Library.*

Common Language Specification

An important goal of the .NET Framework is to support multiple languages. But all languages are not created equal, so it is important to agree upon a common subset that all languages will support. The CLS is an agreement among language designers and class library designers about those features and usage conventions that can be relied upon.

CLS rules apply to public features that are visible outside the assembly where they are defined. (An assembly can be thought of as a logical EXE or DLL and will be discussed later in this chapter.) For example, the CLS requires that public names do not rely on case for uniqueness, because some languages are not case sensitive. For more information, see "Cross Language Interoperability" in "Inside the .NET Framework" in the .NET Framework SDK documentation.

Languages in .NET

A language is a CLS-compliant *consumer* if it can use any CLS-compliant type—that is, if it can call methods, create instances of types, and so on. (A type is basically a class in most object-oriented languages, providing an abstraction of data and behavior, grouped together.) A language is a CLS-compliant *extender* if it is a consumer and can also extend any CLS-compliant base class, implement any CLS-compliant interface, and so on.

Microsoft itself is providing four CLS-compliant languages. VB.NET, C#, and C++ with Managed Extensions are extenders. JScript.NET is a consumer.

Third parties are providing additional languages (more than a dozen so far). Active-State is implementing Perl and Python. Fujitsu is implementing COBOL. It should be noted that at present some of these languages are not .NET languages in the strict sense. For example, ActiveState provides a tool called PerlNET that will create a .NET component from a Perl class. This facility enables .NET applications to call the wealth of Perl modules, but it does not make Perl into either a consumer or an extender. For more information on PerlNET, see the book *Programming Perl in the .NET Environment* (Saltzman, Oberg), another book in The Integrated .NET Series.

Common Language Runtime

In this section, we delve more deeply into the structure of .NET by examining the CLR. We look at the design goals of the CLR and discuss the rationale for using managed code and a runtime. We outline the design of the CLR, including the concepts of MSIL, metadata, and JIT compilation. We compare the CLR with the Java Virtual Machine. We discuss the key concept in .NET of assembly, which is a logical grouping of code. We explore the central role of types in .NET and look at the Common Type System (CTS). We explain the role of managed data and garbage collection. Finally, we use the Intermediate Language Disassembler (ILDASM) tool to gain some insight into the structure of assemblies.

Design Goals of the CLR

The CLR has the following design goals:

- Simplify application development
- Support multiple programming languages
- Provide a safe and reliable execution environment
- Simplify deployment and administration
- Provide good performance and scalability

SIMPLE APPLICATION DEVELOPMENT

With more than 2,500 classes, the .NET Framework class library provides enormous functionality that the programmer can reuse. The object-oriented and component features of .NET enable organizations to create their own reusable code. Unlike COM, the programmer does not have to implement any plumbing code to gain the advantages of components. Automatic garbage collection greatly simplifies memory management in applications. The CLR facilitates powerful tools such as Visual Studio.NET that can provide common functionality and the same UI for multiple languages.

MULTIPLE LANGUAGES

The CLR was designed from the ground up to support multiple languages. This feature is the most significant difference between .NET and Java, which share a great deal in philosophy.

The CTS makes interoperability between languages virtually seamless. The same built-in data types can be used in multiple languages. Classes defined in one language can be used in another language. A class in one language can even inherit from a class in another language. Exceptions can be thrown from one language to another.

Programmers do not have to learn a new language in order to use .NET. The same tools can work for all .NET languages. You can debug from one language into another.

SAFE EXECUTION ENVIRONMENT

With the CLR, a compiler generates MSIL instructions, not native code. It is this managed code that runs. Hence, the CLR can perform runtime validations on this code before it is translated into native code. Types are verified. Subscripts are verified to be in range. Unsafe casts and uninitialized variables are prevented.

The CLR performs memory management. Managed code cannot access memory directly. No pointers are allowed. This means that your code cannot inadvertently write over memory that does not belong to it, possibly causing a crash or other bad behavior.

The CLR can enforce strong security. One of the challenges of the software world of third party components and downloadable code is that you open your system to damage from executing code from unknown sources. You might want to restrict Word macros from accessing anything other than the document that contains them. You want to stop potentially malicious Web scripts. You even want to shield your system from bugs of software from known vendors. To handle these situations, .NET security includes *Code Access Security* (CAS).

SIMPLER DEPLOYMENT AND ADMINISTRATION

With the CLR, the unit of deployment becomes an *assembly,* which is typically an EXE or a DLL. The assembly contains a *manifest,* which allows much more information to be stored.

An assembly is completely self-describing. No information needs to be stored in the registry. All the information is in one place, and the code cannot get out of sync with information stored elsewhere, such as in the registry, a type library, or a header file.

The assembly is the unit of versioning, so that multiple versions can be deployed side by side in different folders. These different versions can execute at the same time without interfering with each other.

Assemblies can be private or shared. For private assembly deployment, the assembly is copied to the same directory as the client program that references it. No registration is needed, and no fancy installation program is required. When the component is removed, no registry cleanup is needed, and no uninstall program is required. Just delete it from the hard drive.

In shared assembly deployment, an assembly is installed in the Global Assembly Cache (or GAC). The GAC contains shared assemblies that are globally accessible to all .NET applications on the machine. A download assembly cache is accessible to applications such as Internet Explorer that automatically download assemblies over the network.

PERFORMANCE

You may like the safety and ease-of-use features of managed code, but you may be concerned about performance. It is somewhat analogous to the concerns of early assembly language programmers when high-level languages came out.

The CLR is designed with high performance in mind. JIT compilation is designed into the CLR. The first time a method is encountered, the CLR performs verifications and then compiles the method into native code (which will contain safety features, such as array bounds checking). The next time the method is encountered, the native code executes directly.

Memory management is designed for high performance. Allocation is almost instantaneous, just taking the next available storage from the managed heap. Deallocation is done by the garbage collector, which Microsoft has tweaked for efficiency.

Why Use a CLR?

Why did Microsoft create a CLR for .NET? Let's look at how well the goals just discussed could have been achieved without a CLR, focusing on the two main goals of safety and performance. Basically, there are two philosophies. The first is compile-time checking and fast native code at runtime. The second is runtime checking.

Without a CLR, we must rely on the compiler to achieve safety. This places a high burden on the compiler. Typically, there are many compilers for a system, including third-party compilers. It is not robust to trust that every compiler from every vendor will adequately perform all safety checking. Not every language has features supporting adequate safety checking. Compilation speed is slow with complex compilation. Compilers cannot conveniently optimize code based on enhanced instructions available on some platforms but not on others. What's more, many features (such as security) cannot be detected until runtime.

Design of Common Language Runtime

So we want a runtime. How do we design it? One extreme is to use an interpreter and not a compiler at all. All the work is done at runtime. We have safety and fast builds, but runtime performance is very slow. Modern systems divide the load between the front-end compiler and the back-end runtime.

INTERMEDIATE LANGUAGE

The front-end compiler does all the checking it can do and generates an intermediate language. Examples include

- P-code for Pascal
- Bytecode for Java

The runtime does further verification based on the actual runtime characteristics, including security checking.

With JIT compilation, native code can be generated when needed and subsequently reused. Runtime performance becomes much better. The native code generated by the runtime can be more efficient, because the runtime knows the precise characteristics of the target machine.

MICROSOFT INTERMEDIATE LANGUAGE

All managed code compilers for Microsoft .NET generate MSIL. MSIL is machine-independent and can be efficiently compiled into native code.

MSIL has a wide variety of instructions:

- Standard operations such as load, store, arithmetic and logic, branch, etc.
- Calling methods on objects
- Exceptions

Before executing on a CPU, MSIL must be translated by a JIT compiler. There is a JIT compiler for each machine architecture supported. The same MSIL will run on any supported machine.

METADATA

Besides generating MSIL, a managed code compiler emits metadata. Metadata contains very complete information about the code module, including the following:

- Version and locale information
- All the types
- Details about each type, including name, visibility, etc.
- Details about the members of each type, such as methods, the signatures of methods, etc.

Types

Types are at the heart of the programming model for the CLR. A type is analogous to a class in most object-oriented programming languages, providing an abstraction of data and behavior, grouped together. A type in the CLR contains the following:

- Fields (data members)
- Methods
- Properties
- Events

There are also built-in primitive types, such as integer and floating point numeric types, strings, etc. In the CLR, there are no functions outside of types, but all behavior is provided via methods or other members. We discuss types under the guise of classes and value types when we cover VB.NET.

Metadata is the "glue" that binds together the executing code, the CLR, and tools such as compilers, debuggers, and browsers. On Windows, MSIL and metadata are packaged together in a standard Windows PE file. Metadata enables "Intellisense" in Visual Studio. In .NET, you can call from one language to another, and metadata enables types to be converted transparently. Metadata is ubiquitous in the .NET environment.

JIT COMPILATION

Before executing on the target machine, MSIL is translated by a JIT compiler to native code. Some code typically will never be executed during a program run. Hence, it may be more efficient to translate MSIL as needed during execution, storing the native code for reuse.

When a type is loaded, the loader attaches a stub to each method of the type. On the first call, the stub passes control to the JIT, which translates to native code and modifies the stub to save the address of the translated native code. On subsequent calls to the method, the native code is called directly.

As part of JIT compilation, code goes through a verification process. Type safety is verified, using both the MSIL and metadata. Security restrictions are checked.

COMMON TYPE SYSTEM

At the heart of the CLR is the Common Type System (CTS). The CTS provides a wide range of types and operations that are found in many programming languages. The CTS is shared by the CLR and by compilers and other tools.

The CTS provides a framework for cross-language integration and addresses a number of issues:

- Similar, but subtly different, types (for example, **Integer** is 16 bits in VB6, but **int** is 32 bits in C++; strings in VB6 are represented as BSTRs and in C++ as **char** pointers or a **string** class of some sort; and so on)
- Limited code reuse (for example, you can't define a new type in one language and import it into another language)
- Inconsistent object models

Not all CTS types are available in all languages. The CLS establishes rules that must be followed for cross-language integration, including which types *must* be supported by a CLS-compliant language. Built-in types can be accessed through the **System** class in the Base Class Library (BCL) and through reserved keywords in the .NET languages.

In Chapter 4, we begin our discussion of data types with the simple data types. We continue the discussion of types in Chapter 11, where we introduce *reference* types such as class and interface. At all times, you should bear in mind that there is a mapping between types in VB.NET, represented by keywords, and the types defined by the CTS, as implemented by the CLR.

Managed Data and Garbage Collection

Managed code is only part of the story of the CLR. A significant simplification of the programming model is provided through *managed data*. When an application domain is initialized, the CLR reserves a contiguous block of storage known as the *managed heap*. Allocation from the managed heap is extremely fast. The next available space is simply returned, in contrast to the C runtime, which must search its heap for space that is large enough.

Deallocation is not performed by the user program but by the CLR, using a process known as *garbage collection*. The CLR tracks the use of memory allocated on the managed heap. When memory is low, or in response to an explicit call from a program, the CLR "garbage collects" (or frees up all unreferenced memory) and compacts the space that is now free into a large contiguous block.

Summary

VB.NET does not exist in isolation, but has a close connection with the underlying .NET Framework. In this chapter, you received an orientation to the overall architecture and features of .NET.

Microsoft .NET is a new platform that sits on top of the operating system and provides many capabilities for building and deploying desktop and Web-based applications. .NET has many features that will create a much more robust Windows operating system.

The .NET Framework includes the Common Language Runtime (CLR), the .NET Framework Class Library, the Common Type System (CTS), the .NET languages, and Visual Studio.NET.

The CLR manages the execution of code and provides useful services. The design goals of the CLR included simple application development, safety, simple deployment, support of multiple languages, and good performance.

.NET uses managed code that runs in a safe environment under the CLR. .NET compilers translate source code into Microsoft Intermediate Language (MSIL), which is translated at runtime into native code by a just-in-time (JIT) compiler.

An assembly is a grouping of types and resources that work together as a logical unit. Types and the CTS are the heart of the CLR. Garbage collection is used by the CLR to automatically reclaim unreferenced data.

In Chapter 2, we will take our first steps in VB.NET programming.

First VB.NET Programs

Visual Basic has evolved tremendously in the days since VB3 was introduced. In its latest version, Visual Basic.NET, or simply VB.NET, is fully object-oriented. It can be used to build many types of applications, including Windows applications, applications for a Web interface, and console applications. In this chapter, we begin to explore how VB.NET can be used to build console applications. First, we examine the basic structure of VB.NET programs and explain the use of namespaces. We then explore how to perform simple calculations and use the .NET Framework Class Library to perform basic input and output. Finally, we begin to explain some of the object-oriented concepts in VB.NET.

Namespaces

Much of the interesting functionality available in Visual Basic.NET is provided by the .NET Framework Class Library. To manage the large number of available classes, they are grouped into *namespaces.*

Console I/O is provided by the .NET **System.Console** class. The **WriteLine** method is used to display a line of text, like this:

```
System.Console.WriteLine("Hello World")
```

References to **System.Console.WriteLine** may be shortened to **Console.WriteLine** if you import the **System** namespace, using the following command:

```
Import System
...
Console.WriteLine("Hello World")
```

The **Import** statement tells the Visual Basic compiler to look in the **System** namespace before generating an error whenever an unknown class or function is referenced.

Console Programs

Visual Basic.NET can be used to build several types of applications, including *console applications*. A console application interacts with the user in a console (or DOS-like window). The .NET Framework Class Library provides support for interacting with console windows, which is available to all .NET languages.

Here's a simple console application in VB.NET that displays "Hello World" to the console:

```
' HelloWorld.vb

Imports System
Module HelloWorld
    Sub Main()
        Console.WriteLine("Hello World")
    End Sub
End Module
```

Code
Example

Although this is a very simple program, it illustrates the structure of a VB.NET application. The preceding program may be found in the **HelloWorld** directory for this chapter.

Compiling and Running Using the Command Line

In this chapter, we use the .NET Framework SDK to compile our programs. It can be accessed via the command line[1] (as we saw in Chapter 1):

```
>vbc HelloWorld.vb
```

An executable file **Hello.exe** will be generated. To execute your program, type the following at the command line:

```
>Hello
```

---

1. For simplicity, we show the command line prompt as simply ">". If you installed the book software in the default directory, the complete prompt will be: "`C:\OI\IntroVb\Chap01\Hello>`".

The program executes, and you should see this greeting displayed:

```
Hello World
```

We will learn how to use the Microsoft Visual Studio.NET IDE (integrated development environment) in Chapter 3. You will probably prefer to work in this integrated environment that provides an integrated source code editor, compiler, and debugger. But it is always useful to learn about all the tools that are available to you, so we will use the command line tools for our first programs.

Program Structure

The first line of code in this program is a *comment:*

```
' HelloWorld.vb

Imports System
Module HelloWorld
...
End Module
```

A comment is used for documentation purposes. It begins with a single quote. All text after the quote is considered documentation. The quote may appear at places other than the beginning of a line; it can be used to add comments to an executable statement. For example:

```
x = x + 1    ' Increment x
y = y + 1    ' Increment y
```

As discussed previously, the second line of code is the **Imports** statement that tells the compiler to look in the specified namespace when it encounters a class name that it does not immediately recognize. In this case, it tells the compiler to look in the **System** namespace.

```
' HelloWorld.vb

Imports System

Module HelloWorld
...
End Module
```

Every VB.NET console application has at least one *module*. A module is a container of data and procedures. All of the module's code will be contained between the **Module** statement and the **End Module** statement. We will discuss modules in detail later.

```
' HelloWorld.vb

Imports System
Module HelloWorld
...
End Module
```

A console application must contain a module with a subroutine (procedure) named **Main.** Subroutines begin with the keyword **Sub** and end with the statement **End Sub.** All code in between those statements belongs to the subroutine. For example:

```
' HelloWorld.vb

Imports System
Module HelloWorld
    Sub Main()
        ...
    End Sub
End Module
```

The subroutine **Main** is the *entry point* of a console application. As such, execution begins with the code inside that subroutine.

Every procedure in VB.NET contains one or more *statements*. A statement must be completely expressed on a single line unless the continuation indicator, which is discussed below, is used.

VB.NET is not case sensitive. However, the editor will convert VB.NET keywords into a consistent case (for example, **Module** instead of module and **End Sub** instead of end sub). We will learn more about case sensitivity issues in Chapter 4.

In the **HelloWorld** program, the .NET Framework class, **Console,** is used to provide standard output. Specifically, the **WriteLine** method is used to display a string, followed by a new line.

```
' HelloWorld.vb

Imports System
Module HelloWorld
    Sub Main()
        Console.WriteLine("Hello World")
    End Sub
End Module
```

If you want to break a statement across two or more lines, each line to be continued must be terminated by a space and then an underscore. The compiler then assumes that the next line is part of the same statement. For example:

```
Console.WriteLine( _
                "Hello World" _
                )
```

In the previous **WriteLine**, the string literal `"Hello World"` must not be broken across two lines. If a string literal is too long to easily fit on one line, it must be broken into two literals and then concatenated using the **&** operator.

```
Console.WriteLine( _
                "Hello out there, you bright " & _
                "and beautiful world" _
                )
```

Finally, all VB.NET files have the extension **.vb.** The code shown here is located in a file named **HelloWorld.vb.**

Variables

In VB.NET, you can define variables to hold data. Variables represent storage locations in memory. In VB.NET, variables are of a specific data type. Common types include **Integer** for integers and **Single** for floating-point numbers.

You must declare variables before you can use them. A variable declaration reserves memory space for the variable. It may also be used to specify an initial value. However, if no initial value is specified, VB.NET initializes numeric types to zero.

```
Dim length As Integer = 10
    ' This reserves space and assigns it an initial value

Dim width As Integer
    ' This reserves space but does not initialize it,
    ' therefore it is initialized to zero
```

Expressions

You can form expressions by combining variables and literals using operators. VB.NET supports a wide range of operators, including basic arithmetic ones:

```
+           addition
-           subtraction
*           multiplication
/           division
\           integer division
^           exponentiation
```

Examples of expressions include:

```
length * width
(fahrenheit - 32) * 5 / 9
3.14159 * radius ^ 2
```

Assignment

You can assign a value to a variable by using the = symbol. The variable whose value is to be updated must be on the left-hand side of the =. The expression to be evaluated must be on the right-hand side of the =.

```
areaOfASquare = width * height
celsius = (fahrenheit - 32) * 5 / 9
areaOfACircle = 3.14159 radius ^ 2
```

The same variable can be used on both sides of an assignment statement. For example, to increment the value of the variable age, you use the following code:

```
age = 42
age = age + 1
```

In this case, age begins with the value 42. The expression "age + 1" evaluates to 43. The value 43 is then assigned to the variable age, replacing any previous value of the variable.

Performing Calculations in VB.NET

You can use VB.NET to perform calculations and display results by adding code to **Main**. Follow these steps:

1. Declare any variables you will need.
2. Create expressions for the calculations you want, and assign them to your variables.
3. Display the answer using **Console.WriteLine**.

Output

We have seen that the .NET Framework Class Library provides the **Console.WriteLine** method for outputting a string followed by a new line character. You may also use the **Console.Write** method, which writes a string without the new line character. You can use both methods to label your output by building a string using the concatenation operator **&**. The .NET Framework, as we will discuss in Chapter 4, automatically converts the number to a string in this context. Thus, you can write the following:

```
Dim total As Integer
total = 35
Console.WriteLine("The total is " & total)
```

It will produce the output shown below:

```
The total is 35
```

Sample Program

Code Example

To illustrate the capabilities of Visual Basic.NET presented thus far, we will examine a program that can calculate the area of a rectangle. See **SquareArea\Version1**.

```
' SquareArea.vb - Version 1

' Calculates the area of a rectangle given its length and
' width (Note: in this version the length and width are
' hardcoded)

Imports System

Module SquareArea
    Sub Main()
        Dim length As Integer
        Dim width As Integer
        Dim area As Integer

        length = 20
        width = 12
        area = length * width

        Console.WriteLine("Area = " & area)
    End Sub
End Module
```

The **Main** subroutine begins by declaring three integer variables. It sets the length variable to 20 and the width variable to 12. It then calculates a value for area based on the length and width. Finally, it displays the results.

This program really isn't very flexible. To calculate the area of a different rectangle, you would have to edit the code and recompile it. It would be much more flexible if it prompted the user at runtime for the values of length and width. The next section describes simple console input.

Input

The .NET Framework Class Library provides the **Console.ReadLine** method to read a string.

```
Console.Write("Enter name: ")
Dim name As String
name = Console.ReadLine()
```

However, in the case of the area calculator, we want to read numeric values. To do this, we must convert the string to the type of data we need. Again, the .NET library comes to our aid. The **System.Convert** class has a variety of methods to convert data for us. For example:

```
Console.Write("Enter rectangle length: ")
Dim buf As String
buf = Console.ReadLine()
Dim length As Integer
length = Convert.ToInt32(buf)
```

Revised Sample Program

Code Example

A more flexible version of the area calculator is shown below. It can be found at **SquareArea\Version2**.

```
' SquareArea.vb - Version 2

' Calculates the area of a rectangle given its length and
' width (Note:  we prompt the user for length and width
' values)

Imports System

Module SquareArea
    Sub Main()
        Dim buf As String
        Dim length As Integer
        Dim width As Integer
        Dim area As Integer

        Console.WriteLine("Enter length: ")
        buf = Console.ReadLine()
        length = Convert.ToInt32(buf)

        Console.WriteLine("Enter width: ")
        buf = Console.ReadLine()
        width = Convert.ToInt32(buf)

        area = length * width
        Console.WriteLine("Area = " & area)
```

```
    End Sub
End Module
```

In this version, the user is prompted for a length and then a width. The user's response is stored in the string variable **buf**, before being converted to the proper type and stored in length or width. If the user enters bad data, such as alphabetic characters instead of a number, the system will throw an *exception*. Exceptions are presented in detail in Chapter 9.

The .NET Framework Class Library

The .NET Framework has a very large class library (over 2,500 classes). In this chapter, we have used the **Console** and **Convert** classes. To make all this functionality more manageable, the classes are partitioned into *namespaces*. The root namespace is **System**, which contains many useful classes, including the following:

- **Console** provides access to standard input, output, and error streams for I/O.
- **Convert** provides conversions among base data types.
- **Math** provides mathematical constants and functions.

Underneath the **System** namespace, other namespaces exist, including these:

- **System.Data** contains classes constituting the ADO.NET architecture for accessing databases.
- **System.Xml** provides standards-based support for processing XML.
- **System.WindowsForms** provides support for creating applications with rich Windows-based interfaces.
- **System.Web** provides support for browser/server communication.

Although we will discuss and use many interesting .NET classes, our focus in this book is on the VB.NET programming language. For much more information about the .NET Framework Class Library, see our book, *Application Development Using Visual Basic and .NET* (Oberg, Thorsteinson, Wyatt).

Summary

In this chapter, we learned the basics of programming in VB.NET. Every console application written in VB.NET has a module with a subroutine called **Main** that represents the entry point into the application. Expressions are formed from literals, variables, and operators, and with the assignment statement, you can assign a value computed by an expression to a variable. The .NET Framework has a large class library that is partitioned into namespaces. The **System** namespace contains the **Console** class, which has methods such as **ReadLine** and **WriteLine** for performing I/O. In the next chapter, we will learn about Visual Studio.NET, which will make our programming easier and more enjoyable.

Visual Studio.NET

Although it is possible to program .NET using only the command line compiler, it is much easier and more enjoyable to use Visual Studio.NET. In this chapter, we cover the basics of using Visual Studio to edit, compile, run, and debug programs. You will then be equipped to use Visual Studio in the rest of the book. We will introduce additional features of Visual Studio later in the book as we encounter a need. This book was developed using beta software, so you may encounter some changes to the information presented here in the final released product. Visual Studio is a highly configurable Windows application. Your installation may be configured differently than ours, in which case, you would encounter variations in the exact layout of windows and other specifications shown here. As you work with Visual Studio, think of yourself as an explorer discovering a rich and varied new country.

Overview of Visual Studio.NET

Open Microsoft Visual Studio.NET 7.0, and you will see a starting window similar to what is shown in Figure 3–1.

What you see on default startup is the main window with an HTML page that can help you navigate among various resources, open or create projects, and change your profile information. (If you close the start page, you can get it back anytime from the menu using Help | Show Start Page.) Clicking on **My Profile** brings up a profile page on which you can change various set-

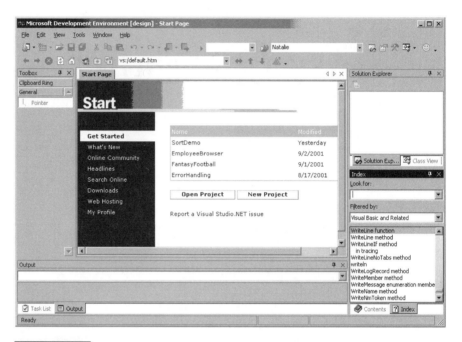

FIGURE 3–1   *Visual Studio.NET main window.*

tings. Several profiles are available in Visual Studio, including a standard one for "typical" work (called the "Visual Studio Developer" profile) and special ones for various languages. Because Visual Studio.NET is the unification of many development environments, programmers used to one particular previous environment may prefer a particular keyboard scheme, window layout, and so on. For example, if you choose the profile "Visual Basic Developer," you will get the Visual Basic 6 keyboard scheme. In this book, we use all the defaults, so go back to the profile "Visual Studio Developer" if you made any changes. See Figure 3–2.

Code
Example

To gain an appreciation for some of the diverse features in Visual Studio.NET, open the **Bank** console solution in this chapter: Choose File | Open Solution..., navigate to the **Bank** directory, and open the file **Bank.sln**. You will see several windows. (See Figure 3–3.)

Starting from the left are icons for the Server Explorer and the Toolbox, followed by the main window area, which currently is just a gray area. Below the main window is the Output Window, which shows the results of builds and so on. On the top right, the Solution Explorer enables you to conveniently see all the files in a "solution," which may consist of several "projects." On the bottom right is the Properties window, which lets you conveniently edit properties on forms for Windows applications.

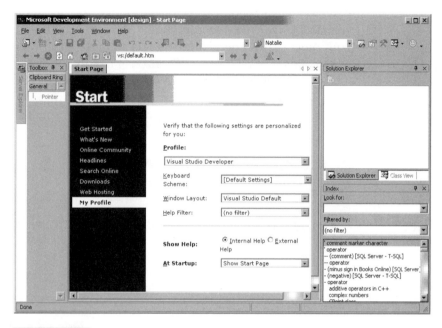

FIGURE 3–2   Visual Studio.NET profile page.

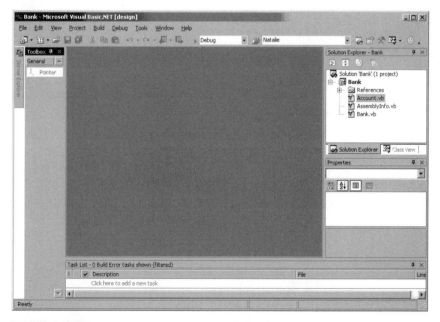

FIGURE 3–3   A console project in Visual Studio.NET.

From the Solution Explorer, you can navigate to files in the projects. In turn, double-click on **Account.vb** and **Bank.vb**, the two source files in the **Bank** project. Text editor windows appear in the main window area. Across the top of the main window are horizontal tabs that let you quickly select any of the open windows. Visual Studio.NET is a Multiple Document Interface (MDI) application, so you can also select the window to show from the Windows menu. Figure 3–4 shows the open source files with the horizontal tabs.

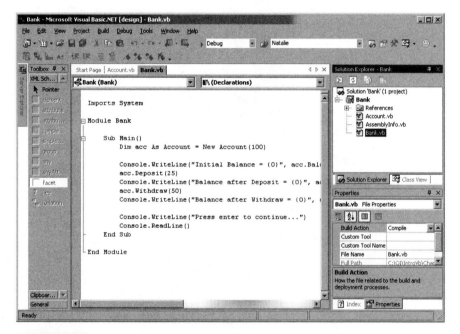

FIGURE 3–4   *Horizontal tabs for open source files.*

Toolbars

Visual Studio comes with many different toolbars. You can configure the toolbars you want displayed, and you can drag toolbars to the position you find most convenient. You can also customize toolbars by adding or deleting buttons that correspond to different commands.To specify which toolbars are displayed, use the menu View | Toolbars. You can also right-click in any empty area of a toolbar. A list of toolbars appears with check marks beside the ones currently displayed. By clicking on an item on this menu, you can make the corresponding toolbar appear or disappear. For your work in this book, add these toolbars:

- Build
- Debug

CUSTOMIZING A TOOLBAR

We want to make sure that the "Start Without Debugging" command is available on the Debug toolbar. If this command (which looks like a red exclamation point) is not already on your Debug toolbar, you can add it using the following procedure, which can be used to add other commands to toolbars:

1. Select menu Tools | Customize... to bring up the Customize dialog.
2. Select the Commands tab.
3. In Categories, select Debug, and in Commands, select Start Without Debugging. See Figure 3–5.
4. Drag the selected command onto the Debug toolbar, positioning it where you desire. For now, place it to the immediate right of the wedge-shaped Start ▶ button.
5. Close the Customize dialog.

FIGURE 3–5   *Adding a new command to a toolbar.*

Creating a Console Application

Code Example

As our first exercise in using Visual Studio, we will create a simple console application. Our program **Bytes** will attempt to calculate how many bytes are in a kilobyte, a megabyte, a gigabyte, and a terabyte. If you want to follow along on your PC as you read, you can use the **Demos** directory for this chapter. The first version is in **Bytes\Version1**. A final version can be found in **Bytes\Version3**.

Creating a VB.NET Project

1. From the Visual Studio main menu, choose File | New | Project.... This will bring up the New Project dialog.
2. For Project Types, choose Visual Basic Projects, and for Templates, choose Empty Project.
3. Click the Browse button, navigate to **Demos**, and click Open. See Figure 3–6.
4. In the Name field, type **Bytes**.
5. Click OK.

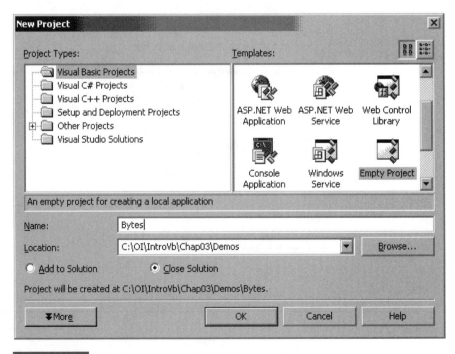

FIGURE 3–6   *Creating an empty VB.NET project.*

Adding a VB.NET Module

At this point, you have an empty VB.NET project. We will now add a file called **Bytes.vb**, which will contain the source code for our program.

1. In the Solution Explorer, right-click over **Bytes**, and choose Add | Add New Item.... This will bring up the Add New Item dialog.
2. For Categories, choose Local Project Items.
3. For Templates, choose Module.
4. For Name, type **Bytes.vb**. See Figure 3–7.
5. Click Open.

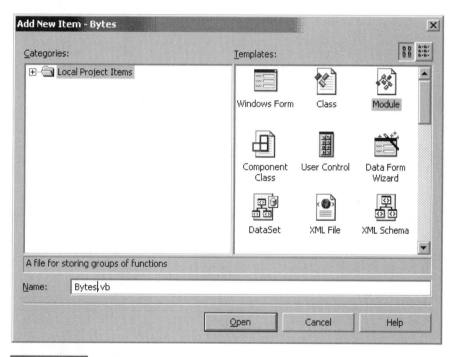

FIGURE 3–7   *Adding a VB.NET module to a VB.NET project.*

Using the Visual Studio Text Editor

In the Solution Explorer, double-click on **Bytes.vb**. This will open the file in the Visual Studio text editor. Notice that a skeleton version of a module already exists because you selected Module as the template for the file. Type the following code in **Bytes.vb**. You should notice that the editor uses color-coded syntax highlighting as you type.

```
' Bytes.vb - Version 1
```

```
Imports System

Module Bytes

    Sub Main()
        Dim bytes As Integer = 1024

        Console.WriteLine("1 kilobyte = {0} bytes", bytes)
        bytes = bytes * 1024
        Console.WriteLine("1 megabyte = {0} bytes", bytes)
        bytes = bytes * 1024
        Console.WriteLine("1 gigabyte = {0} bytes", bytes)

    End Sub

End Module
```

Besides the color syntax highlighting, other features include automatic indenting and automatically adding End statements to various programming constructs. All in all, you should find the Visual Studio editor friendly and easy to use.

Building the Project

You can build the project using one of the following:
- Menu Build | Build
- Toolbar 🖫
- Keyboard shortcut Ctrl + Shift + B

Running the Program

You can run the program using one of the following:
- Menu Debug | Start Without Debugging
- Toolbar ❗
- Keyboard shortcut Ctrl + F5

You won't see any output. This is because the default project type for an "empty project" is a Windows Application. To change it, you must right-click on the project name (**Bytes**) in the Solutions Explorer window and choose Properties. See Figure 3–8. In the Output type drop-down, select Console Application. Using the Project Properties dialog, you can also configure the Startup Object of the applications.

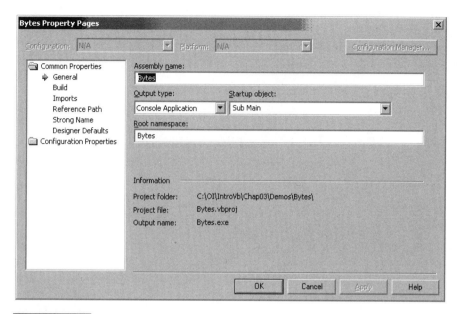

FIGURE 3-8   *Changing project properties.*

Now rebuild your application, and try to run it again. You will see the following output in a console window:

```
1 kilobyte = 1024 bytes
1 megabyte = 1048576 bytes
1 gigabyte = 1073741824 bytes
Press any key to continue
```

If you press any key, as indicated, the console window will close.

Defining the Startup Object

In VB.NET, you must define the startup object. You do this via the project Properties dialog shown in Figure 3-8. Depending on how the project was built and whether you changed the name of the module after it was generated, you may need to set the startup object to Sub Main. The compiler will generate a syntax message if it is unable to find Sub Main.

Running the Program in the Debugger

You can run the program in the debugger using one of the following:

- Menu Debug | Start
- Toolbar ▶
- Keyboard shortcut F5

A console window will briefly open up and then immediately close. If you want the window to stay open, you must explicitly program for it, for example, by asking for input. Add the following two lines to your program right above the "End Sub" statement:

```
Console.WriteLine("Press enter to continue...")
Console.ReadLine()
```

When you run your program, the output will stay on the screen until you press the Enter key. You can also set a breakpoint to stop the execution before the program exits. We will outline features of the debugger later in the chapter.

Project Configurations

A project *configuration* specifies build settings for a project. You can have several different configurations, and each configuration will be built in its own directory, so you can exercise the different configurations independently. Every project in a Visual Studio solution has two default configurations, **Debug** and **Release**. As the names suggest, the **Debug** configuration will build a debug version of the project, in which you can do source level debugging by setting breakpoints, among other things. The **obj\Debug** directory will then contain a *program database* file with a **.pdb** extension that holds debugging and project state information.

You can choose the configuration from the main toolbar ▸ Debug ▾. You can also choose the configuration using the menu Build | Configuration Manager..., which brings up the Configuration Manager dialog. From the Active Solution Configuration drop-down box, choose **Release**. See Figure 3-9.

Build the project again. A second version of the IL language file **Bytes.exe** is created, this time in the **obj\Release** directory. There will be no **.pdb** file in this directory.

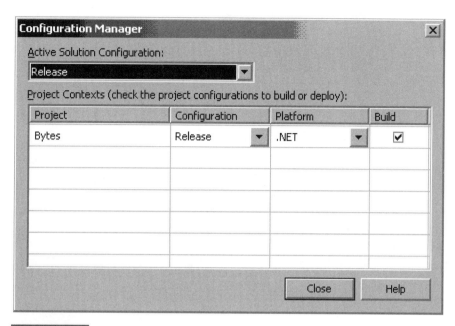

FIGURE 3–9   *Choosing Release in the Configuration Manager.*

Debugging

Some of the most exciting features of any IDE are the debugging features. To take advantage of these features, you must make sure that you built your executable using a Debug configuration. There are two ways to enter the debugger:

1. **Just-in-Time Debugging:** You run as normal, and if an exception occurs, you will be allowed to enter the debugger. The program has crashed, so you will not be able to run it any further. But you will be able to see the value of variables, and you will see the point at which the program failed.

2. **Standard Debugging:** You start the program under the debugger. You may set breakpoints, single step, and so on.

To experiment with the debugger, add the following two lines to your program after the calculation of gigabytes:

```
bytes = bytes * 1024
Console.WriteLine("1 terabyte = {0} bytes", bytes)
```

Code Example

Then rebuild the application. You can find this version of the program in **Bytes\Version2**.

Just-in-Time Debugging

Build and run (without debugging) the **Bytes** program from the preceding section, making sure to use the **Debug** configuration. This time, the program will not run through smoothly to completion, because an exception will be thrown. A Just-In-Time Debugging dialog will appear (see Figure 3–10). Click Yes to debug.

The Attach to Process dialog will then be displayed (see Figure 3–11). Click OK to debug.

Finally, the Microsoft Development Environment dialog will be displayed (see Figure 3–12). Click Break to debug. If you originally executed the program using Start instead of Start Without Debugging, the dialogs in Figures 3–10 and 3–11 will not be displayed.

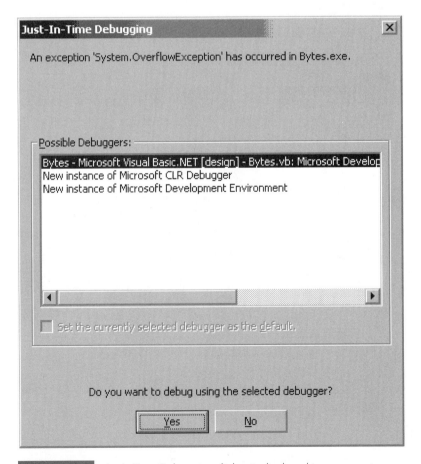

FIGURE 3–10   *Just-In-Time Debugging dialog is displayed in response to an exception.*

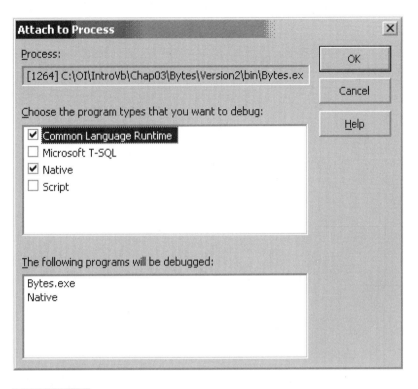

FIGURE 3–11   *The Attach to Process dialog.*

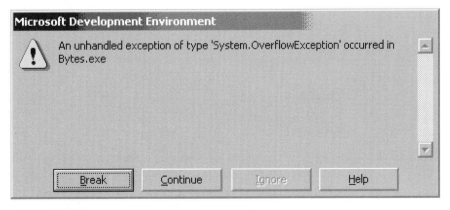

FIGURE 3–12   *Microsoft Developer Environment options for responding to exceptions.*

You will now see a window showing the source code where the problem arose, with an arrow pinpointing the location (see Figure 3–13).

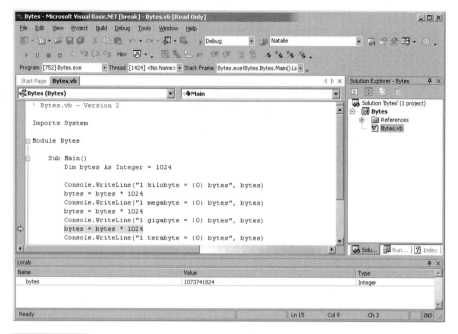

FIGURE 3–13   *Breaking on a System.OverflowException.*

If you look in the Locals window, which is docked across the bottom of the Visual Studio window, you will see that the current value of the variable **bytes** is 1073741824. When the expression **bytes * 1024** was executed, the resulting value was larger than the largest possible integer. This is why the exception indicated that you had an *overflow*.

To stop debugging, you can use the ■ toolbar button or the menu Debug | Stop Debugging.

Standard Debugging

BREAKPOINTS

Typically, when you want to debug, you set a breakpoint at a line in the code where you want to begin to follow the execution. Then you run using the debugger. As an example, set a breakpoint at the first line:

```
bytes = bytes * 1024
```

The easiest way to set a breakpoint is to click in the gray bar to the left of the source code window. You can also set the cursor on the desired line and click the "hand" toolbar button 🖑 to toggle a breakpoint. (It sets a breakpoint if one is not set, and removes the breakpoint if a one is set.)

Now you can run under the debugger. Execution begins in Main, and pauses when the breakpoint is hit. A yellow arrow over the red dot of the breakpoint shows the next line to be executed. See Figure 3–14.

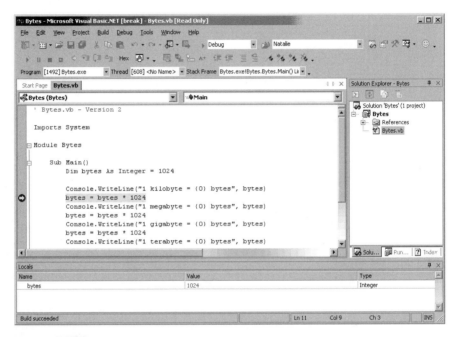

FIGURE 3–14   *A breakpoint has been hit.*

When you are finished with a breakpoint, you can remove it by clicking again in the gray bar or by toggling with the hand toolbar button. If you want to remove all breakpoints, you can use the menu Debug | Clear All Breakpoints, or you can use the toolbar button ⬚ .

WATCHING VARIABLES

At this point, you can inspect variables. Several options are available to accomplish this: Locals window, tool tips, Quick Watch window, and Watch window.

You have already seen in Figures 3–13 and 3–14 the Locals window that is displayed when a breakpoint is encountered. It lists all the variables that are defined in the current procedure, as well as their current values. If you don't see the Locals window, you can use the menu Debug | Windows | Locals to bring up the window.

Another easy way to examine the value of a variable is to hover the mouse over the variable. The value of the variable will be shown as a yellow tool tip, as illustrated in Figure 3–15.

You can also right-click over a variable and choose Quick Watch (or use the eyeglasses toolbar button 🔍). Figure 3–16 shows a typical Quick Watch window. You can also change the value of a variable from this window.

Finally, you can use the Watch window to manage a custom list of variables you want to watch. To add a variable to the Watch window, right-click on it and choose Add Watch. The Watch window is similar to the Locals window, and it stays docked at the bottom of the Visual Studio window. When a variable changes value, the new value is shown in red. Figure 3–17 shows the Watch window. (Note that the display has been changed to hex, as described in the next section.)

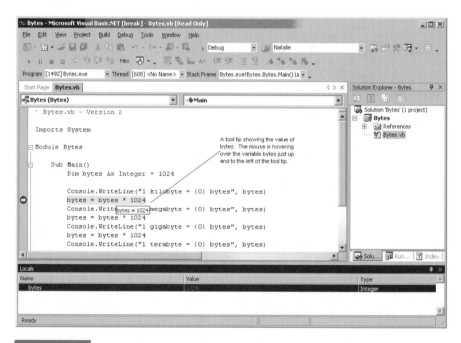

FIGURE 3–15   *Using tool tips to show a variable's value.*

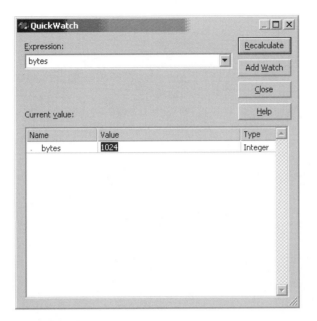

FIGURE 3–16 *The Quick Watch window shows the variable, allowing you to change it.*

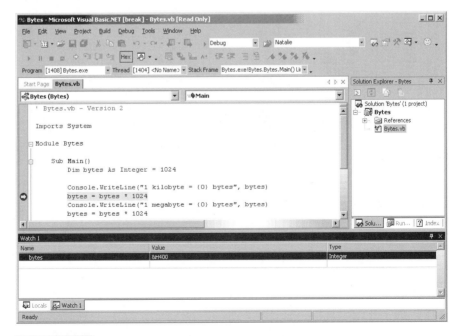

FIGURE 3–17 *The Visual Studio Watch window.*

DEBUGGER OPTIONS

You can change debugger options by choosing from the menu Tools | Options and then selecting Debugging from the list. Figure 3–18 illustrates setting a hexadecimal display. If you then go back to a Watch window, you will see a hex value such as **0x400** displayed.

Another useful debugging option to change under the Edit and Continue category allows you to edit code while you are in Break mode (see Figure 3–19). This option is automatically set for C# projects, but not for VB projects.

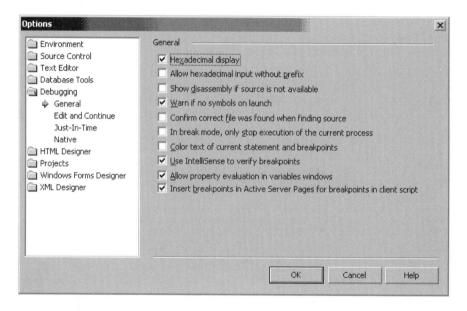

<table>
<tr><td>**FIGURE 3–18**</td><td>*Setting hexadecimal display in Debugging Options.*</td></tr>
</table>

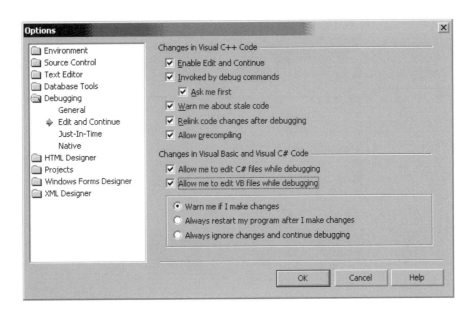

Setting Edit and Continue options.

SINGLE STEPPING

When you are stopped in the debugger, you can *single step* through the code. This means that you can execute one line at a time and examine the results of each statement. You can also begin execution by single stepping. There are a number of single step buttons: 𝄞 . These are the most common (in the order shown on the toolbar):

- Step Into
- Step Over
- Step Out

There is also a Run to Cursor button 𝄞 .

With Step Into, you execute the current statement. If it is a call to a procedure, execution will step into the procedure. With Step Over, you execute the current statement. If it is a call to a procedure, it will execute the entire procedure.

Code
Example

To illustrate Step Into, build the **Bytes\Version3** project, where the expression bytes * 1024 has been replaced by a call to the function **Multiply-ByOneK**. Set a breakpoint at the first function call, and then select Step Into. The result is illustrated in Figure 3–20. Note the red dot at the breakpoint and the yellow arrow in the function.

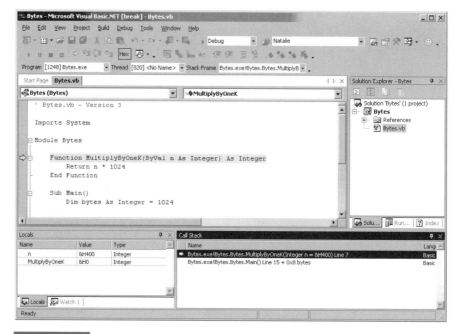

FIGURE 3-20 *Stepping into a function.*

When debugging, Visual Studio maintains a call stack. You can display the call stack by using the menu Debug | Windows | Call Stack. In our example, the Call Stack is just two deep when you used Step Into to step into the function. See the Call Stack pane in Figure 3–20. It shows that the **Main** function called **MultiplyByOneK**.

Stop debugging and start again. But instead of choosing Step Into, choose Step Over. You will see that you are immediately placed on the call to **WriteLine**.

Summary

Visual Studio.NET is a very rich integrated development environment (IDE), with many features to make programming more enjoyable. In this chapter, we covered the basics of using Visual Studio to edit, compile, run, and debug programs so that you will be equipped to use Visual Studio in the rest of the book. Visual Studio.NET has a vast array of features for building database applications, Web applications, components, and many other kinds of projects. It supports many different languages. A project can be built in different configurations, such as Debug and Release, and when you finish an application, you should produce a Release build and use that executable to run the program. In this book, we are using only a tiny fraction of the capabilities of this powerful tool. However, the simple features we employ are very useful and will certainly make your life as a VB.NET programmer easier.

VB.NET AS A VISUAL BASIC LANGUAGE

*P*art Two covers the core features of VB.NET. If you know Visual Basic, you will have a definite leg up in learning VB.NET, and you can quickly skim this section, paying attention to the information in the sidebars. Sidebars alert you to either (1) the first time a concept new to VB.NET is introduced, or (2) a significant change to the VB.NET language that experienced VB programmers should note. If you are not familiar with Visual Basic, this section is for you. It will quickly bring you up to speed on the core topics of data types, operators, and control structures.

Fundamentals of VB.NET

Visual Basic.NET is a welcomed successor to Microsoft's popular Visual Basic 6. It provides developers with a programming language that is very rich in native language capabilities. This chapter describes the basic rules and program structure that you must know to be a VB.NET programmer. It begins to examine the diverse range of data types that can be manipulated in VB.NET and the powerful set of operators that are provided. It explores options that can be set to specify the degree of type-checking performed by the compiler. Finally, it examines console I/O in more detail than what has previously been discussed.

Naming Standards

VB.NET programmers must create variables, procedures, modules, structures, and classes in their quest to produce applications that solve interesting problems. In the course of doing this, they must name these elements. These rules govern the naming of these elements:

- You may use only letters, digits, and the underscore.
- You must begin with either a letter or an underscore.
- You must have at least one letter in the name.

Although VB.NET names are not case-sensitive, the source code editor will convert all instances of the name to the case that was used when the identifier was defined. In addition, the .NET Common Language Runtime uses case-sensitive binding, which means that other .NET languages that interact with your assembly must use the same case that you used when you defined the element. Here are some examples of valid names:

```
grossPay
Sum
X1
_dateOfCompletion
Name_Of_Employer
Employee
CalculateArea
Find_Last_Known_Address
displayData
```

Visual Basic.NET uses keywords to identify certain structural elements of a program.

Keywords include:

```
And     ByRef      ByVal    Case
Catch   Class      Dim      Else
Error   For        If       Inherits
Me      Module     New      Optional
Step    Unicode    Throw    To
Try     WithEvents While    Xor
```

There are over 75 keywords in VB.NET, and the complete list can be found in Visual Basic's Help by searching for "keyword." These keywords are *reserved* by the language, and if you use them as identifiers, you will get syntax errors. However, VB.NET allows you to use keywords as identifiers if you surround every reference to them with square brackets. Thus, the following are valid identifiers:

```
[Single]
[Date]
```

However, with a little work, you can probably think of other identifiers which convey the same meaning without using keywords. For example:

```
Unmarried    instead of    [Single]
aDate        instead of    [Date]
```

Program Structure

VB.NET programs consist of a collection of modules that are used to divide the program into a set of related "chunks." The functionality in each module should be related in some way. For example, one module might contain input and output functions. Another module might contain the business logic of the application. For example, a payroll application would contain functions to calculate gross pay, deductions, and net pay.

Each module in the application is named and resides in a file with a **.vb** extension. It begins with the keyword **Module**, followed by the module name. It ends with the keywords **End Module**.

```
Module module-name

End Module
```

In VB.NET, console applications (which are discussed in the first half of this book) must have a subroutine called **Main**. This defines the *entry point* of the program, or the point at which execution begins.

VB.NET Code Files Use .vb Suffix

VB6 programmers should notice that all VB.NET code files now use the suffix .vb, regardless of the contents of the file.

Code Example

As an example, the following module consists of a collection of subroutines that display different information. It is saved in a file called **DisplayModule.vb** and found in the folder **UsingModules#**.

```
' DisplayModule.vb
' Collection of related procedures

Imports System

Module DisplayModule

    Public Sub SayHello()
        Console.WriteLine("Hello!")
    End Sub

    Public Sub RambleOn()
        Console.WriteLine("How now brown cow...")
    End Sub

    Public Sub SayGoodbye()
        Console.WriteLine("Goodbye!")
    End Sub

End Module
```

Any code in the application can call the **Public** procedures defined in **DisplayModule**. We will describe the exact purpose of **Public**, as well as other access modifiers, in Chapter 6. As an example, the following module contains the application's **Main** subroutine, which calls the subroutines defined in **DisplayModule** to print data to the screen.

```
' UsingModules.vb
' Example of using procedures in another module

Module UsingModules

    Sub Main()
        SayHello()
        RambleOn()
        SayGoodbye()
    End Sub

End Module
```

In addition to the module construct defined above, VB.NET supports the creation of other structural units, including classes and forms. These are somewhat similar to modules, and we will address them in detail in Parts 3 and 4 of this book.

Data Types

Data in a computer is fundamentally just a string of bits. Associating a *data type* with the bits allows them to be interpreted as meaningful data. These are some examples of data types in VB.NET:

- **Char** (a 16-bit character)
- **Integer** (a 32-bit integer)
- **Single** (a 32-bit floating-point number)

The same bit string can represent different data, depending on the type. For example, this is the bit string representation of the integer 43 in VB.NET:

```
0000 002B (hex)
0000 0000 0000 0000 0000 0010 1011 (binary)
```

That same bit string as a **Single** is 6.025583E-44. Many programming errors can occur if bits were assigned using one format and later interpreted using another.

You can group the simple data types provided by VB.NET into several categories, including integer types, floating-point types, decimal types, character types, and Boolean types. We will examine the more sophisticated data types available in VB.NET in Chapter 7.

Variant Data Type Is Not Supported in VB.NET

VB6 programmers should note that the data type **Variant** is no longer supported. The default data type for variables that are not typed is **Object**. The **Object** data type is discussed in Chapter 7.

Integer Types

Integer data types represent whole numbers (for example, 43, -13). VB.NET supports four types of integer data: **Byte**, **Short**, **Integer**, and **Long**. The **Byte** data type is *unsigned,* which means that it can represent only *non-negative* data values. The remaining data types (**Short**, **Integer**, and **Long**) are *signed,* which means that they can represent both *positive* and *negative* values. The integer data types can be differentiated from each other by the amount of memory they require. The fewer bits they consume, the smaller the range of values they support.

The .NET Framework Class Library provides data types that are equivalent to the Visual Basic.NET data types. These types are located in the **System** namespace. **System** also defines data types that have no equivalent *native* VB.NET data type, but are available to all .NET programming languages. These are the data types used in the MSIL intermediate language. It is because of this common type system that .NET languages can interoperate with each other. Table 4–1 lists the integer types and their bit sizes.

TABLE 4–1   *VB.NET and .NET Integer Data Types*

VB.NET Data Type	Size	.NET Data Type
Byte	8 bits	System.Byte
not available	8 bits	System.Sbyte
Short	16 bits	System.Int16
not available	16 bits	System.UInt16
Integer	32 bits	System.Int32
not available	32 bits	System.UInt32
Long	64 bits	System.Int64
not available	64 bits	System.UInt64

Floating-Point Types

Floating-point data types represent numbers that contain fractional parts (for example, 3.14159, 2.8345E-8), in which an exponent can be used to represent very large and very small values. VB.NET supports two types of floating-point numbers, **Single** and **Double**. Table 4–2 lists the floating-point data types available in VB.NET and in the .NET **System** namespace.

TABLE 4–2	*VB.NET and .NET Floating-Point Data Types*	
VB.NET Data Type	**Size**	**.NET Data Type**
Single	32 bits	System.Single
Double	64 bits	System.Double

Microsoft has adopted the IEEE 754 floating-point standard for all .NET languages. This standard specifies that certain operations, which previously might have produced errors, now create special values. These values include the following:

- **Not-a-Number** (also known as **NaN**) values result from dividing 0.0 by 0.0.
- **Positive infinity** values result from dividing a non-zero positive value by 0.0.
- **Negative infinity** values result from dividing a non-zero negative value by 0.0.

The program **IEEE754** demonstrates that VB.NET recognizes these special values and can interact with them in a way that will not cause errors. The program declares two variables, assigns them values, and then prints the result of various division operations.

Code Example

```
' Example of IEEE 754 special values

Imports System

Module IEEE754

    Sub Main()
        Dim top As Single
```

```
        Dim bottom As Single

        top = 0
        bottom = 0
        Console.WriteLine(top / bottom)

        top = 18
        bottom = 0
        Console.WriteLine(top / bottom)

        top = -18
        bottom = 0
        Console.WriteLine(top / bottom)
    End Sub

End Module
```

If you execute the program above, the output illustrates that VB.NET does not generate an error when these operations are performed. Instead, a special value is returned and can be interpreted by any element that interacts with **Single** values. The output of the program looks like this:

```
NaN
Infinity
-Infinity
```

VB.NET also provides functions to test for these values; these functions will be introduced in a subsequent chapter.

Decimal Types

Floating-point data types suffer from a precision problem. They can keep only about 7 digits of accuracy for **Single** values and 15 digits of accuracy for **Double** values. They also suffer from the inherent problems of using the binary numbering system for internal representation. In binary, 1/10 is a repeating decimal. Therefore, a floating-point data type is not typically acceptable for most financial calculations. To solve this problem, VB.NET has a **Decimal** data type that can represent any decimal number with up to 28 digits of precision. It does this by representing the number as a signed integer, scaled by a variable power of 10 (for example, the number of digits to the right of the decimal point). Table 4–3 provides information about the **Decimal** type:

TABLE 4–3	VB.NET and .NET Decimal Data Types	
VB.NET Data Type	**Size**	**.NET Data Type**
Decimal	128 bits	System.Decimal

Currency Data Type Is Not Supported in VB.NET

VB6 programmers should note that the data type **Currency** is no longer supported. It has been replaced by the **Decimal** data type.

Character Types

VB.NET has two data types to represent character data: **Char** and **String**. The **Char** data type represents a single 16-bit Unicode character. The **String** data type represents a sequence of zero or more 16-bit Unicode characters. Table 4–4 lists the character data types available in VB.NET and the .NET Common Language Runtime.

TABLE 4–4	*VB.NET and .NET Character Data Types*	
VB.NET Data Type	**Size**	**.NET Data Type**
Char	16 bits	System.Char
String	80 bits + 16 bits for each character	System.String

Boolean Types

VB.NET uses the **Boolean** data type to represent the values **False** and **True**. This data type is used to represent on/off, yes/no, and true/false values. Table 4–5 provides information about Boolean types:

TABLE 4–5	*VB.NET and .NET Boolean Data Types*	
VB.NET Data Type	**Size**	**.NET Data Type**
Boolean	8 bits	System.Boolean

Date/Time Types

The date/time data type in VB.NET is **Date**. This data type can hold dates, times, or dates and times. Table 4–6 provides more information about the date/time type:

TABLE 4–6	*VB.NET and .NET Date Data Types*	
VB.NET Data Type	**Size**	**.NET Data Type**
Date	8 bytes	System.DateTime

Date Data Type Has New Internal Representation in VB.NET

VB6 programmers should note that the data type **Date** has changed its underlying representation from 4 bytes to the 8-byte .NET DateTime format. There are no implicit conversions between **Date** and **Double** in VB.NET.

Data Type Ranges

Code
Example

A simple program, **DataRanges**, that demonstrates the range of each data type is shown below. It uses the **MinValue** and **MaxValue** properties of each data type to display the type's range.

```
' Displays the ranges of each data type

Imports System

Module DataRanges

    Sub Main()
        Console.WriteLine("Byte Range: {0} to {1}", _
                        Byte.MinValue, Byte.MaxValue)
        Console.WriteLine("Short Range: {0} to {1}", _
                        Short.MinValue, Short.MaxValue)
        Console.WriteLine("Integer Range: {0} to {1}", _
                        Integer.MinValue, Integer.MaxValue)
        Console.WriteLine("Long Range: {0} to {1}", _
                        Long.MinValue, Long.MaxValue)
        Console.WriteLine("Decimal Range: {0} to {1}", _
                        Decimal.MinValue, Decimal.MaxValue)
        Console.WriteLine("Single Range: {0} to {1}", _
                        Single.MinValue, Single.MaxValue)
        Console.WriteLine("Double Range: {0} to {1}", _
                        Double.MinValue, Double.MaxValue)
        Console.WriteLine("Char Range: {0} to {1}", _
                        Char.MinValue, Char.MaxValue)
        Console.WriteLine("Strings have no range")
        Console.WriteLine("Boolean Range: {0} to {1}", _
                        Boolean.FalseString, _
                        Boolean.TrueString)
        Console.WriteLine("Date Range: {0} to {1}", _
                        Date.MinValue, Date.MaxValue)

    End Sub

End Module
```

Output from the program is shown below. The format has been adjusted to make it more readable.

```
Byte Range: 0 to 255
Short Range: -32768 to 32767
Integer Range: -2147483648 to 2147483647
Long Range: -9223372036854775808 to 9223372036854775807
Decimal Range: -79228162514264337593543950335 to
    79228162514264337593543950335
Single Range: -3.402823E+38 to 3.402823E+38
Double Range: -1.79769313486232E+308 to
    1.79769313486232E+308
Char Range:   to ?
Strings have no range
Boolean Range: False to True
Date Range: 1/1/0001 12:00:00 AM to 12/31/9999 11:59:59 PM
```

Literals

A *literal* is a value that is explicitly written in code. For example, in the line below, 13 is a literal and 'a' is a variable.

```
a = 13
```

VB.NET assumes that literals are typed. The type is determined based on the way the value is expressed. If a literal is expressed without any suffix, its data type is either **Integer**, **Double**, **String**, or **Boolean**. For example:

```
12          ' is an Integer literal
9.2         ' is a Double literal
"Hi"        ' is a String literal
False       ' is a Boolean literal
```

To explicitly specify the data type of a literal, you must use a suffix to indicate its type. Table 4–7 lists the allowable suffixes.

TABLE 4–7   *VB.NET Literal Suffixes*

Literal Data Type	Suffix
Short	S
Integer	I
Long	L
Single	F
Double	R
Decimal	D
Char	C

The examples below illustrate the use of suffixes to specify the data types of literals:

```
12S          ' is a Short literal
12I          ' is an Integer literal
12L          ' is a Long literal
12F          ' is a Single literal
12R          ' is a Double literal
12D          ' is a Decimal literal
"L"C         ' is a Char literal
```

VB.NET typically assumes that integer-type (**Short, Integer**, and **Long**) literals are decimal (base 10) representation for numbers. However, a programmer can specify that literals values are octal (base 8) or hexadecimal (base 16). This is done by prefacing the literal with an ampersand (&) and the letter O (for octal) or H (for hexadecimal). For example:

```
70           ' is a base 10 literal
&O70         ' is a base 8 (octal) literal - which equals
             '          the base 10 value 56
&H70         ' is a base 16 (hexadecimal) literal - which
             '          equals the base 10 value 112
```

Date literals are somewhat different. They require the use of a special character (#) to mark both the beginning and the ending of the literal string. This string may include a date, a time, or a date and a time. If any values are omitted, the following defaults are used:

- If the date is omitted, 1/1/0001 is assumed.
- If the time is omitted, 12:00:00 AM is assumed.

These rules apply to **Date** literals:

- A date value may not be two digits.
- A time value may be specified using either a 24-hour or a 12-hour value. If the time omits the AM or PM, it is assumed to be a 24-hour time.
- If a time value omits either the minutes or the seconds, 0 is assumed.
- If a time value omits both the minutes and the seconds, then AM or PM must be specified.

Examples of **Date** literals include the following:

```
#9/5/1958#
#9/5/1958 10:02:00 AM#
#10:02:00 AM#
```

A neat feature of the Visual Studio source code editor is that it can assist you in making your code easy to read via automatic indentation, case correction, etc. However, the side effect of this feature is that you may not be able to enter this date literal:

```
#23:00#
```

without the text editor reformatting it to this:

```
#11:00:00 PM#
```

To stop the editor from doing this, you can use the menu Tools | Options to change the settings for the Text Editor in VB. You must turn off Pretty listing of code. (See Figure 4–1.) However, you should think twice about turning it off because the editor will no longer assist you with indenting, changing the case of text you type, etc.

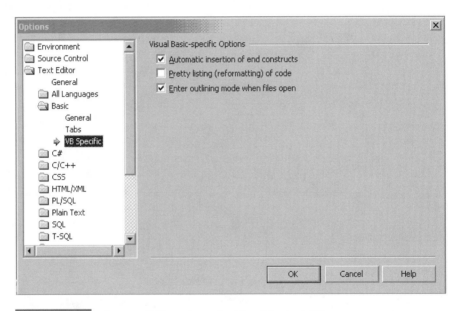

FIGURE 4–1   *Turning off "Pretty listing" in Visual Studio.NET.*

Variables

A programming language allows programmers to define variables. These variables are symbolic names that are used to represent data in a program. For example, the variable **id** could hold an employee ID number, and the variable **pay** could hold an employee's pay rate.

VB.NET programmers generally define variables using one of three techniques. If the variable is defined inside a procedure, it is defined using the **Dim** statement.

```
Sub Main()
   Dim id As Integer
   Dim name As String
   Dim payRate As Decimal
   ...

End Sub
```

The variables **id**, **name**, and **payRate** are local to the subroutine **Main**. That is, they can be referenced only inside that procedure.

VB.NET does not require you to declare each variable using a separate **Dim** statement. Several variables may be declared in one line.

```
Dim grossPay, taxes, netPay As Single
Dim isValid, isWithinRange As Boolean
```

In the case above, **grossPay**, **taxes**, and **netPay** are **Single** variables, and **isValid** and **isWithinRange** are **Boolean** variables.

Multiple Variables, Same Type

VB6 programmers should notice that, when several variables are declared in one statement, they are all of the same type. This was not true in VB6. Only the last variable in the list was of the defined data type. The other variables were **Variants**.

VB.NET automatically *initializes* variables when they are declared. Programmers who have used Visual Basic for a long time can sometimes forget that this is a relatively unique feature among programming languages. Many other languages programming languages leave variables uninitialized when they are declared. This means that they contain garbage (who knows what!) when they are declared. Table 4–8 shows the default values used to initialize variables of different types.

TABLE 4–8 · *Initial Values for Variables*

Variable Type	Initial Value
all integer type variables	0
all floating-point type variables	0.0
Decimal variables	0.0
Char variables	binary 0
String variables	null reference
Boolean variables	False
Date variables	#1/1/0001 12:00:00 AM#

Variables may be explicitly initialized when they are declared. To do this, simply use the assignment statement after the data type to initialize the variable. If a variable is initialized when it is declared, Visual Basic.NET requires that only one variable be declared per statement.

```
Dim unitPrice As Decimal = 12.97

Dim x, y As Integer = 100     ' generates an error
```

Strong Typing

In some programming languages, such as VBScript, you do not declare a data type for variables. These languages are called untyped languages because the interpreter or compiler does not check data types. However, runtime errors will still occur if the value of a variable is inappropriate for an operation.

Most compiled languages are typed. That is, they check the data types of variables when they are used to make sure that the operation is allowed. However, the degree of type-checking varies from language to language. Ada is very strongly typed, and you cannot typically add an integer to a floating-point value. C++ warns if truncation occurs when a numeric value is assigned to a variable and precision will be lost, or if the operation doesn't make sense for the type, it generates an error.

Visual Basic.NET resides somewhere in the middle as a typed language. It introduces a compiler option (**Option Strict**) that can indicate the level of type-checking that should be used. The next two sections show how this option affects a VB.NET program.

OPTION STRICT OFF

Code Example

The program **WithoutOptionStrict** illustrates that, with **Option Strict** set to "off" (which is the default), VB.NET is very flexible about the operations it allows.

```
' Example of Weak Type Checking
' (Option Strict off)

Imports System

Module TypeChecking
   Sub Main()
      Dim someString As String
      Dim someNumber As Integer
      someString = "7"

      ' string-to-integer assignment
      someNumber = someString
      Console.WriteLine("{0}", someString)
      Console.WriteLine("{0}", someNumber)
```

```
      End Sub
End Module
```

VB.NET is able to assign the string containing "7" to the numeric variable. It has performed an implicit conversion for you. Visual Basic was designed as an easy-to-use language, so many "natural" conversions are performed automatically.

OPTION STRICT ON

Code
Example

The program **WithOptionStrict** illustrates that, with **Option Strict** set to "on," VB.NET will not perform most implicit conversions for you and will generate errors instead.

```
' Example of Strong Type Checking
' (Option Strict on)

Option Strict On
Imports System

Module TypeChecking
    Sub Main()
        Dim someString As String
        Dim someNumber As Integer
        someString = "7"

        ' string-to-integer assignment
        someNumber = someString
        Console.WriteLine("{0}", someString)
        Console.WriteLine("{0}", someNumber)
    End Sub
End Module
```

When you compile this program, you receive the error message:

```
"Option Strict disallows implicit conversions from String
to Integer"
```

on this line:

```
someNumber = someString
```

VB.NET generates this error because you are trying to assign a string type to a numeric type.

If **Option Strict** is turned on, the compiler will not necessarily generate error messages on *all* data type mismatches. For example, on numeric assignments, VB.NET is primarily concerned about loss of precision.

```
Dim someFloat As Single
Dim anotherNumber As Integer

' if no loss of precision occurs, "obvious" implicit
' conversions are allowed and the following line is legal
someFloat = 4

' if loss of precision occurs, all implicit conversions
' are disallowed and the following line generates a syntax
' error
anotherNumber = someFloat
```

We discuss many VB.NET conversion functions for simple data types later in this chapter, and we discuss more .NET conversions in Chapter 8.

Constants

When writing code, you are sometimes faced with a decision. For example, assume the local sales tax rate is 8.25 percent. If you are building expressions that include the sales tax rate, how do you represent it? You might choose to represent it as a literal, like this:

```
tax = price * .0825
```

There are two problems with this approach. First, it is difficult to look back and remember that .0825 is the sales tax rate. Second, if the sales tax rate appears in many places in the code and the rate changes, it can be difficult to be sure that you have changed it in every place.

Another approach is to use a variable to represent the sales tax rate. For example,

```
Dim salesTaxRate As Single = .0825
...
tax = price * salesTaxRate
```

The disadvantage of this approach is that, because **salesTaxRate** is a variable, its value might be accidentally (or intentionally!) altered before execution reaches the line that calculates the tax. If the **salesTaxRate** is not changeable, as the use of the literal .0825 suggests, then this approach is risky.

A third approach, the most desirable one, is to use a *constant*. A constant is similar to a variable; it is declared and initialized. However, the compiler generates an error if an attempt is made to change its value.

```
Const salesTaxRate As Single = .0825
...
salesTaxRate = .0850        'error
...
tax = price * salesTaxRate
```

Data Conversions

Frequently, when you are programming, you need to use a value of one data type when a different data type is normally used. This will require that you convert the value expressed in one data type into another data type. VB.NET supports two types of conversions:

- An *implicit* conversion is done silently by the compiler, whenever required.
- An *explicit* conversion occurs when the programmer uses a conversion function.

If **Option Strict** is set to "off," you are instructing the compiler to make implicit conversions in all cases. However, because of the unexpected results, many programmers prefer to set **Option Explicit** to "on" and then control conversions explicitly.

There are a number of rules about conversions, but don't try to memorize them; it is easier to reason from general principles. The basic principle is that it is safe to convert from one type to a "wider" type, such as from **Integer** to **Long** or from **Single** to **Double**. Such a conversion will always be done for you implicitly by the compiler.

But sometimes you will perform a conversion that the compiler cannot determine to be safe. You may know that the possible values for a variable are within an acceptable range, or you may deliberately be willing to accept some loss of precision. In such cases, you can explicitly convert the data type using one of the VB.NET functions or the **System.Convert** class discussed in Chapter 2. See Table 4–9 for a partial list of the conversion functions.

TABLE 4–9	*Type Conversion Options*	
Conversion to...	**VB.NET Conversion Function**	**.NET System.Convert Method**
Byte	CByte	ToByte
Short	CShort	ToInt16
Integer	CInt	ToInt32
Long	CLng	ToInt64
Single	CSng	ToSingle
Double	CDbl	ToDouble
Decimal	CDec	ToDecimal
Char	CChar	ToChar
String	CStr	ToString
Date	CDate	ToDateTime
Boolean	CBool	ToBoolean

For example, with **Option Explicit** set to "on," the first statement of the following is an error. You need to explicitly convert the value.

```
Dim pi As Single = 3.14    ' generates a compiler error
                           ' because 3.14 is a double
Dim pi As Single = CSng(3.14)   ' no error
Dim pi As Single = Convert.ToSingle(3.14) ' no error
```

The first line produces an error message because floating-point literals are always **Double**, unless a type suffix has been applied. You can explicitly convert the value using **CSng** or **Convert.ToSingle** conversion to eliminate the error message. In this case, the conversion loses no precision because the number does not have many significant digits.

Operators

Visual Basic has a set of operators that have been enhanced since VB6. These operators can be classified by the number of operands to which they apply, a property that is sometimes known as operator cardinality.

- *Unary* operators take a single operand. A simple example is unary minus, which changes the sign of a number.
- *Binary* operators are the most common and take two operands. Examples include simple arithmetic operators such as addition and subtraction.

We begin this discussion of operators by exploring the operators for addition, subtraction, multiplication, division, exponentiation, and modulo arithmetic. We then examine the relational operators used to make comparisons between two expressions. Finally, we review the logical and bitwise operators available in VB.NET.

The examples shown in the following section are found in the sample program **OperatorSummary**.

Code Example

Arithmetic Operators

The arithmetic operators may be applied to any of the numerical data types of integer, floating-point, and decimal. The evaluation of any expression will always result in a value that represents the most precise operand. For example, if both operands of a multiply are **Integer**, the result will be **Integer**. However, if one operand is an **Integer** and the other operand is a **Double,** the result will be a **Double** because **Double** is a higher level of precision.

You must be careful with certain mathematical operations. For example, if you multiply two very large numbers together, the result might be so large that it cannot be represented. If an integer operation generates an overflow, by default it will generate a runtime exception of type **OverflowException**. Figure 4–2 shows the configuration options for a typical VB.NET program. You can see that the compiler checks for integer overflows. If you explicitly turn off this check, any overflow bits will be truncated, which will lead to an inaccurate result.

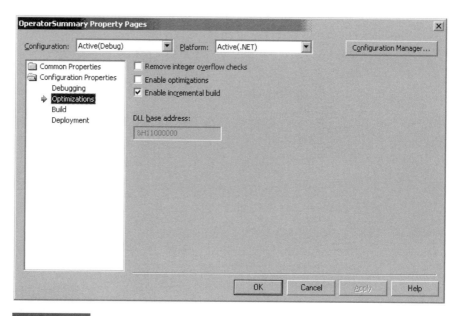

FIGURE 4–2   *Build configuration options for integer overflow checking.*

Floating-point arithmetic is computed according to the rules of IEEE 754 arithmetic discussed earlier in this chapter. Floating-point overflow will produce the special result of positive or negative infinity. Dividing zero by zero will produce the result **NaN**.

The result of decimal arithmetic will also throw an **OverflowException** if the result is too large. If the result is too small, it will be set to zero.

VB.NET provides the unary minus (-) and unary plus (+) for all numeric types. The unary minus negates the operand. The unary plus does not change the value of the operand. For example:

```
Dim n As Integer = 15
Console.WriteLine("(n=15)   -n = {0}", -n)
n = -15
Console.WriteLine("(n=-15) +n = {0}", +n)
Console.WriteLine("(n=-15) -n = {0}", -n)
```

Output from this example is as follows:

```
(n=15)   -n = -15
(n=-15)  +n = -15
(n=-15)  -n = 15
```

VB.NET provides binary arithmetic operators for addition (**+**), subtraction (**-**), multiplication (*****), floating-point division (**/**), and exponentiation (**^**). It also supports binary operators for integer division (****) and remainder (**Mod**) arithmetic. Integer division is defined as the number of times the denominator can be evenly divided into the numerator. The remainder operator is calculated by multiplying the integer quotient by the divisor and subtracting from the original number. The following example shows these operators as they apply to floating point values.

```
Console.WriteLine("2.5 + 1.3 = {0}", 2.5 + 1.3)
Console.WriteLine("2.5 - 1.3 = {0}", 2.5 - 1.3)
Console.WriteLine("2.5 * 1.3 = {0}", 2.5 * 1.3)
Console.WriteLine("2.5 / 1.3 = {0}", 2.5 / 1.3)
Console.WriteLine("2.5 \ 1.3 = {0}", 2.5 \ 1.3)
Console.WriteLine("2.5 Mod 1.3 = {0}", 2.5 Mod 1.3)
Console.WriteLine("2.5 ^ 1.3 = {0}", 2.5 ^ 1.3)
```

Output from this example shows the results of the operations. Because the literals 2.5 and 1.3 are double precision floating-point values, the results of the floating-point division and exponentiation operations show 15 digits of precision.

```
2.5 + 1.3 = 3.8
2.5 - 1.3 = 1.2
2.5 * 1.3 = 3.25
2.5 / 1.3 = 1.92307692307692
2.5 \ 1.3 = 2     ' result is rounded
2.5 Mod 1.3 = 1.2
2.5 ^ 1.3 = 3.29095551083559
```

The same operators can be applied to integer data types. Because the result must be an integer, the result will be truncated if it does not come out even. The rounding will always be in the direction of zero.

```
Console.WriteLine("5 + 3 = {0}", 5 + 3)
Console.WriteLine("5 - 3 = {0}", 5 - 3)
Console.WriteLine("5 * 3 = {0}", 5 * 3)
Console.WriteLine("5 / 3 = {0}", 5 / 3)
Console.WriteLine("5 \ 3 = {0}", 5 \ 3)
Console.WriteLine("5 Mod 3 = {0}", 5 Mod 3)
Console.WriteLine("5 ^ 3 = {0}", 5 ^ 3)
```

The output from the example shows that the only floating-point result is from the floating-point division operator.

```
5 + 3 = 8
5 - 3 = 2
5 * 3 = 15
5 / 3 = 1.66666666666667
5 \ 3 = 1
5 Mod 3 = 2
5 ^ 3 = 125
```

Division by zero for integer types will result in a **DivideByZeroException**. If you happen to divide the largest negative integer by -1, you will get an **OverflowException**, because the most negative number is one greater in magnitude than the most positive number.

You can also apply all of these operators to the **Decimal** data type with similar results.

```
Console.WriteLine("5.25D + 3.24D  = {0}", 5.25D + 3.24D)
Console.WriteLine("5.25D - 3.24D  = {0}", 5.25D - 3.24D)
Console.WriteLine("5.25D * 3.24D  = {0}", 5.25D * 3.24D)
Console.WriteLine("5.25D / 3.24D  = {0}", 5.25D / 3.24D)
Console.WriteLine("5.25D \ 3.24D  = {0}", 5.25D \ 3.24D)
Console.WriteLine("5.25D Mod 3.24D  = {0}", _
                5.25D Mod 3.24D)
Console.WriteLine("5.25D ^ 3.24D  = {0}", 5.25D ^ 3.24D)
```

Output from this example is as follows:

```
5.25D + 3.24D = 8.49
5.25D - 3.24D  = 2.01
5.25D * 3.24D  = 17.01
5.25D / 3.24D  = 1.6203703703703703703703703704
5.25D \ 3.24D  = 1
5.25D Mod 3.24D  = 2.01
5.25D ^ 3.24D  = 215.434941461855
```

String Operators

VB.NET allows you to use both the addition operator (+) and the concatenation operator (&) to perform string concatenation. Although both work, most VB programmers use the ampersand operator to distinguish string operations from numeric ones.

```
Dim s1 As String = "Hello"
Dim s2 As String = "World"
Dim s3 As String
s3 = s1 & " " & s2' result is Hello World
```

Relational Operators

VB.NET has six operators for making comparisons between expressions. Each operator returns a Boolean value, either **True** or **False**. See Table 4–10 for more information.

TABLE 4–10	*Relational Operators*
Operation	**Returns True if...**
x = y	x equals y
x <> y	x is not equal to y
x < y	x is less than y
x <= y	x is less than or equal to y
x > y	x is greater than y
x >= y	x is greater than or equal to y

These operators are most often used when comparing two values to decide what course of action should be taken. We will discuss the use of statements such as **If/Then** and **Do While** in the next chapter. In the meantime, the following example illustrates the use of various relational operators for comparing two values:

```
Console.WriteLine("10 = 5 Is {0}", 10 = 5)
Console.WriteLine("10 <> 5 Is {0}", 10 <> 5)
Console.WriteLine("10 < 5 Is {0}", 10 < 5)
Console.WriteLine("10 <= 5 Is {0}", 10 <= 5)
Console.WriteLine("10 > 5 Is {0}", 10 > 5)
Console.WriteLine("10 >= 5 Is {0}", 10 >= 5)
```

The output from this example is as follows:

```
10 = 5 Is False
10 <> 5 Is True
10 < 5 Is False
10 <= 5 Is False
10 > 5 Is True
10 >= 5 Is True
```

LOGICAL OPERATORS

You can combine Boolean values by using the binary logical operators **And**, **Or**, and **Xor**. The **And** operator returns **True** only if both operands are **True**. The **Or** operator returns **True** if either operand is **True**. You can also use the unary logical operator **Not** to negate, or invert, the operand. For example, if the operand is **True**, then applying **Not** to it will yield **False**. The following truth tables show all possible combinations for the **And** (Table 4–11), **Or** (Table 4–12), **Xor** (Table 4–13), and **Not** (Table 4–14) operators.

TABLE 4–11 | *Truth Table for the And Operator*

operand$_1$	operand$_2$	operand$_1$ And operand$_2$
False	False	False
False	True	False
True	False	False
True	True	True

TABLE 4–12 | *Truth Table for the Or Operator*

operand$_1$	operand$_2$	operand$_1$ Or operand$_2$
False	False	False
False	True	True
True	False	True
True	True	True

TABLE 4–13 | *Truth Table for the Xor Operator*

operand$_1$	operand$_2$	operand$_1$ Xor operand$_2$
False	False	False
False	True	True
True	False	True
True	True	True

TABLE 4–14 | *Truth Table for the Not Operator*

operand$_1$	Not operand$_1$
False	True
True	False

An example of using the VB.NET operators is shown in the following example. It uses an **If/Then** statement to check to see whether the variable **num** is within an acceptable range.

```
If num < minValue Or num > maxValue Then
   Console.WriteLine("Error: number out of range")
End If
```

SHORT CIRCUIT EVALUATION

VB.NET also provides two logical operators, **AndAlso** and **OrElse**, to help evaluate expressions as efficiently as possible. Examine the following example of evaluating an expression:

```
age > 18 And state = "TX"
```

If the value of **age** is less than 18, there is no reason to evaluate the second expression. The only way that **And** can return **True** is if both operands are **True**.

The **AndAlso** operator is used to prohibit the evaluation of the second operand if the result of the expression is known after evaluating the first operand. For example:

```
y <> 0 AndAlso x / y > 3
```

If the value of **y** is equal to 0, the evaluation of the expression stops and the operator returns **False**. In this example, this is the desired behavior to prevent the evaluation of **x / y**, which would return one of the IEEE 754 values.

The truth tables shown in Table 4–15 and Table 4–16 describe the operations of the **AndAlso** and **OrElse** operators based on the value of each operand.

TABLE 4–15   *Truth Table for the AndAlso Operator*

operand$_1$	operand$_2$	operand$_1$ AndAlso operand$_2$
False	not evaluated	False
False	not evaluated	False
True	False	False
True	True	True

TABLE 4–16   *Truth Table for the OrElse Operator*

operand$_1$	operand$_2$	operand$_1$ OrElse operand$_2$
False	False	False
False	True	True
True	not evaluated	True
True	not evaluated	True

BITWISE OPERATORS

VB.NET supports the *bitwise* operators **Not**, **And**, **Xor**, and **Or** for bit manipulation. These operators are similar to the logical operators mentioned above, with one exception. The logical operators require that the operands in the expression are **Boolean** values. The bitwise operators operate upon numeric values.

The unary bitwise **Not** operator performs one's complement arithmetic on the operand. One's compliment "toggles" the bits. For example, if the operand were a 16-bit value that contained all zeros, applying the bitwise **Not** to it would convert it to a 16-bit value that contained all ones.

The bitwise operators **And**, **Or**, and **Xor** operate by comparing bits, one at a time, from two operands. They use the truth tables shown for Boolean values to determine the outcome of each bit comparison. However, you should interpret ones as **True** values and zeros as **False** values. The following example shows the use of bitwise operators:

```
Dim b1, b2 As Byte
b1 = 19      ' Bit pattern of b1 is 0001 0011
b2 = 7       ' Bit pattern of b2 is 0000 0111

' Bit pattern of b1 And b2 is 0000 0011 (or 3)
Console.WriteLine("19 Bitwise And 7 = {0}", b1 And b2)

' Bit pattern of b1 Or b2 is 0001 0111 (or 23)
Console.WriteLine("19 Bitwise Or 7 = {0}", b1 Or b2)

' Bit pattern of b1 Xor b2 is 0001 0100 (or 20)
Console.WriteLine("19 Bitwise Xor 7 = {0}", b1 Xor b2)

' Bit pattern of Not b1 is 1110 1100 (or 236)
Console.WriteLine("Not 19 = {0}", Not b1)
```

Output from the example is as follows:

```
19 Bitwise And 7 = 3
19 Bitwise Or 7 = 23
19 Bitwise Xor 7 = 20
Not 19 = 236
```

ASSIGNMENT OPERATORS

The basic assignment operator (=) in VB.NET is used to assign a value to a variable. It has the following form:

```
variable = expression
```

After the expression is evaluated, its value is assigned to the variable. For example, the following statement assigns the value 8 to the variable **num**.

```
x = 5 + 3
```

One of the newest features of VB.NET is its new *compound assignment* operators that perform arithmetic operations as part of the assignment. Here is an example:

```
x += 2       ' this is equivalent to x = x + 2
x += 2 * b   ' this is equivalent to x = x + (2 * b)
```

There are six new compound assignment operators available in VB.NET. They are demonstrated in the following example:

```
Dim x As Single = 4.6

x *= 2       ' multiply x by 2
x /= 2       ' divide x by 2
x += 2       ' add 2 to x
x -= 2       ' subtract 2 from x
x \= 2       ' divide (integer) x by 2
```

There is also a compound assignment operator for string concatenation. The following expression concatenates an exclamation point to the end of the string contained in the variable **buf**:

```
Dim buf As String = "Hello"
x &= "!"
```

New Operators in VB.NET

VB.NET introduces several operators that are new to VB6 programmers. **OrElse** and **AndAlso** provide shortcut evaluation of conditional expressions. And the assignment operators **^=**, ***=**, **/=**, **\=**, **+=**, **-=**, and **&=** provide shortcuts for common operations.

Operator Precedence

Expressions are built up by combining constants, variables, and operators. When evaluating expressions, the VB.NET compiler follows rules as to the order of operations, and these rules are summarized in the *precedence* table shown in Table 4–17. This table shows the VB.NET operators in order of precedence, from highest to lowest, and includes a few operators we have not discussed yet.

TABLE 4–17   *Operator Precedence in VB.NET*

Category	Operators
Exponentiation	^
Negation	-
Multiplication and division	* /
Integer division	\
Modulo (remainder) arithmetic	Mod
Addition, subtraction, string concatenation	+ - + (string)

TABLE 4–17	Operator Precedence in VB.NET (continued)
Category	**Operators**
String concatenation	&
Comparison	= <> < <= > >= Like Is TypeOf..Is
Negation	Not
Logical/Bitwise conjunction	And AndAlso
Logical/Bitwise disjunction	Or OrElse Xor

A simple example of precedence is addition and multiplication. According to the precedence table, multiplication is done before addition. If you want the order done another way, you must use parentheses to override the standard order. Here is a simple example:

```
x = 5 * 8 + 13        ' multiply first so result is 53
x = 5 * (8 + 13)      ' add first so result is 105
```

As a practical matter, you should learn to use a few of the most common precedence rules. Good use of precedence allows clearer code. Don't feel that you must memorize all of the precedence rules. When in doubt, put parentheses in your expressions.

Console I/O

In Chapter 2, we briefly discussed how to perform simple I/O using the .NET class **Console** and the methods **ReadLine** and **WriteLine**. In this section, we examine console I/O in more detail.

Input

The **ReadLine** method from the **Console** class in the **System** namespace is the primary input method. It is used to read a line of data from the standard input device. The user must press the Enter key before the input is sent to your program. **ReadLine** returns the string that the user typed, up to but not including the carriage return / line feed. Because **ReadLine** always returns a **String,** you must use the conversion functions discussed earlier to convert the data that is entered to the proper data type.

```
Dim inputBuffer As String
Dim payRate As Decimal
Dim hrsWorked As Single
```

```
Console.WriteLine("Enter Pay Rate: ")
inputBuffer = Console.ReadLine()
payRate = CDec(inputBuffer)

Console.WriteLine("Enter Hours Worked: ")
inputBuffer = Console.ReadLine()
hrsWorked = CSng(inputBuffer)
```

Output

The **Console** class in the **System** namespace supports two simple methods for performing output:

- **WriteLine** writes a string followed by a new line character.
- **Write** writes just the string without the new line character.

If you have several values to display, you can use the string concatenation operator **&** to build an output string. If some of the values are not strings, you must convert them to strings. You can do this using the **ToString** method, which exists because all data types in VB.NET are actually subtypes of **System.Object**. **ToString** returns the string representation of any data type. We will discuss the class **System.Object** in Part 3, where you will also see how to override **ToString** for your own custom data types.

```
Dim x As Integer = 24
Dim y As Integer = 5
Dim z As Integer = x * y
Console.Write(x.ToString() & " times " & y.ToString())
Console.WriteLine(" is " + z.ToString())
```

The output (all on one line) of this example is as follows:

```
24 times 5 is 120
```

PLACEHOLDERS

A more convenient way to build an output string is to use *placeholders*, such as {0}, {1}, and so on, in an output string to indicate where actual data should appear. An equivalent way to code the output shown above is as follows:

```
Console.WriteLine("{0} times {1} is {2}", x, y, z)
```

The program **ConsoleIO** demonstrates more sophisticated I/O than we have seen thus far.

```
' Demonstrates input and output functions

Imports System

Module ConsoleIO

    Sub Main()
```

```
        Dim inputBuffer As String
        Dim empID As Integer
        Dim name As String
        Dim payRate As Decimal
        Dim hrsWorked As Single

        ' Read in employee ID
        Console.Write("Enter ID: ")
        inputBuffer = Console.ReadLine()
        empID = CInt(inputBuffer)

        ' Read in name
        Console.Write("Enter Name: ")
        name = Console.ReadLine()

        ' Read in pay rate
        Console.Write("Enter Pay Rate: ")
        inputBuffer = Console.ReadLine()
        payRate = CDec(inputBuffer)

        ' Read in hours worked
        Console.Write("Enter Hours Worked: ")
        inputBuffer = Console.ReadLine()
        hrsWorked = CSng(inputBuffer)

        ' Calculate gross pay
        Dim grossPay As Decimal
        grossPay = hrsWorked * payRate

        ' Print results
        Console.Write("EmpID: {0}   Name: {1}    ", _
                    empID, name)
        Console.WriteLine("Pay: {0}", grossPay)
    End Sub

End Module
```

The program prompts the user for the data using the **Write** method. By using **Write**, the user can enter data directly after the colon is displayed. If the **WriteLine** method had been used, the user enters data on the next line. The **ReadLine** method is used to read a set of data of various types. If the user enters bad input data, an exception will be thrown. We will address this problem in Chapter 9. A sample script of the program session is shown below:

```
Enter ID: 12
Enter Name: Brenda
Enter Pay Rate: 22.50
Enter Hours Worked: 41.75
EmpID: 12   Name: Brenda   Pay: 939.375
```

If you examine the output, you will notice that the pay is not formatted like currency. It is also displayed with too many digits to the right of the decimal, even though the data type of the gross pay variable is **Decimal**. To fix this, we must learn how to format the output of specific variables.

FORMATTING OPTIONS

Placeholders used in the **Write** and **WriteLine** methods may contain formatting information. There are three types of output formatting:

1. Width specification {n,w}, where **n** is the placeholder number and **w** is the width (positive for right justification and negative for left justification). If the width specified is not large enough for the value, it will be ignored.
2. Format specification {n:S}, where **n** is the placeholder number and **S** is a format string.
3. Width and format specification {n,w:S}, where **n** is the placeholder number, **w** is the width, and **S** is a format string.

The format characters that are used are shown in Table 4–18.

TABLE 4–18	*Format Characters*	
Character	**Meaning**	**Notes**
D	Decimal integer	Can only be used with integer values
E	Exponential notation	
F	Fixed-point	
G	General (E or F)	
N	Number with embedded commas	Can only be used with integer values
X	Hexadecimal	
C	Currency (locale specific)	

You can use the width-only specification to build tabular output. In the following example, the name is displayed left-justified in a field ten characters wide, followed by a space, and then the age is displayed right-justified in a field three digits wide.

```
Console.WriteLine("{0,-10} {1,3}", name, age)
```

If the **WriteLine** were placed in a loop, the output might resemble this:

```
Mary       103
Ralph       32
Betty       24
Jessie       1
```

The format specification is used frequently to make numeric output more readable. Specifically, it is very useful to make sure that floating-point values and decimal values are displayed with the desired number of digits after the decimal place.

```
Dim productName As String = "BBQ Ribs (1 lb)"
Dim price As Single = 8.5

Console.WriteLine("{0} is priced at $" _
                & "{1,-8:F2}", productName, price)
Console.WriteLine("{0} is priced at $" _
                & "{1,8:F2}", productName, price)
Console.WriteLine("{0} is priced at " _
                & "{1,8:C}", productName, CDec(price))
```

In this example, the first and second **WriteLine** calls display a floating-point variable. The number 2 following the format specifier F indicates the number of digits to the right of the decimal point that should be displayed. The dollar sign is part of the output string. In the third **WriteLine**, the value is displayed as a decimal value and the dollar sign is part of the formatting. The output of the program above would look like this:

```
BBQ Ribs (1 lb) is priced at $8.50
BBQ Ribs (1 lb) is priced at $    8.50
BBQ Ribs (1 lb) is priced at    $8.50
```

The **Currency** format character "C" formats output in a manner appropriate for currency, including using a currency symbol. Currency formatting is specific to a *locale*. The default locale is the United States, and the currency symbol is the dollar sign ($). Working with other locales is beyond the scope of this book. If globalization issues are of interest to you, you may wish to study the documentation of the **System.Globalization** namespace.

The program **FormattingOptions** illustrates the use of various numeric formats. Specifically, it compares the use of different floating-point format codes.

Code
Example

```
' Displays various options for output formatting

Module FormattingOptions

    Sub Main()
        Console.WriteLine("{0,36:D}", Integer.MaxValue)
        Console.WriteLine("{0,36:N0}", Integer.MaxValue)
        Console.WriteLine("{0,36:N4}", Integer.MaxValue)
        Console.WriteLine("{0,36:X} (hex)", Integer.MaxValue)

        Console.WriteLine("{0,36:F}", 2 ^ 60)
        Console.WriteLine("{0,36:G}", 2 ^ -60)
        Console.WriteLine("{0,36:F26}", 2 ^ -60)
```

```
        Console.WriteLine("{0,36:E26}", 2 ^ -60)
    End Sub

End Module
```

The following represents the output of the program. Each value is displayed right-justified in a field 36 characters wide.

```
                          2147483647
                       2,147,483,647
                   2,147,483,647.0000
                            7FFFFFFF  (hex)
           1152921504606847000.00
                  8.67361737988404E-19
       0.00000000000000000086736174
   8.6736173798840355000000000000E-019
```

A Practical Example

To demonstrate the use of variables, operators, and expressions in a practical example, we will build a VB.NET program that computes accumulations in an Individual Retirement Account with annual deposits and compound interest. The program will accept the following inputs:

- Annual Deposit = A
- Interest Rate = R
- Number of Years = N

The following formula assumes that a deposit is made at the end of each year and that interest is compounded annually:

$$\text{Total Accumulation} = A * ((1 + R)^N - 1) / R$$

This program can be found in **SavingsCalculator**.

Code Example

```
' Computes the total accumulated in a savings account
' when a deposit is made at the end of each year to the
' account and the interest is compounded annually

Imports System

Module SavingsCalculator

    Sub Main()
        Dim depositAmount As Decimal
        Dim interestRate As Single
        Dim numYears As Integer

        Console.Write("Enter amount of deposit: ")
        depositAmount = CDec(Console.ReadLine())

        Console.Write("Enter interest rate: ")
```

```
        interestRate = CSng(Console.ReadLine())

        Console.Write("Enter number of years: ")
        numYears = CInt(Console.ReadLine())

        Dim endingValue As Decimal
        endingValue = depositAmount * _
              (((1 + interestRate) ^ numYears) - 1) / _
              interestRate

        Console.WriteLine("Ending Value = {0:C}", _
                          endingValue)
    End Sub

End Module
```

The following shows the output of one run:

```
Enter amount of deposit: 1000
Enter interest rate: .07
Enter number of years: 20
Ending Value = $40995.49
```

Summary

This chapter discussed the fundamental issues of VB.NET programming. We discussed the simple data types available in VB.NET and examined how they relate to the underlying .NET Common Type System. We examined the syntax for defining variables and constants. We looked at the operators available to a VB.NET programmer for the formulation of complex expressions. We surveyed the data conversion functions that are available natively in Visual Basic, as well as those that are part of the .NET Framework Class Library. We concluded by examining console I/O in more detail. In Chapter 7, we will look at other data types available in VB.NET.

Control Structures

Visual Basic.NET provides a variety of control structures commonly found in languages that support structured programming. In this chapter, we examine these control structures, which include If/Then/Else statements, Select statements, While loops, Do loops, and For loops. If you are experienced with any structured programming language, you should be able to breeze through this chapter. If you are at an early stage in your programming career (or if you're a college student), you should find the step-by-step descriptions and example programs very helpful.

Conditional Statements

Programmers use conditional statements to alter the order in which statements are executed. For example, "If the age of the diner is less than 12, the price of the buffet is $4.50; otherwise, the price of the buffet is $9.95." Decisions are represented in a flowchart by using a diamond symbol (see Figure 5–1).

If/Then Statement

The simplest form of the **If/Then** statement in VB.NET is used to execute a statement, or set of statements, when a condition is true:

```
If conditional-expression Then
    statement(s)
End If
```

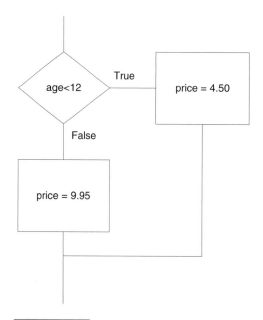

Flowchart representation of a decision.

The statement must begin with the keyword **If.** The *conditional-expression* must evaluate to either **True** or **False,** and the keyword **Then** must follow the expression. Any statements that are to be executed must appear on separate lines. Finally, the **If** is terminated by the keyword **End If.**

```
' Salaried employees are always paid for 40 hours
If employeeType = "Salaried" Then
   grossPay = 40 * payRate
End If
```

The conditional expression may use any of the relational operators discussed in Chapter 4. In addition, the keywords **And, Or,** and **Not** may be used to express compound conditions.

```
' Medical expenses are reimbursed if the patient's
' insurance is in force and the deductible is met
If insuranceInForce And deductibleToDate > 1000 Then
   fullyCovered = True
   coveredAmount = cost
End If
```

In the preceding example, **insuranceInForce** is a **Boolean** variable that either contains the value **True** or **False.**

If a single statement is to be executed when the condition is **True,** it may be placed on the same line as the keyword **Then** and the **End If** must be omitted.

```
If employeeType = "Salaried" Then grossPay = 40 * payRate
```

However, this shortened version does not lend itself well to maintainability. For example, if in the future, a second statement must be added to the condition, then the statement must be moved to its own line, the new statement must be added, and an **End If** must be added. A better pre-emptive approach is to always have an **End If** statement. The code is more readable and can be changed more easily.

In the following program, the user is prompted for an employee's pay rate, whether the employee is eligible for the bonus program, and the number of hours the employee worked that week. The program calculates the employee's gross pay. It pays overtime after 40 hours, and if the employee is eligible for the bonus program *and* has worked at least 40 hours that week, it adds a 5 percent bonus to the gross pay. This program can be found in **Payroll\Version1.**

```
' Payroll calculator
' Calculates pay based on an hourly rate and hrs worked.
' Pays overtime after 40 hours.  If employees are eligible,
' it also calculates a 5% pay bonus for employees that
' work at least 40 hours.

Imports System

Module Payroll

    Sub Main()
        Dim payRate As Decimal
        Dim hrsWorked As Single
        Dim eligibleForBonus As String
        Dim grossPay As Decimal

        Console.Write("Enter pay rate: ")
        payRate = CDec(Console.ReadLine())
        Console.Write("Eligible for bonus (y/n): ")
        eligibleForBonus = Console.ReadLine()
        Console.Write("Enter hours worked: ")
        hrsWorked = CSng(Console.ReadLine())

        grossPay = hrsWorked * payRate
        If hrsWorked > 40 Then
            grossPay += (hrsWorked - 40) * 0.5 * payRate
        End If
        If hrsWorked >= 40 And eligibleForBonus = "y" Then
            grossPay *= 1.05                ' a 5% bonus
```

```
      End If
      Console.WriteLine("Gross pay: {0,8:c}", grossPay)
   End Sub

End Module
```

If this program is run several times varying the input, the output for each run might resemble the following:

```
Enter pay rate: 10
Eligible for bonus (y/n): n
Enter hours worked: 40
Gross pay:   $400.00

Enter pay rate: 10
Eligible for bonus (y/n): y
Enter hours worked: 40
Gross pay:   $420.00

Enter pay rate: 10
Eligible for bonus (y/n): n
Enter hours worked: 45
Gross pay:   $475.00

Enter pay rate: 10
Eligible for bonus (y/n): y
Enter hours worked: 45
Gross pay:   $498.75
```

If/Then/Else Statement

An **If/Then/Else** statement can be used to indicate that different actions must be taken depending on whether a condition is true:

```
If conditional-expression Then
   statement(s)
Else
   statement(s)
End If
```

The statement is similar to the **If/Then** statement. However, the keyword **Else** must appear between two sets of statements. If the *conditional-expression* is true, the first set of statements is executed. If the *conditional-expression* is false, the second set of statements is executed.

```
If employeeType = "Salaried" Then
   grossPay = 40 * payRate
Else
   grossPay = hoursWorked * payRate
End If
```

The following program is a slightly different version of the previous payroll program. The user is prompted for an employee's type, pay rate, and the number of hours worked that week. The program calculates the employee's gross pay using different formulas based on the employee's type. If the employee is salaried, the program always calculates pay based on 40 hours of work, regardless of the actual number of hours. If the employee is paid hourly, the program pays based on actual hours worked and includes overtime after 40 hours. This program can be found in **Payroll\Version2.**

```
' Payroll calculator - version 2

' Calculates pay.  If the employee is salaried, they
' are always paid for 40 hours.  If they are hourly,
' they are paid for each hour worked and are eligible
' for overtime after 40 hours.

Imports System

Module Payroll

    Sub Main()
        Dim employeeType As String
        Dim payRate As Decimal
        Dim hrsWorked As Single
        Dim grossPay As Decimal

        Console.Write( _
            "Enter employee type (salaried/hourly): ")
        employeeType = Console.ReadLine()
        Console.Write("Enter pay rate: ")
        payRate = CDec(Console.ReadLine())
        Console.Write("Enter hours worked: ")
        hrsWorked = CSng(Console.ReadLine())

        grossPay = hrsWorked * payRate
        If employeeType = "hourly" Then
           If hrsWorked > 40 Then
              grossPay += (hrsWorked - 40) * 0.5 * payRate
           End If
        Else
           If hrsWorked >= 40 Then
              grossPay *= 1.05        ' 5% bonus
           End If
        End If
    End Sub

End Module
```

If this program is run several times varying the input, the output for each run might resemble the following:

```
Enter employee type (salaried/hourly): salaried
Enter pay rate: 20
Enter hours worked: 50
Gross pay:  $800.00

Enter employee type (salaried/hourly): hourly
Enter pay rate: 10
Enter hours worked: 10
Gross pay:  $100.00

Enter employee type (salaried/hourly): hourly
Enter pay rate: 10
Enter hours worked: 45
Gross pay:  $475.00
```

Sometimes, decisions are not simply yes/no decisions. Rather, a decision must be made between a set of possible choices. In this case, **If/Then** statements may be nested. When statements are nested, each **If/Then** statement must be considered as being unique and each requires its own **End If.**

```
If studentClassification = "undergraduate" Then
   tuition = creditHours * 80
Else
   If studentClassification = "graduate" Then
      tuition = creditHours * 90
   Else
      If studentClassification = "nondegree" Then
         tuition = creditHours * 65
      End If
   End If
End If
```

An **If/Then/ElseIf** statement is often used in place of the nested **If/Then** statements shown above. The advantage of the **If/Then/ElseIf** is that it is designed to select between a set of choices, and an **End If** is not required for each condition.

```
If conditional-expression Then
   statement(s)
ElseIf conditional-expression Then
   statement(s)
[ElseIf conditional-expression Then
   statement(s) ...]
[Else
   statement(s)]
End If
```

The statement is similar to the **If/Then** statement. However, the keyword **ElseIf** is used for additional conditions. (**ElseIf** must be one word!) You have the option of using only one **Else** condition when none of the other conditions in the **If** statement is true.

An example of the **If/Then/ElseIf** statement is demonstrated in the program **TuitionCalculator.** This tuition calculation program uses a student's classification and the number of credit hours in which he is enrolled to determine his tuition cost. It also demonstrates the use of the **Exit Sub** statement. This statement exits the subroutine. Because the subroutine in this example is **Main**, the program also ends.

```
Imports System

Module TuitionCalculator

    Sub Main()
        Dim classification As String
        Dim creditHours As Integer
        Dim tuition As Decimal

        Console.WriteLine("Enter classification")
        Console.Write( _
          "   (undergraduate, graduate, nondegree): ")
        classification = Console.ReadLine()
        Console.Write("Enter credit hours: ")
        creditHours = CInt(Console.ReadLine())

        If classification = "undergraduate" Then
            tuition = creditHours * 80
        ElseIf classification = "graduate" Then
            tuition = creditHours * 90
        ElseIf classification = "nondegree" Then
            tuition = creditHours * 60
        Else
            Console.WriteLine("Invalid classification!")
            Exit Sub          ' exits the program
        End If
        Console.WriteLine( _
          "Tuition for {0} {1} hours is {2,8:C}", _
          creditHours, classification, tuition)
    End Sub

End Module
```

If this program is run several times varying the input, the output for each run might resemble the following:

```
Enter classification
   (undergraduate, graduate, nondegree): undergraduate
Enter credit hours: 18
```

```
Tuition for 18 undergraduate hours is $1,440.00

Enter classification
   (undergraduate, graduate, nondegree): graduate
Enter credit hours: 12
Tuition for 12 graduate hours is $1,080.00

Enter classification
   (undergraduate, graduate, nondegree): nondegree
Enter credit hours: 6
Tuition for 6 nondegree hours is $360.00

Enter classification
   (undergraduate, graduate, nondegree): senior
Enter credit hours: 15
Invalid classification!
```

Select Case Statement

Another type of decision construct is the **Select** statement. It is used to select from among a set of values:

```
Select Case expression
Case case clause
   statement(s)
[Case case clause
   statement(s)]
[Case Else
   statement(s)]
End Select
```

The statement must begin with the keyword **Select Case.** The *expression* is evaluated, and based on its value, the statements in one **Case** may be executed. The **Select Case** is terminated by the keyword **End Select.**

The selection process begins with the first **Case** in the sequence. If one of the values matches the expression, that **Case** is executed and execution resumes at the bottom of the select statement. There can also be a **Case Else,** which is executed if no other **Case** matches the value of the expression. If no **Case Else** is coded, and the value does not match any of the **Case** conditions, execution "falls through" to the line of code following the select statement.

The following code can be found in the program **CityStateSelection:**

```
Select Case city
Case "Dallas", "Ft. Worth", "Nacogdoches"
   state = "Texas"
Case "Shawnee", "Tulsa"
   state = "Oklahoma"
Case "Los Angeles", "San Francisco", "Stockton"
   state = "California"
```

Code
Example

```
Case "Baltimore", "Greenbelt", "St. Mary's City"
   state = "Maryland"
Case Else
   state = "*Unknown*"
End Select
```

In the preceding example, the variable **city** is examined. If it matches any string in the first case, then **state** is assigned the value "Texas." If it does not match any string in the first case, then the second case is examined. This continues through each case. If no case is matched, then the **Case Else** is executed.

The case clause may list individual values or a range of values, or it may use the **Is** keyword to build a relational expression.

```
Select Case departmentNumber
Case 10, 12 to 15
   building = "Main Center"
Case 11, 18
   building = "Building A"
Case 17, Is >= 19
   building = "Building B"
Case Is < 10
   building = "Building C"
End Select
```

In this example, the numeric variable **departmentNumber** is evaluated. Any department with a number less than 10 is located in Building C. Departments 10, 12, 13, 14, and 15 are located in the Main Center. Departments 11 and 18 are located in Building A. And Department 17, along with Departments 19, 20, 21, etc., are located in Building B.

IIf Function

VB.NET has an ***immediate If*** function that deserves mention at this point. It is used to evaluate a Boolean condition and use the result to select one of two values.

```
value = _
    IIf(conditional-expression, expression1, expression2)
```

The first parameter to the **IIf** is a *conditional-expression* that is evaluated. The second parameter is the value that is returned if the conditional expression is **True.** The third parameter is the value that is returned if the conditional expression is **False.**

```
insuranceCost = IIf(insOption = "Y", 125, 0)
```

In this example, the cost of insurance is $125 if **insOption** contains a "Y" (yes) or $0 if it doesn't.

Looping Statements

When programmers write code to do some task repetitively, some form of looping construct is needed. We have already seen code that calculates a single employee's gross pay. However, it is more likely that the program would have to calculate gross pay for a set of employees. In this case, a loop would be needed.

There are two basic types of loops. Figure 5–2 shows an example of flowcharting a *pre-test* loop. The condition is tested before the body of the loop is executed. It is possible, using a pre-test loop, that the body of the loop might never be executed.

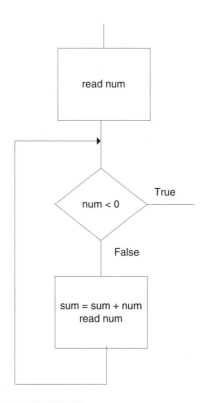

FIGURE 5–2   *Flowchart representation of a pre-test loop.*

Figure 5–3 shows an example of flowcharting a *post-test* loop. The condition is tested after the body of the loop is executed. The number of iterations in a post-test loop is at least one.

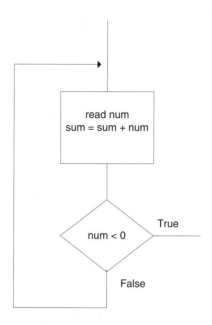

FIGURE 5–3   *Flowchart representation of a post-test loop.*

VB.NET provides several forms of looping constructs that include both pre-test and post-test abilities.

Do/Loop Statement

The **Do/Loop** is the primary looping construct used in VB.NET. There are two forms of the **Do/Loop**. The first version, the **Do While** statement, is used to loop through a set of code *while* some condition is true.

```
Do While conditional-expression
    statement(s)
Loop
```

The *conditional-expression* is evaluated when it is encountered. If the expression evaluates to **False,** the loop is exited immediately; otherwise, if the expression evaluates to **True,** the statements in the loop body are executed. Control then returns to the top of the loop, and the expression is re-evaluated. This continues until the expression evaluates to **False,** and then the loop exits. Execution then continues with the statements after the keyword **Loop.**

Code Example

In the program **SumOfNumbers\Version1,** a set of numbers is read and summed until a negative value is entered:

```
' SumOfNumbers - Version 1

Imports System

Module SumOfNumbers

    Sub Main()
        Dim num, sum As Integer

        Console.WriteLine("CALCULATE SUMS OF NUMBERS")
        Console.WriteLine("Enter a negative number to stop!")
        Console.WriteLine()

        ' Read the first number
        Console.Write("Enter a number: ")
        num = CInt(Console.ReadLine())

        ' If it isn't negative, process it
        Do While num >= 0
            sum += num
            ' Read the next number
            Console.Write("Enter a number: ")
            num = CInt(Console.ReadLine())
        Loop
        Console.WriteLine("The sum is {0}", sum)
    End Sub

End Module
```

This program, found in **SumOfNumbers\Version1,** reads the first number and, assuming it isn't negative, adds it to the sum. It then asks for another number and repeats the process.

The **Do Until** statement can be used to loop through a set of code *until* some condition is true.

```
Do Until conditional-expression
    statement(s)
End Loop
```

Code Example

With the exception of the fact that the termination condition of the **Do Until** statement is opposite of the **Do While** statement, these statements are identical. **SumOfNumbers\Version2** represents an alternate version of the program written using the **Do Until** statement. It looks like this:

```
' SumOfNumbers - Version 2

Imports System

Module SumOfNumbers

    Sub Main()
        Dim num, sum As Integer

        Console.WriteLine("CALCULATE SUMS OF NUMBERS")
        Console.WriteLine("Enter a negative number to stop!")
        Console.WriteLine()

        ' Read the first number
        Console.Write("Enter a number: ")
        num = CInt(Console.ReadLine())

        ' If it isn't negative, process it
        Do Until num < 0
            sum += num
            ' Read the next number
            Console.Write("Enter a number: ")
            num = CInt(Console.ReadLine())
        Loop
        Console.WriteLine("The sum is {0}", sum)
    End Sub

End Module
```

Both the **Do While** and **Do Until** are pre-test loop constructs. The minimum number of times that the loop might be executed is zero. This is why a pre-read (one that appears before the condition) is necessary. If the first number the user enters is negative, we want to immediately stop the loop.

Post-Test Loops

There are post-test versions of the **Do While** and **Do Until** statements. In these versions, the condition is placed after the **Loop** keyword instead of the **Do** keyword.

```
Do
    statement(s)
Loop {While | Until} conditional-expression
```

Code Example

The following program, found in **LeapYear,** calculates whether a given year is a leap year. Any year evenly divisible by 4 is a leap year except those years that are also evenly divisible by 100. An exception to this rule is this: If the year is evenly divisible by 400, it is a leap year. After the program determines whether the year is a leap year, the user is given the opportunity to try another year.

```
' Leap year calculator

Imports System

Module LeapYear

    Sub Main()
        Dim year As Integer
        Dim goAgain As String

        Do
            Console.Write("Enter a year: ")
            year = CInt(Console.ReadLine())
            If year Mod 4 = 0 And _
              (year Mod 100 <> 0 Or year Mod 400 = 0) Then
                Console.WriteLine("{0} is a leap year", year)
            Else
                Console.WriteLine("{0} is not a leap year", _
                    year)
            End If

            Console.Write("Do you want to try another (y/n)? ")
            goAgain = Console.ReadLine()

        Loop While goAgain = "y"
    End Sub

End Module
```

If you run the program, you might end up with output that resembles the following:

```
Enter a year: 1900
1900 is not a leap year
Do you want to try another (y/n)? y
Enter a year: 1995
1995 is not a leap year
Do you want to try another (y/n)? y
Enter a year: 1996
1996 is a leap year
Do you want to try another (y/n)? y
Enter a year: 2000
2000 is a leap year
Do you want to try another (y/n)? n
```

Exiting Do/Loops Prematurely

Any **Do/Loop** may be exited prematurely by using the **Exit Do** statement. When this statement is executed, execution is immediately transferred to the first statement following the **Loop** keyword.

For example, the preceding program could be modified to check for years that are less than 0. If the program detects this condition, it could stop accepting input.

```
Do
    Console.Write("Enter a year: ")
    year = CInt(Console.ReadLine())
    If year < 0 Then
        Console.WriteLine("Invalid year... terminating!")
        Exit Do
    End If

    ' Calculate whether the year is a leap year and
    ' print the results

    Console.Write("Do you want to try another (y/n)? ")
    goAgain = Console.ReadLine()

Loop While goAgain = "y"
```

While Statement

Another version of a pre-test While loop can be found in VB.NET. This **While** statement has roots in earlier versions of VB (before the **Do/Loop** statement existed). It has been retained for compatibility reasons, and you should be familiar with it because you will find that some programmers prefer it.

```
While conditional-expression
    statement(s)
End While
```

This statement functions exactly like its corresponding **Do/Loop** statement. However, instead of terminating with an **End While,** the exit statement that works with this statement is **Exit While.**

End While Terminates a While Loop in VB.NET, Not Wend

Programmers familiar with the While statement in previous versions of Visual Basic should note that the end of the While statement is now End While. In VB6, it was Wend.

Code
Example

A quick example program that demonstrates this statement is found below. You can also find it in **EvenOrOdd.** It reads a set of integers and determines whether the number is odd or even. If the number is zero, it terminates. Notice that it uses a condition of **True** in the **While** loop. This means that the loop is an *infinite* loop. If it did not provide some type of premature exit, it would execute until the computer was shut down or until the user interrupted its execution using the Task Manager.

```
' EvenOrOdd

Imports System

Module EvenOrOdd

    Sub Main()
        Dim number As Integer          '

        While True
            ' Read the number
            Console.WriteLine("Enter a number(0 to stop): ")
            number = CInt(Console.ReadLine())

            ' Process the number
            If number = 0 Then
                Exit While
            ElseIf number Mod 2 = 0 Then
                Console.WriteLine("{0} is even", number)
            Else
                Console.WriteLine("{0} is odd", number)
            End If
        End While
    End Sub

End Module
```

Output from the program above might look like this:

```
Enter a number (0 to stop): 5
5 is odd
Enter a number (0 to stop): -5
-5 is odd
Enter a number (0 to stop): 4
4 is even
Enter a number (0 to stop): 103
103 is odd
Enter a number (0 to stop): 888
888 is even
```

For/Next Statement

The **For/Next** statement is a looping construct that is used when the number of times that the body of the loop executes is fixed.

```
For counter = start-value To end-value [By increment]
   statement(s)
 Next [counter]
```

The **For/Next** statement initializes the counter variable to a starting value. If the increment value is positive, the loop executes if the counter is <= the ending value. If the increment is negative, the loop executes if the counter is >= the ending value. (If the increment is omitted, it is assumed to have the value 1.)

Code
Example

For example, the following program asks the user how many numbers she has to accumulate. It then calculates the sum of the numbers. This program is found in **SumOfNumbers\Version3.**

```
' SumOfNumbers - Version 3

Imports System

Module SumOfNumbers

    Sub Main()
        Dim count, index, num, sum As Integer

        Console.WriteLine("CALCULATE SUMS OF NUMBERS")
        Console.WriteLine()

        ' Determine how many numbers there are
        Console.Write("How many numbers will you enter? ")
        count = CInt(Console.ReadLine())

        ' Read and process the numbers
        For index = 1 To count
            Console.Write("Number: ")
            num = CInt(Console.ReadLine())
            sum += num
        Next
        Console.WriteLine("The sum is {0}", sum)
    End Sub

End Module
```

Loops can be designed to iterate backwards by using a negative increment value:

```
For index = 10 To 1 Step -1
   Console.WriteLine("{0}... ", index)
```

```
Next
Console.WriteLine("Blastoff!")
```

Loops can be designed to iterate using some increments larger than 1:

```
For year = 1776 To 2038 Step 4
   Console.WriteLine("{0} is an election year", year)
Next
```

The **For** statement supports the **Exit For** statement to exit early from a **For** loop. When the **Exit For** statement is encountered, control is immediately transferred to the statement following the **Next**. For example:

```
For i = 1 To 100
   Console.WriteLine("Enter choice (Q to stop): ")
   answer = Console.ReadLine()
   If answer = "Q" Or answer = "q" Then Exit For

   ' calculations go here
Next
' Exit For comes here
```

Code Example

The program **LuckyGuess** selects a random number between 1 and 10 and gives the user three chances to "guess" the number. Hints such as "Too low" and "Too high" are displayed after each guess if the user is unsuccessful.

This program uses three functions we have not discussed yet. The **Rnd()** function calculates a random number between 0 and 1. To scale it to a number in a specified range, you must use the following formula:

Int (lowerbound + Rnd() * upperbound)

Int truncates the fractional part of the number. For example, if we wanted random numbers in the range 1 to 4, we would have to scale the random number (see Table 5–1):

TABLE 5–1	
Value Desired	**Approximate Rnd() Range**
1	0 – .25
2	.25 – .5
3	.5 – .75
4	.75 – 1

Most computer languages, including VB.NET, provide a library routine for calculating random numbers. However, the algorithm generates *pseudo-random* numbers. The numbers that are returned from the function are always in the same sequence if the same *seed* is used. To generate different sequences each time the program is executed, you must initialize the generator by calling the **Randomize()** function.

```
Imports System

Module LuckyGuess

    Sub Main()
        Dim randomNumber As Integer
        Dim chance, guess As Integer

        ' Initialize the random number generator
        Randomize()
        ' Calculate a random number between 1 and 10
        randomNumber = Int(1 + 10 * Rnd())

        ' Give the user three chances
        For chance = 1 To 3
            ' Get their guess
            Console.WriteLine("Enter guess #{0}: ", chance)
            guess = CInt(Console.ReadLine())

            ' Determine how accurate their guess was
            If guess = randomNumber Then
                Console.WriteLine( _
                    "Congratulations! You found it!")
                Exit For
            ElseIf guess < randomNumber Then
                Console.WriteLine("Too low!")
            Else
                Console.WriteLine("Too high!")
            End If
        Next
        Console.WriteLine( _
            "The number was {0}", randomNumber)
    End Sub

End Module
```

One possible set of output from running this program is shown here:

```
Enter guess #1:
6
Too high!
Enter guess #2:
1
Too low!
Enter guess #3:
2
Too low!
The number was 4
```

Another possible set of output from running this program could be:

```
Enter guess #1:
7
Too high!
Enter guess #2:
3
Congratulations! You found it!
The number was 3
```

Visual Basic also supports a **For/Each** statement that can be used to examine items in a collection. However, we will defer a discussion on that topic until Chapter 6.

Summary

This chapter discussed the basic control structures in VB.NET. We examined several programs that utilized various versions of the **If/Then/Else** statement, as well as the **Select** statement. These statements provide the cornerstone of most simple decision logic in Visual Basic.NET, and you will find it very useful to be comfortable using the different forms of the statements.

We have also examined several programs that utilize looping constructs. We have seen that some loops terminate based on the evaluation of some condition (**Do/Loop** and **While**), while other loops perform iterations for a fixed number of intervals (**For/Next**). We also discussed alternative ways of prematurely exiting the various loops using the various forms of **Exit** (**Exit Do**, **Exit For**, and so on).

The next chapter discusses how to organize larger programs into smaller sections of code called procedures for ease of maintenance and increased reusability.

Procedures

Visual Basic.NET provides programmers with several ways to organize their code. Thus far, we have seen that a VB.NET program can consist of a collection of modules. These modules, in turn, are broken down into smaller pieces called procedures. Two of the most common types of procedures are subroutines and functions. Subroutines perform specific tasks. Functions perform specific tasks and then return a value. These procedures are typically defined in the following ways:

- *By a programmer*
- *By the Visual Basic language*
- *By the .NET framework*
- *By a third-party component*

This chapter examines how a programmer can use subroutines and functions to break apart a larger program into smaller, more manageable units of code. It then introduces the concept of properties. Chapter 8 examines some of the predefined procedures available to a VB.NET programmer. Object-oriented programming, in which data and procedures are grouped together in objects, is another technique for breaking an application into smaller units of code, and we will examine this approach in Part 3 of the book.

Subroutines

A *subroutine* is a collection of logically related statements that performs specific tasks. So far in this book, we have seen that console programs have the subroutine **Main,** which represents the starting point of the application. This is a special subroutine and must be named **Main.** Most other subroutines, however, are named by the programmer to describe the task that the subroutine performs. For example, a collection of statements that displays data on the screen might be named **DisplayData.**

The simplest subroutines begin with the keyword **Sub**, followed by the name of the subroutine and a set of parentheses. Subroutines must end with the line **End Sub.** Between the two, the body of the subroutine is defined. For example, a simple subroutine to display help on the console can be coded as follows:

```
Sub DisplayHelp()
    Console.WriteLine("HELP: Press P to play,")
    Console.WriteLine("      O to set options,")
    Console.WriteLine("      H for help,")
    Console.WriteLine("      and Q to quit.")
End Sub
```

The subroutine can be invoked (or called) by another code segment in the program whenever its services are needed. This subroutine is invoked by specifying the name of the subroutine followed by an empty set of parentheses.

```
DisplayHelp()
```

You'll often find that a subroutine needs data to perform its task. This data can be passed to the subroutine when it is called if the subroutine defines a list of *parameters*. Parameters represent placeholders for data that is passed into the procedure. Each time the subroutine is called, the parameter might have a different value.

A parameter list is defined by declaring variables within the parentheses of the function header. For example, a simple subroutine that displays a welcome string that includes a user's name can be coded as follows:

```
Sub DisplayWelcome(ByVal name As String)
    Console.WriteLine("Welcome {0}", name)
    Console.WriteLine("Would you like to play a game?")
End Sub
```

In this example, the parameter **name** is defined as a **String.** The keyword **ByVal** at the beginning of the declaration means that the original value passed in will not change. (We will discuss more about **ByVal** in the next section.)

The statement that invokes the subroutine passes values to the parameters enclosed in parentheses. These values are often called arguments. The **DisplayWelcome** subroutine could be invoked by any of the following statements:

```
DisplayWelcome("Dana")

DisplayWelcome("Bob")

Dim someName As String
someName = Console.ReadLine()
DisplayWelcome(someName)
```

If you examine the previous calls to the subroutine, you will notice that both literals and variables can be used as arguments. If the argument is a variable, the variable name does not have to match the parameter name.

A subroutine can be passed several values. In this case, the parameter list contains several declarations separated by commas. As an example, the subroutine **DisplaySummary** defined below writes summary game information to the console. It displays information in a standard format, but the values it displays must be passed to it when it is invoked.

```
Sub DisplaySummary(ByVal name As String, _
  ByVal numPoints As Integer, ByVal playingTime As Integer)

    Console.WriteLine("Game Summary:")
    Console.WriteLine("   Name:        {0}", name)
    Console.WriteLine("   Points:      {0}", _
              numPoints)
    Console.WriteLine( _
              "   Playing Time: {0} minutes", playingTime)

End Sub
```

The following examples illustrate different ways that the **DisplayTotals** subroutine can be invoked:

```
DisplaySummary("Dana", 125975, 2)


Dim playerName As String
Dim points, gameTime As Integer
. . .
DisplaySummary(playerName, points, gameTime)
```

New Syntax for Calling Subroutines in VB.NET

VB6 programmers must note that parentheses are now required on all subroutine calls. The keyword Call can still be placed in front of the procedure name you want to call, but is not needed.

Functions

A *function* is a collection of logically related statements that perform a specific task and return a value. For example, a procedure named **DisplayData** would probably be implemented as a subroutine because it simply displays data. However, a procedure named **CalculateSalesTax** would probably be implemented as a function because its goal is to calculate and return a value.

The simplest function begins with the keyword **Function**, followed by the name of the function, a set of parentheses, and a return-type specification. Functions must end with the line **End Function.** Between the two, the body of the function is defined. The returned value is specified using a **Return** statement. For example, a simple function to return the value 5 can be coded as follows:

```
Function GetFive() As Integer
    Return 5
End Sub
```

Functions Return an Object if Type Not Specified

The return type of a function in VB.NET is assumed to be an Object unless otherwise specified. Typically, you will specify a return type.

A function is invoked by specifying the name of the function followed by a list of arguments enclosed in parentheses. If no arguments are to be passed, the parentheses are still required.

Because a function returns a value, it must be accommodated for in the calling statement. For example, in the following code, the variable x receives the value (5) returned from the function.

```
Dim x As Integer
x = GetFive()
```

In the following code, the value returned from the function is displayed by the call to the **WriteLine** method.

```
Console.WriteLine("Num = {0}", GetFive())
```

More often, however, functions are more complicated than **GetFive.** They are passed values, which are used in calculating the return values. For example, a function that calculates gross pay given a pay rate and hours worked can be coded as follows:

```
Function CalculatePay(ByVal payRate As Decimal, _
 ByVal hrsWorked As Single) As Decimal

   Dim grossPay As Single
   grossPay = hrsWorked * payRate
   Return grossPay
End Function
```

The **CalculateGrossPay** function can be invoked by any of the following statements:

```
pay = CalculateGrossPay(9.75, 40)

pay = CalculateGrossPay(p, h)

Console.WriteLine("Tax = {0:C}", CalculateSalesTax(p, h))
```

New Return Syntax for Returning Values from Functions in VB.NET

VB6 programmers should note that values are returned from functions in VB.NET using the new Return keyword. However, the VB6 technique of assigning the return value to the name of the function still works.

Example: A Game of Chance

Code Example

The following **GameOfChance** program illustrates the use of simple subroutines and functions. When the program begins, the system prompts the player for her name. The player can then play the game, see how many points she currently has, and quit.

The game is a simple game of chance. The player can accumulate from one to seven points each time she takes a turn. The number of points she receives is calculated using a random number generator. But there is risk. If the number 3 is generated, the player loses all points gained up to that point.

```
Imports System

' This import is for the random number generator
Imports Microsoft.VisualBasic.VBMath

' This import is for time information
Imports Microsoft.VisualBasic.DateAndTime
```

```
Module GameModule

    ' This is the main controlling point of the game. It
    ' prompts the player for their name, accepts commands,
    ' and causes the appropriate action to occur.
    Sub Main()
        Dim cmd, playerName As String
        Dim points, playTime As Integer
        Dim startTime, curTime As Date

        ' Prompt for the player name
        Console.Write("What is your name? ")
        playerName = Console.ReadLine()

        ' Get the starting time of the game
        startTime = Now      ' Now returns the current date/time

        ' Display a welcome message
        DisplayWelcome(playerName)

        ' Repeat until the player chooses quit
        Do While True
            ' Prompt for the command
            Console.Write("Command (H for help): ")
            cmd = Console.ReadLine()

            ' Process the command
            Select Case cmd
                Case "P", "p"
                    points = Play(points)

                Case "S", "s"
                    ' calculate how long the game has lasted
                    ' (in minutes)
                    playTime = DateDiff( _
                     DateInterval.Minute, startTime, Now)
                    DisplaySummary(playerName, points, playTime)

                Case "H", "h"
                    DisplayHelp()

                Case "Q", "q"
                    Exit Sub

                Case Else
                    Console.WriteLine( "Error: unknown command.")
            End Select
```

```
    Loop

End Sub

' Display a welcome message
Sub DisplayWelcome(ByVal name As String)
    Console.WriteLine("Welcome {0}", name)
    Console.WriteLine("Let's play!
End Sub

' Display summary info about the game
Sub DisplaySummary(ByVal name As String, ByVal _
 numPoints As Integer, ByVal playingTime As Integer)

    Console.WriteLine("Game Summary:")
    Console.WriteLine("    Name:          {0}", name)
    Console.WriteLine("    Points:        {0}", numPoints)
    Console.WriteLine("    Playing Time: {0} minutes", _
     playingTime)

End Sub

' Display help
Sub DisplayHelp()
    Console.WriteLine("HELP: Press P to play,")
    Console.WriteLine("      S for game summary,")
    Console.WriteLine("      H for help,")
    Console.WriteLine("      and Q to quit.")
End Sub

' Play receives the player's starting points and returns
' the number of points the player has at the end.
Function Play(ByVal startingPoints As Integer) As Integer
    Dim newPoints As Integer

    ' Randomize initializes the random number generator
    Randomize()
    ' Generate a random number
    newPoints = Rnd() * 6 + 1

    Console.Write("You received a {0}", newPoints)

    ' Check to see how this value impacts the player
    If newPoints = 3 Then
        ' lose all points
        Console.WriteLine( "... too bad! Lose all points!")
        Return 0
    Else
```

```
        ' add points to starting points
        Console.WriteLine("... good choice!")
        Return startingPoints + newPoints
      End If
    End Function

End Module
```

Sample output from this program is shown here:

```
What is your name? Dana
Welcome Dana
Let's play!
Command (H for help): H
HELP: Press P to play,
      S for game summary,
      H for help,
      and Q to quit.
Command (H for help): P
You received a 3... too bad! Lose all points!
Command (H for help): P
You received a 2... good choice!
Command (H for help): P
You received a 7... good choice!
Command (H for help): P
You received a 4... good choice!
Command (H for help): P
You received a 2... good choice!
Command (H for help): P
You received a 7... good choice!
Command (H for help): S
Game Summary:
   Name:         Dana
   Points:       22
   Playing Time: 1 minutes
Command (H for help): Q
```

Pass-by-Value Versus Pass-by-Reference

Programming languages have different mechanisms for passing parameters to procedures. So far, we have seen the keyword **ByVal** used when passing parameters to procedures. In VB.NET, using the keyword **ByVal** on a parameter declaration indicates that the parameter is passed *by value.* Typically, these values are pushed onto a program stack when the procedure is called, and the called function obtains its own independent copy of the values. Any changes made to these values will not be propagated back to the calling program.

The alternative to **ByVal** is **ByRef,** which indicates the parameter is passed *by reference.* Before we can discuss how **ByVal** and **ByRef** work, we must discuss the difference between value types and reference types in .NET. This is because **ByVal** works one way for value types and a different way for reference types.

Some terminology will help us in the following discussion. Storage is allocated on the program stack for a procedure's parameters. This storage area is known as the *activation record.* It is popped (disposed of) when the procedure is no longer active. The *formal parameters* of a procedure are the parameters as seen within the method. They are provided storage in the activation record. The *actual arguments* of a procedure are the expressions between commas in the parameter list of the procedure call.

In VB.NET, ByVal is the Default

VB6 programmers should be aware that ByVal is the default parameter-passing mechanism in VB.NET; ByRef was the default mechanism in VB6.

Value Types Versus Reference Types

In .NET, value types are all the numeric types, the **Char** type, the **Boolean** type, enumerations, and structures. These types are allocated on the program stack. When you assign one value type to another, the system copies all the memory from one location to the other (called a *member-wise,* or *shallow,* copy). For example:

```
Dim num1, num2 As Integer
num2 = 7

num1 = num2    ' all bits in num2 are copied into num1
```

In this case, we have two copies of an integer. This is sufficient for these types.

Reference types are typically class types or arrays. When a variable references a class type, it does just that, it *references* it. The memory for the object is actually stored in a separate location called the heap. When one reference type is assigned to another, the system also performs a *shallow* copy. For example:

```
Public Class Point
    Dim x, y As Integer
End Class
```

. . .

```
Dim p1, p2 As Point        ' creates 2 reference variables
p1 = New Point    ' creates a Point object; p1 references
it
p1 = New Point    ' creates a Point object; p2 references
it

p1 = p2    ' all bits in p2 are copied into p1, which
causes
           ' p1 and p2 to reference the same Point object
```

In this case, we now have only one copy of the **Point** object. .NET will clean up (or perform garbage collection) and release the memory automatically for the **Point** object that **p1** originally referenced.

Don't worry about understanding class types yet. Although we have seen classes from the .NET library, we won't concentrate on building our own classes until Part 3 of this book.

Using ByVal Parameters with Value Types

The **ByVal** keyword is used to indicate that a parameter is passed to a procedure by value. For value types, this means that the parameter receives a *copy* of the actual argument. Therefore, if the parameter is changed in the procedure, it is not reflected in the calling routine. The program **ByVal_vs_ByRef** illustrates a number of scenarios involving passing by value and by reference.

```
Sub Test1(ByVal num As Integer)
   num += 15
   Console.WriteLine("inside sub: num = {0}", num)
End Sub
```

The following code calls this procedure:

```
Dim someNumber As Integer = 33

Console.WriteLine("someNumber = {0}", someNumber)
Test1(someNumber)
Console.WriteLine("inside main (after): someNumber = {0}",
_
 someNumber)
```

The output is as follows:

```
someNumber = 33
inside sub: num = 48
inside main (after): someNumber = 33
```

In this example, you can see that the argument **someNumber** was not modified when it passed to the procedure **Test1** by value, although the local copy (**num**) in **Test1** was modified.

Using ByRef Parameters with Value Types

The **ByRef** keyword is used to indicate that a parameter is passed to a procedure by reference. For value types, this means that the parameter receives a *reference* to the actual argument. Therefore, if the parameter is changed in the procedure, it is reflected in the calling routine. For example:

```
Sub Test2(ByRef num As Integer)
    num += 15
    Console.WriteLine("inside sub: num = {0}", num)
End Sub
```

The following code calls this procedure:

```
Dim someNumber As Integer = 33

Console.WriteLine("someNumber = {0}", someNumber)
Test2(someNumber)
Console.WriteLine("inside main (after): someNumber = {0}", _
 someNumber)
```

The output is as follows:

```
someNumber = 33
inside sub: num = 48
inside main (after): someNumber = 48
```

In this example, you can see that the argument **someNumber** was modified when it passed to the procedure **Test1** by reference. If a literal (for instance, the number 33) is passed to a procedure, the literal argument is not changed.

ByVal Behavior Different for Value and Reference Types

Pay close attention to the ByVal examples for value and reference types. You will see that ByVal does not prohibit actual arguments from being modified if they are reference types.

Using ByVal Parameters with Reference Types

The **ByVal** keyword works differently when the actual argument is a reference type. This is because the parameter receives a *copy of the reference* to the object as opposed to a *copy of the object!* Therefore, if the object that is referenced by the parameter is altered in the procedure, it is reflected in the calling routine. For example, let's define a class called **Point.** Any **Point** object contains two data values, **x** and **y.**

```
Class Point
    Public x, y As Integer
End Class
```

A **Point** object can be passed to a procedure, as shown here:

```
Sub Test3(ByVal p As Point)
    p.x += 13
    p.y += 99
    Console.WriteLine("inside sub: p = {0},{1}", p.x, p.y)
End Sub
```

The following code calls this procedure:

```
Dim aPoint As New Point()
aPoint.x = 100
aPoint.y = 0

Console.WriteLine("aPoint = {0},{1}", aPoint.x, aPoint.y)
Test3(aPoint)
Console.WriteLine("inside main (after): aPoint = {0},{1}", _
    aPoint.x, aPoint.y)
```

The output is as follows:

```
aPoint = 100,0
inside sub: p = 113,99
inside main (after): point = 113,99
```

In this example, you can see that the argument **aPoint** was modified when it passed to the procedure **Test3** by value. Again, this is because when **aPoint** was passed to the parameter **p** in **Test3**, **p** received a copy of the *reference* to the *same* object that **aPoint** referenced.

However, if the procedure had created a new **Point** object and assigned a reference to it to the parameter **p**, the actual argument **aPoint** would not have known about the new object and would reference the same instance of the **Point** that it did when the procedure was called. For example:

```
Sub Test4(ByVal p As Point)
    p = New Point
    p.x += 13
    p.y += 99
    Console.WriteLine("inside sub: p = {0},{1}", p.x, p.y)
End Sub
```

The following code calls this procedure:

```
Dim aPoint As New Point()
aPoint.x = 100
aPoint.y = 0

Console.WriteLine("aPoint = {0},{1}", aPoint.x, aPoint.y)
Test4(aPoint)
Console.WriteLine("inside main (after): aPoint = {0},{1}", _
 aPoint.x, aPoint.y)
```

The output is as follows:

```
aPoint = 100,0
inside sub: p = 13,99
inside main (after): point = 100,0
```

The **Test3** example illustrates that arguments of a reference type, when passed **ByVal,** can be modified if the corresponding parameter modifies the object that it originally referenced. However, the **Test4** example illustrates that the argument will always reference the same instance of the object after the procedure terminates.

Using ByRef Parameters with Reference Types

The **ByRef** keyword is used to indicate that a parameter is passed to a procedure by reference. For value types, this means that the parameter receives a *reference* to the actual argument. Therefore, if the parameter is changed in the procedure, it is reflected in the calling routine. For example:

```
Sub Test5(ByRef p As Point)
   p = New Point
   p.x += 13
   p.y += 99
   Console.WriteLine("inside sub: p = {0},{1}", p.x, p.y)
End Sub
```

The following code calls this procedure:

```
Dim aPoint As New Point()
aPoint.x = 100
aPoint.y = 0

Console.WriteLine("aPoint = {0},{1}", aPoint.x, aPoint.y)
Test5(aPoint)
Console.WriteLine("inside main (after): aPoint = {0},{1}", _
 aPoint.x, aPoint.y)
```

The output is as follows:

```
aPoint = 100,0
inside sub: p = 13,99
inside main (after): point = 13,99
```

In this example, you can see that the argument **aPoint** references the new **Point** object after the procedure **Test5** returns.

Access, Modules, and Scope

Most large applications are not coded in a single module. Instead, the program is broken into a series of logical units that are coded using modules and classes. When this occurs, you must make a decision for each procedure you write as to whether it can be used throughout the program or whether it is a private "helper" procedure.

Access Control

VB.NET addresses this problem by allowing you to specify an access type for each variable, procedure, and type declaration. Using the keyword **Public** indicates that the item is "global" and can be accessed from anywhere in the application. Using the keyword **Private** indicates that the item can be accessed only from within the module in which it is defined. For example, a public subroutine could be declared as follows:

```
Public Function AddTwo(ByVal x As Integer, ByVal y As _
  Integer) As Integer

   Dim retVal As Integer
   retVal = x + y
   Return retVal

End Sub
```

This would indicate that this subroutine is generic and usable throughout the application.

VB.NET supports several types of access: **Public, Protected, Private, Friend,** and **Protected Friend.** These will be addressed again in more detail in Part 3 of the book.

Scope

Until now, we have concentrated primarily on declaring variables with a procedure and passing them as parameters to other procedures. However, the issue of variable and procedure declarations is more complicated than what we have demonstrated.

Code Example

The following example, found in **ScopeExample,** is designed to let us explore the concept of scope. Scope relates to the visibility of names. When the name references a variable, scope also refers to the lifetime of the variable and the lifetime of the referenced object.

```
Module Module2
    ' x is accessible from any procedure within this module
    ' but is not accessible outside of this module; it is
    ' created when the application begins and remains as
    ' long as the application is executing
    Private x As Integer

    ' y is accessible from any procedure in the application;
    ' it has the same lifetime as x because it is a
    ' module-level variable
    Public y As Integer

    ' z has the same characteristics as x;  variables created
    ' via Dim at the module level are private
    Dim z As Integer

    ' AAA can be called by any procedure in the application
    Public Sub AAA()
        ...
    End Sub

    ' BBB can only be called by a procedure in this module
    ' because it was defined as private
    Private Sub BBB()
        ...
    End Sub

    ' CCC can be called by any procedure in the application;
    ' if an access specifier is omitted for procedures in a
    ' module, they are public
    Sub CCC()
        ...
    End Sub

    ' Foo has the same characteristics as AAA and CCC
    Public Sub Foo()
        ...
```

```
      End Sub

End Module
```

Now, we can introduce another module. This module has public and private class types, as well as a public procedure with the same name as a procedure in **Module2.**

```
' The type Rect is accessible from the entire application
Public Class Rect
    Public top, left, bottom, right As Integer
End Class

Module Module3
    ' The type Point is accessible only from procedures in
    ' this module
    Private Class Point
        Public x, y As Integer
    End Class

    ' Foo is accessible from all procedures in the
    ' application, but has a name conflict with a
    ' procedure in another module
    Public Sub Foo()
        Dim x As New Point()

    End Sub
End Module
```

Finally, we examine whether these scoping rules are true by building a third module to try to access variables and modules from other procedures.

```
Module Module1

    Sub Main()
        x = 100        ' Error: the name x is not declared
        y = 100
        z = 100        ' Error: the name z is not declared

        AAA()
        BBB()          ' Error: the name BBB is not declared
        CCC()

        Foo()          ' Error: the name Foo is ambiguous
        Module2.Foo()
        Module3.Foo()
    End Sub

    Private Sub Test()
        Dim y As Integer
        y = 30
```

```
        Console.WriteLine("{0}", y)    ' Displays 30
    End Sub

End Module
```

As you can see, only the public variables and procedures from other modules are accessible in this module. In addition, when we attempt to reference **Foo,** which has implementations in two different modules, we get an error indicating that the name **Foo** is ambiguous. We must use the module name in the call to **Foo** to resolve the ambiguity.

Finally, in the **Test** subroutine, we see that a local variable can be declared that has the same name as a global variable. In this case, the local variable *hides* the global variable and any reference to the variable name within the procedure is a reference to the local version.

Static

When variables are defined within a procedure, they are local to that procedure. Space for the variables is allocated when the procedure is called and is deallocated when the procedure finishes executing. However, this sometimes has interesting side effects.

For example, the following program found in **StaticExample** illustrates the use two procedures. One function is used to generate a random number in the range 1 to 6. Another subroutine displays the result and labels it with the particular roll number (roll 1, roll 2, etc.).

```
Imports System
Imports System.Math
Imports Microsoft.VisualBasic.VBMath

Module StaticExample

    Private Sub DisplayResults(ByVal roll As Byte)
        Dim rollNum As Integer

        ' Keep track of what roll this is
        rollNum += 1

        ' Display the results
        Console.WriteLine("Roll {0} was a {1}", rollNum, roll)
    End Sub

    Public Function Roll() As Byte
        ' Return a number between 1 and 6  -  Floor is a
        ' System.Math function that truncates the number
        Return Floor(rnd() * 6) + 1
    End Function
```

```
Sub Main()
    Dim n, val As Byte
    For n = 1 To 10
        DisplayResults(Roll())
    Next
End Sub

End Module
```

Output from this program might resemble this:

```
Roll 1 was a 5
Roll 1 was a 4
Roll 1 was a 4
Roll 1 was a 2
Roll 1 was a 2
Roll 1 was a 5
Roll 1 was a 1
Roll 1 was a 5
Roll 1 was a 5
Roll 1 was a 5
```

The first thing you notice when examining the output is that the roll number is always 1. This is because the variable **rollNum** in the subroutine **DisplayResult** is reallocated on the stack each time the program is called. Because it is reallocated, the result is reset to the default value 0 each time. To fix this problem, we must declare the variable using **Static.**

Static variables are allocated when the application begins. They are not reallocated each time a procedure is called. However, they are not accessible outside of the procedure within which they are defined. By changing the declaration of **rollNum** to the following:

```
Static Dim rollNum As Integer
```

and executing the program again, the results might become as follows:

```
Roll 1 was a 5
Roll 2 was a 4
Roll 3 was a 4
Roll 4 was a 2
Roll 5 was a 2
Roll 6 was a 5
Roll 7 was a 1
Roll 8 was a 5
Roll 9 was a 5
Roll 10 was a 5
```

This example shows that the roll number is now working as expected.

In VB6, if all variables declared within a procedure were static, the keyword Static could be placed on the procedure. This is no longer supported. In VB.NET, the keyword Static must be placed on the declaration of each static variable.

Overloading

VB.NET supports a feature related to procedures called *overloading*. Overloading means that many procedures may have the same name as long as the parameter lists differ. This technique provides a programmer with a more natural way of invoking a procedure with different sets of arguments.

For example, if you want to code a set of procedures that can determine the minimum values of two, three, or four integers without overloading, you must code the following:

```
Public Function Min2(ByVal n1 As Integer, ByVal n2 _
 As Integer) As Integer

    Dim smallest As Integer = n1
    If n2 < smallest Then smallest = n2
    Return smallest

End Function

Public Function Min3(ByVal n1 As Integer, ByVal n2 _
 As Integer, ByVal n3 As Integer) As Integer

    Dim smallest As Integer = n1
    If n2 < smallest Then smallest = n2
    If n3 < smallest Then smallest = n3
    Return smallest

End Function

Public Function Min4(ByVal n1 As Integer, ByVal n2 _
 As Integer, ByVal n3 As Integer, ByVal n4 As Integer) _
 As Integer

    Dim smallest As Integer = n1
    If n2 < smallest Then smallest = n2
    If n3 < smallest Then smallest = n3
    If n4 < smallest Then smallest = n4
    Return smallest

End Function
```

In the above example, calls to the corresponding three procedures would be as follows:

```
Console.WriteLine("Min of 2 = {0}", Min2(7, 2))
Console.WriteLine("Min of 3 = {0}", Min3(7, 2, 100))
Console.WriteLine("Min of 4 = {0}", Min4(7, 2, 9, 1000))
```

However, it is much more intuitive if any procedure to calculate minimum values were simply called **Min.** In VB.NET, many procedures may have the same name, as long as they have different *signatures*. Procedures have the same signature if they have the same number of parameters and each corresponding parameter has the same data type. The return type is not included in defining the signature of a procedure. At runtime, the compiler will resolve a given invocation of the procedure by trying to match up the actual arguments with formal parameters. A match occurs if the parameters match exactly or if they can match through an implicit conversion.

To overload procedures in VB.NET, the keyword **Overload** is added to the procedure declaration. The program **OverloadingProcedures** illustrates how three overloaded procedures, each named **Min**, can be used to calculate the minimum values of two, three, or four values.

Code
Example

```
Public Overloads Function Min(ByVal n1 As Integer, ByVal _
  n2 As Integer) As Integer

    Dim smallest As Integer = n1
    If n2 < smallest Then smallest = n2
    Return smallest

End Function

Public Overloads Function Min(ByVal n1 As Integer, ByVal _
  n2 As Integer, ByVal n3 As Integer) As Integer

    Dim smallest As Integer = n1
    If n2 < smallest Then smallest = n2
    If n3 < smallest Then smallest = n3
    Return smallest

End Function

Public Overloads Function Min(ByVal n1 As Integer, ByVal _
  n2 As Integer, ByVal n3 As Integer, ByVal n4 As Integer) _
  As Integer

    Dim smallest As Integer = n1
    If n2 < smallest Then smallest = n2
    If n3 < smallest Then smallest = n3
    If n4 < smallest Then smallest = n4
    Return smallest

End Function
```

In the above example, calls to the corresponding three procedures would be as follows:

```
Console.WriteLine("Min of 2 = {0}", Min(7, 2))
Console.WriteLine("Min of 3 = {0}", Min(7, 2, 100))
Console.WriteLine("Min of 4 = {0}", Min(7, 2, 9, 1000))
```

Optional Parameters

VB.NET allows parameters to be defined as optional. That is, the calling statement may or may not pass a value for that parameter. If optional parameters are defined, a default value for them must be specified. When arguments are passed, the actual argument is used. When no argument is passed, the default value for the parameter is used.

To define a parameter as optional, the keyword **Optional** is used. The default value for the parameter is specified using the assignment operator and a value after the declaration. The example **OptionalParameters** illustrates the use of these parameters.

Code
Example

```
' Calculates shipping costs; assumes that the Rapid Express
' is the default shipper. Shipper codes are:
' 1=Rapid Express, 2=Quick Shippers, 3=SS Transport

Private Function CalcCost(ByVal weight As Integer, _
 Optional ByVal shipper As Integer = 1) As Decimal

   Select Case shipper
      Case 1
         ' calculate cost for Rapid Express
         Return 11.5 + (weight - 1) * 7.95
      Case 2
         ' calculate cost for Quick Shippers
         Return 19 + (weight - 1) * 4.25
      Case 3
         ' calculate cost for SS Transport
         Return 2.9 + (weight - 1) * 2.25
   End Select
   Return -1

End Function
```

This function can be called in any of the following ways:

```
Dim sc As Decimal
sc = CalcCost(4)      ' omit optional parameter

sc = CalcCost(4, 1) ' specify default for optional parameter
```

```
sc = CalcCost(4, 3) ' specify any value for optional
```

Optional parameters are most useful when a procedure is typically called with a certain value for a procedure, but may occasionally be called with a different value.

Optional Parameters Must Specify a Default Value

VB6 programmers should be aware that VB.NET requires all optional parameters to specify a default value. In VB6, this was not the case. A VB6 programmer could use the function IsMissing to determine whether a parameter was passed. IsMissing is not supported in VB.NET.

Variable Length Parameter Lists

VB.NET supports the ability to pass a variable number of arguments to a procedure. This is a useful capability when some task is going to be performed on any number of a set of values. For example, you might want to write a procedure that accepts a list of numbers and sums them, or a list of destinations and searches airfare prices to any of them.

VB.NET uses the keyword **ParamArray** to define the variable length parameter list. This list is always passed by value. We will discuss arrays in depth in Chapter 7, but be assured that using **ParamArray** is quite simple. For example, a function that can be used to sum up any number of integers is shown below. Notice that the parameter **num** is defined with a set of parentheses. This indicates that **num** is an array.

```
Public Function SumThemUp(ByVal ParamArray nums() _
 As Integer) As Integer
```

The elements in the array **nums** can be examined using the **For Each** statement in VB.NET. The **For Each** statement is similar to the **For** statement discussed in Chapter 5. It is used to iterate through each element in the list.

```
Dim someList() As Integer
Dim anElement as Integer

For each anElement in someList
   ' anElement contains a different element in the
   ' list on each iteration
Next
```

By putting this all together, we can build a function that sums up a list of integers:

```
Public Function SumThemUp(ByVal ParamArray nums() _
 As Integer) As Integer

   Dim sum, num As Integer

   For Each num In nums
      sum += num
   Next
   Return sum

End Function
```

The following code illustrates several ways that this function could be called:

```
Dim answer As Integer

answer = SumThemUp(12, 15, 3)
Console.WriteLine("Answer = {0}", answer)

answer = SumThemUp(4, 8, 12, 33, 66, 1, 55, 23, 10)
Console.WriteLine("Answer = {0}", answer)

answer = SumThemUp()
Console.WriteLine("Answer = {0}", answer)
```

Output from this code segment is as follows:

```
Answer = 30
Answer = 212
Answer = 0
```

The following illustrates another example of parameter arrays. In this example, a departure city and a list of possible destination cities are passed to the function **LookupLowestAirfare.** It iterates through each destination city and looks up the cheapest airfare for that departure/destination city pair.

```
Public Function LookupLowestAirfare(ByVal departure As _
 String, ByVal ParamArray destinations() As String) _
 As Decimal

   Dim arrivalCity As String
   Dim fare As String

   ' start cheapest fare off so high, something MUST be less
   ' than it!
   Dim cheapestFare As Decimal = Decimal.MaxValue
```

```
    ' loop through each possible destination
    For Each arrivalCity In destinations
        fare = LookupAirFare(departure, arrivalCity)

        ' if fare is cheapest to date, remember it!
        If fare < cheapestFare Then
            cheapestFare = fare
        End If
    Next

    ' return cheapest fare
    Return cheapestFare

End Function

' Looks up airfare for a departure/destination city pair
Public Function LookupAirFare(ByVal departure As String, _
 ByVal arrival As String) As Decimal

    Dim someValue As Decimal
    ' Lookup airfare
    Return someValue

End Function
```

This function might be called by the following:

```
Dim cheapAirFare As Decimal

' Find cheapest airfare from DFW to any NYC airport.
' DFW is the first parameter (departure). JFK,
' LaGuardia, and Newark are the param array (destinations)
cheapAirFare = LookupLowestAirfare( _
 "DFW", "JFK", "LaGuardia", "Newark")

Console.WriteLine("Cheapest airfare is {0}", cheapAirFare)
```

Code Example

The program **ParamArrays** contains the code for the variable length parameter list examples shown in this section.

ParamArray Calling Convention Is Always ByVal

VB6 programmers should note that ParamArrays are always passed by value in VB.NET; in VB6, they were always passed by reference.

Event and Property Procedures

Visual Basic uses two other types of procedures: event procedures and property procedures. These will be discussed in Part 3 of this book.

Example: A Simple Payroll Application

Code
Example

The following example is similar to the payroll application discussed in the previous chapter. However, in this version, we are using modules to group logical parts of the application together and a set of subroutines and functions to achieve maximum reusability. This example can be found in the solution **Payroll.**

The first module contains a set of simple IO functions that convert the incoming data to the requested type. The module **IOFunctions** is shown below:

```
Imports System

' Utility I/O Functions
Module IOFunctions
    Public Function ReadString() As String
        Return Console.ReadLine()
    End Function

    Public Function ReadInt32() As String
        Return Convert.ToInt32(Console.ReadLine())
    End Function

    Public Function ReadSingle() As String
        Return Convert.ToSingle(Console.ReadLine())
    End Function

    Public Function ReadDecimal() As String
        Return Convert.ToDecimal(Console.ReadLine())
    End Function
End Module
```

The second module contains a set of payroll-related procedures. One procedure reads employee data. It uses the .NET **Environment.Exit** method to stop the application. Other functions calculate various employee pay information.

```
Imports System

Module Payroll

    Public Sub ReadEmployeeData(ByRef name As String, _
      ByRef payRate As Decimal, ByRef hrsWorked As Single)

        Console.Write("Enter employee name: ")
        name = ReadString()
        If name = "quit" Then
            Environment.Exit(0)        ' stop the application
        End If

        Console.Write("Enter pay rate: ")
        payRate = ReadDecimal()

        Console.Write("Enter hours worked: ")
        hrsWorked = ReadSingle()
    End Sub

    Public Function CalculateGrossPay(ByVal payRate As _
      Decimal, ByVal hrsWorked As Single, Optional ByVal _
      payOvertime As Boolean = True, Optional ByVal _
      overtimeRate As Single = 1.5) As Decimal

        Dim basePay, overtimePay As Decimal

        ' pay straight pay on all hours worked
        basePay = Convert.ToSingle(payRate * hrsWorked)

        ' pay overtime if allowed
        If hrsWorked > 40 And payOvertime Then
            overtimePay = (hrsWorked - 40) * _
                        payRate * (1 - overtimeRate)
        End If

        ' return value
        Return basePay + overtimePay
    End Function

    Public Function CalculateSSTax(ByVal grossPay As _
      Decimal) As Decimal
        Return grossPay * 0.0765
    End Function

    Public Function CalculateFedTax( _
    ByVal grossPay As Decimal) As Decimal

        If grossPay < 200 Then
```

```
        Return grossPay * 0.1        ' 10% bracket
                                     ' on all pay
    ElseIf grossPay < 500 Then
        Return grossPay * 0.17       ' 17% bracket
                                     ' on all pay
    End If
    Return grossPay * 0.26           ' 26% bracket
                                     ' on all pay
End Function

End Module
```

Finally, the last module is the startup module for the application and contains the subroutine **Main.**

```
Imports System

Module MainApp

    Private Sub DisplayResults(ByVal name As String, ByVal _
        grossPay As Decimal, ByVal ssTax As Decimal, ByVal _
        fedTax As Decimal, ByVal netPay As Decimal)

        Console.WriteLine("Name:         {0,-10}", name)
        Console.WriteLine("Gross Pay:    {0,10:C}", grossPay)
        Console.WriteLine("Soc Sec Tax:  {0,10:C}", ssTax)
        Console.WriteLine("Fed Tax:      {0,10:C}", fedTax)
        Console.WriteLine("Net Pay:      {0,10:C}", netPay)
        Console.WriteLine()
    End Sub

    Sub Main()
        Dim name As String
        Dim hrsWorked As Single
        Dim payRate As Decimal
        Dim grossPay, ssTax, fedTax, netPay As Decimal

        ' ReadEmployee stops if name = "quit"
        Do While True
            ReadEmployeeData(name, payRate, hrsWorked)
            grossPay = CalculateGrossPay(payRate, hrsWorked)
            ssTax = CalculateSSTax(grossPay)
            fedTax = CalculateFedTax(grossPay)
            netPay = grossPay - ssTax - fedTax
            DisplayResults(name, grossPay, ssTax, fedTax, _
                            netPay)
        Loop
    End Sub

End Module
```

Example output from this program is shown here:

```
Enter employee name: Dana
Enter pay rate: 22.50
Enter hours worked: 45
Name:           Dana
Gross Pay:          $956.25
Soc Sec Tax:         $73.15
Fed Tax:            $248.63
Net Pay:            $634.47

Enter employee name: Brenda
Enter pay rate: 18.00
Enter hours worked: 36
Name:           Brenda
Gross Pay:          $648.00
Soc Sec Tax:         $49.57
Fed Tax:            $168.48
Net Pay:            $429.95

Enter employee name: quit
```

Summary

In this chapter, we examined how VB.NET programs can be organized into a series of modules and procedures. VB.NET has two types of procedures: subroutines and functions. Subroutines perform a task, while functions perform a task and explicitly return a result. By default, parameters are passed by value to procedures, but VB.NET also supports pass by reference. Procedures can be overloaded; that is, there can be several versions of a procedure with the same name if the parameter lists are different. VB.NET also supports optional parameters by using the keyword **Optional.** The language also supports procedures that take a variable number of parameters by using **ParamArray.** In Part 3 of this book, we will discuss object-oriented programming and how this will alter the way we structure our programs.

Advanced Data Types

Visual Basic.NET supports a richer set of data types than what we have addressed thus far. In addition to the basic Boolean, character, string, and numeric types, VB.NET supports arrays, enumerations, structures, and classes. In this chapter, we examine how arrays can be defined and used inside a VB.NET program. We also explore the new array features provided by the System.Array class. We then discuss how enumerations can be used to add readability to a program. Finally, we describe how structures can be defined and used inside a VB.NET program. The discussion of class types is deferred until Part 3 of this book.

Arrays

An array is a collection of elements with the following characteristics:

- All array elements are of the same type. The element type of an array can be any type, including an array type. An array of arrays is often referred to as a *jagged* array.
- An array may have one or more dimensions. For example, a two-dimensional array can be visualized as a table of values. The number of dimensions is known as the array's *rank*.
- Array elements are accessed using one or more computed integer values, each of which is known as an *index*. A one-dimensional array has one index.
- The lower bound of any dimension in an array is 0.

135

● The elements of an array are created when the array object is created. The elements are automatically destroyed when references to the array object no longer exist.

Defining and Using Arrays

In VB.NET, an array variable is defined by including parentheses after the variable name. For example:

```
' defines a 1-dimensional array of strings
Dim names() As String

' defines a 2-dimensional array of integers
Dim grid(,) As Integer

' defines a 3-dimensional array of decimals
Dim showPrices(,,) As Decimal
```

The size of the array is not part of its type. By omitting the size, you are defining a variable that is a *reference* to the actual array.

In contrast, one statement may be used to define an array variable and to allocate space for the array. For example:

```
' defines a 1-dimensional array of 10 strings
Dim names(9) As String

' defines a 2-dimensional array of 20 integers
Dim grid(4,3) As Integer

' defines a 3-dimensional array of 300 decimals
Dim showPrices(9,9,2) As Decimal
```

Each number in the parentheses represents the upper bound of that dimension in the array. The lower bound is always 0. In the example above, the variable **names** refers to an array of 10 strings with subscripts 0 to 9. The variable **grid** refers to a two-dimensional array with 5 rows (0 to 4) and 4 columns (0 to 3). And the variable **showPrices** references a three-dimensional array with 10 rows, 10 columns, and a depth (or third dimension) of 3.

Upper Bound of an Array Specified in VB.NET

Please note that the number in parentheses on an array declaration is the upper bound of the dimension. Thus, if the number in parentheses is 10, there are actually 11 elements in that dimension!

You may declare and initialize the elements in an array using the following syntax:

```
Dim names() As String  = _
   {"Greg", "Cindy", "Marty", "Sandy", "Patti"}
```

In this example, **names** references a one-dimensional array of 5 strings. If you want to initialize a two-dimensional array, you must define row 1, then row 2, and so on. For each row, you must define each element in the row. For example:

```
Dim matrix(,) As Integer = {{1, 2, 3}, {4, 5, 6}}
```

You may use the following code to print the contents of the matrix. The **UBound** function is used to determine the upper bound of any specified dimension of an array.

```
For i = 0 To UBound(matrix, 1)
   For j = 0 To UBound(matrix, 2)
      Console.Write("{0,5}", matrix(i, j))
   Next
   Console.WriteLine()
Next
```

Output from this code is as follows:

```
1   2   3
4   5   6
```

Example: Using One-Dimensional Arrays

Code
Example

The following program, found in **SimpleArrays,** illustrates a simple use for one-dimensional arrays. In this example, a set of scores is read. They are averaged, and the result is displayed. Then a count of the number of scores that exceeds the average is displayed.

```
Imports System

Module SimpleArrays

   Sub Main()
      Dim testScores(4) As Integer
      Dim i, sum As Integer
      Dim average As Single
```

```
' Read in the scores
For i = 0 To 4
   Console.Write("Enter score {0}: ", i + 1)
   testScores(i) = _
    Convert.ToInt32(Console.ReadLine())
Next

' Calculate the average
For i = 0 To 4
   sum += testScores(i)
Next
average = sum / 5
Console.WriteLine("Average = {0}", average)

' Find out how many scores exceed the average
Dim count As Integer
For i = 0 To 4
    If testScores(i) > average Then
       count += 1
    End If
Next
Console.WriteLine( _
  "Num scores > average = {0}", count)
   End Sub

End Module
```

Output from this program might be the following:

```
Enter score 1: 89
Enter score 2: 92
Enter score 3: 75
Enter score 4: 94
Enter score 5: 91
Average = 88.2
Num scores > average = 4
```

The above example was very simple. All array bounds were known at the time the program was written. There were going to be 5 test scores—no more, no less. However, there are times when an array bound is not known at the time the program is written and can change depending on what is returned from a function. The next example examines this situation.

Example: Using an Array Reference

Code Example

The **ArrayReferences** example illustrates how arrays can be returned from a function or passed to a subroutine. In the **Main** subroutine is the array variable **family** that can refer to any one-dimensional array of strings. After the call to the function **GetMyFamily, family** references an array of 4 strings. After the call to **GetYourFamily, family** references an array of 6 strings. The subroutine **DisplayFamily** illustrates how arrays can be passed to subroutines.

```
Imports System

Module ArrayReferences

    ' Returns an array of 4 strings
    Private Function GetMyFamily() As String()
       Dim names() As String = _
          {"Ralph", "Betty", "Mark", "Dana"}
       Return names
    End Function

    ' Returns an array of 6 strings
    Private Function GetYourFamily() As String()
       Dim names() As String = {"GK", "Dot", _
          "Debbie", "Brenda", "Glenda", "Thresa"}
       Return names
    End Function

    ' Accepts any 1-dimensional array as a parameter
    Private Sub DisplayFamily(ByVal aFamily() _
     As String)
       Dim name As String
       For Each name In aFamily
          Console.Write(name & " ")
       Next
       Console.WriteLine()
    End Sub

    Sub Main()
       Dim family() As String

       family = GetMyFamily()
       Console.WriteLine("My family: ")
       DisplayFamily(family)

       family = GetYourFamily()
       Console.WriteLine("Your family: ")
       DisplayFamily(family)
    End Sub
End Module
```

Output from this program is shown below:

```
My family:
Ralph Betty Mark Dana
```

```
Your family:
GK Dot Debbie Brenda Glenda Thresa
```

Example: Using Two-Dimensional Arrays

Code Example

The following example, found in **RectangularArrays,** illustrates the use of multi-dimensional arrays in which the number of elements in each row is the same. This program calculates and displays a multiplication table for 0 × 0 up to 5 × 7.

```
Imports System

Module RectangularArrays

    Sub Main()
        Dim matrix(5, 7) As Integer
        Dim i, j As Byte

        ' Initialize the array
        For i = 0 To 5
            For j = 0 To 7
                matrix(i, j) = i * j
            Next
        Next

        ' Write headings
        Console.WriteLine("Multiplication table:")
        Console.Write("      ")
        For j = 0 To 7
            Console.Write("{0,5}", j)
        Next
        Console.WriteLine()
        Console.Write("      ")
        For j = 0 To 7
            Console.Write("{0,5}", "---")
        Next
        Console.WriteLine()

        ' Write table
        For i = 0 To 5
            Console.Write("{0,5} |", i)
            For j = 0 To 7
                Console.Write("{0,5}", matrix(i, j))
            Next
            Console.WriteLine()
        Next
    End Sub

End Module
```

Output from this program is as follows:

```
Multiplication table:
        0   1   2   3   4   5   6   7
        --- --- --- --- --- --- --- ---
    0 | 0   0   0   0   0   0   0   0
    1 | 0   1   2   3   4   5   6   7
    2 | 0   2   4   6   8   10  12  14
    3 | 0   3   6   9   12  15  18  21
    4 | 0   4   8   12  16  20  24  28
    5 | 0   5   10  15  20  25  30  35
```

Jagged Arrays

VB.NET allows you to declare a jagged array. A jagged array is an array of arrays. Each row in the array can have a different number of elements. For example:

```
Dim showParticipants(3)() As String
```

The variable **showParticipants** references an array with 4 rows. Each row references a different one-dimensional array. Elements in the array that the row references can be allocated with the **New** statement. For example:

```
showParticipants(i) = New String(5) {}
```

The number in parentheses after the data type indicates how many elements are allocated for the array. The brackets after the data type are required. You can also omit the number of elements and use the brackets to initialize the array. In this case, the number of elements is determined from the number of initializer elements.

```
showParticipants(i) = New String() {"Mary", _
    "Ethel", "Gothie", "Annabelle", "Jessie", _
    "Fred", "Jack", "Lafe", "Sudie"}
```

Example: Using Jagged Arrays

Code Example

The following program, found in **JaggedArrays,** maintains a list of test scores for 4 students. Each student can have a different number of test scores. The subroutine **GetTestScores** creates an array for each student with his or her unique number of test scores and then returns that array. The average for each student is calculated and displayed.

```
Imports System

Module JaggedArray

    Private Function GetTestScores(ByVal numScores As _
```

```vbnet
   Integer) As Integer()

     Dim testNo As Integer
     Dim scores() As Integer

     ' Create an array with n elements for the
     ' scores
     scores = New Integer(numScores - 1) {}

     ' Prompt for test scores
     For testNo = 0 To numScores - 1
        ' Display score # 1 to # n
        Console.Write("Enter score #{0}: ", testNo + 1)
        scores(testNo) = _
          Convert.ToInt32(Console.ReadLine())
     Next

     ' Return the array
     Return scores
  End Function

  Private Function GetAverage(ByVal scores() As Integer) _
    As Single

     Dim i, sum As Integer

     ' Sum up each element in the array
     For i = 0 To UBound(scores)
        sum += scores(i)
     Next

     ' Return the average
     Return sum / (UBound(scores) + 1)
  End Function

  Sub Main()
     Dim studentNo, numTests As Integer

     ' Create a jagged array with rows for 4 sets of scores
     Dim testScores(3)() As Integer

     ' For each student, ask how many test scores
     ' they have and then accept input for each test
     For studentNo = 0 To 3
        ' Display student # 1 to # 4
        Console.Write( _
          "Student {0}, how many tests do you have? ", _
          studentNo + 1)
```

```
        numTests = Convert.ToInt32(Console.ReadLine())

        ' The function GetTestScores returns an array
        ' with the test scores in it
        testScores(studentNo) = GetTestScores(numTests)
    Next
    Console.WriteLine()

    ' Display each student's average
    For studentNo = 0 To 3
        ' Display student # 1 to # 4
        Console.WriteLine("Student {0}, Average = {1}", _
            studentNo + 1, GetAverage(testScores(studentNo)))
    Next
    End Sub

End Module
```

Output from this program might be as follows:

```
Student 1, how many tests do you have? 2
Enter score #1: 88
Enter score #2: 89
Student 2, how many tests do you have? 1
Enter score #1: 100
Student 3, how many tests do you have? 4
Enter score #1: 90
Enter score #2: 76
Enter score #3: 79
Enter score #4: 84
Student 4, how many tests do you have? 2
Enter score #1: 79
Enter score #2: 94

Student 1, Average = 88.5
Student 2, Average = 100
Student 3, Average = 82.25
Student 4, Average = 86.5
```

Dynamic Arrays

VB.NET supports a unique feature within the language called dynamic arrays. The **ReDim** statement can be used to change the size of an array. For example, the following declaration creates an array with 6 elements in it.

```
Dim list() As Integer = {3, 5, 1, 2, 8, 9}
```

The array size can be reallocated by using **ReDim.** If the existing elements must be preserved, you may use the keyword **Preserve** in the declaration. For example, the following statement changes the array's upper bound to 10, but preserves the existing elements.

```
ReDim Preserve list(10)
For i = 0 To UBound(list)
   Console.Write(list(i) & " ")
Next
Console.WriteLine()
```

The output of this example is as follows:

```
3 5 1 2 8 9 0 0 0 0 0
```

You should notice that the new elements contain the default integer value of 0.

The **ReDim** statement can also be used to shrink the number of elements in the array. Again, you must decide whether you want to keep the previous elements. In the following example, the array size is reduced and the existing elements are not preserved.

```
ReDim list(4)
For i = 0 To UBound(list)
   Console.Write(list(i) & " ")
Next
Console.WriteLine()
```

The output of this example is as follows:

```
0 0 0 0 0
```

When you are finished with the elements of an array, VB.NET allows you to assign the value **Nothing** to the array reference.

```
list = Nothing
```

Alternately, you can use the **Erase** statement to tell VB.NET that you are finished with the array elements.

```
Erase list
```

In either case, the garbage collector becomes free to deallocate the elements of the array.

System.Array

In VB.NET, all arrays are derived from the .NET Framework class **System.Array.** Therefore, all arrays in Visual Basic have additional capabilities not readily apparent. Some of the more useful **System.Array** features include the following:

- **Rank** returns the number of dimensions currently in the array.
- **GetUpperBound** returns the upper bound of a specified dimension of the array; this is similar to the **UBound** function that is part of VB.NET.
- **Length** returns the number of elements currently in the array.
- **BinarySearch** searches for an element in a sorted array using a binary search algorithm.
- **Reverse** reverses the elements of an array.
- **Sort** sorts the elements of an array.

These methods provide utility functions that make arrays simple to work with. For example, to sort a list of numbers, you simply use the **Sort** function and write this:

```
Dim list() As Integer = {8,4,6,0,1,5,3}
System.Array.Sort(list)
```

To search a sorted list for a specific value, you can use the **Binary-Search** function and write this:

```
Dim pos As Integer
pos = System.Array.BinarySearch(list, 7)
If pos < 0 Then
   Console.WriteLine("The value is not in the list")
Else
   Console.WriteLine( _
   "The value is in the list at position {0}", pos)
End If
```

To reverse the elements in a list, you could use the **Reverse** function and write this:

```
System.Array.Reverse(list)
```

Code
Example

The program **SystemArrayExample** contains the code shown above.

Enumerations

Enumerations represent a collection of constants that belong to a named type. They allow you to design more readable code that relies less on literal codes and emphasizes a more readable program design. For example, without enumerations, you might find yourself writing the following:

```
Dim empType as Integer
...
Select Case empType
Case 1
   If hrsWorked < = 40 Then
      grossPay = hrsWorked * payRate
   Else
```

```
      grossPay = hrsWorked * payRate
   End If
Case 2
   grossPay = hrsWorked * payRate
End Select
```

However, if you define an enumeration type representing the different "codes" for types of employees, the program will be more readable. For example, the enumeration type would be defined as:

```
Public Enum EmployeeType
   FullTime = 1
   PartTime = 2
End Enum
```

The program could now be written as follows:

```
Dim empType as EmployeeType
...
Select Case empType
Case EmployeeType.FullTime
   If hrsWorked < = 40 Then
      grossPay = hrsWorked * payRate
   Else
      grossPay = hrsWorked * payRate
   End If
Case EmployeeType.PartTime
   grossPay = hrsWorked * payRate
End Select
```

The **Enum** type declaration may specify the underlying data type that is used when variables of certain types are created. The allowable types are **Byte, Short, Integer,** and **Long.** If no type is specified, **Integer** is assumed. To specify a type, use the keyword **As** followed by the data type in the **Enum** definition.

In addition, a member of the enumeration does not have to be assigned a value. If a value isn't assigned, the member assumes its value is one more than the previous item in the enumeration list. If it is the first item in the list, it assumes its value is 0.

```
Public Enum EmployeeType As Byte
   Retired          ' value 0
   FullTime = 1
   PartTime         ' value 2
   Volunteer = 10
End Enum
```

System.Enum

The .NET Framework provides the class **System.Enum,** which is the base class of all enumeration types. By utilizing this design, enumeration types in VB.NET have additional capability not readily obvious. The **System.Enum** class provides many useful methods, including the following:

- **GetName** returns the name of the constant in the specified enumeration.
- **GetNames** returns an array of the names of the constants in a specified enumeration.
- **GetValues** returns an array of the values of the constants in a specified enumeration.
- **IsDefined** returns a Boolean indicating whether a constant exists in an enumerated type.
- **Parse** returns an enumerated object based on a **String** representation of its name.
- **ToString** returns a string representation of a constant in a specified enumeration.

Using these methods, you can write cleaner code that doesn't "hard-code" the various translations between constants and strings. For example, to convert a particular enumeration variable to a string representation, you could use the **ToString** function as follows:

```
Dim eType As EmployeeType

eType = EmployeeType.FullTime

Console.WriteLine("Type = {0}", eType.ToString())
   ' displays the string "FullTime"
```

Another useful method is **GetNames.** This returns an array containing strings representing all possible choices for an enumeration. As an example:

```
Dim aChoice, choices() As String

choices = System.Enum.GetNames(eType.GetType())

For each aChoice in choices
   Console.Write ("{0} ", aChoice)
Next
Console.WriteLine()
   ' displays the string "FullTime  PartTime"
```

Example: Using Enumerations

Code
Example

The following program, found in **EnumerationsExample,** illustrates a simple use of some of the **Enum** type capabilities. Some of these functions generate runtime exceptions if you enter illegal values. We will discuss how to trap these exceptions in Chapter 9.

```
Public Enum EmployeeType
   FullTime = 1
   PartTime = 2
End Enum

Module EnumerationsExample

   Sub Main()
      Dim aChoice, choices() As String
      Dim empType As EmployeeType
      Dim hrsWorked As Single
      Dim payRate, grossPay As Decimal
      Dim answer As String

      Console.Write("Pay type (H for Help)? ")
      answer = Console.ReadLine()
      If answer = "H" Then
         choices = System.Enum.GetNames(empType.GetType())

         Console.Write("Enter one of the following: ")
         For Each aChoice In choices
            Console.Write(aChoice & " ")
         Next
         Console.WriteLine()

         Console.Write("Pay type? ")
         answer = Console.ReadLine()
      End If
      empType = System.Enum.Parse(empType.GetType(), answer)

      Console.Write("Hours worked? ")
      hrsWorked = Convert.ToSingle(Console.ReadLine())

      Console.Write("Pay Rate? ")
      payRate = Convert.ToSingle(Console.ReadLine())

      Select Case empType
         Case EmployeeType.FullTime
            If hrsWorked <= 40 Then
               grossPay = hrsWorked * payRate
            Else
               grossPay = hrsWorked * payRate
            End If
```

```
        Case EmployeeType.PartTime
            grossPay = hrsWorked * payRate
        End Select
        Console.WriteLine("Pay = {0} for {1} work.", _
          grossPay, empType.ToString())
    End Sub

End Module
```

Output from this program might resemble this:

```
Pay type (H for Help)? H
Enter one of the following: FullTime PartTime
Pay type? FullTime
Hours worked? 45
Pay Rate? 10
Pay = 450 for FullTime work.
```

Structures

VB.NET allows programmers to build user-defined types in one of two manners. In the simplest case, the type is primarily used to group related variables into a unit that can easily be managed. These structure types are discussed in this section. Programmers may also build classes, which represent data and procedures bundled into a single unit. Classes are the basis of object-oriented programming and are discussed in Part 3 of this book.

To define a structure, you must choose a name for the data type and identify the members of the structure. In VB.NET, the **Structure** keyword is used. For example:

```
Public Structure Employee
    Public ID As String
    Public Name As String
    Public Salary As Decimal
End Structure
```

In this example, the data type **Employee** is available throughout the application because it is defined as public. An instance of the structure is declared using the same technique as Integers, Singles, etc.

```
Dim bKaye, nRachel As Employee

bKaye.ID = "79-0610"
bKaye.Name = "Brenda Kaye"
bKaye.Salary = 42000
```

```
nRachel.ID = "84-0214"
nRachel.Name = "Natalie Rachel"
nRachel.Salary = 23750
```

Code
Example

In VB.NET, structure variables are considered value types. This means that when one instance of a structure is assigned to another, all of the memory is copied from one variable to another. The program **StructureExamples** examines how structures are affected by beginning value types.

For example, look at the following structure definition:

```
Structure Point
    Public x, y As Integer
End Structure
```

Two instances of a structure variable can be defined (and initialized) as shown below:

```
Dim aPoint, bPoint As Point
aPoint.x = 10
aPoint.y = 20
```

The following code segment illustrates that after **aPoint** is assigned to **bPoint**, it can be changed. However, **bPoint** remains as an unaltered copy of the original **aPoint** values.

```
bPoint = aPoint
aPoint.x += 25
aPoint.y += 25
Console.WriteLine("{0}, {1}", aPoint.x, aPoint.y)
Console.WriteLine("{0}, {1}", bPoint.x, bPoint.y)
```

Output from this code segment is shown below:

```
35, 45
10, 20
```

In addition, because structures are value types, it means that a structure variable passed **ByVal** to a procedure will not be modified when the procedure finishes executing. We discussed **ByVal** and **ByRef** parameters for both value types and reference types in Chapter 6.

With Statement

The **With** statement in VB.NET allows you to interact with a structure without having to repeat the name of the structure variable before each reference to a member of the structure. It is a convenient language statement. For example:

```
Dim bKaye As Employee

With bKaye
    .ID = "79-0610"
    .Name = "Brenda Kaye"
    .Salary = 42000
End With
```

In the above example, all references that begin with a dot (.) refer to the **bKaye** variable. Without the **With** statement, you would have to write this:

```
Dim bKaye As Employee

bKaye.ID = "79-0610"
bKaye.Name = "Brenda Kaye"
bKaye.Salary = 42000
```

Example: Vehicle Value Estimator

Code Example

The following program, found in **VehicleEstimator,** illustrates the use of structures. In this example, a **VehicleRecord** data type is defined and contains information about a new vehicle. The function **GetVehicleInfo** is used to gather data from the user and return a **VehicleRecord** structure to the main program. The number of miles that the vehicle has been driven is entered, and the subroutine **UpdateVehicleValue** uses age and mileage information to estimate the vehicle's value. Finally, the subroutine **DisplayVehicle** writes the results to the screen.

```
Imports System

Structure VehicleRecord
    Public VIN As Long
    Public Make_Model As String
    Public Year As Short
    Public Miles As Integer
    Public Cost As Decimal
    Public Value As Decimal
```

```
End Structure

Module VehicleEstimator

    ' Read in data and create a vehicle
    Public Function GetVehicleInfo() As VehicleRecord
        Dim v As VehicleRecord
        With v
            Console.Write("Enter VIN: ")
            .VIN = Convert.ToInt64(Console.ReadLine())

            Console.Write("Enter Description: ")
            .Make_Model = Console.ReadLine()

            Console.Write("Enter Model Year: ")
            .Year = Convert.ToInt16(Console.ReadLine())

            Console.Write("Enter Mileage: ")
            .Miles = Convert.ToInt32(Console.ReadLine())

            Console.Write("Enter Cost: ")
            .Cost = Convert.ToDecimal(Console.ReadLine())
            .Value = .Cost
        End With

        Return v
    End Function

    ' Modify the vehicle's value based on age & miles
    Public Sub UpdateVehicleValue(ByRef v As VehicleRecord)
        Dim age As Integer
        Dim percent As Single

        ' account for basic depreciation
        age = Year(Now) - v.Year
        Select Case age
            Case 0 To 2             ' pretty new car
                percent = 1 - ((age + 1) * 0.1)
                v.Value = (v.Cost - 1500) * percent
            Case 3 To 4             ' still relatively new car
                percent = 1 - ((age + 1) * 0.12)
                v.Value = (v.Cost - 1500) * percent
            Case 5 To 10            ' used car
                percent = 1 - age / 11
                v.Value = (v.Cost - 1500) * percent
            Case Is < 20            ' clunker
                v.Value = 1500
            Case Else               ' classic car
                v.Value = v.Cost * 0.65
        End Select
```

```
    ' adjust for high miles
    With v
        If .Miles > 200000 Then
            .Value *= 0.5
        ElseIf .Miles > 100000 Then
            .Value *= 0.75
        End If
    End With
End Sub

' Display data in the structure
Public Sub DisplayVehicle(ByVal v As VehicleRecord)
    Console.WriteLine( _
      "{0} {1} with {2} miles valued at {3:C}", _
      v.Year, v.Make_Model, v.Miles, v.Value)
End Sub

Sub Main()
    Dim aVehicle As VehicleRecord
    ' Initialize the structure with data returned from
    ' the function
    aVehicle = GetVehicleInfo()

    Dim newMiles As Integer
    ' Find out how many miles were added after the vehicle
    ' was purchased
    Console.Write("How many miles did you add? ")
    newMiles = Convert.ToInt32(Console.ReadLine())

    ' Update the value of the vehicle based on age & miles
    aVehicle.Miles += newMiles
    UpdateVehicleValue(aVehicle)

    ' Display an estimate of the vehicle's value
    DisplayVehicle(aVehicle)
End Sub

End Module
```

Output of this program might be as follows:

```
Enter VIN: 27652514326721
Enter Description: Ford Explorer XLT
Enter Model Year: 1993
Enter Mileage: 25
Enter Cost: 22500
How many miles did you add? 225915
1993 Ford Explorer XLT with 225940 miles valued at
$2,863.64
```

Summary

In this chapter, we discussed some of the advanced data types available in VB.NET. Specifically, we addressed the array, enumeration, and structure data types. In VB.NET, arrays are objects. They are a reference data type and are based on the class **System.Array.** Methods from **System.Array** are available to perform operations such as sorting and searching. We also examined the enumeration types. These user-defined types allow you to define meaningful enumeration constants within an application. They are value types and are based on **System.Enum.** This class provides methods for converting between enumeration constants and string descriptions of the constants. Finally, we discussed building user-defined data types using structures. Structures are value types that represent a mechanism of grouping related information into one easy-to-manage structure.

VB.NET Utility Functions

*V*isual Basic has been a powerful and easy-to-use language for many years, in part because many common operations are intrinsic to the language. With VB.NET, these operations have become members of the Microsoft.VisualBasic namespace. This namespace provides many of the functions that were previously built-in to the language. In addition, the .NET System namespace provides many other functions that VB programmers will find useful. This chapter examines several types of utility functions available to VB.NET programmers, including common mathematical operations, financial functions, and character and string manipulation operations.

Math Functions

There are many mathematical functions available in the .NET Framework Class Library. These functions include algebraic functions such as **Log** and **Sqrt,** as well as trigonometric functions such as **Sin** and **Cos.**

In VB.NET, most mathematical functions are provided by the **System.Math**. Many of these functions replace functions that were part of the VB6 language. Table 8–1 lists some of the more useful functions, along with the VB6 function that it replaces, if appropriate.

TABLE 8–1	*Common Math Functions Available in VB.NET*

System.Math Function	Replaces VB6 Function	Description
Abs	Abs	Returns the absolute value of a number.
Acos		Returns the angle whose cosine is the number.
Asin		Returns the angle whose sine is the number.
Atan	Atn	Returns the angle whose tangent is the number.
Ceiling		Returns the smallest integer greater than or equal to the number.
Cos	Cos	Returns the cosine of the angle.
Cosh		Returns the hyperbolic cosine of the angle.
Exp	Exp	Returns e raised to a power.
Floor		Returns the largest integer less than or equal to the number.
IEEERemainder		Returns the remainder obtained by dividing two numbers. (This is the same as the Mod operator.)
Log	Log	Returns the logarithm of a number.
Log10		Returns the base 10 logarithm of a number.
Max		Returns the larger of two numbers.
Min		Returns the smaller of two numbers.
Pow		Returns a number raised to a power. (This is the same as the ^ operator.)
Round	Round	Returns the number nearest to the value.
Sign	Sgn	Returns the sign of the number (-1 for negative numbers, 0 for zero, 1 for positive numbers).
Sin	Sin	Returns the sine of the angle.
Sinh		Returns the hyperbolic sine of the angle.
Sqrt	Sqr	Returns the square root of the number.
Tan	Tan	Returns the tangent of the angle.
Tanh		Returns the hyperbolic tangent of the angle.

The **System.Math** class also defines two constants that are very useful to programmers working with complex mathematical expressions. Table 8–2 lists the constants and their values.

TABLE 8–2	*Math Constants Available in VB.NET*
System.Math Constants	**Value**
E	2.71828182845905
PI	3.14159265358979

The trigonometric functions typically must be passed a **Double** value representing an angle, specified in radians. They return a **Double** value. To convert the angle in degrees to an angle in radians, you must multiply the angle in degrees by PI / 180. For example:

```
Dim angle, result As Double
angle = 45 ' degrees
result = System.Math.Sin(angle * PI / 180)
```

The algebraic functions are typically overloaded for most numeric data types. For example:

```
' A version that accepts Integers
Dim intValue, intResult As Integer
intValue = -3
intResult = System.Math.Abs(intValue)

' A version that accepts Decimals
Dim decValue, decResult As Decimal
decValue = -33.45
decResult = System.Math.Abs(decValue)
```

Code Example

The **MathFunctions** program illustrates the use of some of the mathematical functions available to Visual Basic.NET programmers, as well as the use of the **System.Math** constants. You will notice that, because the exponentiation (^) and remainder (**Mod**) operators are part of the Visual Basic language, the .NET functions **Exp, Pow,** and **IEEERemainder** provide alternate ways of performing operations that are already part of the programming language.

```
' MathFunctions.vb
' Test .NET Math Functions

Imports System
Imports System.Math

Module MathFunctions
```

```
Sub TestAlgebraicFunctions()
   Console.WriteLine("Abs(-13) = {0}", Abs(-13))

   Console.WriteLine("Exp(2) = {0}", Exp(2))
   Console.WriteLine("E^2 = {0}", E ^ 2)

   Console.WriteLine("IEEERemainder(5,2) = {0}", _
                  IEEERemainder(5, 2))
   Console.WriteLine("5 Mod 2 = {0}", 5 Mod 2)

   Console.WriteLine("Log(3) = {0}", Log(3))
   Console.WriteLine("Log10(10) = {0}", Log10(10))

   Console.WriteLine("Pow(2,3) = {0}", Pow(2, 3))
   Console.WriteLine("2^3 = {0}", 2 ^ 3)

   Console.WriteLine("Sqrt(24) = {0}", Sqrt(24))
End Sub

Sub TestTrigonometricFunctions()
   ' Note: angle * PI/180 = radians
   Console.WriteLine("Sin(45 * PI/180) = {0}", _
                  Sin(45 * PI / 180))
   Console.WriteLine("Cos(60 * PI/180) = {0}", _
                  Cos(60 * PI / 180))
   Console.WriteLine("Tan(75 * PI/180) = {0}", _
                  Tan(75 * PI / 180))
End Sub

Sub Main()
   TestAlgebraicFunctions()
   Console.WriteLine()
   TestTrigonometricFunctions()
End Sub

End Module
```

Output from this program illustrates the return values of the functions:

```
Abs(-13) = 13
Exp(2) = 7.38905609893065
E^2 = 7.38905609893065
IEEERemainder(5,2) = 1
5 Mod 2 = 1
Log(3) = 1.09861228866811
Log10(10) = 1
Pow(2,3) = 8
2^3 = 8
Sqrt(24) = 4.89897948556636
Sin(45 * PI/180) = 0.707106781186547
```

```
Cos(60 * PI/180) = 0.5
Tan(75 * PI/180) = 3.73205080756888
```

The functions discussed above are primarily algebraic and trigonometric functions. The **Microsoft.VisualBasic.VBMath** namespace (see Table 8–3) contains functions that are useful when random numbers are required.

TABLE 8–3 *Random Number Generation Functions Available in VB.NET*

Microsoft.VisualBasic.VBMath Functions	Description
Randomize	Initializes the random number generator.
Rnd	Returns a random value between 0 and 1.

Random number generators are used in many types of programs to simulate random behavior in the real world. For example, to simulate the roll of a die, you must randomly calculate a number between 1 and 6. Computer routines that generate random number routines use complex calculations; however, the numbers they generate are not truly random. They are called *pseudorandom numbers* because the algorithm produces the same sequence of numbers each time, given a specific starting point. This is considered a desirable feature because it allows you to reproduce the results of the execution of a program. To introduce true random behavior, these generators allow you to specify a *seed,* or starting point.

In VB.NET, the **Randomize** function is used to initialize the random number generator. If it has passed no arguments, it uses the system's timer as the seed for the generator. The **Rnd** function is used to generate a random number between 0 and 1. It can then be scaled to represent a number within any range using the following formula:

number = Floor (Rnd() * N + S)

where N represents the number of values within the range and S represents the starting point, or lower bound, of the range.

The **RandomNumberFunctions** program illustrates the generation of 10 random numbers between 1 and 6, corresponding to the roll of a die.

Code
Example

```
' RandomNumberFunctions.vb
' Test the random number generation functions

Imports System
Imports System.Math
Imports Microsoft.VisualBasic.VBMath

Module RandomNumberFunctions
```

```
Sub Main()
   ' Seed the random number generator
   ' Randomize()

   ' Generate 6 random numbers between 1 and 6
   Dim randVal As Double
   Dim number, i As Integer
   For i = 1 To 20
      randVal = Rnd()
      number = Floor(randVal * 6 + 1)
      If i = 1 Then Console.Write("First 10 numbers: ")
      If i = 11 Then Console.Write("Last 10 numbers: ")
      Console.Write("{0} ", number)
      If i = 10 Or i = 20 Then Console.WriteLine()
   Next
End Sub

End Module
```

Output from this program is as follows:

```
First 10 numbers: 5 4 4 2 2 5 1 5 5 5
Last 10 numbers: 1 3 6 5 3 6 6 1 6 3
```

If you run it a second time, the output is unchanged:

```
First 10 numbers: 5 4 4 2 2 5 1 5 5 5
Last 10 numbers: 1 3 6 5 3 6 6 1 6 3
```

However, it you uncomment the call to **Randomize** in the **Main** subroutine, the output (for this execution) is as follows:

```
First 10 numbers: 5 1 1 3 2 4 4 5 1 5
Last 10 numbers: 2 2 2 1 3 2 6 4 4 2
```

Running the program a second time yields the following results:

```
First 10 numbers: 4 5 2 3 4 5 1 1 6 6
Last 10 numbers: 5 4 3 3 4 2 5 4 2 1
```

The results you experience will likely be different because the starting point of the random number generator is the system timer.

Financial Functions

Code
Example

There are many financial functions available for use by VB.NET programmers. The **Microsoft.VisualBasic.Financial** namespace is home to many functions that were found in previous versions of Visual Basic. Table 8–4 lists some of the more useful functions. Examples of the use of many of these functions can be found in the program **FinancialFunctions.**

TABLE 8–4	Financial Functions Available in VB.NET
Microsoft.VisualBasic.Financial Functions	**Description**
DDB	Uses the double-declining balance method to find the depreciation of an asset.
FV	Calculates the future value of an annuity.
Ipmt	Finds the interest payment for a given period of an annuity based on periodic, fixed payments and a fixed interest rate.
MIRR	Finds the modified internal rate of return for a series of periodic cash flows (payments and receipts).
NPer	Finds the number of periods for an annuity based on periodic, fixed payments and a fixed interest rate.
NPV	Finds the net present value of an investment based on a series of periodic cash flows (payments and receipts) and a discount rate.
Pmt	Calculates the payment for an annuity.
PPmt	Finds the principal payment for a given period of an annuity based on periodic, fixed payments and a fixed interest rate.
PV	Calculates the present value of an annuity.
SLN	Uses the straight-line method to find the depreciation of an asset.
SYD	Uses the sum-of-years digits method to find the depreciation of an asset.

The **Microsoft.VisualBasic.DueDate Enumeration** contains two constants that are used with many of the financial functions. These constants, shown in Table 8–5, indicate when payments are made to annuities.

TABLE 8–5	Constants for Financial Functions

Microsoft.VisualBasic.DueDate Constants
EndOfPeriod
BegOfPeriod

The financial functions can be useful if you work within certain financial domains. For example, the **Pmt** function can be used to calculate the period payment of a loan. Similarly, **PPmt** calculates the amount of any payment applied to principal, and **IPmt** calculates the amount of any payment applied to interest.

In the following example, the payment of a $53,000 loan at 7.625% interest that spans 15 years is computed.

```
Dim interestRate, numPayments, loanAmount, futureValue, _
 presentValue As Double
Dim payment, prinPmt, intPmt As Double
Dim paymentType As DueDate

interestRate = 0.07625' Interest rate (APR)
numPayments = 15 * 12' Number of payments (15 years)
loanAmount = 53000' Loan amount
futureValue = 0 ' Amount of ending value
paymentType = EndOfPeriod' Payment at the end of month

payment = Pmt(interestRate / 12, numPayments, -loanAmount, _
 futureValue, paymentType)

Console.WriteLine( _
 "For a {0:C} loan at {1}% interest for {2} years, " & _
 vbCrLf & "payment will be {3:C} per month" & vbCrLf, _
 loanAmount, interestRate * 100, numPayments / 12, _
 payment)

Dim i As Byte
' Look at the first 12 payments
For i = 1 To 12
   prinPmt = _
    PPmt(interestRate / 12, i, numPayments, -loanAmount)
   intPmt = _
    IPmt(interestRate / 12, i, numPayments, -loanAmount)

   Console.WriteLine( _
    "Payment {0} : Principal {1:C} Interest {2:C}", _
    i, prinPmt, intPmt)
Next i
```

Output of this code shows the following:

```
For a $53,000.00 loan at 7.625% interest for 15 years,
payment will be $495.09 per month

Payment 1 : Principal $158.32 Interest $336.77
Payment 2 : Principal $159.32 Interest $335.76
Payment 3 : Principal $160.34 Interest $334.75
Payment 4 : Principal $161.36 Interest $333.73
```

```
Payment 5  : Principal $162.38 Interest $332.71
Payment 6  : Principal $163.41 Interest $331.68
Payment 7  : Principal $164.45 Interest $330.64
Payment 8  : Principal $165.50 Interest $329.59
Payment 9  : Principal $166.55 Interest $328.54
Payment 10 : Principal $167.61 Interest $327.48
Payment 11 : Principal $168.67 Interest $326.42
Payment 12 : Principal $169.74 Interest $325.35
```

The **DDB** function calculates depreciation using the double-declining balance method. If an asset costs $20,000 and has a salvage value of $2,000 at the end of a five-year period, then $18,000 must be depreciated over the five-year period. The double-declining balance depreciates a large percentage of the asset in its early years. For example:

```
Dim initialCost, salvageValue, usefulLife, _
  depreciation, remainingBalance As Double

initialCost = 20000    ' $20,000 Cost
salvageValue = 2000    ' $2,000 Salvage Value
usefulLife = 5         ' Years of Useful Life
remainingBalance = initialCost    ' Undepreciated Balance

Dim year As Integer
For year = 1 To usefulLife
   depreciation = _
    DDB(initialCost, salvageValue, usefulLife, year)

   ' Keep running total of balance not depreciated
   remainingBalance -= depreciation

   Console.WriteLine("Year {0} depreciation = {1:C}, " & _
    " balance = {2:C}", year, depreciation, _
    remainingBalance)
Next
```

The output of this program illustrates the results returned from the **DDB** function when calculating the depreciation of the asset over the life of the asset:

```
Year 1 depreciation = $8,000.00, balance = $12,000.00
Year 2 depreciation = $4,800.00, balance = $7,200.00
Year 3 depreciation = $2,880.00, balance = $4,320.00
Year 4 depreciation = $1,728.00, balance = $2,592.00
Year 5 depreciation = $592.00, balance = $2,000.00
```

Using the same asset discussed in the preceding double-declining balance example, the straight-line depreciation function, **SLN,** uses a depreciation algorithm that depreciates the asset evenly throughout its life. For example:

```
Dim initialCost, salvageValue, usefulLife, _
 depreciation, remainingBalance As Double

initialCost = 20000    ' $20,000 Cost
salvageValue = 2000    ' $2,000 Salvage Value
usefulLife = 5         ' Years of Useful Life
remainingBalance = initialCost    ' Undepreciated Balance

Dim year As Integer
For year = 1 To usefulLife
   depreciation = _
    SLN(initialCost, salvageValue, usefulLife)

   ' Keep running total of balance not depreciated
   remainingBalance -= depreciation

   Console.WriteLine("Year {0} depreciation = {1:C}, " & _
    " balance = {2:C}", year, depreciation, _
    remainingBalance)
Next
```

The output of this program illustrates the results returned from the **SLN** function when calculating the depreciation of the asset over the life of the asset:

```
Year 1 depreciation = $3,600.00, balance = $16,400.00
Year 2 depreciation = $3,600.00, balance = $12,800.00
Year 3 depreciation = $3,600.00, balance = $9,200.00
Year 4 depreciation = $3,600.00, balance = $5,600.00
Year 5 depreciation = $3,600.00, balance = $2,000.00
```

Informational Functions

Code Example

There are functions in the **Microsoft.VisualBasic.Information** namespace that can be used to make decisions about the type of contents of a variable. Table 8–6 lists some of the more useful functions. Examples of the use of these functions can be found in the program **InformationalFunctions.**

TABLE 8–6	*Information Functions Available in VB.NET*

Microsoft.VisualBasic.Information Functions	**Description**
IsArray	Indicates whether a variable references an array.
IsDate	Indicates whether an expression can be converted to a date.
IsDbNull	Indicates whether an expression evaluates to System.DBNull.
IsNothing	Indicates whether an expression has an object assigned to it.
IsNumeric	Indicates whether an expression can be converted to a number.
IsReference	Indicates whether an expression evaluates to a reference type.
QBColor	Returns an integer representing the RGB of a specified color number.
RGB	Generates an RGB color value.
UBound	Returns the upper bound of an array.

The functions **IsNumeric** and **IsDate** are useful for testing variables to determine if the data they contain is of the data type specified. For example:

```
Dim inputBuf As String
Dim payRate As Single
Dim hireDate As Date

Console.Write("Enter pay rate: ")
inputBuf = Console.ReadLine()

If IsNumeric(inputBuf) Then
   payRate = CSng(inputBuf)
Else
   Console.WriteLine("Error: Invalid pay rate, " & _
                     "assuming $5.25")
   payRate = 5.25
End If

Console.Write("Enter Hire Date: ")
inputBuf = Console.ReadLine()

If IsDate(inputBuf) Then
   hireDate = CDate(inputBuf)
Else
   Console.WriteLine("Error: Invalid hire date, " & _
```

```
                              "assuming today")
       hireDate = Today()   ' This is a VB.NET function
End If
```

The **IsArray** and **UBound** functions can be used together to produce
code that can accept any type of array and perform some type of generic
action. The following function calculates the number of elements in an array
of any dimension. The array is passed to the function as an **Object** so that an
array of any number of dimensions can be passed.

```
Function NumberOfArrayElements(ByVal numList As Object, _
 Optional ByVal numDim As Integer = 1) As Integer
    If Not IsArray(numList) Then
       Console.WriteLine("Error: the object is not an array")
       Exit Function
    End If

    Console.WriteLine("Number of dimensions: {0}", numDim)

    Dim i, numOfElements, totNumOfElements As Integer

    ' Examine each dimension
    For i = 1 To numDim
       Console.WriteLine(" {0}: LBound - 0 UBound - {1}", _
        i, UBound(numList, i))

       ' Determine how many elements in the iTH dimension
       numOfElements = _
        UBound(numList, i) + 1
       If i = 1 Then
          totNumOfElements = numOfElements
       Else
          totNumOfElements *= numOfElements
       End If
    Next
    Return totNumOfElements
End Function
```

This function can be called using any of the following code. In the first
case, a one-dimensional array is passed. In the second case, a two-dimensional array is passed. In the last case, a variable that is not an array is passed
to illustrate how the **IsArray** function can be used.

```
Dim list1(10) As Integer
Console.WriteLine(" Num of elements: {0}", _
                  NumberOfArrayElements(list1))

Dim list2(4, 6) As Integer
Console.WriteLine(" Num of elements: {0}", _
```

```
                    NumberOfArrayElements(list2, 2))

Console.WriteLine(" Num of elements: {0}", _
                  NumberOfArrayElements("Hello"))
```

Output from this code is as follows:

```
Number of dimensions: 1
 1: LBound- 0 UBound- 10
 Num of elements: 11
Number of dimensions: 2
 1: LBound- 0 UBound- 4
 2: LBound- 0 UBound- 6
 Num of elements: 35
Error: the object is not an array
 Num of elements: 0
```

Conversion Functions

Code Example

Many functions, such as **CInt** and **Convert.ToInt32,** are available to convert data from one type to another. We discussed most of them in Chapter 4. Table 8–7 lists some additional functions available in **Microsoft.VisualBasic.Conversion.** The program **ConversionFunctions** illustrates the use of these functions.

TABLE 8–7	*Information Functions Available in VB.NET*

Microsoft.VisualBasic.Conversion Functions	Description
Fix	Removes the fractional part of *number* and returns the resulting integer. If number is negative, it returns the first negative integer greater than or equal to *number.* For example: -2.1 to -2.
Hex	Returns a string corresponding to the hexadecimal value of the number. If the number passed in is not a whole number, it is rounded before the conversion takes place.
Int	Removes the fractional part of *number* and returns the resulting integer. If number is negative, it returns the first negative integer less than or equal to *number.* For example: -2.1 to -3.

| **TABLE 8–7** | *Information Functions Available in VB.NET (continued)* |

Microsoft.VisualBasic.Conversion Functions	Description
Oct	Returns a string corresponding to the octal value of the number. If the number passed in is not a whole number, it is rounded before the conversion takes place.
Str	Returns a string corresponding to the decimal value of the number. It will be preceded by a blank if the number is positive or by a minus if the number is negative.
Val	Returns the numeric value of a string as a Double.

The **Hex** and **Oct** functions are used to obtain a hexadecimal or octal representation of a base 10 number. For example, the following code:

```
Console.WriteLine("Hex(87) = {0}", Hex(87))
Console.WriteLine("Oct(87) = {0}", Oct(87))
```

produces this output:

```
Hex(87) = 57
Oct(87) = 127
```

The **Int** and **Fix** functions are used to obtain the integer part of a floating-point value. They differ in how they interpret negative numbers. For example, the following code:

```
Console.WriteLine("Int(13.8) = {0}", Int(13.8))
Console.WriteLine("Fix(13.8) = {0}", Fix(13.8))

Console.WriteLine("Int(-13.8) = {0}", Int(-13.8))
Console.WriteLine("Fix(-13.8) = {0}", Fix(-13.8))
```

produces this output:

```
Int(13.8) = 13
Fix(13.8) = 13
Int(-13.8) = -14
Fix(-13.8) = -13
```

Notice that, when the number is positive, **Int** and **Fix** return the same values. However, when the value is negative, **Int** returns the smaller value and **Fix** returns the larger value.

The **Str** function is used to obtain a string representation of a value, while **Val** is used to obtain the numeric value of a string. **Str** varies just a little from the **ToString** method that all types have. For example, this code:

```
Dim someString As String
someString = Str(-82.456)
Console.WriteLine("Str(-82.456) = {0}", _
                  """" & someString & """")
someString = Str(82.456)
Console.WriteLine("Str(82.456) = {0}", _
                  """" & someString & """")

Dim num As Double
num = Val(someString)
Console.WriteLine("Val(""82.456"") = {0}", num)
```

produces this output:

```
Str(-82.456) = "-82.456"
Str(82.456) = " 82.456"
Val("82.456") = 82.456
```

You will notice that the **Str** function leaves space in the string for the sign of the number. If the number is positive, a space is substituted for the sign. In addition, the example above displays a double quote (") in the output. However, the literal "" is the empty string, and """ is a syntax error. To place one double quote in a literal string requires two double quotes in the string (for example: """"). An easier way to do this is to use one of the constants defined for control characters. These are discussed in a later section.

System.Convert Class Replaces Older VB6 Conversion Functions

The functions Str and Val are shown for historical purposes to make it easier for you to read VB6 code and books. The System.Convert class has many methods that can convert data to string and numeric values and is the preferred way of converting data in VB.NET.

In addition, the .NET functions Floor and Ceiling discussed earlier should be used for all new VB.NET code, instead of the VB6 functions Int and Fix.

Control Characters

The **Microsoft.VisualBasic.ControlChars** namespace contains a collection of constants that can be used to build strings. Table 8–8 lists some of the more useful constants.

TABLE 8–8	*Control Character Constants*

Microsoft.VisualBasic.ControlChars Constant
Back
Cr
CrLf
FormFeed
Lf
NewLine
NullChar
Quote
Tab
VerticalTab

Code Example

These constants can be used when creating strings for assignment to variables, as well as creating output strings. The program **ControlChars** illustrates the use of a few of these constants.

```vb
' ControlChars.vb
' Illustrates the use of control characters

Imports System
Imports Microsoft.VisualBasic.ControlChars

Module ControlChars

    Sub Main()
        Dim s As String
        s = "Wes said, " & Quote & "Good morning" & _
            Quote & "!"
        Console.WriteLine("{0}", s)

        s = "Hello" & CrLf & "world"
        Console.WriteLine("{0}", s)

        Dim i As Integer
        Console.WriteLine("Num" & Tab & "Square")
        For i = 1 To 4
            Console.WriteLine("{0}" & Tab & "{1}", i, i ^ 2)
        Next
    End Sub

End Module
```

VB.NET Retains VB6 Constants

The constants vbCrLf and vbTab (among other) that VB6 programmers are familiar with are still available in VB.NET in the namespace Microsoft.VisualBasic.Constants.

Character Manipulation Functions

The **Microsoft.VisualBasic.Strings** namespace contains several functions that can be useful when working with characters. In addition, the **System.Char** data type provides several methods that are useful. Table 8–9 lists some of these functions.

TABLE 8–9 *Character Functions in VB.NET*

Microsoft.VisualBasic.Strings Character Functions	Description
Asc	Given an ASCII character, it returns the character code.
AscW	Given a Unicode character, it returns the character code.
Chr	Given an ASCII character code, it returns the ASCII character.
ChrW	Given a Unicode character code, it returns the Unicode character.
LCase	Converts a character to lowercase.
Len	Returns the number of bytes needed to store a character.
UCase	Converts a character to uppercase.

The **UCase** and **LCase** functions are used to convert a character to a specific case. For example, the following code:

```
Dim someChar as Char

someChar = "a"C ' character literal
Console.WriteLine("{0}",UCase(someChar))

someChar = "A"C
Console.WriteLine("{0}",LCase(someChar))
```

produces this output:

```
A
a
```

Each character in a computer system is identified by an integer referred to as its *character code*. To find the character code of any given ASCII character, you must use the **Asc** function. For example, the following code:

```
Console.WriteLine("Character: {0} Integer code: {1}", _
                  "A"c, Asc("A"))
Console.WriteLine("Character: {0} Integer code: {1}", _
                  "Z"c, Asc("Z"))
Console.WriteLine("Character: {0} Integer code: {1}", _
                  "0"c, Asc("0"))
Console.WriteLine("Character: {0} Integer code: {1}", _
                  "9"c, Asc("9"))
Console.WriteLine("Character: {0} Integer code: {1}", _
                  "a"c, Asc("a"))
Console.WriteLine("Character: {0} Integer code: {1}", _
                  "z"c, Asc("z"))
```

produces this output:

```
Character: A Integer code: 65
Character: Z Integer code: 90
Character: 0 Integer code: 48
Character: 9 Integer code: 57
Character: a Integer code: 97
Character: z Integer code: 122
```

The **Chr** function performs the inverse; that is, given a character code, it returns the ASCII character. For example, the following code:

```
Dim c As Char
Dim i As Integer

For i = 32 To 122
   Console.WriteLine("Integer code: {0} Character: {1}", _
                     i, Chr(i))
Next
```

produces this output:

```
Code: 32 Character:
Code: 33 Character: !
Code: 34 Character: "
Code: 35 Character: #
Code: 36 Character: $
Code: 37 Character: %
Code: 38 Character: &
Code: 39 Character: '
Code: 40 Character: (
Code: 41 Character: )
Code: 42 Character: *
Code: 43 Character: +
```

```
Code: 44 Character: ,
Code: 45 Character: -
Code: 46 Character: .
Code: 47 Character: /
Code: 48 Character: 0
Code: 49 Character: 1
   . . .            These entries not shown
Code: 56 Character: 8
Code: 57 Character: 9
Code: 58 Character: :
Code: 59 Character: ;
Code: 60 Character: <
Code: 61 Character: =
Code: 62 Character: >
Code: 63 Character: ?
Code: 64 Character: @
Code: 65 Character: A
Code: 66 Character: B
   . . .            These entries not shown
Code: 89 Character: Y
Code: 90 Character: Z
Code: 91 Character: [
Code: 92 Character: \
Code: 93 Character: ]
Code: 94 Character: ^
Code: 95 Character: _
Code: 96 Character: `
Code: 97 Character: a
Code: 98 Character: b
   . . .            These entries not shown
Code: 121 Character: y
Code: 122 Character: z
```

Date/Time Functions

In VB.NET you often have a choice between using functions in the **Microsoft.VisualBasic** namespace or new functions that are part of the standard .NET Framework Class Library, often in the **System** namespace. In this section we will look at two ways of working with dates and times.

DATE/TIME IN MICROSOFT.VISUALBASIC NAMESPACE

Code Example

The **Microsoft.VisualBasic.DateTime** namespace contains many functions that can be useful when working with dates. Table 8–10 lists many of these functions and the VB6 functions they replace. The **DateTimeFunctions** program illustrates the use of many of these functions.

| TABLE 8–10 | Date and Time Functions in VB.NET |

Microsoft.VisualBasic. DateTime Function	Replaces VB6 Function	Description
DateAdd		Returns a new Date given a starting date and an interval.
DateDiff		Returns the interval between two dates.
DatePart		Extracts the specified portion from a Date.
DateSerial		Given three integers representing month, day, and year, it returns a Date.
DateString	Date$	Returns the current date as a string.
DateValue		Given a string representation, it returns a Date containing the date portion of the string.
Day		Returns an integer (1-31) representing the day of a given Date.
Hour		Returns an integer (0-23) representing the hour of a given Date.
Minute		Returns an integer (0-59) representing the minute of a given Date.
Month		Returns an integer (1-12) representing the month of a given Date.
MonthName		Returns a string representing the name of a given month number.
Now		Returns the current date/time.
Second		Returns an integer (0-59) representing the second of a given Date.
TimeOfDay	Time	Returns the current time.
TimeString	Time$	Returns the current time as a string.
TimeSerial		Given three integers representing hour, minute, and second, it returns a Date containing that time.
TimeValue		Given a string representation, it returns a Date containing the time portion of the string.
Today	Date	Returns the current date.
Weekday		Returns an integer (1-7) representing the weekday of a given Date.

TABLE 8-10	*Date and Time Functions in VB.NET (continued)*

Microsoft.VisualBasic.DateTime Function	Replaces VB6 Function	Description
WeekdayName		Returns a string representing the name of a given weekday number.
Year		Returns an integer (1-9999) representing the year of a given Date.

VB.NET uses **Now, Today,** and **TimeOfDay** to access the system calendar and clock. These return a value of type **Date.** For example:

```
Dim aDate As Date

aDate = Now        ' Current date/time
Console.WriteLine ("Now is: {0}", aDate)

aDate = Today      ' Current date
Console.WriteLine ("Today is: {0}", aDate)

aDate = TimeOfDay' Current time
Console.WriteLine ("TimeOfDay is: {0}", aDate)
```

Output from the code above might be the following:

```
Now is: 9/28/2001 10:35:57 AM
Today is: 9/28/2001 12:00:00 AM
TimeOfDay is: 1/1/0001 10:35:57 AM
```

VB.NET has several functions that can parse out a specific part of a date. These were listed in Table 8–10 and include **Month, Day, Year, Hour, Minute,** and **Second.** The following example examines these functions and some others that can be used to extract specific parts from a **Date** object:

```
Console.WriteLine ("Month: {0}", Month(Now))
Console.WriteLine ("  also known as: {0}", _
        MonthName(Month(Now)))
Console.WriteLine ("Day: {0}", Day(Now))
Console.WriteLine ("Year: {0}", Year(Now))

Console.WriteLine ("Day of Week: {0}", Weekday(Now))
Console.WriteLine ("  also known as: {0}", _
        WeekdayName(Weekday(Now)))

Console.WriteLine ("Hour: {0}", Hour(Now))
Console.WriteLine ("Minute: {0}", Minute(Now))
Console.WriteLine ("Second: {0}", Second(Now))
```

Output from the preceding code might be as follows:

```
Month: 9
  also known as: September
Day: 28
Year: 2001
Day of Week: 6
  also known as: Friday
Hour: 10
Minute: 35
Second: 57
```

VB.NET also has a function called **DatePart** that can be used to extract parts from a **Date.** It must be passed a parameter that indicates the portion of the date desired. This parameter is of type **DateInterval.** Table 8–11 lists **DateInterval** constants.

TABLE 8–11	*DateInterval Constants in VB.NET*

Microsoft.VisualBasic.DateInterval Constants
Day
DayOfYear
Hour
Minute
Month
Quarter
Second
Weekday
WeekOfYear
Year

The following code illustrates the use of the **DatePart** function:

```
Console.WriteLine ("Month: {0}", _
            DatePart(DateInterval.Month, Now))
Console.WriteLine ("Day: {0}", _
            DatePart(DateInterval.Day, Now))
Console.WriteLine ("Year: {0}", _
            DatePart(DateInterval.Year, Now))

Console.WriteLine ("Quarter of Year: {0}", _
            DatePart(DateInterval.Quarter, Now))
Console.WriteLine ("Week of Year: {0}", _
            DatePart(DateInterval.WeekOfYear, Now))
```

```
Console.WriteLine ("Day of Year: {0}", _
          DatePart(DateInterval.DayOfYear, Now))
Console.WriteLine ("Day of Week: {0}", _
          DatePart(DateInterval.Weekday, Now))

Console.WriteLine ("Hour: {0}", _
          DatePart(DateInterval.Hour, Now))
Console.WriteLine ("Minute: {0}", _
          DatePart(DateInterval.Minute, Now))
Console.WriteLine ("Second: {0}", _
          DatePart(DateInterval.Second, Now))
```

Output of this code might be as follows:

```
Month: 9
Day: 28
Year: 2001
Quarter of Year: 3
Week of Year: 39
Day of Year: 271
Day of Week: 6
Hour: 10
Minute: 35
Second: 57
```

VB.NET also provides functions to do mathematics with dates. The **DateAdd** function can be used to add an interval to a date to calculate a new date, while the **DateDiff** function can determine the interval between two dates. For example:

```
Console.WriteLine ("15 days from today is: {0}", _
          DateAdd(DateInterval.Day, 15, Now))

Dim newYearsDay As Date = #1/1/2002#

Console.WriteLine ("Days until next year: {0}", _
          DateDiff(DateInterval.Day, Now, newYearsDay))
Console.WriteLine ("Hours until next year: {0}", _
          DateDiff(DateInterval.Hour, Now, newYearsDay))
```

Output of this code might be as follows:

```
15 days from today is: 10/13/2001 10:35:57 AM
Days until next year: 94
Hours until next year: 2269
```

DATETIME AND TIMESPAN CLASSES

For compatibility with previous VB code, you can use functions in the **Microsoft.VisualBasic.DateTime** namespace. For new code, you should use the methods and properties of **DateTime** structure in the .NET **System** namespace. (In Chapter 4, we discussed that VB.NET's **Date** type is implemented by the **System.DateTime** structure.)

Recall that **DateTime** represents date and times ranging from 12 midnight, January 1 of the year 1 A.D. to 11:59:59 of December 31 of the year 9999 A.D. Time values are measured in units of 100 nanoseconds, called "ticks." .NET also provides a **TimeSpan** structure that can be used to represent an interval of time. Table 8–12 shows some of the common properties and methods of **DateTime**.

TABLE 8–12	*Selected Methods and Properties of DateTime*	
Member	**Property or Method**	**Description**
Now	Shared Method	Current local date and time.
ToString	Method (several overloads)	String representation, available in a variety of formats.
DayOfYear	Property	Day of the year of this instance.
DayOfWeek	Property	Day of the week of this instance.
Hour	Property	Hour component of this instance.
Minute	Property	Minute component of this instance.
Ticks	Property	Number of 100 nanosecond ticks.
Add	Method	Add a TimeSpan to a DateTime.

The program **DateTimeDemo** illustrates these operations. The current date and time is found and displayed in various ways. The following are a few of the many formats available for displaying a **DateTime** using the **ToString** method:

- d or short date
- D or long date
- t or short time
- T or long time

A **TimeSpan** object is created using one of several overloaded constructors. The constructor in this program takes as parameters a day, hour, minute, and second. We want to find a time 30 days and 1 hour in the future. The date and time at this future moment are displayed. Here is the code:

```
Module DateTimeDemo

   Sub Main()
      Dim dt As DateTime = DateTime.Now
      Console.WriteLine ("Current date and time")
      Console.WriteLine ("DateTime = {0}", dt)
      Console.WriteLine ("Date (short) = {0}", _
         dt.ToString("d"))
```

```vb
      Console.WriteLine ("Date (long) = {0}", _
         dt.ToString("D"))
      Console.WriteLine ("Time (short) = {0}", _
         dt.ToString("t"))
      Console.WriteLine ("Time (long) = {0}", _
         dt.ToString("T"))

      'Some other date and time metrics
      Console.WriteLine ("DayOfYear = {0}", _
         dt.DayOfYear)
      Console.WriteLine ("DayOfWeek = {0}", _
         dt.DayOfWeek)
      Console.WriteLine ("Hour = {0}", _
         dt.Hour)
      Console.WriteLine ("Minute = {0}", _
         dt.Minute)
      Console.WriteLine ("Ticks = {0}", _
         dt.Ticks)

      'TimeSpan of 30 days and 1 hour
      Dim ts As New TimeSpan(30, 1, 0, 0)
      Console.WriteLine("30 days and 1 hour later")
      dt = dt.Add(ts)
      Console.WriteLine("DateTime = {0}", dt)
   End Sub

End Module
```

Here is the output:

```
Current date and time
DateTime = 2/11/2002 5:06:11 PM
Date (short) = 2/11/2002
Date (long) = Monday, February 11, 2002
Time (short) = 5:06 PM
Time (long) = 5:06:11 PM
DayOfYear = 42
DayOfWeek = Monday
Hour = 17
Minute = 6
Ticks = 631490439719857312
30 days and 1 hour later
DateTime = 3/13/2002 6:06:11 PM
```

String Functions

VB.NET's **String** data type is an alias for the .NET **String** class in the **System** namespace. There are many functions, both in the namespace **Microsoft.VisualBasic.Strings,** as well as in the **System.String** class, for manipulating strings. These functions can be used to convert the case of a string, to concatenate strings, and to find substrings. A summary of these is listed Table 8–13.

TABLE 8–13	*String Manipulation Functions in VB.NET*

Microsoft.VisualBasic.Strings Functions	System.String Functions	Description
	Chars	Returns a character at a given position in the string.
	Compare	Compares two strings. Can be configured to perform case-insensitive comparisons.
	EndsWith	Determines whether a string ends with a specified string.
	Format	Returns a string formatted according to specific guidelines.
	Insert	Returns a string representing a substring inserted at a specified position in the original string.
InStr	IndexOf	Returns the position of a substring found within a string.
InStrRev	LastIndexOf	Returns the position of a substring within a string, starting from the right side of the string.
Join	Join	Returns a string constructed from elements in an array.
LCase	ToLower	Returns the string converted to lowercase.
Left		Returns the specified left portion of a string.
Len	Length	Returns the number of characters in a string.
LSet	PadRight	Returns a left-aligned string of a specified length.
LTrim	TrimStart	Returns a copy of a specified string with all leading spaces removed.

| TABLE 8–13 | *String Manipulation Functions in VB.NET (continued)* |

Microsoft.VisualBasic.Strings Functions	System.String Functions	Description
Mid	Substring	Returns the specified portion of a string.
Replace	Replace	Returns a string in which one substring has been replaced with another substring.
Right		Returns the specified right portion of a string.
RSet	PadLeft	Returns a right-aligned string of a specified length.
RTrim	TrimEnd	Returns a copy of a specified string with all trailing spaces removed.
Space		Returns a string containing a specified number of spaces.
Split	Split	Returns an array containing substrings formed from a given string and a delimiter.
	StartsWith	Determines whether a string begins with a specified string.
StrConv		Returns a string converted from a given input string; options include changing case and character sets.
StrDup		Returns a string consisting of repeated characters.
StrReverse		Returns a string containing a reversed copy of a specified string.
Trim	Trim	Returns a copy of a specified string with all leading and trailing spaces removed. The **System.String** version allows the trim characters to be specified.
UCase	ToUpper	Returns the string converted to uppercase.

This section examines many of the VB.NET functions and the **System.String** methods. In some cases, we show two techniques of accomplishing the same behavior. If you are new to Visual Basic, you should use the .NET versions, if possible. However, if you are migrating from VB6, you may find it comforting to know that you do not need to rewrite your existing code.

Code
Example

(You should, however, try to become familiar with the .NET versions and begin to use them in all new code!) To see the code for the following examples, refer to the **StringFunctions** program.

The VB.NET string functions **Left, Right,** and **Mid** are used to extract substrings from a String. These functions assume the first character in the string is at index 1. Therefore, this code:

```
newStr = Mid(someStr, 5,2)
```

would cause VB.NET to begin at the fifth character and extract two characters. A more complete example is listed below:

```
Dim someStr As String

someStr = "Programming is fun!"
Console.WriteLine("String: {0}", someStr)

Console.WriteLine("Left 11 characters are: {0}", _
    Left(someStr, 11))
Console.WriteLine( _
    "2 characters beginning at position 13 are: {0}", _
    Mid(someStr, 13, 2))
Console.WriteLine("Right 4 characters are: {0}", _
    Right(someStr, 4))
```

Output from this program would be as follows:

```
String: Programming is fun!
Left 11 characters are: Programming
2 characters beginning at position 13 are: is
Right 4 characters are: fun!
```

You could also use the **String** method **Substring** to perform this operation. The **String** class assumes the first character is at position 0, so the parameters referencing the starting position must be adjusted. For example:

```
Console.WriteLine( _
  "11 characters beginning at position 0 are: {0}", _
  someStr.Substring(0, 11))
Console.WriteLine( _
  "2 characters beginning at position 12 are: {0}", _
  someStr.Substring(12, 2))
Console.WriteLine( _
  "all characters beginning at position 15 are: {0}", _
  someStr.Substring(15))
```

produces the following output:

```
11 characters beginning at position 0 are: Programming
2 characters beginning at position 12 are: is
all characters beginning at position 15 are: fun!
```

Confusing: The Starting Character in a String May Be Position 0 or 1

As you saw in the preceding example, the older Visual Basic functions assume the first character in a string is at position 1, whereas the newer .NET methods assume the first character is at position 0. You must be vigilant about which type of function you are using if you want to avoid making deadly mistakes!

The .NET **String** class has methods to manipulate the contents of a string, including **Substring, Insert,** and **Remove.**

```
Dim buf As String = "Microsoft Visual Basic 6.0"

Console.WriteLine(buf.Substring(10, 12))

' Removes 6.0 from end of buf
buf = buf.Remove(buf.Length - 4, 4)

' Inserts .NET at end of buf
buf = buf.Insert(buf.Length, ".NET")

Console.WriteLine(buf)
```

This program would produce the following output:

```
Visual Basic
Visual Basic.NET
```

The Visual Basic functions to change the case of characters in a string, **UCase** and **LCase,** work like the **System.String** methods **ToUpper** and **ToLower.** The Visual Basic functions to trim leading and trailing spaces from strings (**LTrim, RTrim,** and **Trim)** also work like the **System.String** methods **Trim, TrimStart,** and **TrimEnd.** However, the **System.String** methods are more flexible because there are versions to trim characters other than spaces.

```
Dim dataLine As String

' Using Visual Basic functions
dateline = UCase(Trim(dataLine))

' Using System.String methods
dataLine = dataLine.Trim().ToUpper()

' Trims specific ending punctuation marks
dataLine = dataLine.TrimEnd(","c, "."c, "?"c, "!"c, ";"c)
```

The easiest way to access individual characters in a string is to use the **System.String** method **Chars.** Alternately, you can use the **Mid** function of Visual Basic to extract individual characters.

```
Dim s As String = "ABCDEFG"
Dim c As Char
Dim i As Integer

' System.String technique
For i = 0 To s.Length - 1
   c = s.Chars(i)
   Console.Write(c & " ")
Next
Console.WriteLine()

' Visual Basic technique
For i = 1 To Len(s)
   c = CChar(Mid(s, i, 1))
   Console.Write(c & " ")
Next
Console.WriteLine()
```

Output from the preceding code segments is the same:

```
A B C D E F G
```

The **String** data type has several methods to help you format information, including the methods **Format, PadLeft,** and **PadRight.** Visual Basic also has some very powerful functions to allow you to format information; those functions are addressed in the next section.

The **Format** method is useful for formatting numbers. It uses the same syntax as that used in the **WriteLine** method. It returns a value representing the formatted string. For example:

```
Dim s As String
Dim n As Decimal = 123.45

s = String.Format("Amount = {0,10:C}", n)
Console.WriteLine(s)
```

The output of this example is as follows:

```
Amount =    $123.45
```

If you want to control only the formatting of string values, that is, to make them align in a specific way, then use the **PadLeft** and **PadRight** methods. These methods require that you specify the total width of the string that you want returned, including the text before padding, and they create a return value padded to the desired with.

In the following code, a string is built by padding two column headings. The pad character is a space.

```
Dim heading1 As String = "Number"
Dim heading2 As String = "Power"
```

```
Dim heading As String = heading1.PadRight(12) & _
                        heading2.PadLeft(13)
Console.WriteLine(heading)

Dim i As Integer
Dim value As Long
For i = 0 To 31
   value = 2 ^ i
   Console.WriteLine("2^{0,-10}{1,13:N0}", i, value)
Next
```

The format for the variable **i** specified a field width of 10 to be left justified. The format for the variable **value** indicates a field width of 13 to be right justified and numeric (N) with 0 digits after the decimal. The column heading for **i** was padded to a width of 12 to correspond to the output of the value **i** (width 10) combined with the two characters in the literal "2^." Output of this example is as follows:

```
Number          Power
2^0                 1
2^1                 2
2^2                 4
2^3                 8
2^4                16
2^5                32
. . .
2^28      268,435,456
2^29      536,870,912
2^30    1,073,741,824
2^31    2,147,483,648
```

The **PadLeft** and **PadRight** methods can also be used to specify a padding character. In the following example, a decimal account is preceded by asterisks:

```
Dim s As String
Dim n As Decimal = 123.45

s = n.ToString()
s = s.PadLeft(9, "*"c)
Console.WriteLine(s)
```

The output is as follows:

```
***123.45
```

Format Functions

We have seen that the .NET Framework can be used to format data for display. However, Visual Basic has historically had very powerful functions for formatting information for display purposes. These functions, listed in Table 8–14, continue in VB.NET and can be found in the namespace **Microsoft.VisualBasic.Strings.**

TABLE 8–14   *Format Functions in VB.NET*

Microsoft.VisualBasic.Strings Function	Description
Format	Returns a string containing a formatted value. Very flexible function that can be controlled to produce almost any output format.
FormatCurrency	Returns a string containing a value formatted as currency. Includes several predefined options for output styles.
FormatDateTime	Returns a string containing a value formatted as a date/time. Includes several predefined options for output styles.
FormatNumber	Returns a string containing a value formatted as a number. Includes several predefined options for output styles.
FormatPercent	Returns a string containing a value formatted as percent.

The **FormatCurrency** function is used to format values representing monetary values. For example, the following code segment:

```
Console.WriteLine(FormatCurrency(135.28))
Console.WriteLine(FormatCurrency(-135.28))
```

produces this output, which shows the behavior for positive and negative monetary values:

```
$135.28
($135.28)
```

The default value of the number of digits displayed is based on the computer's regional settings.

The function has several optional parameters, including the following:

● The numeric value representing the monetary unit to be formatted
● The number of digits after the decimal point (-1 indicates that the regional settings should be used)

- Whether a leading zero is shown if the amount is less than 1
- Whether parentheses are used for negative numbers
- Whether digits are grouped using a delimiter

There are three constants that can be used as parameter values to control formatting in this function. They are:

- Microsoft.VisualBasic.TriState.True
- Microsoft.VisualBasic.TriState.False
- Microsoft.VisualBasic.TriState.UseDefault

For example, to display a delimiter for larger numbers using the regional settings for number of digits and the delimiter, you could write the following code:

```
Console.WriteLine(_
  FormatCurrency(1357651.28, -1, TriState.UseDefault, _
        TriState.UseDefault, TriState.True))

Console.WriteLine(_
  FormatCurrency(-1357651.28, -1, TriState.UseDefault, _
        TriState.UseDefault, TriState.True))
```

The output would be as follows:

```
$1,357,651.28
($1,357,651.28)
```

You could also control whether a leading zero is shown for values less than 1 and/or whether negative numbers are shown in parentheses. For example:

```
Console.WriteLine( _
  FormatCurrency(0.35, -1, TriState.False))
Console.WriteLine( _
  FormatCurrency(0.35, -1, TriState.True))

Console.WriteLine( _
  FormatCurrency(-0.35, -1, TriState.False, TriState.True))
Console.WriteLine( _
  FormatCurrency(-0.35, -1, TriState.False, TriState.True))
Console.WriteLine( _
  FormatCurrency(-0.35, -1, TriState.True, TriState.False))
Console.WriteLine( _
  FormatCurrency(-0.35, -1, TriState.True, TriState.True))
```

The output would be this:

```
$.35
$0.35

-$.35
```

```
($.35)
-$0.35
($0.35)

-.35%
(.35%)
-0.35%
(0.35%)
```

The **FormatPercent** function is used to format values representing percentages. The method has several parameters, including the following:

- The numeric value representing the percentage to be formatted
- The number of digits after the decimal point
- Whether a leading zero is shown if the percent is less than 1
- Whether negative values are shown in parentheses

The following code segment and associated output illustrate various combinations of the parameters.

```
Console.WriteLine(FormatPercent(0.0835))
Console.WriteLine(FormatPercent(0.0835, 1))
Console.WriteLine(FormatPercent(0.0835, 2))

Console.WriteLine(FormatPercent(-0.0835))
Console.WriteLine(FormatPercent(-0.0835, 1))
Console.WriteLine(FormatPercent(-0.0835, 2))
```

The two sets of output show the behavior for positive and negative percentage values:

```
8.35%
8.4%
8.35%

-8.35%
-8.4%
-8.35%
```

You can use the same tri-state constants seen in the **FormatCurrency** examples as parameters for the **FormatPercent** function to control leading zero representation and negative percentage representation. For example, this code:

```
Console.WriteLine( _
  FormatPercent(-0.0035, 2, TriState.False, _
TriState.False))

Console.WriteLine( _
  FormatPercent(-0.0035, 2, TriState.False, TriState.True))
```

```
Console.WriteLine( _
  FormatPercent(-0.0035, 2, TriState.True, TriState.False))

Console.WriteLine( _
  FormatPercent(-0.0035, 2, TriState.True, TriState.True))
```

produces the following output:

```
-.35%
(.35%)
-0.35%
(0.35%)
```

Environment Functions

The **System.Environment** namespace contains a collection of methods that can be used to gather information about the environment in which an application is running. Table 8–15 lists some of the more useful functions:

TABLE 8–15   *Environment Functions in VB.NET*

System.Environment Namespace	Description
CurrentDirectory	Returns a string containing the name of the current working directory.
Exit	Terminates the process.
GetCommandLineArgs	Returns an array of strings representing the command line arguments that were used to launch the program.
GetEnvironmentVariables	Returns all environment variables and their values.
MachineName	Returns a string containing the NetBIOS name of the computer.
OSVersion	Returns an OperatingSystem object that can be queried to determine information about the current operating system.
TickCount	Returns the number of milliseconds that have elapsed since the system started. Useful for benchmarking the execution speed of code.
UserName	Returns a string containing the user name of the person who started the thread.

Code
Example

The program **EnvironmentFunctions** shown below illustrates the use of some of these methods. It uses **TickCount** to benchmark the performance of the application. You will notice from the output that it executes much slower from within the Visual Studio IDE. The program displays the name of the user and the name of the machine on which the program runs. It also demonstrates how command line parameters can be accessed.

```
' EnvironmentFunctions.vb
' Demonstrates the use of the Environment functions

Imports System
Imports Microsoft.VisualBasic.ControlChars

Module EnvironmentFunctions

    Sub Main()
        Dim startTick As Long
        startTick = Environment.TickCount

        Dim userName As String = Environment.UserName
        Dim machineName As String = Environment.MachineName

        Console.WriteLine( _
          "Current user on machine {0} is {1}", _
          machineName, userName)

        Dim args() As String
        Dim anArgument As String

        Console.WriteLine("Command line args were: ")
        args = Environment.GetCommandLineArgs()

        For Each anArgument In args
            Console.WriteLine(Tab & anArgument)
        Next

        Dim endTick As Long
        endTick = Environment.TickCount

        Console.WriteLine( _
          "The code above took {0} milliseconds to execute", _
          endTick - startTick)
    End Sub

End Module
```

To test this code, you must navigate to the directory where your .EXE resides using the command prompt. Then you may execute the program from the command line and enter two arguments, as shown below:

```
> environmentfunctions 11-12-01 Seattle
```

The output of the program will be as follows:

```
Current user on machine LAPTOP is Administrator
Command line args were:
    environmentfunctions
    11-12-01
    Seattle
The code above took 110 milliseconds to execute
```

If you run the program from inside of the Visual Studio environment, the output will be as follows:

```
Current user on machine LAPTOP is Administrator
Command line args were:
    C:\OI\IntroVb\Chap08\EnvironmentFunctions\bin\
EnvironmentFunctions.exe
The code above took 420 milliseconds to execute
```

Of course, your path will be different if your program is in a different location.

Object Browser

Before we conclude this chapter, we think you should be aware of a nifty little tool available to VB.NET programmers. The Object Browser is a utility that displays objects available within a particular application. The information displayed depends upon what has been imported.

To display the Object Browser, use the View menu, select Other Windows, and then select the Object Browser. In the left pane, you see the namespaces that have been imported. Figure 8–1 illustrates the members of the **EnvironmentFunctions** namespace. This program, shown in the preceding section, consisted of the module **EnvironmentFunctions** and a subroutine called **Main.**

Figure 8–2 illustrates the members of the **Microsoft.VisualBasic.Strings** namespace. If you look at the bottom of the Object Browser window, you can gather some information about the selected element shown in the right pane. This diagram illustrates the **Format** function.

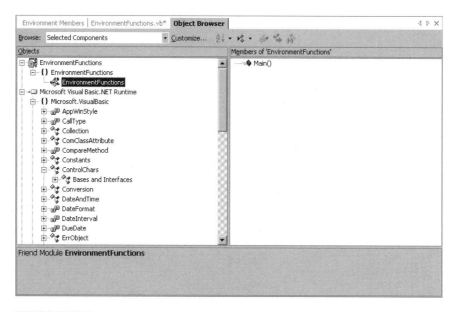

FIGURE 8–1 *Custom namespace in the Object Browser.*

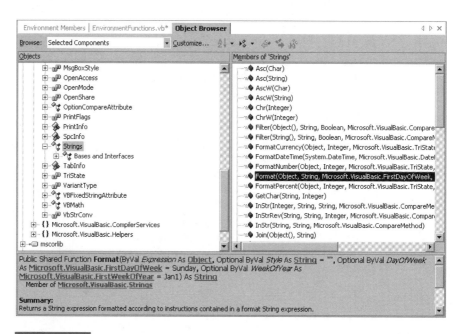

FIGURE 8–2 *Microsoft.VisualBasic.Strings namespace in the Object Browser.*

Summary

In this chapter, we examined many of the utility functions available to VB.NET programmers. As you have seen, some of these functions are provided by classes in the .NET Framework Class Library. Other functions have been provided by previous versions of Visual Basic and are found in the **Microsoft.VisualBasic** namespace. You should take some time using the Object Browser and explore the functions and classes that are available to you. This will make you a more efficient programmer. You will be able to use existing functions, rather than "home growing" functions that duplicate behaviors already available and bug free!

Exception Handling

One of the things all programmers must face is how to handle errors that occur during program execution. This chapter introduces Visual Basic.NET's new exception-handling mechanism and the Try, Catch, and Throw statements. We examine the .NET class, System.Exception, and how it can be used to gather information about the runtime exception. We also explore how to generate application-specific exceptions. Finally, we go over several examples to help you become accustomed to this new technique of error handling.

Error Detection

One problem that all programmers are faced with is how to handle errors. Traditionally, we use conditional statements to test for all known errors. If we recognize an error, we respond to it. If we are calling a function that might fail, the function returns a success code that we must then examine.

This approach suffers from several problems. Code that is needed to detect all the errors can sometimes make it difficult to determine what the code is actually trying to do. For example, study the program **ErrorHandling\Version 1** below. It reads simple mathematical expressions such as 10+3 or 12/6, evaluates them, and displays the result.

Code Example

```
' Example of old-style error handling
' Version 1

Imports System
```

```
Module ErrorHandling

Sub Main()
   Dim success As Boolean
   Dim operand1, operand2, result As Integer
   Dim operator As Char

   ' Read an expression such as 10+3 or 9/4
   Console.Write("Enter operand: ")
   operand1 = Convert.ToInt32(Console.ReadLine())
   Console.Write("Enter operator: ")
   operator = Convert.ToChar(Console.ReadLine())
   Console.Write("Enter operand: ")
   operand2 = Convert.ToInt32 (Console.ReadLine())

   ' Check to make sure the operator is a valid operator
   ' and then call Calculate
   success = False
   If operator = "+"c Or operator = "-"c Or _
    operator = "*"c Or operator = "/"c Then

       If operator <> "/"c Then
          result = Calculate(operand1, operator, _
           operand2)
          success = True
       Else
          ' Detect divide by zero
          If operand2 <> 0 Then
             result = Calculate( _
              operand1, operator, operand2)
             success = True
          Else
             Console.WriteLine("Divide by zero")
          End If
       End If
   Else
       Console.WriteLine("Invalid operator")
   End If
   ' Display the results if all went well
   If success Then
       Console.WriteLine("Result = {0}", result)
   End If
End Sub


Function Calculate(ByVal op1 As Integer, _
  ByVal op As Char, ByVal op2 As Integer) As Integer
    Select Case op
```

```
        Case "+"c
            Return op1 + op2
        Case "-"c
            Return op1 - op2
        Case "*"c
            Return op1 * op2
        Case "/"c
            Return op1 / op2
    End Select
End Function

End Module
```

The example above represents a simple calculator. The **Main** procedure reads the expression, checks to make sure the operator is one of the four basic arithmetic operators, and then calls the function **Calculate** to determine the result. **Main** also recognizes a "divide by zero" situation. The variable **success** is used to determine whether an error was detected so that we know whether we should print the result of the calculation.

The readability of the example program could be improved by shifting some of the error detection to the **Calculate** function. However, the function must now return a success code so that we know whether it was successful in its calculation. If it fails, we also need to know why!

The following example, found in **ErrorHandling\Version 2,** illustrates that the **Calculate** function can gracefully absorb much of the error-detection responsibilities.

```
' Example of old-style error handling
' Version 2 (improved!)

Imports System

Module ErrorHandling

    Sub Main()
        Dim successCode As Integer
        Dim operand1, operand2, result As Integer
        Dim operator As Char

        ' Read an expression such as 10+3 or 9/4
        Console.Write("Enter operand: ")
        operand1 = Convert.ToInt32(Console.ReadLine())
        Console.Write("Enter operator: ")
        operator = Convert.ToChar(Console.ReadLine())
        Console.Write("Enter operand: ")
        operand2 = Convert.ToInt32 (Console.ReadLine())

        ' Calculate the result of the expression
        successCode = Calculate( _
```

```
            operand1, operator, operand2, result)

      ' Display the result (or an error message)
      Select Case successCode
         Case 0
            Console.WriteLine("Result = {0}", result)
         Case 1
            Console.WriteLine("Divide by zero")
         Case 2
            Console.WriteLine("Invalid operator")
      End Select
   End Sub

   Function Calculate(ByVal op1 As Integer, _
     ByVal op As Char, ByVal op2 As Integer, _
     ByRef answer As Integer) As Integer

      ' Check the operator and perform the calculation
      ' (if relevant)
      Select Case op
         Case "+"c
            answer = op1 + op2
         Case "-"c
            answer = op1 - op2
         Case "*"c
            answer = op1 * op2
         Case "/"c
            If op2 = 0 Then Return 1
            answer = op1 / op2
         Case Else
            Return 2
      End Select
      Return 0
   End Function

End Module
```

As you can see, the code is much easier to read. However, we must now return status codes from the function. The meaning of these codes must be known so that they can be used. In addition, VB.NET programmers are not forced to capture the return value of functions. This means that some programmers may not detect that the function failed to calculate the result and may inadvertently use the result. Even more significantly, if we fail to detect all errors, the program will likely crash.

On Error Not Supported in VB.NET

VB6 programmers should note that the previous style of exception handling that includes the use of the On Error statement and the Err object is not supported in VB.NET.

VB.NET Exception Handling

Visual Basic.NET introduces a new exception-handling mechanism that is a significant improvement from that used in previous versions of Visual Basic. The exception-handling mechanism is similar to that found in languages like C#, C++, Java, and Ada. Exceptions are implemented by the .NET Common Language Runtime, so exceptions can be thrown in an assembly written in one .NET language and caught in an assembly written in another.

Exception handling is accomplished via the following:

- An error is generated by *throwing* an exception.
- An error is handled by *catching* the exception.
- Code that might encounter an exception is enclosed in a *try block*.

Code Example

The following program, found in **ExceptionMessagesDemo,** illustrates the basic use of the **Try** and **Catch** blocks:

```
Imports System

Module ExceptionMessagesDemo

    Sub Main()
        Dim num As Integer

        ' This represents the code where an exception
        ' might occur
        Try
            Console.WriteLine("Enter a number: ")
            num = Convert.ToInt32(Console.ReadLine())
            Console.WriteLine("Your number was {0}", num)

        ' This illustrates catching a system generated
        ' exception (probably from input that could not be
        ' converted to an Integer)
        Catch e As System.Exception
            Console.WriteLine("Message:     {0}", e.Message)
            Console.WriteLine("Source:      {0}", e.Source)
            Console.WriteLine("Target Site: {0}", _
                              e.TargetSite)
            Console.WriteLine("Stack Trace: {0}", _
                              e.StackTrace)
            Console.WriteLine("To String:   {0}", e.ToString)
        End Try
    End Sub

End Module
```

System.Exception

System.Exception is the .NET class that contains information about an exception. It contains several properties, including the following:

- **Message** returns a string containing information about the exception.
- **Source** returns a string containing the name of the application or object that threw the exception.
- **TargetSite** returns a string containing the name of the procedure that threw the exception.
- **StackTrace** returns a string with stack trace information identifying the point at which the exception was encountered.
- **InnerException** returns a reference to another exception that was active when the current exception was thrown.

The **ExceptionMessagesDemo** program, shown previously, produces the following output when non-numeric data is entered into the program:

```
Message:      Input string was not in a correct format.
Source:       mscorlib
Target Site: Int32 ParseInt32(System.String,
   System.Globalization.NumberStyles,
   System.Globalization.NumberFormatInfo)
Stack Trace:    at System.Number.ParseInt32(String s,
   NumberStyles style, Number FormatInfo info)
   at System.Convert.ToInt32(String value)
   at ExceptionMessagesDemo.ExceptionMessagesDemo.Main() in
   C:\OI\IntroVb\Chap09
   \ExceptionMessagesDemo\ExceptionMessagesDemo.vb:line 13
To String: System.FormatException: Input string was not
   in a correct format.
   at System.Number.ParseInt32(String s, NumberStyles
   style, NumberFormatInfo info)
   at System.Convert.ToInt32(String value)
   at ExceptionMessagesDemo.ExceptionMessagesDemo.Main() in
   C:\OI\IntroVb\Chap09
   \ExceptionMessagesDemo\ExceptionMessagesDemo.vb:line 13
```

The **Message** property produced an output string that let us know the "input string was not in a correct format." The **Source** property let us know that the exception occurred in the .NET dll "mscorlib." The **TargetSite** property let us know that the function **ParseInt32** generated the exception. And the **StackTrace** property told us that **ParseInt32** was called by the **Convert.ToInt32** procedure, which in turn was called by the **Exception-MessagesDemo.Main** procedure line 13.

Finally, you can see that the **ToString** method generated a string containing a selective combination of most of the other properties.

All Exceptions in .NET Are Types of System.Exception

In VB.NET, the different types of exceptions that can be thrown are derived from, or are types of System.Exception. Sometimes, System.Exception is referred to as the generalized version of an exception and a specific type of exception, such as System.IndexOutOfRange-Exception, is referred to as a specialized exception.

A variable of type InvalidDataException can refer only to that type of exception. However, a variable of type System.Exception can reference any type of exception.

Some of the specialized exceptions will be examined later in this chapter. The concepts of generalization and specialization, sometimes called inheritance, will be discussed in detail in Chapters 11-13.

Exception Flow of Control

The general structure of code which might encounter an exception is shown below:

```
Try
       ' code that might cause an exception to be thrown
Catch variable-name As Exception-data-type1
       ' code to handle this type of exception
[ Catch variable-name As Exception-data-typeN
       ' code to handle this type of exception ...]
[ Finally
     ' code that executes regardless of whether ]
     ' an exception was thrown
End Try
```

Exceptions are caught in one or more **Catch** blocks that immediately follow **Try.** Because there are many types of exceptions, there can be many **Catch** blocks (one for each type of exception expected). Each catch handler has a parameter specifying the data type of the exception that it can handle, and it can use the properties of the parameter to respond to the exception appropriately. If no exception is thrown inside the **Try** block, all the catch handlers are skipped.

For example, the following code segment illustrates the handling of an **IndexOutOfRange** exception and a **FormatException**.

```
Dim numList(99), nextAvail As Integer
...
Do While True
...

    Try
        Console.Write("Enter next number: ")
        numList(nextAvail) = _
                Convert.ToInt32(Console.ReadLine())
```

```
      nextAvail += 1

  Catch boundsErr As IndexOutOfRangeException
      ' respond to an error that indicates nextAvail is
      ' not in the range 0-99

  Catch badDataErr As FormatException
      ' respond to an error that indicates the data
      ' entered was non-numeric

  Catch e As Exception
    ' respond to an unknown error

  End Try
Loop
```

When an exception is thrown, the *first* catch handler that matches the exception data type is executed, and then control passes to the statement just after the catch block(s). In this example, the following things happen:

- If the exception is an **IndexOutOfRangeException,** the code in the first **Catch** handler is executed and execution resumes at the **Loop** statement below **End Try** (if the **Catch** handler did not throw another exception or otherwise alter the execution path).
- If the exception is a **FormatException,** the code in the second **Catch** handler is executed and execution resumes at the **Loop** statement below **End Try** (if the **Catch** handler did not throw another exception or otherwise alter the execution path).
- If the exception is of any other type, the code in the last **Catch** handler is executed and execution resumes at the **Loop** statement below **End Try** (if the **Catch** handler did not throw another exception or otherwise alter the execution path).

This example could have been rewritten as shown below. In this version, **Catch** handlers are built only for the expected exception types:

```
Dim numList(99), nextAvail As Integer
...
Do While True
...

  Try
    Console.Write("Enter next number: ")
    numList(nextAvail) = _
              Convert.ToInt32(Console.ReadLine())
    nextAvail += 1

  Catch boundsErr As IndexOutOfRangeException
      ' respond to an error that indicates nextAvail is not
      ' in the range 0-99
```

```
    Catch badDataErr As FormatException
        ' respond to an error that indicates the data entered
        ' was non-numeric
    End Try
Loop
```

If an exception of some other type is thrown in the **Try** block, no appropriate handler is found. Therefore, the exception is thrown to the next higher "context" (the function that called the current one).

Code that should be executed regardless of whether an exception was encountered is enclosed in a **Finally** block located immediately below the last **Catch** block. For example, if you needed to access a file for data, you might write the following code:

```
Try
    ' Open the file
    ' Read the data
    ' Close the file
Catch e As Exception
    ' Respond to an error
    ' Check the file, and if open, close it
End Try
```

Or, to avoid the duplicated code to close the file, you might write the following code:

```
Try
    ' Open the file
    ' Read the data
Catch e As Exception
    ' Respond to an error
Finally
    ' Check the file, and if open, close it
End Try
```

These examples are similar. However, the second one guarantees that the file will be closed, even if the **Try** block has an **Exit** or **Return** statement in it or if the **Catch** block throws an exception.

Exceptions can be generated by the system or can be specifically thrown with a **Throw** statement. For example, if the user enters non-numeric data at the following prompt:

```
Dim num As Integer
Console.Write("Enter your age: ")
num = Convert.ToInt32(Console.ReadLine())
```

the system will throw an exception. You can also programmatically throw an exception when your application recognizes an error condition. In the following example, the application enforces a pay rate in the range $5.15 to $75.00.

```
Dim payRate As Decimal
Console.Write("Enter a pay rate: ")
payRate = Convert.ToDecimal(Console.ReadLine())
If payRate < 5.15 or payRate > 75 Then
   Throw New Exception("Pay rate is invalid!")
End If
```

By throwing an exception when an application error is detected, the programmer can treat system-generated exceptions and application errors in the same manner. For example:

```
Dim payRate As Decimal
Try
   Console.Write("Enter a pay rate: ")
   payRate = Convert.ToDecimal(Console.ReadLine())
   If payRate < 5.15 or payRate > 75 Then
      Throw New Exception("Pay rate is invalid!")
   End If
Catch e As Exception
   ' The pay rate was not entered correctly
   ' ... either a conversion problem or a range problem
   Console.WriteLine("Pay rate error: {0}", e.Message)
End Try
```

Types of Exceptions

There are actually many types of exceptions in VB.NET. Table 9–1 lists just a few of the ones that are commonly encountered.

TABLE 9–1   *Partial Listing of .NET Exceptions*

Exception	Description
System.FormatException	This exception is thrown when the format of an argument does not meet the parameter specifications of the method.
System.IndexOutOfRangeException	This exception is thrown when an attempt is made to access an element outside the bounds of the array.
System.InvalidCastException	This exception is thrown for invalid conversions.
System.NullReferenceException	This exception is thrown when an attempt is made to use a null object reference.
System.OutOfMemoryException	This exception is thrown when memory is insufficient to continue program execution.

TABLE 9–1	*Partial Listing of .NET Exceptions (continued)*

Exception	Description
System.OverflowException	This exception is thrown when an arithmetic or conversion operation generates an overflow.
System.RankException	This exception is thrown when an array with the wrong number of dimensions is passed to a procedure.
System.StackOverflowException	This exception is thrown when the program stack overflows. It is typically caused by unbounded recursion.

Code
Example

The following program, found in **MultipleExceptionsDemo,** handles several different types of system exceptions. The user may enter one of several commands to add data to a list, view data in the list, or quit.

```
Imports System

Module MultipleExceptionsDemo

    ' Different types of commands
    Private Enum CommandType As Byte
        NewData
        LookupElement
        ShowAll
        Quit
    End Enum

    ' Gets the user's command
    Private Function GetCommand() As CommandType
        Dim cmd As String
        Do While True
            Console.WriteLine("Enter command (H for help): ")
            cmd = Console.ReadLine().ToUpper()

            ' Translate the user's command
            Select Case cmd
                Case "H"
                    Console.WriteLine( _
                            "Enter N=new data, L=lookup value, ")
                    Console.WriteLine( _
                            "         D=display all data, Q=quit ")
                Case "N"
                    Return CommandType.NewData
                Case "L"
                    Return CommandType.LookupElement
                Case "D"
                    Return CommandType.ShowAll
```

```
            Case "Q"
                Return CommandType.Quit
        End Select
    Loop
End Function

Sub Main()
    Dim cmdType As CommandType
    Dim index, value, nums(9) As Integer

    ' Repeats forever (or until Quit is selected!)
    Do While True
        ' Gets the user's command
        cmdType = GetCommand()
        Try
            ' Processes the user's command
            Select Case cmdType
                Case CommandType.NewData
                    Console.Write("Enter index: ")
                    index = _
                        Convert.ToInt32(Console.ReadLine())
                    Console.Write("Enter new value: ")
                    value = _
                        Convert.ToInt32(Console.ReadLine())
                    nums(index) = value
                Case CommandType.LookupElement
                    Console.Write("Enter index: ")
                    index = _
                        Convert.ToInt32(Console.ReadLine())
                    Console.WriteLine( _
                        "{0} is at position {1}", _
                        nums(index), index)
                Case CommandType.ShowAll
                    Console.Write("Values are: ")
                    For index = 0 To 9
                        Console.Write(nums(index) & "  ")
                    Next
                    Console.WriteLine()
                Case CommandType.Quit
                    Exit Sub
            End Select

        ' Handles exceptions
        Catch boundErr As IndexOutOfRangeException
            Console.WriteLine("Error: {0}", _
                boundErr.Message)
            Console.WriteLine( _
                "-----  Valid indices are 0 to 9")

        Catch formatErr As FormatException
```

```
            Console.WriteLine( _
                   "Error: {0}", formatErr.Message)
            Console.WriteLine( _
                   "-----  Must enter an integer value")

        Catch e As SystemException
            Console.WriteLine("Unknown error: {0}", _
                   e.ToString())
        End Try
      Loop
    End Sub

End Module
```

Output from this program might resemble the following:

```
Enter command (H for help):
D
Values are: 0  0  0  0  0  0  0  0  0  0
Enter command (H for help):
N
Enter index: 12
Enter new value: 99
Error: Exception of type System.IndexOutOfRangeException was
      thrown.
-----  Valid indices are 0 to 9
Enter command (H for help):
N
Enter index: 1
Enter new value: 10
Enter command (H for help):
L
Enter index: 1
10 is at position 1
Enter command (H for help):
N
Enter index: abc
Error: Input string was not in a correct format.
-----  Must enter an integer value
Enter command (H for help):
Q
```

Context and Stack Unwinding

Whenever a program executes in VB.NET, it places local variables onto the program stack. If a nested block or another procedure is called, a new "context" is encountered. The system places a new record on the program stack and again places all local variables in the new record on the stack.

Whenever an exception occurs, the system examines the current context to determine whether an exception handler exists for the exception. If so, the exception handler is called. If an exception is not handled in the current context, the exception is passed to successively higher contexts until it is finally handled, or until the top-level procedure fails to catch it and it is handled by a default system handler.

When the higher context is entered, VB.NET adjusts the stack properly, a process known as *stack unwinding*. Stack unwinding involves cleaning up local variables on the program stack so that the garbage collector can deallocate them.

Exception Handling Strategies

It is probably more difficult to learn good exception handling strategies than it is to learn the mechanics of **Try, Catch,** and **Throw.** Among other questions, these come to mind:

- Where should I put the **Try** block?
- How big/small should the **Try** block be?
- Must every procedure have a **Try** statement?
- What should I do in a **Catch** block?

Although the best place for a detailed discussion on exception handling strategies is in a book that discusses software engineering, we will try to answer as many questions as we can here by examining several possible exception handling strategies.

Granularity of the Try Block

Many people say that the code in a **Try** block should represent an atomic transaction. That is, the code in the **Try** block should be completed in its entirety or not at all. You can make mistakes by putting too much code—or too little code—in the **Try** block.

For example, look at the program **FToCExample.** This simple program accepts a number representing a temperature in Fahrenheit, converts it to Celsius, and displays the result.

Code
Example

In version 1 of the program, found in **FToCExample\Version 1,** the programmer placed a **Try** block before almost every statement. If an exception occurs, the temperature conversion is abandoned.

```
Sub Main()
    Dim f, c As Single

    Try
```

```
      Console.Write("Enter temp (in Fahrenheit): ")
      f = Convert.ToSingle(Console.ReadLine())
   Catch e As Exception
      Console.WriteLine("Error:" & e.Message)
      Exit Sub
   End Try

   Try
      c = (f - 32) * 5 / 9
   Catch e As Exception
      Console.WriteLine("Error:" & e.Message)
      Exit Sub
   End Try

   Try
      Console.WriteLine("{0}F = {1}C", f, c)
   Catch e As Exception
      Console.WriteLine("Error:" & e.Message)
      Exit Sub
   End Try
End Sub
```

Code Example

Although this code executes properly and does not fail when the user enters bad data, its design is less than ideal. Regardless of the cause of the exception, the programmer simply displays a message and exits the application when an exception is encountered. If that is the desired behavior, a better version is found in **FToCExample\Version 2.**

```
Public Sub Main()
   Dim f, c As Single

   Try
      Console.Write("Enter temp (in Fahrenheit): ")
      f = Convert.ToSingle(Console.ReadLine())
      c = (f - 32) * 5 / 9
      Console.WriteLine("{0}F = {1}C", f, c)
   Catch e As Exception
      Console.WriteLine("Error:" & e.Message)
      Exit Sub
   End Try
End Sub
```

As you can see, version 2 represents a much cleaner version of the code, yet performs exactly the same as version 1.

Responsibilities of the Catch Block

The **Catch** block of an exception handler can perform many different types of activities. For example, it may simply display an error message. Or it may set some return value to a default value. Or it may repeat the failed activity again. There are several things to consider when writing a **Catch** handler:

- Does the fact that this exception occurred cause us to notify the user with some type of message?
- Could we take corrective action to suppress the exception? (For example, if input was illegal or a calculation failed, could we assume a default value?)
- Is this an exception, or if we tried the action again, might we succeed? (For example, if the user entered bad data, should we let them try again, or if the disk drive wasn't ready, should we access it again?)
- When we finish executing the code in the **Catch** block, have we handled the exception so that we can continue? Or do we need to notify some other block of code that we were unable to resolve some problem?

Code
Example

In this next version of the program, we introduce corrective behavior in our **Catch** statement for user input. The following code, found in **FToCEx-ample\Version 3,** forces the user to enter good data. If an exception is found during the conversion of input data, the program loops back and asks the user for data again.

```
Sub Main()
    Dim f, c As Single
    Dim goodInput As Boolean = False

    ' Loop until the user enters good data
    Do While Not goodInput
        Try
            Console.Write("Enter temp (in Fahrenheit): ")
            f = Convert.ToSingle(Console.ReadLine())
            goodInput = True
        Catch e As Exception
            Console.WriteLine("Error:" & e.Message)
        End Try
    Loop

    ' Process the data
    Try
        c = (f - 32) * 5 / 9
        Console.WriteLine("{0}F = {1}C", f, c)
    Catch e As Exception
        Console.WriteLine("Error:" & e.Message)
        Exit Sub
    End Try
End Sub
```

As you can see in the example, there are two **Try** blocks. The first **Try** block is inside a **Do** loop that does not exit unit the variable **goodData**

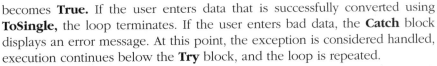

becomes **True.** If the user enters data that is successfully converted using **ToSingle,** the loop terminates. If the user enters bad data, the **Catch** block displays an error message. At this point, the exception is considered handled, execution continues below the **Try** block, and the loop is repeated.

Many people would not be happy with the previous version because it asks for a temperature, in Fahrenheit, over and over until good data is entered. In the program **FToCExample\Version 4,** we introduce a limit to the number of times that user may try to enter a Fahrenheit value.

Code
Example

```
Sub Main()
    Dim f, c As Single
    Dim goodInput As Boolean = False
    Dim numChancesLeft As Byte

    Try
        ' Loop until the user enters good data (max 3 times)
        numChancesLeft = 3
        Do While Not goodInput
            Try
                Console.Write("Enter temp (in Farenheit): ")
                f = Convert.ToSingle(Console.ReadLine())
                goodInput = True
            Catch e As Exception
                Console.WriteLine("Error:" & e.Message)
                numChancesLeft -= 1
                If numChancesLeft <= 0 Then
                    Throw New System.Exception("Failed to " & _
                    " enter good data after 3 attempts")
                End If
            End Try
        Loop
        ' Process the data
        c = (f - 32) * 5 / 9
        Console.WriteLine("{0}F = {1}C", f, c)
    Catch e As Exception
        Console.WriteLine("Error:" & e.Message)
        Exit Sub
    End Try
End Sub
```

In this version, there are nested **Try** blocks. The innermost **Try** block represents the input section. It is in a loop. If bad input data generates an exception, an error message is displayed and the variable **numChancesLeft** is decremented. When **numChancesLeft** becomes 0, the inner **Catch** block throws a new exception with the message:

```
Failed to enter good data after three attempts
```

The outer **Try** block's **Catch** handles exceptions generated by any of the three "tasks" that the **Try** surrounds:

- Prompting for user input
- Converting temperature data from Fahrenheit to Celsius
- Displaying the result

The only thing wrong with this version is that it is becoming difficult to read and should be more modularized.

Where Should We Handle Exceptions?

In the previous versions of the example, all the code was written inside the **Main** subroutine. This will typically not occur with programs of non-trivial size. So we should begin to build a strategy for program decomposition and how it affects the handling of exceptions.

As a general rule, exceptions should be handled very close to where they occur. But this does not mean that every procedure needs a **Try** block. You can't handle an exception unless the procedure has some understanding of how it should respond when the exception occurs.

Code Example

The next version of the **FToCExample** example is found in **FToCExample\Version 5.** As you can see by examining the code, we have become much more modular.

```
Imports System

Module FToCExample

    Sub Main()
        Dim f, c As Single
        ' Convert a temperature in Fahrenheit to Celsius
        Try
            f = GetTemperature()
            c = FToC(f)
            Console.WriteLine("{0}F = {1}C", f, c)
        Catch e As Exception
            Console.WriteLine("Error:" & e.Message)
            Exit Sub
        End Try
    End Sub


    ' Read a single precision value
    Public Function GetSingle() As Single
        Return Convert.ToSingle(Console.ReadLine())
    End Function


    ' Prompt the user for a Fahrenheit value and read the
    ' user's response
    Public Function GetTemperature() As Single
```

```
      Dim f As Single
      Dim numChancesLeft As Byte = 3
      Do While True
         Try
            Console.Write("Enter temp (in Fahrenheit): ")
            f = GetSingle()
            Return f
         Catch e As Exception
            Console.WriteLine("Error:" & e.Message)
            numChancesLeft -= 1
            If numChancesLeft <= 0 Then
               Throw New System.Exception("Failed to " & _
                  " enter good data after 3 attempts")
            End If
         End Try
      Loop
   End Function

   ' Knows the formula to convert Fahrenheit to Celsius
   Public Function FToC(ByVal f As Single) As Single
      Return (f - 32) * 5 / 9
   End Function

End Module
```

The **Main** procedure contains a **Try** block around the three steps of the temperature conversion process. If an exception arises in any step, the process is abandoned and the **Catch** statement is activated.

The function **GetTemperature** is used to prompt the user for a temperature and to read the value entered from the console. It contains the logic to detect input exceptions and respond to them. The function handles all exceptions locally, if possible. However, after three failed attempts to retrieve good data from the user, this function generates an exception, notifying the conversion process that it was unable to perform its task.

The function **GetSingle** is a helper routine used by **GetTemperature.** Although it is the procedure that would encounter an exception if the user entered bad data, it does not handle that exception. The **GetSingle** function has a simple job—to get data from the user and convert it to a single-precision, floating-point number. If it fails, it does not know how to respond to that error (for example, whether to try again or to assume a value). Therefore, it has no **Try** block.

Similarly, the function **FToC** has no **Try** block. If it failed for some reason, it would be up to the calling procedure to decide how to respond.

Inner Exceptions

When we throw an exception from inside a **Catch** statement, we lose information about the original exception. However, we can retain that information by passing it as a parameter while constructing the new exception. The original exception is then available through the **InnerException** property of the new exception.

In the following program, **FToCExample\Version 6,** we have modified the **GetTemperature** function. After the user's third try at entering data, the new version of our program passes the exception back to the **Main** subroutine. The **Catch** handler in the **Main** subroutine has been modified to look for an **InnerException.**

```
Imports System

Module FToCExample

    Sub Main()
        Dim f, c As Single

        ' Convert a temperature in Fahrenheit to Celsius
        Try
            f = GetTemperature()
            c = FToC(f)
            Console.WriteLine("{0}F = {1}C", f, c)
        Catch e As Exception
            Console.WriteLine("Error:" & e.Message)
            If Not (e.InnerException Is Nothing) Then
                Console.WriteLine("  Original Error:" & _
                    e.InnerException.Message)
            End If
            Exit Sub
        End Try
    End Sub

    ' Read a single precision value
    Public Function GetSingle() As Single
        Return Convert.ToSingle(Console.ReadLine())
    End Function

    ' Prompt the user for a Fahrenheit value and read the
    ' user's response
    Public Function GetTemperature() As Single
        Dim f As Single
        Dim numChancesLeft As Byte = 3
        Do While True
            Try
                Console.Write("Enter temp (in Fahrenheit): ")
                f = GetSingle()
```

```
            Return f
        Catch e As Exception
            Console.WriteLine("Error:" & e.Message)
            numChancesLeft -= 1
            If numChancesLeft <= 0 Then
                Throw New System.Exception("Failed to " & _
                    "enter good data after 3 attempts", e)
            End If
        End Try
    Loop
End Function

' Knows the formula to convert Fahrenheit to Celsius
Public Function FToC(ByVal f As Single) As Single
    Return (f - 32) * 5 / 9
End Function

End Module
```

Custom Exceptions

You may create your own exception types using VB.NET by deriving a new class from **System.Exception.** For example, in a payroll application, you might create exceptions such as **InvalidPayException** or **InvalidEmployee-TypeException.** We will discuss this process in detail in Chapter 12.

IEEE 754 Floating-Point Standards

As we mentioned in Chapter 4, VB.NET adheres to the IEEE 754 standards with regard to floating-point arithmetic. Specifically, this means that floating-point division by 0 does not generate a runtime exception. Instead, the **System.Single** type defines three "special" floating-point constants:

- **PositiveInfinity** is the result of dividing a positive number by 0.
- **NegativeInfinity** is the result of dividing a negative number by 0.
- **NaN** (not a number) is the result of dividing 0 by 0.

System.Single also contains methods that allow programmers to test for these special values. These methods include **IsPositiveInfinity, IsNega-tiveInfinity, IsInfinity** (for positive or negative infinity), and **IsNaN.**

The following program, found in **IEEE754Example,** illustrates the use of these methods and constants.

Code Example

```
Imports System

Module IEEE754Example

    Sub Divide(ByVal num As Single, ByVal denom As Single)
        Dim s As Single
        s = num / denom
        If Not Single.IsNaN(s) Then
            Console.WriteLine("{0} / {1} = {2}", num, _
                              denom, s)
        Else
            Console.WriteLine("Error: {0} / {1} " & _
                "(Divide by zero!)", num, denom)
        End If
    End Sub

    Sub Main()
        Divide(5, 2)
        Divide(5, 0)
        Divide(-5, 2)
        Divide(-5, 0)
        Divide(0, 0)
    End Sub

End Module
```

If you run the program, the output is as follows:

```
5 / 2 = 2.5
5 / 0 = Infinity
-5 / 2 = -2.5
-5 / 0 = -Infinity
Error: 0 / 0 (Divide by zero!)
```

Summary

This chapter examined the new exception handling mechanism in VB.NET. The new mechanism uses **Try** blocks and **Catch** handlers to identify where exceptions are expected and how a program should respond to them. Exceptions may be generated by the procedures in the .NET library, or you may raise exceptions using a **Throw** statement. The .NET Framework Class Library provides a **System.Exception** class, which is used to gather information about where exceptions occur. Many types of exceptions, which are derived from **System.Exception,** exist in the .NET library and are thrown by various .NET procedures when an exception occurs. You may also create your own types of exceptions, and we will examine this in more detail in Chapter 12.

PART THREE

OBJECT-ORIENTED PROGRAMMING IN VB.NET

*P*art 3 examines the object-oriented features of VB.NET. This language is now fully object-oriented, which is one of the most significant improvements in VB.NET. In this part, we begin by examining how classes are built. Subsequent chapters discuss implementation and interface inheritance. These topics are covered gradually and thoroughly, making this part of the book accessible to readers without previous object-oriented experience.

Object-Oriented Programming

The most important feature of VB.NET is that it is a thoroughly object-oriented language, built that way from the ground up. VB.NET enjoys the benefits of other object-oriented languages, such as C++ and Java, and has some additional features that enhance the OOP experience. Beyond being object-oriented, VB.NET is also designed to facilitate the creation of components, which can be thought of as black-box entities that can be easily reused in creating software systems. In this chapter, we look at the big picture of what object-oriented programming is. We discuss objects and classes, abstraction and encapsulation, inheritance, and polymorphism. We provide a survey of some of the more important object-oriented languages, and we see where VB.NET fits in this picture. We conclude with an introduction to components, which extend the ideas of object-oriented programming in a manner that facilitates software reuse.

Objects

Objects have both a real-world and a software meaning, and an object model can describe a relationship between the two. This section summarizes the key terminology of objects.

Objects in the Real World

The term *object* has an intuitive real-world meaning. There are concrete, tangible objects, such as a ball, an automobile, and an airplane. There are also more abstract objects that have a definite intellectual meaning, such as a committee, a patent, or an insurance contract.

Objects have both attributes (or characteristics) and operations that can be performed upon them. A ball has a size, a weight, a color, and so on. Operations may be performed on the ball, such as throw, catch, and drop.

There can be various relationships among classes of objects. For example, one relationship is a specialization relationship, such as an automobile is a special kind of vehicle. Another relationship is a whole/part relationship, such as an automobile consists of an engine, a chassis, wheels, and other parts.

Object Models

Objects can also be used in programs. Objects are useful in programming because you can set up a software model of a real-world system. Software objects correspond to objects in the real world. Explicitly describing the real-world system in terms of objects helps you to understand the system more explicitly and precisely. The model can then be implemented as actual software using a programming language. A software system implemented in this way tends to be more faithful to the real system, and it can be changed more readily when the real system is changed.

There are formal languages for describing object models. The most popular language is UML (Unified Modeling Language), which is a synthesis of several earlier modeling languages. Formal modeling languages are beyond the scope of this book, but we will find that informal models are useful.

Reusable Software Components

Another advantage of objects in software is that they can facilitate reusable software components. Hardware has long enjoyed significant benefits from reusable hardware components. For example, computers can be created from power supplies, printed circuit boards, and other components. Printed circuit boards, in turn, can be created from chips. The same chip can be reused in many different computers, and new hardware designs do not have to be created from scratch.

With appropriate software technology, similar reuse is feasible in software systems. Objects provide the foundation for software reuse.

Objects in Software

An *object* is a software entity containing data and related functions as a self-contained module. Objects hold *state* and specify *behavior.* Figure 10–1 illustrates a bank account object. The state of the object consists of the owner of the account, an ID for the account, and the account balance. The behavior of the account consists of functions to deposit or withdraw an amount, to change the owner of the account, and to obtain an account statement. Objects provide the means for *abstraction, encapsulation,* and *instantiation.*

| **FIGURE 10–1** | *A bank account object.* |

State and Behavior

An object has data—a set of properties, or attributes—which are its essential characteristics. The state of an object is the value of these attributes at any point in time. The behavior of an object is the set of operations or responsibilities that it must fulfill for itself and for other objects.

The data and operations are packaged together, as illustrated in Figure 10–2. As part of software design, this packaging aids conceptualization and abstraction. Related items are turned into a conceptual unit.

Data
and
Operations

FIGURE 10-2 *Data and operations are packaged together.*

Abstraction

An *abstraction* captures the essential features of an entity, suppressing unnecessary details. All instances of an abstraction share these common features. Abstraction helps us deal with complexity.

Encapsulation

The implementation of an abstraction should be hidden from the rest of the system, or *encapsulated*. Objects have a public side and a private side, as illustrated in Figure 10-3.

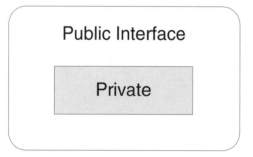

Public Interface

Private

FIGURE 10-3 *Objects have public and private sides.*

The public side is what the rest of the system knows, while the private side implements the public side. Data itself is private, walled off from the rest of the program. Data can be accessed only through functions (or *methods*) with a public interface.

There are two kinds of protection:

● Internal data is protected from corruption.
● Users of the object are protected from changes in the representation.

ENCAPSULATION EXAMPLE

Consider a *Bank* object that has a list of *Account* objects. How do you represent this list of accounts? You could use an array, or a linked list, or several other representations. If you pick a specific representation, say a linked list, and expose this representation to the rest of the system, you will have an overly complicated system. Moreover, the system will be brittle, because with several parts of the system accessing the linked list, it would be possible for a piece of code to make an error in manipulating the links, leaving the list in a corrupted state.

A much better solution is to encapsulate the list within the Bank object and define public methods such as **AddAccount** and **DeleteAccount.** The rest of the system does not need to be concerned with the details of representation of the list, but simply goes through these public methods.

Classes

A *class* groups all objects with common behavior and common structure. A class allows production of new objects of the same type. An object is an instance of some class. We refer to the process of creating an individual object as *instantiation.*

Classes can be related in various ways, such as by *inheritance* and by *containment.*

Inheritance

Inheritance is a key feature of the object-oriented programming paradigm. You abstract out common features of your classes and put them in a high-level base class. You can add or change features in more specialized derived classes, which "inherit" the standard behavior from the base class. Inheritance facilitates code reuse and extensibility.

Consider **Account** as a base class, with derived classes of **CheckingAccount** and **SavingsAccount.** All accounts share some characteristics, such as a balance. Different kinds of accounts differ in other respects. For example, a checking account has a monthly fee, while a savings account earns interest at a certain rate. Figure 10–4 illustrates the relationship among these different kinds of accounts.

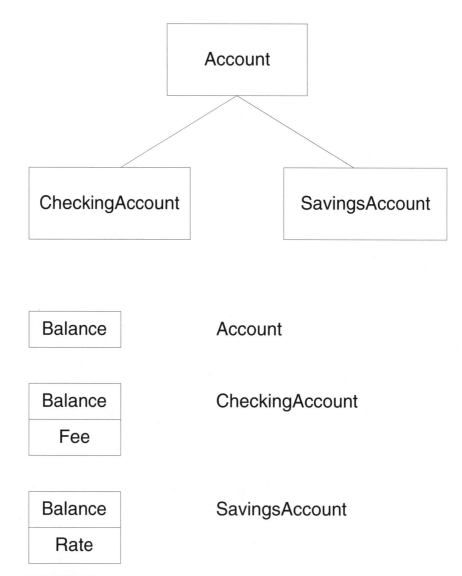

The inheritance relationship among different account classes.

Relationships Among Classes

Classes may be related to each other in various ways.

- The inheritance (IS-A) relationship specifies how one class is a special case of another class. A **CheckingAccount** (subclass or derived class) is a special kind of **Account** (superclass or base class).

- The composition (HAS-A) relationship specifies how one class (the whole) is made up of other classes (the parts). A **Bank** (whole) has a list of **Account** objects.
- A weaker kind of relationship (USES-A) can be identified when one class merely makes use of some other class when carrying out its responsibilities.

Polymorphism

Consider the problem of generating monthly statements for different kinds of accounts. Checking and savings accounts differ, with one possibly resulting in a fee and the other in a posting of interest.

A traditional approach is to maintain a type field in an account structure and to perform processing in a switch statement, with cases for each type. Using switch statements is error prone and requires much maintenance when adding a new account type.

An alternative is to localize the intelligence to generate a statement in each account class, which will support its own **GetStatement** method. Generic monthly statement code can then be written that will handle different types of accounts and will not have to be modified to support additional account types. Provide a **GetStatement** method in the base class and an override of this method in each derived class. Call **GetStatement** through an object reference to a general **Account** object. Depending on the actual account class referred to, the appropriate **GetStatement** method will be called.

The ability for the same method call to result in different behavior depending on the object through which the method is invoked is referred to as *polymorphism*. Although somewhat advanced, polymorphism can greatly simplify complex systems and is an important part of the object-oriented paradigm.

Object-Oriented Languages[1]

How do you write programs that make use of objects? So-called "data hiding" to achieve encapsulation can be implemented fairly easily in many programming languages. For example, in C you can declare data to be static and thus

---

1. The sections "Object-Oriented Languages" and "Components" are taken from the author's book *Understanding and Programming COM+*, Prentice Hall, 2000.

have file scope. Then you implement various functions in this source file that may access the data. The functions can be called from functions in other source files (they are public), but the data itself is private to the file where it is declared.

It is not quite so easy in C to implement class-type behavior, where you can create objects as instances of a class. It can be done through the concept of an opaque "handle" that is used to represent a data object. A special "CreateXXXX" function is implemented to create a particular type of object and return a handle. Internally, a handle table is maintained, which associates a pointer to actual data with a handle. Outside, there is no access to the pointer to the data, only to the handle. All functions that manipulate these "objects" take a handle as a parameter. This type of handle architecture is used extensively in the Windows C style API, including extension systems such as ODBC.

Simula and C++

The first use of the class construct in a programming language occurred in 1967 in Norway, in the language Simula, which was derived from Algol. Bjarne Stroustrup, the inventor of C++, used the language Simula in his doctoral research for coding simulation programs he wrote to model computer systems. He found that the Simula language was very expressive and permitted him to work at a high level of abstraction. But when it came time to run the programs to get the numerical results he needed for his thesis, he found that the performance was far too slow, and he would never be able to complete the work in time! So he recoded his programs in C. But he did something very intelligent. In place of handcoding, he wrote a translator program that would take a C-like program with extensions for classes (modeled after Simula) and translate to pure C. The result was a language initially called "C with Classes," which later became C++. The translator program became the AT&T "cfront" compiler, which would translate C++ to C, thus facilitating the creation of C++ compilers for many different kinds of computers (because C itself is implemented on many machines). Later C++ compilers translated directly to machine language for the particular machine. Whether the translation is via a preliminary translation to C via cfront or directly, the end result is compiled machine language code for the target platform. Besides being compiled code, the design of C++ (remember Stroustrup and his need to complete his thesis!) in several ways was steered toward *efficiency*.

Smalltalk

Another important object-oriented language was Smalltalk. Unlike C++, which derived from C, Smalltalk (designed at the Xerox Parc research facility) was created from the ground up as a "pure" object-oriented language. In Smalltalk, everything, even numbers, was implemented as objects. There was an extensive standard class library that was part of the language. There were also rich program development tools, such as class browsers and debuggers. The result was a very capable program development environment. Smalltalk code was not as efficient as C++, and the programming language was quite different from what most programmers were used to. Smalltalk has remained as a niche language. There have been other object-oriented languages that have remained even more as niche players, such as Objective C and Eiffel.

Java

A popular current language is Java. Java is object-oriented and built from the ground up but, unlike Smalltalk, Java takes a more pragmatic approach to native data types, implementing them directly, not as objects. Java compiles into a portable intermediate language called "bytecode" that runs on a Java Virtual Machine, which interprets the bytecode on a particular platform. The result is that the same compiled Java program will run unchanged on many different computers—a feature very desirable in Internet applications. Java comes with a large and rapidly expanding standard class library. A downside of Java is lower performance.

C#

The new programming language C# is fully object-oriented and in many respects combines the best elements of C++, Smalltalk, Java, and Visual Basic. C# is closest to Java among other programming languages, and the basic structure of the .NET environment is rather close to the Java environment, with C# and other .NET languages generating an intermediate language, which executes on a virtual machine (the Common Language Runtime). But C# contains some important enhancements. The most significant is that in C# "everything is an object," as in Smalltalk. This uniformity greatly simplifies use of the language, enabling numbers to be treated like objects, stored in collections, and so on. But whereas Smalltalk paid a heavy performance penalty for such uniformity, C# has a unique concept of "boxing" and "unboxing," in which a primitive value like a number can be "boxed" into an object wrapper when there is need for the value to be treated as an object. But for usages where an object is not required, simple values can be efficiently manipulated directly.

Another important innovation of C# is its support of *components*, which we discuss in the next major section.

Visual Basic and VB.NET

Visual Basic is not commonly thought of as an object-oriented language, but versions of the language are quite object-oriented. The Visual Basic object model is tied closely to the Microsoft Component Object Model (COM) and works very well in a COM environment, both for using COM objects and for creating them. Originally, Visual Basic was interpreted, but later versions can produce compiled code. Visual Basic is exceptionally easy to program.

The newest version of Visual Basic, VB.NET, is a fully object-oriented language and conforms to the same object model as C#. Like C#, VB.NET provides complete support of software components.

Components

A few years ago, the magazine *BYTE* ran a cover story titled "Is Object-Oriented Programming Dead?" Inside, they made the point that in many ways "objects" have not lived up to their hype. People had talked about how objects would facilitate code reuse. In fact, objects have been compared to hardware chips. Great economy is now achieved in hardware engineering by creating computers from chips rather than implementing custom circuitry. It was hoped that similar reuse could be achieved by software objects. But it never happened.

Meanwhile, Microsoft created a language called Visual Basic to simplify programming Windows applications. Central to the Visual Basic approach was drawing various graphical user interface (GUI) elements, or "controls" (like text boxes, list boxes, buttons, etc.), onto a form. These various controls could be attached to little pieces of code that would handle associated events. From the beginning, Microsoft recognized that the built-in controls were nowhere near comprehensive enough to satisfy the needs of Visual Basic programmers. So Microsoft defined a specification for a "VBX" (Visual Basic Extension) custom control. A VBX would plug into the VB development environment and behave just like an ordinary built-in control, but would do the special features designed for it. Like an ordinary control, a VBX had *properties* that could be set and *events* that could be handled by VB code.

Soon there were hundreds and then thousands of VBXs created and sold by independent software vendors. A VBX could be a simple graphical "widget" of some sort or could implement complex functionality such as Windows sockets. Any VBX could be easily plugged into a Visual Basic program.

The *BYTE* article highlighted VBXs as more successful than objects in implementing the dream of reuse. The article raised the hackles of many in the object-oriented community. VBXs were not object-oriented: They lacked even the concept of a method, and they certainly did not support features such as inheritance and polymorphism. But they did facilitate reuse. They were commercially successful.

A VBX can be considered an example (albeit, a somewhat crude one) of a software *component*. Loosely, a software component can be thought of as a piece of binary code that can be easily plugged into different applications.

VB.NET and Components

Beyond supporting classical object-oriented programming, VB.NET is designed as a *component-oriented* language. In VB.NET, properties, methods, and events are all supported directly by the language, enabling the creation of the easy-to-use pluggable components that have been a characteristic of the Visual Basic environment. Combined with the RAD characteristics of Visual Studio.NET, VB.NET development does indeed offer much of the ease and speed of development of Visual Basic. At the same time, VB.NET is completely object-oriented (even more so than C++), so VB.NET is extremely powerful.

We will discuss the component-oriented features of VB.NET as we elaborate the features of the language in the coming chapters, and in Chapter 23, we will show how to create the black-box class libraries that are components in the .NET world.

Summary

VB.NET is a thoroughly object-oriented language, built that way from the ground up. In this chapter, we surveyed the principle concepts of object-oriented programming, including objects and classes, abstraction and encapsulation, inheritance, and polymorphism. We looked at a number of object-oriented languages and saw the position of VB.NET in this picture. Finally, we briefly examined components, which can be thought of as black-box entities that can be easily reused in creating software systems. VB.NET is a language that is object-oriented and also facilitates creating components. In Chapter 11, we will begin our detailed discussion of object-oriented programming in VB.NET with a careful discussion of classes in VB.NET.

Classes

Visual Basic.NET is a significant improvement over previous versions of Visual Basic in terms of its object-oriented capabilities. For the first time, it represents a fully object-oriented language, complete with implementation and interface inheritance. In this chapter, we explore the use of VB.NET classes for representing program entities. We begin with an examination of how VB.NET supports encapsulation by providing the ability to define private data attributes and public methods. We describe how New is used to create objects, and how constructors can be used to initialize objects. We then introduce Property and Event procedures, as well as shared data and methods. Finally, we describe how garbage collection is accomplished in .NET.

Classes as User-Defined Data Types

The VB.NET programming language has a rich collection of intrinsic data types that were discussed in Chapter 4. Data types such as **Integer, Decimal, Date,** and **String** can be used to represent basic data. VB.NET also provides several advanced data types such as arrays and structures, which were discussed in Chapter 7.

This chapter focuses on one of VB.NET's most interesting data types: **Class.** It allows programmers to build object-oriented programs. Using classes, you can develop complex data entities such as an employee, an invoice, a robot, or a communications packet**.**

Defining a Class

As we discussed in Chapter 10, a class can be used to build complex data types that contain both data and behavior. The data elements, which are called *data members* or *attributes,* are made up of the basic data types of the language. The behavioral elements, which are called *member functions* or *methods,* are implemented as procedures.

When creating an entity, the goal is to capture only the essential features of the entity, suppressing unnecessary details. This helps us deal with complexity. As an example, think about a bank account.

- What data elements would it contain? An account number? An owner's name? The address to which statements are mailed? An account balance? The date the account was opened?
- What behavior would it have? Could you open it? Deposit to it? Withdraw from it? Check the account balance? Would it pay interest? Would it charge a monthly service fee for low balances?

There are many possible features of a bank account, but for our purposes, the only essential data elements are the account number, the owner's name, and the balance. The only essential operations are opening the account, making a deposit, making a withdrawal, and querying the values of the three data members. All instances of a bank account share these common features.

The implementation details of the bank account should be hidden from the rest of the system, or *encapsulated.* Objects have a public and a private side. The public side is what the rest of the system knows about the object, while the private side implements the public side. For example, the public method **Deposit** operates on the private data member **m_balance.** Figure 11–1 illustrates the bank account we have designed.

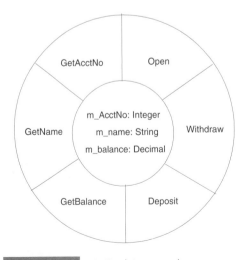

FIGURE 11–1   *A BankAccount class.*

Data itself is typically private and can be accessed through methods in the public interface. Such encapsulation provides two kinds of protection:

- Internal data is protected from corruption. The public methods that change the data can enforce range constraints, formatting constraints, etc., on private data members, while still allowing users access to them.
- Users of the object are protected from changes in the representation of data members. If a private data member is changed from one data type to another, users of the object are not necessarily affected. If **m_balance** (in the example above) is replaced by two private data members, **m_dollars** and **m_cents,** the user is not affected. Only the public methods that interact with **m_balance** must be modified.

To code such a class in VB.NET, you must first add a new class module to your project. You can do this by right-clicking on the name of the project and choosing **Add Class**. Figure 11–2 illustrates the prompt screen that will be displayed. If you name the class **BankAccount,** the environment generates a new file named **BankAccount.vb.**

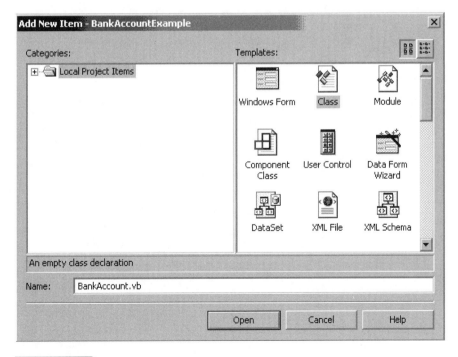

FIGURE 11–2   *Adding a class to a VB.NET project.*

To define a class, you must begin the definition with the keyword **Class** followed by the name of the class. The class is terminated by the **End Class** statement.

```
Class BankAccount

End Class
```

To define data members of a class, you typically add them as *private* data members. A common naming convention is to prefix the variable names with **m_** to indicate that they are members of the class. For example:

```
Public Class BankAccount

    Private m_acctNo As Integer
    Private m_name As String
    Private m_balance As Decimal
    ...

End Class
```

To define the behavioral aspects of the class, you must add methods or procedures. Each method that is accessible by anyone who creates a **BankAccount** object is defined as a *public* procedure. For example:

```
Public Class BankAccount

    ' PRIVATE ATTRIBUTES
    Private m_acctNo As Integer
    Private m_name As String
    Private m_balance As Decimal

    ' PUBLIC METHODS
    Public Sub Open(ByVal acctNo As Integer, ByVal name As _
      String, Optional ByVal initialBalance As Decimal = 0)
        m_acctNo = acctNo
        m_name = name
        m_balance = initialBalance
    End Sub

    Public Function Deposit(ByVal amount As Decimal) _
      As Boolean
        ' Check for a negative deposit
        If amount < 0 Then Return False

        ' Process deposit
        m_balance += amount

        Return True
    End Function
```

```
Public Function Withdraw(ByVal amount As Decimal) _
As Boolean
    ' Check for a negative withdrawal
    If amount < 0 Then Return False

    ' Check for overdraft condition
    If amount > m_balance Then Return False

    ' Process withdrawal
    m_balance -= amount

    Return True
End Function

Public Function GetAcctNo() As Integer
    Return m_acctNo
End Function

Public Function GetName() As String
    Return m_name
End Function

Public Function GetBalance() As Decimal
    Return m_balance
End Function
End Class
```

Code
Example

The preceding code, found in **BankAccountExample\Version 1,** defines a new data type. This **BankAccount** class can be thought of as a template that can be used to create instances of a **BankAccount** (for example: "my" account and "your" account). An instance of a class is called an *object.* When objects of type **BankAccount** are created, they each contain an account number, name, and balance.

Class Syntax and Usage in VB.NET Differs from VB6

One of the most significant changes to Visual Basic from VB6 to VB.NET has been the introduction of complete object-oriented capabilities. Because of this, there are many changes to the language that VB6 programmers should be aware of. Changes range from new syntax for property procedures to the introduction of the Inherits keyword. VB6 programmers should read Chapters 11 through 13 carefully.

Creating and Using Objects

In VB.NET, there is a fundamental distinction between built-in data types, such as **Integer** and **Decimal,** and the extended types that are created using classes. Most built-in data types[1] are *value types*. This means that when you declare a variable of a built-in data type, you are allocating memory and creating the actual instance.

```
Dim x As Integer    ' 4 bytes of memory have been allocated
```

When you declare a variable of a class type, which is a reference type, you are only obtaining memory for a *reference* to an object of the class type. No memory is allocated for the object itself.

```
Dim myAcct as BankAccount    ' myAcct is a reference to a
                             ' BankAccount object; no
                             ' object exists yet
```

To create, or instantiate, an object in VB.NET, you must use the **New** keyword.

```
myAcct = new BankAccount()    ' a BankAccount object now
                              ' exists and myAcct is a
                              ' reference to it
```

Once an object exists, you may interact with it using any public member of the class. In this example, there are six methods that we may invoke.

```
myAcct.Open (101, "Dana")
myAcct.Deposit(1200)
Console.WriteLine("Account {0} has balance of {1:C}", _
        myAcct.GetAcctNo(), myAcct.GetBalance())
```

Set Keyword Not Used in VB.NET

VB6 programmers should note that the Set keyword is no longer used when performing object assignment.

The **New** keyword can be used when the variable is declared if you want to instantiate the object at the same time as you declare the variable.

```
Dim myAcct as New BankAccount    ' myAcct is a reference to a
                                 ' BankAccount object that
                                 ' was created in this
                                 ' declaration
```

The **BankAccount** class can be used to create many account objects. For example, if you wanted to declare two **BankAccount** objects, you can write the following code:

---

1. The type **String,** although a keyword in VB.NET, is in fact a reference type and is defined by the .NET class **System.String**.

```
Dim dlwAcct, mwwAcct as New BankAccount
dlwAcct.Open(158, "Dana", 1250)
mwwAcct.Open(263, "Mark", 1750)
```

To deposit $150 to the first account, you would use this statement:

```
dlwAcct.Deposit(150)
```

To deposit $150 to the second account, you would use this statement:

```
mwwAcct.Deposit(150)
```

If you attempt to reference the private members of an object from outside the implementation of a method, you will get a syntax error. For example, this code:

```
mwwAcct.m_balance = 1000000
```

will generate this syntax error:

```
BankAccount.m_balance is Private, and is not accessible in
this context.
```

Example: Bank Account (Version 1)

A more comprehensive example of using accounts can be found in the **Driver** module of **BankAccountExample\Version 1**. This program manages two accounts, **dlwAcct** and **mwwAcct**. It allows the user to interactively manipulate these two accounts using a series of predefined menu commands. The **BankAccount** class that it references was defined in the section "Defining a Class."

```
Imports System

Module Driver

    Sub Main()
        ' Declare two account references
        Dim dlwAcct, mwwAcct As BankAccount

        ' Create two accounts
        dlwAcct = New BankAccount()
        mwwAcct = New BankAccount()

        ' Open (initialize) the accounts
        dlwAcct.Open(158, "Dana", 1250)
        mwwAcct.Open(263, "Mark", 1750)

        Dim cmd, whichAccount As String
        Dim amount As Decimal
        Dim stat As Boolean
```

```vbnet
' Command loop
Do While True
   Console.Write("Enter command (H for help): ")
   cmd = Console.ReadLine().ToUpper()

   Select Case cmd
      Case "H"                ' help
         DisplayHelp()

      Case "D"                ' deposit
         whichAccount = ChooseAccount()
         amount = ChooseAmount()
         If whichAccount = "D" Then
            dlwAcct.Deposit(amount)
         ElseIf whichAccount = "M" Then
            mwwAcct.Deposit(amount)
         End If

      Case "W"                ' withdraw
         whichAccount = ChooseAccount()
         amount = ChooseAmount()
         If whichAccount = "D" Then
            stat = dlwAcct.Withdraw(amount)
            Console.WriteLine("Withdraw " & _
              IIf(stat, "Successful", "Failed"))
         ElseIf whichAccount = "M" Then
            stat = mwwAcct.Withdraw(amount)
            Console.WriteLine("Withdraw " & _
              IIf(stat, "Successful", "Failed"))
         End If

      Case "S"                ' show acct information
         whichAccount = ChooseAccount()
         If whichAccount = "D" Then
            Display(dlwAcct)
         ElseIf whichAccount = "M" Then
            Display(mwwAcct)
         End If

      Case "Q"                ' quit
         Exit Sub

      Case Else               ' error
         Console.WriteLine("Error: illegal command!")
   End Select
   Console.WriteLine()
Loop
End Sub

Private Sub DisplayHelp()
```

```
            Console.WriteLine( _
                "Legal commands are: H for Help, D for Deposit, ")
            Console.WriteLine( _
                "      W for Withdraw, S for Show Account Info, ")
            Console.WriteLine("      and Q for quit. ")
        End Sub

        Private Function ChooseAccount() As String
            Dim answer As String
            Do
                Console.Write( _
                    "....From which account (D=Dana, M=Mark)? ")
                answer = Console.ReadLine().ToUpper()
            Loop While answer <> "D" And answer <> "M"
            Return answer
        End Function

        Private Function ChooseAmount() As Decimal
            Dim answer As Decimal
            Console.Write("....How much? ")
            answer = Convert.ToDecimal(Console.ReadLine())
            Return answer
        End Function

        Private Sub Display(ByVal anAccount As BankAccount)
            Console.WriteLine("Account No: {0}", _
                            anAccount.GetAcctNo())
            Console.WriteLine("Name:      {0}", _
                            anAccount.GetName())
            Console.WriteLine("Balance:    {0:C}", _
                            anAccount.GetBalance())
        End Sub

End Module
```

Sample output from this program is shown below:

```
Enter command (H for help): S
....From which account (D=Dana, M=Mark)? D
Account No: 158
Name:      Dana
Balance:    $1,250.00

Enter command (H for help): S
....From which account (D=Dana, M=Mark)? M
Account No: 263
Name:      Mark
Balance:    $1750.00

Enter command (H for help): D
```

```
....From which account (D=Dana, M=Mark)? D
....How much? 850

Enter command (H for help): W
....From which account (D=Dana, M=Mark)? M
....How much? 500
Withdraw Successful

Enter command (H for help): W
....From which account (D=Dana, M=Mark)? M
....How much? 1500
Withdraw Failed

Enter command (H for help): S
....From which account (D=Dana, M=Mark)? D
Account No: 158
Name:       Dana
Balance:    $2,100.00

Enter command (H for help): S
....From which account (D=Dana, M=Mark)? M
Account No: 263
Name:       Mark
Balance:    $1250.00
```

Assigning Object References

It is important to have a firm understanding of the way that object references work in order to effectively write object-oriented programs in VB.NET. Figure 11–3 illustrates the object reference **myAcct** and the data it refers to after the following code:

```
Dim myAcct as New BankAccount

myAcct.Open(1551, "Brenda", 2250)
```

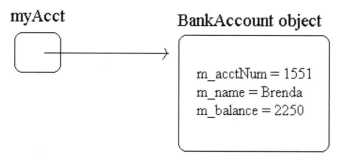

FIGURE 11–3 *An object reference and the data to which it refers.*

A second object variable, as shown below, can be created that references another object. Figure 11–4 illustrates the two object references.

```
Dim yourAcct as New BankAccount

yourAcct.Open(1552, "Glenda", 2000)
```

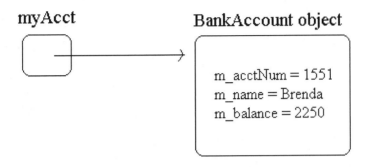

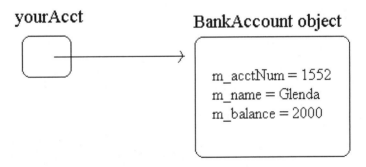

References to two objects.

Because these variables are reference types, when you make an assignment to an object variable, you are only assigning the reference. *There is no copying of data.* Figure 11–5 illustrates both object references and the data after the following assignment:

```
yourAcct = myAcct' yourAcct now refers to same object
                  ' that myAcct does
```

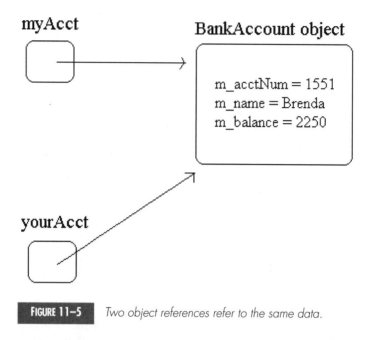

myAcct

BankAccount object

m_acctNum = 1551
m_name = Brenda
m_balance = 2250

yourAcct

FIGURE 11–5   *Two object references refer to the same data.*

Garbage Collection

Assignment of object references in VB.NET can lead to orphaned objects. For example, in Figure 11–5, the variable **myAcct** was assigned to **yourAcct**. Because of this assignment, **yourAcct** became orphaned. Such an object (or "garbage") takes up memory in the computer, which can now never be referenced.

The Common Language Runtime automatically reclaims the memory of unreferenced objects. This process is known as *garbage collection*. Garbage collection takes up some execution time, but it is a great convenience for programmers, helping to avoid a common program error known as a *memory leak*.

Garbage collection is discussed in detail in our book *Application Development Using Visual Basic and .NET.*

Defining Class Behavior

There are several types of procedures that can be defined in a VB.NET class. Subroutines and functions, more commonly called methods, provide the primary interface to a class. However, VB.NET also allows classes to define property and event procedures.

Methods

Methods in a VB.NET class follow, for all practical purposes, the same rules as any module-level procedure that we discussed in Chapter 6.

- They must define an access specifier (typically **Public** or **Private**).
- They may have optional parameters.
- They may be overloaded.
- They may have a variable-length parameter list.

However, there are some differences relating to the fact that these methods are associated with specific object instances. Within any method, the programmer has access to all of the data members of the class, all parameters and local variables defined within the method, and any other global-level variable. For example, inside the **BankAccount**'s **Deposit** method that we saw previously, we had access to **m_balance** even though it wasn't specifically declared inside the function.

```
Public Function Deposit(ByVal amount As Decimal) As Boolean
    ' Check for a negative deposit
    If amount < 0 Then Return False

    ' Process deposit
    m_balance += amount

    Return True
End Function
```

We had access to **m_balance** because it was defined as a data member of the class.

In a similar vein, consider these two bank account objects that are referenced by the variables **myAcct** and **yourAcct**:

```
myAcct.Deposit(100)        ' In this call to the Deposit
                           ' method, m_balance refers to
                           ' myAcct's m_balance

yourAcct.Deposit(100)      ' In this call to the Deposit
                           ' method, m_balance refers to
                           ' yourAcct's m_balance
```

Me

Sometimes, it is convenient to be able to access the current object reference from within a method. VB.NET defines the keyword **Me** for this purpose. **Me** is a special variable that always refers to the current object instance. An alternative implementation of the **Deposit** method shown above might be as follows:

```
Public Function Deposit(ByVal amount As Decimal) As Boolean
    ' Check for a negative deposit
    If amount < 0 Then Return False

    ' Process deposit
    Me.m_balance += amount

    Return True
End Function
```

Me can also be useful when the names of parameters match the names of member variables. For example, assume the **BankAccount** class had been designed without using an **m_** prefix for the variable names of all data members. The implementation of the **Open** method, shown below, is able to distinguish local variables (referenced by name) from instance variables (referenced using **Me**).

```
Class BankAccount

    Private acctNo As Integer
    Private name As String
    Private balance As Decimal

    Public Sub Open(ByVal acctNo as Integer, ByVal name _
     As String, ByVal balance As Decimal)
        Me.acctNo = acctNo
        Me.name = name
        Me.balance = balance
    End Sub

    . . .

End Class
```

Although the code shown above eliminates the need to use unique variable names for your data members and parameters, it is generally preferable to use the **m_** naming convention when building classes.

Properties

VB.NET provides a special type of procedure available to classes, modules, and structures called a *property* procedure. If you have a background as a VB6 programmer, you are probably familiar with properties. They were introduced in early versions of VB as a way to interact with controls on a Windows form. But to the rest of us, they initially have an odd look. For example, to change the caption of a button, you would have written the following code in VB6:

```
cmdCalculate.Caption = "Click here to calculate the answer"
```

However, this statement is actually called the **Set** property procedure for **Caption**. Properties are still used to interact with Windows controls in VB.NET; however, they are also used in user-defined types.

USING PROPERTIES

In VB.NET, a property *looks like* a public data member of an object from the perspective of the user of the object. For example, if the **BankAccount** class has a public property called **Name** that accesses the account's **m_name** data member, you could write the following code:

```
Dim someAcct As New BankAccount
someAcct.Open(1976, "Jean C.", 850)

Dim n As String
n = someAcct.Name            ' Reading the name

someAcct.Name = "Jean M."   ' Changing the name
```

Properties allow the user of an object to interact with the object in a new way. If the property **Name** shown above did not exist, we would have to provide **GetName** and **SetName** methods in the **BankAccount** class and write the following code:

```
Dim someAcct As New BankAccount
someAcct.Open(1976, "Jean C.", 850)

Dim n As String
n = someAcct.GetName()        ' Reading the name

someAcct.SetName("Jean M.") ' Changing the name
```

DEFINING PROPERTIES

To define a property, its name and data type must be specified. In addition, code must be written for both the **Get** and **Set** portions of the property. The following syntax describes a property:

```
[accessSpecifier] Property propertyName() As dataType
    Get
        statement(s) that return a value
    End Get

    Set [(ByVal Value As dataType)]
        statement(s) that assigns Value to some member
    End Set
End Property
```

If the access specifier is omitted for a property, it is assumed to be **Public**.

Properties Have New Syntax in VB.NET

VB6 programmers should note that the syntax for properties has been changed in VB.NET. There are no separate Get, Let, and Set procedures.

A **Name** property for the **BankAccount** class would be implemented as a **String** property because it represents access to data member **m_name**, which is a **String**. The **Name** property would be coded as follows:

```
Public Class BankAccount

    Private m_acctNo As Integer
    Private m_name As String
    Private m_balance As Decimal

    Public Property Name() As String
       Get
           Return m_name
       End Get

       Set(ByVal Value As String)
           m_name = Value
       End Set
    End Property

    ...

End Class
```

Whenever the property **Name** is used on the *left-hand side* of an assignment statement, VB.NET invokes the **set** property. If the property is used in any other context, the **get** property is invoked.

Parameter Optional in Set Property

The VB.NET language definition says that the parameter specified in the Set property is optional. If it is not specified, the implied parameter is named Value and is of the data type specified by the property.

Sometimes, a property must be read-only. That is, it should never be used on the *left-hand side* of an assignment statement. In these cases, the property is designated read-only using the **ReadOnly** keyword, and it does not have a **Set** portion.

For example, consider the **BankAccount** class again. In our version, we have decided that a **BankAccount** object can change its account number after it has been open. In this case, we must provide read-only access to the account number.

```
Public Class BankAccount

    Private m_acctNo As Integer
    Private m_name As String
    Private m_balance As Decimal

    Public ReadOnly Property AcctNo() As Integer
        Get
            Return m_acctNo
        End Get
    End Property

    ...

End Class
```

There are also times when a property must be write-only. That is, you can never use it to get the value of a property. In these cases, the property is designated write-only using the **WriteOnly** keyword and does not have a **Get** portion.

Although a write-only property is fairly rare, we could envision one in a slightly different version of the **BankAccount** class. In this alternate version, the class would define a PIN (personal identification number) that must be passed in for any withdrawal to succeed. The PIN would be defined when the account was opened. It could not be accessed, but it could be changed.

```
Public Class BankAccount

    Private m_acctNo As Integer
    Private m_name As String
    Private m_PIN as String
    Private m_balance As Decimal

    Public WriteOnly Property PIN() As String
        Set(ByVal Value As String)
            m_PIN = Value
        End Set
    End Property

    ...

End Class
```

Property procedures may also have parameters passed to them. Although this is uncommon, it can happen when a property represents an underlying array. For example, if a **Student** object maintained an array of test scores, a property called **Score** could be defined in the **Student** class that allowed the following type of access:

```
Dim zack As New Student
zack.Score(0) = 84
zack.Score(1) = 96
...
For i = 0 to 3
   Console.WriteLine("Test Score #{0} = {1}", _
                     i, zack.Score(i))
Next
```

The **Student** class, as described above, would minimally contain the following code:

```
Public Class Student

    Private m_scores(9) As Integer

    Public Property Score(ByVal index As Byte) As Integer
       Get
           Return m_scores(index)
       End Get
       Set(ByVal Value As Integer)
           m_scores(index) = Value
       End Set
    End Property

    ...

End Class
```

As you can see, the parameter **index** that is passed into the property **Score** is used as an index into the underlying **m_scores** array. Of course, introducing this property introduces the likelihood of a runtime exception if an invalid index value is passed into the **Scores** property.

Example: Bank Account (Version 2)

Code Example

A complete version of the new **BankAccount** class is shown below. It replaces the **GetAcctNo**, **GetName**, and **GetBalance** functions with the property **Name** and the read-only properties **AcctNo** and **Balance**. This code can be found in **BankAccountExample\Version 2**.

```
Public Class BankAccount

    Private m_acctNo As Integer
    Private m_name As String
    Private m_balance As Decimal

    Public Sub Open(ByVal acctNo As Integer, ByVal name As _
      String, Optional ByVal initialBalance As Decimal = 0)
        m_acctNo = acctNo
        m_name = name
        m_balance = initialBalance
    End Sub

    Public Function Deposit(ByVal amount As Decimal) _
     As Boolean
        ' Check for a negative deposit
        If amount < 0 Then Return False

        ' Process deposit
        m_balance += amount

        Return True
    End Function

    Public Function Withdraw(ByVal amount As Decimal) _
     As Boolean
        ' Check for a negative withdrawal
        If amount < 0 Then Return False

        ' Check for overdraft condition
        If amount > m_balance Then Return False

        ' Process withdrawal
        m_balance -= amount

        Return True
    End Function

    Public ReadOnly Property AcctNo() As Integer
        Get
            Return m_acctNo
        End Get
    End Property

    Public Property Name() As String
        Get
            Return m_name
        End Get
        Set(ByVal Value As String)
            m_name = Value
```

```
        End Set
    End Property

    Public ReadOnly Property Balance() As Decimal
        Get
            Return m_balance
        End Get
    End Property

End Class
```

The **Driver** module that allows the user to interactively manipulate two bank accounts has been modified to use these new properties.

```
Imports System

Module Driver

    Sub Main()
        ' Declare two account references
        Dim dlwAcct, mwwAcct As BankAccount

        ' Create two accounts
        dlwAcct = New BankAccount()
        mwwAcct = New BankAccount()

        ' Open (initialize) the accounts
        dlwAcct.Open(158, "Dana", 1250)
        mwwAcct.Open(263, "Mark", 1750)

        Dim cmd, whichAccount, newName As String
        Dim amount As Decimal
        Dim stat As Boolean

        ' Command loop
        Do While True
            Console.Write("Enter command (H for help): ")
            cmd = Console.ReadLine().ToUpper()

            Select Case cmd
                Case "H"                    ' help
                    DisplayHelp()

                Case "D"                    ' deposit
                    whichAccount = ChooseAccount()
                    amount = ChooseAmount()
                    If whichAccount = "D" Then
                        dlwAcct.Deposit(amount)
                    ElseIf whichAccount = "M" Then
                        mwwAcct.Deposit(amount)
```

```
                End If

        Case "W"                ' withdraw
            whichAccount = ChooseAccount()
            amount = ChooseAmount()
            If whichAccount = "D" Then
                stat = dlwAcct.Withdraw(amount)
                Console.WriteLine("Withdraw " & _
                  IIf(stat, "Successful", "Failed"))
            ElseIf whichAccount = "M" Then
                stat = mwwAcct.Withdraw(amount)
                Console.WriteLine("Withdraw " & _
                  IIf(stat, "Successful", "Failed"))
            End If

        Case "S"                ' show acct information
            whichAccount = ChooseAccount()
            If whichAccount = "D" Then
                Display(dlwAcct)
            ElseIf whichAccount = "M" Then
                Display(mwwAcct)
            End If

        Case "N"                ' change owner name
            whichAccount = ChooseAccount()
            newName = ChooseName()
            If whichAccount = "D" Then
                dlwAcct.Name = newName
            ElseIf whichAccount = "M" Then
                mwwAcct.Name = newName
            End If

        Case "Q"                ' quit
            Exit Sub

        Case Else               ' error
            Console.WriteLine("Error: illegal command!")
    End Select
    Console.WriteLine()
  Loop
End Sub

Private Sub DisplayHelp()
   Console.WriteLine( _
      "Legal commands are: H for Help, D for Deposit, ")
   Console.WriteLine( _
      "        W for Withdraw, S for Show Account Info, ")
   Console.WriteLine( _
      "        N for Change Name, and Q for quit. ")
End Sub
```

```
Private Function ChooseAccount() As String
   Dim answer As String
   Do
      Console.Write( _
            "....From which account (D=Dana, M=Mark)? ")
      answer = Console.ReadLine().ToUpper()
   Loop While answer <> "D" And answer <> "M"
   Return answer
End Function

Private Function ChooseAmount() As Decimal
   Dim answer As Decimal
   Console.Write("....How much? ")
   answer = Convert.ToDecimal(Console.ReadLine())
   Return answer
End Function

Private Function ChooseName() As String
   Dim answer As String
   Console.Write("....What is the new name? ")
   answer = Console.ReadLine()
   Return answer
End Function

Private Sub Display(ByVal anAccount As BankAccount)
   Console.WriteLine("Account No: {0}", _
                  anAccount.AcctNo)
   Console.WriteLine("Name:        {0}", _
                  anAccount.Name)
   Console.WriteLine("Balance:     {0:C}", _
                  anAccount.Balance)
End Sub

End Module
```

Sample output from this program is shown below. We issued commands that emphasize the interaction with the properties. The deposit and withdrawal methods were tested extensively in the previous version of this example.

```
Enter command (H for help): H
Legal commands are: H for Help, D for Deposit,
     W for Withdraw, S for Show Account Info,
     N for Change Name, and Q for quit.

Enter command (H for help): S
....From which account (D=Dana, M=Mark)? D
Account No: 158
Name:       Dana
```

```
Balance:    $1,250.00

Enter command (H for help): N
....From which account (D=Dana, M=Mark)? D
....What is the new name? Dana L. Wyatt

Enter command (H for help): S
....From which account (D=Dana, M=Mark)? D
Account No: 158
Name:       Dana L. Wyatt
Balance:    $1,250.00
```

Example: Statistics Calculator

To emphasize the design of classes, let's examine another situation. We need a class that maintains a list of floating-point numbers and can perform basic statistical calculations. **StatisticsManager** has the following methods and properties:

- The **InsertNumber** method is used to add a number to the internal list.
- The **Count** property returns the number of elements in the internal list.
- The **Average** property returns the average of the elements in the internal list.
- The **ItemAt** property returns the value of an item in the internal list given its subscript number. (This property requires a parameter that identifies the subscript of the item in the list that is to be returned.)

The following code, found in the program **Statistics**, contains the class **StatisticsManager** and illustrates how to build methods and properties.

Code
Example

```
Public Class StatisticsManager

    Private m_numbers(99) As Single
    Private m_numCount As Short

    Public Sub InsertNumber(ByVal number As Single)
        m_numbers(m_numCount) = number
        m_numCount += 1
    End Sub

    Public ReadOnly Property Count() As Short
        Get
            Return m_numCount
        End Get
    End Property

    Public ReadOnly Property ItemAt(ByVal index As Short) _
```

```
 As Single
    Get
        If index < 0 Or index >= m_numCount Then
            Throw New IndexOutOfRangeException()
        End If
        Return m_numbers(index)
    End Get
End Property

Public ReadOnly Property Average() As Single
    Get
        Dim sum As Single
        Dim index As Short
        For index = 0 To m_numCount - 1
            sum += m_numbers(index)
        Next
        Return sum / m_numCount
    End Get
End Property

End Class
```

The following simple procedure, also found in **Statistics**, uses the **StatisticsManager** class to find the average of a set of numbers.

```
Sub Main()
    Dim stat As New StatisticsManager()
    stat.InsertNumber(82)
    stat.InsertNumber(91)
    stat.InsertNumber(86)

    Dim index As Short
    For index = 0 To stat.Count - 1
        Console.WriteLine("Item({0}) = {1}", _
                        index, stat.ItemAt(index))
    Next
    Console.WriteLine("Average = {0}", stat.Average)
End Sub
```

Output from this program is shown below:

```
Item(0) = 82
Item(1) = 91
Item(2) = 86
Average = 86.33334
```

Shared Attributes and Procedures

In VB.NET, each instance of a class has its own set of unique values for the data members of the class. That is, each **BankAccount** object would have its own set of unique values for account number, owner's name, and balance. This type of data is called *instance data*.

Sometimes, however, it is useful to have a data value or procedure associated with the entire class, as opposed to individual instances. Such a member is called a **Shared** member.

Shared Attributes

To define a shared data member, simply add the keyword **Shared** to the data declaration. For example, we can modify our **BankAccount** class to keep track of the next available account number by adding a shared data member to the class.

```
Public Class BankAccount

    Private m_acctNo As Integer
    Private m_name As String
    Private m_balance As Decimal

    Private Shared m_nextAccountNum As Integer = 101

    . . .

End Class
```

In the example above, the class defines the variable **m_nextAccountNum**, which contains the next number that should be used for a new account. This variable is associated with the class, not with a particular instance of the class. Therefore, all instances of a **BankAccount** use the *same* variable m_**nextAccountNum**. This shared variable is used inside the **Open** method, which now resembles the following:

```
Public Sub Open(ByVal name As String, _
 Optional ByVal initialBalance As Decimal = 0)
   m_acctNo = m_nextAccountNum
   m_name = name
   m_balance = initialBalance

   m_nextAccountNum += 1
End Sub
```

The **Open** method no longer requires—or allows—the user of an object to specify the account number. Instead, the **BankAccount** class maintains the next available number. The following code illustrates one use of the new **Open** method:

```
Dim dlwAcct As New Account
dlwAcct.Open("Dana", 1250)
```

Like instance data members, shared data members can be either **Public** or **Private**. To access a public shared member, you must use the dot notation with the name of the class replacing the name of the object. For example, a public shared variable is defined as follows:

```
Public Class BankAccount
    Public Shared BankName As String = "First State Bank"
    Private Shared m_nextAccountNum As Integer = 101
    ...
End Sub
```

The variable **BankName** would be referenced outside of the class as follows:

```
Console.WriteLine(BankAccount.BankName)
```

A complete listing of this version of the class can be found in **BankAccount\Version 3**.

Shared Methods and Properties

A class may also declare methods and properties as **Shared**. To do this, simply add the keyword **Shared** to the method or property declaration.

A shared method or property can be called without instantiating the class. You use the dot notation, with the class name in front of the dot. Because you can call a shared procedure without an instance, it can only access local variables, shared variables of the class, and global variables. It cannot access instance data members.

You have been using shared methods since Chapter 2 of this book. The .NET **Console** class contains the shared methods **ReadLine** and **WriteLine**.

Example: Arithmetic Calculator

The following example, found in the program **Calculator**, defines a class that contains nothing but **Shared** methods. This class represents a simple mathematical calculator. However, rather than defining a set of global functions, we have defined a **Calculator** class.

```
Public Class Calculator

    Public Shared Function Add(ByVal op1 As Double, _
    ByVal op2 As Double)
        Return op1 + op2
```

```
End Function

Public Shared Function Subtract(ByVal op1 As Double, _
  ByVal op2 As Double)
     Return op1 - op2
End Function

Public Shared Function Multiply(ByVal op1 As Double, _
  ByVal op2 As Double)
     Return op1 * op2
End Function

Public Shared Function Divide(ByVal op1 As Double, _
  ByVal op2 As Double)
     Return op1 / op2
End Function
End Class
```

The following simple program uses methods in the **Calculator** class to achieve specific mathematical calculations.

```
Imports System

Module Driver

  Sub Main()
     Console.Write("Enter operand 1: ")
     Dim operand1 As Double = _
           Convert.ToDouble(Console.ReadLine())

     Console.Write("Enter operand 2: ")
     Dim operand2 As Double = _
           Convert.ToDouble(Console.ReadLine())

     Console.WriteLine("Add: {0}", _
           Calculator.Add(operand1, operand2))
     Console.WriteLine("Subtract: {0}", _
           Calculator.Subtract(operand1, operand2))
     Console.WriteLine("Multiply: {0}", _
           Calculator.Multiply(operand1, operand2))
     Console.WriteLine("Divide: {0}", _
           Calculator.Divide(operand1, operand2))
  End Sub

End Module
```

An example of the output of this test program is as follows:

```
Enter operand 1: 3
Enter operand 2: 9
Add: 12
```

```
Subtract: -6
Multiply: 27
Divide: 0.333333333333333
```

Constructors and Initialization

We have yet to discuss how an object in VB.NET is initialized. When an object is created, what initial values are assigned to the instance data? In many languages, variables that are not specifically initialized contain garbage. However, this is not a problem in VB.NET because variables are automatically initialized to a default value. These default values were discussed in detail in Chapter 4, but to refresh your memory, numerical data types are initialized to 0.

However, what do you do if you want to perform your own initialization? There are three approaches:

- The user of the class can perform the initialization by calling some special function such as the **BankAccount**'s **Open** method. The drawback is that we must be concerned that the user may have forgotten to call the initialization function.
- The class can initialize data members in the member declarations. The drawback is that all instances of the class are initialized with the same starting values.

```
Public Class BankAccount

    Private m_acctNo As Integer
    Private m_name As String = "Unknown"
    Private m_balance As Decimal

    ...
End Class
```

- The class can provide a special function called the *constructor* that can be used to initialize objects on a per-instance basis.

Defining Constructors

By using a constructor, you can allow the user to initialize individual objects in many different ways. In addition, you can perform other appropriate initializations (for example: open a file) when the object is created.

In VB.NET, a constructor is like a special method that is automatically called when an object is created using the **New** method. The constructor must be defined as a subroutine called **New**. It is typically defined as **Public**, and it may define a parameter list. For example:

```
Public Class BankAccount

    Private m_acctNo As Integer
    Private m_name As String
    Private m_balance As Decimal

    Private Shared m_nextAccountNum As Integer = 101

    Public Sub New(Optional ByVal name As String = "", _
     Optional ByVal initialBalance As Decimal = 0)
        m_acctNo = m_nextAccountNum
        m_name = name
        m_balance = initialBalance

        m_nextAccountNum += 1
    End Sub

    ...

End Class
```

In the routine that creates objects, the **New** keyword is used to instantiate object instances. It is during this **New** operation that you pass arguments to the constructor. For example:

```
Dim natAcct As BankAccount
natAcct = New BankAccount("Natalie", 1700)
```

The **New** keyword can also be used in the same statement that declares the reference variable. For example:

```
Dim britAcct As New BankAccount("Brittany", 1500)
```

Because the **BankAccount** constructor defines optional parameters, it could also be invoked using the following statement:

```
Dim zackAcct As New BankAccount()
```

In this case, the variable **zackAcct** references a **BankAccount** object that had the name initialized to the empty string and the balance initialized to zero.

VB.NET Class Constructors Must Be Named New

VB6 programmers should note that class constructors must now be named New. Class_Initialize is no longer valid.

Just like other procedures in VB.NET, constructors can be overloaded. However, you do not use the keyword **Overloaded** on the procedure definition. For example, we could have defined the following three constructors for the **BankAccount** class:

```
Public Class BankAccount

    Private m_acctNo As Integer
    Private m_name As String
    Private m_balance As Decimal

    Private Shared m_nextAccountNum As Integer = 101

    Public Sub New()
        m_acctNo = m_nextAccountNum
        m_name = ""
        m_balance = 0

        m_nextAccountNum += 1
    End Sub

    Public Sub New(ByVal name As String)
        m_acctNo = m_nextAccountNum
        m_name = name
        m_balance = 0

        m_nextAccountNum += 1
    End Sub

    Public Sub New(ByVal name As String, _
      ByVal initialBalance As Decimal)
        m_acctNo = m_nextAccountNum
        m_name = name
        m_balance = initialBalance

        m_nextAccountNum += 1
    End Sub
    ...

End Class
```

The first constructor listed (with no parameters) allows us to create an object without specifying any initial values:

```
Dim firstAcct As New Account
```

The second constructor listed (with one **String** parameter) allows us to create an object by specifying an owner's name:

```
Dim secondAcct As New Account("Jen")
```

The third constructor listed (with a **String** parameter and a **Decimal** parameter) allows us to create an object by specifying an owner's name and a starting balance:

```
Dim secondAcct As New Account("Jay", 1617)
```

However, through the creative use of optional parameters in our **BankAccount** example, we were able to provide the same functionality with only one constructor.

Default Constructor

If you do not define a constructor in your class, VB.NET will implicitly create one for you. This constructor is called the *default constructor,* and it has no parameters. The compiler-supplied default constructor will initialize member variables with the value specified on the variable declaration. If no value is specified, the default value for that variable's specific data type is used. In versions 1 and 2 of **BankAccount**, we did not specify a constructor, so we were using the compiler-supplied default.

The default constructor is an important constructor, because it is what allows the following declaration to occur:

```
Dim someAcct As New Account
```

Code
Example

However, if you provide any form of a constructor in your class, the compiler no longer supplies a version of the default constructor for you. As an example, consider the following version of a **Stock** class found in the program **StockPortfolio**. It defines one constructor that requires three parameters.

```
Public Class Stock

    Private m_symbol As String
    Private m_totalShares As Integer
    Private m_averageCost As Decimal

    Public Sub New(ByVal symbol As String, _
     ByVal numShares As Integer, ByVal cost As Decimal)
        m_symbol = symbol
        m_totalShares = numShares
        m_averageCost = cost
    End Sub

    . . .

End Class
```

The following line of code compiles successfully:

```
Dim msft as New Stock("MSFT", 100, 70)
```

However, this next declaration generates a compiler error that says the required arguments are not provided:

```
Dim someStock as New Stock()
```

This syntax error occurs because we have provided a constructor. If we had provided no constructors, VB.NET would have provided a default constructor. But because we provided one constructor, we must provide all allowable versions.

The real dilemma in the above example is deciding whether the declaration of **someStock** should generate an error, or whether we should provide an overloaded version of the default constructor. If it does not make sense to have a stock object that does not contain a symbol, then do nothing and allow this to be an error. If it does make sense that stock objects have yet to be assigned a symbol, add a second constructor as shown below:

```
Public Class Stock

    Private m_symbol As String
    Private m_totalShares As Integer
    Private m_averageCost As Decimal

    Public Sub New()
        m_symbol = ""
        m_totalShares = 0
        m_averageCost = 0
    End Sub

    Public Sub New(ByVal symbol As String, _
     ByVal numShares As Integer, ByVal cost As Decimal)
        m_symbol = symbol
        m_totalShares = numShares
        m_averageCost = cost
    End Sub

    . . .

End Class
```

Example: Bank Account (Versions 4A and 4B)

Code Example

The program **BankAccount\Version 4A** illustrates the use of constructors. Code for the **BankAccount** class was examined earlier in the section "Defining Constructors." The following partially illustrates the modifications that must be made to the **Driver** module. It shows that, without the **Open** method, **Driver** must initialize **BankAccount** objects by using the constructor. Because the constructor can be called three ways, there are several approaches that could be taken to initialize an account object.

```
Imports System

Module Driver

    Sub Main()
        ' Create two account references
        Dim dlwAcct, mwwAcct As BankAccount

        ' Create and initialize the two accounts
        ' One approach
        dlwAcct = New BankAccount()
        dlwAcct.Name = "Dana"
        dlwAcct.Deposit(1250)

        ' Another approach
        mwwAcct = New BankAccount("Mark", 1750)

        . . .
    End Sub

End Module
```

For a complete listing of this program, refer to the directory **BankAccount\Version 4A**.

Shared Constructor

Standard constructors are called each time an instance of a class is created. VB.NET also provides a *shared constructor* that is called only once, before any object instances are created. A shared constructor is defined by prefixing the constructor with the keyword **Shared**. A shared constructor can take no parameters and has no access modifier.

You can use a shared constructor to initialize a shared variable. The program **BankAccount\Version 4B** illustrates use of a shared constructor to initialize the shared variable **m_nextAccountNum**. In Version 4A, the variable was initialized to a specific starting value of 101 as part of the declaration of the variable. Using a shared constructor, we can initialize the variable to a starting value that is calculated at runtime, for example from a database. Version 4B of the program illustrates using a random number generator to calculate a starting value.

```
Shared Sub New()
    Dim rand As New Random()
    m_nextAccountNum = 101 + rand.Next(10000)
End Sub
```

In this constructor, we use the .NET **System.Random** class to generate random numbers. The **Next** method returns a random number that is less than the specified maximum. (Our example might result in duplicate account numbers!)

Constant and ReadOnly Members

VB.NET has two constructs to assist you when you want to make sure that a member of a class always has the same value. They keyword **ReadOnly** can be applied to instance variables to force its value to be constant. Look at this example:

```
Public Class BankAccount

    Private ReadOnly m_acctNo As Integer
    Private m_name As String = "Unknown"
    Private m_balance As Decimal

    Private Shared m_nextAccountNum As Integer = 101

    Public Sub New(Optional ByVal name As String = "", _
      Optional ByVal initialBalance As Decimal = 0)
        m_acctNo = m_nextAccountNum
        m_name = name
        m_balance = initialBalance

        m_nextAccountNum += 1
    End Sub

    ...

End Class
```

In the example above, the variable **m_acctNo** is defined as read-only. This means that it can be initialized in the constructor, but it cannot be changed in any other procedure. Any attempt to change it results in a syntax error. Although using **ReadOnly** isn't ever required, using it on variables that cannot change is good design.

VB.NET also provides the ability to define **Const** member declarations of a class. *When a data member is defined as **Const**, it is also a **Shared** member!* If it is **Public,** you can access it from outside the class using dot notation and the class name instead of an object variable. Unlike a **ReadOnly** member, a **Const** member cannot be changed in a constructor.

```
Public Class BankAccount

    Private ReadOnly m_acctNo As Integer
    Private m_name As String = "Unknown"
```

```
Private m_balance As Decimal

Private Shared m_nextAccountNum As Integer = 101
Private Const m_bankName As String = "First State Bank"

...

End Class
```

Events

VB.NET provides the ability for a class to *fire events* that can then be caught by the user using an instance of the class. Events are essentially callbacks to the user's code that occur when certain predefined data transitions occur.

For example, the **BankAccount** class might define the event **TransactionOccurred** that is fired each time a deposit or withdrawal action is successfully completed, or **OverdraftOccurred** is fired whenever a transaction results in a balance less than zero. Or a **Database** class might define the events **ConnectionCompleted** and **ConnectionTerminated** that are fired when connections are made or broken to the underlying data source.

There is an important difference between events and exceptions that must be noted. Events are callbacks to a user's code that can be trapped or ignored. Exceptions *must* be caught. An uncaught exception will terminate the program.

DEFINING EVENTS

Events are defined by adding an event declaration to the class using the **Event** keyword. Events must have a name and an optional list of parameters that will be sent to the event handler. For example, to add the **TransactionOccurred** event to the **BankAccount** class, we make the following changes. The **TransactionOccurred** event passes back to the user's code the type of event that occurred and the amount of the event. To provide a robust solution, we have introduced a set of enumeration values representing the different types of transactions that can occur.

```
Public Class BankAccount

    Public Enum TransactionType
        Deposit
        Withdrawal
    End Enum

    ' EVENTS
    Public Event TransactionOccurred(ByVal transType _
```

```
As TransactionType, ByVal amount As Decimal)

' PRIVATE ATTRIBUTES
Private m_acctNo As Integer
Private m_name As String
Private m_balance As Decimal

...

End Class
```

There are some restrictions on event procedures.

- They cannot have return values.
- They cannot have optional parameters.
- They cannot have a variable length parameter list.

However, events may define **ByVal** and **ByRef** parameters. The subtleties between these will be addressed later in this chapter.

RAISING EVENTS

Events are generated by the class when data transitions happen within an object that indicates the event should occur. To raise a specific event, the **RaiseEvent** statement is used. For example, the **TransactionOccurred** event is raised in the **Deposit** and **Withdraw** methods when they have successfully completed their activities.

```
Public Function Deposit(ByVal amount As Decimal) As Boolean
    ' Check for a negative deposit
    If amount < 0 Then Return False

    ' Process deposit
    m_balance += amount

    ' Fire event
    RaiseEvent TransactionOccurred( _
     TransactionType.Deposit, amount)

    Return True
End Function

Public Function Withdraw(ByVal amount As Decimal) _
 As Boolean
    ' Check for a negative withdrawal
    If amount < 0 Then Return False

    ' Check for overdraft condition
    If amount > m_balance Then Return False

    ' Process withdrawal
```

```
    m_balance -= amount

    ' Fire event
    RaiseEvent TransactionOccurred( _
      TransactionType.Withdrawal, amount)
    Return True
End Function
```

TRAPPING EVENTS USING WITHEVENTS

Events are trapped by the code that creates and uses a particular instance of the class. To indicate that you want to trap events generated for a particular object, you must declare the variable using the **WithEvents** keyword. For example:

```
Private WithEvents dlwAcct As BankAccount
```

To listen for events on a particular object, the variable must not be declared as a local variable in a procedure. It must be declared at the class or module level. After the variable declaration is complete, you will notice that the variable appears in the upper-left dropdown box on the editor window (see Figure 11–6).

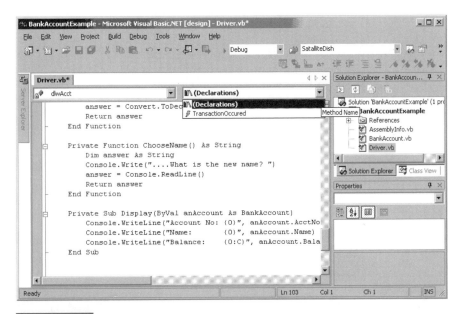

FIGURE 11–6   *The Wizard bar on the editor window.*

You can trap events on any object declared using **WithEvents** by select-ing the appropriate object from the left dropdown box on the wizard bar, and then selecting the appropriate event from the right dropdown box on the wiz-ard bar. Code for the handler function will be generated automatically. For example, by selecting the object **dlwAcct** and the event **TransactionOc-curred**, the following code is generated:

```
Public Sub dlwAcct_TransactionOccurred( _
  ByVal transType As BankAccount.TransactionType, _
  ByVal amount As Decimal) _
  Handles dlwAcct.TransactionOccurred


  . . .
End Sub
```

The **Handles** keyword that follows the subroutine declaration indicates that this procedure is an event handler. The *objectName dot eventName* nota-tion that follows the keyword **Handles** indicates that this function is invoked when the **TransactionOccurred** event is generated for the **dlwAcct** object.

One possible implementation of the **TransactionOccurred** event han-dler is shown below:

```
Public Sub dlwAcct_TransactionOccurred(ByVal transType As _
  BankAccount.TransactionType, ByVal amount As Decimal) _
  Handles dlwAcct.TransactionOccurred

  Select Case transType
    Case BankAccount.TransactionType.Deposit
      Console.WriteLine( _
        "Deposit of {0:C} for account {1} recorded", _
        amount, dlwAcct.AcctNo)

    Case BankAccount.TransactionType.Withdrawal
      Console.WriteLine( _
        "Withdrawal of {0:C} for account {1} recorded", _
        amount, dlwAcct.AcctNo)
  End Select

End Sub
```

This handler displays a message to the console each time a transaction occurs on the **dlwAcct** object.

Event Handlers Use Handles Keyword

VB6 programmers should note that VB.NET code for handling events differs from that in VB6. VB.NET introduces the Handles keyword to identify the object and event that any par-ticular function handles. The name of the function no longer has any required format.

Example: Bank Account (Version 5A)

Code
Example

A complete listing of the **BankAccount** class that implements the **TransactionOccurred** event can be found in the directory **BankAccount\Version 5A**. However, the preceding sections on "Defining Events" and "Raising Events" list all code changes that have been made to the class.

The **Driver** module in this version, partially shown below, has been modified so that it traps the **TransactionOccurred** event on both the **dlwAcct** and **mwwAcct** objects. For a complete listing of this module, refer to the code in **BankAccount\Version 5A.**

```
Imports System

Module Driver
    ' Declare two account references that can trap events
    Dim WithEvents dlwAcct, mwwAcct As BankAccount

    Sub Main()
      ' Initialize the two accounts
      dlwAcct = New BankAccount("Dana", 1250)           '
      mwwAcct = New BankAccount("Mark", 1750)

      ...

    End Sub

    Public Sub dlwAcct_TransactionOccurred(ByVal transType _
      As BankAccount.TransactionType, ByVal amount As _
      Decimal) Handles dlwAcct.TransactionOccurred

        Select Case transType
          Case BankAccount.TransactionType.Deposit
            Console.WriteLine("Deposit of {0:C} for " & _
              "account {1} recorded", amount, _
                dlwAcct.AcctNo)

          Case BankAccount.TransactionType.Withdrawal
            Console.WriteLine("Withdrawal of {0:C} for " _
              & "account {1} recorded", amount, _
                dlwAcct.AcctNo)
        End Select

    End Sub

    Public Sub mwwAcct_TransactionOccurred(ByVal transType _
      As BankAccount.TransactionType, ByVal amount As _
      Decimal) Handles mwwAcct.TransactionOccurred

        Select Case transType
```

```
        Case BankAccount.TransactionType.Deposit
           Console.WriteLine("Deposit of {0:C} for " & _
             "account {1} recorded", amount, _
             mwwAcct.AcctNo)

        Case BankAccount.TransactionType.Withdrawal
           Console.WriteLine("Withdrawal of {0:C} for " _
             & "account {1} recorded", amount, _
             mwwAcct.AcctNo)
      End Select

    End Sub

End Module
```

Sample output from this program that illustrates the messages written by the event handlers is as follows:

```
Enter command (H for help): D
....From which account (D=Dana, M=Mark)? M
....How much? 300
Deposit of $300.00 for account 102 recorded

Enter command (H for help): S
....From which account (D=Dana, M=Mark)? M
Account No: 102
Name:        Mark
Balance:     $2,050.00

Enter command (H for help): W
....From which account (D=Dana, M=Mark)? M
....How much? 900
Withdrawal of $900.00 for account 102 recorded
Withdraw Successful

Enter command (H for help): W
....From which account (D=Dana, M=Mark)? M
....How much? 1400
Withdraw Failed
```

TRAPPING EVENTS DYNAMICALLY

Although trapping events using the **WithEvents** keyword is easy, it is somewhat limiting. The event handler is attached to a specific reference variable via static code. Although the object that the variable references can change, the variable that the event handler references cannot change.

VB.NET allows you to dynamically connect and disconnect events with event handler procedures. This is done via the **AddHandler** and **Remove-Handler** statements.

For example, assume that two variables of type **BankAccount** were defined as follows:

```
Private dlwAcct As New BankAccount
Private mwwAcct As New BankAccount
```

and a handler function for any **TransactionOccurred** event was defined as follows:

```
Public Sub someTransactionOccurred(ByVal transType As _
  BankAccount.TransactionType, ByVal amount As Decimal)

    Select Case transType
       Case BankAccount.TransactionType.Deposit
          Console.WriteLine( _
            "Deposit of {0:C} recorded", amount)

       Case BankAccount.TransactionType.Withdrawal
          Console.WriteLine( _
             "Withdrawal of {0:C} recorded", amount)
       End Select

    End Sub
```

You can use the **AddHandler** statement to indicate that the **dlwAcct.TransactionOccurred** event should be sent to the **someTransactionOccurred** handler:

```
AddHandler dlwAcct.TransactionOccurred, _
            someTransactionOccurred
```

You can use similar logic to send the **mwwTransactionOccurred** event to the same handler:

```
AddHandler mwwAcct.TransactionOccurred, _
            someTransactionOccurred
```

This handler function is now called regardless of whether the **dlwAcct** object or the **mwwAcct** object generated the event. However, because of our event design, we are now unable to determine what object occurred inside our handler function.

Example: Bank Account (Version 5B)

Code
Example

The following program, found in **BankAccount\Version 5B**, represents a slight redesign in the **BankAccount** class. The event **TransactionOccurred** has been redesigned to carry with it information as to which object generated the event.

```vb
Public Class BankAccount

    Public Enum TransactionType
        Deposit
        Withdrawal
    End Enum

    ' EVENTS
    Public Event TransactionOccurred(ByVal transType As _
     TransactionType, ByVal theAccount As BankAccount, _
     ByVal amount As Decimal)

    ' PRIVATE ATTRIBUTES
    Private m_acctNo As Integer
    Private m_name As String
    Private m_balance As Decimal

    Private Shared m_nextAccountNum As Integer = 101

    ' PUBLIC METHODS
    Public Sub New(Optional ByVal name As String = "", _
     Optional ByVal initialBalance As Decimal = 0)
        m_acctNo = m_nextAccountNum
        m_name = name
        m_balance = initialBalance

        m_nextAccountNum += 1
    End Sub

    Public Function Deposit(ByVal amount As Decimal) _
     As Boolean
        ' Check for a negative deposit
        If amount < 0 Then Return False

        ' Process deposit
        m_balance += amount

        ' Fire event
        RaiseEvent TransactionOccurred( _
         TransactionType.Deposit, Me, amount)

        Return True
    End Function

    Public Function Withdraw(ByVal amount As Decimal) _
     As Boolean
        ' Check for a negative withdrawal
        If amount < 0 Then Return False

        ' Check for overdraft condition
```

```
        If amount > m_balance Then Return False

        ' Process withdrawal
        m_balance -= amount

        ' Fire event
        RaiseEvent TransactionOccurred( _
         TransactionType.Withdrawal, Me, amount)

        Return True
    End Function

    Public ReadOnly Property AcctNo() As Integer
        Get
            Return m_acctNo
        End Get
    End Property

    Public Property Name() As String
        Get
            Return m_name
        End Get
        Set(ByVal Value As String)
            m_name = Value
        End Set
    End Property

    Public ReadOnly Property Balance() As Decimal
        Get
            Return m_balance
        End Get
    End Property
End Class
```

You can see in the **Deposit** and **Withdraw** methods that the keyword **Me** is used to reference the current object when generating the event.

The following partial listing of code in **Driver.vb** illustrates how the object passed in the event handler is used to gather information about the source of an event when the **AddHandler** statement is used to trap events.

```
Imports System

Module Driver
    ' Declare two account references that can trap events
    Dim dlwAcct, mwwAcct As BankAccount

    Sub Main()
        ' Initialize the two accounts
        dlwAcct = New BankAccount("Dana", 1250)      '
        mwwAcct = New BankAccount("Mark", 750)
```

```
      AddHandler dlwAcct.TransactionOccurred, _
               AddressOf someTransactionOccurred
      AddHandler mwwAcct.TransactionOccurred, _
               AddressOf someTransactionOccurred


      ...

   End Sub

   Public Sub someTransactionOccurred(ByVal transType _
    As BankAccount.TransactionType, ByVal theAccount _
    As BankAccount, ByVal amount As Decimal)

      Select Case transType
         Case BankAccount.TransactionType.Deposit
            Console.WriteLine( _
              "Deposit of {0:C} recorded for {1}", _
              amount, theAccount.AcctNo)

         Case BankAccount.TransactionType.Withdrawal
            Console.WriteLine( _
              "Withdrawal of {0:C} recorded for {1}", _
              amount, theAccount.AcctNo)
      End Select

   End Sub

End Module
```

Output from this program might be as follows:

```
Enter command (H for help): W
....From which account (D=Dana, M=Mark)? M
....How much? 100
Deposit of $100.00 recorded for 102

Enter command (H for help): D
....From which account (D=Dana, M=Mark)? M
....How much? 200
Deposit of $200.00 recorded for 102

Enter command (H for help): W
....From which account (D=Dana, M=Mark)? D
....How much? 10000
Withdraw Failed
```

ToString Available in User-Defined Classes

The **ToString** method that is found in all data types, such as **Integer**, **Decimal**, and **Date,** is also available in *every* class you define yourself. As an example, consider the previous version 5 of the **BankAccount** class:

```
Public Class BankAccount

    Private m_acctNo As Integer
    Private m_name As String
    Private m_balance As Decimal

    ...
End Class
```

In a test program, we can create two instances of a **BankAccount** and display them using the **WriteLine** method. In the first case, we directly call **ToString**. In the second case, we rely upon the implicit call to **ToString** to obtain the string representation for us.

```
Imports System

Module Driver

    Sub Main()
        Dim natAcct As New BankAccount("Natalie", 1700)
        Dim britAcct As New BankAccount("Brittany", 1500)

        Console.WriteLine(natAcct.ToString())
        Console.WriteLine(britAcct)
    End Sub

End Module
```

The program compiles and runs, but the output is a little disappointing:

```
BankAccountExample.BankAccount
BankAccountExample.BankAccount
```

The **ToString** method being used in the previous example is the one defined in the .NET class **Object** from which our **BankAccount** class implicitly inherits. The base class **Object** knows nothing about our class, so it displays the name of the class. (It is able to determine the name of our class using the .NET reflection capabilities, which will be discussed in Chapter 22.)

The **ToString** method is an *overridable* method, which means that we may provide a version of it in our own class to display a more meaningful representation. The new version of our class is implemented in **BankAccount\Version 6**.

Code Example

```
Public Class BankAccount

    Private m_acctNo As Integer
    Private m_name As String
    Private m_balance As Decimal

    ...

    ' OVERRIDDEN METHODS
    Public Overrides Function ToString() As String
        Dim retVal As String
        retVal = String.Format( _
          "Account: {0}, Owner: {1}, Balance: {2:C}", _
          m_acctNo, m_name, m_balance)
        Return retVal
    End Function

End Class
```

As you can see, the **ToString** method is defined using the keyword **Overrides** to indicate that this method overrides an inherited one. The implementation of the method uses the **Format** method of the **String** class to construct a string that is then returned from the function.

The test program remains the same, but the output is what we expected:

```
Account: 101, Owner: Natalie, Balance: $1,700.00
Account: 102, Owner: Brittany, Balance: $1,500.00
```

Summary

In this chapter, we explored the use of classes in VB.NET for representing user-defined data types. A class can be thought of as a template from which individual instances, or *objects*, can be created. Classes support encapsulation through *attributes* and *methods*. Typically, attributes are defined as **Private** members of a class, and methods are defined as **Public** members of a class. Because classes are reference types, when you declare a variable of a class type, you are obtaining memory only for a *reference* to an object of the class type. No memory for the object is allocated itself until **New** is invoked. The Common Language Runtime automatically reclaims the memory of orphaned, or *unreferenced,* objects. This process is known as *garbage collection.* Initialization of objects is performed in special procedures called *constructors.*

Classes provide functionality via the properties and methods that are implemented within the class. When an object is created, only the **Public** members of a class can be accessed. **Shared** members can be defined within a class and are shared by all instances of that class. Public shared members are accessed via the class name, a dot, and the member name. VB.NET also provides the ability for objects to generate events to notify users of that event that some predefined action occurred.

Inheritance

With the release of this latest version of Visual Basic, Microsoft has transformed Visual Basic into a fully object-oriented programming language. It not only supports the concept of objects, as we discussed in Chapter 11, but it also now supports the concepts of implementation and interface inheritance. Inheritance allows programmers to build new classes by extending previously coded ones. This chapter illustrates how a VB.NET programmer can effectively design classes that can be extended. It explores the concept of polymorphism and how it is achieved in VB.NET. This chapter also examines how inheritance introduces the need for a new access specifier, Protected. Finally, it addresses the relationship of all VB.NET classes and the .NET class Object.

Inheritance Fundamentals

Inheritance is a key feature of the object-oriented programming paradigm. It is based upon the concept that categories of objects share common features and that these common features can be abstracted out of your classes and placed in a high-level base class. You can build more specialized *derived* classes that *inherit* the standard behavior from the base class, allowing you to focus only on additional features that the specialized class provides. These derived classes can also *override*, or replace, features that are inherited from a base class.

For example, consider the banking community. There are many types of accounts that can probably be opened: checking accounts, savings accounts, certificates of deposit, IRAs, and so on. Each of these types of accounts has certain minimal characteristics, such as an account number and balance, in common. These accounts differ in other respects. For example, a checking account may have a monthly fee. When a language supports inheritance, we can build a base class called **Account** that contains the common features of all accounts and build derived classes, such as **CheckingAccount**, that contain the unique behavior of that type of account. Figure 12–1 illustrates the relationship between **Account** and different types of accounts.

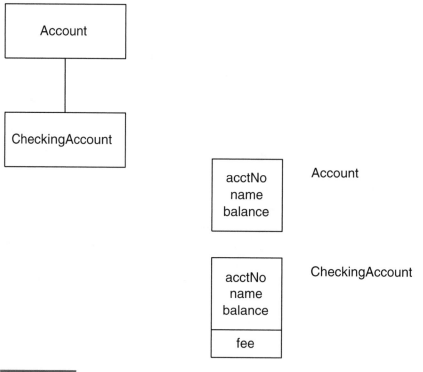

FIGURE 12–1   *The inheritance relationship between types of accounts.*

Inheritance in VB.NET

VB.NET supports inheritance through the use of the keyword **Inherits**. For example, the class **CheckingAccount** would inherit features from the class **Account** by writing the following code:

```
Public Class Account

    ' code the features of an account here

End Class


Public Class CheckingAccount
    Inherits Account

    ' code the additional features of a checking account
here

End Class
```

The keyword **Inherits** must appear after the declaration of the class and before the declaration of any members of the class. In this example, the class **CheckingAccount** inherits, or now has, the same data members, properties, methods, and events that are defined in the class **Account**.

Example: Types of People

Code Example

The following program, found in **PeopleExample\Version 1**, examines the construction of a set of classes that represent people. Specifically, we have designed two classes: **WorkingPerson** and **RetiredPerson**. However, because both classes had the person's name and date of birth in common, that information was abstracted out and placed in a third class called **Person**.

The **Person** class has two private data members, **m_name** and **m_dob**. It also defined the public properties **Name** and **DOB** that allow access to the private data members.

```
Public Class Person

    Private m_name As String
    Private m_dob As Date

    Public Property Name() As String
        Get
            Return m_name
        End Get
        Set(ByVal Value As String)
            m_name = Value
        End Set
    End Property

    Public Property DOB() As Date
        Get
            Return m_dob
        End Get
```

```
      Set(ByVal Value As Date)
         m_dob = Value
      End Set
   End Property

End Class
```

To construct and initialize a **Person** object, you can write the following code:

```
Dim jen As New Person
jen.Name = "Jen"
jen.DOB = #12/21/1982#
```

The **WorkingPerson** class has all the features of the class **Person**, plus it defines an additional data member **m_pay** and the public property **Pay**, which provides access to **m_pay.**

```
Public Class WorkingPerson
   Inherits Person

   Private m_pay As Decimal

   Public Property Pay() As Decimal
      Get
         Return m_pay
      End Get
      Set(ByVal Value As Decimal)
         m_pay = Value
      End Set
   End Property

End Class
```

To construct and initialize a **WorkingPerson** object, you can write the following code. The *public* features of the class **Person** may also be accessed. Inheritance defines an *is-a* relationship; that is, **WorkingPerson** is a **Person**, so all the features of **Person** are available in **WorkingPerson**.

```
Dim dick As New WorkingPerson
dick.Name = "Dick"
dick.DOB = #3/21/1953#
dick.Pay = 65750
```

Just like the class **WorkingPerson**, a **RetiredPerson** class can also be built that defines features unique to retired people. In this case, the class defined two public properties, **MonthlyIncome** and **YearRetired**, as well as private variables used in the implementation of these methods.

```
Public Class RetiredPerson
   Inherits Person

   Private m_monthlyIncome As Decimal
   Private m_yearRetired As Short

   Public Property MonthlyIncome() As Decimal
      Get
         Return m_monthlyIncome
      End Get
      Set(ByVal Value As Decimal)
         m_monthlyIncome = Value
      End Set
   End Property

   Public Property YearRetired() As Short
      Get
         Return m_yearRetired
      End Get
      Set(ByVal Value As Short)
         m_yearRetired = Value
      End Set
   End Property

End Class
```

To construct and initialize a **RetiredPerson** object, you can write the following code. Again, because **RetiredPerson** *is a* **Person,** all the features of **Person** are available in **RetiredPerson**.

```
Dim sue As New RetiredPerson
sue.Name = "Sue"
sue.DOB = #8/21/1956#
sue.Pay = 55000
sue.YearRetired = 2002
```

.NET's Object Class

All classes in VB.NET are ultimately derived from the .NET class **Object.** You do not need to use the **Inherits** keyword to indicate this; the compiler does that for you automatically. This means that your base class, **Person** in the preceding example, inherited methods such as **ToString** from **Object**. When derived classes are built, they pick up the methods of their immediate base class plus the methods from classes further up the hierarchy. Figure 12–2 illustrates the three-level hierarchy of our **PersonExample** application.

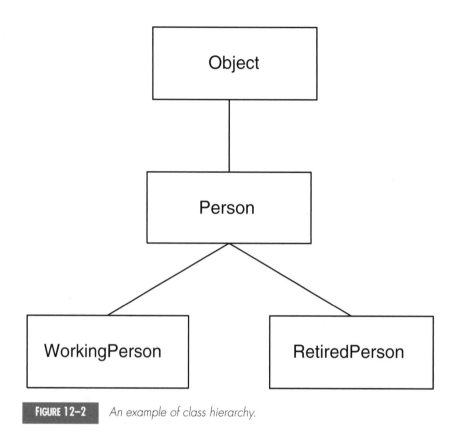

Figure 12-2
An example of class hierarchy.

Controlling Base Class Construction

We have yet to add any constructors to our **Person**, **WorkingPerson**, and **RetiredPerson** classes. Therefore, the constructor that we are using is the compiler-supplied default constructor. If you will recall from Chapter 11, it allows us to create objects without specifying any initialization information when the object is instantiated.

```
Dim jen As New Person()
Dim dick As New WorkingPerson()
Dim sue As New RetiredPerson()
```

We could modify the **Person** class so that the person's name and date of birth information must be provided when the object is instantiated as shown below:

```
Dim jen As New Person("Jen", #12/21/1982#)
```

Code
Example

This will require us to modify the **Person** class, as well as the **Working-Person** and **RetiredPerson** classes. The new version of our program can be found in **PersonExample\Version 2.**

To begin with, we must add the constructor to the **Person** class:

```
Public Class Person

    Private m_name As String
    Private m_dob As Date

    Public Sub New(ByVal name As String, ByVal dob As String)
        m_name = name
        m_dob = dob
    End Sub

    . . .

End Class
```

Derived Class Construction

When derived classes are constructed, they must call their base class constructor to initialize the base class part of the derived class object. The compiler does this implicitly. However, the implicit call uses the *default* constructor in the base class. Until now, the **Person** class has had a default constructor. But with the introduction of the new parameterized constructor in the **Person** class, there is no longer a default constructor in **Person**.

(Recall from Chapter 11 that, if any constructor is provided in a class, the compiler no longer provides the default constructor.)

As soon as we add the parameterized constructor to the **Person** class, **WorkingPerson** and **RetiredPerson** have syntax errors. The error message for the **WorkingPerson** class states the following:

```
Cannot implicitly create a constructor for 'Class
WorkingPerson' because its base class 'Person' doesn't
declare a public constructor that has no parameters. Either
define a constructor on 'Class WorkingPerson' or a
parameterless constructor on base 'Class Person'.
```

This must be one of the best syntax error messages ever! It not only identifies the problem, it tells us what we have to do to fix the problem! We have two choices:

- Build a new default (parameter-less) constructor in the class **Person** so that the compiler-supplied default constructors in **WorkingPerson** and **RetiredPerson** will work.
- Build new constructors in the classes **WorkingPerson** and **Retired-Person** that call the parameterized constructor in the class **Person**.

We are going to choose the second option, because choosing the first option would violate our original statement: "The person's name and date of birth information *must* be provided when the object is instantiated."

MYBASE

VB.NET provides the keyword **MyBase** in derived classes that can be used to refer to an object reference to access any base class member. In the **Working-Person** class, **MyBase** refers to the **Person** class.

DERIVED CLASS CONSTRUCTORS

Derived class constructors typically require the same parameters as the base class, plus additional ones to satisfy the needs of the derived class. For example, if a **Person** object requires a name and date of birth at the time of instantiation, then so should a **WorkingPerson** object and a **RetiredPerson** object because they are derived from the **Person** class. The **WorkingPerson** class may decide whether the additional attribute **pay** is or is not required. Similarly, the **RetiredPerson** class may decide whether the additional attributes **monthly income** and **year of retirement** are or are not required.

To define a derived class constructor, you must build the subroutine **New**. The derived class constructor should explicitly call the base class constructor using the **MyBase** keyword. For example, the constructor for **WorkingPerson** would be defined as follows:

```
Public Class WorkingPerson
   Inherits Person

   Private m_pay As Decimal

   Public Sub New(ByVal name As String, ByVal dob As Date, _
     ByVal pay As Decimal)
     MyBase.New(name, dob)

     m_pay = pay
   End Sub

   ...
End Class
```

You should notice that the **WorkingPerson** constructor requires three parameters. The parameters **name** and **dob** are used to initialize the base class portion of **WorkingPerson.** The parameter **pay** is used to initialize the data defined in the **WorkingPerson** class. To create an instance of a **WorkingPerson,** you must code as follows:

```
Dim dick As New WorkingPerson("Dick", #3/21/1953#, 65750)
```

Derived Classes Have No Privileged Access to Base Class

As we have said, a derived class inherits all members of its immediate base class, as well as any members that class inherited. However, it has no privileged access to the private members of its base class (even though, theoretically, those members are in the derived class!).

For example, if the **WorkingPerson** constructor attempted to access the private data members **m_name** and **m_dob** that were inherited from **Person**, the compiler would generate syntax errors.

```
Public Sub New(ByVal name As String, ByVal dob As Date, _
  ByVal pay As Decimal)
    m_name = name
    m_dob = dob
    m_pay = pay
End Sub
```

The error messages would state the following:

```
'PeopleExample.Person.m_name' is Private, and is not
accessible in this context.

'PeopleExample.Person.m_dob' is Private, and is not
accessible in this context.
```

The solution to this problem lies in understanding access modifiers, which are described in the next section.

Access Control

Access to individual class members can be controlled by placing an access modifier such as **Public** or **Private** in front of the member. VB.NET provides five types of access specifiers that may be applied to data members, methods, properties, and events of a class.

- A **Public** member can be accessed from outside the class.
- A **Private** member can be accessed only from within the class.
- A **Protected** member can be accessed from within the class and from within any derived classes.
- A **Friend** member can be accessed from within classes in the same assembly but not from outside the assembly. (Recall from Chapter 1 that an assembly is roughly equivalent to the current program. Assemblies will be discussed in more detail in Chapter 23.)
- A **Protected Friend** member can be accessed from any class within the assembly and from derived classes outside the assembly.

Access specifers may also be applied to a class itself. The meaning is similar. That is, a class defined as **Public** is accessible from inside or outside the assembly. A class defined as a **Friend** is accessible to any code within the same assembly.

Applying access specifiers to members of a class can only further restrict access to a class, not widen it. For example, if you have a class with **Friend** accessibility, making a member **Public** will not make it accessible from outside the assembly. A common use of the **Friend** modifier is for helper classes that are intended to be used only within the current assembly.

Note that if you omit the access modifier in front of a member, the compiler will assume **Public**. If you omit the access modifier in front of a class, **Friend** will be the default used by the compiler.

Example: Using Protected Access

Code
Example

For a derived class to be able to access certain implementation details of its base class, provisions must be made when coding the base class. In this section, we examine extensions to our **Person**, **WorkingPerson**, and **RetiredPerson** classes. This program is found in **PeopleExample\Version 3**.

The **Person** class will be given a third member variable called **m_password**. This member is initialized when the **Person** object is created. However, there is no **Public** property that would allow a **Person** object to expose the password—for security reasons, of course!

```
Public Class Person

    Private m_name As String
    Private m_dob As Date
    Private m_password As String

    Public Sub New(ByVal name As String, ByVal dob As Date, _
      ByVal password As String)
        m_name = name
        m_dob = dob
        m_password = password
    End Sub

    . . .

End Class
```

The **RetiredPerson** class will be given an additional member variable named **m_savings**. This member is initialized when the **RetiredPerson** object is created. And because a **RetiredPerson** is a **Person,** its constructor must be modified to require a password to be specified when a **RetiredPerson** object is instantiated. There is also a read-only **Public** property **Savings** that returns the value of **m_savings**. To "spend" any savings, the person's password must be specified; therefore, **RetiredPerson** also introduces the method **SpendSavings.** If the password provided matches the person's password, **m_savings** is modified; otherwise, an exception is thrown. This new feature would be used as follows:

```
' The following RetiredPerson is named Jay, was born on
' 7/29/1958, has a password of "Baseball", has a savings
' of 12000000, a monthly income of 0 and retired in 2001
Dim jay As New RetiredPerson("Jay", #7/29/1958#, _
 "Baseball", 12000000, 0, 2001)
...

Dim secretWord As String
Console.Write("Enter password: ")
secretWord = Console.ReadLine()
Try
   jay.SpendSavings(someAmount,secretWord)
   Console.WriteLine("{0} withdrawn from savings", _
    someAmount)
Catch e As Exception
   Console.WriteLine(e.Message())
End Try
```

When we code the **RetiredPerson**'s **SpendSavings** method, we will probably write code that resembles the following:

```
Public Sub SpendSavings(ByVal amt As Decimal, _
 ByVal password As String)
   If password = m_password Then
     m_savings -= amt
   Else
     Throw New Exception( _
       "Invalid password! Savings may not be spent!")
   End If
End Sub
```

However, we will get a syntax error when we reference **m_password** because it is a private member of **Person**. Private members of a class are accessible only to other members of the *same* class. To solve this problem, we must add a **Protected** property to the **Person** class that allows its derived classes read-only access to the value of **m_password**. The final solution follows.

Base Class: Person

The code for **Person** provides the following:

- A new constructor that accepts a password
- Protected read-only access to the password for derived classes

```
Public Class Person

    Private m_name As String
    Private m_dob As Date
    Private m_password As String

    Public Sub New(ByVal name As String, ByVal dob As Date, _
     ByVal password As String)
        m_name = name
        m_dob = dob
        m_password = password
    End Sub

    Public Property Name() As String
        Get
            Return m_name
        End Get
        Set(ByVal Value As String)
            m_name = Value
        End Set
    End Property

    Public Property DOB() As Date
        Get
            Return m_dob
        End Get
        Set(ByVal Value As Date)
            m_dob = Value
        End Set
    End Property

    Protected ReadOnly Property Password() As String
        Get
            Return m_password
        End Get
    End Property

End Class
```

Derived Class: RetiredPerson

The code for **RetiredPerson** provides the following:

- A new constructor that accepts a password and an initial value for savings
- A read-only property to provide access to savings
- A **SpendSavings** method that uses the password to make sure that the modification of savings is allowed

```
Public Class RetiredPerson
    Inherits Person

    Private m_monthlyIncome As Decimal
    Private m_yearRetired As Short
    Private m_savings As Decimal

    Public Sub New(ByVal name As String, ByVal dob As Date, _
     ByVal password As String, ByVal savings As Decimal, _
     ByVal monthlyIncome As Decimal, _
     ByVal yearRetired As Short)
        MyBase.New(name, dob, password)

        m_savings = savings
        m_monthlyIncome = monthlyIncome
        m_yearRetired = yearRetired
    End Sub

    Public Property MonthlyIncome() As Decimal
        Get
            Return m_monthlyIncome
        End Get
        Set(ByVal Value As Decimal)
            m_monthlyIncome = Value
        End Set
    End Property

    Public Property YearRetired() As Short
        Get
            Return m_yearRetired
        End Get
        Set(ByVal Value As Short)
            m_yearRetired = Value
        End Set
    End Property

    Public ReadOnly Property Savings() As Decimal
        Get
            Return m_savings
        End Get
```

```
   End Property

   Public Sub SpendSavings(ByVal amt As Decimal, _
    ByVal password As String)

      If password = MyBase.Password Then
         m_savings -= amt
      Else
         Throw New Exception( _
           "Invalid password! Savings may not be spent!")
      End If
   End Sub

End Class
```

Derived Class: WorkingPerson

The code for **WorkingPerson** provides the following:

- A new constructor that accepts a password and an initial value for savings

```
Public Class WorkingPerson
   Inherits Person

   Private m_pay As Decimal

   Public Sub New(ByVal name As String, ByVal dob As Date, _
    ByVal password As String, ByVal pay As Decimal)
      MyBase.New(name, dob, password)

      m_pay = pay
   End Sub

   Public Property Pay() As Decimal
      Get
         Return m_pay
      End Get
      Set(ByVal Value As Decimal)
         m_pay = Value
      End Set
   End Property

End Class
```

Test Program

The test program illustrates the use of these new features. Specifically, it examines how to use exception handling to interact with the **SpendSavings** method in **RetiredPerson**.

```vbnet
Imports System

Module Driver

    Sub Main()
        Dim jay As New RetiredPerson("Jay", #7/29/1958#, _
        "Baseball", 12000000, 0, 2001)

        Dim cmd As String
        Do While True
            Console.Write("Enter command (S-spend, Q-quit): ")
            cmd = Console.ReadLine().ToUpper()

            Select Case cmd
                Case "S"
                    Dim amount As Decimal
                    Dim pwd As String
                    Console.Write( _
                     "How much do you want to spend? ")
                    amount = Convert.ToDecimal( _
                     Console.ReadLine())
                    Console.Write("What is your password? ")
                    pwd = Console.ReadLine()
                    Try
                        jay.SpendSavings(amount, pwd)
                        Console.WriteLine("Savings left: {0:C}", _
                         jay.Savings)
                    Catch e As Exception
                        Console.WriteLine(e.Message)
                    End Try

                Case "Q"
                    Exit Sub

                Case Else
                    Console.WriteLine("Error: Bad command!")
            End Select

            Console.WriteLine()
        Loop
    End Sub

End Module
```

Output of the program is as follows:

```
Enter command (S-spend, Q-quit): s
How much do you want to spend? 40
What is your password? baseball
Invalid password! Savings may not be spent!

Enter command (S-spend, Q-quit): s
How much do you want to spend? 40
What is your password? Baseball
Savings left: $11,999,160.00

Enter command (S-spend, Q-quit): q
```

Example: Exception Handling

Another example of the use of inheritance can be found in the .NET base class library. Chapter 9 discussed how VB.NET's exception handling mechanism can be used to generate and/or trap exceptions. One of the more common uses of inheritance is for applications to define their own set of custom exceptions. Before exception handling was around, applications used to define custom error codes. (The infamous 0c7 was a common error code on the IBM platform.)

In the next example, found in **PeopleExample\Version 4**, we define the custom exception type **IllegalSpendingException** that will be thrown by **RetiredPerson** when a bad password is received in the **SpendSavings** method.

The .NET class defines three basic exception classes as shown in Figure 12–3. **ApplicationException** is typically the base class for application-specific exceptions, whereas **SystemException** is typically the base class for .NET exceptions.

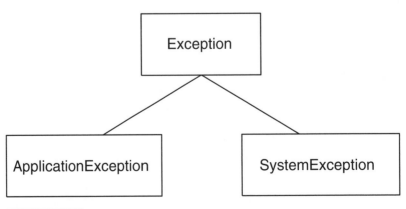

FIGURE 12–3   *The .NET exception class hierarchy.*

In this example, **IllegalSpendingException** is derived from **ApplicationException**. It defines an additional property not available in other exceptions. This property, **Password**, contains the password used for any failed spending attempt. It specified that the generic message string "Invalid password on spending request" will be used on all instances of this exception type.

```
Public Class IllegalSpendingException
   Inherits System.ApplicationException

   Private m_badPassword As String
   Public Sub New(ByVal password As String)
     MyBase.New("Invalid password on spending request")

     m_badPassword = password
   End Sub

   Public ReadOnly Property Password() As String
     Get
        Return m_badPassword
     End Get
   End Property

End Class
```

The code for **RetiredPerson's SpendSavings** method is then recoded to throw the **IllegalSpendingException** instead of a generic exception. It does not have to specify a message string because the **IllegalSpendingException** class defines a message string.

```
Public Sub SpendSavings(ByVal amt As Decimal, _
 ByVal password As String)
   If password = MyBase.Password Then
      m_savings -= amt
   Else
      Throw New IllegalSpendingException(password)
   End If
End Sub
```

The portion of the test program that changes is shown below. First, you should notice that the **Try** block has been expanded to encompass the entire "spending" process. If an exception occurs because invalid data is entered at the **ReadLine**, we will trap that exception. There are now two **Catch** handlers: One is called if our new **IllegalSpendingException** is thrown, and the other is called if anything else is thrown.

```
Dim amount As Decimal
Dim pwd As String
Try
   Console.Write("How much do you want to spend? ")
```

```
       amount = Convert.ToDecimal(Console.ReadLine())
       Console.Write("What is your password? ")
       pwd = Console.ReadLine()
       jay.SpendSavings(amount, pwd)
       Console.WriteLine("Savings left: {0:C}", jay.Savings)

Catch ex As IllegalSpendingException
   Console.WriteLine("{0} - Password supplied: {1}", _
     ex.Message, ex.Password)
Catch e As Exception
   Console.WriteLine(e.Message)
End Try
```

Output from this program illustrates the different exception messages that are generated:

```
Enter command (S-spend, Q-quit): s
How much do you want to spend? dfgdf
Input string was not in a correct format.

Enter command (S-spend, Q-quit): s
How much do you want to spend? 40
What is your password? mustangs
Invalid password on spending request - Password supplied:
mustangs

Enter command (S-spend, Q-quit): s
How much do you want to spend? 40
What is your password? Baseball
Savings left: $11,999,160.00

Enter command (S-spend, Q-quit): q
```

Shadowing Base Class Methods

When a derived class implements a method with the same signature as the base class, the method is said to *shadow*, or obscure, the base class implementation. This is an error unless you explicitly use the keyword **Shadows** on the derived class method.

Code Example

The program **Bank\Version 1** defines an **Account** similar to the one we examined in Chapter 11:

```
Public Class Account

    Private m_acctNo As Integer
    Private m_name As String
    Private m_balance As Decimal
```

```
Private Shared m_nextAccountNum As Integer = 101

Public Sub New(Optional ByVal name As String = "", _
 Optional ByVal initialBalance As Decimal = 0)
   m_acctNo = m_nextAccountNum
   m_name = name
   m_balance = initialBalance

   m_nextAccountNum += 1
End Sub

Public Function Deposit( ByVal amount As Decimal) _
 As Boolean
   ' Check for a negative deposit
   If amount < 0 Then Return False

   ' Process deposit
   m_balance += amount

   Return True
End Function

Public Function Withdraw(ByVal amount As Decimal) _
 As Boolean
   ' Check for a negative withdrawal
   If amount < 0 Then Return False

   ' Check for overdraft condition
   If amount > m_balance Then Return False

   ' Process withdrawal
   m_balance -= amount

   Return True
End Function

Public ReadOnly Property AcctNo() As Integer
   Get
       Return m_acctNo
   End Get
End Property

Public Property Name() As String
   Get
       Return m_name
   End Get
   Set(ByVal Value As String)
      m_name = Value
   End Set
```

```
      End Property

      Public ReadOnly Property Balance() As Decimal
         Get
             Return m_balance
         End Get
      End Property

      Protected Function SetBalance(ByVal newValue As Decimal)
         m_balance = newValue
      End Function

   End Class
```

This code is similar to the versions we saw in Chapter 11, except that it provides the protected method **SetBalance** that can be used by derived classes to modify the **m_balance** variable without using **Deposit** and **Withdraw**.

We can now build a derived class called **CheckingAccount** that is an **Account**, except that it allows the withdrawal amounts up to the current balance plus $200. That is, there is a $200 overdraft credit line on the account. Each time a withdrawal is made that leaves the balance less than zero, a $25 fee is charged to the account. To achieve the overdraft behavior that a **CheckingAccount** needs, it must reimplement the **Withdraw** method.

```
Public Class CheckingAccount
   Inherits Account

   Public Sub New(Optional ByVal name As String = "", _
    Optional ByVal initialBalance As Decimal = 0)
      MyBase.New(name, initialBalance)
   End Sub

   Public Shadows Function Withdraw(ByVal amount As _
    Decimal) As Boolean
      ' Replaces the base class version! Check for
      ' allowable withdrawal (200 overdraft
      ' protection)

      If (Balance - amount) < -200 Then _
         Return False

      ' Process withdrawal
      SetBalance(Balance - amount)

      ' Charge a $25 fee if the balance is < 0
      If Balance < 0 Then
         SetBalance(Balance - 25)
      End If
```

```
        Return True
    End Function

End Class
```

If you examine the **Withdraw** method, you will see that it uses the keyword **Shadows** after the access specifier on the method declaration. Because the derived class cannot access any private data member of **Account**, it uses **Account's** protected **SetBalance** method to modify the account balance.

We will also define a **SavingsAccount** class that works like the **CheckingAccount** class, except that **SavingsAccount** objects have a minimum balance of $2,500 and do not allow any withdrawals to take the balance below that level.

```
Public Class SavingsAccount
    Inherits Account

    Public Sub New(Optional ByVal name As String = "", _
      Optional ByVal initialBalance As Decimal = 0)
        MyBase.New(name, initialBalance)
    End Sub

    Public Shadows Function Withdraw(ByVal amount As _
      Decimal) As Boolean
        ' Replaces the base class version.  Check for
        ' allowable withdrawal (min balance = 2500)
        If (Balance - amount) < 2500 Then Return False

        ' Process withdrawal
        SetBalance(Balance - amount)

        Return True
    End Function

End Class
```

The test program for these classes is shown below. It creates both a **CheckingAccount** and a **SavingsAccount** object, and deposits and withdraws amounts from those accounts to test their limits. It uses the **DisplayAccount** subroutine to display both types of accounts.

```
Imports System

Module Driver

    ' Display any account's data
    Private Sub Display(ByVal anAccount As Account)
        Console.Write("Acct: {0,-5}", anAccount.AcctNo)
```

```
            Console.Write("   Name: {0, -7}", anAccount.Name)
            Console.WriteLine("   Balance: {0:C}", _
              anAccount.Balance)
        End Sub

        Public Sub Main()
            Dim success As Boolean
            Dim mollyeAcct As New SavingsAccount("Mollye", 4000)
            Console.WriteLine("Initially:")
            Display(mollyeAcct)

            Console.WriteLine(vbCrLf & "Deposit $800:")
            mollyeAcct.Deposit(800)
            Display(mollyeAcct)

            Console.WriteLine(vbCrLf & "Withdraw $1:")
            mollyeAcct.Withdraw(1)
            Display(mollyeAcct)

            Console.WriteLine(vbCrLf & "Withdraw all:")
            mollyeAcct.Withdraw(mollyeAcct.Balance)
            Display(mollyeAcct)

            Console.WriteLine(vbCrLf & _
              "Withdraw all except $2500:")
            mollyeAcct.Withdraw(mollyeAcct.Balance - 2500)
            Display(mollyeAcct)

            Dim ranseAcct As New CheckingAccount("Ranse", 4000)
            Console.WriteLine(vbCrLf & "Initially:")
            Display(ranseAcct)

            Console.WriteLine(vbCrLf & "Deposit $800:")
            ranseAcct.Deposit(800)
            Display(ranseAcct)

            Console.WriteLine(vbCrLf & "Withdraw $1:")
            ranseAcct.Withdraw(1)
            Display(ranseAcct)

            Console.WriteLine(vbCrLf & "Withdraw all + $10:")
            ranseAcct.Withdraw(ranseAcct.Balance + 10)
            Display(ranseAcct)

            Console.WriteLine(vbCrLf & "Withdraw $500:")
            ranseAcct.Withdraw(500)
            Display(ranseAcct)
        End Sub

    End Module
```

You may be wondering about how both **CheckingAccount** and **SavingsAccount** objects can be passed to the same subroutine using the same parameter. It is because **CheckingAccounts** and **SavingsAccounts** are **Accounts**, and inheritance implements an *is-a* relationship. However, from within the **DisplayAccount** subroutine, the compiler allows the parameter **anAccount** to reference only members defined in the **Account** class.

Output from this program is shown below:

```
Initially:
Acct: 101      Name: Mollye     Balance: $4,000.00

Deposit $800:
Acct: 101      Name: Mollye     Balance: $4,800.00

Withdraw $1:
Acct: 101      Name: Mollye     Balance: $4,799.00

Withdraw all:
Acct: 101      Name: Mollye     Balance: $4,799.00

Withdraw all except $2500:
Acct: 101      Name: Mollye     Balance: $2,500.00

Initially:
Acct: 102      Name: Ranse      Balance: $4,000.00

Deposit $800:
Acct: 102      Name: Ranse      Balance: $4,800.00

Withdraw $1:
Acct: 102      Name: Ranse      Balance: $4,799.00

Withdraw all + $10:
Acct: 102      Name: Ranse      Balance: ($35.00)

Withdraw $500:
Acct: 102      Name: Ranse      Balance: ($35.00)
```

Polymorphism

So far, inheritance has primarily been about reusing code. That is, we have been able to define a base class and inherit an implementation for features common to certain types. This saves us from having to write the code over and over. But this is only part of the story of inheritance. The other part of the story involves the ability to build generic client code that interacts with different types of objects in some common manner.

Traditionally, calls to methods are bound to the underlying method by the compiler at compile time. That is, if you write the following code:

```
Dim myAcct As Account
...
myAcct.Withdraw(100)
```

the compiler generates code to call the **Account** class implementation of **Withdraw**. This is called *static binding*.

Most object-oriented languages, including VB.NET, support *polymorphism*. Polymorphism is a term that is best described with an example. If you were to write the following code:

```
Dim myAcct As Account
...
If someOption = 1 Then
   myAcct = New CheckingAccount("Dana", 1200)
Else
   myAcct = New SavingsAccount("Dana", 1200)
End If
myAcct.Withdraw(100)
```

we would experience unwanted behavior. The compiler, by default, binds the variable **myAcct** to the **Withdraw** method at compile time because **myAcct** is of type **Account**. However, if we could configure VB.NET to wait until runtime to decide whether to bind the call to **Account's Withdraw**, or one of the **Withdraw** methods implemented in a derived class, then we could write very generic, or *polymorphic*, code. This type of binding is called *dynamic binding*.

Example: Static Binding

Code Example

The program **Bank\Version 2** illustrates static binding passing both **CheckingAccount** and **SavingsAccount** objects to the subroutine **WithdrawFromAcct**. This subroutine defines the parameter **anAccount** to be an **Account** reference.

```
Imports System

Module Driver

   ' Displays account information
   Private Sub Display(ByVal anAccount As Account)
      Console.Write("Acct: {0,-5}", anAccount.AcctNo)
      Console.Write("   Name: {0, -7}", anAccount.Name)
      Console.WriteLine("   Balance: {0:C}", _
         anAccount.Balance)
   End Sub
```

```
' Withdraws any amount of money from any account and
' then displays the new account stats
Private Sub WithdrawFromAcct(ByVal amt As Decimal, _
  ByRef anAcct As Account)
    Console.WriteLine(vbCrLf & "Withdraw {0:C}:", amt)
    anAcct.Withdraw(amt)
    Display(anAcct)
End Sub

Public Sub Main()
    Dim mollyeAcct As New SavingsAccount("Mollye", 4000)
    Console.WriteLine("Initially:")
    Display(mollyeAcct)

    Console.WriteLine(vbCrLf & "Deposit $800:")
    mollyeAcct.Deposit(800)
    Display(mollyeAcct)

    WithdrawFromAcct(1, mollyeAcct)
    WithdrawFromAcct(mollyeAcct.Balance, mollyeAcct)

    Dim ranseAcct As New CheckingAccount("Ranse", 4000)
    Console.WriteLine(vbCrLf & "Initially:")
    Display(ranseAcct)

    Console.WriteLine(vbCrLf & "Deposit $800:")
    ranseAcct.Deposit(800)
    Display(ranseAcct)

    WithdrawFromAcct(1, ranseAcct)
    WithdrawFromAcct(ranseAcct.Balance + 10, ranseAcct)
End Sub

End Module
```

Recall that the **CheckingAccount** class has a **Withdraw** method that shadows the **Withdraw** method in **Account**. **CheckingAccount's Withdraw** allows the balance to be -$200. **SavingsAccount** also has a **Withdraw** method that allows the balance to be no less than $2,500.

When we examine the output, we notice some peculiar behavior:

```
Initially:
Acct: 101     Name: Mollye     Balance: $4,000.00

Deposit $800:
Acct: 101     Name: Mollye     Balance: $4,800.00

Withdraw $1.00:
Acct: 101     Name: Mollye     Balance: $4,799.00
```

```
Withdraw $4,799.00:
Acct: 101      Name: Mollye      Balance: $0.00

Initially:
Acct: 102      Name: Ranse       Balance: $4,000.00

Deposit $800:
Acct: 102      Name: Ranse       Balance: $4,800.00

Withdraw $1.00:
Acct: 102      Name: Ranse       Balance: $4,799.00

Withdraw $4,809.00:
Acct: 102      Name: Ranse       Balance: $4,799.00
```

In this program, **anAcct** in the subroutine is an object reference of type **Account**, and calling **Withdraw** through this object reference will *always* result in **Account.Withdraw** being called, no matter what kind of object **anAcct** may actually be referring to. **Account's Withdraw** uses zero as the minimum value of an account.

Overridable Methods

In VB.NET, you can designate a method in a base class as *overridable*. The compiler will then generate code to *dynamically* bind all calls to that overridable method. Using this technique, you can build generic procedures that work with a variety of types of objects.

Follow these steps to define a method as overridable:

- Define the method in the base class as overridable using the **Overridable** keyword.
- On the method in the derived class that is overridden, use the keyword **Overrides** on its declaration.

Example: Dynamic Binding (Polymorphism)

The program **Bank\Version 3** illustrates a polymorphic version of **Bank\Version 2**. The case class **Account** defines both the **Deposit** and **Withdraw** methods as **Overridable**.

```
Public Class Account

    Private m_acctNo As Integer
    Private m_name As String
    Private m_balance As Decimal

    Private Shared m_nextAccountNum As Integer = 101
```

```vbnet
Public Sub New(Optional ByVal name As String = "", _
 Optional ByVal initialBalance As Decimal = 0)
   m_acctNo = m_nextAccountNum
   m_name = name
   m_balance = initialBalance

   m_nextAccountNum += 1
End Sub

Public Overridable Function Deposit(ByVal amount As _
 Decimal) As Boolean
    ' Check for a negative deposit
    If amount < 0 Then Return False

    ' Process deposit
    m_balance += amount

    Return True
End Function

Public Overridable Function Withdraw(ByVal amount As _
 Decimal) As Boolean
    ' Check for a negative withdrawal
    If amount < 0 Then Return False

    ' Check for overdraft condition
    If amount > m_balance Then Return False

    ' Process withdrawal
    m_balance -= amount

    Return True
End Function

Public ReadOnly Property AcctNo() As Integer
    Get
        Return m_acctNo
    End Get
End Property

Public Property Name() As String
    Get
        Return m_name
    End Get
    Set(ByVal Value As String)
       m_name = Value
    End Set
End Property

Public ReadOnly Property Balance() As Decimal
```

```
      Get
          Return m_balance
      End Get
   End Property

   Protected Function SetBalance(ByVal newValue As Decimal)
      m_balance = newValue
   End Function

End Class
```

The **CheckingAccount** class uses the keyword **Overrides** on its **Deposit** method:

```
Public Class CheckingAccount
   Inherits Account

   Public Sub New(Optional ByVal name As String = "", _
    Optional ByVal initialBalance As Decimal = 0)
      MyBase.New(name, initialBalance)
   End Sub

   Public Overrides Function Withdraw(ByVal amount As _
    Decimal) As Boolean
      ' Replaces the base class version. Check for
      ' allowable withdrawal (200 overdraft protection)
      If (Balance - amount) < -200 Then Return False

      ' Process withdrawal
      SetBalance(Balance - amount)

      ' Charge a $25 fee if the balance is < 0
      If Balance < 0 Then
         SetBalance(Balance - 25)
      End If

      Return True
   End Function

End Class
```

The **SavingsAccount** class also uses **Overrides** when defining **Withdraw**:

```
Public Class SavingsAccount
   Inherits Account

   Public Sub New(Optional ByVal name As String = "", _
    Optional ByVal initialBalance As Decimal = 0)
      MyBase.New(name, initialBalance)
   End Sub
```

```
Public Overrides Function Withdraw(ByVal amount As _
  Decimal) As Boolean
    ' Replaces the base class version
    ' Check for allowable withdrawal (min balance = 2500)
    If (Balance - amount) < 2500 Then Return False

    ' Process withdrawal
    SetBalance(Balance - amount)

    Return True
  End Function
End Class
```

The test program from **Bank\Version 2** has not changed, and yet the output now is quite different:

```
Initially:
Acct: 101      Name: Mollye     Balance: $4,000.00

Deposit $800:
Acct: 101      Name: Mollye     Balance: $4,800.00

Withdraw $1.00:
Acct: 101      Name: Mollye     Balance: $4,799.00

Withdraw $4,799.00:
Acct: 101      Name: Mollye     Balance: $4,799.00

Initially:
Acct: 102      Name: Ranse      Balance: $4,000.00

Deposit $800:
Acct: 102      Name: Ranse      Balance: $4,800.00

Withdraw $1.00:
Acct: 102      Name: Ranse      Balance: $4,799.00

Withdraw $4,809.00:
Acct: 102      Name: Ranse      Balance: ($35.00)
```

When examining the output, you will see that VB.NET performed dynamic binding on the call to deposit in the **WithdrawFromAcct** procedure; that is, it called the Withdraw method that was appropriate for the type of *object* that was passed into the procedure. Account 101 was a **SavingsAccount** and its request to withdraw $4799 was refused (see the 4th transaction) because it would leave the balance below $2500. This means that the **Withdraw** method of **SavingsAccount** processed this transaction. Account 102's request to withdraw $4809 was allowed (see last transaction) because it was a

CheckingAccount, which also resulted in a $25 overdraft charge.   This means that the **Withdraw** method of **CheckingAccount** processed this transaction.

Efficiency

Overloaded invocation is slightly less efficient than calling an ordinary non-overloaded method. With overridable method calls, there is some overhead at runtime associated with determining which class's method will be invoked.

Benefits of Polymorphism

The machinery of virtual functions makes it easy to write polymorphic code in VB.NET. As an example of polymorphic code, consider an application that processed many types of bank accounts. How will you write and maintain code that deals with all these different account types?

A traditional approach has been to have a "type field" in an account structure. Code that manipulates an account uses this type field to determine the correct processing to perform. Although straightforward, this approach can be quite tedious and error-prone. Introducing a new kind of account can require substantial maintenance.

Polymorphism can offer a cleaner solution. You organize the different kinds of accounts in a class hierarchy, and you structure your program so that you write general purpose methods that act upon an object reference whose type is that of the base class. Your code calls virtual methods of the base class. The call will be automatically dispatched to the appropriate class, depending on what kind of account is actually being referenced.

Abstract Classes

Sometimes, it does not make sense to instantiate a base class. Instead, the base class exists just to provide a set of common features that are used by the various derived classes. Such a base class is said to be *abstract,* and it cannot be instantiated. In VB.NET, you designate a base class as abstract by using the keyword **MustInherit** in the class definition.

```
Public MustInherit Class Account
   ...
End Class
```

Code Example

The compiler will then flag an error if you try to instantiate the class. In **Bank\Version 4**, we attempt to define the following variable:

```
Dim erma As New Account("Erma", 1635)
```

The syntax error indicates:

```
New may not be used on a class declared with 'MustInherit'.
```

An abstract class may have abstract methods, which are not implemented in the class but only in derived classes. The purpose of an abstract method is to provide a template for polymorphism. The method is called through an object reference to the abstract class, but at runtime the object reference will actually be referring to one of the concrete derived classes. The keyword **MustOverride** is also used to declare abstract methods. In place of the body of the method, you provide nothing.

```
Public MustInherit Class Account
   ...

   Public MustOverride Function Withdraw(ByVal amount As _
      Decimal) As Boolean

   ...
End Class
```

In this abstract **Account** class, other methods and properties may have implementations specified, but the **Withdraw** method has no code associated with it. Derived classes must override this method.

Not Inheritable Classes

At the opposite end of the spectrum from abstract classes are *not inheritable* classes. Although you *must* derive from an abstract class, you *cannot* derive from a class designated as not inheritable. A not inheritable class provides functionality that you can use as is, but you cannot derive from the class and hide or override some of the methods. Marking a class as not inheritable protects against unwarranted class derivations. It can also make the code a little more efficient, because any overridable functions in the not inheritable class are automatically treated by the compiler as non-overridable.

In VB.NET, you use the keyword **NotInheritable** to mark a class as not inheritable. The example **NotInheritableClasses** illustrates this point:

```
Public NotInheritable Class Point
     Public x, y As Integer
End Class
```

When you attempt to define the following class:

```
Public Class ThreeDPoint
    Inherits Point
    Public z As Integer
End Class
```

the compiler generates the following syntax error:

```
'ThreeDPoint' cannot inherit from 'class Point' because
'Point' is marked as 'NotInheritable'.
```

In the .NET Framework Class Library, the **System.String** is a not inheritable class. You must use the **String** class as-is. You may not build your own type of string derived from **System.String**.

Type Conversions in Inheritance

When class hierarchies are developed, the need arises for type checking and type conversion. Type checking refers to the ability to ask an object "What are you?" Type conversion involves converting the type of an object reference from one class type to another.

TypeOf...Is Operator

VB.NET provides the ability to ask an object what type it is via the **TypeOf...Is** operator. For example, given the class hierarchy that we have been working with containing **Account**, **CheckingAccount**, and **SavingsAccount** classes, you could ask the following question:

```
If TypeOf myAcct Is SavingsAccount Then
    ...
ElseIf TypeOf myAcct Is CheckingAccount Then
    ...
Else
    ...
End If
```

This operator is useful when you are interacting with a base class variable and you need to know what type of object it references.

CType

VB.NET also provides a function called **CType** that allows a programmer to convert any expression to another type. This can be used when working with object references to explicitly convert an object reference to another type.

CType throws an exception when the conversion cannot be done. For example:

```
Dim someAcct As Account
Dim savAcct As SavingsAccount

' code that is not shown creates an account object and
' assigns it to someAcct

Try
    savAcct = CType(someAcct, SavingsAccount)
Catch e As Exception
    ' process exception because someAcct is not
    ' a SavingsAccount
End Try

' use the variable savAcct to interact with the account
```

This code examines the variable **someAcct** to see if it references a **SavingsAccount**. If it does, it returns a reference to the account object as a **SavingsAccount** reference. Otherwise, it throws an exception.

Type Conversions

Class hierarchies introduce the need for two types of conversions with respect to object references. The first, casting up the class hierarchy, is inherently safe. The second, casting down the class hierarchy is unsafe.

CONVERTING UP THE HIERARCHY

Converting up the class hierarchy means that a derived class reference is converted to a base class reference. This is okay because of the *is-a* relationship of inheritance. A checking account "is" an account. It is a special kind of account. Everything that applies to an account also applies to a checking account. There can be no "extra member" in the **Account** class that is not also present in the **CheckingAccount** class. Thus:

```
Dim acct As Account

Dim savAcct As SavingsAccount

...

acct = savAcct
```

is perfectly legal. We are converting "up the hierarchy."

CONVERTING DOWN THE HIERARCHY

Converting down a class hierarchy means that a base class reference is converted to a derived class reference. This can be dangerous because there is no guarantee that the base class reference actually references an object of the specific derived class type. For example:

```
Dim acct As Account
Dim chkAcct As CheckingAccount
Dim savAcct As SavingsAccount

If someCondition Then
   acct = New CheckingAccount( )
Else
   acct = New SavingsAccount( )
End If

savAcct = acct
```

is unsafe. Depending on the value of the variable **someCondition** at runtime, **acct** might reference a **CheckingAcount** or a **SavingsAccount**. If **acct** references a **CheckingAccount** object, the assignment of **acct** to **savAcct** will fail. In this example, we are converting "down the hierarchy."

Example: Type Conversions

Code Example

The program **Bank\Version 5** illustrates the use of the conversion features shown in this section. This program has modified the **CheckingAccount** class to include an overdraft limit that can be specified on a per-account basis. The **CheckingAccount** class now resembles the following:

```
Public Class CheckingAccount
   Inherits Account

   Private m_overdraftLimit As Decimal

   Public Sub New(Optional ByVal name As String = "", _
    Optional ByVal initialBalance As Decimal = 0, _
    Optional ByVal odLimit As Decimal = 200)
     MyBase.New(name, initialBalance)
     m_overdraftLimit = odLimit
   End Sub

   Public Property OverdraftLimit() As Decimal
     Get
         Return m_overdraftLimit
     End Get
     Set(ByVal Value As Decimal)
         m_overdraftLimit = Value
     End Set
   End Property

   Public Overrides Function Withdraw(ByVal amount As _
```

```
Decimal) As Boolean
   ' Replaces the base class version.
   ' Check for allowable withdrawal (does not exceed
   ' overdraft protection)
   If (Balance - amount) < -m_overdraftLimit Then
      Return False
   End If

   ' Process withdrawal
   SetBalance(Balance - amount)

   ' Charge a $25 fee if the balance is < 0
   If Balance < 0 Then
      SetBalance(Balance - 25)
   End If

   Return True
End Function

End Class
```

The program builds an array of accounts. As you can see, the creation of the account objects and assignment to the array variable is an example of "upcasting" because **CheckingAccount** and **SavingsAccount** objects are assigned to an **Account** reference variable. The program then passes the account objects to the **Display** procedure. This procedure needs to recognize **CheckingAccount** objects because it must write out the overdraft limit for those accounts. It cannot use the **Account** reference to access the property **OverdraftLimit** so it must "downcast" the reference by assigning only **CheckingAccount** references to the variable **ca**.

```
Imports System

Module Driver

   Private Sub Display(ByVal anAccount As Account)
      Console.Write("Acct: {0,-5}", anAccount.AcctNo)
      Console.Write("   Name: {0, -7}", anAccount.Name)
      Console.Write("   Balance: {0:C}", anAccount.Balance)

      ' Check the type of the account to see if it is
      ' a CheckingAccount
      If TypeOf anAccount Is CheckingAccount Then
         Dim ca As CheckingAccount
         ca = anAccount
         Console.Write( "   OD Limit: {0:C}", _
           ca.OverdraftLimit)
      End If
      Console.WriteLine()
```

```
      End Sub

      Public Sub Main()
         Dim acct(6) As Account

         acct(0) = New SavingsAccount("Mollye", 1225)
         acct(1) = New CheckingAccount("Brit", 1550, 200)
         acct(2) = New SavingsAccount("Nat", 1750)
         acct(3) = New CheckingAccount("Jen", 1875, 400)
         acct(4) = New SavingsAccount("Zack", 1150)
         acct(5) = New CheckingAccount("Ranse", 1625, 0)
         acct(6) = New SavingsAccount("Jay", 1675)

         Dim i As Integer
         For i = 0 To 6
            Display(acct(i))
         Next
      End Sub

   End Module
```

Output from this program is as follows:

```
Acct: 101  Name: Molly  Bal: $1,225.00
Acct: 102  Name: Brit   Bal: $1,550.00   OD Limit: $200.00
Acct: 103  Name: Nat    Bal: $1,750.00
Acct: 104  Name: Jen    Bal: $1,875.00   OD Limit: $400.00
Acct: 105  Name: Zack   Bal: $1,150.00
Acct: 106  Name: Ranse  Bal: $1,625.00   OD Limit: $0.00
Acct: 107  Name: Jay    Bal: $1,675.00:
```

An alternative implementation of the **If** statement inside the **Display** procedure might be:

```
If TypeOf anAccount Is CheckingAccount Then
  Console.Write("   OD Limit: {0:C}", _
    CType(anAccount,CheckingAccount).OverdraftLimit)
End If
```

Single Inheritance

As you begin to think about the class hierarchies you see around you, remember that VB.NET supports only *single inheritance*. That is, a class can have at most one immediate base class.

When you think about the **Person** class that we discussed at the beginning of this chapter and the derived classes **WorkingPerson** and **Retired-Person**, you probably see other possibilities. What about a **CollegeStudent** class that is derived from **Person,** but has features relating to grades? Or a **MinorChild**? It is not unreasonable to think about a **CollegeStudent** who is also a **WorkingPerson** or a **RetiredPerson**.

Like C# and Java, VB.NET supports the concept of an interface that is a collection of methods. Classes can then implement one or more interfaces. Interfaces will help us solve these challenging multiple classification problems. We will discuss interfaces in detail in Chapter 13.

Summary

In this chapter, we examined how VB.NET supports inheritance. We saw how the **Inherits** keyword can be used to build a class that extends the behavior of an existing class. We discussed how derived classes can use the keyword **MyBase** to interact with their base class, specifically to control initialization of the base class part. We also saw that derived classes have no privileged access to private features of their base class, necessitating the introduction of the **Protected** access modifiers. We explored how derived classes could reimplement the behavior of their base classes, either using shadowing or polymorphism. We also discussed the **TypeOf...Is** operator and the **CType** functions in VB.NET, and how they can be used to provide safe type conversions. We will continue our study of inheritance in Chapter 13, taking up the idea of interfaces.

Interfaces

*T*he concept of an interface is a fundamental concept of object-oriented programming. Interfaces allow programmers to specify common behaviors among a set of different types of objects, without knowing exactly how these objects will implement this behavior. In this chapter, we examine the concept of interface-based programming and how it can be used to define behaviors for intricate class libraries. We begin by explaining how interfaces are defined and continue by exploring how classes can be used to implement these interfaces. We also examine client-side issues. We discuss how interface references can be used to build generic, robust client code and how TypeOf...Is and CType can be used to determine whether a class supports a particular interface. We conclude the chapter with a glimpse of how .NET interfaces can be used to extend the functionality of user-defined classes, a topic that will be discussed in greater detail in Chapter 18.*

Interface Fundamentals

Interfaces are similar to classes. They define a generic set of properties, methods, and events that are common to many types of objects. However, interfaces do not provide any implementation for these members. Instead, interfaces must ultimately be implemented by classes.

An interface represents a contract, in that a class that implements an interface must implement every aspect of that interface exactly as it is defined.

Although interface implementations can evolve (the code inside the implementation can be modified to run faster or more accurately), the interface itself cannot be changed once it has been *published*. An interface is considered to be published after it has been released to other programmers, classes that implement it have been built, and users are building objects from these classes. Changes to a published interface may break existing user code. That is, a client application may suddenly fail to work because a property, method, or event that was used is no longer supported!

Using Interfaces in VB.NET

In VB.NET, interfaces are a full-fledged part of the language, supported by the keyword **Interface**. (In previous versions of Visual Basic, you could program with COM interfaces, but you had to represent them by classes. Working with interfaces is greatly improved in VB.NET.) The interface itself lists properties, methods, and events that must be defined by any object implementing the interface.

Defining Interfaces

The interface **IAsset** shown below represents a set of properties, methods, and events that define an asset. It represents the minimal set of features that all assets must implement. We must still define one or more classes that implement this interface. As a naming convention, interface names normally begin with a capital I. However, this is not a requirement.

```
Interface IAsset
   Event ValueChanged(ByVal oldValue As Decimal, _
      ByVal newValue As Decimal)

   ReadOnly Property Description() As String
   Property Value() As Decimal
End Interface
```

As you can see, the keyword **Interface** is used instead of **Class** when defining interfaces. The interface definition contains property, method, and event declarations. You may not declare any access specifiers such as **Public** or **Private.** And there can be no procedure implementations; that is, the **End Sub**, **End Function**, and **End Property** statements are illegal in an interface.

Two additional interfaces that might be found in a financial application are **IRealEstate** and **IDepreciable**:

```
Interface IRealEstate
   Property TaxRollValue() As Decimal
End Interface

Interface IDepreciable
   ReadOnly Property YearAcquired() As Short
   ReadOnly Property Cost() As Decimal
   Property UsefulLife() As Short
   Sub DepreciateValue()
End Interface
```

An interface in VB.NET may inherit features from another interface using the keyword **Inherits**. The **IRentalProperty** interface shown here inherits from the two interfaces **IRealEstate** and **IDepreciable**, which means it actually defines the properties, methods, and events from these two interfaces, in addition to those listed in its definition.

```
Interface IRentalProperty
   Inherits IRealEstate, IDepreciable
   Property EstimatedMonthlyIncome() As Decimal
End Interface
```

The **IDisplayable** interface (shown below) has nothing to do with financial applications, but can be implemented by any class that wants to have a display method.

```
Interface IDisplayable
   Sub Display()
End Interface
```

The interfaces just described are used in the next section as we illustrate the implementation of these interfaces. This code may be found in the **AssetsExample** solution.

Implementing Interfaces

A class that implements an interface indicates that it does so by using the keyword **Implements.** In VB.NET, a class can implement one or more interfaces. In the following example, the class **Point** simply implements the behavior defined in **IDisplayable**.

```
Public Class Point
   Implements IDisplayable
   Public x, y As Integer

   Public Sub Display() Implements IDisplayable.Display
      Console.WriteLine("Point: ({0},{1})", x, y)
   End Sub
End Class
```

You can see that the class **Point** uses the **Implements** statement to indicate that it implements the interface **IDisplayable**:

```
Public Class Point
   Implements IDisplayable
```

The class **Point** then provides an implementation of the method **Display** defined in **IDisplayable**. VB.NET requires that any method in a class implementing an inherited interface method must indicate that it does so using the keyword **Implements** on the procedure declaration. For example:

```
Public Sub Display() Implements IDisplayable.Display
   Console.Write("({0},{1}}", x, y)
End Sub
```

A VB.NET Class Must Implement an Interface in Its Entirety

VB.NET requires a class to completely implement any interface that it defines. This means that all methods in the interface must have a corresponding implementation in the class, and it cannot silently rely on an implementation provided by a base class. It can still take advantage of code in a base class, but it must explicitly call the base class method or property through MyBase.

Classes can implement several interfaces. The class **Jewelry** defined below implements the interfaces **IAsset** and **IDisplayable.** Note these interesting features as you examine the example:

- It defines two private variables, **m_description** and **m_value**, to help it implement the properties **Description** and **Value** inherited from **IAsset**.
- The class inherits the event **ValueChanged** from **IAsset**. It must redefine the event using the phrase **Implements IAsset.ValueChanged** on the definition.
- The class provides implementations of properties **Description** and **Value** inherited from **IAsset** and uses the **Implements** keyword on those procedures as well.
- The implementation of the **Set** property **Value** uses **RaiseEvent** to cause the **ValueChanged** event to occur.
- The class provides an implementation of method **Display** inherited from **IDisplayable** and uses the **Implements** keyword to indicate the method implements **IDisplayable.Display**.

```
Public Class Jewelry
   Implements IAsset, IDisplayable

   Private m_description As String
   Private m_value As String
```

```
Event ValueChanged(ByVal oldValue As Decimal, _
   ByVal newValue As Decimal) _
   Implements IAsset.ValueChanged

Public Sub New(ByVal descr As String, _
 ByVal value As Decimal)
   m_description = descr
   m_value = value
End Sub

Public ReadOnly Property Description() As String _
 Implements IAsset.Description
    Get
       Return m_description
    End Get
End Property

Public Overridable Property Value() As Decimal _
 Implements IAsset.Value
    Get
       Return m_value
    End Get
    Set(ByVal Value As Decimal)
       Dim oldValue As Decimal = m_value
       m_value = Value
       RaiseEvent ValueChanged(oldValue, Value)
    End Set
End Property

Public Sub Display() Implements IDisplayable.Display
   Console.WriteLine("{0} - Valued at {1:C}", _
     Description, Value)
End Sub
End Class
```

Other classes may implement several interfaces as well as provide unique features of their own. In the following example, the class **BankAccount** defines basic bank account behavior that we have seen earlier in this book, and it implements the interfaces **IAsset** and **IDisplayable**. As you examine the code below, be sure to observe these things:

- The class provides implementations of its own methods **Deposit** and **Withdraw**, as well as properties **AcctNo**, **Name**, and **Balance**.
- The class provides implementations of properties **Description** and **Value** inherited from **IAsset**, as well as the event **ValueChanged**.
- The **ValueChanged** event is raised in the **Deposit** and **Withdraw** methods.

- The **Set** part of the **Value** property throws an exception because the value of an account can only be changed via calls to **Deposit** and **Withdraw**.
- The class provides an implementation of the method **Display** inherited from **IDisplayable**.

```
Public Class BankAccount
    Implements IAsset, IDisplayable

    Private m_acctNo As Integer
    Private m_name As String
    Private m_balance As Decimal

    Private Shared m_nextAcctNum As Integer = 101

    Event ValueChanged(ByVal oldValue As Decimal, _
        ByVal newValue As Decimal) _
        Implements IAsset.ValueChanged

    Public Sub New(ByVal name As String, Optional ByVal _
      initialBalance As Decimal = 0)
        m_acctNo = m_nextAcctNum
        m_name = name
        m_balance = initialBalance

        m_nextAcctNum += 1
    End Sub

    ReadOnly Property AcctNo() As Integer
        Get
            Return m_name
        End Get
    End Property

    ReadOnly Property Name() As String
        Get
            Return m_name
        End Get
    End Property

    ReadOnly Property Balance() As Decimal
        Get
            Return m_balance
        End Get
    End Property

    Public Overridable Sub Deposit(ByVal amount As Decimal)
        Dim oldBalance As Decimal = m_balance

        m_balance += amount
```

```
        RaiseEvent ValueChanged(oldBalance, m_balance)
    End Sub

    Public Overridable Sub Withdraw(ByVal amount As Decimal)
        Dim oldBalance As Decimal = m_balance

        m_balance -= amount
        RaiseEvent ValueChanged(oldBalance, m_balance)
    End Sub

    Public ReadOnly Property Description() As String _
      Implements IAsset.Description
        Get
            Return "Bank Account #" & m_acctNo.ToString()
        End Get
    End Property

    Public Overridable Property Value() As Decimal _
      Implements IAsset.Value
        Get
            Return m_balance
        End Get
        Set(ByVal Value As Decimal)
            Throw New Exception( _
              "An account must be changed via Deposit/Withdraw")
        End Set
    End Property

    Public Sub Display() Implements IDisplayable.Display
        Console.WriteLine( _
            "{0} contains {1:C}", Description, Value)
    End Sub
End Class
```

The classes **Jewelry** and **BankAccount** must both independently implement the basic behavior defined in **IAsset**. In their cases, the implementations of the properties and methods are different. However, in another scenario, you might find that a generic implementation of an interface is possible.

For example, assume that we have an interface called **IAccount** that defines basic bank account behavior as follows:

```
Interface IAccount
    ReadOnly Property AcctNo() As Integer
    Property Name() As String
    ReadOnly Property Balance() As Decimal

    Sub Deposit(ByVal amt As Decimal)
    Sub Withdraw(ByVal amt As Decimal)
End Interface
```

We might decide to implement basic account behavior in a class called **Account** and inherit that support in other classes. For example:

```
Public Class Account
   Inherits IAccount

   ' Implements basic account behavior
   ...

   ' But can also define inherited methods as Overridable
   Public Overridable Sub Deposit(ByVal amt As Decimal)
      ...
   End Sub
   Public Overridable Sub Withdraw(ByVal amt As Decimal)
      ...
   End Sub
End Class

Public Class CDAccount
   Inherits IAccount
   Implements IInterestBearing

   ...
End Class

Public Class CheckingAccount
   Inherits IAccount
   Implements ITransactionHistory

   ...
End Class
```

In these cases, the **Account** class implements the basic behavior of **IAccount**, and those methods do not have to be implemented again when they are inherited into **CDAccount** and **CheckingAccount**.

Using an Interface

There are two ways to interact with objects. We may use a variable of the class type. For example, the variable **herAcct** represents a reference to any **BankAccount** object. Using this variable, we can access any method in the **BankAccount** class.

```
Dim herAcct As New BankAccount("Mary", 1250)
herAcct.Display()
```

Interfaces, however, now give us a second technique for interaction. We can use variables of an interface type to refer to any object that implements the interface. For example, the subroutine **DisplayItem** below can display any object that implements the **IDisplayable** interface.

```
Sub DisplayItem(ByVal something As IDisplayable)
   something.Display()
End Sub
```

This subroutine can then be called and passed to a **Point** object or a **BankAccount** object, because they both implement **IDisplayable**.

```
Dim aPoint As New Point()
aPoint.x = 10
aPoint.y = 15
DisplayItem(aPoint)

Dim herAcct As New BankAccount("Mary", 1250)
DisplayItem(herAcct)
```

Output from the two calls to **DisplayItem** is very different because the two classes implement the **Display** method quite differently. This is an example of the polymorphic nature of the methods in an interface.

```
Point: (10,15)
Bank Account #101 contains $1,250.00
```

However, not all objects can be passed to the **DisplayItem** method. Consider the following class **Blob**:

```
Public Class Blob
   Public stuff As String
End Class
```

It is not a very exciting class, but it definitely doesn't implement the **IDisplayable** interface! If you create an instance of a **Blob** and try to pass it to the **DisplayItem** subroutine:

```
Dim b As New Blob()
b.stuff = "xklsdflakdl"
DisplayItem(b)
```

the following runtime exception is generated:

```
Unhandled Exception: System.InvalidCastException: Exception
of type System.InvalidCastException was thrown.
```

An **InvalidCastException** is generated when you attempt to convert an object reference to an interface reference that the object doesn't support. You can protect against the exception by using **Try** and **Catch.**

```
Try
   DisplayItem(b)
Catch e As InvalidCastException
```

```
        Console.WriteLine("Item does not support IDisplayable")
End Try
```

An alternative approach is to use the **TypeOf...Is** operator in VB.NET. This operator allows us to ask if an object is of a specific type, or if it is derived from a specific class or interface. For example:

```
If TypeOf b Is IDisplayable Then
    DisplayItem(b)
Else
    Console.WriteLine("Item does not support IDisplayable")
End If
```

Although this second solution avoids having to handle exceptions, it pays a performance penalty of checking for the **IDisplayable** interface *twice*: once when evaluating the **TypeOf...Is** operator, and again in the method call when the conversion to **IDisplayable** is made. On the other hand, if you are making a method call inside a loop, it may be best to check once before entering the loop to see whether the object being passed to the method supports a desired interface.

Code Example

The following **AssetsExample** program illustrates some simple instrumentation of a program using the **TickCount** property of the **System.Environment** class. In some of our other code examples, we use a similar technique to do some simple empirical performance analysis.

To understand interfaces a little more, think about building a generic collection of assets. The solution **AssetsExample** defines four types of assets that implement the **IAsset** interface: **Jewelry**, **BankAccount**, **Home**, and **Car.** We can build a collection of assets using the following code:

```
Dim list(19) As IAsset
Dim curNum As Integer

list(0) = New Jewelry("2 ct diamond ring", 1300)
list(1) = New BankAccount("Linda's Checking", 900)
list(2) = New Car("Ford Explorer", 23000, 12, _
    1993)
list(3) = New Home("3329 Duchess Hill Rd", 53000)
list(4) = New BankAccount("Linda's Savings", 1800)
list(5) = New BankAccount("Linda's Piggy Bank", _
    92)

curNum = 6
```

We can write code to determine the value of all these assets by simply using the polymorphic property **Value** defined in **IAsset**:

```
Dim value As Decimal
Dim index As Integer
```

```
For index = 0 To curNum - 1
   Console.WriteLine("{0,-25} {1,10:C}", _
      list(index).Description, list(index).Value)
   value += list(index).Value
Next

Console.WriteLine("Total Value: {0:C}", value)
```

Output from this code is as follows:

```
2 ct diamond ring          $1,300.00
Bank Account #101            $900.00
Ford Explorer              $5,750.00
3329 Duchess Hill Rd      $58,300.00
Bank Account #102          $1,800.00
Bank Account #103            $92.00
Total Value:              $68,142.00
```

Because all of the objects in the list implement **IAsset,** we are able to invoke the property **Value** directly. Upon close inspection of the output, you may notice that the value of Linda's vehicle is less than what she originally specified. This is because the **Car** class implements the interface **IDepreciable** and depreciates a portion of the vehicle for each year that it has been in service. The opposite is true for the house. It has appreciated in the time Linda has owned it.

If we want to deposit $100 to each **BankAccount** object, we must be careful. Not all assets are **BankAccounts**. One solution is to use the **TypeOf...Is** operator to recognize **BankAccount** objects. We cannot use an **IAsset** variable to access **BankAccount** methods, so we must assign the object reference to a variable of type **BankAccount**:

```
For index = 0 To curNum - 1
   If TypeOf list(index) Is BankAccount Then
      Dim ba As BankAccount
      ba = list(index)
      ba.Deposit(100)
   End If
Next
```

We can also use the **CType** function that we discussed in Chapter 12. It can be used to explicitly convert an object reference of one type into an object reference of a different type. Using **CType**, you can rewrite the code this way:

```
For index = 0 To curNum - 1
   If TypeOf list(index) Is BankAccount Then
      CType(list(index), BankAccount).Deposit(100)
   End If
Next
```

If you are experienced with COM (Component Object Model), the operation of finding out whether an interface is supported should be very familiar to you.

Example: Transmitters and Receivers

The following example examines how interfaces can be used to define a collection of behaviors that may or may not be implemented by objects in our system. It builds collections of objects that have minimal features in common and provides generic versions of procedures that can work with many types of objects.

Code Example

This application, found in **Machines**, defines three interfaces that may be implemented by various types of transmitting and receiving devices. These interfaces are then used while building two devices: a pager and a satellite dish. Finally, the client application builds a collection of various devices and controls them via an interactive program.

DEFINING THE INTERFACES

The first interface, **IMachine**, defines two methods. **On** is used to turn the device on. **Off** is used to turn the device off.

```
Interface IMachine
    Sub [On]()
    Sub Off()
End Interface
```

Using VB.NET Keywords as Names

You probably noticed that the subroutine named On is surrounded by square brackets. This is because On is a keyword in the VB.NET language. However, this does not preclude its use as a method, property, event, or variable name. VB.NET allows you to surround with square brackets any identifiers that collide with keywords.

The second interface, **ITransmitter**, defines features that are implemented by any device that transmits data. The **Transmit** method is called to send the data. The **TransmitComplete** event is generated when the transmission of data is complete.

```
Interface ITransmitter
    Sub Transmit(ByVal data As String)
    Event TransmitComplete()
End Interface
```

The last interface, **IReceiver**, defines features that are implemented by any device that can poll to receive data. The **GetData** method is called to read any available data the device receives.

```
Interface IReceiver
    Function GetData() As String
End Interface
```

DEFINING THE CLASSES

The first class, **Pager**, represents a machine that can be turned on and off and receives data. Therefore, it implements the interfaces **IMachine** and **IReceiver**.

Pager defines a private variable, **m_state**, to track whether the pager is on or off. If **GetData** is called when the device is off, an exception is thrown. The implementation of **Pager** shown here does not actually communicate with any hardware to receive data, so we emulate the receipt of data by generating a random number between 1 and 100,000 and return that value.

```
Public Class Pager
    Implements IMachine, IReceiver

    Private m_state As Boolean

    Sub [On]() Implements IMachine.On
       m_state = True
    End Sub

    Sub Off() Implements IMachine.Off
       m_state = False
    End Sub

    Function GetData() As String Implements IReceiver.GetData
       If m_state = False Then
          Throw New Exception("Device off")
       End If

       ' Random Number Generator emulates received data
       Static rng As New System.Random()

       If m_state = False Then
          Throw New Exception("Device off")
       End If

       Dim s As String
       ' access some device to get data.
       ' in this example, we use rng to "get" some data.
       s = rng.Next(1, 100000).ToString()
       Return s
    End Function

End Class
```

SatelliteDish is a little more complicated. It defines the private variable **m_ID** to keep track of the satellite ID. This ID is assigned when a **Satellite-Dish** is instantiated. It also defines the private variable **m_state** to track whether the satellite dish is on or off.

SatelliteDish implements receiver capabilities in a manner similar to the **Pager** class. **SatelliteDish** also implements **ITransmitter** behavior, which means that it defines the method **SendData** to transmit data. Again, our implementation does not communicate with any satellite hardware, so we emulate the transmission of data by writing it to the console. **ITransmitter** also defines the event **TransmitComplete**, which **SatelliteDish** generates at the end of the **SendData** method.

```
Public Class SatelliteDish
    Implements IMachine, IReceiver, ITransmitter

    Private m_state As Boolean
    Private m_id As Integer

    Public Event TransmitComplete() _
        Implements ITransmitter.TransmitComplete

    Public Sub New(ByVal id As Integer)
        m_id = id
    End Sub

    Sub [On]() Implements IMachine.On
        m_state = True
    End Sub

    Sub Off() Implements IMachine.Off
        m_state = False
    End Sub

    Function GetData() As String Implements IReceiver.GetData
        If m_state = False Then
            Throw New Exception("Device off")
        End If

        ' Random Number Generator emulates received data
        Static rng As New System.Random()

        If m_state = False Then
            Throw New Exception("Device off")
        End If

        Dim s As String
        ' access some device to get data.
        ' in this example, we use rng to "get" some data.
        s = rng.Next(-1024, 1024).ToString()
```

```
      Return s
   End Function

   Sub Transmit(ByVal data As String) _
      Implements ITransmitter.Transmit

      ' access some device to send data
      Console.WriteLine( _
         "Transmitter {0}: sending {1}", m_id, data)
      RaiseEvent TransmitComplete()
   End Sub

End Class
```

WRITING THE CLIENT

The client application that we have built to illustrate interface-based programming manages a list of machines. Specifically, in this example, it manages a list of two **Pagers** and two **SatelliteDishes**, using the following:

```
Const lastDevice As Integer = 3

Dim myDevices(lastDevice) As IMachine

myDevices(0) = New Pager()
myDevices(1) = New SatelliteDish(1)
myDevices(2) = New Pager()
myDevices(3) = New SatelliteDish(3)
```

Using the array variable **myDevices**, we can only call methods defined in the interface **IMachine** directly. However, we can use the **CType** function to cast any **myDevices** reference to a **Pager** reference or a **SatelliteDish** reference, as appropriate.

This interactive program allows users to:

- Turn any specified machine on
- Turn any specified machine off
- List the machines that are available
- Send data via any transmitter
- Request all receivers to read incoming data
- Display help
- Quit the application

Code for the client program follows:

```
Module Driver

   Sub Main()
      Const lastDevice As Integer = 3

      ' Define the list of devices
```

```
Dim myDevices(lastDevice) As IMachine
myDevices(0) = New Pager()
myDevices(1) = New SatelliteDish(1)
myDevices(2) = New Pager()
myDevices(3) = New SatelliteDish(3)

' Add event handlers to catch the TransmitComplete
' event for all SatelliteDish objects
AddHandler CType(myDevices(1), _
   ITransmitter).TransmitComplete, _
   AddressOf NotifyTransmitComplete
AddHandler CType(myDevices(3), _
   ITransmitter).TransmitComplete, _
   AddressOf NotifyTransmitComplete

' Process commands
Dim cmd As String
Dim index As Integer

Do While True
   ' Prompt the user
   Console.Write("Enter command (H for help): ")
   cmd = Console.ReadLine().ToUpper()

   Select Case cmd
      Case "N"     ' turn device on
         Console.Write("Enter device id: ")
         index = CInt(Console.ReadLine())
         myDevices(index).On()

      Case "F"     ' turn device off
         Console.Write("Enter device id: ")
         index = CInt(Console.ReadLine())
         myDevices(index).Off()

      Case "S"     ' show all devices
         For index = 0 To upperDevice
            DisplayDeviceInfo(index, myDevices(index))
         Next

      Case "C"     ' check for received data
         For index = 0 To lastDevice
            ReceiveInfoFromDevice(index, _
             myDevices(index))
         Next

      Case "T"     ' transmit data
         Console.Write("Enter transmitter id: ")
         index = CInt(Console.ReadLine())
         Console.Write("Enter data: ")
```

```vb
            cmd = Console.ReadLine()
            Try
                CType(myDevices(index), _
                    ITransmitter).Transmit(cmd)

            Catch badCast As InvalidCastException
                Console.WriteLine( _
                    "Device {0} cannot transmit", index)
            Catch e As Exception
                Console.WriteLine("Error: {0}", e.Message)
            End Try

        Case "H"   ' display help
            Console.WriteLine( _
                "Choices include: N-Turn on device, ")
            Console.Write("F-Turn off device, ")
            Console.WriteLine(_
                "          C-Check receivers, ")
            Console.Write("T-Transmit data, ")
            Console.WriteLine( _
                "          S-Show all devices, ")
            Console.Write("H-Help, ")
            Console.WriteLine("Q-Quit")

        Case "Q"
            Exit Sub

        Case Else
            Console.WriteLine("Invalid command.")
        End Select
        Console.WriteLine()
    Loop
End Sub

' Displays info about a single device
Private Sub ShowDeviceInfo(ByVal id As Integer, _
 ByVal dev As IMachine)
    Console.Write("Device {0} is a ", id)
    If TypeOf dev Is Pager Then
        Console.WriteLine("pager")
    ElseIf TypeOf dev Is SatelliteDish Then
        Console.WriteLine("satellite dish")
    Else
        Console.WriteLine("*unknown*")
    End If
End Sub

' Displays info about a single device
Private Sub ReceiveInfoFromDevice(ByVal id As Integer, _
 ByVal dev As IMachine)
```

```
        Dim info As String
        Try
            info = CType(dev, IReceiver).GetData()
            Console.WriteLine( _
                "Device {0} received {1}", id, info)

        Catch badCast As InvalidCastException
            Console.WriteLine("Device {0} cannot receive", id)
        Catch e As Exception
            Console.WriteLine("Error: {0}", e.Message)
        End Try
    End Sub

    ' Event handler called when any SatelliteDish
    ' completes transmission of data
    Sub NotifyTransmitComplete()
        Console.WriteLine("...transmission complete")
    End Sub
End Module
```

Sample output from this program is as follows:

```
Enter command (H for help): S
Device 0 is a pager
Device 1 is a satellite dish
Device 2 is a pager
Device 3 is a satellite dish

Enter command (H for help): N
Enter device id: 0

Enter command (H for help): N
Enter device id: 3

Enter command (H for help): C
Device 0 received 8713
Error: Device off
Error: Device off
Device 3 received -754

Enter command (H for help): T
Enter transmitter id: 0
Enter data: Unit 3 at position (7,R144)
Device 0 cannot transmit

Enter command (H for help): T
Enter transmitter id: 3
Enter data: Unit 3 at position (7,R144)
Transmitter 3: sending Unit 3 at position (7,R144)
...transmission complete
```

Resolving Ambiguity in Interfaces

When working with interfaces, an ambiguity can arise if a class implements two interfaces and each has a method with the same name and signature. As an example, consider the following versions of the interfaces **IAccount** and **IStatement**. Each interface contains the method **Show**.

```
Interface IAccount
    Sub Deposit(ByVal amount As Decimal)
    Sub Withdraw(ByVal amount As Decimal)
    ReadOnly Property Balance() As Decimal
    Sub Show()
End Interface

Interface IStatement
    ReadOnly Property Transactions() As Integer
    Sub Show()
End Interface
```

How can a class that implements both of these interfaces specify implementations for both of the **Show** methods that have the same name? The answer is to use an alias for each of the method implementations in the derived class. You can use the interface name to qualify the method, as illustrated in the program **Ambiguous.**[1] In the **Ambiguous** example, the **IAccount** version of **Show** is named **IAccount_Show**, and the **IStatement** version of **Show** is named **IStatement_Show**. These method names are typically not used explicitly by client code. Rather, the client code usually calls on the name of the method as it is defined in the interface. **IAccount_Show** implements **IAccount.Show** and displays only the balance. **IStatement_Show** implements **IStatement.Show** and displays both the number of transactions and the balance.

```
Public Class Account
    Implements IAccount, IStatement

    Private m_name As String
    Private m_balance As Decimal
    Private m_numXact As Integer = 0

    Public Sub New(ByVal name As String, ByVal balance _
      As Decimal)
        m_name = name
        m_balance = balance
    End Sub
```

---

1. Actually, any distinct names will do, but using the interface name as part of the method name helps make it more recognizable and meaningful.

```
Public Sub Deposit(ByVal amount As Decimal) _
 Implements IAccount.Deposit
   m_balance += amount
   m_numXact += 1
End Sub

Public Sub Withdraw(ByVal amount As Decimal) _
 Implements IAccount.Withdraw
   m_balance -= amount
   m_numXact += 1
End Sub

Public ReadOnly Property Balance() As Decimal _
 Implements IAccount.Balance
   Get
       Return m_balance
   End Get
End Property

Public Sub IAccount_Show() Implements IAccount.Show
   Console.WriteLine("Name = {0}   Balance = {1}", _
     m_name, Balance)
End Sub

Public ReadOnly Property Transactions() As Integer _
 Implements IStatement.Transactions
   Get
       Return m_numXact
   End Get
End Property

Public Sub IStatement_Show() Implements IStatement.Show
   Console.WriteLine("{0} Transactions - " & _
     "Name = {1}   Balance = {2}", _
     m_numXact, m_name, Balance)
End Sub
End Class
```

Here is the client code that exercises the **IAccount** and **IStatement** interfaces. For comparison, we show making the call both through an interface reference and an object reference.

```
Imports System

Module Ambiguous
   Sub Main()
      Dim acc As Account = New Account("Bob", 100)
      Dim iacc As IAccount = acc
      Dim istat As IStatement = acc
```

```
        iacc.Show()        'calls IAccountShow
        istat.Show()       'calls IStatementShow

        acc.IAccount_Show()
        acc.IStatement_Show()
    End Sub
End Module
```

.NET Interfaces

The real power of VB.NET and the .NET Framework rests in the interfaces that are defined in the .NET class library. A VB.NET developer can implement any one or more of the predefined interfaces and have a wealth of predefined capabilities at his fingertips.

We saw in Chapter 7 that the .NET **System.Array** class contains many useful methods, including **Sort**. And we saw how **Sort** can be used to sort arrays of integers or strings. But what about sorting an array of a user-defined type such as **Account**? How would **Sort** know how to compare two instances of an **Account**? By simply implementing the .NET-defined **IComparable** interface in your **Account** class, which defines the method **CompareTo**, arrays of **Account** objects can be sorted using **System.Array**'s **Sort** method.

Chapter 18 of this book will cover many of the .NET interfaces that can be used to allow your classes to work with .NET classes.

Summary

The term *interface* is widely used in computer programming to describe how parts of a large system fit together. In VB.NET, the keyword **Interface** is used to define a closely related set of properties, methods, and events. Classes in VB.NET can then implement these interfaces. By taking advantage of this feature, we can build very dynamic programs. These programs can query sets of objects using **CType** to determine whether they support a particular interface, and if so, the programs can interact with the object in a specific way. Interfaces in VB.NET are conceptually very similar to interfaces in Microsoft's Component Object Model (COM), but are *much* easier to work with. In this chapter, we examined how the definition of interfaces helps us to specify the behavior of our system more precisely and succinctly.

The VB.NET Type System

*I*n *VB.NET, there is a fundamental distinction between value types, in which storage is allocated immediately when the variable is declared, and reference types, in which storage is allocated elsewhere and the variable is only a reference to the actual data. In previous chapters, we have examined both value types and reference types. In this chapter, we survey the entire VB.NET type system. We review the .NET class Object and examine how all VB.NET types are rooted in that class. In VB.NET, "everything is an object" and simple types are transparently converted to objects as needed through a process known as boxing. An object can be converted back to the simple value from which it originated, through a process known as unboxing.*

.NET Class Library

The .NET class library contains classes that correspond to all the data types that are available in VB.NET. Together, they make up the .NET Common Type System and are the reason that assemblies written in one .NET language may communicate seamlessly with code in another .NET assembly.

Object

The .NET class library defines **System.Object**, which is the ultimate base class of all data types in .NET. Any class that you define is implicitly derived from **Object**. This is why we can say that, in VB.NET, "everything is an object."

Object defines several methods that can be used directly, or overridden in derived classes, including the following:

- **ToString** returns a **String** representing the data in the object.
- **GetType** returns the type of the current object.
- **GetHashCode** returns an **Integer** that would be a suitable hash code for the current object. (We discuss the use of hash codes in Chapter 19.)

To see these methods in action, examine the **ObjectDemo\Version 1** program shown below. It uses the generic function **DisplayInfo** to display information about *any* object.

```vb
' A Point Class
Public Class Point
    Private m_x, m_y As Integer

    Public Sub New(ByVal x As Integer, ByVal y As Integer)
        m_x = x
        m_y = y
    End Sub
End Class

' The main program
Module ObjectDemo

    Private Sub DisplayInfo(ByVal o As Object)
        Console.WriteLine("ToString: {0}", o.ToString())
        Console.WriteLine("HashCode: {0}", o.GetHashCode())
        Console.WriteLine("Type:     {0}", _
                        o.GetType().ToString())
    End Sub

    Sub Main()
        Dim anInt As Integer = 43
        Console.WriteLine("An integer variable...")
        DisplayInfo(anInt)
        Console.WriteLine()

        Dim aSingle As Single = 91.375
        Console.WriteLine("A single variable...")
        DisplayInfo(aSingle)
        Console.WriteLine()

        Dim aString As String = "Howdy"
        Console.WriteLine("A string variable...")
        DisplayInfo(aString)
        Console.WriteLine()
```

```
        Dim aPoint As New Point(45, 70)
        Console.WriteLine("A point variable...")
        DisplayInfo(aPoint)
    End Sub
End Module
```

Output from this program is shown below:

```
An integer variable...
ToString: 43
HashCode: 43
Type:     System.Int32

A single variable...
ToString: 91.375
HashCode: 1119272960
Type:     System.Single

A string variable...
ToString: Howdy
HashCode: 222645448
Type:     System.String

A point variable...
ToString: ObjectDemo.Point
HashCode: 4
Type:     ObjectDemo.Point
```

If you examine the output, you will see that the **ToString** method returns a reasonable string representation of the value of the object in all cases except when the variable **aPoint** is used. The **Point** class does not provide an overridden version of the **ToString** method.

Code Example

The solution to this problem is to add a **ToString** method to all user-defined classes. It must return the data for the object in a reasonable format. The **Point** class in the **ObjectDemo\Version 2** program has been extended with an overridden **ToString** function.

```
' A Point Class
Public Class Point
   Private m_x, m_y As Integer

   Public Sub New(ByVal x As Integer, ByVal y As Integer)
      m_x = x
      m_y = y
   End Sub

   Public Overrides Function ToString() As String
      Return String.Format("({0},{1})", m_x, m_y)
   End Function
End Class
```

And calls are made to the **ToString** method as before:

```
Dim aPoint As New Point(45, 70)
Console.WriteLine("A point variable...")
DisplayInfo(aPoint)
```

The **ToString** displays the data for **Point** objects in traditional (x,y) point representation:

```
A point variable...
ToString: (45,70)
HashCode: 4
Type:     ObjectDemo.Point
```

Value Types

.NET supports value types via the **System.ValueType** class. Each variable of a value type has its own copy of the data. Value type objects are typically allocated on the stack when the variable is declared and are automatically destroyed when the variable goes out of scope. Value types include the simple types discussed in Chapter 4, structures, and enumeration types.

SIMPLE TYPES

The simple data types are general-purpose value data types, including numeric, character, and Boolean.

- The VB.NET **Byte** data type is an 8-bit unsigned integer that corresponds to the **System.Byte** data type.
- The VB.NET **Short** data type is a 16-bit signed integer that corresponds to the **System.Int16** data type.
- The VB.NET **Integer** data type is a 32-bit signed integer that corresponds to the **System.Int32** data type.
- The VB.NET **Long** data type is a 64-bit signed integer that corresponds to the **System.Int64** data type.
- The VB.NET **Decimal** data type is a decimal type with 28 significant digits (typically used for financial purposes) that corresponds to the **System.Decimal** data type.
- The VB.NET **Single** data type is a single-precision floating point that corresponds to the **System.Single** data type.
- The VB.NET **Double** data type is a double-precision floating point that corresponds to the **System.Double** data type.
- The VB.NET **Char** data type is a Unicode character (16 bits) that corresponds to the **System.Char** data type.
- The VB.NET **Boolean** data type is a Boolean (**True** or **False**) that corresponds to the **System.Boolean** data type.

STRUCTURES

Code Example

A **Structure** is a value type that can be used to group several objects together. It can optionally have constructors, methods, and properties associated with it. The following code, found in **StructureDemo**, illustrates the typical use of a structure in VB.NET.

```
Public Structure MailingAddress
    Public street As String
    Public city As String
    Public state As String
    Public zip As Integer
End Structure

Module StructureDemo
    Public Sub DisplayLabel(ByVal name As String, _
    ByVal addr As MailingAddress)
        Console.WriteLine(name)
        With addr
            Console.WriteLine(.street)
            Console.WriteLine("{0}, {1}   {2}", _
                            .city, .state, .zip)
        End With
    End Sub

    Sub Main()
        Dim anAddress As MailingAddress
        With anAddress
            .street = "3329 Blue Ridge Rd"
            .city = "Dallas"
            .state = "TX"
            .zip = 75229
        End With
        DisplayLabel("Ralph Westley", anAddress)
    End Sub
End Module
```

When working with structures, VB.NET provides the **With** statement. Using **With,** a programmer may omit the reference to the name of the structure variable when referencing the members of a structure. Output of the program above is as follows:

```
Ralph Westley
3329 Blue Ridge Rd
Dallas, TX 75229
```

We discussed structures in detail in Chapter 7.

ENUMERATIONS

The enumeration type, discussed in Chapter 7, is a distinct type with named constants. Every enumeration type is a **Byte**, a **Short**, an **Integer** (the default), or a **Long**. By default, the first **Enum** member is assigned the value of 0, the second member is assigned a value of 1, and so on. Constant values can be explicitly assigned.

```
Public Enum BookingStatus As Byte
    ReservationComplete         ' implicitly 0
    HotelNotFound = 5
    DateNotAvailable            ' implicitly 6
End Enum
```

You can use an enumeration type by declaring a variable of that type. You then refer to the enumerated values using dot notation. For example:

```
Dim status As BookingStatus
status = hotel.ReserveRoom(name, startingDate, numDays)
Select Case status
    Case BookingStatus.HotelNotFound
        Console.WriteLine("Hotel not found")

    Case BookingStatus.DateNotAvailable
        . . .

    Case BookingStatus.ReservationComplete
        . . .

End Select
```

Reference Types

.NET supports reference types via the **System.ReferenceType** class. Reference types do not contain data directly; they merely refer to data. They store references to objects. Two different variables can reference the same object. Reference types are allocated on the *managed heap* and eventually are destroyed through a process known as *garbage collection*.

Reference types include class types (such as **String** and **Object**), interfaces, array types, and delegates. Reference types have a special value called **Nothing**, which indicates the absence of an instance.

CLASS TYPES

Code
Example

A class type defines a data structure that has attributes, methods, properties, events, and constants. Class types support extension through the use of *inheritance*. Through inheritance, a derived class can extend (or specialize) a base class. We discussed classes and inheritance thoroughly in Chapters 11, 12, and 13. An example of classes and inheritance can be found in the program **Class-Demo**.

```vb
Public Class Person
    Private m_Name As String
    Private m_DOB As Date

    Public Sub New(ByVal name As String, ByVal dob As Date)
        m_Name = name
        m_DOB = dob
    End Sub

    Public ReadOnly Property Name() As String
        Get
            Return m_Name
        End Get
    End Property

    Public ReadOnly Property DOB() As Date
        Get
            Return m_DOB
        End Get
    End Property
End Class

Public Class WorkingPerson
    Inherits Person

    Private m_jobTitle As String
    Private m_payRate As Decimal

    Public Sub New(ByVal name As String, ByVal dob As Date, _
      ByVal jobTitle As String, ByVal payRate As Decimal)
        MyBase.New(name, dob)

        m_jobTitle = jobTitle
        m_payRate = payRate
    End Sub

    Public Property JobTitle() As String
        Get
            Return m_jobTitle
        End Get
        Set(ByVal Value As String)
            m_jobTitle = Value
        End Set
    End Property

    Public Property PayRate() As Decimal
        Get
            Return m_payRate
        End Get
        Set(ByVal Value As Decimal)
```

```
            m_payRate = Value
        End Set
    End Property
End Class

Module ClassDemo
    Sub Main()
        Dim you As WorkingPerson
        you = New WorkingPerson("Betty Littletree", _
            #8/12/1934#, "Secretary", 17)

        you.PayRate = you.PayRate * 1.07          ' 7% pay raise

        Console.WriteLine("{0} makes {1:C} as a {2}", _
            you.Name, you.PayRate, you.JobTitle)
    End Sub
End Module
```

Output from this program is as follows:

```
Betty Littletree makes $18.19 as a Secretary
```

INTERFACES

The purpose of an interface is to specify a contract independently of implementation. Like a class, an interface has methods. But whereas a class provides an implementation of its methods, an interface only specifies them. A class may implement one or more interfaces, specified by using the **Implements** keyword. A class may also inherit from another class, which implements other interfaces.

```
Public MustInherit Class Account
    Implements IAccount
...

Public Class CheckingAccount
    Inherits Account
    Implements IStatement, IChecking
...
```

We studied interfaces in detail in Chapter 13.

ARRAYS

An array is a collection of homogeneous elements; that is, they are all of the same type. In VB.NET, all array indices start at 0 and the declaration of the array specifies the subscript of the upper bound. Arrays may be single-dimensioned, multi-dimensioned, or jagged. For example:

```
Dim i, j As Integer

' Declare the array at the time the variable is declared
Dim list1(3, 3) As Integer      ' Builds a 4 x 4 array

' Build a multiplication table
For i = 0 To 3
   For j = 0 To 3
      list1(i, j) = i * j
   Next
Next

' Declare an array reference
Dim list2() As Integer

' Declare the array
list2 = New Integer() {4, 3, 2, 1, 0}

For i = 0 To 4
   list2(i) += 1
Next
```

We discussed arrays in Chapter 7.

DELEGATES

The purpose of a delegate is to provide "callback" behavior in an object-oriented, type-safe manner. Whereas in C/C++ you would use a function pointer, in VB.NET you can encapsulate a reference to a method inside a delegate object. You can then pass this delegate object to other code, which can then call your method. The code that calls your method does not have to know at compile time which method is being called. We will study delegates in detail in Chapter 18.

Classes and Structures

Although the concepts of **Class** and **Structure** are very close in VB.NET, there are fundamental differences between them.

- Members of a class have default visibility of **Private**, and members of a structure have default visibility of **Public**.
- A class is a *reference* type, and a structure is a *value* type.
- A class must be instantiated explicitly using **new**; the new instance is then created on the heap, and memory is managed by the system through a garbage collection process.

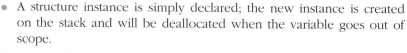

- A structure instance is simply declared; the new instance is created on the stack and will be deallocated when the variable goes out of scope.

There are different semantics for assignment, whether done explicitly or via the pass by value mechanism in a method call. For a class, you get a second object reference, and both object references refer to the same data. For a structure, you get a completely independent copy of the data in the structure. The program **StructureVsClass** illustrates this point.

```
Public Class PointClass
   Public x, y As Integer
      ' Using Dim would result in Private data
End Class

Public Structure PointStruct
   Dim x, y As Integer
      ' Using Dim results in Public data
End Structure


Module StructureVsClass
   Sub Main()
      Dim cp1, cp2 As PointClass
      cp1 = New PointClass()
      cp1.x = 100
      cp1.y = 100

      cp2 = New PointClass()
      cp2.x = 200
      cp2.y = 200

      Console.WriteLine("Before assignment:")
      Console.WriteLine("CP1 - ({0},{1})", cp1.x, cp1.y)
      Console.WriteLine("CP2 - ({0},{1})", cp2.x, cp2.y)

      cp2 = cp1
      cp1.x = 333
      Console.WriteLine("After assignment:")
      Console.WriteLine("CP1 - ({0},{1})", cp1.x, cp1.y)
      Console.WriteLine("CP2 - ({0},{1})", cp2.x, cp2.y)

      Console.WriteLine()
      Dim sp1, sp2 As PointStruct
      sp1.x = 100
      sp1.y = 100

      sp2.x = 200
      sp2.y = 200
      Console.WriteLine("Before assignment:")
```

```
        Console.WriteLine("SP1 - ({0},{1})", sp1.x, sp1.y)
        Console.WriteLine("SP2 - ({0},{1})", sp2.x, sp2.y)

        sp2 = sp1
        sp1.x = 333
        Console.WriteLine("After assignment:")
        Console.WriteLine("SP1 - ({0},{1})", sp1.x, sp1.y)
        Console.WriteLine("SP2 - ({0},{1})", sp2.x, sp2.y)
    End Sub
End Module
```

Output from the program is as follows:

```
Before assignment:
CP1 - (100,100)
CP2 - (200,200)
After assignment:
CP1 - (333,100)
CP2 - (333,100)

Before assignment:
SP1 - (100,100)
SP2 - (200,200)
After assignment:
SP1 - (333,100)
SP2 - (100,100)
```

Boxing and Unboxing

One of the strong features of VB.NET is its unified type system. Every type, including the simple built-in types such as **Integer**, derive from **System.Object**. Remember that in VB.NET, "everything is an object."

The language Smalltalk also has this feature but is inefficient when using simple types. Languages such as C++ and Java treat simple built-in types differently than objects, thus obtaining efficiency but at the loss of a unified type system.

VB.NET enjoys the best of both worlds through a process known as *boxing*. Boxing converts a value type such as **Integer** or a **Structure** to an object reference, and does so implicitly. *Unboxing* converts a boxed value type (stored on the heap) back to an unboxed simple value (stored on the stack). Unboxing is done using a type conversion.

```
Dim x As Integer = 5
Dim o As Object = x        ' boxing
x = Convert.ToInt32(o)     ' unboxing
```

Summary

In this chapter, we discussed the overall type system of VB.NET. There is a fundamental distinction between *value* types, in which storage is allocated immediately when the variable is declared, and *reference* types, in which storage is allocated elsewhere and the variable is only a reference to the actual data. We saw that all types in VB.NET are rooted in the .NET base class **Object**. We reviewed the various kinds of value types, including the simple types, structures, and enumerations. We then examined several reference types, including classes, arrays, and delegates. In VB.NET, value types are transparently converted to objects as needed through a process known as boxing. The inverse process, unboxing, returns an object to the value type from which it came.

PART FOUR

Windows Programming in VB.NET

*P*art Four covers Windows programming in VB.NET. Microsoft has adopted a new approach to developing Windows applications that will be readily apparent to previous VB programmers. Systematic coverage is presented on the core topics in Windows Forms, including form design, controls, events, menus, toolbars, and dialogs. The rich variety of useful controls provided by Windows Forms is covered in detail.

Introduction to Windows Forms

*I*n this chapter, we introduce how to build graphical user interfaces for programs using the .NET Windows Forms classes in the
.NET Framework. We demonstrate how to use Visual Studio.NET to
build a simple graphical user interface with Windows Forms and
basic controls. During this demonstration, we learn about labels,
text boxes, and buttons, as well as the principles of event handling
in Windows Forms. We also take a peek at the code that is generated by the Windows Forms Designer. We conclude by examining
some of the controls that are commonly used to build graphical
applications, including radio buttons, check boxes, list boxes, and
the tool tip control.

Windows Forms

Windows Forms is that part of the .NET Framework that supports building traditional GUI applications on the Windows platform. Windows Forms provides
a large set of classes that make it easy to create sophisticated user interfaces.
These classes are available to all .NET languages.

Your VB.NET Windows application will typically have a main window
that is implemented by building a class derived from **System.Win-
dows.Forms.Form**. Figure 15–1 illustrates a simplified version of the Windows Forms class library and how your main window will inherit basic
windowing support.

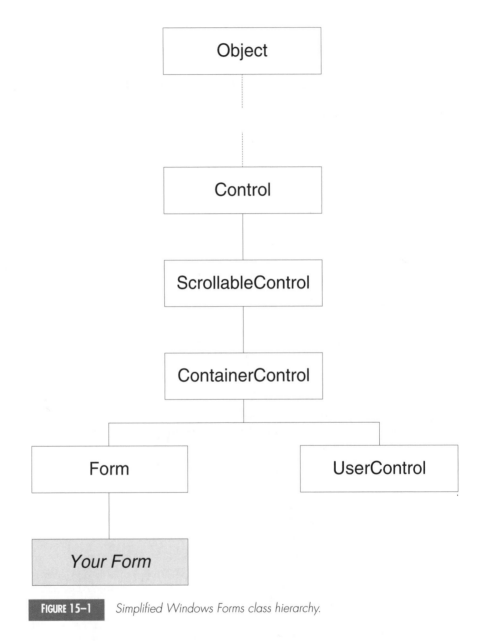

FIGURE 15–1   *Simplified Windows Forms class hierarchy.*

The functionality provided by these classes will be examined after a brief demonstration of the process of building a Windows application using Visual Studio.NET.

Building a Windows Application

VB.NET can build sophisticated applications that contain elaborate graphical user interfaces using two techniques.

- The application can be designed manually using an editor such as Notepad, by creating a class derived from **System.Windows.Forms.Form**, instantiating control variables, writing code to control their size and placement, and then writing event handlers to respond to events from the user.
- The application can be designed using Visual Studio.NET, which provides a visual drag-and-drop tool known as the Windows Forms Designer. You can also connect events to the controls using this tool. The only programming needed is the coding of the event handler.

This book focuses on the second approach and uses Visual Studio.NET in the development of all Windows applications. However, we show you the code that the designer generated. This is the code you must write if you did not want to use the visual design tool.

The following section describes the creation of a simple Windows application that allows the user to enter his name and then displays a basic greeting when the user presses a button. The completed program is found in **GreetingDemo**.

Building the Application

The first step in building a Windows application is to use the File | New menu to create the application as a "Windows Application" (see Figure 15–2). If you want to follow along and do the demonstration yourself, navigate to the **Demos** directory for this chapter.

You will notice that this program generates an initial startup form named **Form1** that serves as your main window (see Figure 15–3). It should also display the Toolbox, which contains all of the basic .NET controls that can be placed on your form. If your Toolbox is not visible, use the View menu to display it.

Behind the scenes, code has been generated that defines a class called **Form1** that is stored in a file called **Form1.vb**. We want to change the name of this class and the file to **MainForm** and **MainForm.vb**, respectively. The name of the class can be changed using the Properties window by setting the **Name** property to **MainForm**. You can confirm that this changed the name of the class by pressing the View Code button ⊞ on the Solutions Explorer toolbar. When the code window is displayed, you see all of the code that has been generated thus far:

```
Public Class MainForm
    Inherits System.Windows.Forms.Form

...

End Class
```

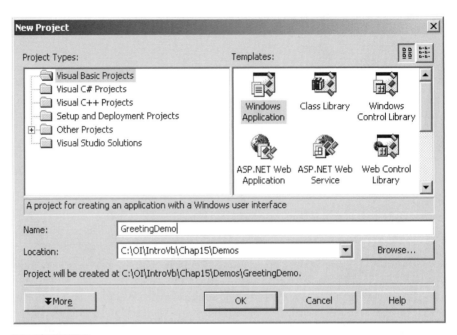

FIGURE 15–2 *Building the Windows application.*

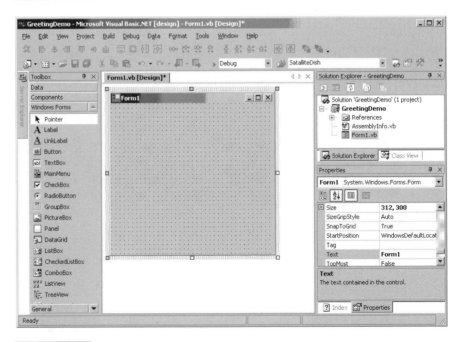

FIGURE 15–3 *A basic Windows application.*

You can change the name of the file in the Solutions Explorer window to **MainForm.vb** by right-clicking on the name of the file and choosing "rename." This is the same process you use to change the names of files in console applications.

Finally, you must change the Startup Object in the project's properties from **Form1** to **MainForm**. You may right-click on the project name in the Solutions Explorer window and choose Properties, or you may use the Project | Properties menu. Again, this is the same process you use to change Startup Object in console applications.

Using the Windows Forms Designer

You can use the Windows Forms Designer to design the graphical user interface of a Windows application by using a mouse to select controls from the Toolbox and place them on a form. The Toolbox is a scrollable window that contains a variety of controls that can be placed on a form in order to interact with a user. Figure 15–4 shows all of the controls.

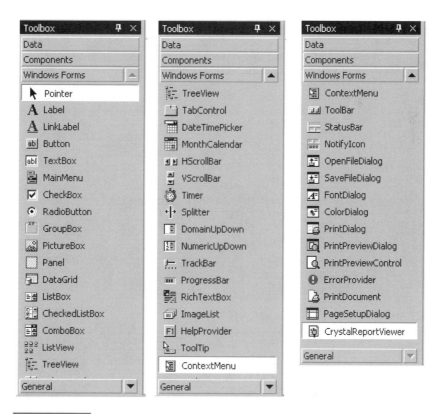

FIGURE 15–4   *The Controls Toolbox.*

.NET Introduces New Controls and Alters Familiar Ones

Programmers familiar with programming Windows will notice several new controls, such as the ErrorProvider and Panel, introduced with .NET. Even controls that resemble standard Windows controls have been changed somewhat. So it behooves everyone (novice to experienced developer) to examine the MSDN description of each control for a few minutes before using it for the first time!

Double-clicking on a control's icon in the Toolbox drawn the control on the form in a default position. It can then be moved to any position you desire. You may also drag a control from the toolbox and drop it where you want. Figure 15–5 shows our main form after three controls have been added. It identifies the types of the controls that were drawn and the properties that were changed for each control.

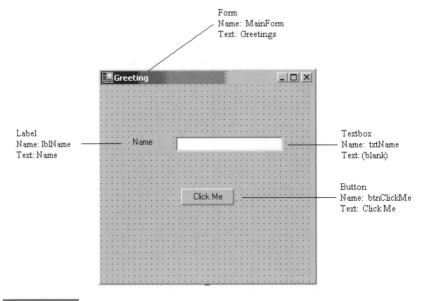

FIGURE 15–5   *Using the Windows Form Designer.*

Aligning Controls

You can use the Layout toolbar in the Windows Forms Designer to improve the appearance of your forms. The Layout toolbar can be used to align two or more controls, to make two or more controls the same size, to control the distance between two or more controls, and so on. Figure 15–6 illustrates the Layout toolbar.

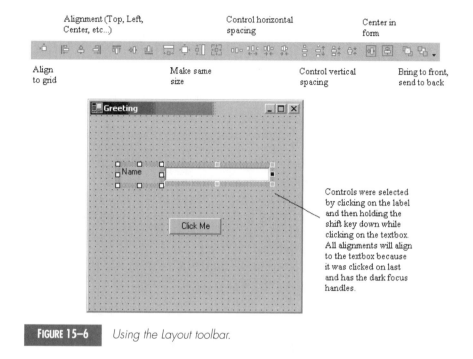

FIGURE 15–6   *Using the Layout toolbar.*

For Figure 15–5, we aligned the controls using the following process:

- We selected both the label and the text box, and chose "Align Top."
- With the label and the text box still selected, we chose "Center Horizontally."
- We selected the button, and chose "Center Horizontally."

Setting the Tab Order

You can set the tab order of the controls on the form using the View | Tab Order menu. (Your form must have the focus for the Tab Order option to appear on the View menu.) It displays the form and places numbers representing the current tab order over each control (see Figure 15–7). As you click on the controls, the tab order changes. The first control you click on becomes number 0, the second control you click on becomes number 1, and so on. When you are finished, use the View | Tab Order menu to make the numbers go away.

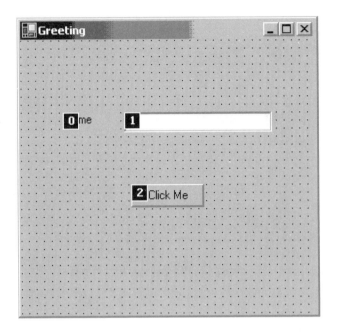

FIGURE 15–7 *Setting the tab order.*

Trapping Events

In order to respond to a user's actions, Windows applications must trap events. For example, if a user clicks on a button, a program might calculate a value. Or if a user selects an item from a list box, a program might retrieve data from a database.

As you recall from Chapter 11, classes in VB.NET can generate events. When variables of that class type are declared using **WithEvents,** events can be trapped and responded to. In the case of a Windows application, all controls placed on the form have variables associated with them that are declared using **WithEvents.** Look at this example:

```
Public Class MainForm
    Inherits System.Windows.Forms.Form

    . . .

    Friend WithEvents lblName As System.Windows.Forms.Label
    Friend WithEvents txtName As System.Windows.Forms.TextBox
    Friend WithEvents btnClickMe As _
        System.Windows.Forms.Button
```

. . .

```
End Class
```

Visual Studio.NET makes trapping the events easy. The code window has two drop-down list boxes attached to the top of the window:

- The left list box lists the objects in the *current* class that can trap events.
- The right list box lists the events that are valid for the *selected* object.

To trap the **Click** event on the **btnClickMe** button, you must choose **btnClickMe** from the left list box and **Click** from the right list box (see Figure 15–8).

An event handler is automatically generated:

```
Private Sub btnClickMe_Click(ByVal sender As Object, _
  ByVal e As System.EventArgs) Handles btnClickMe.Click



End Sub
```

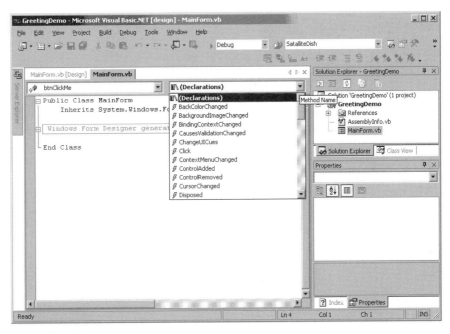

FIGURE 15–8   *Trapping events.*

Writing Event Handlers

The purpose of the demonstration program that we are building is to display a greeting string for the person whose name appears in the text box. To do this, we must extract the value from the text box when the user clicks the button and display that value in a message box. For our program, the following code must appear in the **btnClickMe_Click** procedure.

```
Private Sub btnClickMe_Click(ByVal sender As Object, _
 ByVal e As System.EventArgs) Handles btnClickMe.Click

    Dim s As String
    s = "Welcome, " & txtName.Text & _
        ", to the world of VB.NET"
    MessageBox.Show(s, "Greeting", _
        MessageBoxButtons.OK, MessageBoxIcon.Exclamation)

End Sub
```

The **MessageBox** object used above will be discussed in more detail in Chapter 16, but it basically is used to display a message box with the message contained in the variable **s** and a title of "Greeting." The message box has an OK button and displays an exclamation icon. The **Show** method has various overloaded versions, and a simple message can be displayed by using only the first parameter.

Running the Application

First, you must build the application. When an **.EXE** has been produced, you can run it from within the Visual Studio.NET environment or from the command line. The program initially displays the form shown in Figure 15–9.

After entering a name and pressing the "Click Me" button, the message box shown in Figure 15–10 appears.

FIGURE 15–9   *The initial GreetingDemo form.*

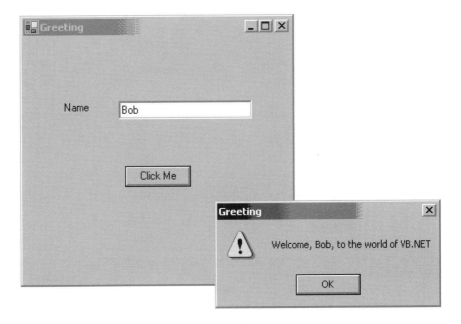

FIGURE 15–10   *The results of clicking the "Click Me" button.*

Under the Hood of a Windows Application

When you create a Windows Application project, it provides starter code for the main form and sets up references to the required .NET libraries. You are then presented with the Windows Forms Designer interface. A similar designer is available for visually drawing Web Forms, which is discussed in our book *Application Development Using Visual Basic and .NET.*

Code Generated by Windows Form Designer

As you can see from Figure 15–11, the code window hides the code that was generated by the Windows Forms Designer. It uses a **Region** directive to place a + (plus) next to a code segment. When the + is clicked, the editor window expands the code.

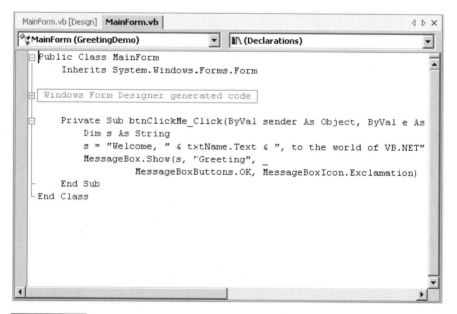

FIGURE 15–11   *The code window hides generated code.*

Region Directive Improves Code Readability

You can add the Region directive to code you write so that the editor window collapses the code and displays a comment instead. To see the code, you simply click the + next to the comment and the code is displayed. A Region directive begins with #Region and contains the comment seen in the editor window. A Region directive ends with #End Region.

The code generated by the Windows Forms Design defines a class that was derived from **System.Windows.Forms.Form**, as shown in this example:

```
Public Class MainForm
    Inherits System.Windows.Forms.Form
...
```

It also uses the **Region** directive to hide code generated by Windows Forms Designer:

```
#Region " Windows Form Designer generated code "
...
```

The constructor makes a call to **InitializeComponent**, which is a method defined in this class and discussed in an upcoming paragraph. You can initialize any variables in this constructor, or you can initialize them in the form's **Load** event, which is called as a form is being loaded and displayed.

```
Public Sub New()
    MyBase.New()

    'This call is required by the Windows Form Designer.
    InitializeComponent()

    'Add any initialization after the
    'InitializeComponent() call

End Sub
```

The class also defines the **Dispose** method, which is used to clean up the form's contents before the form is destroyed.

```
'Form overrides dispose to clean up the component list.
Protected Overloads Overrides Sub Dispose(ByVal _
 disposing As Boolean)

    If disposing Then
        If Not (components Is Nothing) Then
            components.Dispose()
        End If
    End If
    MyBase.Dispose(disposing)
End Sub
```

It defines variables that reference the control objects that were placed on the form:

```
Friend WithEvents lblName As System.Windows.Forms.Label
Friend WithEvents txtName As System.Windows.Forms.TextBox
Friend WithEvents btnClickMe As System.Windows.Forms.Button
```

as well as a container that is used to manage the controls:

```
'Required by the Windows Form Designer
Private components As System.ComponentModel.Container
```

Finally, we see the **InitializeComponent** method that was called in the constructor. It instantiates each control and initializes each property that has a non-default value. It also adds each control to a container that manages the collection of controls. As the comment states, the code in this method should not be modified because it is updated by the Windows Form Designer.

```
'NOTE: The following procedure is required by the
'      Windows Form Designer
'It can be modified using the Windows Form Designer.
'Do not modify it using the code editor.
<System.Diagnostics.DebuggerStepThrough()> _
 Private Sub InitializeComponent()

   Me.lblName = New System.Windows.Forms.Label()
   Me.txtName = New System.Windows.Forms.TextBox()
   Me.btnClickMe = New System.Windows.Forms.Button()
   Me.SuspendLayout()
   '
   'lblName
   '
   Me.lblName.Location = New System.Drawing.Point(44, 72)
   Me.lblName.Name = "lblName"
   Me.lblName.Size = New System.Drawing.Size(56, 23)
   Me.lblName.TabIndex = 0
   Me.lblName.Text = "Name"
   '
   'txtName
   '
   Me.txtName.Location = New System.Drawing.Point(108, 72)
   Me.txtName.Name = "txtName"
   Me.txtName.Size = New System.Drawing.Size(152, 20)
   Me.txtName.TabIndex = 1
   Me.txtName.Text = ""
   '
   'btnClickMe
   '
   Me.btnClickMe.Location = New System.Drawing.Point( _
      115, 144)
   Me.btnClickMe.Name = "btnClickMe"
   Me.btnClickMe.TabIndex = 2
   Me.btnClickMe.Text = "Click Me"
   '
   'MainForm
   '
   Me.AutoScaleBaseSize = New System.Drawing.Size(5, 13)
```

```
Me.ClientSize = New System.Drawing.Size(304, 273)
Me.Controls.AddRange( _
   New System.Windows.Forms.Control() { _
   Me.btnClickMe, Me.txtName, Me.lblName})
Me.Name = "MainForm"
Me.Text = "Greeting"
Me.ResumeLayout(False)

End Sub
```

The end statement of the **Region** directive follows this method definition.

```
#End Region
...
```

And then the class definition terminates with any event handlers and other code you wrote.

```
...
End Class
```

It is not necessary to use Visual Studio.NET to generate a Windows application, but it is much easier if you do so!

Common Properties

The **System.Windows.Forms.Control** class implements the basic functionality required of any class that can be displayed as a window. It defines several properties that will be useful, including those listed in Table 15–1.

TABLE 15–1	*Commonly Used Control Properties*
Property	**Description**
Name	Gets or sets the name of the Control object.
Top, Left, Bottom, Right	Gets or sets the top-left and bottom-right coordinates (location) of the Control object.
Width, Height	Gets or sets the width and height of the Control object.
BackColor, ForeColor	Gets or sets the background and foreground colors of the Control object.
BackgroundImage	Gets or sets the background image displayed in the Control.
Font	Gets or sets the font used by the Control object.
Text	Gets or sets the text associated with this Control.
Created	Gets a Boolean indicating whether the Control object has been created.

TABLE 15–1	*Commonly Used Control Properties (continued)*
Property	**Description**
Visible	Gets or sets a Boolean indicating whether the Control object is visible.
Enabled	Gets or sets a Boolean indicating whether the Control is enabled.
Focused	Gets a value indicating whether the Control has focus.
Dock	Gets or sets the edge of the parent container to which a Control is docked.
TabIndex	Gets or sets the tab order of this Control within its container.
TabStop	Gets or sets a value indicating whether the Tab key can cause this Control object to gain focus.

These properties can be used by any object derived from the Control class. This means they can be used with the form and all controls. For example, to change the text in the title of the **MainForm** object of the previous demo to "Demo Program," you could write this:

```
MainForm.Text = "Demo Program"
```

To change the text in the **Name** text box control of the previous demo, you could write this:

```
txtName.Text = "Dana"
```

Windows Forms Properties May Be Different Than VB6 Properties

VB6 programmers must note that several of the properties used in VB6 have been changed. For example, in VB6 most controls had a Caption property, while the text box had a Text property. In Windows Forms, all controls use the Text property to control the text in the window. Also, unlike VB6, you must explicitly use the Text property; it cannot be omitted by simply using a default value.

Common Events

GUI applications are event-driven. That is, the application executes code in response to user events, such as clicking a button, choosing a menu item, and so on. Each form or control has a predefined set of events that it generates when specific things happen to it. For example, every control has a **Click** event. Table 15–2 shows some commonly used control events.

TABLE 15–2	*Commonly Used Control Events*

Events	Description
Click, DoubleClick	Occurs when a Control object is clicked or double-clicked.
TextChanged	Occurs when the text associated with a Control object is changed.
GotFocus, LostFocus	Occurs when a Control object gains or loses focus.
KeyDown, KeyUp	Occurs when any key is pressed down or released when a Control object has focus.
KeyPress	Occurs when a key associated with a displayable character is pressed and the Control object has focus.
MouseDown, MouseUp, MouseMove	Occurs when the mouse button is pressed down or released or when the mouse is moved over a Control object.
MouseEnter, MouseLeave, MouseHover	Occurs when the mouse pointer enters, leaves, or hovers over a Control object.
Move	Occurs when a Control object is moved.
Resize	Occurs when a Control object is resized.
Paint	Occurs when a Control object is redrawn.
EnableChanged	Occurs when a Control object's Enabled property is changed.
VisibleChanged	Occurs when a Control object's Visible property is changed.

Event Handling

Typically, event handlers for controls indicate the control and event with which they are associated using the **Handles** keyword. For example, the following **IWasPressed** subroutine handles the **Click** event on the control **btnClickMe**.

```
Private Sub IWasPressed(ByVal sender As Object, _
 ByVal e As System.EventArgs) Handles btnClickMe.Click

   . . .

End Sub
```

If you add an event handler to a form class by selecting the control and event from the code window, VB.NET uses *controlName_eventName* as the procedure name. However, it is the **Handles** keyword at the end of the procedure that actually associates the procedure as the specific event handler.

```
Private Sub btnClickMe_Click(ByVal sender As Object, _
    ByVal e As System.EventArgs) Handles btnClickMe.Click

End Sub
```

Each event handler receives a set of parameters that are associated with that event. The first parameter is a reference to the control that generated the event. It can be referenced if an event handler handles events from two or more controls to determine which control generated the event. Additional parameters vary based on the type of event.

Windows Forms Event Handlers Use Handles Keyword

VB6 programmers should note that event handlers may have any name you desire. The VB6 convention that an event handler must use the name controlName_eventName is no longer applicable.

A Quick Look at Simple Controls

We have just barely scratched the surface of programming with Windows Forms. We briefly worked with the simplest controls:

- Labels
- Text boxes
- Buttons

To be able to develop sophisticated Windows applications, you must become familiar with the capabilities of a variety of controls and support classes available in .NET. We begin by examining some of the simplest controls in more detail in this chapter. We will continue in Chapter 16 by examining how to display other dialogs and how menus, toolbars, and status bars can be used to enhance the appearance of your GUI. We will conclude our discussion of Windows Forms in Chapter 17, where we continue to investigate controls such as progress bars, data grids, and tree views. But your investigation shouldn't end after you read these chapters. You should spend time reading the MSDN Help that is provided with VB.NET.

Code
Example

The forms shown below can be found in the application **Samples**. Each example is implemented by a different form class (for example: **LabelExample**, **TextBoxExample**, and so on). A driver form allows you to choose the desired example by clicking a button.

Using a Label

Label controls are typically used to provide descriptive text for controls on a form. For example, our demonstration program uses a label to place the description "Name" next to the text box. Controls cannot receive focus, but they should be included in the tab order of a form directly before the control that they describe. When they are tabbed to, the control following them in the tab order receives focus.

The **Label** class has additional properties not inherited from the **Control** class, including the following:

- The **Autosize** property can be used to cause the size of a label to snap to the size of the **Text** property.
- The **BorderStyle** property can be used to manage the label's border.
- The **Image** property can be used to assign a graphical image to the label.
- The **UseMnemonic** can be used to assign a mnemonic character to a label that allows a user to tab to the control that the label identifies.

The form shown in Figure 15–12 illustrates **UseMnemonic**. At any point, the user can press ALT+N, ALT+S, or ALT+P to change focus. The ALT+S shifts focus to the address text box because the address label has the tab order number 2, the address text box has the tab order number 3, and the label cannot gain focus.

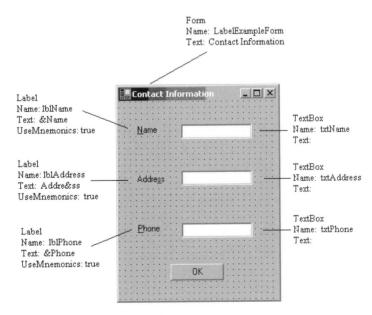

Form
Name: LabelExampleForm
Text: Contact Information

Label
Name: lblName
Text: &Name
UseMnemonics: true

TextBox
Name: txtName
Text:

Label
Name: lblAddress
Text: Addre&ss
UseMnemonics: true

TextBox
Name: txtAddress
Text:

Label
Name: lblPhone
Text: &Phone
UseMnemonics: true

TextBox
Name: txtPhone
Text:

TAB ORDER: Left-to-right, top-to-bottom with the name label having tab order 0, the name textbox 1, ... and the OK button 7

FIGURE 15–12 *Example of using a label.*

Using a Text Box

The **TextBox** control is typically used to allow a user to enter data into an application. It can also be used to display data. The **TextBox** class has additional properties not inherited from the **Control** class, including the following:

- The **Multiline** property allows multiple lines of text to be entered or displayed by the text box.
- The **AcceptsReturn** property is usually used in conjunction with a multiline TextBox object to indicate that the Enter key may be pressed and the keystroke will be recorded as data in the text box.
- The **WordWrap** property is used in a multiline TextBox object to cause the text in the box to wrap when the right edge of the text box is encountered.
- The **Scrollbars** property can be used to set horizontal and vertical scrollbars on a multiline text box.
- The **TextAlign** property can be used to specify whether text is left, right, or center aligned within the text box.
- The **MaxLength** property can be used to limit the number of characters that will be accepted by a text box.
- The **PasswordChar** property can be used to tell the text box to display the specified character instead of the actual character entered.
- The **CharacterCasing** property can be used to indicate whether the text box modifies the case of data entered.
- The **SelectedText**, **SelectionStart**, and **SelectionLength** properties can be used to interact with the highlighted, or selected, portion of the text box's text.
- The **ReadOnly** property can be used to restrict data entry in a text box.

The form shown in Figure 15–13 illustrates a multiline text box.

The **TextBox** class also includes several methods unique to text box controls, including the following:

- **Copy** copies the current selection from the text box to the Clipboard.
- **Cut** copies the current selection from the text box to the Clipboard and then deletes the selection.
- **Paste** replaces the current selection in the text box with the text from the Clipboard.

The form shown in Figure 15–14 is an extension of the multiline text box shown above. We have added three buttons to cause cut, copy, and paste behavior.

Form:
Name: TextBoxExampleForm
Text: Mini-Notepad

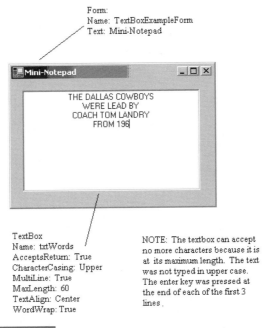

TextBox
Name: txtWords
AcceptsReturn: True
CharacterCasing: Upper
MultiLine: True
MaxLength: 60
TextAlign: Center
WordWrap: True

NOTE: The textbox can accept
no more characters because it is
at its maximum length. The text
was not typed in upper case.
The enter key was pressed at
the end of each of the first 3
lines .

FIGURE 15–13   Using a multiline TextBox Control.

Form
Name: TextBoxExample
Text: Mini-Notepad

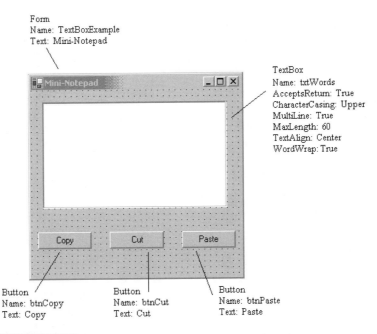

TextBox
Name: txtWords
AcceptsReturn: True
CharacterCasing: Upper
MultiLine: True
MaxLength: 60
TextAlign: Center
WordWrap: True

Button
Name: btnCopy
Text: Copy

Button
Name: btnCut
Text: Cut

Button
Name: btnPaste
Text: Paste

FIGURE 15–14   Example of interacting with the Clipboard.

The code in each of the button's **Click** events is shown below:

```
Private Sub btnCopy_Click(ByVal sender As System.Object, _
  ByVal e As System.EventArgs) Handles btnCopy.Click

    txtWords.Copy()

End Sub

Private Sub btnCut_Click(ByVal sender As Object, ByVal e _
  As System.EventArgs) Handles btnCut.Click

    txtWords.Cut()

End Sub

Private Sub btnPaste_Click(ByVal sender As Object, ByVal _
  e As System.EventArgs) Handles btnPaste.Click

    txtWords.Paste()

End Sub
```

Using a Button

A **Button** is used by the user to initiate some action. It may be clicked by using the mouse or by pressing the Enter key if the button has focus. The **Button** class has additional properties not inherited from the **Control** class, including the following:

- The **DialogResult** property is used to add predefined behaviors such as OK or Cancel to a form. (This property will be discussed in Chapter 16.)
- The **FlatStyle** property may be used to change the button's appearance. (**FlatStyle.Flat** makes it appear flat for a Web look; **FlatStyle.Popup** makes it appear flat until the mouse passes over the button and it takes on the standard Windows appearance.)

A form also has two properties that relate to the behavior of buttons:

- The **AcceptButton** property can be set to a specific button to indicate that the button can be clicked by pressing the Enter key in any control on the form that does not have its own **AcceptReturn** property set to True.
- The **CancelButton** property can be set to a specific button to indicate that the button can be clicked by pressing the Esc key in any control on the form.

Figure 15–15 illustrates a GUI that uses the **AcceptButton** property. This form allows a user to enter two numbers that are then added together

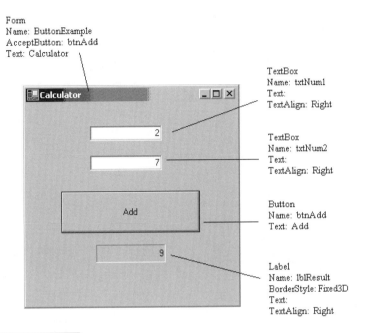

Form
Name: ButtonExample
AcceptButton: btnAdd
Text: Calculator

TextBox
Name: txtNum1
Text:
TextAlign: Right

TextBox
Name: txtNum2
Text:
TextAlign: Right

Button
Name: btnAdd
Text: Add

Label
Name: lblResult
BorderStyle: Fixed3D
Text:
TextAlign: Right

FIGURE 15–15   *Example of using a form's AcceptButton property.*

when the Add button is clicked. Pressing the Enter key will also cause the numbers to be added.

The code in **btnAdd's Click** event is shown below:

```
Private Sub btnAdd_Click(ByVal sender As System.Object, _
 ByVal e As System.EventArgs) Handles btnAdd.Click

   lblResult.Text = Convert.ToSingle(txtNum1.Text) _
      + Convert.ToSingle(txtNum2.Text)

End Sub
```

Using a Radio Button with a Group Box

The **RadioButton** control is used to allow users to select an option from a set of mutually exclusive options. When the user selects one radio button within a group, the other radio buttons clear automatically. The radio button may display text, an image, or both.

All radio button controls within a given container constitute a group. If they reside on a form, all radio buttons in the form constitute one group. More often, a programmer will use a **GroupBox** or **Panel** control to hold a set of mutually exclusive radio buttons.

The **RadioButton** class has additional properties not inherited from the **Control** class, including the following:

● The **Appearance** property determines the appearance of a radio button.
● The **Checked** property indicates whether the radio button is selected.
● The **Image** property identifies the image that is displayed on a radio button.

The **RadioButton** control also defines the **CheckedChanged** event that can be handled by the form in order to perform some action.

Figure 15–16 illustrates a GUI that uses a set of radio buttons to allow the user to select which greeting should be displayed. To design this form, first draw the **GroupBox** control, then draw each radio button and move it into the area within the group box.

Radio Buttons Do Not Have to Be Drawn Originally Inside the GroupBox

VB6 programmers had to be very careful to draw their radio buttons inside the group box. This is not the case in VB.NET. They can be moved into the group box from outside the control.

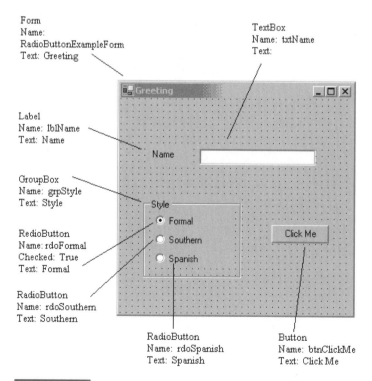

FIGURE 15–16   *Example of using a RadioButton control.*

The code in **btnClickMe's Click** event is shown below:

```
Private Sub btnClickMe_Click(ByVal sender As Object, _
ByVal e As System.EventArgs) Handles btnClickMe.Click

    Dim s As String

    If rdoFormal.Checked = True Then
        s = "Hello "
    ElseIf rdoSouthern.Checked = True Then
        s = "Howdy "
    Else
        s = "Hola "
    End If

    s = s & txtName.Text
    MessageBox.Show(s, "Greeting")

End Sub
```

Figure 15–17 illustrates the message box that the program generates when the "Click Me" button is clicked and the "Southern" radio button is checked.

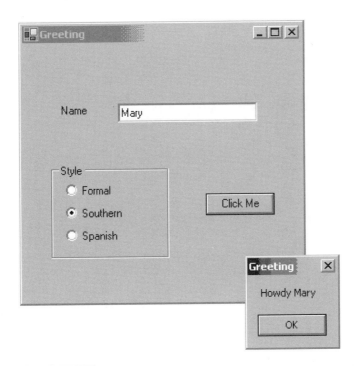

FIGURE 15–17 *Output from radio button example.*

Using a Check Box

A **CheckBox** control is used to allow the user to choose an option using a true/false or yes/no type of box. The **CheckBox** control can be displayed using a text description or an image. It is similar to the **RadioButton** control, except that each check box can be checked or unchecked individually without affecting another check box. The **CheckBox** class has properties that are similar to the **RadioButton** and include the following:

- The **Appearance** property determines the appearance of a check box.
- The **Checked** property indicates whether the check box is in the checked state.
- The **Image** property identifies the image that is displayed on a check box.

The **CheckBox** control also defines the **CheckedChanged** event that can be handled by the form in order to perform some action.

Figure 15–18 illustrates a GUI that uses a check box to control whether a greeting can be personalized with a name. When "Personalize" is checked, the user can enter a name. When it is not checked, the text box and label for "Name" is invisible.

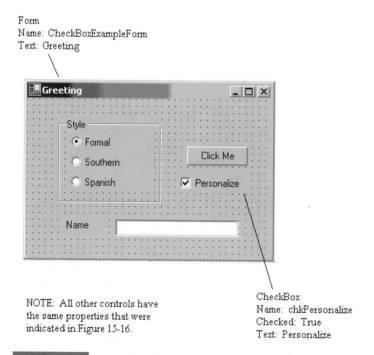

Form
Name: CheckBoxExampleForm
Text: Greeting

NOTE: All other controls have the same properties that were indicated in Figure 15-16.

CheckBox
Name: chkPersonalize
Checked: True
Text: Personalize

FIGURE 15–18   *Example of using a CheckBox control.*

The two event handlers written for this form are shown below:

```
Private Sub btnClickMe_Click(ByVal sender As Object, _
  ByVal e As System.EventArgs) Handles btnClickMe.Click

    Dim s As String

    If rdoFormal.Checked = True Then
        s = "Hello "
    ElseIf rdoSouthern.Checked = True Then
        s = "Howdy "
    Else
        s = "Hola "
    End If

    s = s & txtName.Text
    MessageBox.Show(s, "Greeting")
    txtName.Text = ""

End Sub

Private Sub chkPersonalize_CheckedChanged(ByVal sender _
  As System.Object, ByVal e As System.EventArgs) _
  Handles chkPersonalize.CheckedChanged

    If chkPersonalize.Checked Then
        txtName.Visible = True
        lblName.Visible = True
    Else
        txtName.Visible = False
        lblName.Visible = False
    End If

End Sub
```

Figure 15–19 illustrates the message boxes that can be displayed both with and without the check box checked.

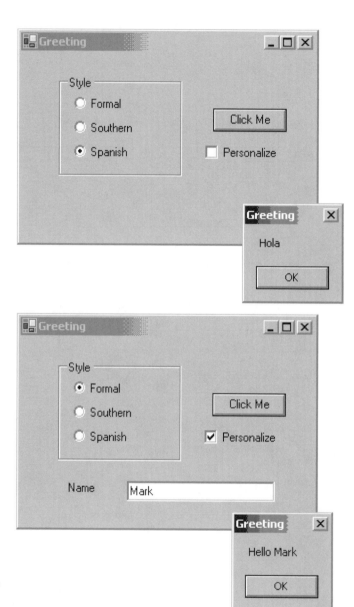

FIGURE 15–19 *Output from check box example.*

Using the ToolTip Control

The **ToolTip** control can be used to display tool tip text when the mouse hovers over a control on a form. The **ToolTip** control is an *invisible* control; that is, when it is added to a form, it is not visible. The **ToolTip** class has several properties that are not defined in the **Control** class, including the following:

- The **Active** property indicates whether the **ToolTip** control is active.
- The **InitialDelay** property indicates the initial delay (in milliseconds) for the first time that tool tip text appears.
- The **ReshowDelay** property indicates the length of time it takes for subsequent displays of the tool tip text to appear.

The **ToolTip** control also has several methods that are used to manage the text displayed on a per-control basis, including the following:

- The **SetToolTip** method is used to set the tool tip text for a specific control.
- The **GetToolTip** method is used to get the tool tip text for a specific control.
- The **RemoveAll** method is used to remove all tool tips associated with the tool tip object.

Figure 15–20 illustrates the process of designing a form that contains a **ToolTip** control. When you draw the **ToolTip** control, it appears in a separate area of the designer window. This area shows all invisible controls on a form.

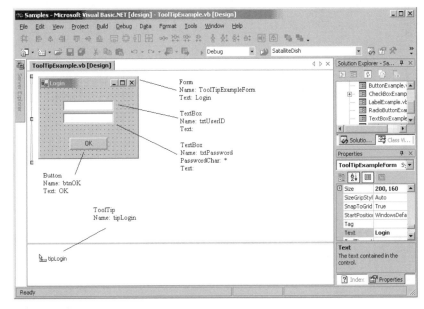

FIGURE 15–20   *Using the ToolTip control.*

The form's **Load** event is used to initialize the tool tip text for the two TextBox controls. The code for this handler is shown below:

```
Private Sub ToolTipExampleForm_Load(ByVal sender As _
  System.Object, ByVal e As System.EventArgs) _
  Handles MyBase.Load

    tipLogin.SetToolTip(txtUserID, "Enter your user id.")
    tipLogin.SetToolTip(txtPassword, "Enter your password.")

End Sub
```

Figure 15–21 illustrates the tool tip text when the mouse is hovered over the first text box.

FIGURE 15–21   *Example of tool tip text.*

Using a ListBox Control

The **ListBox** control can be used to allow the user to enter data by selecting an item from a list. It can be a single-selection or multiple-selection **ListBox** control, and it can display multiple columns of data.

The **ListBox** control is more sophisticated than the other controls discussed here. It manages three collections:

- The **Items** property is used to access all of the items listed within the list box. The **Items** property can be used to access properties such as **Count** and **Item**, and methods such as **Add**, **AddRange**, **Clear**, **Insert**, **Remove**, and **RemoveAt**.
- The **SelectedItems** property is used to access the selected items in the list box. It can also be used to access properties such as **Count** and **Item**.
- The **SelectedIndices** property is used to access the indices of the selected items in the list box. It can also be used to access properties such as **Count** and **Item**.

Although we don't discuss collections until Chapter 19, you should find their use quite intuitive.

The **ListBox** class also has many other properties and methods that can be used to manipulate the control, including these interesting properties:

- The **Sorted** property indicates whether the list box is sorted.
- The **MultiColumn** property indicates whether the list box supports multiple columns.
- The **SelectionMode** property indicates the selection mode (single selection or multiple selection) of the list box.
- The **Text** property indicates the value of the currently selected item in the list box.
- The **SelectedIndex** property indicates the index of the item currently selected in the list box.

The **ListBox** control also contains methods that can be used to manipulate the control, including the following:

- The **FindString** method locates the first item in a list box that begins with the specified string.
- The **FindStringExact** method locates the first item in a list box that exactly matches the specified string.
- The **GetSelected** method returns a Boolean indicating whether the specified item in a list box is selected.
- The **SetSelected** method selects the specified item in the list box.
- The **ClearSelected** method deselects all items in a list box.
- The **BeginUpdate** and **EndUpdate** methods can be used to delineate activities that update the contents of a list box; painting is suspended during these activities to enhance performance.

The **ListBox** control also generates events that can be handled to provide functionality, including the following:

- **SelectedIndexChanged** indicates that the selected index changed.
- **SelectedValueChanged** indicates that the selected text changed.

ADDING AND REMOVING ITEMS

Items can be added to a list box either statically (at design time) or dynamically (at run time). To add the items at design time, you must use the Properties window for the list box. Click the ellipsis button for the **Items** property to display an editor that can be used to add items to the list box (see Figure 15–22). Enter strings that are to be placed in the list box, and then click OK.

To add items to a list box dynamically at run time, you must use the **Items.Add** method, as in this example:

```
lstAnimals.Items.Add("Cat")
lstAnimals.Items.Add("Horse")
```

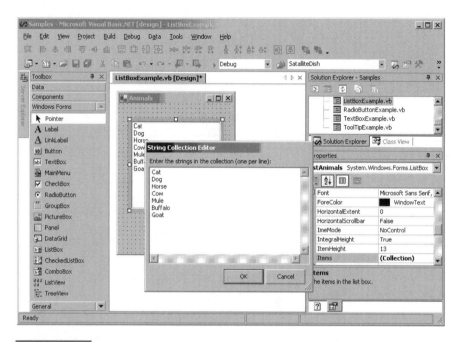

FIGURE 15–22 *Adding items to a list box at design time.*

If you have a large number of items to add to the list box, you could turn off repainting of the control until all items have been added using the **BeginUpdate** and **EndUpdate** methods, as in this example:

```
Dim animals(49) As String
...
Dim i As Integer
lstAnimals.BeginUpdate()
For i = 0 To Ubound(elements)
   lstAnimals.Items.Add(animals(i))
Next
lstAnimals.EndUpdate()
```

Whereas the **Add** method adds a string to the end of the list box, the **Items.Insert** method can be used to specify the location of the string. (The **Insert** method is irrelevant if the **Sorted** property of the list box is True.) Here's an example:

```
lstAnimals.Items.Insert (3, "Mule")
```

The **Add** method and **Insert** method each add one string to an array at a time. The **Items.AddRange** method can be used to assign an entire array to the list box, as in this example:

```
Dim AnimalList(9) As String
...
lstAnimals.Items.AddRange = AnimalList
```

To remove items from a list box, the **Remove** method can be used to remove the first occurrence of a specified string. Here's an example:

```
Dim AnimalList(9) As String
```

The **RemoveAt** method can be used to remove the occurrence at a specified index, as shown here:

```
Dim AnimalList(9) As String
```

To remove all items from the list box, the **Items.Clear** method is used, as shown here:

```
lstAnimals.Items.Clear()
```

Selecting an Item in a List Box

An item in a list box is selected by clicking on the item. This action generates a **SelectedIndexChanged** event. The properties **SelectedIndex** and **SelectedItem** are set by the user's clicking action. When no item is selected, **SelectedIndex** is − 1, as in this example:

```
Private Sub lstAnimals_SelectedIndexChanged(ByVal _
 sender As System.Object, ByVal e As System.EventArgs) _
 Handles lstAnimals.SelectedIndexChanged

   Dim s As String
   If lstAnimals.SelectedIndex <> - 1 Then
     s = lstAnimals.SelectedItem
   End If
   ...
End Sub
```

If the item is a multi-select list box, the code is more complicated. The **SelectedItems** property maintains the collection of selected items. Its property **Count** identifies the number of items selected. These may then be accessed through the subscriptable property **Item**, as in this example:

```
Dim s As String
Dim index As Integer
s = lstAnimals.SelectedItems.Item(0)
For index = 1 To lstAnimals.SelectedItems.Count - 1
   s &= ", " & lstAnimals.SelectedItems.Item(index)
Next
```

LISTBOX: PUTTING IT ALL TOGETHER

Many of the snippets of code we saw previously can be found in the **ListBox-ExampleForm** in the **Samples** project. Figure 15–23 illustrates the controls and their properties that are on this form.

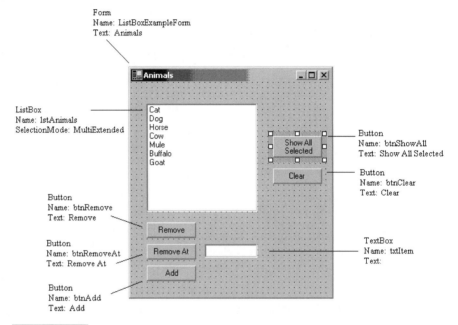

FIGURE 15–23 *Example of using a multi-select ListBox control.*

The behavior of each button is as follows:

- The Remove button is used to remove the item whose string is found in the text box to the right.
- The Remove At button is used to remove the item whose index is found in the text box to the right.
- The Add button is used to add the item whose string is found in the text box to the right.
- The Show All Selected button is used to display the values of all items selected in the list box.
- The Clear button empties the list box.

Additionally, when you click on the list box, a message identifies the item you clicked on. The code to achieve this behavior is as follows:

```
Private Sub btnRemove_Click(ByVal sender As System.Object, _
   ByVal e As System.EventArgs) Handles btnRemove.Click

    lstAnimals.Items.Remove(txtItem.Text)
```

```
End Sub

Private Sub btnRemoveAt_Click(ByVal sender As Object, _
 ByVal e As System.EventArgs) Handles btnRemoveAt.Click

    lstAnimals.Items.RemoveAt(Convert.ToInt16(txtItem.Text))

End Sub

Private Sub btnAdd_Click(ByVal sender As Object, ByVal e _
 As System.EventArgs) Handles btnAdd.Click

    lstAnimals.Items.Add(txtItem.Text)

End Sub

Private Sub btnClear_Click(ByVal sender As Object, _
 ByVal e As System.EventArgs) Handles btnClear.Click

    lstAnimals.Items.Clear()

End Sub

Private Sub lstAnimals_SelectedIndexChanged(ByVal sender _
 As System.Object, ByVal e As System.EventArgs) _
 Handles lstAnimals.SelectedIndexChanged

    Dim s As String
    s = String.Format( _
        "You selected item {0}, which was {1}", _
        lstAnimals.SelectedIndex, lstAnimals.SelectedItem)
    MessageBox.Show(s, "Animal Selection")

End Sub

Private Sub btnShowAll_Click(ByVal sender As _
 System.Object, ByVal e As System.EventArgs) _
 Handles btnShowAll.Click

    If lstAnimals.SelectedItems.Count < 1 Then
       Exit Sub
    End If

    Dim s As String
    Dim index As Integer
    s = lstAnimals.SelectedItems.Item(0)
    For index = 1 To lstAnimals.SelectedItems.Count - 1
       s &= ", " & lstAnimals.SelectedItems.Item(index)
    Next

    MessageBox.Show(s, "Selected Animals")

End Sub
```

Using a ComboBox Control

The **ComboBox** control is very similar to the **ListBox** control, except that users can also type text into the **ComboBox** control, as well as choose from a list. The **ComboBox** control uses the **Items** collection to manage the items in the combo box list. Properties, methods, and events of the two controls are very similar. However, the **ComboBox** control supports only single selection; therefore, the **SelectedItem** property references a single item.

The **ComboBox** control also has a **DropDownStyle** property that allows the control to be used in one of three modes (see Figure 15–24).

- **DropDown** (the default) displays an edit control with an arrow next to it that can be used to drop down the list. An item can be selected from the list or typed into the edit control.
- **Simple** displays an edit control with a list just below it that is always visible. An item can be selected from the list or typed into the edit control.
- **DropDownList** displays a non-editable edit control with an arrow next to it that can be used to drop down the list. An item must be selected from the list.

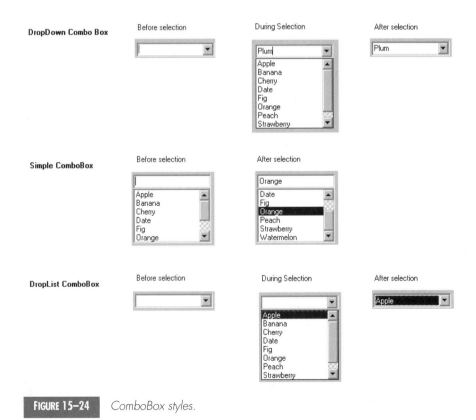

FIGURE 15–24   *ComboBox styles.*

More about Events

VB.NET's event-handling mechanism is very flexible. The language allows one handler to be created to handle events from similar controls. To do this, use the **Handles** keyword to list the events that the procedure handles.

In the following example, found in the **EventHandling** project, there are three buttons that manipulate one label (see Figure 15–25). We have designed this program to use one event handler for all three buttons. In the event handler, we must reference the **sender** parameter to determine which button's **Click** event the handler is processing.

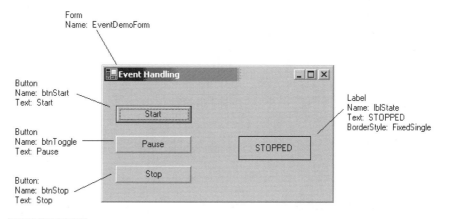

FIGURE 15–25   *GUI for the EventHandling demo.*

```
Private Sub ProcessChanged(ByVal sender As _
  System.Object, ByVal e As System.EventArgs) _
  Handles btnStart.Click, btnStop.Click, btnToggle.Click

    Dim btn As Button
    btn = CType(sender, Button)
    Select Case btn.Text
       Case "Start"
          lblState.Text = "EXECUTING"
       Case "Pause"
          lblState.Text = "PAUSED"
          btn.Text = "Resume"
       Case "Resume"
          lblState.Text = "EXECUTING"
          btn.Text = "Pause"
       Case "Stop"
          lblState.Text = "STOPPED"
    End Select
End Sub
```

VB.NET Does Not Support Control Arrays

VB6 programmers should note that VB.NET does not support control arrays. However, by using the approach shown in this section, you can achieve the benefits of control arrays— one handler for several controls.

Summary

We have seen that Windows Forms is a set of .NET classes that allow you to create Windows applications. The same library may be used by all .NET languages. By using Visual Studio.NET and the Windows Forms Designer, you can build a simple graphical user interface. The designer hides the complexities of building a form and connecting the controls to the form. The Forms Designer lets you drag controls from the Toolbox onto your forms. You can set properties of the controls at design time using the Properties window, or you may set them at run time in code. You can also easily add event handlers. There are many controls available to Windows Forms programmers. We examined some of the basic controls in this chapter, and we will examine many more in Chapters 16 and 17.

Windows Forms, Part II

In this chapter, we continue our discussion of Windows Forms. Now that we know how to design a main window, we must examine other aspects of building Windows applications. We begin by discussing the different types of dialogs. The .NET MessageBox class displays simple message-oriented dialogs. The Windows Form Designer can be used to design custom dialogs. Finally, the CommonDialog control can be used to display dialogs, such as the common color dialog and the file dialog, that are part of the Windows operating system. We conclude by exploring how menus, toolbars, and status bars can be added to a VB.NET Windows application.

Dialog Boxes

Dialog boxes provide an easy way for a user to interact with a Windows application. A dialog box provides a number of controls to facilitate data input and/or data output. A message box that allows a user to answer a yes or no question is the simplest type of dialog.

Dialog boxes often have special characteristics as forms. For example, they typically do not have a system menu, they have no minimize or maximize buttons, and they have a border that does not permit them to be resized. These can be set using the **ControlBox**, **MinimizeBox**, **MaximizeBox**, and **FormBorderStyle** properties.

A dialog box can be a *modal* dialog or a *modeless* dialog. When a modal dialog is displayed, the user cannot work elsewhere in the application until the dialog is closed. If the user tries to do something else on the main form while the dialog is open, he hears a beep. When a modeless dialog is displayed, the user can work elsewhere in the application while the dialog is open.

MessageBox

The .NET **MessageBox** class can be used to manage simple modal dialogs that primarily display information to the user. These message boxes contain text, buttons, and symbols that inform and instruct the user. Figure 16–1 illustrates a sample message box dialog that is displayed in the **MessageBox-Demo** project. The No button is outlined because it was specified as the default button.

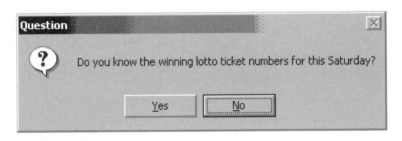

FIGURE 16–1   *A sample message box.*

You cannot create a new instance of the **MessageBox** class; it has a private constructor. To display a message box, call the shared method **Show**. The **Show** method has several parameters that define:

- The message text
- The title of the message box window
- The buttons that are displayed (a value from the **MessageBoxButtons** enumeration)
- The icon that is displayed (a value from the **MessageBoxIcon** enumeration)
- The identity of the default button displayed (a value from the **MessageBoxDefaultButton** enumeration)

The **MessageBoxButtons** enumeration defines the following options:

- OK
- OkCancel
- RetryCancel
- YesNo

- YesNoCancel
- AbortRetryIgnore

The **MessageBoxIcon** enumeration defines the following options:

- **None**, which displays no icon.
- **Question**, which displays a question mark in a circle.
- **Information**, which displays the lowercase *i* in a circle. Can also be referred to as **Asterisk**.
- **Exclamation**, which displays an exclamation point in a triangle with a yellow background. Can also be referred to as **Warning**.
- **Error**, which displays a white *X* in a circle with a red background. Can also be referred to as **Stop** or **Hand**.

The **MessageBoxDefaultButton** enumeration defines the following options:

- **Button1**, which indicates that the first button is the default.
- **Button2**, which indicates that the second button is the default.
- **Button3**, which indicates that the third button is the default.

Each of the following represents a valid call to the **MessageBox's Show** method:

```
MessageBox.Show("Welcome " & txtName.Text, "Greeting")

MessageBox.Show("Name is required.", "Data Error", _
   MessageBoxButtons.OK, MessageBoxIcon.Error)

Dim answer As DialogResult
answer = MessageBox.Show("Do you want to proceed?", _
   "Continue", MessageBoxButtons.YesNo, _
   MessageBoxIcon.Error, MessageBoxDefaultButton.Button2)
If answer = DialogResult.Yes Then
   ...
Else
   ...
End If
```

MessageBox Class Replaces MsgBox Function

VB6 programmers will notice that the MessageBox class encapsulates the same functionality as the MsgBox function and is the preferred way of displaying a message box dialog. However, the MsgBox function still exists.

Custom Dialogs

Custom dialogs can be created and used by performing any of the following functions:

- Add a second form to an existing project, and configure various properties on the new dialog to control its appearance.
- Configure the **DialogResult** properties so that you can return a dialog result through the use of OK and Cancel buttons.
- Write code to display the dialog.
- Write code to respond to the dialog result.

We demonstrate the process of using modal dialogs in the project **CustomDialogExample**. First, we must design the main window. Figure 16–2 illustrates our main window.

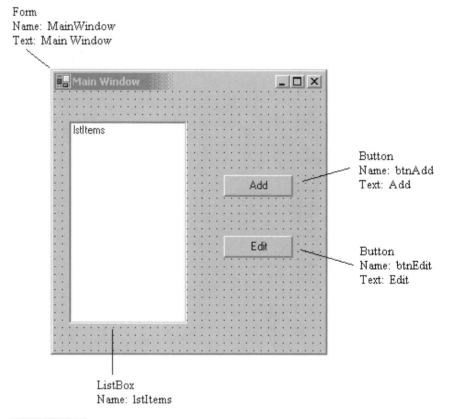

Form
Name: MainWindow
Text: Main Window

ListBox
Name: lstItems

Button
Name: btnAdd
Text: Add

Button
Name: btnEdit
Text: Edit

FIGURE 16–2 *The main window design for CustomDialogExample.*

CREATING A NEW DIALOG

- To create a new dialog, we begin by using the Project | Add Windows Form menu. It prompts us for a form name, and we choose **ListItemForm**. This new form is inserted in our project and is now shown in the Solutions Explorer window (see Figure 16–3).

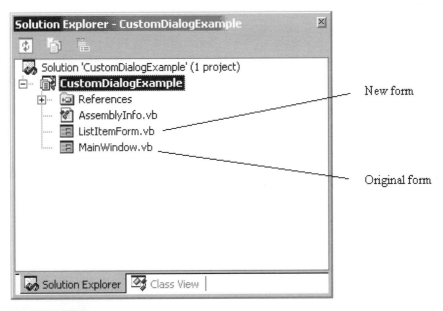

New form

Original form

FIGURE 16-3 *Solutions Explorer showing two forms.*

This new form is designed by placing controls on it from the Toolbox and configuring the properties as needed. For this example, we have designed our form as shown in Figure 16–4 and set the properties as indicated.

USING DIALOGRESULT

- The **DialogResult** property of a button can be used to provide predetermined behavior for buttons. The **DialogResult** property can be set to **None**, or any of the following values:
- OK
- Cancel
- Yes
- No
- Abort
- Retry
- Ignore

For each of the values (except **None**), the button automatically closes the dialog and assigns the button's **DialogResult** property to the form's **DialogResult** property. The form's **DialogResult** property is returned from the form's **ShowDialog** method and can be used to determine which button was pressed to close the form.

Form
Name: ListItemForm
ControlBox: False
FormBorderStyle: FixedDialog
MaximizeButton: False
MinimizeButton: False
Text: Item Information

Label
Name: lblItem
Text: Item

TextBox
Name: txtItem
Text:

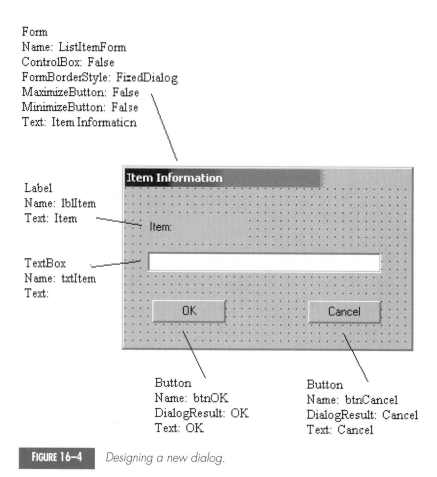

Button
Name: btnOK
DialogResult: OK
Text: OK

Button
Name: btnCancel
DialogResult: Cancel
Text: Cancel

FIGURE 16–4 *Designing a new dialog.*

In our **ListItemForm**, we set the **DialogResult** properties for **btnOK** to **OK** and **btnCancel** to **Cancel**. When the dialog is displayed, the user will enter an item value. The user can close the dialog by pressing either the OK button or the Cancel button. In the code that displays the dialog, the programmer can test the form's **DialogResult** property. If it is OK, the programmer can retrieve the data from the **ListItemForm.** If it is Cancel, the programmer can ignore the data.

DISPLAYING A DIALOG

● To display a dialog, we must remember that any window in VB.NET is an instance of a class derived from **System.Windows.Forms.Form**. Therefore, to create a new window, we use the keyword **New** to create an instance of the class.

```
Dim infoForm As New ListItemForm
```

The form's **ShowDialog** method can then be used to display the dialog as a modal dialog. It returns the value of the **DialogResult** property.

```
Dim buttonPressed As DialogResult

buttonPressed = infoForm.ShowDialog()
If buttonPressed = DialogResult.OK Then
    ' Process the data in the form
End If
```

In the **CustomDialogExample** project, our Add button is going to display the **ListItemForm** in order to gather data that will be added to the list box on the main form. The code to implement this is found in the **Click** event of the **btnAdd** button.

```
Private Sub btnAdd_Click(ByVal sender As _
  System.Object, ByVal e As System.EventArgs) _
  Handles btnAdd.Click

    Dim infoForm As New ListItemForm()
    Dim ans As DialogResult

    ' Display the dialog
    ans = infoForm.ShowDialog()

    ' Process the data collected
    If ans = DialogResult.OK Then
        lstItems.Items.Add(infoForm.txtItem.Text)
    End If

End Sub
```

You can see from the code above that the controls on the form are accessible after the **ShowDialog** method has returned and the window has disappeared. These controls are accessible as long as the instance of the form exists. In this case, this instance of the form exists until the **btnAdd_Click** procedure terminates.

The Edit button in this project is going to take the currently selected item in the list box and place it in text box on the **ListItemForm** so that it may be edited. In the previous button example, we saw an example of retrieving a value from a dialog. This example illustrates the process of placing an initial value in a dialog.

```
Private Sub btnEdit_Click(ByVal sender As Object, _
  ByVal e As System.EventArgs) Handles btnEdit.Click

    ' Make sure there is data to be edited
    If lstItems.SelectedIndex < 0 Then
      MessageBox.Show( _
        "You must select an item to edit first!", _
```

```
      "Edit Error", MessageBoxButtons.OK, _
      MessageBoxIcon.Warning)
    Exit Sub
End If

Dim infoForm As New ListItemForm()
Dim ans As DialogResult

' Put the data on the dialog before it is displayed
infoForm.txtItem.Text = lstItems.SelectedItem

' Display the dialog
ans = infoForm.ShowDialog()

' Process the result
If ans = DialogResult.OK Then
  Dim curLoc As Integer

    ' Prohibit repainting the listbox while it is modified
    lstItems.BeginUpdate()

    ' Remove the old version
    curLoc = lstItems.SelectedIndex
    lstItems.Items.RemoveAt(curLoc)

    ' Reinsert the item
    lstItems.Items.Insert(curLoc, infoForm.txtItem.Text)

    ' Resume painting the listbox
    lstItems.EndUpdate()
  End If
End Sub
```

CHANGING THE BEHAVIOR OF A BUTTON'S DIALOGRESULT

Many dialogs do not blindly accept all data. Instead, they enforce rules relating to the content, format, and range of data before allowing the user to successfully choose an OK button.

In our **CustomDialogExample** program, we are going to enforce the rule that a user may not add blank data to our list box. We will also enforce the rule that the user may not edit an item in a list box so that it becomes blank.

To implement these data validation requirements, we must write code in the **Click** event of **btnOK** on the **ListItemForm** to check the contents of **txtItem**. If we find that the data is invalid, we must prohibit the closing of the dialog. To do this, we can assign the form's **DialogResult** property the value **None**.

```
Private Sub btnOK_Click(ByVal sender As System.Object, _
 ByVal e As System.EventArgs) Handles btnOK.Click

    ' Validate data
   If Trim(txtItem.Text) = "" Then
      MessageBox.Show( _
         "A non-blank item must be provided!", "Error", _
         MessageBoxButtons.OK, MessageBoxIcon.Stop)

      ' Prohibit closing of the dialog
      Me.DialogResult = DialogResult.None
   End If
End Sub
```

RUNNING CUSTOMDIALOGEXAMPLE

Figure 16–5 illustrates what the windows might look like when running the **CustomDialogExample** program.

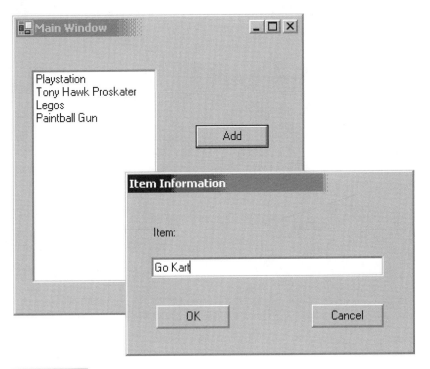

FIGURE 16–5   *Displaying the modal dialog.*

Modeless Dialogs

VB.NET supports modeless dialogs as well as modal dialogs. You can typically identify modeless dialogs from their design; modal dialogs have OK and Cancel buttons, while modeless dialogs have Apply and Close buttons. A few programming differences must be noted:

- The **Show** method is used to display the modeless dialog (instead of the **ShowDialog** method).
- A **DialogResult** is not returned from the **Show** method; programmers must implement their own strategy for providing behavior for the Apply and Close buttons in the modeless dialog.

In the program **ModelessDialogExample**, we use a modeless dialog to add items to a list box. Figure 16–6 illustrates the main window design for this program.

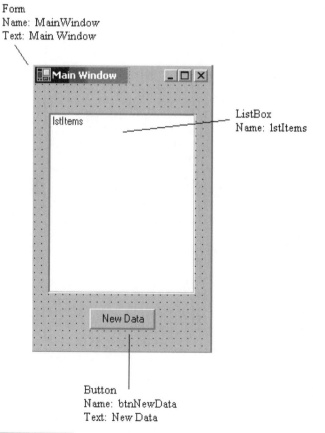

Form
Name: MainWindow
Text: Main Window

ListBox
Name: lstItems

Button
Name: btnNewData
Text: New Data

FIGURE 16–6 *The main window for ModelessDialogExample.*

We must add another form to our project to design the modeless dialog. Again, we can do this using the Project | Add Windows Form menu. Figure 16–7 illustrates the design of the modeless dialog.

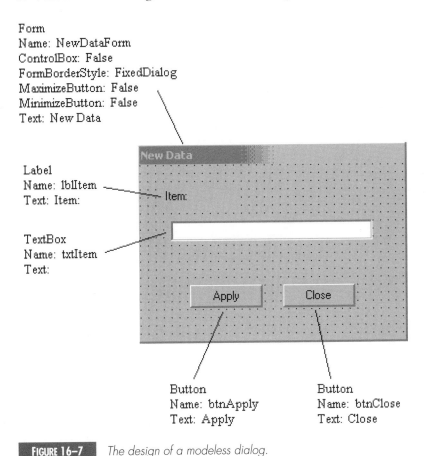

Form
Name: NewDataForm
ControlBox: False
FormBorderStyle: FixedDialog
MaximizeButton: False
MinimizeButton: False
Text: New Data

Label
Name: lblItem
Text: Item:

TextBox
Name: txtItem
Text:

Button
Name: btnApply
Text: Apply

Button
Name: btnClose
Text: Close

FIGURE 16–7   *The design of a modeless dialog.*

MANAGING THE RELATIONSHIP BETWEEN FORMS

A modeless dialog must know about the instance of the form that displayed it so the code in the **Click** event of the Apply button can copy data back to the parent form. We must add a variable to the modeless dialog to manage this relationship. For example, the following variable can be added:

```
Private m_myParent As MainWindow
```

A form that displays the dialog must pass a reference to itself when the modeless dialog is instantiated:

```
Dim infoForm As New ItemInfoForm(Me)
```

This means that the modeless dialog constructor must be modified to accept a reference to a **MainWindow** object and store it in the member variable:

```
Public Sub New(ByVal parent As MainWindow)
   MyBase.New()

   ' Remember the parent window
   m_myParent = parent

   ...

End Sub
```

PROGRAMMING THE APPLY AND CLOSE BUTTONS

Now that the modeless dialog can be displayed, we must provide code for the Apply and Close buttons. The Apply button must copy the data in its controls back to controls on the parent form. For example, the Apply button's **Click** event handler might resemble this:

```
Private Sub btnApply_Click(ByVal sender As Object, _
 ByVal e As System.EventArgs) Handles btnApply.Click

   If Trim(txtItem.Text) <> "" Then
      m_myParent.lstItems.Items.Add(txtItem.Text)
      txtItem.Text = ""
   End If

End Sub
```

The Close button's **Click** event handler should call the form's **Close** method to close the form.

```
Private Sub btnClose_Click(ByVal sender As System.Object, _
 ByVal e As System.EventArgs) Handles btnClose.Click

   Me.Close()

End Sub
```

ENABLING AND DISABLING THE APPLY BUTTON

Many modeless dialogs enable and disable the Apply button as a user interacts with them. Only when the Apply button is enabled would the user be able to move data back to the parent form.

To add this behavior to our dialog, we must make several changes:

- When the modeless dialog is first displayed, the Apply button must be disabled. The easiest way to do this is to set the **Enabled** property for **btnApply** to **False** in the Property window.

- When the user changes the data in **txtItem**, we must monitor it to determine whether the Apply button should be enabled or disabled. This can be done in the **Change** event of the text box. Based on our decision, we must programmatically enable or disable **btnApply**.
- We no longer need to check the contents of **txtItem** in the Apply button, because it won't be enabled if the text box is empty.

The final version of the event handler procedures for **ModelessDialogExample** is shown below:

```
Private Sub btnApply_Click(ByVal sender As Object, _
 ByVal e As System.EventArgs) Handles btnApply.Click

   m_myParent.lstItems.Items.Add(txtItem.Text)
   txtItem.Text = ""

End Sub

Private Sub btnClose_Click(ByVal sender As System.Object, _
 ByVal e As System.EventArgs) Handles btnClose.Click

   Me.Close()

End Sub

Private Sub txtItem_TextChanged(ByVal sender As _
 System.Object, ByVal e As System.EventArgs) _
 Handles txtItem.TextChanged

   If Trim(txtItem.Text) <> "" Then
      btnApply.Enabled = True
   Else
      btnApply.Enabled = False
   End If

End Sub
```

RUNNING CUSTOMDIALOGEXAMPLE

Figure 16–8 illustrates what the windows might look like when running the **ModelessDialogExample** program.

VB6 Statements for Loading and Unloading Forms Replaced

VB6 programmers should note that the entire process of creating and loading a form, as well as unloading a form, has changed. Form objects must be instantiated using the New keyword rather than the Load statement. A Show and ShowDialog method in the Form class replace the Show method and the vbModal parameter. A Close method has been added to allow a form to be closed; however, it is not unloaded until the form object itself is destroyed.

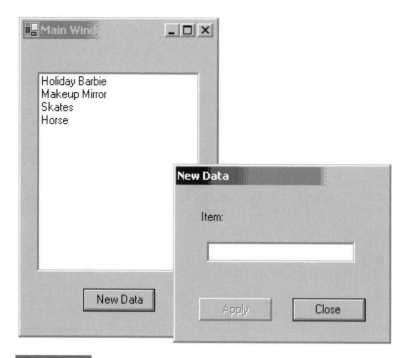

FIGURE 16–8   *Displaying the modeless dialog.*

Common Dialogs

VB.NET supports the Windows Common Dialogs. These dialogs are part of the Windows operating systems and are available for all applications to use. In VB.NET, they are provided as controls and include the following:

- OpenFileDialog
- SaveFileDialog
- ColorDialog
- FontDialog
- PrintDialog
- PrintPreviewDialog
- PageSetupDialog

These dialogs provide part of the consistency that you find in the look and feel of all Windows applications.

USING THE COMMON DIALOG CONTROLS

Code
Example

To use the any of the common dialog controls, you must place them on your form. However, they are invisible controls and are drawn in a separate area of the form by the Windows Form Designer. The Form Designer for the program **CommonDialogExample** is shown in Figure 16–9.

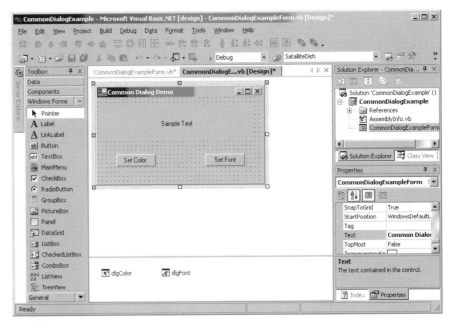

FIGURE 16–9 *The Common Color Dialog.*

Each of these controls has different properties that can be used to interact with the data they collect. For example, the **ColorDialog** has a **Color** property to access the color the user selected and the **FontDialog** has a **Font** property to access the font the user selected. Table 16–1 summarizes some of these properties and methods.

TABLE 16–1 *Properties and Methods of the Common Dialogs*

Dialog	Selected Properties	Methods
OpenFileDialog	AddExtension, CheckFileExists, CheckPathExists, DefaultExt, FileName, FileNames, Filter, InitialDirectory, ReadOnlyChecked, ShowReadOnly	ShowDialog
SaveFileDialog	AddExtension, CheckFileExists, CheckPathExists, DefaultExt, FileName, FileNames, Filter, InitialDirectory	OpenFile, ShowDialog
ColorDialog	AnyColor, Color, CustomColors, SolidColorOnly	ShowDialog
FontDialog	Color, Font, MaxSize, MinSize, ShowApply, ShowColor, ShowEffects	ShowDialog
PrintDialog	AllowPrintToFile, AllowSelection, AllowSomePages, PrintToFile, PrinterSettings, ShowNetwork	ShowDialog

Dialog	Selected Properties	Methods
TABLE 16-1	*Properties and Methods of the Common Dialogs (continued)*	
PrintPreviewDialog		ShowDialog
PageSetupDialog	Bounds, Color, Landscape, Margins, PaperSize, PaperSource, PrinterResolution	ShowDialog

The code that would allow the buttons on the form shown in Figure 16–9 to change the color and font of the label is shown here:

```
Private Sub btnColor_Click(ByVal sender As System.Object, _
  ByVal e As System.EventArgs) Handles btnColor.Click

    Dim answer As DialogResult
    answer = dlgColor.ShowDialog()
    If answer = DialogResult.OK Then
        lblText.BackColor = dlgColor.Color
    End If

End Sub

Private Sub btnFont_Click(ByVal sender As System.Object, _
  ByVal e As System.EventArgs) Handles btnFont.Click

    Dim answer As System.Windows.Forms.DialogResult
    answer = dlgFont.ShowDialog
    If answer = DialogResult.OK Then
        lblText.Font = dlgFont.Font
    End If

End Sub
```

Menus

Menus are one of the primary ways that users interact with some applications. Each form can display its own menu, although it is more common to find a menu only on the main window. Each form can also display a context menu, if the programmer so chooses. A context menu is one that is displayed when the user right-clicks with the mouse to display a popup menu.

MainMenu Control

The **MainMenu** control can be used to design, display, and manage a menu that is attached to the top of the client area of the window. We demonstrate the use of menus, toolbars, and status bars by building a simple calculator program, named **Calculator**. In this example, we have the following menu structure:

```
File          Calculation          Help
Exit          Add                  About Calculator
              Subtract
              Multiply
              Divide
```

The underscore under a letter of the menu caption identifies it as a shortcut. In Windows, you can press the ALT key and a letter to produce the menu containing that shortcut, without using the mouse. After the menu is displayed, an item can be selected using only its shortcut key. For example, the key sequence ALT+C+M generates the same event as if you select the Multiply menu using the mouse.

Menu items may also have an accelerator key attached to them. For example, F4 might be the equivalent of Add, or CTL+E might be the equivalent of Exit. Whereas a shortcut must use a letter from the caption as the shortcut key, an accelerator is free to use a combination of CTL, ALT, SHIFT, and keys from the keyboard.

Before we begin using the menu, we will design the form as shown in Figure 16–10.

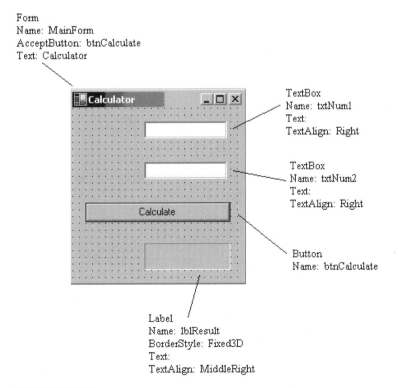

Form
Name: MainForm
AcceptButton: btnCalculate
Text: Calculator

TextBox
Name: txtNum1
Text:
TextAlign: Right

TextBox
Name: txtNum2
Text:
TextAlign: Right

Button
Name: btnCalculate

Label
Name: lblResult
BorderStyle: Fixed3D
Text:
TextAlign: MiddleRight

FIGURE 16–10   *The main window of the calculator.*

USING THE MAINMENU CONTROL

The **MainMenu** control is used to design menus. As you can see in Figure 16–11, we have added a **MainMenu** control to the form and named it **mnuMain**. When it is drawn on the form, an icon appears in a separate window where invisible controls are placed. It has attached a menu to the form that we can now modify.

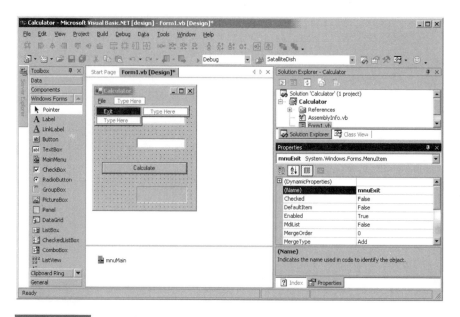

FIGURE 16–11   *Using the MainMenu control.*

Each item on the menu has a set of properties associated with it that can be manipulated using the Properties window. The properties include the following:

- **Name** represents that name by which we can refer to that menu item.
- **Text** represents the caption of that menu item. You can place an ampersand (&) in the caption before the letter that you want to indicate is the shortcut key. For example, "E&xit" would underline the letter *x* on the menu and associate it as the shortcut key.
- **Checked** indicates whether a check mark is next to menu caption.
- **RadioChecked** indicates whether a round check mark is next to the menu caption.
- **Enabled** indicates whether the menu item can be clicked.
- **Visible** indicates whether the menu item is visible.
- **Shortcut** indicates the accelerator key that should be assigned to the menu item.

- **ShortcutVisible** indicates whether the accelerator identity is displayed next to the menu caption.

Table 16–2 shows the property assignments made to the menu shown at the beginning of this section for the calculator program:

TABLE 16–2	*Property Assignments for the Calculator Program*		
Text	**Name**	**Checked**	**Shortcut**
&File	MnuFile		
&Exit	MnuExit		Ctrl+D
&Calculation	MnuCalculation		
&Add	MnuAdd	True	
&Subtract	MnuSubtract		
&Multiply	MnuMultiply		
&Divide	MnuDivide		
&Help	MnuHelp		
&About Calculator	MnuAbout		

RESPONDING TO MENU EVENTS

Each menu item has a **Click** event associated with it. It must be handled in order to provide a response to the user's selection of that menu item. For example, the **Click** event handlers for the Exit and About menus are shown below:

```
Private Sub mnuExit_Click(ByVal sender As System.Object, _
 ByVal e As System.EventArgs) Handles mnuExit.Click

    Me.Close()

End Sub

Private Sub mnuAbout_Click(ByVal sender As System.Object, _
 ByVal e As System.EventArgs) Handles mnuAbout.Click

    MessageBox.Show("Calculator v1.0", "About", _
        MessageBoxButtons.OK, MessageBoxIcon.Information)

End Sub
```

In our calculator program, the user can perform basic math operations on two numbers by clicking the Calculate button. The user uses the menu to set the type of math operation that is performed the next time the button is clicked.

In the event handlers for each of the four items on the Calculation menu (Add, Subtract, Multiply, and Divide), we place a check mark next to the item that was selected and remove any other check marks from other Calculation menu items.

We have written the subroutine **SetChecks** to assist us. It unchecks all menus and then accepts a **MenuItem** parameter that represents the selected menu item. Using a **MenuItem**, we can access menu item properties such as **Text**, **Checked**, **Enabled**, and **Visible** to manipulate the appearance of the menu item.

```
Private Sub SetChecks(ByVal selectedMenu As MenuItem)
   ' Uncheck all menus
   mnuAdd.Checked = False
   mnuSubtract.Checked = False
   mnuMultiply.Checked = False
   mnuDivide.Checked = False

   ' Check the new menu item
   selectedMenu.Checked = True
End Sub

' Event handlers for each menu Click event
Private Sub mnuAdd_Click(ByVal sender As System.Object, _
 ByVal e As System.EventArgs) Handles mnuAdd.Click

   SetChecks(mnuAdd)

End Sub

Private Sub mnuSubtract_Click(ByVal sender As _
 System.Object, ByVal e As System.EventArgs) _
 Handles mnuSubtract.Click

   SetChecks(mnuSubtract)

End Sub

Private Sub mnuMultiply_Click(ByVal sender As _
 System.Object, ByVal e As System.EventArgs) _
 Handles mnuMultiply.Click

   SetChecks(mnuMultiply)

End Sub

Private Sub mnuDivide_Click(ByVal sender As _
 System.Object, ByVal e As System.EventArgs) _
 Handles mnuDivide.Click

   SetChecks(mnuDivide)

End Sub
```

ContextMenu Control

The **ContextMenu** control can be used to display a floating popup menu that is displayed when the user right-clicks on a control or other area of the form. Typically, context menus provide shortcuts to commonly used items on the main menu. To utilize a context menu for a form, you must perform the following actions:

- Add the **ContextMenu** control to the form, and set its **Name** property.
- Set the **ContextMenu** property of the form to the **ContextMenu** control.
- Add menu items to the context menu, and associate them with an event handler.
- If the menu item's **Click** event cannot be associated with an existing handler, you must write the handler function.

We will add a context menu to our calculator program that has menu items for About and Exit. To do this, we must perform these actions:

- Add a **ContextMenu** control to the form, and set its **Name** property to **mnuContext**.
- Set the **ContextMenu** property of the form **MainWindow** to **mnuContext**.

We initialize our context menu when the form loads because the items in the menu are always the same, regardless of the data on the form or the user's actions. The code for this is shown below:

```
Private Sub MainWindow_Load(ByVal sender As Object, _
 ByVal e As System.EventArgs) Handles MyBase.Load

    mnuContext.MenuItems.Add("About...", _
      New EventHandler(AddressOf mnuAbout_Click))
    mnuContext.MenuItems.Add("Exit", _
      New EventHandler(AddressOf mnuExit_Click))

End Sub
```

Because the About and Exit menus already have event handlers associated with their entry in the main menu, we have assigned them as the handlers for the corresponding context menu items. Refer to Chapter 11 if you need to refresh your memory of event handling.

If you do not have existing handler functions that you can associate with the context menu's **Click** event, you must build a standard **Click** event handler and associate that as the handler procedure. In this version of the **Load** event handler, we associate the **ClickedOnContextMenu** procedure as the event handler for both menus.

```
Private Sub MainWindow_Load(ByVal sender As Object, _
  ByVal e As System.EventArgs) Handles MyBase.Load

  mnuContext.MenuItems.Add("About...", _
     New EventHandler(AddressOf ClickedOnContextMenu))
  mnuContext.MenuItems.Add("Exit", _
     New EventHandler(AddressOf ClickedOnContextMenu))

End Sub
```

A **Click** handler is passed a **System.Object** parameter and a **System.EventArgs** parameter. In this handler, we can convert the **sender** parameter to a **MenuItem** parameter using **CType** and extract the **Text** property of the menu item to determine which item from the context menu was selected.

```
Private Sub ClickedOnContextMenu(ByVal sender As _
  System.Object, ByVal e As System.EventArgs)

  Dim mnuSelected As MenuItem = CType(sender, MenuItem)

  If mnuSelected.Text = "About..." Then
     MessageBox.Show("Calculator v1.0", "About", _
       MessageBoxButtons.OK, MessageBoxIcon.Information)
  ElseIf mnuSelected.Text = "Exit" Then
     Me.Close()
  End If

End Sub
```

If we want to know when the context menu is being displayed so that we may set check marks or disable menu items, we must handle the content menu's **PopUp** event. Inside this handler, we can determine the state of the application and modify the menu's appearance as needed.

For example, in our calculator program, we code behavior so that the user may not use the context menu to exit the program if the Divide menu is checked. The **PopUp** event handler follows:

```
Private Sub mnuContext_Popup(ByVal sender As _
  System.Object, ByVal e As System.EventArgs) _
  Handles mnuContext.Popup

  If mnuDivide.Checked = True Then
     mnuContext.MenuItems(1).Enabled = False
  Else
     mnuContext.MenuItems(1).Enabled = True
  End If

End Sub
```

The **MenuItems** collection of a **ContextMenu** control gives us access to the individual **MenuItem** objects in the menu. Using a **MenuItem**, we can access menu properties such as **Text**, **Checked**, **Enabled**, and **Visible** to manipulate the appearance of the context menu.

Figure 16–12 illustrates the appearance of the context menu when it is displayed and the current mathematical operation is division.

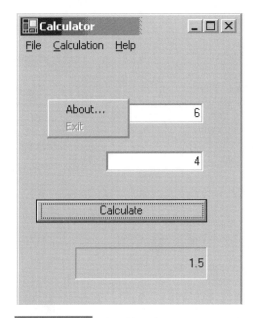

FIGURE 16–12   *Disabling the context menu.*

Status Bars

The **StatusBar** control can be used to display a status bar on a form. The status bar consists of a collection of panels that can be individually controlled. The status bar is primarily used to display information to the user.

Using the StatusBar Control

To add a status bar to a program, use the **StatusBar** control. The **StatusBar** control is a visible control that positions itself as an empty window aligned with the bottom of the form (see Figure 16–13).

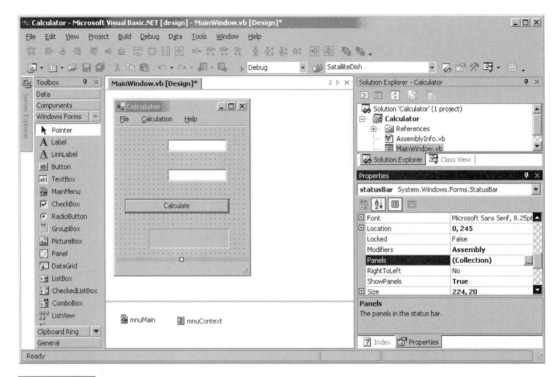

FIGURE 16-13   *Using the StatusBar control.*

Displaying Information in the Status Bar

The **StatusBar** control has a **Panels** property that can be accessed at run time. It represents a collection of individual **StatusBarPanel** objects. The **StatusBarPanel** class defines several properties that can be used to manipulate the panels, including the following:

- **Alignment** controls whether text in a panel is left, center, or right aligned.
- **BorderStyle** controls the type of border used for the panel.
- **Text** controls the contents of the panel.
- **ToolTipText** controls tool tip information that is displayed when the mouse hovers over the panel.
- **Width** controls the width of the panel.

To configure the individual panels on the status bar, you must modify the **Panels** collection. When you use the Properties window to modify the **Panels** collection, an editor appears (see Figure 16–14).

In our example, we made the following changes:

- We named our **StatusBar** control **statusBar**.

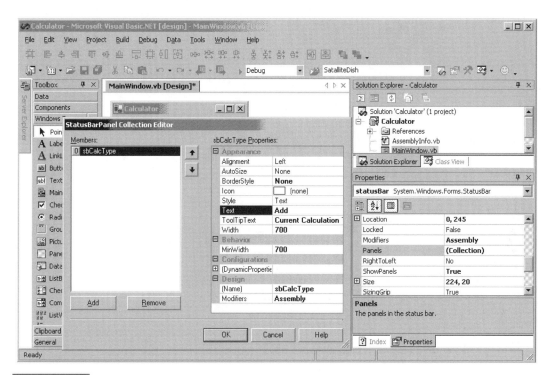

FIGURE 16-14   *The StatusBarPanel Collection Editor.*

- We added one panel to our status bar that has the name **sbCalcType**. It will display the words "Add," "Subtract," and so on, to correspond to the type of calculation that is being performed by the Calculate button.
- We set the **sbCalcType** panel's **ToolTipText** property to "Current Calculation Type."
- We set the **sbCalcType** panel's **Width** property to 700 twips. There are 1,440 twips per inch, so this is just less than 1/2 inch wide.
- We set the **sbCalcType** panel's **Text** property to "Add."
- We set the **statusBar's ShowPanels** property to **True**.

To programmatically place the text "Subtract" in panel 0, you can write the following code:

```
statBar.Panels(0).Text = "Subtract"
```

Figure 16-15 shows us what the status bar on our form looks like when we execute our program.

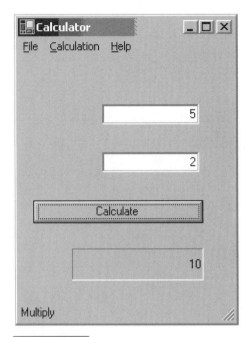

FIGURE 16–15   *Displaying information in the calculator's status bar.*

Toolbars

The **ToolBar** control is used on forms to display a row of buttons that invoke commands. Clicking one of these buttons is similar to clicking a menu item. VB.NET toolbars generally use an **ImageList** control to maintain the images displayed by the toolbar. Each button on the toolbar is associated with an image from the image list. The **ToolBar** class contains several useful methods, including these:

- **Appearance** indicates the appearance (raised or flat) of the toolbar buttons.
- **Autosize** indicates whether the toolbar automatically adjusts its size based upon the size of the buttons.
- **Buttons** manages a collection of **ToolBarButton** objects representing the buttons on the toolbar.
- **ButtonSize** indicates the size of the buttons on the toolbar.
- **ImageList** indicates the **ImageList** object with which the toolbar is associated.
- **Wrapable** indicates whether the toolbar buttons can wrap to another line if the toolbar becomes too small.

In addition, the **ToolBarButton** class contains properties to allow access to individual buttons on the toolbar, including the following:

- **ImageIndex** indicates the image number from the **ImageList** control of the image associated with this button.
- **Enabled** indicates whether the button is enabled.
- **Pushed** indicates whether the button is pushed.
- **Visible** indicates whether the button is visible.
- **Text** indicates the text displayed on a button.
- **ToolTipText** indicates the tool tip text displayed for the button.
- **Style** indicates the style of the button and can include **PushButton**, **Separator**, **ToggleButton**, and **DropDownButton**.

The **ToolBar** class also has methods to add and remove buttons at run time.

Figure 16–16 illustrates the calculator program after the **ImageList** control and the **ToolBar** control were added to the form. The **ImageList** is an invisible control; however, the toolbar is visible and appears as an empty window docked to the top of the parent window.

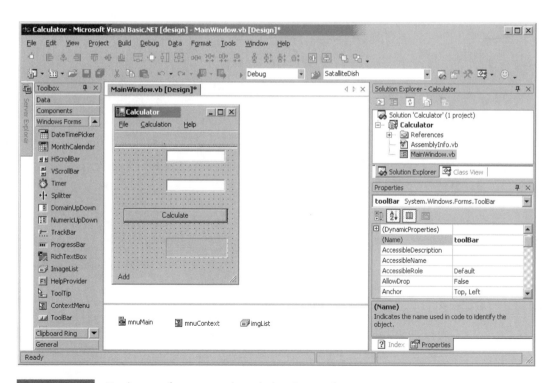

FIGURE 16–16   *Displaying information in the calculator's status bar.*

As you can see from the figure, we used the name **imgList** for the **ImageList** control and **toolBar** for the **ToolBar** control.

Using the ImageList Control

The **Images** collection of the **ImageList** control is used to manage the images in the list. When you click on the **Images** property in the Properties window, the Image Collection Editor is displayed. You can press the Add button to load various images. As you can see in Figure 16–17, we used the image list to load mathematical icons into the list from the **Microsoft Visual Studio.NET\Common7 \Graphics** directory.

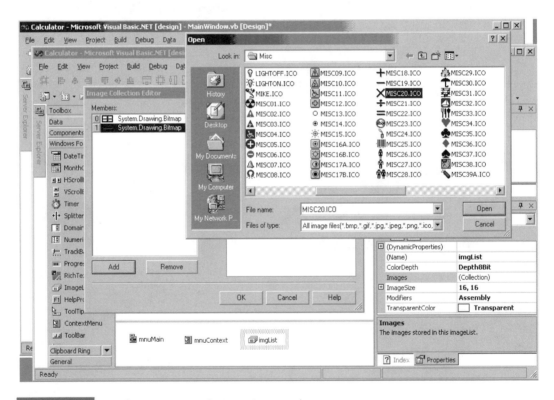

FIGURE 16–17   *Loading images into the ImageList control.*

Using the Toolbar Control

To configure the toolbar control for our calculator program, we must set its **ImageList** property to **imgList**. The toolbar that we want to design will have icons for add (+), subtract (-), multiply (*), and divide (/). These were loaded into the **ImageList** in positions 0, 1, 2, and 3, respectively.

We must then modify the **Buttons** collection of the toolbar. If we select the toolbar's **Buttons** property from the Properties window, we will see the editor shown in Figure 16–18. It will help us create buttons, associate them with images in the image list, and configure their properties as needed.

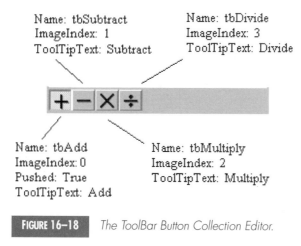

Name: tbSubtract
ImageIndex: 1
ToolTipText: Subtract

Name: tbDivide
ImageIndex: 3
ToolTipText: Divide

Name: tbAdd
ImageIndex: 0
Pushed: True
ToolTipText: Add

Name: tbMultiply
ImageIndex: 2
ToolTipText: Multiply

FIGURE 16–18   *The ToolBar Button Collection Editor.*

You must press the Add button in the ToolBar Button Collections Editor for each of the four buttons you want to add. Their properties should be set to the values shown in Figure 16–19.

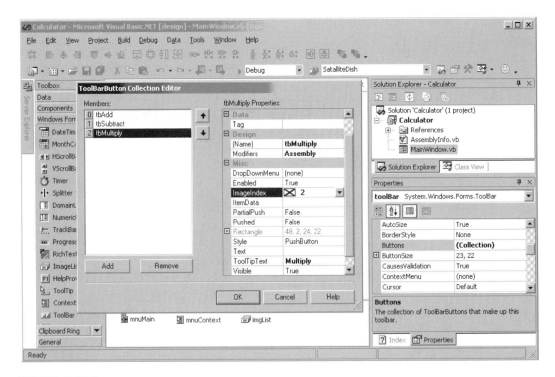

FIGURE 16–19   *The toolbar used by the calculator.*

Responding to Toolbar Events

The **ToolBar** control generates a **ButtonClick** event any time any of the buttons on the toolbar is selected. The event handler for this event is passed a **ToolBarButtonClickEventArgs** parameter that contains information about which button was selected. For example:

```
Private Sub toolBar_ButtonClick(ByVal sender As _
  System.Object, ByVal e As ToolBarButtonClickEventArgs) _
  Handles toolBar.ButtonClick

    Select Case e.Button.ImageIndex
    Case 0
      ... ' process button with image in ImageList(0)
    Case 1
      ... ' process button with image in ImageList(1)
    Case 2
      ... ' process button with image in ImageList(2)
    Case 3
      ... ' process button with image in ImageList(3)
    End Select
End Sub
```

There is a more readable alternative to using the **ImageIndex** property in the handler procedure shown above. Each control in Windows Forms has a **Tag** property. This property isn't used by .NET and provides a convenient placeholder for data. By placing a descriptive string in the Tag property of each button, you can write code similar to that shown below. (In the example, we assume the text in each Tag property is ...) For example:

```
Private Sub toolBar_ButtonClick(ByVal sender As _
  System.Object, ByVal e As ToolBarButtonClickEventArgs) _
  Handles toolBar.ButtonClick

    Select Case e.Button.Tag
    Case "Add"
        ... ' process button with tag "Add"
    Case "Subtract"
        ... ' process button with tag "Subtract"
    Case "Multiply"
        ... ' process button with tag "Multiply"
    Case "Divide"
        ... ' process button with tag "Divide"
    End Select
End Sub
```

Example: Calculator (completed)

Let's reexamine the calculator application that we have developed in this chapter:

- There is an Exit menu that closes the application.
- There is an About menu that displays basic information about our application.
- There is a context menu that displays the About and Exit items; it disables Exit if division is the current mathematical operation.
- There is a Calculation menu that has Add, Subtract, Multiply, and Divide items that are used to keep track of the "current" type of mathematical operation performed by the Calculate button.
- There is a toolbar that provides the same features as the Calculation menu.
- The "current" mathematical operation is indicated in three ways: (1) It is displayed in the status bar, (2) the corresponding toolbar item is pressed, and (3) the corresponding menu item is checked.
- There is a Calculate button that takes the values from the first two text boxes, performs a mathematical operation on them, and then places the result in a label.

To prevent writing the same code for both menu **Click** events and the toolbar **Click** event, we are going to redesign our program.

Handling the Exit and About Menu Clicks

Our event handlers for the Exit and About menus are straightforward:

```
Private Sub mnuExit_Click(ByVal sender As System.Object, _
  ByVal e As System.EventArgs) Handles mnuExit.Click

    Me.Close()

End Sub

Private Sub mnuAbout_Click(ByVal sender As System.Object, _
  ByVal e As System.EventArgs) Handles mnuAbout.Click

    MessageBox.Show("Calculator v1.0", "About", _
        MessageBoxButtons.OK, MessageBoxIcon.Information)

End Sub
```

Populating the Context Menu

Our handler for the form **Load** event adds the Exit and About items to our context menu. It also assigns the existing menu **Click** event handlers as the handlers for the context menu **Click** events.

```
Private Sub MainWindow_Load(ByVal sender As Object, _
  ByVal e As System.EventArgs) Handles MyBase.Load

    mnuContext.MenuItems.Add("About...", _
        New EventHandler(AddressOf mnuAbout_Click))
    mnuContext.MenuItems.Add("Exit", _
        New EventHandler(AddressOf mnuExit_Click))

End Sub
```

Manipulating the Menu, Toolbar, and StatusBar

Now we will provide a private helper procedure to take care of the visual appearance of all menus, toolbar buttons, and the status bar whenever the current mathematical operation changes. We will pass to this procedure references to the menu item that should be checked and the toolbar button that should be pushed. It will perform the following actions:

- Uncheck all menu items.
- Unpush all toolbar buttons.

- Check the proper menu item.
- Push the proper toolbar button.
- Write a descriptive string to the status bar.

```
Private Sub SetGUIChecks(ByVal mnu As MenuItem, _
 ByVal btn As ToolBarButton)

    ' Uncheck all menus
    mnuAdd.Checked = False
    mnuSubtract.Checked = False
    mnuMultiply.Checked = False
    mnuDivide.Checked = False

    ' Unselect all buttons
    Dim i As Integer
    For i = 0 To 3
        toolBar.Buttons(i).Pushed = False
    Next

    ' Update menu, toolbar, and statusbar
    mnu.Checked = True
    btn.Pushed = True

    ' Remove the & (hotkey indicator) from the caption
    ' (use Add instead of &Add) before placing it in the
    ' status bar panel
    statusBar.Panels(0).Text = Replace(mnu.Text, "&", "")

End Sub
```

Handle Menu and Toolbar Click Events

We must handle the menu and toolbar **Click** events, but we will simply call **SetGUIChecks** to achieve the desired behavior for our calculator program.

```
' MENU EVENT HANDLERS
Private Sub mnuAdd_Click(ByVal sender As System.Object, _
 ByVal e As System.EventArgs) Handles mnuAdd.Click

    SetGUIChecks(mnuAdd, toolBar.Buttons(0))

End Sub

Private Sub mnuSubtract_Click(ByVal sender As _
 System.Object, ByVal e As System.EventArgs) _
 Handles mnuSubtract.Click

    SetGUIChecks(mnuSubtract, toolBar.Buttons(1))

End Sub
```

```
Private Sub mnuMultiply_Click(ByVal sender As _
  System.Object, ByVal e As System.EventArgs) _
  Handles mnuMultiply.Click

    SetGUIChecks(mnuMultiply, toolBar.Buttons(2))

End Sub

Private Sub mnuDivide_Click(ByVal sender As _
  System.Object, ByVal e As System.EventArgs) _
  Handles mnuDivide.Click

    SetGUIChecks(mnuDivide, toolBar.Buttons(3))
End Sub

' TOOLBAR EVENT HANDLER
Private Sub toolBar_ButtonClick(ByVal sender As _
  System.Object, ByVal e As _
  System.Windows.Forms.ToolBarButtonClickEventArgs) _
  Handles toolBar.ButtonClick

    Select Case e.Button.Tag
       Case "Add"
          SetGUIChecks(mnuAdd, _
             toolBar.Buttons(e.Button.ImageIndex))
       Case "Subtract"
          SetGUIChecks(mnuSubtract, _
             toolBar.Buttons(e.Button.ImageIndex))
       Case "Multiply"
          SetGUIChecks(mnuMultiply, _
             toolBar.Buttons(e.Button.ImageIndex))
       Case "Divide"
          SetGUIChecks(mnuDivide, _
             toolBar.Buttons(e.Button.ImageIndex))
    End Select
End Sub
```

Handle Calculate Button Click Event

The actual mathematical behavior of our calculator program is programmed in the **Click** event of the Calculate button. Here we must determine which mathematical operation is current and then "do the math." In our version, we determine which operation is current by determining which menu item is checked.

```
Private Sub btnCalculate_Click(ByVal sender As _
  System.Object, ByVal e As System.EventArgs) _
  Handles btnCalculate.Click
```

```
Dim n1 As Double = Val(txtNum1.Text)
Dim n2 As Double = Val(txtNum2.Text)
If mnuAdd.Checked = True Then
    lblResult.Text = n1 + n2
ElseIf mnuSubtract.Checked = True Then
    lblResult.Text = n1 - n2
ElseIf mnuMultiply.Checked = True Then
    lblResult.Text = n1 * n2
Else
    lblResult.Text = n1 / n2
End If

End Sub
```

Disabling Exit on the Context Menu

This program has a requirement that the Exit item on the context menu must be disabled if the current mathematical operation is division. To achieve this, we must write code in the **PopUp** event of the context menu:

```
Private Sub mnuContext_Popup(ByVal sender As _
 System.Object, ByVal e As System.EventArgs) _
 Handles mnuContext.Popup

   If mnuDivide.Checked = True Then
      mnuContext.MenuItems(1).Enabled = False
   Else
      mnuContext.MenuItems(1).Enabled = True
   End If

End Sub
```

It Runs!

Our program is fully functional according to the requirements we specified. Figure 16–20 illustrates its appearance.

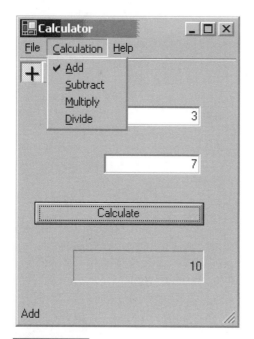

FIGURE 16–20   *The completed calculator project.*

Summary

In this chapter, we examined how VB.NET can manipulate different types of dialogs. The .NET **MessageBox** class is the simplest way to display dialog informational messages to the user and to ask simple yes/no type questions. Custom dialogs may be created by adding a new form to a project and designing the dialog using the Windows Form Designer. They may be displayed in both a modal manner, using **ShowDialog**, and in a modeless manner, using **Show**. The **DialogResult** type is returned by most modal dialogs and is a simple technique for determining the button that was pressed on a dialog to make it close. In this chapter, we also examined how to build a basic user interface consisting of a menu, a status bar, and a toolbar. In Chapter 17, we will examine other types of Windows controls and how they can be used to enhance our GUI appearance.

Windows Forms, Part III

*V*isual Basic.NET supports a wide variety of controls that can be
used on a Windows Forms application. By being familiar with the
appearance, purpose, and capabilities of the various controls,
your desktop applications can be written to be visually appealing
and easy to use. This chapter continues our examination of the
controls. We explore controls available for Date/Time data. We follow with an examination of some of the range controls that are
available, such as the new NumericUpDown control. Controls that
manage lists, such as the DomainUpDown and TreeView controls,
are then presented. The new ErrorProvider control is also examined to see how it can be used to display data validation error
messages. We conclude with a brief discussion of miscellaneous
features of .NET forms.

Calendar Controls

VB.NET supports two types of calendars: the **MonthCalendar** and the
DateTimePicker. Each allows the user to select a date or time from a graphical control. They are useful because they reduce the chance of data entry
errors (such as entering February 31). This section examines the similarities of
and differences between the two controls.

MonthCalendar

The **MonthCalendar** control allows a user to select a date, or range of dates, from a graphical calendar. Interesting properties of the **MonthCalendar** that are not inherited from the **Control** class include the following:

- **FirstDayOfWeek** indicates the first day of the week that is displayed.
- **ShowToday** indicates whether the current day is shown at the bottom of the calendar.
- **ShowTodayCircle** indicates whether the current day is circled.
- **ShowWeekNumbers** indicates whether the week number is shown next to each week.
- **MinDate** and **MaxDate** indicate the minimum and maximum allowable dates.
- **MaxSelectionCount** indicates the maximum number of days that can be selected in the calendar.
- **AnnuallyBoldedDates** is an array of **Date** objects that represents the dates that are bolded every year.
- **MonthlyBoldedDates** is an array of **Date** objects that represents the dates that are bolded every month.
- **BoldedDates** is an array of **Date** objects that represents specific dates that are bolded.
- **CalendarDimensions** indicates the number of rows and columns of months displayed.

Methods of the **MonthCalendar** control include the following:

- **AddAnnuallyBoldedDate** and **RemoveAnnuallyBoldedDate** add and remove dates that are bolded every year.
- **AddMonthlyBoldedDate** and **RemoveMonthlyBoldedDate** add and remove dates that are bolded every month.
- **AddBoldedDate** and **RemoveBoldedDate** add and remove dates that are bolded.
- **UpdateBoldedDates** repaints the control after any change to bolded dates.
- **SetDate** sets a date as the selected date.

Events generated by the **MonthCalendar** control include the following:

- **DateChanged** occurs when the date changes.
- **DateSelected** occurs when a date is selected.

EXAMPLE: USING THE MONTHCALENDAR

The following program, found in **BirthdayGreetings**, displays a birthday greeting to Mary when March 6 is clicked. It also bolds January 9 every year. See Figure 17–1.

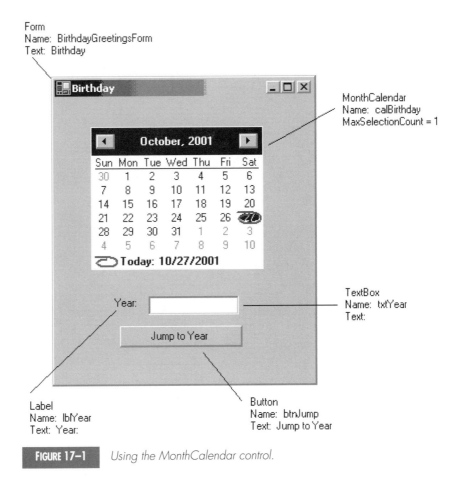

Form
Name: BirthdayGreetingsForm
Text: Birthday

MonthCalendar
Name: calBirthday
MaxSelectionCount = 1

TextBox
Name: txtYear
Text:

Label
Name: lblYear
Text: Year:

Button
Name: btnJump
Text: Jump to Year

FIGURE 17-1   *Using the MonthCalendar control.*

```
Private Sub BirthdayGreetings_Load(ByVal sender As _
  System.Object, ByVal e As System.EventArgs) _
  Handles MyBase.Load

    calBirthday.AddAnnuallyBoldedDate(#1/9/1988#)
      ' You must enter a valid date, which is why a
      ' year is specified in this example

End Sub

Private Sub btnJump_Click(ByVal sender As Object, _
  ByVal e As System.EventArgs) Handles btnJump.Click

    calBirthday.SetDate(DateSerial(txtYear.Text, 1, 1))
    txtYear.Text = ""
```

```
End Sub

Private Sub calBirthday_DateSelected( _
 ByVal sender As Object, _
 ByVal e As System.Windows.Forms.DateRangeEventArgs) _
 Handles calBirthday.DateSelected

   If calBirthday.SelectionStart.Month = 3 And _
        calBirthday.SelectionStart.Day = 6 Then

     MessageBox.Show("Happy Birthday, Mary", "Birthday", _
         MessageBoxButtons.OK,
MessageBoxIcon.Exclamation)
     End If

End Sub
```

DateTimePicker

The **DateTimePicker** control allows the user to select a date and/or time from a graphical control. The format of the date/time displayed can be controlled. Interesting properties of the **DateTimePicker** that are not inherited from the **Control** class include the following:

- **CalendarFont** indicates the font used to show text in the control.
- **MinDate** and **MaxDate** indicate the minimum and maximum allowable dates.
- **Format** indicates the format of date/time values.
- **DropDownAlign** indicates the alignment of the dropdown.
- **ShowUpDown** indicates whether an up control or a down control is used to move through dates.
- **Value** indicates the date/time assigned to the control.

Events generated by the **DateTimePicker** control include the following:

- **DropDown** occurs when the dropdown calendar is displayed.
- **CloseUp** occurs when the dropdown calendar is closed.
- **ValueChanged** occurs when the **Value** property changes.

EXAMPLE: USING THE DATETIMEPICKER

The following program, found in **ImportantDates**, allows you to track a set of appointments. The date and time of the appointment are selected from two **DateTimePicker** controls. See Figure 17–2.

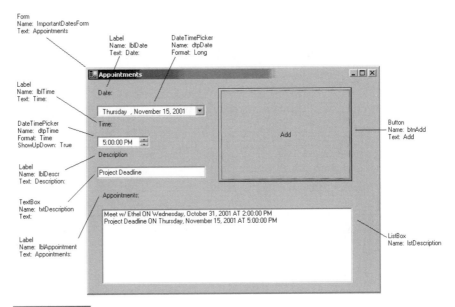

Form
Name: ImportantDatesForm
Text: Appointments

Label
Name: lblDate
Text: Date:

DateTimePicker
Name: dtpDate
Format: Long

Label
Name: lblTime
Text: Time:

DateTimePicker
Name: dtpTime
Format: Time
ShowUpDown: True

Label
Name: lblDescr
Text: Description:

TextBox
Name: txtDescription
Text:

Label
Name: lblAppointment
Text: Appointments:

Button
Name: btnAdd
Text: Add

ListBox
Name: lstDescription

FIGURE 17–2 *Using the DateTimePicker control.*

```
Private Sub ImportantDatesForm_Load(ByVal sender As _
  System.Object, ByVal e As System.EventArgs) _
  Handles MyBase.Load

    ' Only show dates in the future
    dtpDate.MinDate = Now

End Sub

Private Sub btnAdd_Click(ByVal sender As System.Object, _
  ByVal e As System.EventArgs) Handles btnAdd.Click

    Dim d As Date = dtpDate.Value
    Dim t As Date = dtpTime.Value
    Dim s As String = txtDescription.Text
    s &= " ON " & FormatDateTime(d, DateFormat.LongDate)
    s &= " AT " & Format(t, "Medium Time")

    lstAppointments.Items.Add(s)

End Sub
```

Timer Control

The **Timer** control is used to trigger an event at a user-specified interval. Interesting properties of the **Timer** control include the following:

- **Enabled** indicates whether the timer is currently generating events.
- **Interval** indicates the interval between events in milliseconds.

When the **Timer** is enabled, a **Tick** event is triggered in n milliseconds, where n is the value of the **Interval** property.

Example: Using the Timer

The following program, found in **Clock**, displays the current time. It keeps itself current by checking the system time every second. See Figure 17–3.

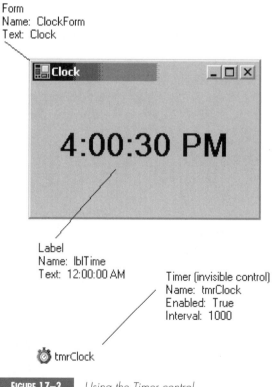

Form
Name: ClockForm
Text: Clock

Label
Name: lblTime
Text: 12:00:00 AM

Timer (invisible control)
Name: tmrClock
Enabled: True
Interval: 1000

FIGURE 17–3   *Using the Timer control.*

```
' Common routine to update the time in the label
Private Sub SetTime()
   Dim t As Date
   t = Now
   lblTime.Text = Format(t, "Medium Time")
End Sub

Private Sub ClockForm_Load(ByVal sender As Object, _
 ByVal e As System.EventArgs) Handles MyBase.Load

   ' start form with correct time
   SetTime()

End Sub

Private Sub tmrClock_Tick(ByVal sender As System.Object, _
 ByVal e As System.EventArgs) Handles tmrClock.Tick

   ' update time every second (interval = 1000)
   SetTime()

End Sub
```

Range Controls

There are several types of range controls in VB.NET. These controls allow the user to pick some value (or display some value) within a specified range. The numeric range controls include the **ProgressBar**, **ScrollBar**, **TrackBar**, and **NumericUpDown** controls. All of the numeric controls have certain properties in common, including the following:

- **Minimum** represents the minimum value in the range of numbers.
- **Maximum** represents the maximum value in the range of numbers.
- **Value** represents the control's current value (between minimum and maximum).

This section examines each of the range controls and the properties, methods, and events that make them unique.

ProgressBar

The **ProgressBar** is a control that allows you to display the progress of an operation. It is an output-only control—that is, the user does not directly interact with it. It displays a value by filling in a specified percentage of its client area. Interesting properties of the **ProgressBar** control that are not inherited from the **Control** class include **Minimum**, **Maximum**, and **Value**, as well as this additional property:

- **Step** indicates the amount of a displayable "step" in the control's value.

Methods of the **ProgressBar** control include the following:

- **PerformStep** advances the current value by the amount of the Step property and redraws the control.

EXAMPLE: USING THE PROGRESSBAR

Code
Example

The following program, found in **SimpleProgress\Version 1**, displays a progress bar as it moves toward completion. It demonstrates how a programmer can use the control to indicate progress toward the completion of some task. See Figure 17–4.

In this simple example, we have a **For** loop that executes 32,000 times. It writes the square root of 1 to 32,000 to a file. The progress bar illustrates completion in steps of 10 percent. In other words, there will not be any progress display until the loop has iterated 3,200 times (10 percent of 32,000). So another bar in the progress control appears after every 3,200 iterations.

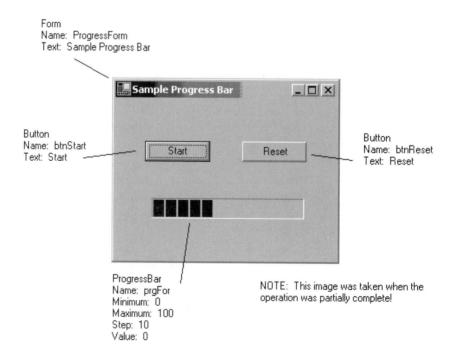

FIGURE 17–4   *Using the ProgressBar control.*

```
Private Sub btnStart_Click(ByVal sender As System.Object, _
 ByVal e As System.EventArgs) Handles btnStart.Click

    ' Write square roots to a file (file i/o is slow!)
    Dim fileNum As Integer
    fileNum = FreeFile()
    FileOpen(fileNum, "sqrt.txt", OpenMode.Output)

    Dim index As Integer
    Dim s As Single
    Dim outLine As String

    For index = 1 To 32000
        s = Math.Sqrt(index)
        outLine = index.ToString() & " - Sqrt = " _
                & s.ToString()
        Print(fileNum, outLine)

        ' update the progress bar  (% completion)
        prgFor.Value = (index / 32000) * 100
    Next

    FileClose(fileNum)

End Sub

Private Sub btnReset_Click(ByVal sender As Object, _
 ByVal e As System.EventArgs) Handles btnReset.Click

    prgFor.Value = 0

End Sub
```

ScrollBar

The **ScrollBar** base class represents a scrollable control that is used to input numeric data within a range. The **HScrollBar** control is displayed horizontally, and the **VScrollBar** control is displayed vertically. Useful properties of this control include **Minimum**, **Maximum**, and **Value** that were previously mentioned, as well as these additional properties:

- **LargeChange** is the increment or decrement to the value when the user clicks to either side of the scroll bar.
- **SmallChange** is the increment or decrement to the value when the user moves the scroll box a small distance.

Events generated by the **ScrollBar** control include the following:

- **Scroll** indicates that the scroll bar was moved via mouse or keyboard activity.

● **ValueChanged** indicates whether the value was changed either through mouse or keyboard activity, or by programmatically changing the **Value** property.

EXAMPLE: USING THE SCROLLBAR

The following program, found in **ColorChanges\Version 1**, automatically displays various shades of red. It begins by setting the intensity of red to 0 (black) and increases it by 5 until it ultimately reaches 255 (full red). A scroll bar adjusts the speed of the color change. Slow indicates that the color changes every 3 seconds; fast indicates the color changes every .25 seconds. The color is displayed using a label's **BackColor** property. The .NET Color structure is used to generate an appropriate color constant from an RGB value. See Figure 17–5.

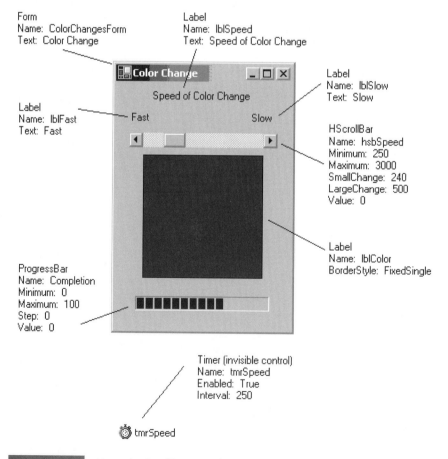

FIGURE 17–5 *Using the ScrollBar control.*

```
Private Sub tmrSpeed_Tick(ByVal sender As System.Object, _
  ByVal e As System.EventArgs) Handles tmrSpeed.Tick

    Static lastRed As Integer
    lblColor.BackColor = Color.FromArgb(lastRed, 0, 0)

    prgCompletion.Value = lastRed / 255 * 100

    lastRed = lastRed + 5
    If lastRed > 255 Then
       lastRed = 255
    End If

End Sub

Private Sub hsbSpeed_ValueChanged(ByVal sender As Object, _
  ByVal e As System.EventArgs) Handles hsbSpeed.ValueChanged

    tmrSpeed.Interval = hsbSpeed.Value

End Sub
```

The **Color** class referenced in the **Tick** event above is a .NET class that assists in defining color values. The shared method **FromArbg** builds a color value "from an RGB value." RGB colors are specified by identifying a red, green, and blue intensity within the range 0 to 255. For example:

- RGB of 0,0,0 is black
- RGB of 255,0,0 is red
- RGB of 0,255,0 is green
- RGB of 0,0,255 is blue
- RGB of 255,255,255 is white
- RGB of 255,255,0 is yellow

TrackBar

The **TrackBar** control is similar to the **ScrollBar** control. It is a scrollable control used to input numeric data within a range. It may be displayed vertically or horizontally. Useful properties of this control include **Minimum**, **Maximum**, and **Value** that were previously mentioned, as well as these additional properties:

- **LargeChange** is the increment or decrement to the value when the user clicks to either side of the slider.
- **SmallChange** is the increment or decrement to the value when the user moves the scroll box a small distance.
- **Orientation** indicates whether the control is displayed horizontally or vertically.

- **TickFrequency** indicates the frequency of ticks.
- **TickStyle** indicates whether tick marks are displayed on the bottom or top of the control.

Events generated by the **TrackBar** control include the following:

- **Scroll** indicates whether the track bar was moved via mouse or keyboard activity.
- **ValueChanged** indicates whether the value was changed either through mouse or keyboard activity, or by programmatically changing the **Value** property.

EXAMPLE: USING THE TRACKBAR

The following program, found in **ColorChanges\Version 2**, is similar to the example used for the **ScrollBar** control. In this version, a **TrackBar** control replaces the **ScrollBar** control. See Figure 17–6.

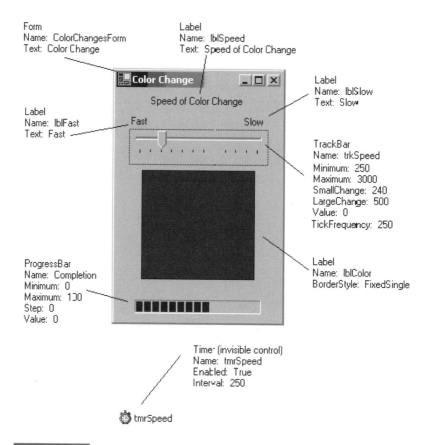

FIGURE 17–6 *Using the TrackBar control.*

```
Private Sub tmrSpeed_Tick(ByVal sender As System.Object, _
 ByVal e As System.EventArgs) Handles tmrSpeed.Tick

    Static lastRed As Integer
    lblColor.BackColor = Color.FromArgb(lastRed, 0, 0)

    prgCompletion.Value = lastRed / 255 * 100

    lastRed = lastRed + 5
    If lastRed > 255 Then
        lastRed = 255
    End If

End Sub

Private Sub trkSpeed_ValueChanged(ByVal sender As Object, _
 ByVal e As System.EventArgs) Handles trkSpeed.ValueChanged

    tmrSpeed.Interval = trkSpeed.Value

End Sub
```

NumericUpDown

The **NumericUpDown** control is a scrollable control that allows a user to select a value by clicking the up and down buttons of the control. The user can also enter text in the control, unless the **ReadOnly** property is set to **True**. Useful properties of this control include **Minimum**, **Maximum**, and **Value** that were previously mentioned, as well as these additional properties:

- **ReadOnly** indicates whether the user may use the keyboard to enter a value in the control.
- **Increment** indicates the amount by which the value is changed when scrolling through the range.
- **DecimalPlaces** indicates the number of decimal points shown.
- **ThousandsSeparator** indicates whether a thousands separator is used.
- **Hexadecimal** indicates whether the value is shown in hexadecimal.

Events generated by the **NumericUpDown** control include the following:

- **ValueChanged** indicates whether the value was changed either through mouse or keyboard activity, or by programmatically changing the **Value** property.

EXAMPLE: USING THE NUMERICUPDOWN

The following program, found in **SimpleProgress\Version 2**, is a version of the example used to illustrate the progress control. However, rather than hard-coding the upper limit for the index, a **NumericUpDown** control is used to allow the user to set the upper limit. See Figure 17–7.

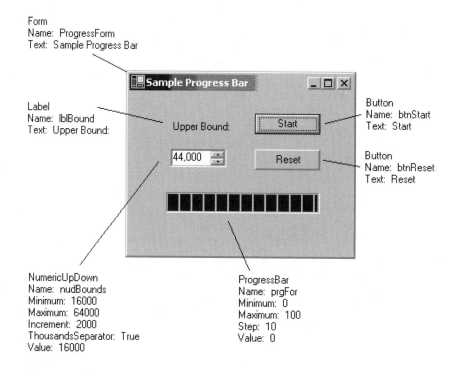

FIGURE 17–7   *Using the NumericUpDown control.*

```
Private Sub btnStart_Click(ByVal sender As System.Object, _
  ByVal e As System.EventArgs) Handles btnStart.Click

   ' Write square roots to a file (file i/o is slow!)
   Dim fileNum As Integer
   fileNum = FreeFile()
   FileOpen(fileNum, "sqrt.txt", OpenMode.Output)

   Dim index As Integer
   Dim s As Single
   Dim outLine As String

   Dim limits As Integer = nudBounds.Value
   For index = 1 To limits
```

```
        s = Math.Sqrt(index)
        outLine = index.ToString() & " - Sqrt = " _
                & s.ToString()
        Print(fileNum, outLine)

        ' update the progress bar  (% completion)
        prgFor.Value = (index / limits) * 100
    Next

    FileClose(fileNum)

End Sub

Private Sub btnReset_Click(ByVal sender As Object, ByVal _
    e As System.EventArgs) Handles btnReset.Click

    prgFor.Value = 0

End Sub
```

This program uses file I/O so that the progress bar moves slowly enough that it can be seen moving. The **FreeFile** function returns a file number that can be used to interact with a file. The **FileOpen** procedure opens a file so that we can write to it. The **Print** procedure writes to the file. And, finally, the **FileClose** procedure closes the file and releases the file number for reuse on other files. File I/O is discussed in more detail in Chapter 21.

List Controls

Several controls in VB.NET can be used to manage lists of information. These controls include the **ListBox**, **ComboBox**, **DomainUpDown**, **CheckedList-Box**, **ListView**, and **TreeView**. These controls display lists and allow the user to select items from the lists.

Domain UpDown

The **DomainUpDown** control is a scrollable control that displays a string value from a list. The user can also enter text in the control if the **ReadOnly** property is set to **False**, but the text entered must match an item in the collection. Interesting properties of the **DomainUpDown** control that were not inherited from the **Control** class include the following:

- **Items** represents the collection of items in the control's list. This property is a collection and has its own properties (for example:

Count) and methods (for example: **Add**, **AddRange**, **Clear**, **Remove**, and **RemoveAt**).

- **SelectedIndex** indicates the index of the item in the list that is selected. If nothing is selected, the value is -1.
- **Text** represents the text that is displayed in the control next to the up/down buttons.

Events generated by the **DomainUpDown** control include the following:

- **SelectedItemChanged** occurs when the **SelectedItem** property is changed.
- **TextChanged** occurs when the **Text** property is changed.

EXAMPLE: USING THE DOMAINUPDOWN

The following program, found in **Contacts**, uses a **DomainUpDown** control to select a value for data entry from a finite set of possibilities. See Figure 17–8.

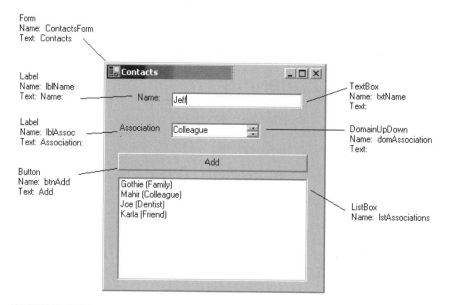

| **FIGURE 17–8** | *Using the DomainUpDown control.* |

```
Private Sub ContactsForm_Load(ByVal sender As _
   System.Object, ByVal e As System.EventArgs) _
Handles MyBase.Load

   Dim assocTypes() As String = _
      {"Colleague", "Friend", "Family", "Doctor", "Dentist"}
   domAssociation.Items.AddRange(assocTypes)
```

```
End Sub

Private Sub btnAdd_Click(ByVal sender As System.Object, _
 ByVal e As System.EventArgs) Handles btnAdd.Click

   Dim s As String
   s = txtName.Text & " (" & domAssociation.Text & ")"
   lstContacts.Items.Add(s)

   txtName.Text = ""
   domAssociation.Text = ""

End Sub
```

CheckedListBox

The **CheckedListBox** control lists items that the user selected by checking the check box next to the item(s) she wants. It has the three properties that represent the collection of items in the control:

- **Items** represents all the items listed in the control.
- **CheckedItems** represents the items checked in the control.
- **CheckedIndices** represents the indices of the items checked in the control.

These properties, because they encapsulate collections, have their own set of properties (for example: **Count** and **Item**) and methods (for example: **Add**, **AddRange**, **Clear**, **Contains**, **Remove**, and **RemoveAt**) that are similar to the **ListBox** control discussed in Chapter 15.

The **CheckedListBox** also has other interesting properties not inherited from the **Control** class, including the following:

- **CheckOnClick** indicates whether the check box is toggled when the item is selected.
- **ThreeDCheckBoxes** indicates the appearance of the check box.
- **Sorted** indicates whether items in the control are sorted.
- **MultiColumn** indicates whether the control supports multiple columns.
- **ColumnWidth** indicates the width of columns if the control is **MultiColumn**.
- **SelectedItem** indicates the currently selected item in the control.
- **SelectedIndex** indicates the index of the currently selected item.

Methods include the following:

- **BeginUpdate** and **EndUpdate** pause and resume painting of the control so that changes can be efficiently made to it.
- **ClearSelected** clears all selections (not checks!) in the control.
- **SetItemChecked** sets the specified item to the checked state.

- **GetItemChecked** indicates the checked state of the specified item.

Events on the **CheckedListBox** control include the following:

- **ItemCheck** occurs when the checked state of an item changes.
- **SelectedIndexChanged** occurs when the **SelectedIndex** property changes.

ADDING ITEMS TO THE CONTROL

To add items to the **CheckedListBox** control, you can use the **Add** or **AddRange** method of the **Items** collection. The **Add** method adds items one at a time:

```
chkLBEmployees.Items.Add("Roland")
```

The **AddRange** method adds items to the control from an array:

```
Dim frontOffice As String() = {"Jeannie", "Sandra", "Susan"}
chkLBEmployees.Items.AddRange(frontOffice)
```

ACCESSING ITEMS IN THE CONTROL

You can use the **Contains** method of either the **Items** or **CheckedItems** property to determine whether a specific string is found in the control:

```
If chkLBEmployees.CheckedItems.Contains("Pat") Then
   ' do something
End If
```

You can access the individual elements in the **Items** collection by specifying the index of the desired item:

```
For index = 0 To chkLBEmployees.Items.Count - 1
   MessageBox.Show(chkLBEmployees.Items(index))
Next
```

You can access the individual elements in the **CheckedItems** collection by specifying the index of the desired item:

```
For index = 0 To chkLBEmployees.CheckedItems.Count - 1
   MessageBox.Show(chkLBEmployees.CheckedItems(index))
Next
```

You can also access the individual elements selected by using the **CheckedIndices** collection:

```
Dim n As Integer
For index = 0 To chkLBEmployees.CheckedIndices.Count - 1

   n = chkLBEmployees.CheckedIndices(index)
   MessageBox.Show(chkLBEmployees.Items(n) )

Next
```

CHECKING/UNCHECKING ITEMS IN THE CONTROL

To programmatically check or uncheck items in a **CheckedListBox** control, you can use the **SetItemChecked** property:

```
chkLBEmployees.SetItemChecked(index, True)
```

EXAMPLE: USING THE CHECKEDLISTBOX

Code
Example

The following example, found in the project **Employees**, illustrates the use of the **CheckedListBox**. It displays an initial list of employees. Employees may be added to and removed from the list via a series of buttons (see Figure 17–9).

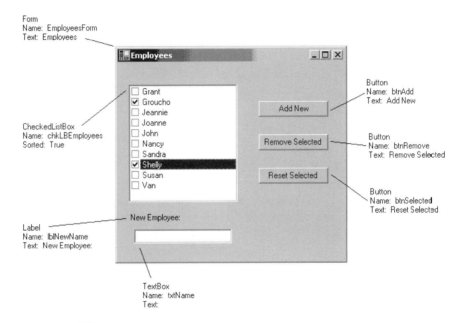

FIGURE 17–9 *Using the CheckedListBox control.*

```
Private Sub EmployeeForm_Load(ByVal sender As _
  System.Object, ByVal e As System.EventArgs) _
  Handles MyBase.Load

    chkLBEmployees.Items.Add("Roland")

    Dim frontOffice() As String = _
        {"Jeannie", "Sandra", "Susan"}
    chkLBEmployees.Items.AddRange(frontOffice)

    Dim backOffice() As String = {"Joanne", "Nancy", "John"}
    chkLBEmployees.Items.AddRange(backOffice)
```

```
End Sub

Private Sub btnNew_Click(ByVal sender As Object, _
 ByVal e As System.EventArgs) Handles btnNew.Click

   If Trim(txtName.Text) <> "" Then
      chkLBEmployees.Items.Add(txtName.Text)
      txtName.Text = ""
   End If

End Sub

Private Sub btnRemove_Click(ByVal sender As Object, _
 ByVal e As System.EventArgs) Handles btnRemove.Click

   Dim index, sel As Integer
   chkLBEmployees.BeginUpdate()
   ' go backwards thru items because deleting one
   ' changes indices
   For index = _
      chkLBEmployees.CheckedIndices.Count - 1 To 0 Step -1

      sel = chkLBEmployees.CheckedIndices(index)
      chkLBEmployees.Items.RemoveAt(sel)
   Next
   chkLBEmployees.EndUpdate()

End Sub

Private Sub btnReset_Click(ByVal sender As Object, _
 ByVal e As System.EventArgs) Handles btnReset.Click

   Dim index, sel As Integer
   chkLBEmployees.BeginUpdate()
   ' go backwards thru items because unchecking one
   ' changes indices
   For index = _
      chkLBEmployees.CheckedIndices.Count - 1 To 0 Step -1

      sel = chkLBEmployees.CheckedIndices(index)
      chkLBEmployees.SetItemChecked(sel, False)
   Next
   chkLBEmployees.EndUpdate()

End Sub
```

ListView

The **ListView** control is a more flexible version of the **ListBox** control and can display its list in four different ways:

- Using large icons
- Using small icons
- Displaying a list
- Displaying list details

The right-hand pane of Windows Explorer is essentially a **ListView** control. When displaying list details, the **ListView** control can display multiple columns for each list item.

The **ListView** control has several interesting properties not inherited from the **Control** class, including the following:

- **Items** represents the items in the control.
- **MultiSelect** indicates whether the control supports multiple selection.
- **Sorting** indicates how items in the control are sorted.
- **View** indicates the current viewing style of items in the control.
- **LargeImageList** displays the **ImageList** with large icons.
- **SmallImageList** displays the **ImageList** with small icons.
- **LabelEdit** indicates whether the user can edit the label on an item in the list.
- **Columns** provides access to the collection of columns.
- **GridLines** indicates whether gridlines are drawn between items and subitems.
- **FocusedItem** indicates the item with focus.
- **FullRowSelect** indicates whether clicking an item selects the item or the whole row.

Methods of the **ListView** control include the following:

- **BeginUpdate** and **EndUpdate** to pause/resume painting of the control so that the control can be efficiently maintained.
- **GetItemAt** returns the item at a specific x,y location.
- **ArrangeIcons** arranges icons according to a specified behavior.

Events generated by the **ListView** control include the following:

- **ColumnClick** occurs when the user clicks a column.
- **ItemActivate** occurs when an item is activated.
- **SelectedIndexChanged** occurs when the selection changes.

ADDING COLUMNS TO THE CONTROL

To add columns to the **ListView** control, first set its **View** property to **Details**. You can then interact with the **Columns** property to add items as needed. For example, the code below adds the two columns indicated here:

- "Name," 70 pixels wide, and with the text left aligned
- "Department," 70 pixels wide, and with the text left aligned

```
lswPeople.Columns.Add( _
    "Name", 70, HorizontalAlignment.Left)
lswPeople.Columns.Add( _
    "Department", 70, HorizontalAlignment.Left)
```

ADDING ITEMS TO THE CONTROL

To add an item, you must use the **Add** method of the **Items** collection and you must specify the following:

- The item label
- An index from the associated **ImageList**
- The subitems associated with the item

Here's what that code would look like:

```
' Adds a new item with ImageIndex 1 and no subitems
lswPeople.ListItems.Add("Dana", 1, Nothing)
```

If the item being added to the list view has subitems, you can create a **ListViewItem** object and configure it before adding it to the **ListView** control. For example:

```
' Adds a subitem to an item
Dim it As New ListViewItem()
it.Text = "Dana"
it.ImageIndex = 1
it.SubItems.Add("IT")

lswPeople.Items.Add(it)
```

EXAMPLE: USING THE LISTVIEW

Code Example

The following example, found in the project **ListView**, illustrates the use of this control. It manages a collection of employees. It supports addition to, and removal from, the list. It also has a menu that can be used to change the view of the **ListView** control (see Figure 17–10).

```
' Declare 3 variables associated with the image lists
Private Const EngIcon As Byte = 0
Private Const ITIcon As Byte = 1
Private Const MgmtIcon As Byte = 2

' Initializing the ListView
Private Sub ListViewForm_Load(ByVal sender As _
  System.Object, ByVal e As System.EventArgs) _
  Handles MyBase.Load

    lswPeople.View = View.Details
```

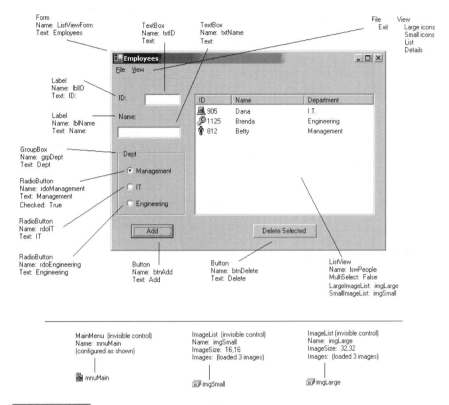

FIGURE 17-10 *Using the ListView control.*

```
' Add 3 columns:  1st is 20% of area, others are 40%
' of the area
lswPeople.Columns.Add("ID", lswPeople.Width / 5, _
   HorizontalAlignment.Center)
lswPeople.Columns.Add("Name", lswPeople.Width / 5 * 2, _
   HorizontalAlignment.Left)
lswPeople.Columns.Add("Department", _
   lswPeople.Width / 5 * 2 - 4, _
   HorizontalAlignment.Left)

' Add initial data
Dim x As New ListViewItem()
x.Text = "905"
x.ImageIndex = ITIcon
x.SubItems.Add("Dana")
x.SubItems.Add("I.T.")
lswPeople.Items.Add(x)

x = New ListViewItem()
```

```
      x.Text = "1125"
      x.ImageIndex = EngIcon
      x.SubItems.Add("Brenda")
      x.SubItems.Add("Engineering")
      lswPeople.Items.Add(x)

End Sub

' Handle the menu commands
Private Sub mnuExit_Click(ByVal sender As System.Object, _
 ByVal e As System.EventArgs) Handles mnuExit.Click

   Me.Close()

End Sub

Private Sub mnuLarge_Click(ByVal sender As System.Object, _
 ByVal e As System.EventArgs) Handles mnuLarge.Click

   lswPeople.View = View.LargeIcon

End Sub

Private Sub mnuSmall_Click(ByVal sender As Object, _
 ByVal e As System.EventArgs) Handles mnuSmall.Click

   lswPeople.View = View.SmallIcon

End Sub

Private Sub mnuList_Click(ByVal sender As Object, _
 ByVal e As System.EventArgs) Handles mnuList.Click

   lswPeople.View = View.List

End Sub

Private Sub mnuDetails_Click(ByVal sender As Object, _
 ByVal e As System.EventArgs) Handles mnuDetails.Click

   lswPeople.View = View.Details

End Sub

' Check items as the user clicks on them
Private Sub lswPeople_MouseDown(ByVal sender As Object, _
 ByVal e As System.Windows.Forms.MouseEventArgs) _
 Handles lswPeople.MouseDown

   Dim x As ListViewItem = lswPeople.GetItemAt(e.X, e.Y)
```

```
    If Not IsNothing(x) Then
        MessageBox.Show("You clicked on employee: " & x.Text)
    End If

End Sub

' Process the Add button click
Private Sub btnAdd_Click(ByVal sender As System.Object, _
 ByVal e As System.EventArgs) Handles btnAdd.Click

    Dim x As New ListViewItem()
    Dim dept As String

    x.Text = txtID.Text
    If rdoManagement.Checked Then
        x.ImageIndex = MgmtIcon
        dept = "Management"
    ElseIf rdoIT.Checked Then
        x.ImageIndex = ITIcon
        dept = "IT"
    Else
        x.ImageIndex = EngIcon
        dept = "Engineering"
    End If
    x.SubItems.Add(txtName.Text)
    x.SubItems.Add(dept)
    lswPeople.Items.Add(x)

    ' Blank out data entry fields
    txtID.Text = ""
    txtName.Text = ""

End Sub

' Process the Delete button click
Private Sub btnDelete_Click(ByVal sender As Object, _
 ByVal e As System.EventArgs) Handles btnDelete.Click

    ' Find the item with focus and delete it
    Dim x As ListViewItem = lswPeople.FocusedItem
    If Not IsNothing(x) Then
        lswPeople.Items.Remove(x)
    End If

End Sub
```

TreeView

The **TreeView** control displays a list of information in a hierarchical manner. Each item in the control is a **TreeNode**. Each **TreeNode** can, in turn, consist of a collection of other **TreeNodes**. In Windows Explorer, the left pane is represented in a **TreeControl**. Interesting properties of the **TreeView** that are not inherited from the **Control** class include the following:

- **Nodes** manages the collection of nodes in the tree. This collection has its own set of properties and methods to manage the individual nodes.
- **SelectedNode** indicates which node is currently selected.
- **ShowLines** indicates whether lines connect the nodes in the tree.
- **ShowLinesAtRoot** indicates whether there are lines at the root of the tree.
- **ShowPlusMinus** indicates whether + (plus) and - (minus) indicators are shown next to collapsed and expanded nodes, respectively.
- **Sorted** indicates whether the nodes are sorted.
- **ImageList** manages the images associated with the nodes.
- **FullRowSelect** indicates whether the selection highlighted is as wide as the tree control.

Methods of the **TreeView** control include the following:

- **BeginUpdate** and **EndUpdate** pause and resume repainting of the control so that the control may be manipulated efficiently.
- **CollapseAll** collapses all nodes in the tree.
- **ExpandAll** expands all nodes in the tree.
- **GetNodeCount** returns the number of nodes in the tree.
- **GetNodeAt** retrieves a node at a specified *x,y* coordinate.

Events generated by the **TreeView** control include the following:

- **BeforeExpand** and **AfterExpand** occur before and after any node is expanded.
- **BeforeCollapse** and **AfterCollapse** occur before and after any node is collapsed.
- **BeforeSelect** and **AfterSelect** occur before and after any node is selected.

ADDING NODES TO THE CONTROL

Because the **TreeView** control displays nodes in a hierarchical manner, you must indicate the parent node when adding any other node. To add a root node and obtain a reference to it, you must use the **Add** method of the **Nodes** collection:

```
Dim root As TreeNode
root = trePeople.Nodes.Add("Leslye & Randy")
```

To add child nodes to the root node above, you could write this:

```
root.Add(New TreeNode("Mollye")
root.Add(New TreeNode("Ranse")
```

To add a new node as a child node of the currently selected node, you must write this:

```
trePeople.SelectedNode.Nodes.Add(New TreeNode("Freddy"))
```

ITERATING THROUGH THE NODES OF THE CONTROL

The easiest way to iterate through each node in a **TreeView** is to use a recursive procedure. To begin with, you would examine each node at the root level.

```
Dim node As TreeNode
For Each node In someTree.Nodes
    ExamineNode(node)
Next
```

Each node, however, can itself have child nodes. So you must examine each child node in that node. This recursive process continues until the node being examined has no child nodes of its own.

```
Sub ExamineNode(ByVal node As TreeNode)
   ' Process node
   ...

   ' Examine child nodes
   Dim childNode As TreeNode
   For Each childNode In node.Nodes
      ExamineNode (childNode)
   Next
End Sub
```

REMOVING NODES FROM THE CONTROL

To remove the currently selected node, you must use the **Remove** method. It removes the current selection from the **TreeView:**

```
trePeople.Nodes.Remove(trePeople.SelectedNode)
```

In addition, all nodes in the **TreeView** control can be removed using the **Clear** method:

```
trePeople.Nodes.Clear()
```

EXAMPLE: USING THE TREEVIEW

The following example, found in the project **TreeView**, illustrates the use of this control. It manages a collection of employees. It supports addition to, and removal from, the list via a context menu (see Figure 17–11).

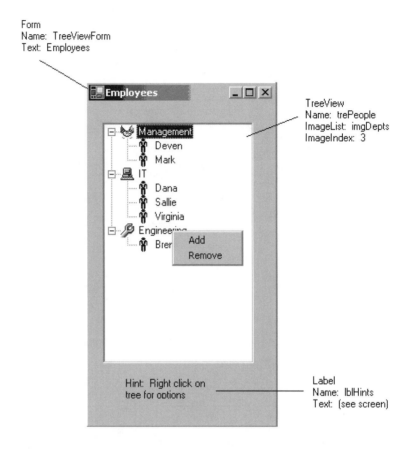

FIGURE 17-11 *Using the TreeView control.*

```
' Declare 3 variables to manage the root nodes and one item
' maintains the item that was clicked on to bring up the
' context menu
Dim MgmtRoot, ITRoot, EngRoot As TreeNode
Dim contextMenuNode As TreeNode

' Initialize the context menu and the tree control
Private Sub TreeViewForm_Load(ByVal sender _
```

```
As System.Object, ByVal e As System.EventArgs) _
Handles MyBase.Load

    ' Associate AddOne and RemoveOne as the handlers
    ' for the context menu
    mnuContext.MenuItems.Add("Add", AddressOf AddOne)
    mnuContext.MenuItems.Add("Remove", AddressOf RemoveOne)

    ' Add three departments
    Dim n As Integer
    n = trePeople.Nodes.Add(New TreeNode("Management", 2, 2))
    MgmtRoot = trePeople.Nodes(n)

    n = trePeople.Nodes.Add(New TreeNode("IT", 1, 1))
    ITRoot = trePeople.Nodes(n)

    n = trePeople.Nodes.Add( _
            New TreeNode("Engineering", 0, 0))
    EngRoot = trePeople.Nodes(n)

    ' Add two employees
    ITRoot.Nodes.Add(New TreeNode("Dana"))
    EngRoot.Nodes.Add(New TreeNode("Brenda"))

End Sub

Private Sub trePeople_MouseDown(ByVal sender As Object, _
 ByVal e As System.Windows.Forms.MouseEventArgs) _
 Handles trePeople.MouseDown

    ' If the right button is down
    If e.Button = MouseButtons.Right Then

        ' Find the item that was clicked on
        contextMenuNode = trePeople.GetNodeAt(e.X, e.Y)

        ' If found, display the context menu
        If Not IsNothing(contextMenuNode) Then
            mnuContext.Show(trePeople, e.X, e.Y)
        End If
    End If

End Sub

' Process the Add context menu
Private Sub AddOne(ByVal sender As System.Object, _
 ByVal e As System.EventArgs)

    Dim parent As TreeNode = contextMenuNode.Parent()
```

```
' Prompt for a name using the InputBox function (it is
' a simple dialog similar to the MessageBox dialog)
Dim name As String
name = InputBox("Enter new name:", "Name", "")

' If the user clicked on a person, add under department
If Not IsNothing(parent) Then
   parent.Nodes.Add(New TreeNode(name))
Else   ' ... clicked on a department, add here
   contextMenuNode.Nodes.Add(New TreeNode(name))
End If

End Sub

' Process the Add context menu
Private Sub RemoveOne(ByVal sender As System.Object, _
 ByVal _e As System.EventArgs)

   Dim parent As TreeNode = contextMenuNode.Parent()

   ' If the user clicked on a person, remove them
   If Not IsNothing(parent) Then
      trePeople.Nodes.Remove(contextMenuNode)
   Else ' ... clicked on a department, display error
      MessageBox.Show("Cannot delete entire department!")
   End If

End Sub
```

ErrorProvider

The **ErrorProvider** control provides a simple way of indicating data errors to the end user of a form. It displays an error icon next to controls that have invalid data. Tool tips on the error icon are used to show the error messages. Interesting properties of the **ErrorProvider** control that are not inherited from the **Control** class include the following:

- **BlinkStyle** indicates the style of blinking used for the error icon.
- **BlinkRate** indicates the rate at which the icon blinks.
- **Icon** indicates the icon used for the error indicator.

Methods of the **ErrorProvider** class include the following:

- **SetError** associates or disassociates an error message with a control.
- **GetError** returns the error message associated with a specified control.

Associating an Error Message with a Control

To associate an error message with a data entry control, use the **ErrorProvider's SetError** method, as shown in this example:

```
errProvider.SetError(txtName, "A name is required")
```

Clearing an Error Message

To clear an error message associated with a data entry control, use the **ErrorProvider's SetError** method and specify a blank error message, as shown in this example:

```
errProvider.SetError(txtName, "")
```

Example: Using an ErrorProvider

Code
Example

The following program, found in **DataValidation**, uses the **ErrorProvider** control to display error messages. On the Main Form, the code in the **Click** event of the Add button prompts the user for new data. If the user chooses OK, the data is added to the tree view (see Figure 17–12).

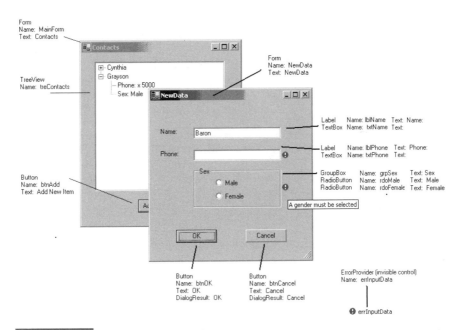

FIGURE 17–12 *Using the ErrorProvider control.*

```
Private Sub btnAdd_Click(ByVal sender As System.Object, _
   ByVal e As System.EventArgs) Handles btnAdd.Click

   Dim answer As DialogResult

   ' Display the data entry dialog
   Dim f As New NewData()
   answer = f.ShowDialog()

   ' Check the return result
   If answer = DialogResult.OK Then
      ' If the user chose OK, add the info to the tree view
      Dim node As New TreeNode()
      node.Text = f.txtName.Text
      node.Nodes.Add("Phone: " & f.txtPhone.Text)
      If f.rdoFemale.Checked Then
         node.Nodes.Add("Sex: Female")
      Else
         node.Nodes.Add("Sex: Male")
      End If
      treContacts.Nodes.Add(node)
   End If

End Sub
```

On the Data Entry Dialog, we use an **ErrorProvider** control to provide visual feedback, as shown in Figure 17–12, when data is incorrect. One **ErrorProvider** control can be used to set multiple error messages. The code in the **Click** event of the OK button validates the data. If there is a problem, it displays error(s) and sets the form's **DialogResult** property to **None**. We have provided code in the change events of the data fields to clear the error message when good data is input.

```
Private Sub btnOK_Click(ByVal sender As System.Object, _
 ByVal e As System.EventArgs) Handles btnOK.Click

   Dim success As Boolean = True

   If Trim(txtName.Text) = "" Then
      errInputData.SetError(txtName, "Must enter a name")
      success = False
   End If

   If Trim(txtPhone.Text) = "" Then
      errInputData.SetError(txtPhone, _
                  "Must enter a phone number")
      success = False
   End If

   If Not rdoMale.Checked And Not rdoFemale.Checked Then
```

```vb
        errInputData.SetError(grpSex, _
                    "A gender must be selected")
        success = False
    End If

    If Not success Then
        Me.DialogResult = DialogResult.None
    End If

End Sub

Private Sub txtName_TextChanged(ByVal sender As _
 System.Object, ByVal e As System.EventArgs) _
 Handles txtName.TextChanged

    If Trim(txtName.Text) <> "" Then
        errInputData.SetError(txtName, "")
    End If

End Sub

Private Sub txtPhone_TextChanged(ByVal sender As Object, _
 ByVal e As System.EventArgs) Handles txtPhone.TextChanged

    If Trim(txtPhone.Text) <> "" Then
        errInputData.SetError(txtPhone, "")
    End If

End Sub

Private Sub rdoFemale_CheckedChanged(ByVal sender As _
 Object, ByVal e As System.EventArgs) _
 Handles rdoFemale.CheckedChanged

    errInputData.SetError(grpSex, "")

End Sub

Private Sub rdoMale_CheckedChanged(ByVal sender As _
 Object, ByVal e As System.EventArgs) _
 Handles rdoMale.CheckedChanged

    errInputData.SetError(grpSex, "")

End Sub
```

More Controls and Visual Inheritance

VB.NET supports several other controls that we have not examined, including the following:

- **PictureBox** is a control that can display an image (.bmp, .gif, .jpeg, etc.).
- **LinkLabel** is a label that can display a hyperlink.
- **HelpProvider** provides popup or online help for controls.
- **Panel** represents a control that may contain other controls. It can be used to enable and disable or make visible or invisible a collection of controls. A **Panel** may also contain scroll bars.
- **Splitter** allows a user to resize docked controls using a mouse. These represent the logical concept of splitter windows.
- **TabControl** is a control used to build tabbed dialogs. Tabbed dialogs are also called property pages.
- **DataGrid** is a data-bound control that can display data from a database.
- **CrystalReportViewer** allows a Crystal Report to be viewed within a VB.NET application.

In addition, a VB.NET programmer can use custom controls developed specifically for .NET applications, as well as the older ActiveX controls. VB.NET supports an exciting new feature called Visual Inheritance in which new forms can be created based on existing forms. You can refer to our book *Application Development Using Visual Basic and .NET* for information on these useful features.

Summary

VB.NET supports a variety of controls that can be used on a Windows Forms application. When you are familiar with the appearance, purpose, and capabilities of the various controls, you can ensure that your desktop applications are written to be visually appealing and easy to use. This chapter concludes our examination of the controls available to VB.NET programmers. Several interesting controls were explored, including the **DomainUpDown**, the **TreeView**, and the **ErrorProvider** controls. You should continue your examination of the .NET controls, and be aware that third-party controls are being rapidly produced and marketed.

PART FIVE

VB.NET and the .NET Framework

Part 5 explores the relationships between VB.NET and the .NET Framework. .NET collection classes are introduced. We also examine the .NET interfaces that classes must implement for fundamental operations such as copying and comparing objects. Delegates, a .NET callback mechanism, are discussed. We also introduce both VB.NET file I/O and database programming using ADO.NET. We look at multiple thread programming and attributes. Attributes are powerful in .NET, enabling the programmer to accomplish tasks declaratively, even while writing very little code. You can implement custom attributes in VB.NET. You can read information about custom attributes, or any other metadata, by a mechanism known as "reflection." The book concludes with an introduction to components and assemblies.

Using the .NET Framework

In Chapter 13, we saw how useful interfaces can be in specifying contracts for our own classes. Interfaces can help us program at a higher level of abstraction, enabling us to see the essential features of our system without being bogged down in implementation details. In this chapter, we examine the role of interfaces in the .NET Framework, where they are ubiquitous. Many of the standard classes implement specific interfaces, and we can call into the methods of these interfaces to obtain useful services.

We begin our discussion with a general examination of "frameworks," which are more than class libraries. We then take another look at arrays, which we first studied in Chapter 7. We show you that the class System.Array implements a number of standard interfaces that are common to all "collection" classes. We will examine many other types of collections in Chapter 19. In order to effectively work with arrays or any other kind of collection, you need to override certain methods of the Object base class.

Besides calling into interfaces that are implemented by library classes, many .NET classes call standard interfaces. If we provide our own implementation of such interfaces, we can have .NET library code call our own code in appropriate ways, customizing the behavior of library code. We look at examples, including object cloning and comparison of objects, in this chapter. This behavior of your program being called into has traditionally been provided by "callback" functions. In VB.NET, there is a type-safe, object-oriented kind of callback known as a *delegate,* which we illustrate with a simple example.

Understanding Frameworks

Effective VB.NET programming requires knowledge of both the VB.NET language and the rich services available through the .NET Framework class library. We have seen many examples in this book of useful functionality that we can add to our program by calling methods of classes in the .NET Framework class library.

A framework is more than a library. In a typical library, you are concerned with your code calling library functions. In a framework, you call into the framework *and the framework calls you.* Your program can be viewed as the middle layer of a sandwich.

- Your code calls the bottom layer.
- The top layer calls your code.

The .NET Framework is an excellent example of such an architecture. There is rich functionality that you can call directly. There are many interfaces, which you can optionally implement to make your program behave appropriately when called by the framework. As a simple illustration, consider sorting an array. The **System.Array** class provides a shared method **Sort** that can be used to sort the elements of an array. But not just any array can be sorted—you need to be able to compare the elements. The .NET Framework provides an interface **IComparable** with a method **Compare** for performing comparisons. The **IComparable** interface is not implemented by the framework for you. Rather, your own class must provide an implementation of **IComparable**, if you want the framework's **Sort** method to be able to work on an array of objects belonging to your class.

Arrays

The .NET Framework class library provides an extensive set of classes for working with collections of objects. These classes are all in the **System.Collections** namespace and implement a number of different kinds of collections, including lists, queues, stacks, arrays, and hash tables. The collections contain **Object** instances. Because all types derive ultimately from **Object**, any built-in or user-defined type may be stored in a collection. We will examine several of the diverse collection classes in Chapter 19.

In this section, we look at a particularly simple kind of collection, the **Array**. The **Array** class is so fundamental that it is provided in the **System** namespace. Several of the interfaces implemented by **Array** are defined in the **System.Collections** namespace. Part of our task in using arrays and similar collections is to properly implement our class whose instances are to be stored in the collection. In particular, our class must generally override certain methods of **Object**.

Array Example

Code Example

To get our bearings, let's begin with a simple example of using the **Array** class. Our example program is **StringList\Version 1**. It initializes a list of strings and then lets the user display the list, add strings, and remove strings. A simple "help" method displays the commands that are available:

```
The following commands are available:
   show      -- show strings in list
   dump      -- dump array contents
   add       -- add a string to list
   removeat -- remove string at index
   remove    -- remove a string
   quit      -- exit the program
```

Here's the code of our example program:

```vb
' StringList.vb

Imports System
Imports System.Collections

Module StringList
    Private arr(9) As String
    Private list As IList
    Private nexti As Integer = 0
    Sub Main()
        list = arr
        ShowList()
        AddString("Bob")
        AddString("Dana")
        AddString("Richard")
        ShowList()
        CommandLoop()
    End Sub

    Private Sub CommandLoop()
        Dim iw As New InputWrapper()
        Dim cmd As String
        Dim buf As String
        Dim index As Integer
        Console.WriteLine("Enter command, quit to exit")
        cmd = iw.getString("> ")
        While Not cmd.Equals("quit")
            Try
                If cmd.Equals("show") Then
                    ShowList()
```

```
            ElseIf cmd.Equals("dump") Then
                DumpArray()
            ElseIf cmd.Equals("add") Then
                buf = iw.getString("string: ")
                AddString(buf)
            ElseIf cmd.Equals("removeat") Then
                index = iw.getInt("index: ")
                RemoveAt(index)
            ElseIf cmd.Equals("remove") Then
                buf = iw.getString("string: ")
                RemoveString(buf)
            Else
                Help()
            End If
        Catch e As Exception
            Console.WriteLine(e.Message)
            If Not e.InnerException Is Nothing Then
                Console.WriteLine(e.InnerException.Message)
            End If
        End Try
        cmd = iw.getString("> ")
    End While
End Sub

Private Sub Help()
    Console.WriteLine( _
        "The following commands are available:")
    Console.WriteLine( _
        "  show     -- show strings in list")
    Console.WriteLine("  dump     -- dump array contents")
    Console.WriteLine( _
        "  add      -- add a string to list")
    Console.WriteLine( _
        "  removeat -- remove string at index")
    Console.WriteLine("  remove   -- remove a string")
    Console.WriteLine("  quit     -- exit the program")
End Sub

Private Sub ShowCounts()
    Console.WriteLine("list.Count = {0}", list.Count)
    Console.WriteLine("number of strings = {0}", nexti)
End Sub

Private Sub ShowList()
    Dim strg As String
    For Each strg In arr
        If strg <> "" Then
            Console.WriteLine(strg)
        End If
    Next
```

```
        ShowCounts()
    End Sub

    Private Sub DumpArray()
        Dim i As Integer
        For i = 0 To list.Count - 1
            If arr(i) <> "" Then
                Console.WriteLine("arr({0}) = {1}", i, arr(i))
            End If
        Next
        ShowCounts()
    End Sub

    Private Sub AddString(ByVal strg As String)
        If list.Contains(strg) Then
            Throw New Exception("List contains " & strg)
        End If
        'list.Add(strg)
        arr(nexti) = strg
        nexti += 1
    End Sub

    Private Sub RemoveAt(ByVal index As Integer)
        'list.RemoveAt(index)
        If nexti = 0 Then
            Throw New Exception("List is empty")
        End If
        If index >= nexti Or index < 0 Then
            Throw New Exception("Index is out of range")
        End If
        Dim i As Integer
        For i = index To nexti - 1
            arr(i) = arr(i + 1)
        Next
        nexti -= 1
    End Sub

    Private Sub RemoveString(ByVal strg As String)
        'list.Remove(strg)
        Dim index As Integer
        index = Array.IndexOf(arr, strg)
        If index = -1 Then
            Throw New Exception("String not found in list")
        End If
        RemoveAt(index)
    End Sub
End Module
```

String Comparisons

VB.NET's String type is implemented by the .NET String class. Until now, we have used only the = operator for comparisons. However, the String type also supports the equals method for comparisons. Use of the equals method has been demonstrated in the previous example.

For the most part, this program is quite plain vanilla programming with arrays, similar to code we saw in Chapter 7. Significant features are shown in bold. Pay particular attention to these items:

- **System.Collections** namespace: This namespace is imported to allow us to use the **IList** interface that is implemented by many collections, including arrays.
- **IList** interface variable: A variable **list** of type **IList** is declared and initialized to the array **arr**. Through this interface variable, we can access properties and methods of the **IList** interface, such as **Count**[1] and **Contains,** which cannot be called through an object reference to the class.

We have commented out several lines of code invoking other methods of **IList**, such as **Add** and **Remove**. Although this code will compile, we will get runtime errors[2]. These methods are not properly supported by the Array class' implementation of **IList**, so with arrays we must resort to lower level coding. We will see in Chapter 19 that these methods work properly for other collection classes, such as **ArrayList.**

Here's a sample run of the program:

```
list.Count = 10
number of strings = 0
Bob
Dana
Richard
list.Count = 10
number of strings = 3
Enter command, quit to exit
> add
string: Ellen
> dump
```

---

1. **Count** is a property of the **ICollection** interface, from which **IList** inherits. We will discuss the main interfaces associated with collections in Chapter 19.
2. When a class implements an interface, the contract is that the class provide members that match the signatures of the interface member. There is no semantic contract of behavior that must be supported. Thus, it is permissible for a class to give only a stub implementation (which might even fail at run time). In the case of an **Array,** it is reasonable for the class to provide stubs only for **Add** and **Remove,** because an array does not have a natural linked list structure that facilitates these operations.

```
arr(0) = Bob
arr(1) = Dana
arr(2) = Richard
arr(3) = Ellen
list.Count = 10
number of strings = 4
> remove
string: Richard
> removeat
index: 0
> dump
arr(0) = Dana
arr(1) = Ellen
list.Count = 10
number of strings = 2
> remove
string: Bob
string not found in list
> removeat
index: 2
index is out of range
```

Dynamic Instantiation of an Array

The **Array** class has a method named **CreateInstance** that supports dynamic programming of arrays. You can define a variable of type **Array** without giving any specifics, such as data type, rank, and dimension(s). Then, in a call to **CreateInstance**, you provide the specifics, and an object instance is created. Version 2 of the **StringList** program provides an illustration:

```
Module StringList
    Private arr As Array
    Private list As IList
    Private nexti As Integer = 0
    Sub Main()
        arr = Array.CreateInstance(GetType(String), 10)
        ...
```

An Array of User-Defined Objects

Now, we want to look at an example of an array of user-defined objects. The mechanics of calling the various collection properties and methods is very straightforward and is essentially identical to the usage for collections of built-in types. In your class, you must override at least the **Equals** method in order to obtain proper behavior in your collection. But for built-in types, you did not have to worry about this issue, because **Equals** is provided by the class library for you.

Code
Example

Our example program is **AccountArray**, which comes in two versions. Version 1 illustrates a very simple **Account** class, with no methods of **Object** overridden:

```
' Account.vb

Imports System

Public Class Account
   Private m_id As Integer
   Private m_balance As Decimal
   Private m_owner As String

   Public Sub New(ByVal balance As Decimal, ByVal owner _
   As String, ByVal id As Integer)
     m_balance = balance
     m_owner = owner
     m_id = id
   End Sub

   Public ReadOnly Property Info() As String
      Get
         ' PadRight is used to format the output
         Return m_id.ToString().PadRight(4) _
            & m_owner.PadRight(12) _
            & String.Format("{0:C}", m_balance)
      End Get
   End Property
End Class
```

The test program **AccountArray.vb** contains code to initialize an array of **Account** objects, to show the initial accounts, and then to perform a command loop. A simple **Help** method gives a brief summary of the available commands:

```
The following commands are available:
   show      -- show accounts in list
   add       -- add an account to list
   quit      -- exit the program
```

The code is very straightforward, so we won't give a complete listing. You can examine the code online.

```
' AccountArray.vb

Imports System
Imports System.Collections

Module AccountArray
   Private arr(9) As Account
   Private list As IList
```

```
Private nexti As Integer = 0

Sub Main()
    list = arr
    AddAccount(100, "Bob", 1)
    AddAccount(200, "Mary", 2)
    AddAccount(300, "Charlie", 3)
    ShowList()
    CommandLoop()
End Sub

    ...


Private Sub AddAccount(ByVal bal As Decimal, _
    ByVal owner As String, ByVal id As Integer)

    Dim acc As New Account(bal, owner, id)
    If list.Contains(acc) Then
        Throw New Exception( _
          "List contains account with id " & id)
    End If
    arr(nexti) = acc
    nexti += 1
End Sub

End Module
```

This is a sample run of the program:

```
1    Bob          $100.00
2    Mary         $200.00
3    Charlie      $300.00
> add
id: 1
owner: Bob
balance: 100
> show
1    Bob          $100.00
2    Mary         $200.00
3    Charlie      $300.00
1    Bob          $100.00
```

The salient point is that the "add" command is not protected against adding a duplicate element ("Bob"). Our code is similar to what we used before in the **StringList** program, but now the **Contains** method does not work properly. The default implementation of **Equals** in the **Object** root class is to check for reference equality, and the two "Bob" elements have the same data but different references.

Code
Example

AccountArray\Version 2 contains corrected code for the **Account** class:

```
' Account.vb

Imports System

Public Class Account

    ...

    Public Overloads Overrides Function Equals( _
    ByVal obj As Object) As Boolean
        Dim acc As Account
        acc = CType(obj, Account)
        Return (acc.m_id = m_id)
    End Function

End Class
```

Our test for equality involves just the account ID. For example, two people with the same name could have an account at the same bank, but their account IDs should be different. If you have "Option Strict On" (and you should!), you need to do an explicit conversion of an **Object** to an **Account** using the **CType** function.

Here is the code for implementing the "add" command:

```
Private Sub AddAccount(ByVal bal As Decimal, _
 ByVal owner As String, ByVal id As Integer)
    Dim acc As New Account(bal, owner, id)
    If list.Contains(acc) Then
        Throw New Exception( _
            "List contains account with id " & id)
    End If
    arr(nexti) = acc
    nexti += 1
End Sub
```

Notice how easy it is to check whether an element is contained in a collection implementing the **IList** interface. Just call the **Contains** method.

This sample run illustrates that the "add" command functions correctly. Note that the error message for an illegal "add" comes from normal exception handling in the test program:

```
1    Bob         $100.00
2    Mary        $200.00
3    Charlie     $300.00
Enter command, quit to exit
> add
id: 1
```

```
owner: Bob
balance: 100
list contains account with id 1
```

Copy Semantics and ICloneable

When programming, you often have occasion to make a copy of a variable. When you program in VB.NET, it is important that you have a firm understanding of exactly what happens when you copy various kinds of data. In this section, we look carefully at the copy semantics of VB.NET. We compare reference copy, shallow memberwise copy, and deep copy. We show you that by implementing the **ICloneable** interface in your class, you can enable deep copy.

Copy Semantics in VB.NET

Recall that VB.NET has value types and reference types. A *value type* contains all its own data, while a *reference type* refers to data stored somewhere else. If a reference variable gets copied to another reference variable, both refer to the same object. If the object referenced by the second variable is changed, the first variable also reflects the new value.

As an example, consider what happens when you copy an array, which is a reference type. Consider the program **ArrayCopy**:

```vbnet
' ArrayCopy.vb

Imports System

Module ArrayCopy
    Sub main()
        Dim arr1() As Integer = {1, 4, 9}
        Dim arr2() As Integer = arr1
        show(arr1, "first array")
        show(arr2, "second array")
        arr1(1) = 444        ' this will change BOTH arrays!
        show(arr1, "first array")
        show(arr2, "second array")
    End Sub

    Private Sub show(ByVal arr() As Integer, _
      ByVal caption As String)
        Console.WriteLine("----{0}----", caption)
        Dim i As Integer
        For i = 0 To arr.Length - 1
            Console.Write("{0} ", arr(i))
```

```
        Next
        Console.WriteLine()
    End Sub
End Module
```

When we make the assignment **arr2 = arr1**, we wind up not with two independent arrays, but rather with two references to the same array. When we make a change to an element of the first array, both arrays wind up changed. Here is the output:

```
----first array----
1 4 9
----second array----
1 4 9
----first array----
1 444 9
----second array----
1 444 9
```

Shallow Copy and Deep Copy

A structure in VB.NET automatically implements a "memberwise copy", sometimes known as a "shallow copy." The **Object** root class has a protected method, **MemberwiseClone**, which performs a memberwise copy of members of a class.

If one or more members of a class are of reference types, this memberwise copy may not be good enough. The result is two references to the same data, not two independent copies of the data. To actually copy the data itself and not merely the references, you need to perform a "deep copy." Deep copy can be provided at either the language level or the library level. In C++, deep copy is provided at the language level through a *copy constructor*. In VB.NET, deep copy is provided by the .NET Framework through a special interface, **ICloneable**, which you can implement in your classes to enable them to perform deep copy.

Example Program

Code Example

We illustrate all these ideas in the program **CopyDemo**. This program makes a copy of a **Course** object. The **Course** class consists of a title and an array **Roster** of students.

```
' Course.vb

Imports System
Imports System.Collections

Public Class Course
```

```vb
Implements ICloneable
Private Const MAXSIZE As Integer = 10
Private m_title As String
Public Roster(MAXSIZE) As String

Public Sub New(ByVal title As String)
   m_title = title
End Sub

Public Property Title() As String
   Get
      Return m_title
   End Get
   Set(ByVal Value As String)
      m_title = Value
   End Set
End Property

Private ReadOnly Property NumStudent() As Integer
   Get
      Dim stud As String
      Dim count As Integer = 0
      For Each stud In Roster
         If stud <> "" Then
            count += 1
         End If
      Next
      Return count
   End Get
End Property

Public Sub AddStudent(ByVal name As String)
   Dim nexti As Integer = FindNextAvailable()
   Roster(nexti) = name
End Sub

Public Sub Show(ByVal caption As String)
   Console.WriteLine("-----{0}-----", caption)
   Console.WriteLine("Course : {0} with {1} students", _
      Title, NumStudent)
   Dim i As Integer
   For i = 0 To MAXSIZE - 1
      If Roster(i) <> "" Then
         Console.WriteLine(Roster(i))
      End If
   Next
End Sub

Public Function ShallowCopy() As Course
   Return CType(Me.MemberwiseClone(), Course)
```

```
      End Function

      Public Function Clone() As Object _
            Implements ICloneable.Clone
         Dim c As New Course(Title)
         c.Roster = CType(Roster.Clone(), String())
         Return c
      End Function

      Private Function FindNextAvailable() As Integer
         Dim i As Integer
         For i = 0 To MAXSIZE - 1
            If Roster(i) = "" Then
               Return i
            End If
         Next
         Return -1
      End Function
End Class
```

The following test program constructs a **Course** instance **c1** and then makes a copy **c2** by various methods.

REFERENCE COPY

The first way the copy is performed is by the straight assignment **c2 = c1**. Now we get two references to the same object, and if we make any change through the first reference, we see the same change through the second reference. The first part of the test program illustrates such an assignment:

```
' CopyDemo.vb

Imports System

Module CopyDemo
   Private c1 As Course
   Private c2 As Course
   Sub Main()
      Console.WriteLine("Copy is done via c2 = c1")
      InitializeCourse()
      c1.Show("original")
      c2 = c1
      c2.Show("copy")
      c2.Title = ".NET Programming"
      c2.AddStudent("Charlie")
      c2.Show("copy with changed title and new student")
      c1.Show("original")
      ...
```

```
Private Sub InitializeCourse()
   c1 = New Course("Intro to VB.NET")
   c1.AddStudent("John")
   c1.AddStudent("Mary")
End Sub

End Module
```

We initialize with the title "Intro to VB.NET" and two students. We make the assignment **c2 = c1** and then change the title and add another student for **c2**. We then show both **c1** and **c2**, and we see that both reflect these changes. This is the output from this first part of the program:

```
Copy is done via c2 = c1
-----original-----
Course : Intro to VB.NET with 2 students
John
Mary
-----copy-----
Course : Intro to VB.NET with 2 students
John
Mary
-----copy with changed title and new student-----
Course : .NET Programming with 3 students
John
Mary
Charlie
-----original-----
Course : .NET Programming with 3 students
John
Mary
Charlie
```

MEMBERWISE CLONE

The next way we illustrate doing a copy is a memberwise copy, which can be accomplished using the **MemberwiseClone** method of **Object**. Because this method is **Protected**, we cannot call it directly from outside our **Course** class. Instead, in **Course**, we defined a method, **ShallowCopy**, which is implemented using **MemberwiseClone**.

```
' Course.vb

Imports System
Imports System.Collections

Public Class Course
   ...

   Public Function ShallowCopy() As Course
```

```
       Return CType(Me.MemberwiseClone(), Course)
    End Function

    ...
End Class
```

Here is the second part of the test program, which calls the **Shallow-Copy** method. Again, we change the title and a student in the second copy:

```
' CopyDemo.vb

Imports System

Module CopyDemo

    ...
      Console.WriteLine()
      Console.WriteLine( _
       "Copy is done via c2 = c1.ShallowCopy()")
      InitializeCourse()
      c2 = c1.ShallowCopy()
      c2.Title = ".NET Programming"
      c2.AddStudent("Charlie")
      c2.Show("copy with changed title and new student")
      c1.Show("original")
    ...

End Module
```

Here is the output of this second part of the program. Now the **Title** field has its own independent copy, but the **Roster** array is just copied by reference, so each copy refers to the same collection of students.

```
Copy is done via c2 = c1.ShallowCopy()
-----copy with changed title and new student-----
Course : .NET Programming with 3 students
John
Mary
Charlie
-----original-----
Course : Intro to VB.NET with 3 students
John
Mary
Charlie
```

USING ICLONEABLE

The final version of copy relies on the fact that our **Course** class supports the **ICloneable** interface and implements the **Clone** method. To clone the **Roster** array, we use the fact that **Array** implements the **ICloneable** interface, as discussed earlier in the chapter. Note that the **Clone** method returns an **Object**, so we must cast to **String()** before assigning to the **Roster** field.

```vb
' Course.vb

Imports System
Imports System.Collections

Public Class Course
   Implements ICloneable
   ...

   Public Function Clone() As Object _
    Implements ICloneable.Clone
      Dim c As New Course(Title)
      c.Roster = CType(Roster.Clone(), String())
      Return c
   End Function

End Class
```

Here is the third part of the test program, which calls the **Clone** method. Again, we change the title and a student in the second copy:

```vb
' CopyDemo.vb

Imports System

Module CopyDemo
   ...
        Console.WriteLine( _
           "    Copy is done via c2 = c1.Clone()")
        InitializeCourse()
        c2 = c1.Clone()
        c2.Title = ".NET Programming"
        c2.AddStudent("Charlie")
        c2.Show("copy with changed title and new student")
        c1.Show("original")
        ...
```

Here is the output from the third part of the program. Now we have completely independent instances of **Course**. Each has its own title and set of students:

```
Copy is done via c2 = c1.Clone()
-----copy with changed title and new student-----
Course : .NET Programming with 3 students
John
Mary
Charlie
-----original-----
```

```
Course : Intro to VB.NET with 2 students
John
Mary
```

Comparing Objects

We have quite exhaustively studied issues involved in *copying* objects. We now examine the issues involved in *comparing* objects. To compare objects, the .NET Framework uses the interface **IComparable**. In this section, we examine the use of the interface **IComparable** through an example of sorting an array.

Sorting an Array

Code Example

The **System.Array** class provides the shared method, **Sort**, that can be used for sorting an array. The program **ArrayName\Version 0** illustrates an attempt to apply this **Sort** method to an array of **Name** objects, where the **Name** class simply encapsulates a **String** through a read-only property **Text**.

```
' ArrayName.vb

Imports System

Public Class Name
   Private m_text As String

   Public Sub New(ByVal text As String)
      m_text = text
   End Sub

   Public ReadOnly Property Text() As String
      Get
          Return m_text
      End Get
   End Property
End Class

Module ArrayName

   Sub Main()
      Dim arr() As Name = New Name(10) {}
      arr(0) = New Name("Michael")
      arr(1) = New Name("Charlie")
      arr(2) = New Name("Peter")
      arr(3) = New Name("Dana")
      arr(4) = New Name("Bob")
```

```
        Array.Sort(arr)
    End Sub

End Module
```

ANATOMY OF ARRAY.SORT

What do you suppose will happen when you run this program? Here's the result:

```
Unhandled Exception: System.InvalidOperationException:
Specified IComparer threw an exception. --->
System.ArgumentException: At least one object must
implement
 IComparable.
```

The shared method **Sort** of the **Array** class relies on some functionality of the objects in the array. That is, the array objects must implement **IComparable**.

Suppose we don't know whether the objects in our array support **IComparable**. How can we find out programmatically at runtime?

THE USE OF DYNAMIC TYPE CHECKING

There are two ways we have seen so far to dynamically check whether an interface is supported:

- Use exceptions.
- Use the **TypeOf ... Is** operator.

In this case, the most direct solution is to use the **TypeOf ... Is** operator, which is applied to an object, not to a class. See **ArrayName\Version 1**.

```
' ArrayName.vb

...
Module ArrayName
    Sub Main()
        Dim arr() As Name = New Name(10) {}
        arr(0) = New Name("Michael")
        arr(1) = New Name("Charlie")
        arr(2) = New Name("Peter")
        arr(3) = New Name("Dana")
        arr(4) = New Name("Bob")
        If TypeOf arr(0) Is IComparable Then
            Array.Sort(arr)
        Else
            Console.WriteLine( _
                "Name does not implement IComparable")
        End If
    End Sub
End Module
```

Here is the output from running the program. We're still not sorting the array, but at least we fail more gracefully.

```
Name does not implement IComparable
```

We can use dynamic type checking of object references to make our programs more robust. We can degrade gracefully rather than fail completely. For example, in our array program the desired outcome is to print the array elements in sorted order. We could check whether the objects in the array support **IComparable**, and if not, we could go ahead and print out the array elements in unsorted order, obtaining at least some functionality.

Implementing IComparable

By consulting the .NET documentation for **System**, we will find that **IComparable** is defined as follows:

```
Public Interface IComparable
    Function CompareTo(ByVal obj As Object) As Integer
End Interface
```

Now, let's implement **IComparable** in the class **Name**. This code is found in **ArrayName\Version 2**. Let's also add a simple loop in **Main** to display the array elements after sorting:

```
' ArrayName.vb

Imports System

Public Class Name
    Implements IComparable
    Private m_text As String

    Public Sub New(ByVal text As String)
        m_text = text
    End Sub

    Public ReadOnly Property Text() As String
        Get
            Return m_text
        End Get
    End Property

    Public Function CompareTo(ByVal obj As Object) _
      As Integer Implements IComparable.CompareTo
        Dim s1 As String = m_text
        Dim s2 As String = CType(obj, Name).Text
        Return String.Compare(s1, s2)
    End Function
```

```
End Class

Module ArrayName

    Sub Main()
        Dim arr() As Name = New Name(10) {}
        arr(0) = New Name("Michael")
        arr(1) = New Name("Charlie")
        arr(2) = New Name("Peter")
        arr(3) = New Name("Dana")
        arr(4) = New Name("Bob")
        If TypeOf arr(0) Is IComparable Then
            Array.Sort(arr)
        Else
            Console.WriteLine( _
                "Name does not implement IComparable")
        End If
        Dim name As Name
        For Each name In arr
            Console.WriteLine(name)
        Next
    End Sub

End Module
```

The **Compare** method used in the implementation of **CompareTo** is a **String** method that returns:

- If string1 is less than string2, it returns a negative number
- If string1 is equal to string2, it returns 0
- If string1 is greater than string2, it returns a positive number

This corresponds exactly to the values that the Sort method expects **CompareTo** to return.

AN INCOMPLETE SOLUTION

If we run the above program, we do not exactly get the desired output:

```
ArrayName.Name
ArrayName.Name
ArrayName.Name
ArrayName.Name
ArrayName.Name
```

The first five lines of output are blank, and in place of the string in **Name**, the class name **ArrayName.Name** is displayed. The unassigned elements of the array are **Nothing**, and they compare successfully with real elements, always being less than a real element.

COMPLETE SOLUTION

We should test for the value **Nothing** before displaying our output. The most straightforward way to correct the issue of the strings in **Name** not displaying is to use the **Text** property. A more interesting solution is to override the **ToString** method in our **Name** class. Here's the complete solution, in the directory **ArrayName\Version 3**:

```
' ArrayName.vb

Imports System

Public Class Name
    Implements IComparable
    Private m_text As String

    Public Sub New(ByVal text As String)
        m_text = text
    End Sub

    Public ReadOnly Property Text() As String
        Get
            Return m_text
        End Get
    End Property

    Public Function CompareTo(ByVal obj As Object) _
     As Integer Implements IComparable.CompareTo
        Dim s1 As String = m_text
        Dim s2 As String = CType(obj, Name).Text
        Return String.Compare(s1, s2)
    End Function

    Public Overrides Function ToString() As String
        Return Text
    End Function

End Class

Module ArrayName
    Sub Main()
        Dim arr() As Name = New Name(10) {}
        arr(0) = New Name("Michael")
        arr(1) = New Name("Charlie")
        arr(2) = New Name("Peter")
```

```
        arr(3) = New Name("Dana")
        arr(4) = New Name("Bob")
        If TypeOf arr(0) Is IComparable Then
            Array.Sort(arr)
        Else
            Console.WriteLine( _
                "Name does not implement IComparable")
        End If
        Dim name As Name
        For Each name In arr
            If Not name Is Nothing Then
                Console.WriteLine(name)
            End If
        Next
    End Sub
End Module
```

Here is the output:

```
Bob
Charlie
Dana
Michael
Peter
```

Interfaces and Delegates

We have examined interfaces in some detail, beginning with our discussion in Chapter 13. In this chapter, we have looked at some of the important generic interfaces defined by the .NET Framework. Interfaces facilitate writing code in such a way that your program is called back by some other code. This style of programming has been available for a long time, under the guise of "callback" functions.

VB.NET provides another mechanism for callback behavior, known as *delegates,* which can be thought of as type-safe and object-oriented callback functions. Delegates are the foundation for a higher-level callback protocol, known as events. We examined events in Chapter 11. Events are a cornerstone of COM, the predecessor of .NET, and are widely used in Windows programming, as we saw in Chapters 15, 16, and 17. You do not need to know that the underlying implementation of events is based on delegates; that is the beauty of abstraction.

In VB.NET, you can encapsulate a reference to a method inside a delegate object. A function pointer can reference only a shared function, but a delegate can refer to either a shared method or an instance method. When a delegate refers to an instance method, it stores both an object instance and an entry point to the instance method. The instance method can then be called through this object instance. When a delegate object refers to a shared method, it stores just the entry point of this shared method.

You can then pass this delegate object to other code, which can then call your method. The code that calls your delegate method does not have to know at compile time which method is being called.

Delegate Example

Code Example

As an example of the use of delegates, consider the problem of writing a general-purpose sort procedure. We would like to have different ways of comparing objects, which affect their sort order. For instance, we can have a comparer that leads to sorting in ascending order, and another comparer for sorting in descending order. This is the same idea as the **IComparable** interface. Delegates provide an alternate solution. Our example program is **DelegateExample**.

VB.NET provides the keyword **Delegate** that can be used for defining a delegate type, which provides a signature for a function. We begin by declaring the delegate **SortComparison**:

```
' DelegateExample.vb

Module DelegateExampleModule

    ' Definition of delegate type
    Delegate Function SortComparison(ByVal n1 As Integer, _
     ByVal n2 As Integer) As Boolean


    . . .
```

Next, we provide two procedures of the delegate type:

```
' Functions of the delegate type
Public Function AscendingSorter(ByVal n1 As Integer, _
 ByVal n2 As Integer) As Boolean
    If n1 > n2 Then Return True
    Return False
End Function

Public Function DescendingSorter(ByVal n1 As Integer, _
 ByVal n2 As Integer) As Boolean
    If n2 > n1 Then Return True
    Return False
End Function


    . . .
```

Now we can provide the general-purpose procedure, which takes a delegate as a parameter. Depending on which delegate instance we pass, we get different behavior:

```
' Comparer is the delegate object of type SortComparison
Public Sub Sort(ByRef list() As Integer, _
  ByVal comparer As SortComparison)
    Dim i, j, tmp As Integer
    For i = 0 To UBound(list) - 1
       For j = i + 1 To UBound(list)
          If comparer(list(i), list(j)) Then
             tmp = list(i)
             list(i) = list(j)
             list(j) = tmp
          End If
       Next j
    Next i
End Sub
```

. . .

Finally, we provide the main procedure, which tests our general purpose **Sort** procedure by performing a sort with two different instances of our delegate, namely **AscendingSorter** and **DescendingSorter**. To pass a delegate object to a procedure taking a delegate parameter, use the VB.NET **AddressOf** operator:

```
Sub Main()
    Dim nums() As Integer = {4, 7, 6, 1, 8, 0, 3}

    Sort(nums, AddressOf AscendingSorter)
    ShowList(nums)

    Sort(nums, AddressOf DescendingSorter)
    ShowList(nums)
End Sub

Public Sub ShowList(ByVal nums As Integer())
    Dim i As Integer
    For i = 0 To nums.GetUpperBound(0)
       Console.Write("{0}  ", nums(i))
    Next
    Console.WriteLine()
End Sub

End Module
```

Here is the output from the program:

```
0  1  3  4  6  7  8
8  7  6  4  3  1  0
```

We will see several additional examples of delegates in Chapter 22.

Summary

In this chapter, we examined the ubiquitous role of interfaces in the .NET Framework. Many of the standard classes implement specific interfaces, and we can call into the methods of these interfaces to obtain useful services. Arrays are an example of collections, which support a well-defined set of interfaces that provide useful functionality. Collections support generic interfaces such as **IList** and **ICloneable**. The **ICloneable** interface is used to implement a deep copy of a class. To work with collections effectively, you need to override certain methods of the **Object** base class, such as **Equals**. We also looked at comparison of objects, which is implemented through the **IComparable** interface.

Interfaces facilitate writing code in such a way that your program is called back by some other code. VB.NET provides the special *delegate* type that can be used to encapsulate a reference to "callback" functions.

In Chapter 19, we will look at other useful collection classes, such as **ArrayList**, **Hashtable**, and others.

NET Collections

The .NET Framework class library provides an extensive set of classes for working with collections of objects. These classes are in the System.Collections namespace and implement a number of different kinds of collections, including lists, queues, stacks, arrays, and hash tables. The collections contain Object instances. Because all types ultimately derive from Object, any built-in or user-defined type may be stored in a collection.

In Chapter 18, we looked at arrays, which are a particular kind of collection. In this chapter, we study several other kinds of collections. We examine the interfaces implemented by the collection classes and see how to use collections in programs. We provide examples of array lists, hash tables, queues, stacks, and sorted lists. When a collection contains elements of a user-defined class, we must be sure to provide overrides for certain methods of the Object root class, such as Equals. Some classes, such as Hashtable and SortedList, contain key/value pairs. If the key belongs to a user-defined class, we must provide an override of GetHashCode.

Collections are widely used throughout the .NET Framework, so it is important to have a good understanding of them. In particular, as we will see in Chapter 20, the .NET database classes contain numerous collections.

ArrayList

We begin our survey of .NET collections with the **ArrayList** class. This class is easy to use. An array list, as the name suggests, is a list of items stored like an array. An array list can be dynamically sized and grows as necessary to accommodate new elements being added.

As mentioned, collection classes are made up of instances of type **Object**. We illustrate creating and manipulating a collection of **String**. We could also easily create a collection of any other built-in or user-defined type. If our type is a value type, such as **Integer**, the instance is boxed before being stored in the collection. When the object is extracted from the collection, it is unboxed back to **Integer**.

Code Example

Our example program is **StringList**. It initializes a list of strings and then lets the user display the list, add strings, and remove strings. A simple "help" method displays the commands that are available:

```
The following commands are available:
  show      -- show strings in list
  array     -- show strings in array format
  add       -- add a string to list
  remove    -- remove a string
  removeat  -- remove string at index
  count     -- show count and capacity
  quit      -- exit the program
```

This program is very similar to the **StringList** example from Chapter 18, but the code is simpler.

```
' StringList.vb

Imports System
Imports System.Collections

Module StringList
   Private arr As ArrayList

   Sub Main()
      arr = New ArrayList(4)
      ShowCounts()
      AddString("Bob")
      AddString("Dana")
      AddString("Richard")
      ShowList()
      ShowCounts()
      CommandLoop()
   End Sub

   Private Sub CommandLoop()
```

```vbnet
        Dim iw As New InputWrapper()
        Dim cmd As String
        Dim buf As String
        Dim index As Integer
        Console.WriteLine("Enter command, quit to exit")
        cmd = iw.getString("> ")
        While Not cmd.Equals("quit")
            Try
                If cmd.Equals("show") Then
                    ShowList()
                ElseIf cmd.Equals("array") Then
                    DumpArray()
                ElseIf cmd.Equals("add") Then
                    buf = iw.getString("string: ")
                    AddString(buf)
                ElseIf cmd.Equals("remove") Then
                    buf = iw.getString("string: ")
                    RemoveString(buf)
                ElseIf cmd.Equals("removeat") Then
                    index = iw.getInt("index: ")
                    RemoveAt(index)
                ElseIf cmd.Equals("count") Then
                    ShowCounts()
                Else
                    Help()
                End If
            Catch e As Exception
                Console.WriteLine(e.Message)
                If Not e.InnerException Is Nothing Then
                    Console.WriteLine(e.InnerException.Message)
                End If
            End Try
            cmd = iw.getString("> ")
        End While
End Sub

Private Sub Help()
    ...
End Sub

Private Sub ShowCounts()
    Console.WriteLine("Capacity = {0}", arr.Capacity)
    Console.WriteLine("Count = {0}", arr.Count)
End Sub

Private Sub ShowList()
    Dim strg As String
    For Each strg In arr
        Console.WriteLine(strg)
    Next
```

```
    End Sub

    Private Sub DumpArray()
        Dim i As Integer
        For i = 0 To arr.Count - 1
            Console.WriteLine("arr({0}) = {1}", i, arr(i))
        Next
    End Sub

    Private Sub AddString(ByVal strg As String)
        If arr.Contains(strg) Then
            Throw New Exception("List contains " & strg)
        End If
        arr.Add(strg)
    End Sub

    Private Sub RemoveAt(ByVal index As Integer)
        arr.RemoveAt(index)
    End Sub

    Private Sub RemoveString(ByVal strg As String)
        If Not arr.Contains(strg) Then
            Throw New Exception(strg & " not on list")
        End If
        arr.Remove(strg)
    End Sub

End Module
```

Here is a sample run of the program:

```
Capacity = 4
Count = 0
Bob
Dana
Richard
Capacity = 4
Count = 3
Enter command, quit to exit
> add
string: Peter
> add
string: Michael
> add
string: Bob
list contains Bob
> count
Capacity = 8
Count = 5
> array
arr(0) = Bob
```

```
arr(1) = Dana
arr(2) = Richard
arr(3) = Peter
arr(4) = Michael
> remove
string: Richard
> array
arr(0) = Bob
arr(1) = Dana
arr(2) = Peter
arr(3) = Michael
> removeat
index: 2
> array
arr(0) = Bob
arr(1) = Dana
arr(2) = Michael
> removeat
index: Peter
Input string was not in a correct format.
> remove
string: Peter
Peter not on list
> removeat
index: 3
Index was out of range.  Must be non-negative and less than
the size of the collection. Parameter name: index
```

Count and Capacity

An array list has properties **Count** and **Capacity**. **Count** is the current number of elements in the list, and **Capacity** is the number of available "slots." If you add a new element when the capacity has been reached, the **Capacity** is automatically increased. The default starting capacity is 16, but it can be adjusted by passing a starting size to the constructor. In our example, we initialized the **Capacity** to be 4.

```
Module StringList
   Private arr As New ArrayList(4)

   . . .
```

The **Capacity** doubles when necessary. The "count" command in the sample program displays the current values of **Count** and **Capacity**, and you can observe how these change by adding new elements.

For Each Loop

The **System.Collections.ArrayList** class implements the **IEnumerable** interface, which we discuss later in the chapter, which means that you can use a **For Each** loop to iterate through the collection.

```
Private Sub ShowList()
   Dim strg As String
   For Each strg In arr
      Console.WriteLine(strg)
   Next
End Sub
```

Array Notation and Item Property

ArrayList implements the **IList** interface, which has the default property **Item**. The **Item** property takes an **Integer** parameter, so you can use array notation to access elements of an array list. The "array" command demonstrates accessing the elements of the list using an index. The element at index 0 is displayed by explicitly using the **Item** property, and the remaining elements are displayed without explicit use of **Item**, relying on the property being default. (We discuss the **IList** interface shortly.)

```
Private Sub DumpArray()
   Dim i As Integer
   Console.WriteLine("arr({0}) = {1}", i, arr.Item(i))
   For i = 1 To arr.Count - 1
      Console.WriteLine("arr({0}) = {1}", i, arr(i))
   Next
End Sub
```

Default Properties in VB.NET

Classic Visual Basic made extensive use of default properties. For example, the Text property of a text box control was the default, so you assigned a String value by using just the name of the control, for example, txtName = "Bob." In VB.NET, simple properties (ones having no parameters) cannot be made default, so this common operation would be written txt-Name.Text = "Bob."

Properties cannot be default in VB.NET because of the need for strict type checking. You are not allowed to assign a String when you want to assign an object. Thus, when you use just txtName on the left side of an assignment, you are required to have another object of the same type on the right side, or you must have one that can be converted. A String cannot be converted into a text box control, so the assignment txtName = "Bob" is not allowed.

Default properties are very useful in one situation—when the default property takes parameters, as is the case with the ArrayList's Item property. Then the problem of ambiguity does not arise, and the benefit of more concise notation comes without cost. A default property is declared using the keyword Default.

Adding to the List

The **Add** method allows you to append an item to an array list. If you want to make sure that you do not add a duplicate item, you can use the **Contains** method to check whether the proposed new item is already contained in the list.

```
Private Sub AddString(ByVal strg As String)
    If arr.Contains(strg) Then
        Throw New Exception("List contains " & strg)
    End If
    arr.Add(strg)
End Sub
```

Remove Method

The **Remove** method allows you to remove an item from an array list. Again, you can use the **Contains** method to check whether the item to be deleted is on the list.

```
Private Sub RemoveString(ByVal strg As String)
    If Not arr.Contains(strg) Then
        Throw New Exception(strg & " not on list")
    End If
    arr.Remove(strg)
End Sub
```

RemoveAt Method

The **RemoveAt** method allows you to remove an item at a specified integer index. If the item is not found, an exception of type **ArgumentOutOfRange-Exception** will be thrown. (In our program, we just let the normal test program exception handling pick up the exception.)

```
Private Sub RemoveAt(ByVal index As Integer)
    arr.RemoveAt(index)
End Sub
```

Collection Interfaces

The classes **ArrayList**, **Array**, and many other collection classes implement a set of four fundamental interfaces, as shown in this snippet of code:

```
Public Class ArrayList
    Implements IList, ICollection, IEnumerable, ICloneable
```

The first three interfaces form a simple interface hierarchy, as shown in Figure 19–1. As you go down the hierarchy, additional methods are added, until **IList** specifies a fully featured list.

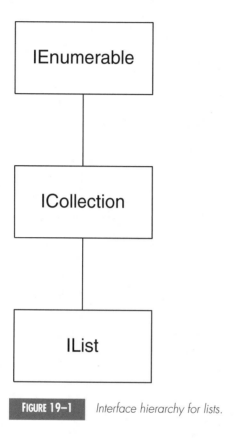

Interface hierarchy for lists.

The fourth interface, **ICloneable**, is independent and is used to support deep copying, which is a topic we studied in Chapter 18.

Interface Documentation

Interfaces are documented in the online .NET Framework SDK Documentation. Figure 19–2 illustrates the documentation of the **IEnumerable** interface. The right pane has a language filter button 🔽, which we have used to show only VB.NET versions. If you are using the interface in one of the .NET Framework classes that implement the interface, you do not need to implement any of the methods yourself. If you are creating your own class that supports an interface, you must provide implementations of all the methods of the interface. In either case, the documentation describes the methods for you.

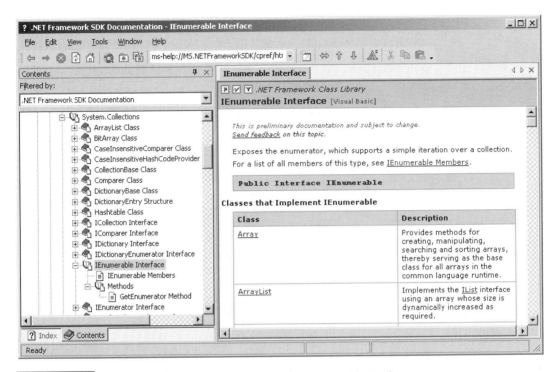

.NET Framework SDK documentation for IEnumerable interface.

IEnumerable and IEnumerator

The basic interface that must be supported by collection classes is **IEnumerable**, which has a single method, **GetEnumerator**.

```
Interface IEnumerable
    Function GetEnumerator() As IEnumerator
End Interface
```

GetEnumerator returns an interface reference to **IEnumerator**, which is the interface used for iterating through a collection. This interface has the property **Current** and the methods **MoveNext** and **Reset**.

```
Public Interface IEnumerator
    ReadOnly Property Current As Object
    Function MoveNext() As Boolean
    Sub Reset()
End Interface
```

The enumerator is initially positioned *before* the first element in the collection, and it must be advanced before it is used. The program **AccountList**, which we discuss in detail later, illustrates using an enumerator to iterate through a list:

```
Private Sub EnumList(ByVal list As ArrayList)
   Dim iter As IEnumerator = list.GetEnumerator()
   Dim more As Boolean = iter.MoveNext()
   Dim acc As Account

   While more
      acc = CType(iter.Current, Account)
      Console.WriteLine(acc.Info)
      more = iter.MoveNext()
   End While
End Sub
```

This pattern of using an enumerator to iterate through a list is so common that VB.NET provides a special kind of loop, **For Each**, that can be used for iterating through the elements of *any* collection. Here is the comparable code using **For Each**:

```
Private Sub ShowList(ByVal list As ArrayList)
   Dim acc As Account
   For Each acc In list
      Console.WriteLine(acc.Info)
   Next
End Sub
```

ICollection

The **ICollection** interface is derived from **IEnumerable** and adds a **Count** property and a **CopyTo** method, as well as **IsSynchronized** and **SyncRoot** properties.

```
Public Interface ICollection
   Inherits IEnumerable

   ReadOnly Property Count As Integer
   ReadOnly Property IsSynchronized As Boolean
   ReadOnly Property SyncRoot As Object
   Sub CopyTo(ByVal array As Array, ByVal index As Integer)
End Interface
```

The synchronization properties **IsSynchronized** and **SyncRoot** can help you deal with thread safety issues. "Is it thread-safe?" is a question frequently asked about library code. The short answer to this question for the .NET Framework class library is "No." This does not mean that the designers of the Framework did not think about thread safety issues. On the contrary, there are many mechanisms to help you write thread-safe code when you need to. However, collections are not automatically thread-safe because your code should not have to pay the performance penalty to enforce synchronization when it is not running in a multithreading scenario. If you do need thread safety, you may use the thread-safety properties as required. We introduce multithreading in Chapter 22.

ILIST

The **IList** interface is derived from **ICollection** and provides methods for adding an item to a list, removing an item, and so on. As we discussed, the default **Item** property lets you use array notation to access elements of the list:

```
Public Interface IList
    Inherits ICollection, IEnumerable

    ReadOnly Property IsFixedSize As Boolean
    ReadOnly Property IsReadOnly As Boolean
    Default Property Item(ByVal index As Integer) As Object
    Function Add(ByVal value As Object) As Integer
    Sub Clear()
    Function Contains(ByVal value As Object) As Boolean
    Function IndexOf(ByVal value As Object) As Integer
    Sub Insert(ByVal index As Integer, ByVal value As Object)
    Sub Remove(ByVal value As Object)
    Sub RemoveAt(ByVal index As Integer)
End Interface
```

Our sample code illustrates using the **Item** property and the **Add**, **Contains**, **Remove**, and **RemoveAt** methods.

A Collection of User-Defined Objects

Now, let's look at an example of a collection of user-defined objects. The mechanics of calling the various collection properties and methods is straightforward and is essentially identical to the usage for collections of built-in types. What's different is that in your class, you must override at least the **Equals** method to obtain proper behavior in your collection. For built-in types, you did not have to worry about this issue, because **Equals** is provided by the class library for you. As we see later in the chapter when we discuss hash tables, you may also have to override the **GetHashCode** method. And you usually should override the **ToString** method. In Chapter 18, we looked at an example of what goes wrong when we don't override **Equals** and **ToString**. In this chapter, we do the right thing from the beginning.

Our example program is **AccountList**, which is similar to the **Accoun-tArray** program from Chapter 18. However, it uses an array list instead of an array. As with the **StringList** example, using the array list simplifies our code. The class is somewhat minimalist, providing an override of only the **Equals** method of **Object**. Nonetheless, the class will do what we expect of it:

```
' Account.vb

Imports System

Public Class Account
   Private m_id As Integer
   Private m_balance As Decimal
   Private m_owner As String

   Public Sub New(ByVal balance As Decimal, ByVal owner _
   As String, ByVal id As Integer)
      m_balance = balance
      m_owner = owner
      m_id = id
   End Sub

   Public ReadOnly Property Info() As String
      Get
         Return m_id.ToString().PadRight(4) & _
            m_owner.PadRight(12) & _
            String.Format("{0:C}", m_balance)
      End Get
   End Property

   Public Overloads Overrides Function Equals( _
   ByVal obj As Object) As Boolean
      Dim acc As Account
      acc = CType(obj, Account)
      Return (acc.m_id = m_id)
   End Function

End Class
```

As in Chapter 18, our test for equality involves just the account ID. For example, two people with the same name could have an account at the same bank, but their account IDs should be different. The test program **Accoun-tList.vb** contains code to initialize an array list of **Account** objects, show the initial accounts, and then perform a command loop. A simple **Help** method gives a brief summary of the available commands:

```
The following commands are available:
   show     -- show accounts in list
   enum     -- enumerate accounts in list
```

```
add     -- add an account to list
remove  -- remove an account from list
quit    -- exit the program
```

The code for **AccountList** follows:

```vb
' AccountList.vb

Imports System
Imports System.Collections

Module AccountList
    Private accounts As ArrayList

    Sub Main()
        accounts = New ArrayList()
        AddAccount(100, "Bob", 1)
        AddAccount(200, "Mary", 2)
        AddAccount(300, "Charlie", 3)
        ShowList(accounts)
        CommandLoop()
    End Sub

    Private Sub CommandLoop()
        Dim iw As New InputWrapper()
        Dim cmd As String
        Dim buf As String
        Dim index As Integer
        Console.WriteLine("Enter command, quit to exit")
        cmd = iw.getString("> ")
        While Not cmd.Equals("quit")
            Try
                If cmd.Equals("show") Then
                    ShowList(accounts)
                ElseIf cmd.Equals("enum") Then
                    EnumList(accounts)
                ElseIf cmd.Equals("add") Then
                    Dim id As Integer = iw.getInt("id: ")
                    Dim owner As String = iw.getString("owner: ")
                    Dim bal As Decimal = _
                        iw.getDecimal("balance: ")
                    AddAccount(bal, owner, id)
                ElseIf cmd.Equals("remove") Then
                    Dim id As Integer = iw.getInt("id: ")
                    RemoveAccount(id)
                Else
                    Help()
                End If
            Catch e As Exception
                Console.WriteLine(e.Message)
```

```vb
            If Not e.InnerException Is Nothing Then
                Console.WriteLine(e.InnerException.Message)
            End If
        End Try
        cmd = iw.getString("> ")
    End While
End Sub

Private Sub Help()
    ...
End Sub

Private Sub ShowList(ByVal list As ArrayList)
    Dim acc As Account
    For Each acc In list
        Console.WriteLine(acc.Info)
    Next
End Sub

Private Sub EnumList(ByVal list As ArrayList)
    Dim iter As IEnumerator = list.GetEnumerator()
    Dim more As Boolean = iter.MoveNext()
    Dim acc As Account

    While more
        acc = CType(iter.Current, Account)
        Console.WriteLine(acc.Info)
        more = iter.MoveNext()
    End While
End Sub

Private Sub AddAccount(ByVal bal As Decimal, _
 ByVal owner As String, ByVal id As Integer)
    Dim acc As New Account(bal, owner, id)
    If accounts.Contains(acc) Then
        Throw New Exception( _
          "List contains account with id " & id)
    End If
    accounts.Add(acc)
End Sub

Private Sub RemoveAccount(ByVal id As Integer)
    Dim acc As New Account(0, "", id)
    'accounts.Remove(acc)
    Dim index As Integer = accounts.IndexOf(acc)
    If index = -1 Then
        Throw New Exception("Account " & id & " not found")
    End If
    accounts.RemoveAt(index)
```

```
    End Sub

End Module
```

To remove an element from an array list, you may construct an element that "equals" to the element to be removed. You can then just call the **Remove** method to remove it (this is shown in a comment in **RemoveAccount**). The drawback to this simple approach is that you get no notification as to whether the element was found in the list. You could test whether the element is on the list by first calling the **Contains** method, but then you would be searching the list twice. A more efficient procedure, as shown in the sample code, is to call the **IndexOf** method, which returns –1 if the element is not found. If it is found, you may then remove it without a search by calling **RemoveAt.**

Here is a sample run illustrating that "add" and "remove" function correctly:

```
1    Bob          $100.00
2    Mary         $200.00
3    Charlie      $300.00
Enter command, quit to exit
> add
id: 1
owner: Bobby
balance: 5
list contains account with id 1
> add
id: 7
owner: Bobby
balance: 5
> enum
1    Bob          $100.00
2    Mary         $200.00
3    Charlie      $300.00
7    Bobby        $5.00
> remove
id: 1
> show
2    Mary         $200.00
3    Charlie      $300.00
7    Bobby        $5.00
> remove
id: 1
Account 1 not found
```

Hashtable

The **ArrayList** class is versatile and easy to use, but it can be inefficient for long lists because a linear search must be made through the list for operations such as **Contains** and **Remove**. More sophisticated data structures can be used to provide better performance. A *dictionary* can provide fast access to a desired element based on a *key*. The key may be either a built-in type or a user-defined type. The .NET Framework specifies the behavior of a dictionary through the interface **IDictionary**. Several classes, such as **Hashtable** and **SortedList**, are provided that implement this interface.

IDictionary Interface

The **IDictionary** interface represents a collection of associated keys and values. By using the key, you can obtain fast access to the corresponding value. Like **IList**, it inherits from **ICollection** and **IEnumerable**:

```
Public Interface IList
    Inherits ICollection, IEnumerable

    ReadOnly Property IsFixedSize As Boolean
    ReadOnly Property IsReadOnly As Boolean
    Default Property Item(ByVal key As Object) As Object
    ReadOnly Property Keys As ICollection
    ReadOnly Property Values As ICollection
    Sub Add(ByVal key As Object, ByVal value As Object)
    Sub Clear()
    Function GetEnumerator() As IDictionaryEnumerator
    Sub Remove(ByVal key As Object)
End Interface
```

There are several noteworthy differences from **IList**. Instead of an integer index, there is a key, which may be of any type. There are no **Contains**, **IndexOf**, **Insert**, or **RemoveAt** methods. The **Item** property takes an **Object** parameter rather than an **Integer** parameter. The **Add** method requires a key as well as the value that is to be inserted into the collection. A special kind of enumerator, **IDictionaryEnumerator**, is returned by **GetEnumerator**. The **Remove** method expects a key instead of a value. And finally, there are two collection properties, **Keys** and **Values**.

The best way to understand the **IDictionary** interface is to study classes that implement the interface. We look first at **Hashtable** and then at **SortedList**.

Hashtable Class

One of the most efficient known data structures for fast lookup is a hash table. Any key can be used for lookup, but rather than use the original key, which may be a long string or even some user-defined type, a "hash" is made of the key, producing an integer. A hash function provides the mapping from the key type to an integer type. It is quite possible for two different keys to hash to the same integer, but a desirable hash function minimizes this occurrence. In the event that multiple keys map to the same integer, the corresponding values are said to reside in the same "bucket." When a search is made for a value in the bucket, a linear search must be made, but this search should be much faster than a search of the original list, because the bucket is small.

The .NET Framework **Hashtable** class, part of the **System.Collections** namespace, provides an implementation of a hash table and supports the **IDictionary** interface.

We illustrate the use of the **Hashtable** class with three sample programs. The first program uses built-in types for both the key and the value. The second program uses a user-defined type for the key. The third program employs user-defined types for both the key and the value.

BUILT-IN KEY AND VALUE

Code Example

Our first example illustrates using a hash table for a lookup of strings by using an integer key. Since both **Integer** and **String** are built-in types, the code is very straightforward. Our sample program is **StringHash\Version 1**. As usual, a "help" command gives a short list of the available commands.

```
The following commands are available:
  show      -- show strings in list
  add       -- add a string to list
  remove    -- remove a string
  find      -- find a string
  quit      -- exit the program
```

A **Hashtable** object is instantiated and initialized with some sample data, and a command loop is entered:

```
' StringHash.vb

Imports System
Imports System.Collections

Module StringHash
    Private hash As New Hashtable()

    Sub Main()
        AddString(1, "Bob")
```

```
      AddString(2, "Dana")
      AddString(3, "Richard")
      AddString(4, "Peter")
      ShowList()
      CommandLoop()
   End Sub
   ...
```

The **CommandLoop** and **Help** procedures provide the basic user interface:

```
Private Sub CommandLoop()
   Dim iw As New InputWrapper()
   Dim cmd As String
   Dim buf As String
   Dim key As Integer
   Console.WriteLine("Enter command, quit to exit")
   cmd = iw.getString("> ")

   While Not cmd.Equals("quit")
      Try
         If cmd.Equals("show") Then
            ShowList()
         ElseIf cmd.Equals("add") Then
            buf = iw.getString("string: ")
            key = iw.getInt("key: ")
            AddString(key, buf)
         ElseIf cmd.Equals("remove") Then
            key = iw.getInt("key: ")
            RemoveString(key)
         ElseIf cmd.Equals("find") Then
            key = iw.getInt("key: ")
            buf = FindString(key)
            If buf Is Nothing Then
               Console.WriteLine("Key {0} not found", _
                  key)
            Else
               Console.WriteLine(buf)
            End If
         Else
            Help()
         End If
      Catch e As Exception
         Console.WriteLine(e.Message)
         If Not e.InnerException Is Nothing Then
            Console.WriteLine(e.InnerException.Message)
         End If
      End Try
      cmd = iw.getString("> ")
   End While
```

```
   End Sub

   Private Sub Help()
      ...
   End Sub
```

The "add" command is implemented by the **AddString** procedure. It adds a string with a specified key to the hash table. A check is made on whether the key is already in the table:

```
Private Sub AddString(ByVal key As Integer, _
  ByVal strg As String)
     If hash.Contains(key) Then
        Throw New Exception( _
           "Hashtable contains key " & key)
     End If
     hash.Add(key, strg)
End Sub
```

The "show" command is implemented by the **ShowList** procedure. It iterates through the hash table and displays the keys and values. This code is slightly more complex than for an array list, because we must use the special enumerator **IDictionaryEnumerator**:

```
Private Sub ShowList()
     Dim iter As IDictionaryEnumerator = _
        hash.GetEnumerator()
     Dim more As Boolean = iter.MoveNext()
     Dim strg As String
     Dim key As Integer

     While more
        key = CType(iter.Key, Integer)
        strg = CType(iter.Value, String)
        Console.WriteLine("{0,4}    {1}", key, strg)
        more = iter.MoveNext()
     End While
End Sub
```

The "remove" command is implemented by the **RemoveString** procedure. We can use a call to **Contains** to check whether the key is present in the list and then call **Remove**, without significant performance loss, because the hash table lookup is so fast. Here's the code for this:

```
Private Sub RemoveString(ByVal key As Integer)
     If Not hash.Contains(key) Then
        Throw New Exception("Key " & key & " not found")
     End If
     hash.Remove(key)
End Sub
```

Finally, the "find" command is implemented by using the **Item** property to lookup a value based on the key:

```
Private Function FindString(ByVal key As Integer) _
  As String
    Return CType(hash.Item(key), String)
End Function
```

```
End Module
```

A USER-DEFINED KEY

New considerations arise when the key belongs to some user-defined class. All of the built-in data types are provided with an implementation of the **GetHashCode** method of the **Object** base type. When you implement your own class to be used for keys, you should implement **GetHashCode**, to provide an appropriate hash function. There is an implementation provided in the root **Object** class, but it is unlikely to be appropriate.

Code Example

The program **StringHash\Version 2** illustrates a hash table lookup of strings, where the key now belongs to the user-defined type **AccountId**. The **AccountId** class represents IDs that might be used for bank accounts. The ID is a string consisting of a single character, followed by an integer. The character can be used to encode the account type, such as "C" for checking and "S" for savings. A constructor creates an **AccountId** from a string representation, and **ToString** converts the other way. Our code for **GetHashCode** relies on the implementation provided by the .NET Framework for the **String** class. Converting first to a **String** and then calling **GetHashCode** is not the fastest solution, but it avoids having to come up with a good hashing function ourselves.

```
' AccountId.vb

Imports System

Public Class AccountId
   Public m_code As Char
   Public m_id As Integer

   Public Sub New(ByVal sid As String)
      m_code = sid.Chars(0)
      m_id = Convert.ToInt32(sid.Substring(1))
   End Sub

   Public Overrides Function ToString() As String
      Return m_code & m_id.ToString()
   End Function

   Public Overloads Overrides Function Equals( _
     ByVal obj As Object) As Boolean
```

```
      Dim aid As AccountId
      aid = CType(obj, AccountId)
      Return (aid.m_code = m_code) And (aid.m_id = m_id)
   End Function

   Public Overrides Function GetHashCode() As Integer
      Return Me.ToString().GetHashCode()
   End Function

End Class
```

The Version 2 main program **StringHash.vb** is very similar to Version 1, but the **AccountId** class is used for a key in place of the **String** class. A complete listing of the code can be found online.

```
' StringHash.vb

Imports System
Imports System.Collections

Module StringHash
   Private hash As New Hashtable()

   Sub Main()
      ShowList()
      AddString("S1", "Bob")
      AddString("C2", "Dana")
      AddString("D3", "Richard")
      AddString("C4", "Peter")
      ShowList()
      CommandLoop()
   End Sub

   Private Sub CommandLoop()
      ...
   End Sub

   Private Sub Help()
      ...
   End Sub

   Private Sub ShowList()
      Dim iter As IDictionaryEnumerator = _
        hash.GetEnumerator()
      Dim more As Boolean = iter.MoveNext()
      Dim strg As String
      Dim key As AccountId

      While more
         key = CType(iter.Key, AccountId)
```

```
         strg = CType(iter.Value, String)
         Console.WriteLine("{0,4}   {1}", key, strg)
         more = iter.MoveNext()
      End While
   End Sub

   Private Sub AddString(ByVal skey As String, _
    ByVal strg As String)
      Dim key As New AccountId(skey)
      If hash.Contains(key) Then
         Throw New Exception( _
            "Hashtable contains key " & skey)
      End If
      hash.Add(key, strg)
   End Sub

   Private Sub RemoveString(ByVal skey As String)
      Dim key As New AccountId(skey)
      If Not hash.Contains(key) Then
         Throw New Exception("Key " & skey & " not found")
      End If
      hash.Remove(key)
   End Sub

   Private Function FindString(ByVal skey As String) _
    As String
      Dim key As New AccountId(skey)
      Return CType(hash.Item(key), String)
   End Function

End Module
```

The following is a sample run in which a new key/value pair is added. Notice that the first attempt to add a new key/value pair fails, because the key ("bar") was not in the proper format. An exception was thrown by the call to **Convert.ToInt32** in the **AccountId** constructor. Here's the sample output:

```
   S1    Bob
   D3    Richard
   C2    Dana
   C4    Peter
Enter command, quit to exit
> add
string: foo
key: bar
Input string was not in a correct format.
> add
string: foo
key: S4
> show
```

```
S1      Bob
D3      Richard
C2      Dana
S4      foo
C4      Peter
```

USER-DEFINED KEY AND VALUE

The most general situation for using a hash table is a user-defined key and a user-defined value, illustrated by the program **AccountHash**. The **Account** class now uses an **AccountId** object as the ID of an account:

```
' Account.vb

Imports System

Public Class Account
    Private m_id As AccountId
    Private m_balance As Decimal
    Private m_owner As String

    Public Sub New(ByVal balance As Decimal, _
     ByVal owner As String, ByVal sid As String)
        m_balance = balance
        m_owner = owner
        m_id = New AccountId(sid)
    End Sub

    Public ReadOnly Property Info() As String
        Get
            Return m_id.ToString().PadRight(10) _
                & _m_owner.PadRight(12) _
                & String.Format("{0,-4:C}", m_balance) _
                & m_id.GetHashCode().ToString().PadLeft(14)
        End Get
    End Property

    Public ReadOnly Property Id() As AccountId
        Get
            Return m_id
        End Get
    End Property

    Public Overloads Overrides Function Equals( _
     ByVal obj As Object) As Boolean
        Dim acc As Account
        acc = CType(obj, Account)
        Return acc.m_id.Equals(m_id)
    End Function

End Class
```

The main program instantiates a hash table, sets up and displays some initial accounts, and goes into a command loop:

```vb
' AccountHash.vb

Imports System
Imports System.Collections

Module AccountHash
    Private hash As New Hashtable()

    Sub Main()
        ShowList()
        AddAccount(100, "Bob", "S1")
        AddAccount(200, "Dana", "C2")
        AddAccount(300, "Richard", "D3")
        AddAccount(400, "Peter", "C4")
        ShowList()
        CommandLoop()
    End Sub
    ...

    Private Sub ShowList()
        Dim iter As IDictionaryEnumerator = _
            hash.GetEnumerator()
        Dim more As Boolean = iter.MoveNext()
        Dim acc As Account
        Dim key As AccountId

        While more
            key = CType(iter.Key, AccountId)
            acc = CType(iter.Value, Account)
            Console.WriteLine("{0}", acc.Info)
            more = iter.MoveNext()
        End While
    End Sub

    Private Sub AddAccount(ByVal bal As Decimal, _
      ByVal owner As String, ByVal skey As String)
        Dim key As New AccountId(skey)
        If hash.Contains(key) Then
            Throw New Exception( _
                "Hashtable contains key " & skey)
        End If
        Dim acc As New Account(bal, owner, skey)
        hash.Add(key, acc)
    End Sub

    Private Sub RemoveAccount(ByVal skey As String)
        Dim key As New AccountId(skey)
```

```
        If Not hash.Contains(key) Then
            Throw New Exception("Key " & skey & " not found")
        End If
        hash.Remove(key)
    End Sub

    Private Function FindAccount(ByVal skey As String) _
      As Account
        Dim key As New AccountId(skey)
        Return CType(hash.Item(key), Account)
    End Function

End Module
```

Here is a sample run of the program. Notice that we print out the hash codes:

```
S1        Bob          $100.00       5862535
D3        Richard      $300.00       5861938
C2        Dana         $200.00       5862036
C4        Peter        $400.00       5862034
Enter command, quit to exit
> remove
key: S1
> remove
key: S1
key S1 not found
> show
D3        Richard      $300.00       5861938
C2        Dana         $200.00       5862036
C4        Peter        $400.00       5862034
> find
key: C2
C2        Dana         $200.00       5862036
> add
balance: 500
owner: Michael
key: S5
> show
S5        Michael      $500.00       5862531
D3        Richard      $300.00       5861938
C2        Dana         $200.00       5862036
C4        Peter        $400.00       5862034
```

Performance of ArrayList and Hashtable

We can do a simple performance comparison of **ArrayList** versus **Hashtable** by using the shared **TickCount** property of the **Environment** class, which returns the number of milliseconds since the system was started. By recording the tick count at the start of an operation and again at the end of the operation, you can obtain a measurement of how many milliseconds were required to perform the operation.

The programs **BankList** and **BankHash** generate simulated account data that can be used for making performance comparisons with different sized lists. For short lists, there is no measurable differences, but for long lists, the hash table is much faster, as would be anticipated.

Generating Random Data

Both programs use the module **NameGen.vb** to generate simulated data:

```
' NameGen.vb
' Generate a random name

Imports System

Module NameGen
   Private rangen As New Random()
   Private first() As String = {"Amy", "Bob", "Carol", _
      "Dana", "Ed", "Fran", "Gwen", "Holly", "Ike", "Joe", _
      "Kim", "Mary", "Nan", "Orin", "Peter", "Ron", "Sam", _
      "Tom", "Una", "Vic"}
   Private last() As String = {"Adams", "Burns", "Chad", _
      "Davis", "Entin", "Fuchs", "Gates", "Hunt", "Ives", _
      "Jones", "Kelly", "Moore", "Niles", "Oberg", "Post", _
      "Reese", "Soong", "Twist", "Vuona", "Wyatt", _
      "Young", "Zhu"}

   Public Function GetRandomName() As String
      Dim ifirst As Integer = rangen.Next(first.Length)
      Dim ilast As Integer = rangen.Next(last.Length)
      Return first(ifirst) & " " & last(ilast)
   End Function

   Public Function GetRandomBalance() As Decimal
      Return 100 * (rangen.Next(9) + 1)
   End Function
```

```
Public Function GetRandomCode() As Char
    Dim codes() As Char = {"C"c, "S"c}
    Return codes(rangen.Next(2))
End Function

End Module
```

Performance of ArrayList

Let's first look at the **BankList** project. The file **Bank.vb** implements a class encapsulating an **ArrayList** of **Account** objects. The integer ID part of an **AccountId** is generated sequentially, and "C" or "S" prefixes are assigned randomly. Methods are provided to add an account, show the list of accounts, remove an account, find an account, and clear the accounts. A **CreateAccounts** method creates a specified number of accounts, according to an integer input parameter.

```
' Bank.vb

Imports System
Imports System.Collections

Public Class Bank
    Private Shared m_nextID As Integer = 1
    Private accounts As New ArrayList()

    Public Function AddAccount(ByVal bal As Decimal, _
     ByVal owner As String, ByVal code As Char) As String
        Dim skey As String = code & m_nextID.ToString()
        m_nextID += 1
        Dim acc As New Account(bal, owner, skey)
        Dim key As AccountId = acc.Id
        accounts.Add(acc)
        Return key.ToString()
    End Function

    Public Sub RemoveAccount(ByVal skey As String)
        Dim key As New AccountId(skey)
        Dim acc As New Account(0, "", skey)
        If Not accounts.Contains(acc) Then
            Throw New Exception( _
                "Account " & skey & " not found")
        End If
        accounts.Remove(acc)
    End Sub

    Public Sub ShowAccounts()
        Dim acc As Account
        For Each acc In accounts
```

```
          Console.WriteLine(acc.Info)
      Next
   End Sub

   Public Sub CreateAccounts(ByVal count As Integer)
      Dim i As Integer
      For i = 1 To count
         AddAccount(GetRandomBalance(), _
            GetRandomName(), GetRandomCode())
      Next
   End Sub

   Public Function FindAccount(ByVal skey As String) _
    As Account
      Dim key As New AccountId(skey)
      Dim target As New Account(0, "", skey)
      Dim acc As Account
      For Each acc In accounts
         If acc.Equals(target) Then
            Return acc
         End If
      Next
      Return Nothing
   End Function

   Public Sub ClearAccounts()
      accounts.Clear()
      m_nextID = 1
   End Sub

End Class
```

The file **TestBank.vb** contains an interactive test program to exercise the various methods of the **Bank** class. The "find" command:

```
...
ElseIf cmd.Equals("find") Then
   Dim sid As String = iw.getString("id: ")

   Dim startTick As Integer = Environment.TickCount
   Dim acc As Account = mybank.FindAccount(sid)
   Dim numTicks As Integer = _
      Environment.TickCount - startTick
   If acc Is Nothing Then
      Console.WriteLine("Account {0} not found", sid)
   Else
      Console.WriteLine(acc.Info)
   End If
   Console.WriteLine("{0} ticks", numTicks)
...
```

Here is a sample run of the program. We first create and show five accounts, and then we look for an account in the middle of the list. Because of the pattern used in generating account IDs, if an account beginning with "C" is found, there will be no corresponding account beginning with "S" and vice versa. We can use this pattern when we try looking for accounts in lists that are too long to display.

```
Enter command, quit to exit
> create
how many: 5
> show
C1          Joe Niles     $100.00                  6
C2          Carol Ives    $200.00                  7
C3          Vic Reese     $900.00                  8
C4          Mary Niles    $800.00                  9
S5          Fran Post     $700.00                 10
> find
id: C3
C3          Vic Reese     $900.00                  8
0 ticks
> find
id: S3
Account S3 not found
0 ticks
```

As is to be expected, there is no measurable elapsed time for searching in such a short list. Next, we clear the list, and create 100,000 accounts. Then, we search for accounts in the middle of the list:

```
> clear
> create
how many: 100000
> find
id: C50000
C50000      Mary Soong  $800.00                    7
10 ticks
> find
id: S50000
Account S50000 not found
20 ticks
```

This time, there is a measurable amount of time required. The successful search for an account in the middle of the list required 10 ticks. An unsuccessful search required twice as long, 20 ticks, because the entire list had to be searched. As our final experiment with this program, we clear the list and create 1,000,000 accounts. Again, we search for accounts in the middle of the list:

```
> clear
> create
how many: 1000000
```

```
> find
id: C500000
C500000    Bob Jones    $300.00                      7
110 ticks
> find
id: S500000
Account S500000 not found
221 ticks
```

The results are similar, with the unsuccessful search taking twice as long as the successful search. Also, the search time for a list 10 times as long is approximately 10 times the duration, reflecting the linear nature of the search.

Performance of Hashtable

The program **BankHash** implements the identical simulation, only using a **Hashtable** data structure in place of an **ArrayList**.

```
' Bank.vb

Imports System
Imports System.Collections

Public Class Bank
    Private Shared m_nextID As Integer = 1
    Private accounts As New Hashtable()

    Public Function AddAccount(ByVal bal As Decimal, _
     ByVal owner As String, ByVal code As Char) As String
        Dim skey As String = code & m_nextID.ToString()
        m_nextID += 1
        Dim acc As New Account(bal, owner, skey)
        Dim key As AccountId = acc.Id
        accounts.Add(key, acc)
        Return key.ToString()
    End Function

    Public Sub RemoveAccount(ByVal skey As String)
        Dim key As New AccountId(skey)
        If Not accounts.Contains(key) Then
            Throw New Exception("Account " & skey & _
            " not found")
        End If
        accounts.Remove(key)
    End Sub

    Public Sub ShowAccounts()
        Dim iter As IDictionaryEnumerator = _
            accounts.GetEnumerator()
        Dim more As Boolean = iter.MoveNext()
```

```
      Dim acc As Account
      While more
         acc = CType(iter.Value, Account)
         Console.WriteLine(acc.Info)
         more = iter.MoveNext()
      End While
   End Sub

   Public Sub CreateAccounts(ByVal count As Integer)
      Dim i As Integer
      For i = 1 To count
         AddAccount(GetRandomBalance(), _
            GetRandomName(), GetRandomCode())
      Next
   End Sub

   Public Function FindAccount(ByVal skey As String) _
    As Account
      Dim key As New AccountId(skey)
      Return CType(accounts.Item(key), Account)
   End Function

   Public Sub ClearAccounts()
      accounts.Clear()
      m_nextID = 1
   End Sub

End Class
```

For this example, we do identical runs, with trials of 100,000 and 1,000,000 accounts. We skip the preliminary trial of five accounts.

```
Enter command, quit to exit
> create
how many: 100000
> find
id: C50000
C50000    Ron Jones    $200.00    -1643386989
0 ticks
> find
id: S50000
Account S50000 not found
0 ticks
> clear
> create
how many: 1000000
> find
id: C500000
Account C500000 not found
0 ticks
```

```
> find
id: S500000
S500000    Nan Reese    $700.00    -424044077
0 ticks
```

The hash table is *much* faster. Even with 1,000,000 accounts, there was no measurable elapsed time for either successful or unsuccessful searches. These results were obtained on a 1.4GHz PC with 512MB of memory.

Other .NET Collection Classes

After you understand the principles of working with .NET collection classes, you can easily use additional classes as required by your application. In this section, we provide sample programs illustrating three more collection classes, **Queue**, **Stack**, and **SortedList**. These classes are all in the **System.Collections** namespace.

Queue

The **Queue** class supports three standard interfaces, as indicated here:

```
Public Class Queue
    Implements ICollection, IEnumerable, ICloneable
```

It maintains a first-in, first-out (FIFO) collection of objects, stored in a circular array. It supports typical operations on a queue, including **Enqueue** and **Dequeue**.

Code
Example

Our sample program is **QueueExample**. A queue stores **Object** references. In this example, we store **DictionaryEntry** objects, which have **Key** and **Value** properties:

```
' QueueExample.vb

Module QueueExampleModule

    Sub Main()
        Dim col As New Queue()
        Dim entry As DictionaryEntry

        col.Enqueue(New DictionaryEntry("Natalie", 17))
        col.Enqueue(New DictionaryEntry("Brittany", 15))
        col.Enqueue(New DictionaryEntry("Zachary", 11))
        col.Enqueue(New DictionaryEntry("Jennifer", 18))
        col.Enqueue(New DictionaryEntry("Jason", 16))

        While col.Count > 0
```

```
            entry = CType(col.Dequeue(), DictionaryEntry)
            Console.WriteLine("{0} is {1} ... {2} " _
            & "items left", entry.Key, entry.Value, _
            col.Count)
        End While
    End Sub

End Module
```

In the following output, notice that objects are dequeued in the same order in which they were enqueued:

```
Natalie is 17 ... 4 items left
Brittany is 15 ... 3 items left
Zachary is 11 ... 2 items left
Jennifer is 18 ... 1 items left
Jason is 16 ... 0 items left
```

Stack

The **Stack** class supports three standard interfaces, as indicated here:

```
Public Class Stack
    Implements ICollection, IEnumerable, ICloneable
```

It maintains a last-in, first-out (LIFO) collection of objects, stored in a circular buffer. It supports typical operations on a stack, including **Push** and **Pop.**

Code Example

Our sample program is **StackExample**. A stack stores **Object** references. In this example, we store **DictionaryEntry** objects, as in our queue example.

```
' StackExample.vb

Module StackExampleModule

    Sub Main()
        Dim col As New Stack()
        Dim entry As DictionaryEntry

        col.Push(New DictionaryEntry("Natalie", 17))
        col.Push(New DictionaryEntry("Brittany", 15))
        col.Push(New DictionaryEntry("Zachary", 11))
        col.Push(New DictionaryEntry("Jennifer", 18))
        col.Push(New DictionaryEntry("Jason", 16))

        While col.Count > 0
            entry = CType(col.Pop(), DictionaryEntry)
            Console.WriteLine("{0} is {1} ... {2} " _
            & "items left", entry.Key, entry.Value, _
            col.Count)
```

```
      End While
   End Sub

End Module
```

In the following output, notice that objects are popped in the opposite order to which they were pushed:

```
Jason is 16 ... 4 items left
Jennifer is 18 ... 3 items left
Zachary is 11 ... 2 items left
Brittany is 15 ... 1 items left
Natalie is 17 ... 0 items left
```

SortedList

The **SortedList** class supports four standard interfaces. In addition to the interfaces supported by **Stack** and **Queue**, the **IDictionary** interface is supported (as in **Hashtable**):

```
Public Class SortedList
   Implements IDictionary, ICollection, IEnumerable, _
              ICloneable
```

It maintains a sorted key/value collection of objects, stored in two arrays—one for the keys and another for the indexes. The entries are sorted according to the keys, and they are accessible through either the key or an index. Operations on a sorted list are somewhat slower than on a hash table, because of the sorting. But a sorted list offers the added flexibility of access through an index as well as a key.

The **Capacity** property of a **SortedList** is the number of entries that the list can hold. As with an array list, a sorted list can grow as required when new elements are added. The capacity can be decreased by calling **TrimTo-Size** or by setting the **Capacity** property.

A sorted list supports typical insertion/removal operations such as **Add**, **Remove**, and **RemoveAt**. Search/lookup operations include **GetKey**, **GetBy-Index**, **IndexOfKey**, and **IndexOfValue**.

Our sample program is **SortedListExample**. Like the other examples, the program stores names and ages. This time, we provide an interactive test program. As usual, the commands can be displayed by typing "help":

```
The following commands are available:
   show     -- show strings in list
   birthday -- increment age of birthday kid
   add      -- add a person to list
   remove   -- remove a person
   removeat -- remove person at index
   quit     -- exit the program
```

Here is the code of our example program:

```vb
' SortedListExample.vb

Imports System
Imports System.Collections

Module SortedListExampleModule
    Private col As New System.Collections.SortedList()

    Sub Main()
        AddPerson("Natalie", 17)
        AddPerson("Brittany", 15)
        AddPerson("Zachary", 11)
        AddPerson("Jennifer", 18)
        AddPerson("Jason", 16)
        ShowList()
        CommandLoop()
    End Sub

    ...

    Private Sub ShowList()
        Dim index As Integer
        Dim nameKey As String
        Dim ageValue As Integer
        For index = 0 To col.Count - 1
            nameKey = CStr(col.GetKey(index))
            ageValue = CInt(col.GetByIndex(index))
            Console.WriteLine("{0} (is {1}) ... at " _
              & "position {2}", nameKey, ageValue, index)
        Next
    End Sub

    Private Sub AddPerson(ByVal name As String, _
      ByVal age As Integer)
        col.Add(name, age)
    End Sub

    Private Sub Birthday()
        Dim index As Integer
        Dim searchName As String
        Dim ageValue As Integer
        ' Search for a name and add one to that age
        Console.Write("Enter birthday kid's name: ")
        searchName = Console.ReadLine()
        index = col.IndexOfKey(searchName)
        If index >= 0 Then
            ageValue = CInt(col.GetByIndex(index)) + 1
            col.SetByIndex(index, ageValue)
            Console.WriteLine("{0} is now {1}!",
```

```
                    searchName, ageValue)
        Else
            Console.WriteLine("Person not found!")
        End If
    End Sub

    Private Sub RemovePerson(ByVal name As String)
        col.Remove(name)
    End Sub

    Private Sub RemovePersonAt(ByVal index As Integer)
        col.RemoveAt(index)
    End Sub

End Module
```

Here is a run of our program:

```
Brittany (is 15) ... at position 0
Jason (is 16) ... at position 1
Jennifer (is 18) ... at position 2
Natalie (is 17) ... at position 3
Zachary (is 11) ... at position 4
Enter command, quit to exit
> birthday
Enter birthday kid's name: Jason
Jason is now 17!
> remove
name: Natalie
> removeat
index: 0
> show
Jason (is 17) ... at position 0
Jennifer (is 18) ... at position 1
Zachary (is 11) ... at position 2
> add
name: George
age: 10
> show
George (is 10) ... at position 0
Jason (is 17) ... at position 1
Jennifer (is 18) ... at position 2
Zachary (is 11) ... at position 3
```

Summary

In this chapter, we surveyed a number of collection classes provided by the .NET Framework. Collections are an example of classes in the .NET Framework that support a well-defined set of interfaces that provide useful functionality. Collections support the interfaces **IEnumerable**, **ICollection**, **IList**, and **ICloneable**. The first three interfaces provide the standard methods for iterating the elements of a list, obtaining a count of the number of elements, adding and removing elements, and so on. The **ICloneable** interface is used to implement a deep copy of a class. To work with collections effectively, you need to override certain methods of the **Object** base class, such as **Equals**, **ToString**, and sometimes **GetHashCode**.

We looked at several specific examples of collection classes, including **ArrayList**, **Hashtable**, **Queue**, **Stack**, and **SortedList**. **Hashtable** and **SortedList** store key/value pairs and provide fast lookup. They implement the **IDictionary** interface.

Database Access

*D*atabase access is an important part of many computer applications, and the .NET Framework provides database support with
a new database technology known as ADO.NET. Over the years,
Microsoft has provided many different database access technologies, and the question of which to use and when to use it has
sometimes been confusing. ADO.NET adds another piece to this
puzzle.

*In this chapter, we begin with a survey of database access technol-
ogies. We then guide you through the steps of setting up a database testbed using Visual Studio.NET. We then discuss ADO.NET
and its use for both connected access to a database and disconnected access. The disconnected scenario is becoming more important as e-commerce types of applications push the limits of
scalability. ADO.NET provides a new data structure, known as a
data set, for disconnected database access. For both connected
and disconnected access, you can program in a largely database-
independent fashion by making use of interfaces provided by the
.NET Framework class library. We illustrate by showing how to
access both SQL Server and Access databases using almost identical code, which must be modified in only a few places to accommodate a different data source. Many database applications have
a Windows client as a user interface. We examine how databound
controls can help you create Windows user interfaces to your
data. Finally, we take a peek at how the ADO.NET classes can
work with XML data as well as relational data.*

Overview of Microsoft Database Access Technologies

Over the years, Microsoft has introduced an alphabet soup of database access technologies, with acronyms such as ODBC, OLEDB, DAO, RDO, ADO, and DOA (just kidding with that last one!). The overall goal is to provide a consistent set of programming interfaces that can be used by a variety of clients to talk to a variety of data sources, including both relational and non-relational data. In this section, we survey some of the most important ones and provide an orientation to where ADO.NET fits in the scheme of things, which we begin discussing in the next section.

ODBC

Microsoft's first initiative in this direction was ODBC, or Open Database Connectivity. ODBC provides a C interface to relational databases. Figure 20–1 illustrates the overall architecture of ODBC.

Using this architecture, applications can talk to different relational databases using the same C interface. The ODBC standard has been widely adopted, and all major relational databases have provided ODBC drivers. In addition, some ODBC drivers have been written for non-relational data sources, such as Excel spreadsheets.

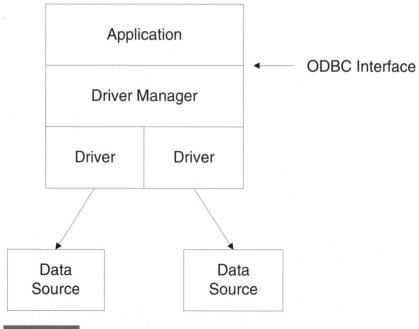

FIGURE 20–1   *The ODBC architecture.*

Although successful, there are two main drawbacks to this approach. The first is the restriction to relational databases. As was pointed out, some ODBC drivers have been written to support ODBC talking to non-relational data, but this approach puts a great burden on the driver to in effect emulate a relational database engine. And this code would have to be replicated in each such driver.

The second drawback is the C interface, which requires a programmer in any other language to first interface to C before being able to call ODBC.

OLE DB

Microsoft's improved strategy is based on the Component Object Model (COM), which provides a language-independent interface, based on a binary standard. Thus, any solution based on COM improves the flexibility from the standpoint of the client program. Microsoft's set of COM database interfaces is referred to as "OLE DB," the original name when OLE was the all-embracing technology, and this name has stuck.

The other big feature is that OLE DB is not specific to relational databases. Any data source that wishes to expose itself to clients through OLE DB must implement an OLE DB provider. OLE DB itself provides much database functionality, including a cursor engine and a relational query engine. This code does not have to be replicated across many providers, as is true with ODBC drivers. Clients of OLE DB are referred to as consumers.

The first OLE DB provider was for ODBC. This immediately gave OLE DB consumers access to all data sources supporting ODBC. The gain was a COM interface for clients. However, this solution imposed an additional layer between the client and the database.

A number of native OLE DB providers have been implemented, including ones for SQL Server and Oracle. There is also a native provider for Microsoft's Jet database engine, which provides efficient access to desktop databases such as Access and dBase. Some object databases such as ObjectStore are also starting to furnish native OLE DB providers.

ActiveX Data Objects (ADO)

Although COM is based on a binary standard, all languages are not created equal with respect to COM. In its heart, COM "likes" C++. It is based on the C++ vtable interface mechanism, and C++ deals effortlessly with structures and pointers. But that's not so with many other languages, such as Visual Basic. If you provide an Automation interface, which restricts itself to Automation-compatible data types, your components are much easier to access from Visual Basic.

OLE DB was designed for maximum efficiency for C++ programs. To provide an easy to use interface for Visual Basic, Microsoft created ActiveX

Data Objects (or ADO). The look and feel of ADO is somewhat similar to the popular Data Access Objects[1] (DAO) that provides an easy-to-use object model for accessing Jet. The ADO model has two advantages: (1) It is somewhat flattened and easier to use, without so much traversing down an object hierarchy, and (2) it is based on OLE DB and gives programmers very broad reach in terms of data sources.

The end result of this technology is a flexible range of interfaces available to the programmer. If you are accessing SQL Server, you have a choice of five main programming interfaces. One is embedded SQL, which is preprocessed from a C program. The other four interfaces are all runtime interfaces and are shown in Figure 20–2.

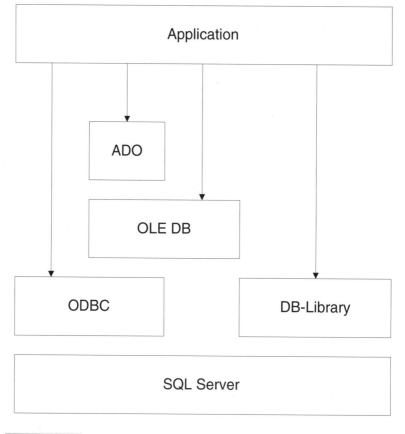

FIGURE 20-2   *Interfaces for accessing SQL Server before ADO.NET.*

---

1. Data Access Objects (DAO) is Mirocosoft's data model that is used for Interacting with Access databases via the Jet Engine.

DB-Library is the original runtime library for SQL Server. It is a layer on top of the SQL Server engine itself, which has a private interface not exposed to applications. An application can call DB-Library. This code is specific to SQL Server, and will not run on other databases or on non-relational data sources. It is a C interface. The second interface is ODBC. As we have seen, ODBC is also a C interface, but it enables you to talk to many relational databases.

If an application is written to OLE DB, it can access a variety of relational and non-relational data sources. The range of data sources you can reach through OLE DB is a superset of ones that can be reached through ODBC, because there is an OLE DB provider for ODBC. SQL Server is a native provider, so your application using OLE DB has a quite direct path to SQL Server. As indicated above, there are a number of native OLE DB providers to other databases, such as Oracle, and more are appearing.

ADO is the highest level interface. It is easy to use and has been widely used in Visual Basic programs. We do not review ADO in detail, but we give a brief sketch of the ADO object model. Some of the ADO objects have analogues in ADO.NET.

ADO Object Model

ADO is structured as a family of COM classes ("objects") supporting dual interfaces. ADO can be accessed through scripting languages, as well as early binding programming languages. This means that ADO can be used in Active Server Pages and works well in the middle tier of Web applications, providing the means of talking to the data tier.

The classes in ADO are arranged in a hierarchy, as illustrated in Figure 20–3, which is somewhat simplified for clarity. Unlike previous hierarchies, such as the one for DAO, this hierarchy is flatter and is not strict. Thus, it is possible (and quite common, in fact) in ADO to instantiate a lower-level object by itself, and the required higher-level object is instantiated behind the scenes. The result is a programming model that is very easy to use.

The object model contains both individual objects and collections of objects. In the diagram, collections are shown as shaded boxes.

CONNECTION OBJECT

You need a connection object to connect to a data source. Either you create one explicitly, or some other object implicitly creates one for you. The most important property of a connection object is **ConnectionString**, which is used by the underlying OLE DB provider to connect to the actual data source.

After it's created, the **Connection** object may either be used directly by means of the **Execute** method, or the **Connection** object may be passed to a **Recordset** object or a **Command** object.

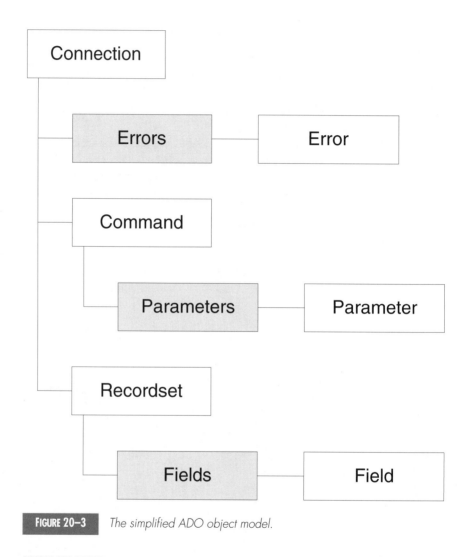

FIGURE 20-3   *The simplified ADO object model.*

RECORDSET OBJECT

In ADO, as in other Microsoft database interfaces, a *recordset* is used for returning data from a database. A recordset may consist of multiple rows and multiple columns (fields). Thus, a **Recordset** object contains a collection of **Field** objects. The collection is referred to as **Fields**. Sometimes, you may want to refer to the **Fields** collection explicitly, such as interrogating a data source when you don't know the names of the fields. The **Fields** collection is also useful if you want to create your own recordset to store data, rather than populate a recordset with data from a database. Often, you don't need to explicitly work with the **Fields** collection. You can reference a particular field by using its name as a key.

A recordset may contain multiple rows, and you can navigate among these rows using methods like **MoveFirst** and **MoveNext**. When iterating through a recordset in this fashion, you are employing a database *cursor*, which is supplied by the underlying OLE DB provider.

ADO.NET

As part of the .NET Framework class library, Microsoft has created a new set of data access classes, known collectively as ADO.NET. Why has Microsoft introduced a new data access technology? For one thing, they *had* to. OLE DB and ADO.NET are based on COM. Because .NET provides a new object infrastructure, it is necessary to provide .NET data access classes. (It is quite possible in .NET to call legacy COM components, a subject we will discuss in Chapter 23. Hence .NET applications can call ADO through an interoperability layer. But it is clearly desirable to provide native .NET interfaces for something as basic as data access.)

Moreover, there has been a significant evolution in application development since ADO was designed. Many of today's applications are oriented toward the Web and have a much more loosely coupled structure than traditional desktop or client/server applications. Many modern applications use XML to encode data that is passed over a network. After the needed data has been extracted from the data source and converted to XML, the connection to the data source can be closed. An application that does not require all its clients to simultaneously maintain database applications can be much more scaleable.

To facilitate programming in this disconnected scenario, ADO.NET provides a new class, **DataSet**, which holds in memory a representation of data that was retrieved from some data source. Unlike the **Recordset** of the ADO model, which could hold only a single table, the **DataSet** can hold many tables; it also holds constraints and relationships among the tables. Thus, a data set can be viewed as an in-memory database.

To obtain data from a database, ADO.NET supplies a **Connection** class. A **Connection** object can be used to support connection-oriented programming of a database, if that is what is desired. Or, through a **DataAdapter** object, a data set can be populated with data from the data source, and the connection can be closed.

Later in this chapter, we discuss how to program ADO.NET using VB.NET, in both the connected and disconnected scenarios. But first, we set up a simple testbed for doing database programming using Visual Studio.NET.

A Visual Studio.NET Database Testbed

In the main part of this chapter, we write programs to access databases. We work with both SQL Server and Access databases, and we see how easy it is to write programs that access different data sources in a consistent manner. An Access database is self-contained in an **.mdb** file. Our sample Access database is **SimpleBank.mdb** in the directory **OI\Databases**. A script, **CreateSimpleBank.sql**, is provided for creating a SQL Server database **SimpleBank**. We discuss running this script later in this section. To gain practice in working with the database tools provided with Visual Studio, let's create this database by hand.

Sample Database

Our sample database stores account information for a small bank. There are three tables:

- **Account** stores information about bank accounts. Columns are **AccountId, Owner, AccountType,** and **Balance.** The primary key is **AccountId.**
- **IdGen** has one column, **NextAccountId,** and only one row. This table is used to provide a simple mechanism for generating IDs for new accounts, in a manner that works the same for both the Access database and the SQL Server database.
- **Transaction** stores information about account transactions. Columns are **XactType, AccountId,** and **Amount.** There is a parent/child relationship between the **Account** and **Transaction** tables. (This relationship is deliberately omitted from the Access database for demonstration purposes.)

If you have Access installed on your system, you can open **SimpleBank.mdb** and investigate this simple database.

The Visual Studio.NET Server Explorer

Visual Studio.NET Server Explorer is a useful tool for working with databases. Although not as powerful as the SQL Server Enterprise Manager, it can give you the basic functionality you need when writing or debugging database applications. It will be very useful when we work with the examples in this chapter.

To access the Server Explorer, use the View | Server Explorer menu item. The Server Explorer is a dockable window that can be moved around as required. Figure 20–4 illustrates the Server Explorer.

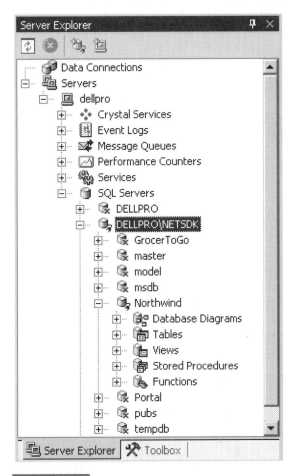

FIGURE 20—4 *The Visual Studio.NET Server Explorer window.*

You can find information about all the fields in a table, or look at and edit the data in the tables. You can create or edit stored procedures and design tables. We use the Server Explorer to create the SQL Server version of our simple bank database. The first thing to notice in the left-panel tree view is a list of SQL Servers installed on your system. If MMMM is the name of your machine, you may have a SQL Server named MMMM, if you have SQL Server itself installed. In any event, you likely have a SQL Server named MMMM\NETSDK, which corresponds to a stripped down version of SQL Server called the Microsoft Database Engine or MSDE. The MSDE is bundled free with the .NET SDK.

Below a particular SQL Server is a list of the databases on that server. Some sample databases ship with SQL Server or MSDE, including the **North-**

wind database. If you click the plus (+) next to a particular database, you see Database Diagrams, Tables, Views, etc., which you can further expand by clicking the corresponding +.

We will see further features of the Server Explorer when we go through the steps of creating our sample database.

Creating a Database

It is extremely easy to create a database using SQL Server. You don't have to worry about a "database device" or initially allocating enough storage for the database, because SQL Server, beginning with version 7.0, can automatically "grow" databases as required. Follow these steps to create one database, **SimpleBank**.

1. In Server Explorer, expand the tree view to show the databases on your server, as shown previously in Figure 20–4.
2. Right-click over "Databases."
3. From the context menu that comes up, choose New Database.
4. Enter "SimpleBank" as the name of your new database.
5. Select "Use SQL Server Authentication," enter "sa" for the Login Name, and leave the Password blank. (Naturally, you would **NEVER** have such open security for a real database). See Figure 20–5.
6. Click OK.

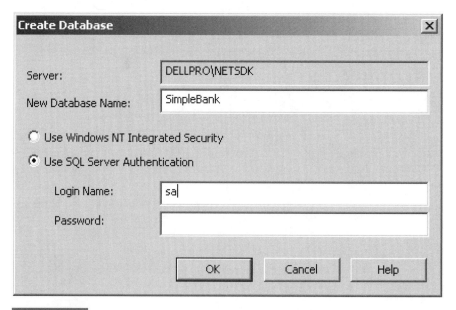

FIGURE 20–5   *Creating a new database using Server Explorer.*

Creating Tables

You can also create tables using Server Explorer. Follow these easy steps:

1. Right-click over your new database **SimpleBank.**
2. From the context menu, choose New | Table.
3. Enter the name "Account" for the new table.
4. Enter information as shown in Figure 20–6 to define four columns.
5. Clear the check mark from the Allow Nulls, except for the **AccountType** field.
6. Enter 0 as a default value for **Balance.**
7. Right-click over the first column, **AccountId,** and choose "Set Primary Key" from the context menu.

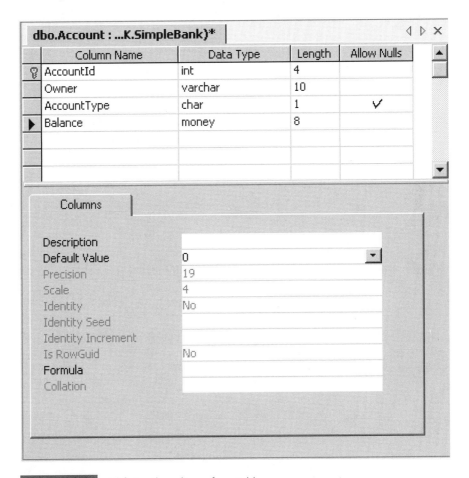

FIGURE 20–6   *Defining the schema for a table.*

Close the window you were using to define the new table, and say "Yes" to saving the changes, and enter "Account" for the name of your new table.

In a similar manner, create tables **IdGen** and **Transaction**. The **IdGen** table has a single column called **NextAccountId** of data type **int**. The **Transaction** table has three columns, as defined in Table 20–1. Allow Nulls is cleared for each column, and there is no primary key.

TABLE 20-1	Schema for Transaction Table	
Column Name	**Data Type**	**Length**
XactType	char	1
AccountId	int	4
Amount	money	8

Creating a Relationship

Next, we set up a parent/child relationship between the **Account** table and the **Transaction** table, using the **AccountId** column as a foreign key in the **Transaction** table. With Server Explorer, you can easily create a relationship through a database diagram following these steps:

1. Right-click over "Database Diagrams" below the **SimpleBank** database.
2. Choose New Diagram from the context menu. The Add Table dialog comes up.
3. Holding down the Ctrl key, select the **Account** and **Transaction** tables, and click the Add button. Click Close.
4. Position the tables the way you want by dragging with the mouse. For now, position the **Account** table to the left of the **Transaction** table.

You can now create the desired relationship using the following procedure:

1. In the **Account** table, click the row selector ▯ next to the column you desire to relate to another table, in this case **AccountId**.
2. Click and drag to the related table, in this case **Transaction**.
3. Release the mouse button. You see the Create Relationship dialog that lets you set up a relationship between a primary key and a foreign key. Because the **AccountId** column matches in both tables, you see that column selected. Accept the default options in the check boxes. See Figure 20–7. Click OK to create the relationship.

The parent/child relationship has now been created and is shown in the database diagram. See Figure 20–8. Each account can now have a list of transactions associated with it. (In our example, the transactions are deposits and withdrawals of various amounts.)

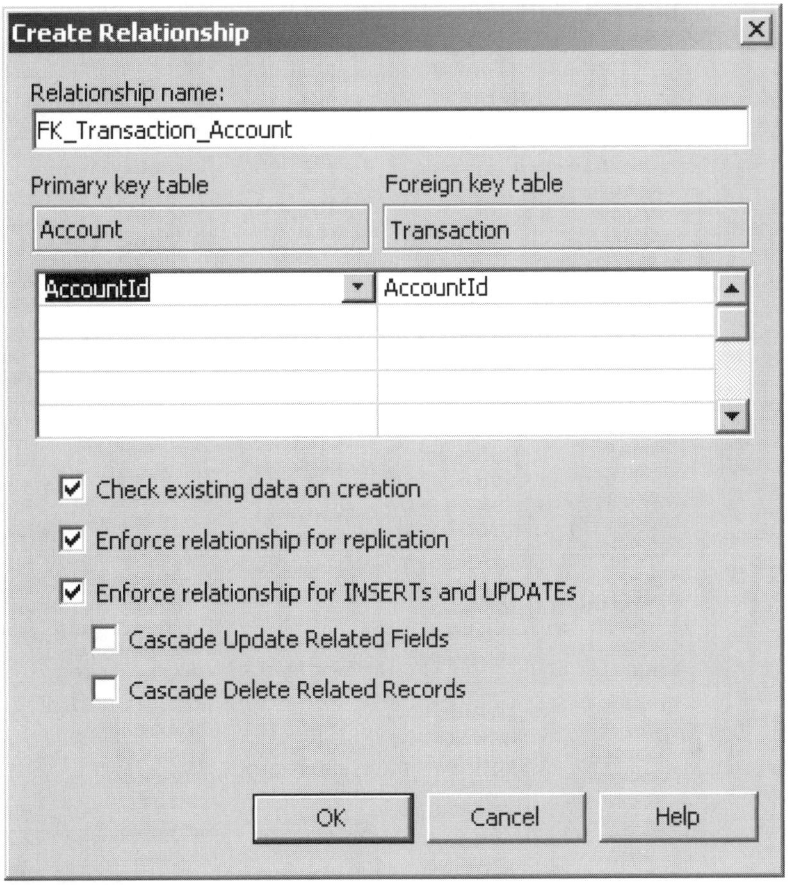

Create Relationship

Relationship name:

FK_Transaction_Account

Primary key table	Foreign key table
Account	Transaction
AccountId ▼	AccountId ▲
	▼

☑ Check existing data on creation

☑ Enforce relationship for replication

☑ Enforce relationship for INSERTs and UPDATEs

   ☐ Cascade Update Related Fields

   ☐ Cascade Delete Related Records

[OK]　[Cancel]　[Help]

FIGURE 20–7　*The Create Relationship dialog box.*

FIGURE 20–8　*The Database diagram showing a parent/child relationship.*

As you close the database diagram window, you are prompted to save and to supply a name. Be sure to save.

Inserting Data into a Table

You can insert data into a new table using Server Explorer. We will enter data into the **Account** table. In the left pane, right-click over the table and choose "Retrieve Data from Table" from the context menu. You can now type some sample data, like that shown in Figure 20–9. Don't enter anything into the **AccountType** column; leave it as <NULL>.

dbo.Account-Tra...SDK.SimpleBank)	**dbo.Account : ...SDK.SimpleBank)**		
AccountId	Owner	AccountType	Balance
101	Bob	<NULL>	100
102	Mary	<NULL>	200
103	Charles	<NULL>	300
▶			

FIGURE 20–9   *Entering data into a table using Server Explorer.*

Performing Queries

After your database is set up, you can start to perform queries against it, making use of SQL. For example, to retrieve all the data from the **Account** table, you can perform the following query.

```
select * from Account
```

In this chapter, our focus is on writing database *programs* using VB.NET and the ADO.NET classes. But it is useful to perform a simple query now as a quick check that your database has been set up properly. Also, as you go along in the chapter, you may want to test your SQL by using a query tool.

USING QUERY ANALYZER

If you have SQL Server installed on your system (not merely MSDE), you can make use of the Query Analyzer tool. This GUI program is easy to use. You can launch this tool by going to Start | Programs | Microsoft SQL Server | Query Analyzer. A login window appears. Select the SQL Server against which you want to perform queries, and enter the Login name and Password. Click OK.

From the database dropdown list, choose "SimpleBank." You can now type your query, and then click the ▶ toolbar button (or from the menu, choose Query | Execute). The results of your query are displayed in a lower pane, as illustrated in Figure 20–10.

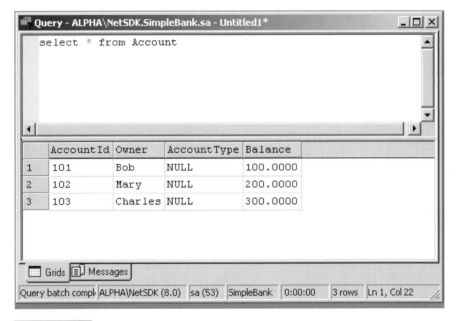

FIGURE 20–10 *Performing a query with Query Analyzer.*

USING OSQL COMMAND LINE TOOL

An alternative to Query Analyzer is a command line tool, which is invoked with the command **osql**. You can enter the following at the command prompt, to execute the same simple select:

```
C:\OI\Databases>osql /Usa /P /S ALPHA\NETSDK /Q "select *
from SimpleBank..Account"
```

where we have used the following options:

```
/U   user name
/P   password
/S   server
/Q   query
```

In the SQL code for the query, we have prefixed the table name by the name of the database followed by two periods. Here is the result of this query:

```
AccountId    Owner        AccountType Balance
-----------  -----------  ----------- --------------------
        101 Bob           NULL                   100.0000
        102 Mary          NULL                   200.0000
        103 Charles       NULL                   300.0000
```

ADO.NET Architecture

ADO.NET is a set of classes that provide consistent access to multiple data sources, which may be either relational data from a database or hierarchical data expressed in XML. A driving factor in ADO.NET is a provision for disconnected access to data, which is much more scalable and flexible than the connection-oriented database access that is traditional in client/server systems.

The **DataSet** class is the central component of the disconnected architecture. A data set can be populated from either a database or from an XML stream. From the perspective of the user of the data set, the original source of the data is immaterial. A consistent programming model is used for all application interaction with the **DataSet**.

The second key component of ADO.NET architecture is the .NET Data Provider, which provides access to a database and can be used to populate a data set. A data provider can also be used directly by an application to support a connected mode of database access.

Figure 20–11 illustrates the overall architecture of ADO.NET.

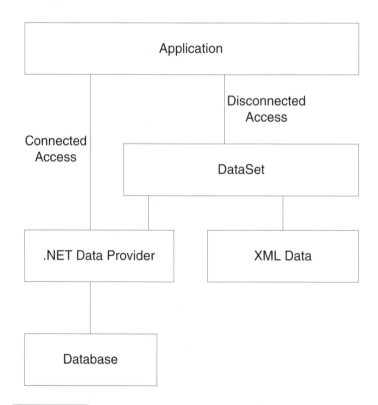

FIGURE 20–11   *The ADO.NET architecture block diagram.*

.NET Data Providers

A .NET data provider is used for connecting to a database. It provides classes that can be used to execute commands and to retrieve results. The results are either used directly by the application, or they are placed in a data set. A .NET data provider implements four key interfaces:

- **IDbConnection** is used to establish a connection to a specific data source.
- **IDbCommand** is used to execute a command at a data source.
- **IDataReader** provides an efficient way to read a stream of data from a data source. The data access provided by a data reader is forward-only and read-only.
- **IDbDataAdapter** is used to populate a data set from a data source.

The ADO.NET architecture specifies these interfaces, and different implementations can be created to facilitate working with different data sources. A .NET data provider is analogous to an OLE DB provider, but the two should not be confused. An OLE DB provider implements COM interfaces, and a .NET data provider implements .NET interfaces.

When OLE DB first came out, it immediately supplied a provider for ODBC. This single provider offered access to an array of data sources, to any data source with an ODBC driver. A native OLE DB provider was offered for SQL Server. As time passed, more OLE DB providers became available.

The situation today is similar for .NET data providers. Currently, there are two .NET data providers. The **OleDb** data provider goes through the COM interop layer to talk to OLE DB. Thus, any data source with an OLE DB provider can be accessed through ADO.NET. The **SqlServer** data provider uses the native SQL Server wire protocol (which is a private protocol, at a lower level even than the DB-Library interface mentioned earlier in the chapter). As time passes, we can anticipate that additional native .NET data providers will be offered by different database vendors.

To make your programs more portable, you should endeavor to program with the interfaces rather than using specific classes directly. In our example programs, we illustrate using interfaces to talk to an Access database (using the OleDb data provider) and a SQL Server database (using the SqlServer data provider).

Classes of the OleDb provider have a prefix of OleDb, and classes of the SqlServer provider have a prefix of Sql. Table 20–2 shows a number of parallel classes between the two data providers and the corresponding interfaces.

	Comparison of Classes in the OleDb and SqlServer Data Providers

TABLE 20-2

Interface	OleDb	SQL Server
IDbConnection	OleDbConnection	SqlConnection
IDbCommand	OleDbCommand	SqlCommand
IDataReader	OleDbDataReader	SqlDataReader
IDbDataAdapter	OleDbDataAdapter	SqlDataAdapter
IDbTransaction	OleDbTransaction	SqlTransaction
IDataParameter	OleDbDataParameter	SqlDataParameter

Classes such as **DataSet**, which are independent of any data provider, do not have a prefix.

.NET Namespaces

ADO.NET classes are found in the following namespaces:

- **System.Data** consists of classes that constitute most of the ADO.NET architecture.
- **System.Data.OLEDB** contains classes that provide database access using the OLE DB data provider.
- **System.Data.SQLClient** contains classes that provide database access using the SQL Server data provider.
- **System.Data.SQLTypes** contains classes that represent data types used by SQL Server.
- **System.Data.Common** contains classes that are shared by data providers.

Connected Data Access

Although much of the design of ADO.NET is geared to supporting disconnected database applications, there is also support for the connected model. Because connected applications are more familiar, we begin our detailed discussion of ADO.NET programming with the connected scenario.

Using a Connection

The connection class (**OleDbConnection** or **SQLConnection**) is used to manage the connection to the data source. It has properties for **Connection-String**, **ConnectionTimeout**, and so forth. There are methods for **Open**, **Close**, transaction management, etc.

A *connection string* is used to identify the information the object needs to connect to the database. You can specify the connection string when you construct the connection object, or you may specify it by setting its properties. A connection string contains a series of **argument = value** statements separated by semicolons.

To program in a manner that is independent of the data source, you should obtain an interface reference of type **IDbConnection** after creating the connection object, and you should program against this interface reference.

CONNECTING TO A SQL SERVER DATA PROVIDER

Let's begin by writing a small program to connect to the SQL Server database **SimpleBank** that you created earlier in the chapter. If you would like to create this program yourself, follow the instructions. Do your work in the **Demos** directory for Chapter 20. If you just want to look at the finished program, examine the project in **SqlConnectOnly**. Follow these steps to create it yourself:

1. Use Visual Studio to create a new VB.NET console application called "SqlConnectOnly."
2. Type the code shown in bold. Note that we obtain an interface reference of type **IDbConnection**, so that our code is more independent of the data source.

```
Imports System.Data.SqlClient

Module SQLConnectOnly

    Sub Main()
        Dim connStr As String = _
            "server=localhost;uid=sa;pwd=;database=SimpleBank"
        Dim sqlConn As New SqlConnection()
        Dim conn As IDbConnection = sqlConn
        conn.ConnectionString = connStr
        Console.WriteLine( _
            "Using SQL Server to access SimpleBank")
        Console.WriteLine("Database state: " & _
            conn.State.ToString())
        conn.Open()
        Console.WriteLine("Database state: " & _
            conn.State.ToString())
    End Sub

End Module
```

3. Build and run the program. You should get the following output:

```
Using SQL Server to access SimpleBank
Database state: Closed
Database state: Open
```

This program illustrates the correct connect string for connecting to a SQL Server database. Note the use of the database "localhost." When SQL Server is installed on your system, a SQL Server is created having the name of your computer. You could use either this name or "localhost." If you are on a network and there is a remote SQL Server running, you could connect to that SQL Server by substituting the name of the remote server. If you are running MSDE instead of SQL server, you could use "MMMM\NETSDK," where MMMM is the name of your machine. This assumes that you are using the MSDE that is installed with the .NET Framework SDK.

The program illustrates the **ConnectionString** and **State** properties of the connection object and the **Open** method.

ADO.NET CLASS LIBRARIES

To run a program that uses the ADO.NET classes, you must be sure to set references to the appropriate class libraries. The following libraries should usually be included:

- System.dll
- System.Data.dll
- System.Xml.dll

The last one is needed when we are working with data sets; it is not required for the current examples.

References to these libraries are set up automatically when you create a console project in Visual Studio. If you create an empty project, you need to specifically add these references. Figure 20–12 shows the references in our console project, as created by Visual Studio.

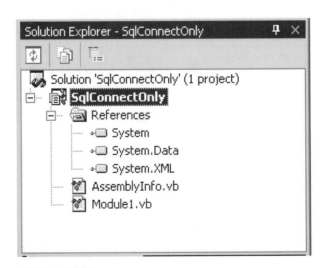

References in console project created by Visual Studio.

CONNECTING TO AN OLE DB DATA PROVIDER

To connect to an OLE DB data provider instead, you need to change the namespace you are importing and instantiate an object of the **OleDbConnection** class. You must provide a connection string appropriate to your OLE DB provider. We are going to use the Jet OLE DB provider, which can be used for connecting to an Access database. The program **JetConnectOnly** illustrates connecting to the Access database **SimpleBank.mdb**. Note that database files for this book are installed in the directory **C:\OI\Databases** when you install the sample programs. The lines in bold are the only ones that are different from the corresponding SQL Server example.

```
Imports System.Data.OleDb

Module JetConnectOnly

   Sub Main()
      Dim connStr As String = _
        "Provider=Microsoft.Jet.OLEDB.4.0;" _
        & "Data Source=C:\OI\Databases\SimpleBank.mdb"
      Dim jetConn As New OleDbConnection()
      Dim conn As IDbConnection = jetConn
      conn.ConnectionString = connStr
      Console.WriteLine("Using Access DB SimpleBank.mdb")
      Console.WriteLine("Database state: " & _
         conn.State.ToString())
      conn.Open()
      Console.WriteLine("Database state: " & _
         conn.State.ToString())
   End Sub

End Module
```

Using Commands

After we have opened a connection to a data source, we can create a command object, which executes a query against a data source. Depending on our data source, we create either a **SqlCommand** object or an **OleDbCommand** object. In either case, we initialize an interface reference of type **IDbCommand**, which is used in the rest of our code, again promoting relative independence from the data source.

The code fragments shown below are from the **ConnectedSql** program, which illustrates performing various database operations on the **SimpleBank** database. We look at the complete program and a sample run a little later.

Table 20–3 summarizes some of the principle properties and methods of **IDbCommand**.

TABLE 20-3	*Common Properties and Methods of IDbCommand*
Property or Method	**Description**
CommandText	Text of command to run against the data source
CommandTimeout	Wait time before terminating command attempt
CommandType	How CommandText is interpreted (e.g. Text, StoredProcedure)
Connection	The IDbConnection used by the command
Parameters	The parameters collection
Cancel	Cancels the execution of an IDbCommand
ExecuteReader	Obtains an IDataReader for retrieving data (SELECT)
ExecuteNonQuery	Executes a SQL command such as INSERT, DELETE, etc.

CREATING A COMMAND OBJECT

The following code illustrates creating a command object and returning an **IDbCommand** interface reference.

```
Private Function CreateCommand(ByVal query As String) _
 As IDbCommand
   Return New SqlCommand(query, sqlConn)
End Function
```

EXECUTENONQUERY

The following code illustrates executing a SQL DELETE statement using a command object. We create a query string for the command, and obtain a command object for this command. The call to **ExecuteNonQuery** returns the number of rows that were updated.

```
Private Sub RemoveAccount(ByVal id As Integer)
   Dim query As String = _
      "delete from Account where AccountId = " & id
   Dim command As IDbCommand = CreateCommand(query)
   Dim numrow As Integer = command.ExecuteNonQuery()
   Console.WriteLine("{0} rows updated", numrow)
End Sub
```

Using a Data Reader

After we have created a command object, we can call the **ExecuteReader** method to return an **IDataReader**. With the data reader, we can obtain a read-only, forward-only stream of data. This method is suitable for reading large amounts of data, because only one row at a time is stored in memory. When you are finished with the data reader, you should explicitly close it. Any output parameters or return values of the command object are not available until after the data reader has been closed.

Data readers have an **Item** property that can be used for accessing the current record. The **Item** property accepts either an integer (representing a column number) or a string (representing a column name). The **Item** property is the default property and can be omitted if desired.

The **Read** method is used to advance the data reader to the next row. When it is created, a data reader is positioned *before* the first row. You must call **Read** before accessing any data. **Read** returns **true** if there are more rows; otherwise, it returns false.

Here is an illustration of code using a data reader to display results of a SELECT query.

```
Private Sub ShowList()
   Dim query As String = "select * from Account"
   Dim command As IDbCommand = CreateCommand(query)
   Dim reader As IDataReader = command.ExecuteReader()
   While reader.Read()
      Console.WriteLine("{0}  {1,-10}  {2:C}", _
         reader("AccountId"), reader("Owner"), _
         reader("Balance"))
   End While
   reader.Close()
End Sub
```

Sample Database Application Using Connected Scenario

Our sample application opens a connection, which remains open during the lifetime of the application. Command objects are created to carry out typical database operations, such as retrieving rows from the database, adding rows, deleting rows, and changing rows. There are two versions of the application, one for the SQL Server version of our **SimpleBank** database, and one for the Access version. We first look at the SQL Server version and then examine the small amount of code that must be changed for the Access version.

USING SQL SERVER DATA PROVIDER

Code Example

The first version of our program uses the SQL Sever data provider. The program is called **ConnectedSql**. Assuming that you have set up the **Simple-Bank** database as described earlier in the chapter, you should be able to build and run the program. The **SqlConnectOnly** program is a short program that you can use to help debug any connection problems you might have.

The program is an interactive command line program. Typing "help" gives a list of the available commands:

The following commands are available:
```
  show      -- show accounts in database
  add       -- add an account to database
  remove    -- remove an account from database
  change    -- change owner name
  clear     -- clear accounts from database
  init      -- initialize with starting accounts
  quit      -- exit the program
```

Here is the source code:

```vb
' ConnectedSql.vb

Imports System
Imports System.Data
Imports System.Data.SqlClient

Module ConnectedSql
    Private connStr As String = _
        "server=localhost;uid=sa;pwd=;database=SimpleBank"
    Private conn As IDbConnection
    Dim sqlConn As New SqlConnection()

    Sub Main()
        OpenSql()
        CommandLoop()
    End Sub

    Private Sub OpenSql()
        conn = sqlConn
        conn.ConnectionString = connStr
        Console.WriteLine( _
            "Using SQL Server to access SimpleBank")
        Console.WriteLine("Database state: " & _
            conn.State.ToString())
        conn.Open()
        Console.WriteLine("Database state: " & _
            conn.State.ToString())
    End Sub

    Private Sub CommandLoop()
        ...
    End Sub

    Private Sub ShowList()
        Dim query As String = "select * from Account"
        Dim command As IDbCommand = CreateCommand(query)
        Dim reader As IDataReader = command.ExecuteReader()
        While reader.Read()
            Console.WriteLine("{0}  {1,-10}  {2:C}", _
                reader("AccountId"), reader("Owner"), _
```

```
            reader("Balance"))
        End While
        reader.Close()
    End Sub

    Private Sub AddAccount(ByVal bal As Decimal, _
      ByVal owner As String, ByVal id As Integer)
        Dim query As String = "insert into Account values(" _
          & id & ", '" & owner & "', ' ', " & bal & ")"
        Dim command As IDbCommand = CreateCommand(query)
        Dim numrow As Integer = command.ExecuteNonQuery()
        Console.WriteLine("{0} rows updated", numrow)
    End Sub

    Private Sub RemoveAccount(ByVal id As Integer)
        Dim query As String = _
          "delete from Account where AccountId = " & id
        Dim command As IDbCommand = CreateCommand(query)
        Dim numrow As Integer = command.ExecuteNonQuery()
        Console.WriteLine("{0} rows updated", numrow)
    End Sub

    Private Sub ChangeAccount(ByVal id As Integer, _
      ByVal owner As String)
        Dim query As String = _
          "update Account set Owner = '" _
          & owner & "' where AccountId = " & id
        Dim command As IDbCommand = CreateCommand(query)
        Dim numrow As Integer = command.ExecuteNonQuery()
        Console.WriteLine("{0} rows updated", numrow)
    End Sub

    Private Sub ClearAccounts()
        Dim query As String = "delete from Account"
        Dim command As IDbCommand = CreateCommand(query)
        Dim numrow As Integer = command.ExecuteNonQuery()
        Console.WriteLine("{0} rows updated", numrow)
    End Sub

    Private Function CreateCommand(ByVal query As String) _
      As IDbCommand
        Return New SqlCommand(query, sqlConn)
    End Function
End Module
```

Here is a sample run:

```
Using SQL Server to access SimpleBank
Database state: Closed
Database state: Open
Enter command, quit to exit
```

```
> clear
3 rows updated
> init
1 rows updated
1 rows updated
1 rows updated
> show
1   Bob          $100.00
2   Mary         $200.00
3   Charles      $300.00
> remove
id: 2
1 rows updated
> change
id: 1
new owner: Robert
1 rows updated
> add
id: 4
owner: David
balance: 400
1 rows updated
> show
1   Robert       $100.00
3   Charles      $300.00
4   David        $400.00
```

USING OLE DB DATA PROVIDER

Code Example

The program **ConnectedJet** illustrates using the OLE DB data provider for the Jet database engine to talk to an Access database. This program is functionally equivalent to the program **ConnectedSql** that we just examined. Here is selected source code. We show in bold all the places where the program was changed:

```vbnet
' ConnectedJet.vb

Imports System
Imports System.Data
Imports System.Data.OleDb

Module ConnectedJet
    Private connStr As String = _
      "Provider=Microsoft.Jet.OLEDB.4.0;" _
      & "Data Source=C:\OI\Databases\SimpleBank.mdb"
    Private conn As IDbConnection
    Dim jetConn As New OleDbConnection()

    Sub Main()
        OpenJet()
```

```
      CommandLoop()
   End Sub

   Private Sub OpenJet()
      conn = jetConn
      conn.ConnectionString = connStr
      Console.WriteLine("Using Access DB SimpleBank.mdb")

      ...

   Private Function CreateCommand(ByVal query As String) _
   As IDbCommand
      Return New OleDbCommand(query, jetConn)
   End Function

End Module
```

Disconnected Data Sets

A **DataSet** stores data in memory and provides a consistent relational programming model that is the same, whatever the original source of the data. Thus, a **DataSet** contains a collection of tables and relationships between tables. Each table contains a primary key and collections of columns and constraints, which define the schema of the table, and a collection of rows, which make up the data stored in the table. The object model of the **DataSet** class is illustrated in Figure 20–13.

There are several ways you can populate a data set with a schema and data:

- Read the schema and data from a database, using a **DataAdapter**.
- Programmatically create the schema, and populate it with data.
- Load the data set from an XML representation.

Data Adapters

A *data adapter* provides a bridge between a disconnected data set and its data source. Each .NET data provider provides its own implementation of the interface **IDbDataAdapter**. The OLE DB data provider has the class **OleDbDataAdapter**, and the SQL data provider has the class **SqlDataAdapter**.

A data adapter has properties for **SelectCommand**, **InsertCommand**, **UpdateCommand**, and **DeleteCommand**. These properties identify the SQL needed to retrieve, add, change, or remove data from the data source.

A data adapter has the **Fill** method to place data into a data set. It has the **Update** command to update the data source using data from the data set.

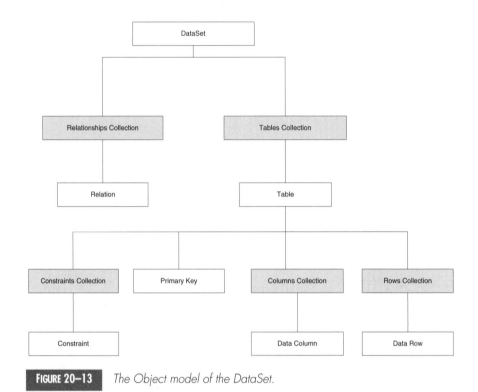

FIGURE 20–13   *The Object model of the DataSet.*

COMMAND BUILDER

You could explicitly initialize the various command properties to appropriate SQL text, in a manner similar to what we did in the connected scenario. The SQL is a little more elaborate, because the commands are parameterized. An alternative is to use the **SqlCommandBuilder** class to automatically generate appropriate commands. (There is a comparable class for OLE DB data providers.) Our sample program illustrates this automatic command building.

Sample Application Using Disconnected Scenario

We illustrate the disconnected scenario with another version of our bank application. This time, rather than keeping a connection open, we use a data adapter to populate a data set. We perform various operations on this data set. When we are finished, we update the data source from the data set.

To emphasize the disconnected nature of this scenario, we supply several parallel commands, so that the data set and database can be updated and displayed independently.

Again, we have two versions. **BankDbSql** uses a SQL Server data adapter, and **BankDbJet** uses an OLE DB data adapter to talk to an Access

Code Example

database. We use the **BankDbSql** version for this example. As with the programs illustrating the connected scenario, only a few lines of code have to be changed to port the program from data provider to another.

MAIN PROGRAM

We initialize the connect string and declare several global variables that will be used, including interface references for the connection and data adapter. We also instantiate a data set object. The initial database state (closed) is displayed, and a command loop is entered.

```
' BankDb.vb

Imports System
Imports System.Data
Imports System.Data.SqlClient

Module BankDb
   Private connStr As String = _
      "server=localhost;uid=sa;pwd=;database=SimpleBank"
   Private conn As IDbConnection
   Private sqlConn As New SqlConnection()
   Private adapter As IDbDataAdapter
   Private ds As New DataSet()

   Sub Main()
      conn = sqlConn
      conn.ConnectionString = connStr
      Console.WriteLine( _
         "Using SQL Server to access SimpleBank")
      Console.WriteLine( _
         "Database state: " & conn.State.ToString())
      CommandLoop()
   End Sub

   ...
```

OPENING AND CLOSING THE DATABASE

Procedures are required to open and close the database. After each operation, we display the current state. Here's the code:

```
Private Sub OpenDb()
   conn.Open()
   Console.WriteLine("Database state: " & _
      conn.State.ToString())
End Sub

Private Sub CloseDb()
   conn.Close()
```

```
    Console.WriteLine("Database state: " & _
        conn.State.ToString())
End Sub
```

CREATING A DATA ADAPTER AND GENERATING COMMANDS

A procedure is supplied that creates a data adapter. A command builder is also instantiated, passing a reference to the adapter to the constructor of the builder. The constructor of the command·builder then generates the required commands and stores them in the adapter. Our procedure displays these generated commands:

```
Private Function CreateAdapter(ByVal query As String) _
  As IDbDataAdapter
    Dim adapter As New SqlDataAdapter(query, connStr)
    Dim builder As New SqlCommandBuilder(adapter)

    ShowCommand(builder.GetDeleteCommand)
    ShowCommand(builder.GetInsertCommand)
    ShowCommand(builder.GetUpdateCommand)
    Return adapter
End Function
```

FILLING THE DATA SET

We have a procedure for filling the data set. We open the database. We set up a SELECT query, call our procedure for creating the data adapter, and call the **Fill** method of the data adapter, passing it a reference to our data set. Because this is a disconnected scenario, we then close the database. Here's the code:

```
Private Sub FillDataSet()
    OpenDb()
    Dim query As String = "select * from Account"
    adapter = CreateAdapter(query)
    adapter.Fill(ds)
    CloseDb()
End Sub
```

DISPLAYING THE DATA SET

We provide a procedure that displays the data set whenever desired. We first instantiate a **DataTable** object. We then use a **DataRow** object to iterate through the **Rows** collection. We display the contents of each row, using the default **Item** property, which can be passed a column name. Because **Item** is a default property, it can be omitted.

Note the use of a table called "Table." This table was created when we called the **Fill** method of **IDbDataAdapter**. Here, we pay a price for our generic coding of using an interface pointer. If we had used a **SqlData-Adapter** instance instead, we could have passed a table name, such as

"Account," as a parameter to our call of the **Fill** method. Then the name of the table in the data set would match the name of the corresponding table in the database. This would be nice, but the generic method works fine.

```
Private Sub ShowAccountsDs()
   Dim dt As DataTable = ds.Tables("Table")
   Dim row As DataRow
   For Each row In dt.Rows
      Console.WriteLine("{0}   {1,-10}   {2:C}", _
         row("AccountId"), row("Owner"), row("Balance"))
   Next
End Sub
```

ADDING A ROW TO THE DATA SET

We provide a procedure to add a row of data to the data set. We obtain a **DataTable** object from the **Tables** collection of the data set. Note again the use of the generic name "Table" for our table in the data set. We call the **NewRow** method of **DataTable** to create an empty row, which we populate with the data that is passed as parameters into our procedure. We then call the **Add** method of the **Rows** collection to add our new row to the collection.

```
Private Sub AddAccountDs(ByVal bal As Decimal, _
 ByVal owner As String, ByVal id As Integer)
   Dim dt As DataTable = ds.Tables("Table")
   Dim row As DataRow = dt.NewRow()
   row("AccountId") = id
   row("Owner") = owner
   row("Balance") = bal
   dt.Rows.Add(row)
End Sub
```

DELETING A ROW

We provide another procedure to delete a row having a specific ID. We again create a **DataTable** object, from which we select the row having the specified ID, obtaining a collection consisting of one row. Because collections are indexed beginning at 0, we can reference this row by **rows(0)**. We call the **Delete** method to delete this row from the data set.

```
Private Sub DeleteAccountDs(ByVal id As Integer)
   Dim dt As DataTable = ds.Tables("Table")
   Dim rows() As DataRow = dt.Select("AccountId = " & id)
   rows(0).Delete()
End Sub
```

CHANGING A ROW

Next, we provide a procedure that allows us to change a row in the data set. Specifically, we will change the owner name. Again, we instantiate a **DataT-**

able using the generic name "Table" for the table in our data set. We use the same code as in the delete procedure to select a row matching the ID that was passed in as a parameter. This time, instead of deleting the row, we update the "Owner" column.

```
Private Sub ChangeOwnerDs(ByVal owner As String, _
 ByVal id As Integer)
   Dim dt As DataTable = ds.Tables("Table")
   Dim rows() As DataRow = dt.Select("AccountId = " & id)
   rows(0)("Owner") = owner
End Sub
```

UPDATING THE DATABASE

All the changes we have made affect only the data set, not the original database from which we obtained the data. To propagate our changes back to the database, we call the **Update** method of the data adapter. This method returns the number of rows that were updated in the database (as is done by the **ExecuteNonQuery** method of a command object). Here's the code for this:

```
Private Sub UpdateAccount()
   OpenDb()
   Dim numrow As Integer
   numrow = adapter.Update(ds)
   Console.WriteLine("{0} rows updated", numrow)
   CloseDb()
End Sub
```

DIRECT ACCESS TO THE DATABASE

For demonstration purposes, we also implement a few procedures that allow us to access the database directly using the connected scenario. These procedures allow us to independently update the database and the data set, nailing the point that the data set is disconnected from the database. We content ourselves with procedures to show the contents of the **Account** table of the database and to add a row to this table. These procedures rely on a function to create a command object. Look at the code used:

```
Private Sub ShowAccountsDb()
   OpenDb()
   Dim query As String = "select * from Account"

   Dim command As IDbCommand = CreateCommand(query)
   Dim reader As IDataReader = command.ExecuteReader()
   While reader.Read()
     Console.WriteLine("{0}  {1,-10}  {2:C}", _
        reader("AccountId"), reader("Owner"), _
        reader("Balance"))
   End While
```

```
    reader.Close()
    CloseDb()
End Sub

Private Sub AddAccountDb(ByVal bal As Decimal, _
  ByVal owner As String, ByVal id As Integer)
    OpenDb()
    Dim query As String = "insert into Account values(" _
      & id & ", '" & owner & "', '','" & bal & ")"

    Dim command As IDbCommand = CreateCommand(query)
    Dim numrow As Integer = command.ExecuteNonQuery()
    Console.WriteLine("{0} rows updated", numrow)
    CloseDb()
End Sub

Private Function CreateCommand(ByVal query As String) _
  As IDbCommand
    Return New SqlCommand(query, sqlConn)
End Function
```

Running the Sample Program

Here is a sample run of the program. Note that we have provided statements showing the state of the database whenever it is opened or closed. We populate a data set and do some manipulations. We compare the contents of the database and the data set. We then update the database from the data set and verify that now they are in sync. Note that our exception handling in the main command loop neatly catches exceptions. You could try out many more exceptional conditions if you wished. Notice that you are not allowed to display information about a row that has been deleted from a data set. Here's the output:

```
Using SQL Server to access SimpleBank
Database state: Closed
Enter command, quit to exit
> fill
Database state: Open
DELETE FROM Account WHERE ( AccountId = @p1 AND Owner = @p2
AND AccountType = @p3 AND Balance = @p4 )
INSERT INTO Account( AccountId , Owner , AccountType ,
Balance ) VALUES ( @p1 ,@p2 , @p3 , @p4 )
UPDATE Account SET AccountId = @p1 , Owner = @p2 ,
AccountType = @p3 , Balance = @p4 WHERE ( AccountId = @p5
AND Owner = @p6 AND AccountType = @p7 AND Balance = @p8 )
Database state: Closed
> show
1   Robert       $100.00
3   Charles      $300.00
```

```
4  David        $400.00
> remove
id: 2
Exception of type System.IndexOutOfRangeException was
thrown.
> remove
id: 3
> change
id: 4
new owner: Donovan
> show
1  Robert       $100.00
Deleted row information can't be accessed through the row.
> showdb
Database state: Open
1   Robert      $100.00
3   Charles     $300.00
4   David       $400.00
Database state: Closed
> update
Database state: Open
2 rows updated
Database state: Closed
> show
1  Robert       $100.00
4  Donovan      $400.00
> showdb
Database state: Open
1   Robert      $100.00
4   Donovan     $400.00
Database state: Closed
```

Databound Controls

All of our demonstration programs so far have been console applications. We have done this to focus on the coding of database functionality, without being distracted by issues concerning user interface. Also, by catching exceptions in our command loop, we are able to conveniently display exception information, making it easy for you to experiment and observe the results, even for exceptional situations.

Naturally, in practice you want to create an attractive user interface, either as a Windows application or a Web application. (Web applications are beyond the scope of this book. See *Application Development Using Visual Basic and .NET* and *Fundamentals of Web Applications Using .NET and XML* for coverage of Web applications. Both of these books are in The Integrated .NET Series.)

In this section, we give a brief introduction to providing a graphical user interface to a database application using Windows Forms. There are two approaches that can be followed. The first is to write specific code to populate controls with data that has been retrieved from a database. The second is to use *databound* controls. We illustrate this second approach by showing how to bind a data set to a data grid control.

Binding a Data Grid to a Data Set

An exceptionally easy and effective way to both display and manipulate data in a database is through a *data grid* control. The basic steps are simple:

1. Create a data set, and populate it with data using a data adapter.
2. Bind the data set to a data grid control on a form.
3. The user sees the data displayed in the grid and can change data, delete rows, and add rows.
4. Update the data source using the data adapter.

The program **DataBoundExample** provides an illustration. A form provides a data grid to display the **Account** table from the **SimpleBank** database. There are buttons to fill the data set (and hence, the data grid) and to update the database. Figure 20–14 illustrates the user interface.

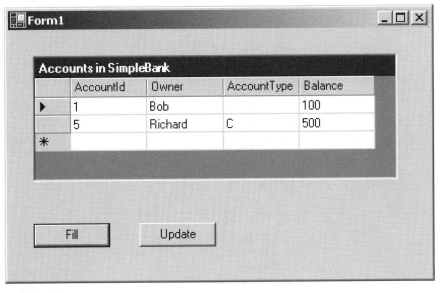

FIGURE 20–14 *A graphical user interface for displaying and updating Account table.*

The code is in two files. The database code is in **BankDb.vb**, and the user interface code is in **Form1.vb**. Here is the database code. It is basically the code we had before in our command-line example. We have converted the module to a class, exposed the data set as a public member, made the procedures public, and stripped out the command-line input/output. A constructor is provided to initialize the connection string. Code that is called by our user interface is highlighted.

```vb
' BankDb.vb

Imports System
Imports System.Data
Imports System.Data.SqlClient

Public Class BankDb
    Private connStr As String =   _
        "server=localhost;uid=sa;pwd=;database=SimpleBank"
    Private conn As IDbConnection
    Private sqlConn As New SqlConnection()
    Private adapter As IDbDataAdapter
    Public ds As New DataSet()

    Public Sub New()
        conn = sqlConn
        conn.ConnectionString = connStr
    End Sub

    Private Sub OpenDb()
        conn.Open()
    End Sub

    Private Sub CloseDb()
        conn.Close()
    End Sub

    Public Sub FillDataSet()
        OpenDb()
        Dim query As String = "select * from Account"
        adapter = CreateAdapter(query)
        adapter.Fill(ds)
        CloseDb()
    End Sub

    ...

    Public Function UpdateAccount() As Integer
        OpenDb()
        Dim numrow As Integer
        numrow = adapter.Update(ds)
        CloseDb()
```

```
        Return numrow
    End Function


    ...


    Private Function CreateAdapter(ByVal query As String) _
      As IDbDataAdapter
        Dim adapter As New SqlDataAdapter(query, connStr)
        Dim builder As New SqlCommandBuilder(adapter)
        Return adapter
    End Function

End Class
```

Here is the user interface code:

```
Public Class MainForm
    Inherits System.Windows.Forms.Form


    ...


    Private m_bank As New BankDb()

    Private Sub cmdFill_Click(ByVal sender As _
      System.Object, ByVal e As System.EventArgs) _
      Handles cmdFill.Click
        m_bank.FillDataSet()
        dgAccounts.SetDataBinding( _
          m_bank.ds.Tables(0), Nothing)
    End Sub

    Private Sub cmdUpdate_Click(ByVal sender As _
      System.Object, ByVal e As System.EventArgs) _
      Handles cmdUpdate.Click
        Dim numrow As Integer
        numrow = m_bank.UpdateAccount()
        MessageBox.Show(numrow & " rows updated")
    End Sub

End Class
```

The key line of code is the call to the data grid's **SetDataBinding** method, which binds the data grid to a table of a data set. Now, when the user interacts with the data grid, all changes made by the user in the data grid are propagated back to the data set automatically (but not to the database). The handler for clicking the "Update" button updates the database.

Creating a Data Set Manually

Code
Example

Although it is common to populate a data set from a database, you can also create a data set programmatically. You provide code to define the tables and columns of the data set (the schema). You can then use this data set as a temporary store for program data, enjoying the full relational capabilities of a data set. The program **ManualDataSet** provides an example:

```
'ManualDataSet.vb

Imports System.Data
Imports System.Data.OleDb

Module DataSetModule

    Sub Main()
        Dim tbl As DataTable
        Dim row As DataRow
        Dim col As DataColumn

        ' Create a DataSet
        Dim ds As New DataSet("SampleDB")

        ' Create a Products table
        tbl = New DataTable("Products")
        ds.Tables.Add(tbl)

        ' Create the schema for the Products table
        col = New DataColumn("ProductName")
        col.DataType = _
         System.Type.GetType("System.String")
        col.DefaultValue = ""
        col.Unique = True
        tbl.Columns.Add(col)

        col = New DataColumn("Price")
        col.DataType = _
         System.Type.GetType("System.Single")
        col.DefaultValue = 0
        tbl.Columns.Add(col)

        col = New DataColumn("SupplierID")
        col.DataType = _
         System.Type.GetType("System.String")
        col.DefaultValue = ""
        tbl.Columns.Add(col)

        ' Add data to the Products table
        row = ds.Tables("Products").NewRow
```

```
ds.Tables("Products").Rows.Add(row)
row("ProductName") = "Bean Bag Chair"
row("Price") = 38.29
row("SupplierID") = "LIMA"

row = ds.Tables("Products").NewRow
ds.Tables("Products").Rows.Add(row)
row("ProductName") = "Rocking Chair"
row("Price") = 123.95
row("SupplierID") = "ACME"

row = ds.Tables("Products").NewRow
ds.Tables("Products").Rows.Add(row)
row("ProductName") = "Bar Stool"
row("Price") = 29.99
row("SupplierID") = "ACME"

' Create the Suppliers table
tbl = New DataTable("Suppliers")
ds.Tables.Add(tbl)

' Create the schema for the Suppliers table
col = New DataColumn("SupplierID")
col.DataType = _
 System.Type.GetType("System.String")
col.DefaultValue = ""
col.Unique = True
tbl.Columns.Add(col)

col = New DataColumn("SupplierName")
col.DataType = _
 System.Type.GetType("System.String")
col.DefaultValue = ""
tbl.Columns.Add(col)

' Add data to the Suppliers table
row = ds.Tables("Suppliers").NewRow
ds.Tables("Suppliers").Rows.Add(row)
row("SupplierID") = "LIMA"
row("SupplierName") = "Beans, Beans, Beans, LLC"

row = ds.Tables("Suppliers").NewRow
ds.Tables("Suppliers").Rows.Add(row)
row("SupplierID") = "ACME"
row("SupplierName") = "ACME Products, Inc."

' Display all data in all tables
Console.WriteLine("-------------------------")
For Each tbl In ds.Tables
    Console.WriteLine(tbl.TableName & ": ")
    Console.WriteLine("-------------------------")
```

```
      For Each row In ds.Tables(tbl.TableName).Rows
         For Each col In s.Tables(tbl.TableName).Columns
            Console.WriteLine("{0} : {1}   ", _
            col.ColumnName, -
            row(col.ColumnName).ToString())
         Next
         Console.WriteLine()
      Next
      Console.WriteLine("----------------------------")
   Next
End Sub

End Module
```

Here is the output from running the program:

```
----------------------------
Products:
----------------------------
ProductName : Bean Bag Chair
Price : 38.29
SupplierID : LIMA

ProductName : Rocking Chair
Price : 123.95
SupplierID : ACME

ProductName : Bar Stool
Price : 29.99
SupplierID : ACME


----------------------------
Suppliers:
----------------------------
SupplierID : LIMA
SupplierName : Beans, Beans, Beans, LLC

SupplierID : ACME
SupplierName : ACME Products, Inc.


----------------------------
```

Data Binding and a Manual Data Set

After the data set is created, you can bind it to a data grid, as illustrated previously for a data set that was populated from a database. The manual data set example has two tables. Our user interface provides buttons so that either the **Products** table or the **Suppliers** table can be displayed. Figure 20–15 shows the user interface.

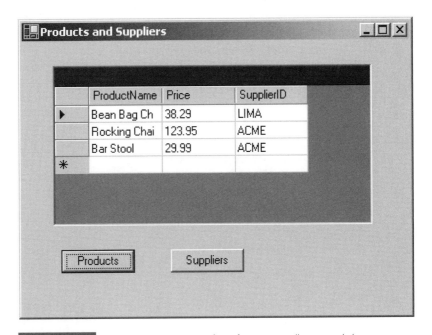

FIGURE 20-15 *A graphical user interface for a manually created data set.*

Code Example

Code for this program can be found in **ManualDataSetGUI**. It contains **DataSetModule**, which is responsible for creating the manual data set and returning a reference to it.

```
Imports System.Data
Imports System.Data.OLEDB

Module DataSetModule

    Public Function CreateDataSet() As DataSet
        Dim tbl As DataTable
        Dim row As DataRow
        Dim col As DataColumn

        ' Create a DataSet
        Dim ds As New DataSet("SampleDB")

        ...

        Return ds
    End Function

End Module
```

The form creates the data set when it is loaded, and then the binds **DataGrid** to either the **Products** table or the **Suppliers** table dynamically by calling the grid's **SetDataBindings** method.

```
Public Class MainForm
    Inherits System.Windows.Forms.Form

    ...

    Friend WithEvents DataGrid1 As _
        System.Windows.Forms.DataGrid
    Friend WithEvents cmdSuppliers As _
        System.Windows.Forms.Button
    Friend WithEvents cmdProducts As _
        System.Windows.Forms.Button

    ...

    Private m_ds As DataSet

    Private Sub MainForm_Load(ByVal sender As _
        System.Object, ByVal e As System.EventArgs) _
        Handles MyBase.Load
        m_ds = CreateDataSet()
    End Sub

    Private Sub cmdProducts_Click(ByVal sender As _
        System.Object, ByVal e As System.EventArgs) _
        Handles cmdProducts.Click
        DataGrid1.SetDataBinding(m_ds, "Products")
    End Sub

    Private Sub cmdSuppliers_Click(ByVal sender As _
        System.Object, ByVal e As System.EventArgs) _
        Handles cmdSuppliers.Click
        DataGrid1.SetDataBinding(m_ds, "Suppliers")
    End Sub

End Class
```

Using XML Data

XML is becoming the standard for transmitting data on the Internet. It is similar to HTML in that it is based on tags. However, unlike HTML, its tags are not predefined. It is capable of representing a self-describing collection of data. For example, we might define an Employee in XML as follows:

```
<Employee>
       <ID>95-0413</ID>
       <Name>Betty Smalltree</Name>
       <Salary>48000.00</Salary>
</Employee>
```

Because the data is text-based, it can be passed through firewalls and does not require the use of protocols such as DCOM.

ADO.NET uses XML internally to manage the data in a **DataSet** object. The **DataSet** class has methods that can be used to read and write XML schema and data information.

XML Schema and Data

An XML document may describe schema information as well as contain data. XML schemas are written in XML. XML can be used to describe both the tables and columns in a relational database.

The following describes the Products table built manually using the **DataSet** object earlier in the chapter:

- The three columns are ProductName, Price, and SupplierID.
- ProductName must be unique.

Here is the XML schema description:

```
<xsd:element name="Products">
   <xsd:complexType content="elementOnly">
      <xsd:all>
         <xsd:element name="ProductName" default=""
            type="xsd:string"/>
         <xsd:element name="Price" default="0"
            type="xsd:float"/>
         <xsd:element name="SupplierID" default=""
            type="xsd:string"/>
      </xsd:all>
   </xsd:complexType>
   <xsd:unique name="Constraint1">
      <xsd:selector>.</xsd:selector>
      <xsd:field>ProductName</xsd:field>
   </xsd:unique>
</xsd:element>
```

Here is the data from the Products table:

```
<Products>
   <ProductName>Aroma Therapy Candles</ProductName>
   <Price>2.95</Price>
   <SupplierID>SMELL</SupplierID>
```

```
</Products>
<Products>
   <ProductName>Bean Bag Chair</ProductName>
   <Price>18.29</Price>
   <SupplierID>LIMA</SupplierID>
</Products>
<Products>
   <ProductName>Carpet Cleaner</ProductName>
   <Price>9.95</Price>
   <SupplierID>SPILL</SupplierID>
</Products>
```

Using XML with a DataSet

The **DataSet** class has several methods to read and write XML data:

- **WriteXml** generates an XML file containing both the data and schema information from the **DataSet**.
- **ReadXml** reads in an XML file, and translates both the data and the schema information as needed to populate the **DataSet**.
- **WriteXmlData** generates an XML file containing the **DataSet**'s data.
- **ReadXmlData** reads in an XML file and translates the data as needed to populate the **DataSet**.
- **WriteXmlSchema** generates an XML file containing the **DataSet**'s schema.
- **ReadXmlSchema** reads in an XML file and translates the schema as needed for **DataSet**.

Code
Example

The program **XMLExample** illustrates writing and reading XML data. We create the data set programmatically, as in our earlier **ManualDataSet** example. We then write the XML data and read the XML data:

```
Module XMLModule

   Sub BuildXMLData()
      ' Create a DataSet
      ...

      ' Write the data file
      ds.WriteXml("SampleDB.xml")
   End Sub

   Sub ReadXMLData()
      Dim ds As New DataSet("SampleDB")
      ds.ReadXml("SampleDB.xml")

      ' Display all data in all tables
      ...
```

```
    End Sub

    Sub Main()
        BuildXMLData()
        ReadXMLData()
    End Sub

End Module
```

Summary

ADO.NET provides a set of classes that can be used to interact with data providers. You can access data sources in either a connected or disconnected mode. The **DataReader** can be used to interact with a data source in a connected mode. The **DataSet** can be used to interact with data from a data source without maintaining a constant connection to the data source. The **DataSet** can be populated from a database using a **DataAdapter**. You can easily display data from a data set on a form by binding the data set to a data grid control. XML can be used to pass data between application tiers without worrying about data type conversions. Methods are provided in the **DataSet** class to facilitate reading and writing data as XML.

File I/O

*I*nput and output is a fundamental aspect of computer programming. In Chapter 20, we discussed databases. In this chapter, we discuss the subject of file I/O, including working with both files and directories. In the first part of the chapter, we discuss file I/O using familiar functions and objects from earlier versions of Visual Basic. In the last part of the chapter, we cover the new I/O model in the .NET Framework, which provides a flexible I/O model based on the concept of a stream. We also discuss the topic of serialization, which makes it easy to read and write complex data structures.

Visual Basic File Processing Functions

VB.NET provides built-in file processing functions that can be used to read and write text files and binary files. In previous versions of VB, these features were provided as VB *statements*, but in VB.NET they are provided as functions. For example:

```
' VB 6 code to open a file for input
Open "data.dat" For Input As #1

'Equivalent VB.NET code
FileOpen(1, "data.dat", OpenMode.Input)
```

Managing Files

The file processing features of VB.NET that are native to the language are found in the **Microsoft.VisualBasic.FileSystem** namespace. Here, you will find functions that manipulate the directory system, such as those listed in Table 21-1.

TABLE 21–1	*VB.NET File System Functions*

Function	**Description**
ChDrive	Changes the active drive
ChDir	Changes the active directory
CurDir	Returns the active path
SetAttr	Sets the file attributes of a specified drive, directory, or file
GetAttr	Gets the file attributes of a specified drive, directory, or file
MkDir	Builds a directory
RmDir	Removes a directory
Rename	Renames a file or directory
Kill	Deletes a file
FileCopy	Copies a file or directory
FileDateTime	Gets the date and time of when a file was created or last modified

These functions are very straightforward. However, because you are working with the file system, you should make judicious use of exception handling. For example, the following code fragment deletes a file from the root directory.

```
Try
   Kill("c:\backup.dat")
Catch e As IO.FileNotFoundException
   Console.WriteLine("File not found!")
Catch e As Exception
   Console.WriteLine("File error!")
End Try
```

If the file exists when you run this code, it is deleted. If you run this code again, the file will not be found!

You can programmatically copy a file using the **FileCopy** function. You can also set a file's attributes to values such as **ReadOnly**, **Normal**, **Hidden**, or **Archive** using the **SetAttr** function. For example::

```
Try
   FileCopy("c:\data.dat", "c:\backup.dat")
   SetAttr("c:\backup.dat", FileAttribute.ReadOnly)
```

```
Catch e As IO.FileNotFoundException
   Console.WriteLine("File not found!")
Catch e As Exception
   Console.WriteLine("File error!")
End Try
```

Code
Example

The program **FunWithFiles** makes a copy of your autoexec.bat file and then manipulates the *copy* of the file.

```
Imports Microsoft.VisualBasic.FileSystem

Module FunWithFiles

    Sub Main()

        Try
            Console.WriteLine("Copying file...")
            FileCopy("C:\autoexec.bat", "c:\deleteMe.txt")
            Console.WriteLine("...file copied!")
        Catch e As IO.FileNotFoundException
            Console.WriteLine("Error: File not found!")
            Exit Sub
        Catch e As Exception
            Console.WriteLine("Error: Unable to copy file!")
            Exit Sub
        End Try

        Try
            Console.WriteLine( _
                "Setting file attribute to ReadOnly...")
            SetAttr("c:\deleteMe.txt", FileAttribute.ReadOnly)
            Console.WriteLine( _
                "...attributes set successfully!")
        Catch e As IO.FileNotFoundException
            Console.WriteLine("Error: File not found!")
        Catch e As Exception
            Console.WriteLine( _
                "Error: Unable to change attributes!")
        End Try

        Try
            Console.WriteLine("Deleting file...")
            Kill("c:\deleteMe.txt")
            Console.WriteLine("...Deleted!")
        Catch e As IO.FileNotFoundException
            Console.WriteLine("Error: File not found!")
        Catch e As Exception
            Console.WriteLine("Error: Unable to delete file!")
        End Try
```

```
    Try
        Console.WriteLine( _
            "Setting file attribute to Normal...")
        SetAttr("c:\DeleteMe.txt", FileAttribute.Normal)
        Console.WriteLine( _
            "...attributes set successfully!")
    Catch e As IO.FileNotFoundException
        Console.WriteLine("Error: File not found!")
    Catch e As Exception
        Console.WriteLine( _
            "Error: Unable to change attributes!")
    End Try

    Try
        Console.WriteLine("Deleting file...")
        Kill("c:\DeleteMe.txt")
        Console.WriteLine("...Deleted!")
    Catch e As IO.FileNotFoundException
        Console.WriteLine("Error: File not found!")
    Catch e As Exception
        Console.WriteLine("Error: Unable to delete file!")
    End Try
    End Sub

End Module
```

Output of this program is as follows:

```
Copying file...
...file copied!
Setting file attribute to ReadOnly...
...attributes set successfully!
Deleting file...
Error: Unable to delete file!
Setting file attribute to Normal...
...attributes set successfully!
Deleting file...
...Deleted!
```

Reading and Writing Files

The **Microsoft.VisualBasic.FileSystem** namespace also provides a collection of functions for doing sequential and random file I/O. Table 21–2 summarizes some of the more interesting functions.

TABLE 21-2	VB.NET File I/O Functions

Function	Description
FreeFile	Obtains a file number that is used to reference files
FileOpen	Opens a file
FileClose	Closes a file
Lock	Denies access to a file, either at the file level or record level, by other processes
Unlock	Re-enables access to a file after it has been locked
Print	Writes data to a sequential file
PrintLine	Writes data to a sequential file, followed by a carriage return and line feed
Write	Writes data to a sequential file (NOTE: Write encloses each data element written to the file in quotes and separates data elements with commas.)
WriteLine	Writes data to a sequential file, followed by a carriage return and line feed (See note about Write above.)
Input	Reads data from a sequential file
InputString	Reads a specified number of characters from a file
LineInput	Reads a line of data (up to the carriage return and line feed) from a sequential file
FilePut	Writes data to a file at a specified location
FileGet	Reads data from a file at a specified location
LOF	Returns the length of the file
EOF	Detects the end of file

VB uses a file number to interact with files. You can specify the number yourself, or you can ask VB to give you the next available file number that isn't in use by calling **FreeFile**.

```
Dim fileNum As Integer
fileNum = FreeFile()
```

After a file number has been obtained, you must use the **FileOpen** function to open a file. This function requires you to select a mode (for example: input or output); whether the file is a sequential, binary, or random file; and the type of access allowed. For example, to open a sequential file for input, you can write this:

```
FileOpen(fileNum, "Data.Dat", OpenMode.Input)
```

To open a file in binary mode for input that locks the file, you can write this:

```
FileOpen(fileNum, "Data.Dat", OpenMode.Binary, _
    OpenAccess.Read, OpenShare.Locked)
```

To use random files, you must write fixed length records to the file. Typically, this is done by building a structure that describes the data that will be read or written. For example:

```
Structure Employee
   Dim ID As Integer
   <VBFixedString(25)> Dim Name As String
   Dim Pay As Single
End Structure
```

You can see that we had to use a .NET attribute identifying the string as fixed length to make this work. This is because the size of each **Employee** record in a random file must be the same so that the system can calculate the byte offset of any given record number.

When opening a random file that contains **Employee** records, you must specify the length of each record. In our case, the **Employee** structure is 33 bytes (4 for the **Integer**, 25 for the **String**, and 4 for the **Single**). But we will use the **Len** function, which calculates this for us. Here's an example:

```
Dim e As Employee
Dim recLen As Integer = Len(e)
FileOpen(fileNum, "data.dat", OpenMode.Random, , , recLen)
```

When you are finished accessing a file, it should be closed using the **FileClose** function, as shown here:

```
FileClose(fileNum)
```

SEQUENTIAL FILES

VB has historically had two styles of sequential file I/O. One style (using **Print** or **PrintLine**) writes data to the file exactly as the program specifies. The other style (using **Write** or **WriteLine**) separates elements written to the file with commas and encloses string elements in quotes. The program **SequentialFiles** illustrates this:

```
Imports System
Imports Microsoft.VisualBasic.FileSystem

Module SequentialFileIO

   Sub Main()
      Dim i As Integer
      Dim s As String

      Dim fileNum As Integer
      fileNum = FreeFile()
```

```
        FileOpen(fileNum, "PrintData.txt", OpenMode.Output)
        For i = 1 To 5
            FileSystem.Print(fileNum, "Data: ")
            FileSystem.PrintLine(fileNum, i)
        Next
        FileClose(fileNum)

        FileOpen(fileNum, "WriteData.txt", OpenMode.Output)
        For i = 1 To 5
            FileSystem.Write(fileNum, "Data: ")
            FileSystem.WriteLine(fileNum, i)
        Next
        FileClose(fileNum)

        FileOpen(fileNum, "PrintData.txt", OpenMode.Input)
        Console.WriteLine("Data written using Print...")
        For i = 1 To 5
            s = FileSystem.LineInput(fileNum)
            Console.WriteLine(s)
        Next
        FileClose(fileNum)

        FileOpen(fileNum, "WriteData.txt", OpenMode.Input)
        Console.WriteLine("Data written using Write...")
        For i = 1 To 5
            s = FileSystem.LineInput(fileNum)
            Console.WriteLine(s)
        Next
        FileClose(fileNum)
    End Sub

End Module
```

Output from this program is shown below:

```
Data written using Print...
Data:   1
Data:   2
Data:   3
Data:   4
Data:   5
Data written using Write...
"Data: ",1
"Data: ",2
"Data: ",3
"Data: ",4
"Data: ",5
```

The **Input** function in VB.NET understands the format of file written using calls to **Write**. It can be used to read in the various elements in a file produced using the **Write** function. For example:

```
FileOpen(fileNum, "WriteData.txt", OpenMode.Input)
Console.WriteLine( _
   "Data written using Write and read using Input...")

Dim inString As String
Dim inCount As Integer
For i = 1 To 5
   Input(fileNum, inString)    ' read the first field
   Input(fileNum, inCount)     ' read the second field
   Console.WriteLine(inString & inCount)
Next
FileClose(fileNum)
```

As you can tell from the following output, the **Input** function knew how to interpret the quotes and commas:

```
Data written using Write and read using Input...
Data: 1
Data: 2
Data: 3
Data: 4
Data: 5
```

RANDOM FILES

Random files are more practical when the data for your application is stored in a file and you need to be able to interact with the file on a per-record basis. That is, you want to look up a particular record without reading the entire file or change a record without rewriting the entire file.

When using random files, we use the **FilePut** and **FileGet** functions. These allow you to specify the record number of the record with which you want to interact.

The following example, found in **RandomFiles**, builds a simple random file with four employees. Each employee's ID is also his or her record number in the file. Using this program, you can look up an employee's data and change his or her pay. This program checks the disk to see whether the data file is there. If the file is there, it is used. If the file isn't there, the program rebuilds the file.

Code
Example

```
Imports System
Imports Microsoft.VisualBasic.FileSystem

Module RandomFiles
   Structure Employee
      Dim ID As Integer
```

```vb
   <VBFixedString(25)> Dim Name As String
   Dim Pay As Single
End Structure

Private Sub BuildFile()
   Dim fileNum As Integer
   fileNum = FreeFile()

   Dim e As Employee
   Dim recLen As Integer = Len(e)
   FileOpen(fileNum, "employees.dat", OpenMode.Random, _
      , , recLen)

   ' Load the file with 4 records
   e.ID = 1
   e.Name = "Dana"
   e.Pay = 4501
   FilePut(fileNum, e)

   e.ID = 2
   e.Name = "Bob"
   e.Pay = 4900
   FilePut(fileNum, e)

   e.ID = 3
   e.Name = "Brenda"
   e.Pay = 4600
   FilePut(fileNum, e)

   e.ID = 4
   e.Name = "Richard"
   e.Pay = 4500
   FilePut(fileNum, e)
   FileClose(fileNum)
End Sub

Sub Main()
   Dim fileNum As Integer
   fileNum = FreeFile()

   Dim e As Employee
   Dim recLen As Integer = Len(e)

   Try
      ' See if the file exists
      Dim builtOn As Date
      builtOn = FileDateTime("employees.dat")
      Console.WriteLine( _
         "Accessing file built on {0}", builtOn)
```

```
        Catch notFound As IO.FileNotFoundException
            ' The first time we run this, the file
            ' isn't there so we build it
            BuildFile()
            Console.WriteLine("Building file...")
        Catch ex As Exception
            Console.WriteLine("Error: {0}", ex.Message)
            Exit Sub
        End Try

        FileOpen(fileNum, "employees.dat", OpenMode.Random, _
            , , recLen)

        ' Allow the user to request a particular record
        Dim EID As Integer
        Console.Write("Which employee do you want? ")
        EID = Convert.ToInt32(Console.ReadLine())

        ' Use EID as record number to find the record
        FileGet(fileNum, e, EID)
        Console.WriteLine( _
            "Employee {0} makes {1}", e.Name, e.Pay)

        Dim newPay As Integer
        Console.Write("Enter a new value for pay: ")
        newPay = Convert.ToSingle(Console.ReadLine())
        e.Pay = newPay

        ' Rewrite the record
        FilePut(fileNum, e, EID)

        FileClose(fileNum)
    End Sub

End Module
```

The first time we run the program, we will have the following output:

```
Building file...
Which employee do you want? 3
Employee Brenda                    makes 4600
Enter a new value for pay: 4650
```

If we run the program again, the file exists and we will use that copy.

```
Accessing file built on 12/17/2001 10:46:14 PM
Which employee do you want? 3
Employee Brenda                    makes 4650
Enter a new value for pay: 4675
```

File System Objects

Microsoft introduced the concept of File System Objects in VB6. They provided a set of objects that could be used to read and write files, as well as manipulate the file system. File System Objects were provided in VB6 by adding a reference to the "Microsoft Scripting Runtime" COM server. However, in VB.NET, a better solution is to use the .NET file capabilities. These capabilities are discussed in the following section. However, if you are a VB6 programmer determined to use the File System Objects, read Chapter 22 to learn how to use COM servers from VB.NET.

Input and Output in .NET

The .NET Framework provides a very flexible and consistent framework for performing input and output. The classes supporting input and output are in the **System.IO** namespace. In this section, we first examine how the .NET Framework handles directories. Then we look at file I/O, which makes use of an intermediary called a stream. We conclude with a discussion of serialization.

Directories

The classes **Directory** and **DirectoryInfo** contain routines for working with directories. All the methods of **Directory** are shared, so you can call them without having a directory instance (see Table 21-3). The **DirectoryInfo** class contains instance methods (see Table 21-4). In many cases, you can accomplish the same objective using methods of either class. The methods of **Directory** always perform a security check. If you are going to reuse a method several times, it may be better to obtain an instance of **DirectoryInfo** and use its instance methods, because a security check may not always be necessary. (We do not discuss security in this book. For a discussion of security in .NET, you may wish to refer to our book *Application Development Using Visual Basic and .NET.*)

TABLE 21-3	Interesting Directory Members

Method	Description
GetLogicalDrives	Gets a string representation of the logical drives on the computer
GetCurrentDirectory	Gets the current directory
SetCurrentDirectory	Sets the directory to the one specified

TABLE 21-3	Interesting Directory Members (continued)
Method	**Description**
GetDirectories	Gets an array of directories in the current directory
GetFiles	Gets an array of files in the current directory
CreateDirectory	Creates the directory specified
Delete	Deletes the specified directory
SetCreationTime	Sets the creation time of the current directory
SetLastAccessTime	Sets the last access time of the current directory
SetLastWriteTime	Sets the last write time of the current directory

TABLE 21-4	Interesting DirectoryInfo Members
Properties and Method	**Description**
New	The constructor that creates a DirectoryInfo object from a path
Create	(method) Creates a directory
CreateSubdirectory	(method) Creates a subdirectory on the specified path
GetDirectories	Gets the subdirectories in the current directory
GetFiles	Gets the files in the current directory
CreationTime	(property) Gets or sets the creation time of the current directory
LastAccessTime	(property) Gets or sets the last access time of the current directory
LastWriteTime	(property) Gets or sets the last write time of the current directory

Code
Example

We illustrate both classes with a simple program **DirectoryDemo\Version 1**, which contains DOS-like commands to show the contents of the current directory ("dir") and to change the current directory ("cd"). A directory can contain both files and other directories. The method **GetFiles** returns an array of **FileInfo** objects, and the method **GetDirectories** returns an array of **DirectoryInfo** objects. In this program, we use only the **Name** property of **FileInfo**. In the following section, we examine how to read and write files using streams.

```
' DirectoryDemo.vb

Imports System
Imports System.IO
```

```
Module DirectoryDemo
    Private path As String
    Private dir As DirectoryInfo

    Public Sub Main()
        path = Directory.GetCurrentDirectory()
        Console.WriteLine("path = {0}", path)

        dir = New DirectoryInfo(path)

        Dim iw As New InputWrapper()
        Dim cmd As String
        Console.WriteLine("Enter command, quit to exit")
        cmd = iw.getString("> ")
        While Not cmd.Equals("quit")
            Dim id As Integer
            Try
                If cmd.Equals("cd") Then
                    path = iw.getString("path: ")
                    dir = New DirectoryInfo(path)
                    Directory.SetCurrentDirectory(path)
                ElseIf cmd.Equals("dir") Then
                    Dim files() As FileInfo = dir.GetFiles()
                    Console.WriteLine("Files:")
                    Dim f As FileInfo
                    For Each f In files
                        Console.WriteLine("   {0}", f.Name)
                    Next
                    Dim dirs() As DirectoryInfo = _
                        dir.GetDirectories()
                    Console.WriteLine("Directories:")
                    Dim d As DirectoryInfo
                    For Each d In dirs
                        Console.WriteLine("   {0}", d.Name)
                    Next
                Else
                    Help()
                ...
```

Here is a sample run of the program. Notice that the current directory starts out as the directory containing the program's executable.

```
path = C:\OI\IntroVb\Chap21\DirectoryDemo\Version 1\bin
Enter command, quit to exit
> dir
Files:
   DirectoryDemo.exe
   DirectoryDemo.pdb
Directories:
> cd
```

```
path: ..
> dir
Files:
   DirectoryDemo.sln
   DirectoryDemo.vb
   DirectoryDemo.vbproj
   InputWrapper.vb
Directories:
   bin
   obj
> cd
path: c:\OI\IntroVb\Chap21
> dir
Files:
Directories:
   DirectoryDemo
   FileDemo
   SerializeAccount
```

Path Class

The **System.IO** namespace contains the class **Path** that provides fields and methods for working with directory strings in a cross-platform manner. For example, the public field **DirectorySeparatorChar** returns the character that is used for separating directories in a path string. In Windows, this character is a backslash (\);on Unix systems, it is a slash (/). There are methods for performing operations such as finding a complete path name, finding the root name of a file, finding the extension of a file, and so forth. There are also methods for working with temporary files and the temporary directory.   Refer to Table 21-5.

TABLE 21–5	*Interesting Path Members*
Properties and Methods	**Description**
DirectorySeparatorChar	Gets the platform-specific directory separator
InvalidPathChars	Gets the platform-specific list of invalid path characters
GetFullPath	Expands a specified path to a fully qualified path
GetPathRoot	Gets the root portion of the specified path
GetFileNameWithoutExtension	Gets the file name, without any extension, from a specified path
GetFileName	Gets the file name from a specified path
GetTempFileName	Generates a unique temporary file name
ChangeExtension	Changes the file extension given a specified path

Code
Example

The program **DirectoryDemo\Version 2** adds two commands, "path" and "temp," to illustrate using the **Path** class. Notice that we have renamed the variable holding the current directory path from **path** to **dirPath**, to avoid a name clash with the class name **Path**.

```vb
' DirectoryDemo.vb

Imports System
Imports System.IO

Module DirectoryDemo
    Private dirPath As String
    Private dir As DirectoryInfo
    Private tempPath As String
    Public Sub Main()
        dirpath = Directory.GetCurrentDirectory()
        Console.WriteLine("path = {0}", dirpath)

        dir = New DirectoryInfo(dirpath)

        tempPath = Path.GetTempPath()
        Console.WriteLine("Temp path = {0}", tempPath)

        Dim iw As New InputWrapper()
        Dim cmd As String
        Console.WriteLine("Enter command, quit to exit")
        cmd = iw.getString("> ")
        While Not cmd.Equals("quit")
            ...
            ElseIf cmd.Equals("path") Then
                Console.WriteLine("Dir. Separator = {0}", _
                    Path.DirectorySeparatorChar)
                Dim fn As String = iw.getString("filename: ")
                ShowFilePathInfo(fn)
            ElseIf cmd.Equals("temp") Then
                Dim tempfile As String
                tempfile = Path.GetTempFileName()
                Console.WriteLine("Temp file = {0}", _
                    tempfile)
                dir = New DirectoryInfo(tempPath)
                Directory.SetCurrentDirectory(tempPath)
            Else
                Help()
                ...

    Private Sub ShowFilePathInfo(ByVal fn As String)
        Console.WriteLine("Full path = {0}", _
            Path.GetFullPath(fn))
        Console.WriteLine("File root = {0}", _
```

```
            Path.GetFileNameWithoutExtension(fn))
        Console.WriteLine("Extension = {0}", _
            Path.GetExtension(fn))
    End Sub

    ...
End Module
```

Here is a sample run of the program. Note that when you use the "temp" command, you are placed into the temporary directory. You might be surprised to find how many files can accumulate there. When I ran this program, I discovered more than 6,000 files in my temporary directory!

```
path = C:\OI\IntroVb\Chap21\DirectoryDemo\Version 2\bin
Temp path = C:\DOCUME~1\ADMINI~1\LOCALS~1\Temp\
Enter command, quit to exit
> dir
Files:
   DirectoryDemo.exe
   DirectoryDemo.pdb
Directories:
> path
DiretorySeparator = \
filename: DirectoryDemo.exe
Full path = C:\OI\IntroVb\Chap21\DirectoryDemo\Version 2
\bin\DirectoryDemo.exe
File root = DirectoryDemo
Extension = .exe
> temp
Temp file = C:\DOCUME~1\ADMINI~1\LOCALS~1\Temp\tmpBF.tmp
> dir
Files:
   tmpBC.tmp
   tmpBF.tmp
Directories:
   msoclip1
```

Files and Streams

Programming languages have undergone an evolution in how they deal with the important topic of file I/O. Early languages, such as FORTRAN, COBOL, and the original BASIC, had I/O statements built into the language. Later languages have tended not to have I/O built into the language, but instead rely on a standard library for performing I/O, such as the **stdio** library in C.

Still later languages, such as C++ and Java, introduced a further abstraction called a *stream*. A stream serves as an intermediary between the program and the file. Read and write operations are done to the stream, which is tied to a file. This architecture is very flexible, because the same kind of read and write operations can apply not only to a file, but to other kinds of I/O, such as network sockets. This added flexibility introduces a slight additional complexity in writing programs, because you have to deal not only with files but also with streams, and considerable variety of stream classes exists. But the added complexity is well worth the effort, and VB.NET strikes a nice balance, with classes that make performing common operations quite simple.

As with directories, the **System.IO** namespace contains two classes for working with files. The **File** class has all shared methods, and the **FileInfo** class has instance methods. Refer to Table 21–6 for a list of the more interesting members of the **File** class.

TABLE 21–6	*Interesting File Members*
Methods	**Description**
Open	Opens a **FileStream** on a specified path
OpenText	Creates a **StreamReader** that can read from a text file at the specified path
CreateText	Creates a **StreamWriter** that can write a text file at the specified path
Copy	Copies an existing file to a new file
Delete	Deletes a file at a specified path

The File class contains methods to manage the file, but use **StreamReader** and **StreamWriter** objects to do the actual file I/O. Tables 21–7 and 21–8 outline some of the interesting methods of the **StreamReader** and **StreamWriter** classes.

TABLE 21–7	*Interesting StreamReader Members*
Methods	**Description**
Read	Reads the next character from the input stream
ReadLine	Reads a line from the input stream
ReadToEnd	Reads to the end of the input stream
Close	Closes the StreamReader

TABLE 21–8	*Interesting StreamWriter Members*
Methods	**Description**
Write	Overloaded method which writes data to the stream
WriteLine	Overloaded method writes data followed by the line terminator to the stream
Flush	Flushes the buffer and causes all buffered data to be written to the stream
Close	Closes the StreamWriter

Code Example

The program **FileDemo** extends the **DirectoryDemo** example program to illustrate reading and writing text files. We illustrate binary file I/O later in this chapter, when we discuss serialization. The directory commands are retained so that you can easily exercise the program on different directories. The two new commands are "read" and "write." The "read" command illustrates using the **File** class. The "dir" command, already present in the **DirectoryDemo** program, illustrates using the **FileInfo** class.

Here is the code for the "read" command. The user is prompted for a file name. The shared **OpenText** method returns a **StreamReader** object, which is used for the actual reading. The **ReadLine** method for reading a line of text is similar to the **ReadLine** method of the **Console** class. **ReadLine** returns **Nothing** (or a null reference) when at end of file. Our program simply displays the contents of the file at the console. When done, we close the **StreamReader**.

```
...
ElseIf (cmd.Equals("read")) Then
   Dim fileName As String = iw.getString("file name: ")
   Dim reader As StreamReader = File.OpenText(fileName)

   Dim strg As String
   strg = reader.ReadLine()
   While strg <> Nothing
      Console.WriteLine(strg)
      strg = reader.ReadLine()
   End While

   reader.Close()
...
```

Here is the code for the "write" command. Again, we prompt for a file name. This time, we also prompt for whether to append to the file. There is a special constructor for the **StreamWriter** class that directly returns a **StreamWriter** without first getting a file object. The first parameter is the name of the file, and the second is a **Boolean** flag specifying the append mode. If **True**, the writes will append to the end of an already existing file. If **False**, the writes will overwrite an existing file. In both cases, if a file of the specified name does not exist, a new file will be created.

```
...
ElseIf cmd.Equals("write") Then
   Dim fileName As String = iw.getString("file name: ")
   Dim strAppend As String = _
      iw.getString("append (yes/no): ")
   Dim append As Boolean = _
      CBool(IIf(strAppend.Equals("yes"), True, False))

   Dim writer As New StreamWriter(fileName, append)
```

```
Console.WriteLine("Enter text, blank line to terminate")
Dim strg As String = iw.getString(">> ")
While strg <> ""
    writer.WriteLine(strg)
    strg = iw.getString(">> ")
End While

writer.Close()
...
```

Here is a sample run of the program. We first obtain a listing of existing files in the current directory. We then create a new text file, **one.txt**, and enter a couple of lines of text data. We again do "dir," and our new file shows up. We try out the "read" command. You could also open the file in a text editor to verify that it has been created and has the desired data. Next, we write out another line of text to this same file, this time saying "yes" to append mode. We conclude by reading the contents of the file.

```
path = C:\OI\IntroVb\Chap21\FileDemo\bin
Enter command, quit to exit
> dir
Files:
    FileDemo.exe
    FileDemo.pdb
Directories:
> write
file name: one.txt
append (yes/no): no
Enter text, blank line to terminate
>> hello, world
>> this is second line
>>
> dir
Files:
    FileDemo.exe
    FileDemo.pdb
    one.txt
Directories:
> read
file name: one.txt
hello, world
this is second line
> write
file name: yes
append (yes/no): yes
Enter text, blank line to terminate
>> and a third line
>>
> read
file name: one.txt
```

```
hello, world
this is second line
```

Serialization

Using the **File** and **Stream** classes can be quite cumbersome if you have to save a complicated data structure with linked objects. You have to save the individual fields to disk, remembering which field belongs to which object, and which object instance was linked to another object instance. When restoring the data structure, you have to reconstitute that arrangement of fields and object references.

The serialization technology provided by the .NET Framework does this for you. "Serialize" means to convert a graph of objects into a linear sequence of bytes. This sequence of bytes can then be written to a stream or otherwise used to transmit all the data associated with the object instance. Objects can be serialized without writing special code, because the metadata knows the object's memory layout.

To hook into the serialization mechanism provided by the .NET Framework, you mark your class with a special *attribute*. We will discuss attributes in Chapter 22, but for now, you can easily use attributes by placing a special tag in front of a class.

Code
Example

The program **SerializeAccount** illustrates serialization of the **Account** class by means of an attribute. The code for the **Account** class is shown below, and only one line of code is involved: The attribute **<System.Serializable>** is placed before the class. In this case, *all* the data members of the class will be serialized. If you want to exclude a data member from being serialized (for example, because it contained some kind of temporary cache of data), you can place the attribute **<System.NonSerialized>** in front of the member you want excluded. Serialization applies only to instance data members; shared members are never serialized.

```
' Account.vb

Imports System

<System.Serializable()> Public Class Account
    Private m_id As Integer
    Protected m_balance As Decimal
    Private m_owner As String
    ...
```

The **SerializeAccount** class illustrates serializing and deserializing a collection of **Account** objects. What is powerful about the serialization mechanism is that you can serialize complex graphs of objects simply by making each object serializable, which in turn can be done in the .NET Framework by using an attribute. A composite object is serialized by serializing each of its constituent objects. The .NET Framework collection classes, such as **ArrayList**, have serialization support built in.

Although making a class serializable is simply a matter of using an attribute, you must write a little code to cause an object graph to serialize itself. If you are using serialization to implement persistence, you need to perform the following basic steps to save the data:

1. Instantiate a **FileInfo** object where the data will be saved.
2. Open a **Stream** object for writing to the file.
3. Instantiate a formatter object for laying out the objects in a suitable format.
4. Apply the formatter's **Serialize** method to the root object and the stream.

The code for deserializing is similar. There are two built-in formatters provided by the .NET Framework:

- **BinaryFormatter** lays out object data in a binary format.
- **SOAPFormatter** lays out object data in an XML format.

If you use a binary formatter, you need the following two namespaces in order to perform the serialization:

- System.Runtime.Serialization
- System.Runtime.Serialization.Formatters.Binary

The following code is for a test program that provides commands to save and load a collection of accounts. Some test accounts are created initially, and commands are provided to add and remove accounts, in addition to saving and loading accounts.

```
' SerializeAccount.vb

Imports System
Imports System.Collections
Imports System.IO
Imports System.Runtime.Serialization
Imports System.Runtime.Serialization.Formatters.Binary

Module SerializeAccount
   Private accounts As New ArrayList()

   Public Sub Main()
      accounts = New ArrayList()
      AddAccount(100, "Bob", 1)
      AddAccount(200, "Mary", 2)
      AddAccount(300, "Charlie", 3)
      ShowAccounts(accounts)

      Dim iw As New InputWrapper()
      Dim cmd As String
      Console.WriteLine("Enter command, quit to exit")
```

```
        cmd = iw.getString("> ")
        While Not cmd.Equals("quit")
            Dim id As Integer
            Try
                If cmd.Equals("add") Then
                    Dim bal As Decimal = iw.getDecimal( _
                        "starting balance: ")
                    Dim owner As String = iw.getString("owner: ")
                    id = iw.getInt("id: ")
                    If AddAccount(bal, owner, id) Then
                        Console.WriteLine("Account opened")
                    End If
                ElseIf cmd.Equals("remove") Then
                    id = iw.getInt("account id: ")
                    RemoveAccount(id)
                ElseIf cmd.Equals("show") Then
                    ShowAccounts(accounts)
                ElseIf (cmd.Equals("save")) Then
                    Dim f As New FileInfo("accounts.bin")
                    Dim s As Stream = f.Open(FileMode.Create)
                    Dim b As New BinaryFormatter()
                    b.Serialize(s, accounts)
                    s.Close()
                ElseIf (cmd.Equals("load")) Then
                    Dim f As New FileInfo("accounts.bin")
                    Dim s As Stream = f.Open(FileMode.Open)
                    Dim b As New BinaryFormatter()
                    accounts = CType(b.Deserialize(s), ArrayList)
                    s.Close()
                Else
                    help()
                End If
            Catch e As Exception
                Console.WriteLine(e.Message)
                If Not e.InnerException Is Nothing Then
                    Console.WriteLine(e.InnerException.Message)
                End If
            End Try
            cmd = iw.getString("> ")
        End While
    End Sub
    ...
```

Here are two consecutive sample runs of the program. In the first run, we add two accounts and remove one. We save the new data. In the second run, we load and verify that we have gotten back the modified collection of accounts.

```
1    Bob           $100.00
2    Mary          $200.00
3    Charlie       $300.00
Enter command, quit to exit
> add
balance: 400
owner: David
id: 4
> add
balance: 500
owner: Ellen
id: 5
> remove
id: 3
> save
> quit

---- Second run ----
1    Bob           $100.00
2    Mary          $200.00
3    Charlie       $300.00
Enter command, quit to exit
> load
> show
1    Bob           $100.00
2    Mary          $200.00
4    David         $400.00
5    Ellen         $500.00
> quit
```

Summary

In this chapter, we looked at the file I/O. In the first part of the chapter, we examined how to do file I/O using the functions and methods in the **Microsoft.VisualBasic** namespace. In the second part of the chapter, we examined how to use the new I/O features provided by the .NET Framework **System.IO** namespace. .NET provides classes to manipulate both directories and files. Reading and writing a file is done through an intermediate object called a stream. You can do both text and binary I/O with a stream. With the serialization mechanism provided by the .NET Framework, it is easy to serialize a complex data structure into a linear stream of bytes, write the stream out to a file, and then read the data back and recreate the data structure.

Advanced Features

*I*n this chapter, we discuss a number of advanced features of VB.NET programming using the .NET Framework. These topics are important in their own right, and they provide further examples of important VB.NET concepts that we have been studying. The first topic is the StringBuilder class, which can be much more efficient than the String class in certain situations. Next, we examine programming with multiple threads. The .NET Framework provides a clean threading model based on delegates, and there is a flexible set of classes to support thread lifetime management and synchronization. The .NET Framework makes it easier to create thread-safe classes without any programming whatsoever, through the use of a synchronization attribute. We examine another important built-in attribute, Serializable, which makes it easy to save complex data structures to persistent storage with minimal coding. We then see how to implement custom attributes. Next, we introduce the powerful reflection API, which gives programmatic access to metadata.

StringBuilder Class

As we have discussed, instances of the **String** class are immutable. As a result, when you manipulate instances of **String**, you are frequently obtaining new **String** instances. Depending on your applications, creating all these instances may be expensive. The .NET library provides a special class, **String-**

Builder (located in the **System.Text** namespace), in which you may directly manipulate the underlying string without creating a new instance. When you are finished, you can create a **String** instance out of an instance of **String-Builder** by using the **ToString** method.

StringBuilder Properties and Methods

Table 22–1 summarizes some of the important properties of the **String-Builder** class.

TABLE 22–1	Properties of the StringBuilder Class

Property	Description
Capacity	Gets or sets the capacity of the current StringBuilder, which is the number of characters the current StringBuilder is capable of holding.
Chars	Gets or sets the character at a specified position.
Length	Gets or sets the length of the current StringBuilder.
MaxCapacity	Gets the maximum capacity of the current StringBuilder.

A **StringBuilder** instance has a capacity and a maximum capacity. These capacities can be specified in a constructor when the instance is created. By default, an empty **StringBuilder** instance starts out with a capacity of 16. As the stored string expands, the capacity increases automatically.

Table 22–2 summarizes some of the important methods of the **String-Builder** class.

TABLE 22–2	Methods of the StringBuilder Class

Method	Description
Append	Appends an object to the end of the current StringBuilder.
Insert	Inserts a specified object into the StringBuilder at a specified position.
Remove	Removes the specified characters from the current StringBuilder.
Replace	Replaces all instances of a specified character with a new character.
ToString	Converts a StringBuilder to a String.

Code Example

The program **StringBuilderDemo** provides a simple demonstration of using the **StringBuilder** class. It shows the starting capacity and the capacity after strings are appended. Also, the maximum capacity, which is the largest capacity to which a **StringBuilder** object can grow, is displayed. At the end, a **String** is returned.

```vb
' StringBuilderDemo.vb

Imports System
Imports System.Text

Module StringBuilderDemo

    Public Sub Main()
        Dim build As New StringBuilder()
        ShowCapacity(build)
        build.Append( _
            "This is the first sentence." & vbNewLine)
        ShowCapacity(build)
        build.Append( _
             "This is the second sentence." & vbNewLine)
        ShowCapacity(build)
        build.Append("This is the last sentence." & vbNewLine)
        ShowCapacity(build)
        Dim strg As String = build.ToString()
        Console.Write(strg)
    End Sub

    Private Sub ShowCapacity(ByVal build As StringBuilder)
        Console.WriteLine( _
            "capacity = {0}, max. capacity = {1}", _
            build.Capacity, build.MaxCapacity)
    End Sub

End Module
```

Here is the output:

```
capacity = 16, max. capacity = 2147483647
capacity = 34, max. capacity = 2147483647
capacity = 70, max. capacity = 2147483647
capacity = 142, max. capacity = 2147483647
This is the first sentence.
This is the second sentence.
This is the last sentence.
```

StringBuilder Performance

Code Example

The performance gain from using **StringBuilder** in place of **String** can be striking. To illustrate, the program **StringBuilderTicks** counts the number of ticks (milliseconds) when strings are built using **String** and **StringBuilder**. Two implementations are provided for the delegate **GetString**, which describes a function that returns a string of a specified length. Each implementation generates the string character by character, using a random uppercase character.

GetString1 uses the **String** class, which can result in tremendous overhead, because **String** objects are continually being created, while the old **String** object becomes garbage. Eventually, the garbage collector must collect all the wasted memory, taking up further time.

```
Private Function GetString1(ByVal count As Integer) _
 As String
   Dim strg As String
   Dim i As Integer
   For i = 1 To count
       strg += GetChar()
   Next
   Return strg
End Function
```

GetString2 uses the **StringBuilder** class. Individual characters are appended to a **StringBuilder** object. Only when the maximum capacity needs to be increased will a new **StringBuilder** object be created. At the end, the **StringBuilder** is converted into a **String** by the **ToString** method.

```
Private Function GetString2(ByVal count As Integer) _
 As String
   Dim strg As New StringBuilder()
   Dim i As Integer
   For i = 1 To count
       strg.Append(GetChar())
   Next
   Return strg.ToString()
End Function
```

Individual characters are created randomly by the **GetChar** function:

```
Private Function GetChar() As Char
   Dim i As Integer = rand.Next(26)
   Return Chr(&H41 + i)
End Function
```

A function **ComputeTicks** is provided to calculate how many ticks are required to create a string of specified length. **ComputeTicks** takes as a parameter a function, which is an instance of the delegate **GetString**, such as the functions **GetString1** and **GetString2**. (We discussed delegates in Chapter 18.) The number of ticks required is determined by taking a snapshot before and after calling the instance of **GetString**, using the **TickCount** property of the **Environment** class. (We used the **TickCount** property earlier for doing performance measurements, such as in our evaluation of hash table performance in Chapter 19.)

```
Private Function ComputeTicks(ByVal func As GetString, _
 ByVal count As Integer) As Integer
   Dim startTick As Integer = Environment.TickCount
   Dim strg As String = func(count)
   Return Environment.TickCount - startTick
End Function
```

The main program sets up an array of different lengths that we can use in our experiment. Then the number of ticks required is computed by each method for these different lengths, and the results are displayed.

```
Module StringBuilderTicks
   Private rand As New Random()

   Private Delegate Function GetString(ByVal count As _
      Integer) As String

   Sub Main()
      'Calculate time to build strings of various lengths
      'String and StringBuilder
      Dim lengths() As Integer = {100, 1000, 10000, 100000}
      Console.WriteLine( _
         " Length        String    StringBuilder")
      Dim i As Integer
      For i = 0 To lengths.Length - 1
         Dim strCount As Integer = _
            ComputeTicks(AddressOf GetString1, lengths(i))
         Dim bldCount As Integer = _
            ComputeTicks(AddressOf GetString2, lengths(i))
         Console.WriteLine("{0,8}{1,14}{2,16}", _
            lengths(i), strCount, bldCount)
      Next
   End Sub

   ...
End Module
```

Here are the results of running this program (on a computer with a clock speed of 1.4 GHz and 512MB of memory). You can see that as the number of characters is increased, the **StringBuilder** class performs significantly better than the **String** class.

Length	String	StringBuilder
100	0	0
1000	10	0
10000	160	10
100000	26338	20

StringBuilder Outperforms String For Mutable Strings

The performance of the StringBuilder class is significantly better than the String class when strings are modified, as we saw in this section. A simple way to improve the performance of your application is to remember to use the StringBuilder class instead of the String class in these situations!

Multiple Thread Programming

Modern programming environments allow you to program with multiple threads. Threads run inside of processes and allow multiple concurrent execution paths. If there are multiple CPUs, you can achieve parallel processing through the use of threads. On a single processor machine, you can often achieve greater efficiency by using multiple threads, because when one thread is blocked (waiting on an I/O completion, for example), another thread can continue execution. Also, using multiple threads can make a program more responsive to shorter tasks, such as tasks requiring user responses.

Along with the potential benefit of programming with multiple threads, there is greater program complexity, because you have to manage the issues of starting up threads, controlling their lifetimes, and synchronizing among threads. Because threads are within a common process and share an address space, it is possible for two threads to concurrently access the same data. Such concurrent access, known as a "race condition," can lead to erroneous results when non-atomic operations are performed, a topic we discuss in detail later in this section.

.NET Threading Model

The .NET Framework provides extensive support for multiple thread programming in the **System.Threading** namespace. The core class is **Thread**, which encapsulates a thread of execution. This class provides methods to start and suspend threads, to sleep, and to perform other thread management functions. The method that executes for a thread is encapsulated inside a delegate of type **ThreadStart**. We introduced delegates in Chapter 18. When starting a thread, it is frequently useful to define an associated class, which contains instance data for the thread, including initialization information. A designated method of this class can be used as the **ThreadStart** delegate method.

CONSOLE LOG DEMONSTRATION

Code
Example

The **ThreadDemo** program provides an illustration of this architecture. The **ConsoleLog** class encapsulates a thread ID and parameters specifying a sleep interval and a count of how many lines of output are written to the console. It provides the method **ConsoleLog** that writes out logging information to the console, showing the thread ID and number of elapsed (millisecond) ticks. Here is the program code:

```vb
' ThreadDemo.vb

Imports System
Imports System.Threading

Class ConsoleLog
   Private m_delta As Integer
   Private m_count As Integer
   Private m_ticks As Integer = 0
   Private m_threadId As Integer
   Private Shared nextThreadId As Integer = 1

   Public Sub New(ByVal delta As Integer, _
    ByVal count As Integer)
     m_delta = delta
     m_count = count
     m_threadId = nextThreadId
     nextThreadId = nextThreadId + 1
   End Sub

   Public Sub ConsoleThread()
     Dim i As Integer
     For i = 0 To m_count - 1
        Console.WriteLine("Thread {0}: ticks = {1}", _
          m_threadId, m_ticks)
        Thread.Sleep(m_delta)
        m_ticks = m_ticks + m_delta
     Next
     Console.WriteLine("Thread {0} is terminating", _
       m_threadId)
   End Sub

End Class

Module ThreadDemo

   Sub Main()
     Dim slowLog As New ConsoleLog(1000, 5)
     Dim fastLog As New ConsoleLog(400, 5)

     Dim slowStart As New _
       ThreadStart(AddressOf slowLog.ConsoleThread)
     Dim fastStart As New _
       ThreadStart(AddressOf fastLog.ConsoleThread)
```

```
        Dim slowThread As New Thread(slowStart)
        Dim fastThread As New Thread(fastStart)

        Console.WriteLine("Starting threads ...")
        slowThread.Start()
        fastThread.Start()
        Console.WriteLine("Threads have started")
    End Sub

End Module
```

The program is configured with a "slow" thread and a "fast" thread. The slow thread will sleep for one second between outputs, and the fast thread will sleep for only 400 milliseconds. A **ConsoleLog** object is created for each of these threads, initialized with appropriate parameters. Both will do five lines of output.

Next, appropriate delegates are created of type **ThreadStart**. Notice that we use an instance method, **ConsoleThread**, as the delegate method. Use of an instance method rather than a shared method is appropriate in this case, because we want to associate parameter values (sleep interval and output count) with each delegate instance.

We then create and start the threads. We write a message to the console just before and just after starting the threads. When do you think the message "Threads have started" is displayed, relative to the output from the threads themselves? Here is the output from running the program. You will notice a slight delay as the program executes, reflecting the sleep periods.

```
Starting threads ...
Threads have started
Thread 1: ticks = 0
Thread 2: ticks = 0
Thread 2: ticks = 400
Thread 2: ticks = 800
Thread 1: ticks = 1000
Thread 2: ticks = 1200
Thread 2: ticks = 1600
Thread 1: ticks = 2000
Thread 2 is terminating
Thread 1: ticks = 3000
Thread 1: ticks = 4000
Thread 1 is terminating
```

The "Threads have started" message is displayed immediately, reflecting the asynchronous nature of the two threads. The **Start** calls return immediately, and the second message prints. Meanwhile, the other thread gets started by the system, which takes a little bit of time, and then each thread starts producing output.

RACE CONDITIONS

A major issue in concurrency is shared data. If two computations access the same data, different results can be obtained depending on the timing of the different accesses, a situation known as a race condition. Race conditions present a programming challenge because they can occur unpredictably. Careful programming is required to ensure that they do not occur.

Race conditions can easily arise in multithreaded applications, because threads belonging to the same process share the same address space and, thus, can share data. Consider two threads making deposits to a bank account, where the deposit operation is not atomic. These threads might perform the following functions:

- Get balance.
- Add amount to balance.
- Store balance.

The following sequence of actions then produces a race condition, with invalid results:

1. Balance starts at $100.
2. Thread 1 makes deposit of $25 and is interrupted after getting balance and adding amount to balance, but before storing balance.
3. Thread 2 makes deposit of $5,000 and goes to completion, storing $5,100.

Thread 1 now finishes, storing $125, overwriting the result of thread 2. The $5,000 deposit has been lost!

The program **ThreadAccount\Race** illustrates this race condition. The **Account** class has a method **DelayDeposit**, which updates the balance non-atomically. The thread sleeps for five seconds in the middle of the update operation, leaving open a window of vulnerability for another thread to come in.

```
' Account.vb

Imports System.Threading

Public Class Account
   Protected m_balance As Decimal

   Public Sub New(ByVal balance As Decimal)
      m_balance = balance
   End Sub

   Public Sub Deposit(ByVal amount As Decimal)
      m_balance = m_balance + amount
   End Sub

   Public Sub DelayDeposit(ByVal amount As Decimal)
      Dim newbal As Decimal = m_balance + amount
```

```
        Thread.Sleep(5000)
        m_balance = newbal
     End Sub

     Public ReadOnly Property Balance() As Decimal
        Get
            Return m_balance
        End Get
     End Property

  End Class
```

The test program launches threads in a manner similar to that used in the **ThreadDemo** program. The **AsynchAccount** class contains the thread methods that are used by thread 1 (to call **DelayDeposit**) and thread 2 (to call **Deposit**).

```
' ThreadAccount.vb

Imports System
Imports System.Threading

Class AsynchAccount
   Private m_amount As Decimal

   Public Sub New(ByVal amount As Decimal)
      m_amount = amount
   End Sub

   Public Sub AsynchDelayDeposit()
      ThreadAccount.account.DelayDeposit(m_amount)
   End Sub

   Public Sub AsynchDeposit()
      ThreadAccount.account.Deposit(m_amount)
   End Sub

End Class

Module ThreadAccount
   Public account As Account

   Public Sub Main()
      account = New Account(100)

      Dim asynch1 As New AsynchAccount(25)
      Dim asynch2 As New AsynchAccount(5000)

      Dim start1 As New ThreadStart( _
         AddressOf asynch1.AsynchDelayDeposit)
```

```
        Dim start2 As New ThreadStart( _
            AddressOf asynch2.AsynchDeposit)

        Console.WriteLine("balance = {0:C}", _
            account.Balance)
        Console.WriteLine( _
            "delay deposit of {0:C} on thread 1", 25)

        Dim t1 As New Thread(start1)
        Dim t2 As New Thread(start2)

        t1.Start()
        Console.WriteLine("deposit of {0:C} on thread 2", _
            5000)
        t2.Start()
        t2.Join()
        Console.WriteLine( _
            "balance = {0:C} (thread 2 done)", account.Balance)
        t1.Join()
        Console.WriteLine("balance = {0:C} (thread 1 done)", _
            account.Balance)
    End Sub

End Module
```

The call **t2.Join** blocks the current thread until thread **t2** finishes. This technique enables us to show the balance after a thread has definitely completed. Below is the output. As you can see, we have exactly replicated the race condition scenario outlined at the beginning of this section.

```
balance = $100.00
delay deposit of $25.00 on thread 1
deposit of $5,000.00 on thread 2
balance = $5,100.00 (thread 2 done)
balance = $125.00 (thread 1 done)
```

Thread Synchronization Programming

Such race conditions can be avoided by serializing access to the shared data. Suppose that only one thread at a time is allowed to access the bank account. Then the first thread that starts to access the balance completes the operation before another thread begins to access the balance; in other words, the second thread is blocked. In this case, threads synchronize based on accessing data.

Another way threads can synchronize is for one thread to block until another thread has completed. The **Join** method is a means for accomplishing this kind of thread synchronization, as illustrated above.

The **System.Threading** namespace provides a number of thread synchronization facilities. In this section, we illustrate use of the **Monitor** class.

MONITOR

You can serialize access to shared data using the **Enter** and **Exit** methods of the **Monitor** class.

- **Monitor.Enter** obtains the monitor lock for an object. An object is passed as a parameter. This call blocks if another thread has entered the monitor of the same object. It does not block if the current thread has previously entered the monitor.
- **Monitor.Exit** releases the monitor lock. If one or more threads are waiting to acquire the lock, and the current thread has executed **Exit** as many times as it has executed **Enter**, one of the threads is unblocked and allowed to proceed.

An object reference is passed as the parameter to **Monitor.Enter** and **Monitor.Exit**. This is the object on which the monitor lock is acquired or released. To acquire a lock on the current object, pass **Me**.

Code Example

The program **ThreadAccount\Monitor** illustrates the use of monitors to protect the critical section where the balance is updated. In this program, we also place the calls to **ShowBalance** just before exiting the monitor. This technique ensures that we see the balance as soon as it is updated.

```vb
' Account.vb

Imports System.Threading

Public Class Account
   Protected m_balance As Decimal

   Public Sub New(ByVal balance As Decimal)
      m_balance = balance
   End Sub

   Public Sub Deposit(ByVal amount As Decimal)
      Monitor.Enter(Me)
      m_balance = m_balance + amount
      ShowBalance()
      Monitor.Exit(Me)
   End Sub

   Public Sub DelayDeposit(ByVal amount As Decimal)
      Monitor.Enter(Me)
      Dim newbal As Decimal = m_balance + amount
      Thread.Sleep(5000)
      m_balance = newbal
      ShowBalance()
      Monitor.Exit(Me)
```

```
   End Sub

   Public ReadOnly Property Balance() As Decimal
      Get
         Return m_balance
      End Get
   End Property

   Private Sub ShowBalance()
      Console.WriteLine("balance = {0:C} ({1})", _
         m_balance, Thread.CurrentThread.Name)
   End Sub

End Class
```

The test program is similar to the one in the previous example, except we are now doing the display of the new balance immediately after the thread has updated the balance. Below is the output. Notice that the synchronization is successful—the $5,000 deposit wasn't wiped out!

```
balance = $100.00
delay deposit of $25.00 on thread 1
deposit of $5,000.00 on thread 2
balance = $125.00 (Thread 1)
balance = $5,125.00 (Thread 2)
```

INDEPENDENT, READ-ONLY DATA

When implementing thread synchronization you should not paint with too broad a brush stroke. You should only lock the data you need to, so that access to independent data can proceed uninterrupted. The program **Thread-Account\Independent** introduces the property **Owner**. The owner is completely independent of the balance, so we do not need a lock around the code to get the owner. Here is the relevant code for the modified **Account** class:

```
' Account.vb

Imports System.Threading

Public Class Account
   Protected m_balance As Decimal
   Protected m_owner As String

   Public Sub New(ByVal balance As Decimal)
      m_balance = balance
      m_owner = "Tom Thread"
   End Sub

   Public Sub Deposit(ByVal amount As Decimal)
```

```
        Monitor.Enter(Me)
        m_balance = m_balance + amount
        ShowBalance()
        Monitor.Exit(Me)
    End Sub

    Public Sub DelayDeposit(ByVal amount As Decimal)
        Monitor.Enter(Me)
        Dim newbal As Decimal = m_balance + amount
        Thread.Sleep(5000)
        m_balance = newbal
        ShowBalance()
        Monitor.Exit(Me)
    End Sub

    Public ReadOnly Property Balance() As Decimal
        Get
            Return m_balance
        End Get
    End Property

    Public ReadOnly Property Owner() As String
        Get
            Return m_owner
        End Get
    End Property

    Private Sub ShowBalance()
        Console.WriteLine("balance = {0:C} ({1})", _
            m_balance, Thread.CurrentThread.Name)
    End Sub

End Class
```

The test program is similar to our previous test programs, but it adds code at the end of **Main** to get the owner name, after sleeping briefly to make sure the threads have started and have hit the locks.

```
' ThreadAccount.vb

...

Module ThreadAccount
    Public account As Account

    Public Sub Main()
        account = New Account(100)

        Dim asynch1 As New AsynchAccount(25)
        Dim asynch2 As New AsynchAccount(5000)
```

```
    Dim start1 As New ThreadStart( _
        AddressOf asynch1.AsynchDelayDeposit)
    Dim start2 As New ThreadStart( _
        AddressOf asynch2.AsynchDeposit)

    Console.WriteLine("balance = {0:C}", account.Balance)
    Console.WriteLine( _
        "delay deposit of {0:C} on thread 1", 25)
    Dim t1 As New Thread(start1)
    t1.Name = "Thread 1"
    Dim t2 As New Thread(start2)
    t2.Name = "Thread 2"
    t1.Start()
    Console.WriteLine("deposit of {0:C} on thread 2", _
        5000)
    t2.Start()
    Thread.Sleep(100)     ' allow time for threads to start
    Console.WriteLine("Owner = {0}", account.Owner)
  End Sub

End Module
```

Below is the output. It is the same as for the previous example, with an additional line of output showing the owner. This extra line of output is displayed almost immediately, with very little pause. The output from the threads comes afterwards.

```
balance = $100.00
delay deposit of $25.00 on thread 1
deposit of $5,000.00 on thread 2
owner = Tom Thread
balance = $125.00 (Thread 1)
balance = $5,125.00 (Thread 2)
```

Attributes

We have seen various ways to *program* proper synchronization so that we avoid a race condition. Although the code in our example was quite straightforward, in more elaborate situations, code involving multiple threads may become quite complex, especially when exceptional conditions are taken into account. A different approach to implementing complex code is to let the system do it for you. There must be a way for the programmer to inform the system of what is desired. In the .NET Framework, such cues can be given to the system by means of *attributes*.

Microsoft introduced attribute-based programming in Microsoft Transaction Server. The concept was that MTS, not the programmer, would implement complex tasks such as distributed transactions. The programmer would "declare" the transaction requirements for a COM class, and MTS would implement it. This use of attributes was greatly extended in the next generation of MTS, known as COM+. In MTS and COM+, attributes are stored in a separate repository, distinct from the program itself.

Attributes are also used in Interface Definition Language (IDL), which is used to give a precise specification of COM interfaces, including the methods and signatures. Part of the function of IDL is to make it possible for a tool to generate proxies and stubs for remoting a method call across a process boundary or even across a network. When parameters are passed remotely, it is necessary to give more information than when they are passed with the same process. For example, within a process, you can simply pass a reference to an array. But in passing an array across a process boundary, you must inform the tool of the size of the array. This information is communicated in IDL by means of attributes, which are specified using a square bracket notation. Again, attribute information is stored in a location separate from program code.

A problem with attributes in both MTS/COM+ and IDL is that they are separate from the program source code. When the source code is modified, the attribute information may become out of sync with the code.

In VB.NET, attributes are declared with angle brackets. The attributes are part of the program source code. When compiled into intermediate language, the attributes become part of the metadata.

Synchronization Attribute

What does all this have to do with synchronization? The .NET Framework provides many different kinds of attributes, which your source code may use to obtain automatic use of services of the Framework. An example is the **Synchronization** attribute, which is applied to a class and automatically synchronizes method calls, allowing only one thread to call into the class at a time.

Code Example

The program **ThreadAccount\Attribute** illustrates synchronization of the **Account** class by means of an attribute. The code is shown below, and only three lines of code are involved:

- A new namespace, **System.Runtime.Remoting.Contexts**
- The attribute **<Synchronization(SynchronizationAttribute. REQUIRED)>**
- The class derives from **ContextBoundObject**.

The base class **ContextBoundObject** extracts the attribute information from the metadata, using a mechanism known as *reflection*. It then provides the appropriate code to ensure serial invocation of methods. You do not need to understand how the base class carries out its work; it is abstracted for you.

Later in this chapter, we show how you can implement your own custom attributes, and we also introduce reflection. We illustrate how you can define a base class, which enables use of the custom attribute in any derived class. In the code that follows, observe that the attribute is on the same line as the entity to which it applies, in this case, a **Class**.

```vb
' Account.vb

Imports System.Threading
Imports System.Runtime.Remoting.Contexts

<SynchronizationAttribte( _
SynchronizationAttribute.REQUIRED)> Public Class Account
    Inherits ContextBoundObject
    Protected m_balance As Decimal
    Protected m_owner As String

    Public Sub New(ByVal balance As Decimal)
        m_balance = balance
        m_owner = "Tom Thread"
    End Sub

    Public Sub Deposit(ByVal amount As Decimal)
        m_balance = m_balance + amount
        ShowBalance()
    End Sub

    Public Sub DelayDeposit(ByVal amount As Decimal)
        Dim newbal As Decimal = m_balance + amount
        Thread.Sleep(5000)
        m_balance = newbal
        ShowBalance()
    End Sub

    Public ReadOnly Property Balance() As Decimal
        Get
            Return m_balance
        End Get
    End Property

    Public ReadOnly Property Owner() As String
        Get
            Return m_owner
        End Get
    End Property

    Private Sub ShowBalance()
        Console.WriteLine("balance = {0:C} ({1})", _
            m_balance, Thread.CurrentThread.Name)
    End Sub
```

```
End Class
```

Here is the output:

```
balance = $100.00
delay deposit of $25.00 on thread 1
deposit of $5,000.00 on thread 2
balance = $125.00 (Thread 1)
balance = $5,125.00 (Thread 2)
owner = Tom Thread
```

As you can see, the race condition has been avoided, and there is no explicit thread synchronization code using monitors or a similar construct. However, the behavior is somewhat different from our previous program, **ThreadAccount\Independent**. Now *all* method calls into **Account** are serialized, including calling the property to obtain the owner. When you ran the program, you should have noticed a pronounced delay before the owner was displayed, whereas this happened almost immediately in the **Independent** example. This automatic synchronization is coarse grained, so we obtained greater concurrency in this example by implementing the synchronization ourselves.

Custom Attributes

We have seen two examples, synchronization and serialization, of useful attributes provided by the system. The .NET Framework makes the attribute mechanism entirely extensible, allowing you to define custom attributes, which cause information to be written to the metadata. Using *reflection,* you can then extract this information from the metadata at runtime and modify the behavior of your program appropriately. To simplify the use of the custom attribute, you may declare a base class to do the work of invoking the reflection API to obtain the attribute information stored in the metadata. We illustrate getting custom attribute information using reflection in this section, and in the following discussion, we discuss reflection in more generality.

Code
Example

We illustrate this whole process of defining and using custom attributes with a simple example, **AttributeDemo**, which uses the custom attribute **InitialDirectory** to control the initial current directory when the program is run. As we saw in Chapter 21, by default the current directory is the directory containing the program's executable. In the case of a Visual Studio VB.NET project, this directory is **bin**, relative to the project source code directory.

Using a Custom Attribute

First, let's see an example of using the **InitialDirectory** custom attribute. We then see how to define and implement it. To control the initial directory for a class, we derive the class from the base class **DirectoryContext**. We may then apply to the class the attribute **InitialDirectory**, which takes a **string** parameter giving a path to what the initial directory should be. The property **DirectoryPath** extracts the path from the metadata. If our class does not have the attribute applied, this path is the default. Here's the code for our test program:

```
' AttributeDemo.vb

Imports System
Imports System.IO

Class Normal
    Inherits DirectoryContext
End Class

<InitialDirectory("c:\OI\IntroVb\Chap22")> Class Special
    Inherits DirectoryContext
End Class


Module AttributeDemo

   Public Sub Main()
      Dim objNormal As New Normal()
      Console.WriteLine("path = {0}", _
         objNormal.DirectoryPath)
      ShowDirectoryContents(objNormal.DirectoryPath)

      Dim objSpecial = New Special()
      Console.WriteLine("path = {0}", _
         objSpecial.DirectoryPath)
      ShowDirectoryContents(objSpecial.DirectoryPath)
   End Sub

   Private Sub ShowDirectoryContents(ByVal path As String)
      Dim di As New DirectoryInfo(path)
      Dim files() As FileInfo = di.GetFiles()
      Console.WriteLine("Files:")
      Dim f As FileInfo
      For Each f In files
         Console.WriteLine("   {0}", f.Name)
      Next

      Dim dirs() As DirectoryInfo = di.GetDirectories()
      Console.WriteLine("Directories:")
      Dim d As DirectoryInfo
```

```
    For Each d In dirs
        Console.WriteLine("    {0}", d.Name)
    Next
End Sub

End Module
```

Here is the output:

```
path = C:\OI\IntroVb\Chap22\AttributeDemo\bin
Files:
    AttributeDemo.exe
    AttributeDemo.pdb
Directories:
path = c:\OI\IntroVb\Chap22

Files:
Directories:
    AttributeDemo
    ReflectionDemo
    SerializeAccount
    ThreadAccount
    ThreadDemo
```

Defining an Attribute Class

To create a custom attribute, you must define an attribute class, derived from the base class **Attribute**. The convention is to give your class a name ending in "Attribute." The name of your class without the "Attribute" suffix can then be used as the name of the custom attribute, as well as the complete class name. In our example, the name of our class is **InitialDirectoryAttribute**, and the name of the corresponding attribute is either **InitialDirectory** or **InitialDirectoryAttribute**.

You may provide one or more constructors for your attribute class. The constructors define how to pass positional parameters to the attribute (in other words, provide a parameter list, separated by commas). It is also possible to provide "named parameters" for a custom attribute, where the parameter information is passed using syntax **name = value**.

The attribute class itself has an attribute **AttributeUsage** used to specify to what kinds of entities the attribute can be applied.

You may also provide properties to read the parameter information. In our example, we have a property **Path**, which is initialized in the constructor:

```
' DirectoryAttribute.vb

Imports System

<AttributeUsage(AttributeTargets.Class)> _
```

```
Public Class InitialDirectoryAttribute
   Inherits Attribute
   Private m_path As String

   Public Sub New(ByVal path As String)
      m_path = path
   End Sub

   Public ReadOnly Property Path() As String
      Get
         Return m_path
      End Get
   End Property

End Class
```

Defining a Base Class

The last step in working with custom attributes is to provide a means to extract the custom attribute information from the metadata. As explained in the next section, the .NET Framework provides an elaborate API, the Reflection API, for precisely this purpose. The root class for metadata information is **Type**, and you can obtain the **Type** of any object by calling the method **GetType**, which is provided in the root class **object**. To read custom attribute information, you need only one method, **Type.GetCustomAttributes**.

Although it would be quite feasible for the program using the custom attribute to perform this operation directly, you usually want to make the coding of the client program as simple as possible. Hence, it is useful to provide a base class to do the work of reading the custom attribute information from the metadata. In the previous section, we saw an example of such a base class, **ContextBoundObject**, which was used when we wanted a class to be able to use the **Synchronization** attribute.

In our case, we provide a base class **DirectoryContext**, which is used by a class wishing to take advantage of the **InitialDirectory** attribute. This base class provides the property **DirectoryPath** to return the path information stored in the metadata. Here is the code for the base class:

```
' DirectoryContext.vb

Imports System
Imports System.Reflection
Imports System.IO

Public Class DirectoryContext

   Public Overridable ReadOnly Property DirectoryPath() _
   As String
      Get
```

```
      Dim t As Type = Me.GetType()
      Dim a As Attribute
      For Each a In t.GetCustomAttributes(True)
         Dim da As InitialDirectoryAttribute
         Try
            da = CType(a, InitialDirectoryAttribute)
            Return da.Path
         Catch e As Exception
         End Try
      Next
      Return Directory.GetCurrentDirectory()
    End Get
  End Property

End Class
```

We require the **System.Reflection** namespace. **GetType** returns the current **Type** object, and we can then use the **GetCustomAttributes** method to obtain a collection of **Attribute** objects from the metadata. This collection is heterogeneous, consisting of different types. We can use the VB.NET **CType** function to test whether a given element in the collection is of type **Initial-DirectoryAttribute**. If we find such an element, we return the **Path** property. Otherwise, we return the default current directory, obtained from **GetCurrentDirectory**.

Reflection

At the heart of .NET is metadata, which stores very complete type information. The Reflection API permits you to query this information at runtime. You can also dynamically invoke methods, and through the **System.Reflection.Emit** namespace, you can even dynamically create and execute MSIL code. In the preceding section, we saw an illustration of using reflection to obtain custom attribute information. In this section, we provide a further example of dynamically obtaining a listing of all types defined in an assembly. (A program's EXE file is an example of an assembly. We will discuss assemblies in Chapter 23 and see some further examples, such as dynamic link libraries or DLLs.) We are only scratching the surface of a large subject, but our example should help you get started.

As befits the name "reflection," our demo program **ReflectionDemo** shows information about itself. The program contains two classes, **Dog** and **ReflectionDemo**. The program calls the **Bark** method of **Dog**. It then calls **Assembly.GetExecutingAssembly** to obtain its assembly. It shows all the types in the assembly and all the methods of each type.

```
' ReflectionDemo.vb

Imports System
Imports System.Reflection

Public Class Dog
   Public Shared Sub Bark()
      Console.WriteLine("woof, woof!!")
   End Sub
End Class

Module ReflectionDemo

   Public Sub Main()
      Dog.Bark()
      Dim assem As System.Reflection.Assembly
      assem = _
         System.Reflection.Assembly.GetExecutingAssembly()
      ShowAssemblyName(assem)
      ShowAssemblyTypes(assem)
   End Sub

   Public Sub ShowAssemblyTypes( _
      ByVal a As System.Reflection.Assembly)
      Dim types() As Type = a.GetTypes()
      Dim t As Type
      For Each t In types
         Console.WriteLine(t)
         ShowMethods(t)
      Next
   End Sub

   Public Sub ShowAssemblyName( _
      ByVal a As System.Reflection.Assembly)
      Console.WriteLine("assembly name = {0}", a.FullName)
   End Sub

   Public Sub ShowMethods(ByVal t As Type)
      Dim methInfo() As MethodInfo = t.GetMethods()
      Dim m As MethodInfo
      For Each m In methInfo
         Console.WriteLine("   {0}", m.Name)
      Next
   End Sub

End Module
```

Here is the output from running the program:

```
woof, woof!!
assembly name = ReflectionDemo, Version=0.0.0.0,
```

```
Culture=neutral, PublicKeyToken=null
ReflectionDemo.Dog
   GetHashCode
   Equals
   ToString
   Bark
   GetType
ReflectionDemo.ReflectionDemo
   GetHashCode
   Equals
   ToString
   Main
   ShowAssemblyTypes
   ShowAssemblyName
   ShowMethods
   GetType
```

You can examine information about any assembly by using the **ILDASM** utility. To run **ILDASM,** simply enter **ildasm** at a command prompt or use Start | Run. To examine a particular assembly, use the File | Open command. Figure 22–1 shows the types for **ReflectionDemo.exe,** which compares with the output from our **ReflectionDemo** program.

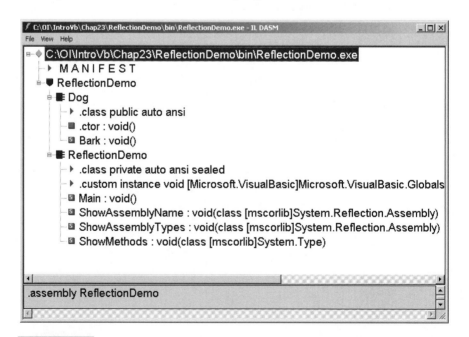

The ILDASM top window shows the types in an assembly.

Summary

This chapter examined a number of advanced features. The **StringBuilder** class can offer much better performance than the **String** class in some situations where strings are created dynamically. We examined multiple threading in detail. The .NET threading model is built on delegates. Synchronization can be accomplished through .NET Framework classes such as **Monitor**. Attributes are a powerful concept in .NET, making it possible to accomplish much without writing code. We looked at the built-in attributes **Synchronized** and **Serializable**, and we saw how to create a custom attribute. Custom attribute information can be read from metadata using the Reflection API.

Components and Assemblies

Until now, we have built exclusively monolithic applications, consisting of a single executable file. Our applications have been logically modular, consisting of several classes, typically distributed among a number of files. But these files have all been compiled together, forming a single EXE. Modern large applications are rarely monolithic; instead, they are made up of a number of executable units. In the Windows environment, an application normally consists of an EXE and a number of DLLs. In this chapter, we show you how to create class library DLLs, or components, which expose classes and their methods to external programs. We begin by using command-line tools, and later in the chapter, we use Visual Studio.NET. We also examine assemblies, which are the unit of deployment in .NET. An assembly can be a single EXE or DLL, or it can consist of several files, called modules. An assembly also contains a manifest, which describes how the elements of the assembly relate to each other and to external elements. An application in .NET can be composed of assemblies built using different languages, and you can even inherit across languages. We conclude the chapter by showing how to call a COM component from .NET.

Building Components Using .NET SDK

Prior to .NET, there was a big divide between using classes within an application and creating "software components" that implemented classes but could be called from independent executable units. With Microsoft software, the mechanism for creating such independent components was the Component Object Model or COM. Implementing a COM component is nontrivial, because much "plumbing" code must be provided to facilitate proper operation across executable boundaries. Tools were developed in individual languages to simplify the process. Visual Basic provided an easy way to create COM components, but this was specific to Visual Basic, and not all COM features were supported.

.NET changes the picture completely. It is totally trivial to create a component from a class. You just need to build a different kind of project, a "class library." The .NET Framework takes care of the plumbing for you automatically. This approach applies uniformly to all .NET languages.

In this section, we see how to create a component using the .NET SDK command-line compiler. Although we generally create components using Visual Studio.NET, not all features are available under Visual Studio, so we do some work with the SDK.

Creating a Component: A Demonstration

Code Example

We begin with a simple demonstration. Do your work in the **Demos** directory for this chapter. A completed version of the demonstration is available in **HelloSDK**.

CLASS LIBRARY

Using any text editor, create the file **HelloLib.vb**:

```
' HelloLib.vb

Imports System

Class Hello
   Private m_greeting As String = "Hello, I'm a DLL"

   Public Property Greeting() As String
      Get
         Return m_greeting
      End Get
      Set(ByVal Value As String)
         m_greeting = Value
      End Set
   End Property

End Class
```

This program should be typed exactly as shown, including the lack of any access specifier before **Class Hello**. This class simply exposes the property **Greeting**. Notice that there is no **Main** procedure. This class is not intended to be used in an EXE file. To compile the file as a class library, enter the following at the command line:

```
vbc /t:library HelloLib.vb
```

The command switch **/t,** or **/target,** specifies the kind of file to create. There are four options, as shown in Table 23–1.

TABLE 23-1	/target Output File Options
Option	**Meaning**
/target:exe	Console application EXE
/target:winexe	Windows application EXE
/target:library	Class library DLL
/target:module	Module (no assembly)

The default is **/target:exe** or console. We are now building a class library DLL. If you did not make any typing mistakes, you should get a clean compilation. If you use the DOS **dir** command, you should see that the file **HelloLib.dll** has been created.

Compiling at the Command Line in VB.NET

In this chapter we compile at the command line extensively. Most of your work as a VB.NET programmer can be done within Visual Studio, but some features are only available at the command line. Also, it can be more instructive to compile at the command line, because the compiler options must be specified explicitly.

Remember to set the environment variables properly, as explained in Chapter 2.

CLIENT PROGRAM

To exercise our class library, we need to create a client program. This could be either a console application or a Windows application. We create a simple console application as a test program. Type the following program, and save in the file **TestHello.cs**:

```
' TestHello.vb

Imports System

Module TestHello

    Public Sub Main()
        Dim obj As New Hello()
```

```
        Console.WriteLine(obj.Greeting)
    End Sub

End Module
```

Compile this program using the following command:

```
vbc /r:HelloLib.dll TestHello.vb
```

The compiler option **/r** or **/reference** is used to import metadata from the specified class library. This makes any public classes in the class library available to the current compilation unit. You get a compiler error message:

```
C:\OI\IntroVb\Chap23\Demos\TestHello.vb(7) : error BC30389:
'Hello' is Private,
and is not accessible in this context.

    Dim obj As New Hello()
        ~~~~~
```

FRIEND AND PUBLIC ACCESS

The problem comes from the fact that, in the file **HelloLib.vb**, we did not place any access modifier on the **Hello** class. The default access is **Friend**, which means that the class can be accessed within the current assembly. We mentioned **Friend** access in Chapter 12 but were not able to demonstrate its implications, because until now, all our programs have consisted of only a single assembly. We discuss assemblies in detail in the next section.

The fix to our compiler error is simply to make the **Hello** class **Public**.

```
' HelloLib.vb

Public Class Hello
    ...
```

Make this change, and then recompile both files. Now, you should get a clean compilation. You can then run the file **TestHello.exe** and obtain the expected output.

```
C:\OI\IntroVb\Chap23\Demos>testhello
Hello, I'm a DLL
```

MONOLITHIC PROGRAM

Code Example

The directory **HelloMonolithic** contains a monolithic version of this program. There is a Visual Studio project consisting of the two files. The **Hello** class is left with no access modifier, so the default **Friend** access is in place. This time, there is no problem because we are building only a single assembly. You can easily build this example by running the **build.bat** batch file at the command line.

Assemblies

In this section, we take a closer look at assemblies. We begin by examining the structure of assemblies in some detail, and then we work through an example that illustrates creating and using different types of assemblies.

Assembly Structure

An assembly is a grouping of types and resources that work together as a logical unit. An assembly consists of one or more physical files, called *modules*, which may be code files or resources (such as bitmaps). An assembly forms the boundary for security, deployment, type resolution, and versioning.

Logically, an assembly holds three kinds of information:

- MSIL (Microsoft Intermediate Language) implementing one or more types
- Metadata
- A *manifest* describing how the elements in the assembly relate to each other and to external elements

The general structure of an assembly is shown in Figure 23–1.

All the information in an assembly could be stored in a single file, or it could be distributed among a number of files called modules. All the assemblies we have built so far, including the DLL we built in the preceding section, have been single-file assemblies. In a multiple-file assembly, the manifest could be a standalone file or it could be contained in one of the modules.

MANIFEST

The manifest contains comprehensive information about the contents of an assembly and facilitates other assemblies using the assembly. The manifest contains a number of elements:

- **Assembly identity**: The name of the assembly, version information (consisting of four parts for fine-grained versioning), and culture (containing locale information suitable for globalization).
- **Files**: A list of files in the assembly.
- **Referenced assemblies**: A list of external assemblies that are referenced.
- **Types**: A list of all types in the assembly, a mapping to the modules containing the types, and visibility information about the types.
- **Security permissions**: Details needed by client programs that will determine whether they have rights to run the assembly.
- **Product information**: Information such as company, trademark, and copyright.

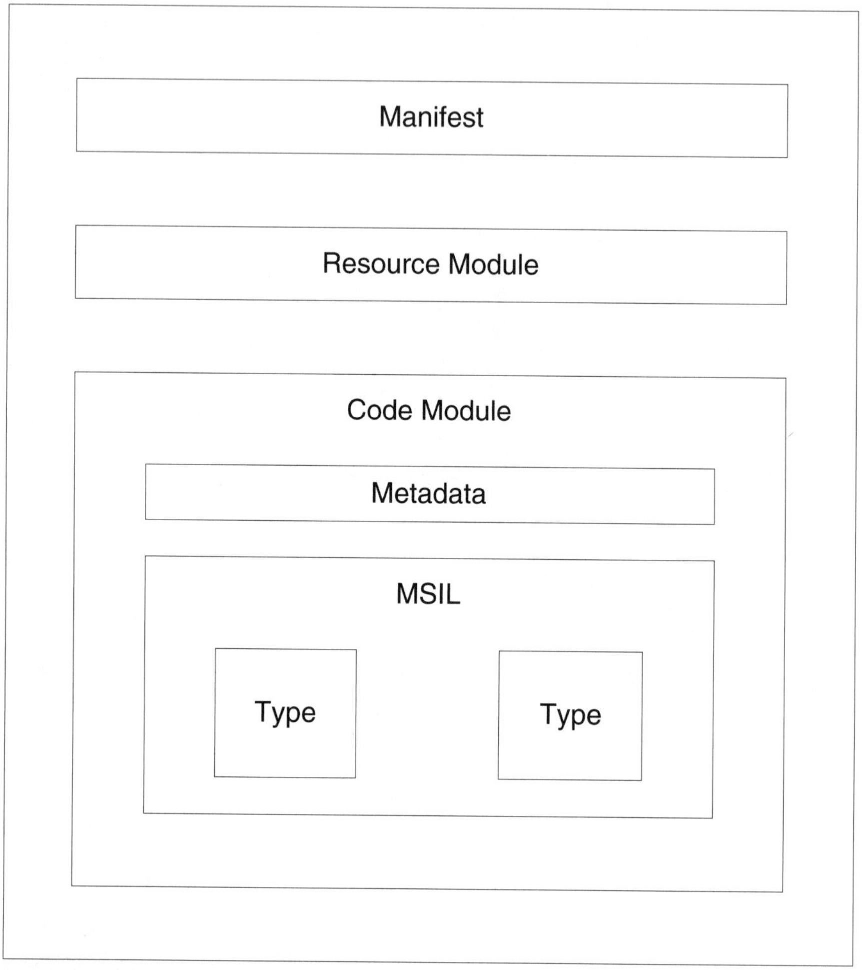

FIGURE 23–1   *The structure of an assembly.*

- **Custom attributes**: Special attribute information specific to this assembly. We discussed attributes in Chapter 22.
- **An (optional) shared name and hash**: This information facilitates running the assembly from a common location where multiple programs may access it. The hash protects client programs from running a corrupted version of the assembly.

Assembly Example

We illustrate assemblies, including an assembly with multiple modules, with a simple bank account example. The general logic of this program is simple. Our example is intended to focus on different ways of packaging the units of the program. There are two assemblies in the example, as illustrated in Figure 23–2:

- **Account.dll** is an assembly consisting of two modules, built from **Account.vb** and **SimpleMath.vb**.
- **SimpleTest.exe** is a test program.

Account.DLL

Account.cs

SimpleMath.netmodule

SimpleTest.EXE

FIGURE 23–2   *A bank application consisting of two assemblies.*

MONOLITHIC VERSION

We begin with a monolithic version, consisting of a single assembly. A Visual Studio solution is provided in the directory **AccountMonolithic**. Because all the classes are in the same program, we can utilize **Friend** accessibility. There are three files in the program, which compile into the same assembly.

The first file is **SimpleMath.vb**, which has the class **SimpleMath** with **Friend** accessibility. There is a single shared method **Add**.

```
' SimpleMath.vb

Friend Class SimpleMath

    Public Shared Sub Add(ByRef sum As Decimal, _
    ByVal term As Decimal)
        sum = sum + term
    End Sub

End Class
```

The second file is **Account.vb**, which encapsulates a balance as a private member variable with a public property **Balance**. There is a public method **Deposit**, which is implemented using the **SimpleMath** class.

```
' Account.vb

Public Class Account
   Private m_balance As Decimal

   Public Sub New(ByVal balance As Decimal)
      m_balance = balance
   End Sub

   Public ReadOnly Property Balance() As Decimal
      Get
          Return m_balance
      End Get
   End Property

   Public Sub Deposit(ByVal amount As Decimal)
      SimpleMath.Add(m_balance, amount)
   End Sub

End Class
```

The third file is **SimpleTest.vb**, which contains a test program that exercises both the **Account** class and the **SimpleMath** class.

```
' SimpleTest.vb

Imports System

Module Test
   Dim acc As Account

   Public Sub Main()
      acc = New Account(100)
      Console.WriteLine("balance = {0}", acc.Balance)
      acc.Deposit(25)
      Console.WriteLine("balance = {0}", acc.Balance)

      'Test using SimpleMath directly
      Dim number As Decimal = acc.Balance
      SimpleMath.Add(number, 25)
      Console.WriteLine("number = {0}", number)
   End Sub

End Module
```

The three files are part of a Visual Basic console project in the solution **AccountMonolithic.sln**. The project can be built using Visual Studio, creating the assembly **AccountMonolithic.exe**. Running this assembly produces the following output:

```
balance = 100
balance = 125
number = 150
```

MULTIPLE ASSEMBLIES

Code
Example

AccountAssembly illustrates building multiple assemblies, one of which contains multiple modules. No Visual Studio solution is provided because Visual Studio does not support building a module that is not an assembly. You may compile at the command line.

First, create a module from the file **SimpleMath.vb**:

```
vbc /t:module /out:SimpleMath.mod SimpleMath.vb
```

This step illustrates the **/t:module** option for compiling **SimpleMath.vb**. This creates a module that is not an assembly. The compiler creates a file with the special extension **.netmodule**, called **SimpleMath.netmodule**.

The next step is to create an assembly from the source file **Account.vb** and the module **SimpleMath.netmodule**:

```
 vbc /t:library /addmodule:SimpleMath.mod Account.vb
```

The VB.NET compiler provides the **/addmodule** option for this purpose. As the name suggests, this option adds a module to the current assembly that is being built. The target is a library, so the output file will be a DLL. We don't specify a name for the output file, so it is **Account.dll**.

Finally, we build **SimpleTest.exe** using the following command:

```
vbc /t:exe /r:Account.dll SimpleTest.vb
```

The build is automated by the batch file **build.bat**. You can run this batch file at the command line simply by typing **build**.

The source code is identical to that in **AccountMonolithic**, except for the file **SimpleMath.vb**. Now we are creating separate programs, so the **Friend** access type doesn't work for the **SimpleMath** class. We must use **Public**, as shown here:

```
' SimpleMath.vb

Public Class SimpleMath

   Public Shared Sub Add(ByRef sum As Decimal, _
   ByVal term As Decimal)
```

```
        sum = sum + term
    End Sub

End Class
```

Multiple Language Applications

Code
Example

A great feature of .NET is the ease with which you can create .NET applications using multiple languages. You can even implement a class using one language and inherit from this class in another language. **AccountMixed** illustrates a mixed language application using VB.NET and C#. The class **CheckingAccount**, implemented in VB.NET, inherits from the class **Account** implemented in C#. We continue to work at the command line, and the batch file **build.bat** builds the assemblies.

In case you are curious about C#, here is the code for **Account.cs**. The code should be easy to understand, although the syntax is a little different from VB.NET.

```csharp
// Account.cs

using System;

public class Account
{
    protected decimal m_balance;

    public Account(decimal balance)
    {
        m_balance = balance;
    }

    public decimal Balance
    {
        get
        {
            return m_balance;
        }
    }

    public void Deposit(decimal amount)
    {
        m_balance += amount;
    }
}
```

The file **CheckingAccount.vb** contains VB.NET code implementing a class **CheckingAccount** that inherits from **Account**. The derived class implements a new property **Fee** and a new method **Post**. Note that the derived VB.NET class can use the protected member variable **m_balance** from the C# base class.

```
' CheckingAccount.vb

Imports System

Public Class CheckingAccount
    Inherits Account

    Private m_fee As Decimal = 2D

    Public Sub New(ByVal balance As Decimal)
       MyBase.New(balance)
    End Sub

    Public ReadOnly Property Fee() As Decimal
       Get
            Return m_fee
       End Get
    End Property

    Public Sub Post()
       m_balance = m_balance - Fee
    End Sub

End Class
```

The class **SimpleTest.vb** contains a test program to exercise the two kinds of account classes:

```
' SimpleTest.vb

Imports System

Module Test

    Public Sub Main()
       Dim acc As New Account(100)
       Dim chk As New CheckingAccount(500)

       ShowBalance(acc)
       acc.Deposit(25)
       ShowBalance(acc)

       ShowBalance(chk)
       chk.Deposit(25)
```

```
        ShowBalance(chk)

        Console.WriteLine("fee = {0}", chk.Fee)
        chk.Post()
        ShowBalance(chk)
    End Sub

    Private Sub ShowBalance(ByVal acc As Account)
        Console.WriteLine("balance = {0}", acc.Balance)
    End Sub

End Module
```

You can use the batch file **build.bat** to build the class library **Account.dll** and the console program **SimpleTest.exe**:

```
csc /t:library Account.cs
vbc /t:exe /r:Account.dll /out:SimpleTest.exe *.vb
```

Running the program **SimpleTest.exe** produces the following output:

```
balance = 100
balance = 125
balance = 500
balance = 525
fee = 2
balance = 523
```

Building Components Using Visual Studio.Net

So far in this chapter, we have done all our component building at the command line. By using the various command-line compiler options, you should by now be fairly familiar with the build process, including especially the use of references via the **/reference** option. In this section, we see how to use Visual Studio for building class libraries and client programs. The class library and the client program are separate projects within one solution. If you would like to look at the complete solution, see **AccountClientAnswer**.

Demonstration: Solution with Multiple Projects

To learn how to create a multiple-project solution, including a class library, go through the following demonstration. Do your work in the **Demos** directory for this chapter. To save typing, you may copy source files from **AccountAssembly**.

CREATING THE FIRST PROJECT

1. From the Visual Studio main menu, choose File | New | Project. This brings up the New Project dialog.
2. For Project Types, choose "Visual Basic Projects" and for Templates choose "Empty Project."
3. Click the Browse button, navigate to **Demos**, and click Open.
4. In the Name field, type **AccountClient**. See Figure 23–3. Click OK.

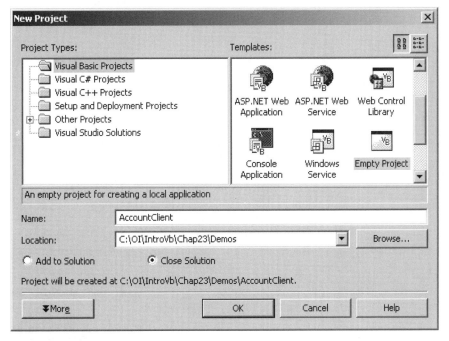

FIGURE 23–3   *Creating an empty VB.NET project.*

ADDING THE SOURCE FILES

1. Using Windows Explorer, copy the files **Account.vb**, **SimpleMath.vb**, and **SimpleTest.vb** from **AccountAssembly** into the current directory, **Demos\AccountClient**.
2. In the Solution Explorer, right-click over **AccountClient**, and from the context menu, choose Add | Add Existing Item. In the dialog that appears, select the three files **Account.vb**, **SimpleMath.vb**, and **SimpleTest.vb**. (You may use multiple selection by holding down the Ctrl key.) Click Open.
3. Review the code for the test program **SimpleTest.vb**. A new **Account** object is created, initialized with a starting balance of 100. A deposit is

made. The balance is displayed at the beginning and after the transaction. The **SimpleMath.Add** method is tested. (The prompt to read a string at the end prevents a quick close of the application if you run it in the debugger.)

4. Review the code for the **Account** class in the file **Account.vb**. There is a constructor that initializes the starting balance. There is a method **Deposit** and a property **Balance**.

5. Build the project (remember to change the Output Type of the project to Console Application, if necessary). Run the program. You should see the following output:

```
balance = 100
balance = 125
number = 150
Press return to exit
```

CHANGING THE OUTPUT PATH

Until now, when we have built a project in Visual Studio, we have always accepted the default location for the executable. If we are building a Debug version of our project, the executable is located in the **bin** directory. When we are working with an application that consists of several assemblies, it is convenient for the executable and component files to reside in the same directory. At runtime, our application can then easily find its components. We can achieve this goal by changing the output path of our executable to be the source directory. Later, we will build our component to reside in the same directory.

1. In Solution Explorer, right-click on the **AccountClient** project, and choose Properties.

2. In the Property Pages window that appears, click on Configuration Properties and then on Build.

3. Clear the Output Path area. See Figure 23-4. Click OK.

4. Build and run. The executable **AccountClient.exe** should be in the same folder as the source files.

ADDING A SECOND PROJECT

1. In Solution Explorer, right-click over the solution and choose Add | New Project. The Add New Project dialog comes up.

2. Choose "Visual Basic Projects" as the Project Type and "Class Library" as the template. Click the Browse button and navigate to the **Demos\AccountClient** directory. Click Open. Type **AccountLib** as the name of the project. See Figure 23–5. Click OK. Observe that a subdirectory **AccountLib** will be created below **AccountClient**.

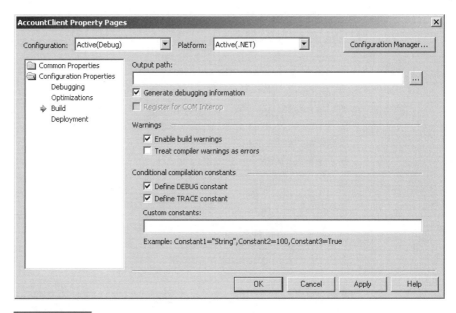

FIGURE 23–4   *Changing the output path for the executable.*

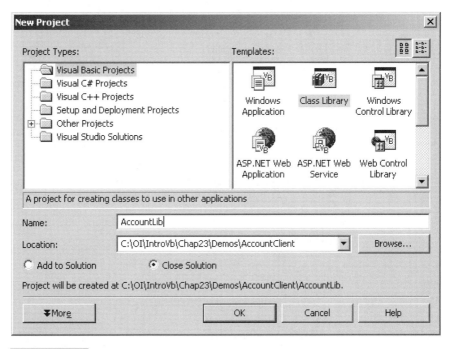

FIGURE 23–5   *The Add New Project dialog.*

MOVE CODE TO THE SECOND PROJECT

1. The file **AssemblyInfo.cs** contains code that can be used to customize the manifest in the assembly. For simplicity, remove the two files **AssemblyInfo.vb** and **Class1.vb** from the new project. (Use the Delete key, or right-click on the files and choose Delete.)

2. Move the files **Account.vb** and **SimpleMath.vb** from the **AccountClient** project to the **AccountLib** project. (You can drag inside Solution Explorer.)

3. Change the output path for **AccountLib** to be the **AccountClient** source directory. Right-click on the **AccountLib** project, and choose Properties. In the Property Pages window that appears, click on Configuration Properties and then on Build. Click on the three dots next to the Output Path area, and navigate to the **AccountClient** directory. See Figure 23–6. Click OK. Now when we build both projects, the files **AccountClient.exe** and **AccountLib.dll** wind up in the same directory.

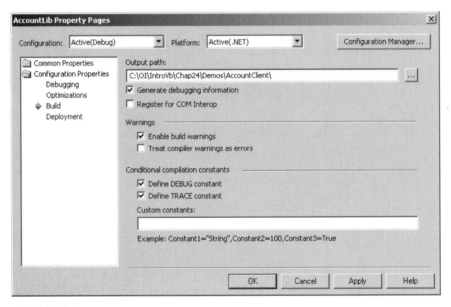

FIGURE 23–6 *Changing the output path for the class library.*

4. Build the class library by right-clicking on **AccountLib** and choosing Build.

5. Try to build the client test program by right-clicking on **AccountClient** and choosing Build. You get a number of error messages pertaining to the type **Account** not being defined.

ADDING A REFERENCE

1. In Solution Explorer, right-click on **AccountClient** and choose Add Reference.

2. Click Browse, and navigate to **AccountLib.dll** in the directory **Demos\AccountClient**. Click Open. See Figure 23–7.

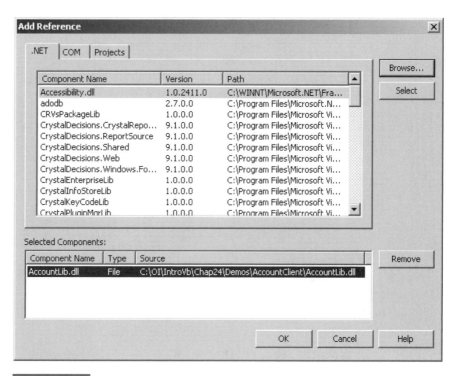

FIGURE 23–7   *Adding a reference.*

3. Click OK. You now see a Reference in Solution Explorer. Note also the two projects in our solution.

4. Now build the client again. You get the same errors! Open the Object Browser (View | Other Windows | Object Browser). See Figure 23–8. Notice that the **Account** class is in the namespace **AccountLib**, which was created for you when you built the class library project generated by Visual Studio.

5. In the file **SimpleTest.vb**, add an **Imports** statement to bring in the namespace **AccountLib**.

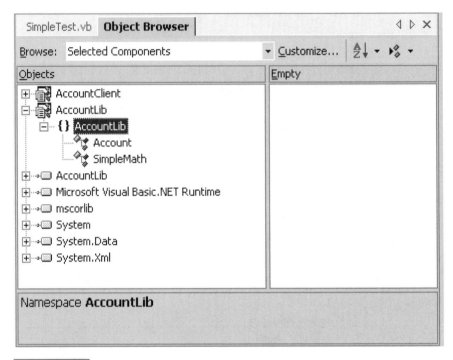

FIGURE 23–8   *The Object Browser shows the class is inside a namespace.*

```
' SimpleTest.vb

Imports System
Imports AccountLib

Module Test
...
```

6. Build the **AccountClient** project. This time it should work! Run the client.

Solutions and Projects

We have now constructed a solution with two projects. Figure 23–9 shows Solution Explorer with this solution and its two projects.

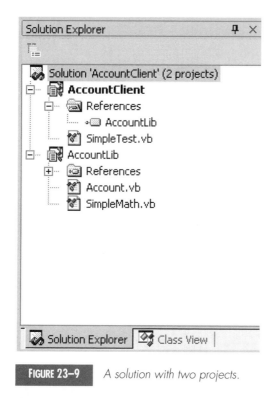

FIGURE 23-9   *A solution with two projects.*

BUILDING A SOLUTION

There are two build buttons on the toolbar: 🏗 🏗 . The first button builds the currently selected project. You can select a project by clicking on it in Solution Explorer. The second button builds the entire solution.

PROJECT DEPENDENCIES

Continuing our demonstration, close the solution (menu File | Close Solution) and delete the **bin** and **obj** directories for both projects and all the **DLL** and **EXE** files. (If you have trouble deleting the directories, close Visual Studio.) Open the solution again and build the entire solution. You get build errors because the client program is built first and the class library does not yet exist. To fix this problem, open the Project Dependencies dialog from the menu using Project | Project Dependencies. With the **AccountClient** project selected from the Project dropdown, check **AccountLib** in the Depends On list. See Figure 23–10. Click OK.

Now try building the solution again. This time, the build should succeed because the library is built first.

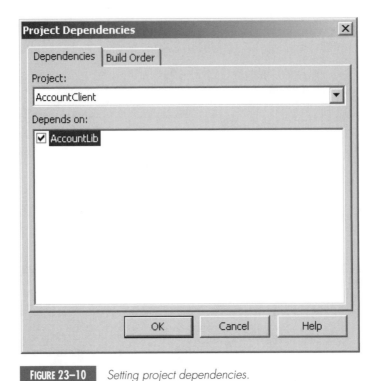

FIGURE 23–10   *Setting project dependencies.*

Working with References

Working with a project that has references can sometimes be tricky. If you get into a situation in which your client program does not build and you suspect the problem is that the reference to a dependent library is not found, try first removing the reference. Then add the reference again.

Interoperating with COM

We have seen that .NET components can be built in different languages, such as VB.NET and C#, and interoperate with each. It is also possible for .NET components to interoperate with COM components in these ways:

- You can call a COM component from .NET.
- You can call a .NET component from COM.

The .NET Framework supports both of these kinds of interoperability, and tools are provided. We illustrate the first scenario (the common one) of a .NET application calling a legacy COM component. We use the **Type Library**

Importer tool **Tlbimp.exe**, which imports a type library for a COM component and generates a .NET proxy (or "wrapper") for calling a COM component from .NET. This tool is transparently invoked by Visual Studio when you add a reference to a COM component.

The subject of Microsoft's Component Object Model or COM is beyond the scope of this book. For a discussion of COM and COM+, you can refer to *Understanding and Programming COM+* by Robert J. Oberg.

Wrapping a Legacy COM Server

The interoperability scenario we examine is managed code calling COM components. The .NET Framework makes it easy to create a Runtime Callable Wrapper (RCW), which acts as a bridge between managed and unmanaged code. The RCW is illustrated in Figure 23–11.

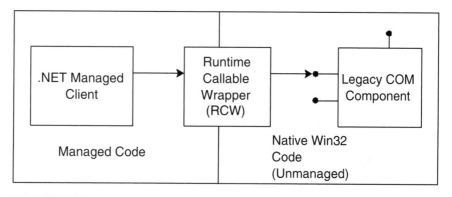

FIGURE 23–11   *A Runtime Callable Wrapper between managed and unmanaged code.*

It is not necessary for you to implement an RCW yourself, because the **Tlbimp.exe** tool can read type library information and automatically generate the appropriate RCW for you. Visual Studio.NET makes it even easier when you add a reference to a COM object in Solution Explorer. We examine both of these facilities as we look at some examples of COM components and .NET clients.

Demonstration: Wrapping a Legacy COM Server

The best way to get a feel for how this wrapping process works is to perform the operations yourself. The .NET client program is in the directory **NetClient**. The directory **LegacyComServer** contains the following files:

```
BankDual.dll        COM server DLL
BankDual.tlb        Type library
reg_bankdual.bat    Batch file to register the server
unreg_bankdual.bat  Batch file to unregister the server
BankConsole.exe     Client executable file
```

The source code for the client and server are in the directories **Client-Source** and **ServerSource** respectively. Both programs are written in Visual C++, and project files are provided for Visual C++ 6.0. Unless you have Visual C++ 6.0 installed on your system in addition to Visual Studio.NET, you cannot build these projects, but you can still run the program and create a .NET client.

We could also have implemented the legacy COM server and client programs using Visual Basic 6, and the code would have been much simpler. But to run the programs, you would need the Visual Basic 6 runtime installed on your computer. In this book, we only assume that you have Visual Studio.NET installed on your computer, which includes the CLR as a runtime, but not the VB6 runtime. In any event, the source code for the legacy server and client does not matter, because we are coding a client program using VB.NET.

This COM server implements a simple bank account class that has **Deposit** and **Withdraw** methods and a **Balance** property.

REGISTER THE COM SERVER

The first step is to register the COM server. You can do that by running the batch file **reg_bankdual.bat,** which executes this command:

```
regsvr32 bankdual.dll
```

You can now see the registration entries using the Registry Editor (**regedit.exe**) or the OLE/COM Object Viewer (**oleview.exe**). The latter program is provided on the Tools menu of Visual Studio.NET. It groups related registry entries together, providing a convenient display. You can also perform other operations, such as instantiating objects. Figure 23–12 shows the entries for the **Account2** class that is implemented by this server. We have clicked the little plus (+) in the left pane, which instantiates an object and queries for the standard interfaces. You can release the object by right-clicking over the class and choosing Release Instance from the context menu.

RUN THE COM CLIENT

You can now run the legacy COM client by double-clicking on **BankConsole.exe** in Windows Explorer. The starting balance is shown, followed by a withdrawal of $25, and the balance is shown again. Here is the output from running the client program:

```
balance = 150
balance = 125
Press Enter to quit:
```

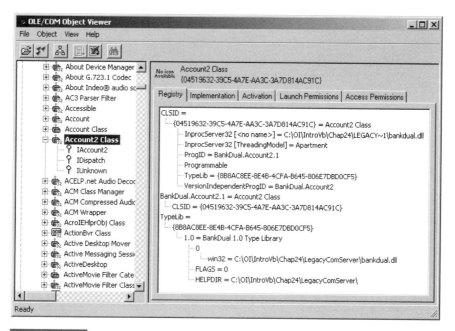

FIGURE 23–12   *The OLE/COM Object Viewer showing registry entries.*

IMPORT THE TYPE LIBRARY (TLBIMP.EXE)

To call the COM component from managed code, we must create an RCW. We can do that by running the **TlbImp.exe** utility that we discussed. We run this utility from the command line, in the directory **NetClient**, where we want the RCW assembly to wind up. We provide a relative path to the type library file[1] BankDual.tlb in the directory LegacyComServer. What we have to type is shown in bold.

```
tlbimp ..\legacycomserver\bankdual.tlb
TlbImp - Type Library to .NET Assembly Converter Version
1.0.2914.16
Copyright (C) Microsoft Corp. 2001. All rights reserved.

Type library imported to BANKDUALLib.dll
```

The RCW assembly that is created is **BANKDUALLib.dll**, taking its name from the name of the type library, as discussed earlier.

---

1. The file **BankDual.dll** also contains the type library and could have been used in place of **BankDual.tlb**.

IMPLEMENT THE .NET CLIENT PROGRAM

It is now easy to implement the .NET client program. The code is in the file **NetClient.vb** in the directory **NetClient**.

```
' NetClient.vb

Imports System
Imports BANKDUALLib

Module NetClient

   Public Sub Main()
      Dim acc As New Account2()
      Console.WriteLine("balance = {0}", acc.Balance)
      acc.Withdraw(25)
      Console.WriteLine("balance = {0}", acc.Balance)
   End Sub

End Module
```

For simplicity, we do no error checking. In the .NET version, we should use exception handling to check for errors. The RCW uses the namespace **BANKDUALLib**, based on the name of the type library.

You must add a reference to **BANKDUALLib.dll**. In the Visual Studio Solution Explorer, you can right-click over References, choose "Add Reference," and use the ordinary .NET tab of the Add Reference dialog.

Build and run the project inside of Visual Studio. You should see the following output:

```
balance = 150
balance = 125
```

After you have added a reference to an RCW, you have all the features of the IDE available for .NET assemblies, including Intellisense and the Object Browser. You can bring up the Object Browser using View | Other Windows | Object Browser. Figure 23–13 illustrates the information shown.

IMPORT A TYPE LIBRARY USING VISUAL STUDIO

When you are using Visual Studio, you can import a COM type library directly, without first running **TlbImp.exe**. To see how to do this, use Solution Explorer to delete the reference to **BANKDUALLib.dll**. In fact, delete the file itself, and delete the **bin** and **obj** directories of **NetClient**. Now, right-click over References, choose "Add Reference," and then select the COM tab from the Add Reference dialog. The list box shows all the COM components with a registered type library. Select "BankDual 1.0 Type Library," as illustrated in Figure 23–14.

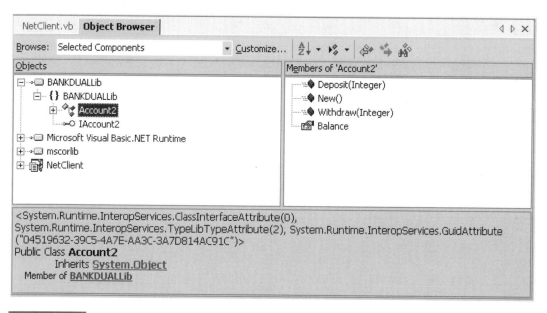

FIGURE 23-13 The Object Browser showing information about the RCW.

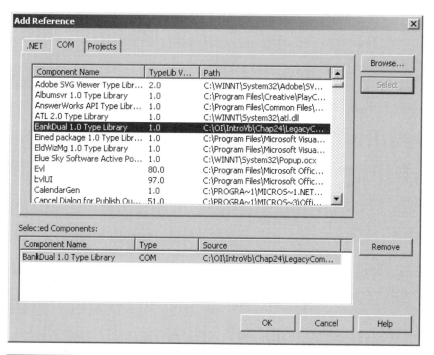

FIGURE 23-14 Adding a reference to a COM component in Visual Studio.

Now click OK. You see a message telling you that a "primary interop assembly" is not registered for this type library. You are invited to have a wrapper generated for you, as illustrated in Figure 23–15. Click "Yes." The generated RCW is the file **Interop.BANKDUALLib_1_0.dll** in the directory **bin**. You should be able to build and run the .NET client program.

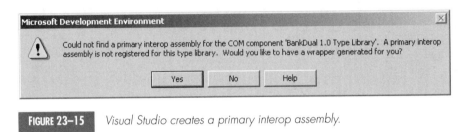

FIGURE 23–15   *Visual Studio creates a primary interop assembly.*

The *primary interop assembly* created by Visual Studio is normally created by the publisher of the COM component. This can be done using the **TlbImp.exe** utility with the **/primary** option.

Summary

Modern large applications are rarely monolithic; instead, they are made up of a number of executable units. In the Windows environment, an application normally consists of an EXE and a number of DLLs. In this chapter, we saw how to create class library DLLs or *components* that expose classes and their methods to external programs. We began by using command-line tools; later in the chapter, we used Visual Studio.NET. We also examined *assemblies,* which are the unit of deployment in .NET. An assembly can be a single EXE or DLL, or it can consist of several files, called *modules.* An assembly also contains a *manifest,* which describes how the elements of the assembly relate to each other and to external elements. An application in .NET can be composed of assemblies built using different languages, and you can even inherit across languages. We concluded the chapter by showing how you can call a COM component from .NET.

Case Study: Object-Oriented Programming

When learning a new programming language or technology, it is a good idea to begin with small examples. You can then stay focused on the key concepts without being distracted by lots of programming details. We have tried to follow that principle in this book. However, in real projects, you naturally have to deal with a larger scale. Making the transition can sometimes be a little difficult. Nowhere is that more true than in learning object-oriented programming, which is central in the new Visual Basic.NET. In this appendix, we present a case study to try to bridge between the little examples in the text and the larger examples you must deal with in your applications. The example is still pretty small, with a focus on instruction rather than reality. The case study is intended to illustrate in particular the principles of object-oriented programming, including inheritance and the use of interfaces.

The subject of the case study is a small banking system. In the text, we have often used a bank account example. We now elaborate on it a bit to demonstrate a small object-oriented system. We illustrate both a command-line user interface and a graphical user interface. We first present a monolithic version of the program, and then we break it into components. Because the original program was designed with interfaces and classes, the job of breaking it into components is easy.

The sample code is in the **CaseStudy** directory, which is directly below **IntroVb** at the same level as the chapter directories. There are subdirectories for various versions and components of the case study. The first version we study is **BankMonolithic**, which has all the source code in one project. Although the project is monolithic, the code is not. It is naturally divided into several classes, which are packaged in several files.

Code Example

The Contract

Our bank manages a number of accounts for customers. There are different types of accounts, such as checking accounts and savings accounts. Some functionality concerns management of the accounts, such as adding an account and deleting an account. Other functions pertain to individual accounts, such as making a deposit or withdrawal, which are general to all types of accounts. Other functions are specific to a particular type of account, such as a fee for a checking account.

The contract is specified by a number of interfaces. Some belong to the bank itself, others are common interfaces applicable to all types of accounts, and some interfaces are specific to a particular kind of account.

Bank Interface

Functions carried out directly by the bank itself are grouped into the **IBank** interface. This interface is defined in the file **Bank.vb**:

```
Public Interface IBank
    Function AddAccount(ByVal type As AccountType, ByVal _
    bal As Decimal, ByVal owner As String) As Integer
    Function GetAccounts() As ArrayList
    Sub DeleteAccount(ByVal id As Integer)
    Function FindAccount(ByVal id As Integer) As Account
    Function GetStatements() As ArrayList
End Interface
```

AccountType is an enumeration that is used for specifying the type of an account:

```
Public Enum AccountType
    Checking
    Savings
    Invalid
End Enum
```

Common Account Interfaces

The general methods and properties pertaining to accounts divide fairly naturally into two groups. The first group is concerned with operations on an account object (deposit or withdraw) and getting and setting fields. This group of methods and properties constitutes the **IAccount** interface. These interfaces are defined in **AccountDefinitions.vb**, which also contains the definitions of the specialized interfaces used by checking and savings accounts.

```
Public Interface IAccount
    Sub Deposit(ByVal amount As Decimal)
    Sub Withdraw(ByVal amount As Decimal)
    ReadOnly Property Balance() As Decimal
    Property Owner() As String
    ReadOnly Property Id() As Integer
End Interface
```

You may wonder about properties in the **IAccount** interface. Does this mean that somehow an interface can contain data? Not at all. The properties specify *behavior*—how you can read and write a property value using a convenient notation. The implementation of a property, where the data is stored, is in a class that implements the interface.

The second group is concerned with getting a statement of an account and constitutes the **IStatement** interface.

```
Public Interface IStatement
    Function FormatBalance() As String
    Function GetStatement() As String
    ReadOnly Property Transactions() As Integer
    Sub Post()
    Sub MonthEnd()
    ReadOnly Property Prompt() As String
End Interface
```

Here's an explanation of the methods of **IStatement:**

- **FormatBalance** returns a string representation of the balance in proper currency format.
- **GetStatement** returns a string giving a complete statement for the account, including items such as the owner, ID, balance, and number of transactions. Specific kinds of accounts append supplementary information.
- **Transactions** returns a count of the number of transactions so far in the current month.
- **Post** applies credits or debits for the current month. A checking account may have a debit of a fee, and a savings account may have a credit of interest.
- **MonthEnd** initializes the account for the next month. The transactions count is set to 0. For a savings account, the minimum balance (used for calculating interest) is set to the current balance.
- **Prompt** returns a string indicating the type of account. The prompt string can be an aid to a user interface, giving a cue to the user about which kind of account is being worked on.

IChecking Interface

The **IChecking** interface is an additional interface supported only by checking accounts:

```
Public Interface IChecking
    ReadOnly Property Fee() As Decimal
End Interface
```

There is a single property, **Fee**, which is computed as the monthly fee owed for this account. (Note that the fee is not actually debited from the balance until the **Post** method is invoked.)

ISavings Interface

The **ISavings** interface is an additional interface supported only by savings accounts:

```
Interface ISavings
    ReadOnly Property Interest() As Decimal
    Property Rate() As Decimal
End Interface
```

There are two properties. **Rate** is an annual interest rate. **Interest** is the amount of interest paid in a given month. (**Interest** might be computed by multiplying **Rate/12** by the minimum balance.)

Class Definitions

The interfaces described above can fairly naturally be implemented in four different classes. The **Bank** class implements **IBank**. An abstract class **Account** implements the interface **IAccount**. The concrete class **CheckingAccount** implements **IChecking**, and the class **SavingsAccount** implements **ISavings**. The code files are all in the project **BankMonolithic**.

Bank Class

The **Bank** class is defined in the file **Bank.vb**:

```
Public Class Bank
    Implements IBank

    Private m_accounts As ArrayList
    Private m_nextid As Integer = 1
```

```
Public Sub New()
   m_accounts = New ArrayList()
   AddAccount(AccountType.Checking, 1000, "Bob")
   AddAccount(AccountType.Savings, 200, "Mary")
   AddAccount(AccountType.Checking, 300, "Charlie")
End Sub

Public Function AddAccount(ByVal type As AccountType, _
 ByVal bal As Decimal, ByVal owner As String) _
 As Integer Implements IBank.AddAccount

   Dim acc As Account
   Dim id As Integer = m_nextid
   m_nextid = m_nextid + 1
   Select Case type
      Case AccountType.Checking
         acc = New CheckingAccount(bal, owner, id)
      Case AccountType.Savings
         acc = New SavingsAccount(bal, owner, id)
      Case Else
         Console.WriteLine("Unexpected AccountType")
         Return -1
   End Select

   m_accounts.Add(acc)
   Return id
End Function

Public Function GetAccounts() As ArrayList _
 Implements IBank.GetAccounts
   Return m_accounts
End Function

Public Sub DeleteAccount(ByVal id As Integer) _
 Implements IBank.DeleteAccount
   Dim acc As CheckingAccount
   acc = New CheckingAccount(0D, "", id)
   If Not m_accounts.Contains(acc) Then
      Throw New Exception( _
         "Account " & id & " not found")
   End If
   m_accounts.Remove(acc)
End Sub

Public Function FindAccount(ByVal id As Integer) _
 As Account Implements IBank.FindAccount
   Dim acc As Account
   For Each acc In m_accounts
      If acc.Id = id Then
         Return acc
```

```
            End If
        Next acc
        Return Nothing
    End Function

    Public Function GetStatements() As ArrayList _
      Implements IBank.GetStatements
        Dim array As ArrayList
        array = New ArrayList(m_accounts.Count)

        Dim acc As Account
        For Each acc In m_accounts
            acc.Post()
            Dim strg As String = acc.GetStatement()
            acc.MonthEnd()
            array.Add(strg)
            strg = "----------------------------------------"
            array.Add(strg)
        Next acc
        Return array
    End Function
End Class
```

Account Class

Account is an abstract base class. It implements behavior that is generic to all account classes, as is defined in the interface **IAccount**. It also defines several **Overridable** (or **MustOverride**) methods that are implemented in derived classes. By providing the definition in the base class, we can achieve polymorphic behavior. The class's code is in the file **Account.vb**:

```
' Account.vb

Imports System

Public MustInherit Class Account
    Implements IAccount

    Private m_id As Integer
    Protected m_balance As Decimal
    Private m_owner As String
    Protected m_numXact As Integer = 0

    Public Sub New(ByVal balance As Decimal, _
      ByVal owner As String, ByVal id As Integer)
        m_balance = balance
        m_owner = owner
        m_id = id
    End Sub
```

```
Public Overridable Sub Deposit( _
 ByVal amount As Decimal) Implements IAccount.Deposit
    If amount < 0D Then
        Throw New Exception( _
           "The transaction amount cannot be negative.")
    End If

    m_balance += amount
    m_numXact = m_numXact + 1
End Sub

Public Overridable Sub Withdraw( _
 ByVal amount As Decimal) Implements IAccount.Withdraw
    If amount < 0D Then
        Throw New Exception( _
           "The transaction amount cannot be negative.")
    End If

    Dim newbal As Decimal = Balance - amount
    If newbal < 0D Then
        Throw New Exception( _
           "The balance cannot be negative.")
    End If
    m_balance = newbal
    m_numXact = m_numXact + 1
End Sub

Public ReadOnly Property Balance() As Decimal _
 Implements IAccount.Balance
    Get
        Return m_balance
    End Get
End Property

Public ReadOnly Property Id() As Integer Implements _
 IAccount.Id
    Get
        Return m_id
    End Get
End Property

Public Property Owner() As String _
 Implements IAccount.Owner
    Get
        Return m_owner
    End Get

    Set(ByVal Value As String)
        m_owner = Value
```

```
        End Set
   End Property

   Public Overridable ReadOnly Property Transactions() _
    As Integer
      Get
          Return m_numXact
      End Get
   End Property

   Public Overridable Function FormatBalance() As String
       Return String.Format("{0:C}", m_balance)
   End Function

   Public Overridable Function GetStatement() As String
      Dim s As String
      s = "Statement for " & Owner & " id = " & Id &  -
          Chr(10) & Transactions & _
            " transactions, balance = " & FormatBalance()
      Return s
   End Function

   Public MustOverride Sub Post()

   Public MustOverride ReadOnly Property Prompt() As String

   Public Overridable Sub MonthEnd()
      m_numXact = 0
   End Sub

   Public Overloads Overrides Function Equals( _
    ByVal obj As Object) As Boolean
      Dim acc As Account
      acc = CType(obj, Account)
      Return (acc.Id = Me.Id)
   End Function

   Public Overrides Function GetHashCode() As Integer
       Return (Id.GetHashCode())
   End Function

End Class
```

CheckingAccount Class

The **CheckingAccount** class aids behavior specific to checking accounts, namely a monthly fee. It implements the interface **IChecking**. It also implements the interface **IStatement**. Some of the methods of **IStatement** behave the same for all kinds of accounts, and so a complete implementation is provided in the base class. The derived classes merely have to call the base class implementation. In other cases, we customize the behavior of the method in the derived class. The **CheckingAccount** class inherits the implementation of **IAccount** from the base class. The code file is **CheckingAccount.vb**:

```vb
Public Class CheckingAccount
    Inherits Account
    Implements IStatement, IChecking

    Private m_fee As Decimal = 5D
    Private Const FREEXACT As Integer = 2

    Public Sub New(ByVal balance As Decimal, ByVal owner _
      As String, ByVal id As Integer)
        MyBase.New(balance, owner, id)
    End Sub

    Public ReadOnly Property Fee() As Decimal _
      Implements IChecking.Fee
        Get
            If m_numXact > FREEXACT Then
                Return m_fee
            Else
                Return 0D
            End If
        End Get
    End Property

    Public Overrides Function GetStatement() _
      As String Implements IStatement.GetStatement
        Dim s As String
        s = MyBase.GetStatement()
        s = s + ", fee = " + String.Format("{0:C}", Fee)
        Return s
    End Function

    Public Overrides Sub Post() Implements IStatement.Post
        m_balance = m_balance - Fee
    End Sub

    Public Overrides ReadOnly Property Prompt() As String _
      Implements IStatement.Prompt
        Get
            Return "C: "
        End Get
    End Property

    Public Overrides Sub MonthEnd() _
      Implements IStatement.MonthEnd
        MyBase.MonthEnd()
```

```
      End Sub

      Public Overrides ReadOnly Property Transactions() _
       As Integer Implements IStatement.Transactions
          Get
              Return MyBase.Transactions
          End Get
      End Property

      Public Overrides Function FormatBalance() _
       As String Implements IStatement.FormatBalance
          Return MyBase.FormatBalance()
      End Function

  End Class
```

SavingsAccount Class

The **SavingsAccount** class aids behavior specific to savings accounts, namely interest. It implements the interface **ISavings**. Like **CheckingAccount**, it also implements the interface **IStatement**, in some cases, by calling the base class implementation, and in other cases, by providing a custom implementation in the derived class. The **SavingsAccount** class inherits the implementation of **IAccount** from the base class. The code file is **SavingsAccount.vb**:

```
Public Class SavingsAccount
    Inherits Account
    Implements IStatement, ISavings

    Private m_minBalance As Decimal
    Private m_rate As Decimal = 0.06D

    Public Sub New(ByVal balance As Decimal, _
     ByVal owner As String, ByVal id As Integer)
        MyBase.New(balance, owner, id)
        m_minBalance = balance
    End Sub

    Public ReadOnly Property Interest() _
     As Decimal Implements ISavings.Interest
        Get
            Return m_minBalance * m_rate / 12
        End Get
    End Property

    Public Overloads Sub Withdraw(ByVal amount As Decimal)
        MyBase.Withdraw(amount)
        If m_balance < m_minBalance Then
            m_minBalance = m_balance
```

```
      End If
   End Sub

   Public Overrides Sub Post() Implements IStatement.Post
      m_balance = m_balance + Interest
   End Sub

   Public Overrides Function GetStatement() _
    As String Implements IStatement.GetStatement
      Dim s As String
      s = MyBase.GetStatement()
      s = s & ", Interest = " & _
          String.Format("{0:C}", Interest)
      Return s
   End Function

   Public Property Rate() As Decimal _
    Implements ISavings.Rate
      Get
         Return m_rate
      End Get
      Set(ByVal Value As Decimal)
         m_rate = Value
      End Set
   End Property

   Public Overrides ReadOnly Property Prompt() _
    As String Implements IStatement.Prompt
      Get
         Return "S: "
      End Get
   End Property

   Public Overrides Sub MonthEnd() _
    Implements IStatement.MonthEnd
      MyBase.MonthEnd()
      m_minBalance = Balance
   End Sub

   Public Overrides Function FormatBalance() _
    As String Implements IStatement.FormatBalance
      Return MyBase.FormatBalance()
   End Function

   Public Overrides ReadOnly Property Transactions() _
    As Integer Implements IStatement.Transactions
      Get
         Return MyBase.Transactions
      End Get
   End Property

End Class
```

Console Test Program

The classes perform no user interface operations, and so they can be called from either a console program or a Windows program. The **BankMonolithic** project provides an interactive test program for exercising the classes. The code is straightforward, similar to many such driver programs we used in this book. You can examine the code online. The file **TestBank.vb** exercises the **Bank** class. The "account" command invokes another command loop, provided in the file **Atm.vb**, to exercise an individual account object. Here is a sample run:

```
Enter command, quit to exit
> help
The following commands are available:
  open      -- open an account
  close     -- close an account
  show      -- show all accounts
  account   -- perform transactions on an account
  month     -- prepare monthly statements for all accounts
  quit      -- exit the program
> show
Bob            C:    1    $1,000.00
Mary           S:    2    $200.00
Charlie        C:    3    $300.00
> open
account type: savings
starting balance: 2000
owner: Dana
Account opened, id = 4
> account
account id: 4
balance = $2,000.00
Enter command, quit to exit
S: help
The following commands are available:
  deposit  -- make a deposit
  withdraw -- make a withdrawal
  owner    -- change owner name
  show     -- show account information
  quit     -- exit the ATM
S: deposit
amount: 500
balance = $2,500.00
S: withdraw
amount: 1000
balance = $1,500.00
S: show
Statement for Dana id = 4
```

```
2 transactions, balance = $1,500.00, Interest = $10.00
S: quit
> show
Bob             C:    1    $1,000.00
Mary            S:    2    $200.00
Charlie         C:    3    $300.00
Dana            S:    4    $1,500.00
> month
Statement for Bob id = 1
0 transactions, balance = $1,000.00, fee = $0.00
-------------------------------------------------
Statement for Mary id = 2
0 transactions, balance = $201.00, Interest = $1.00
-------------------------------------------------
Statement for Charlie id = 3
0 transactions, balance = $300.00, fee = $0.00
-------------------------------------------------
Statement for Dana id = 4
2 transactions, balance = $1,510.00, Interest = $10.00
-------------------------------------------------
> show
Bob             C:    1    $1,000.00
Mary            S:    2    $201.00
Charlie         C:    3    $300.00
Dana            S:    4    $1,510.00
```

Class Libraries

One of the great virtues of .NET is the ease with which you can create components, otherwise known as class libraries. Such components are compiled into separate assemblies, as discussed in Chapter 23, and can be used as "black boxes" by other assemblies. To create a class library, you simply use Visual Studio to create a class library project. You can copy the files defining the classes into the directory for the new project and add them to the projects. In any calling project, you must add a reference to the class library.

AccountLib

Code Example

Our first class library is created in the project **AccountLib**, in the directory of the same name. It contains the **Account**, **CheckingAccount**, and **SavingsAccount** classes. The project is built from the files **Account.vb**, **AccountDefinitions.vb**, **CheckingAccount.vb**, and **SavingsAccount.vb**.

When the project is built, the assembly **AccountLib.dll** is created. We can copy this file to any project where we want to use it.

BankLib

Our second class library is created in the project **BankLib**. It contains the **Bank** class and a reference to **AccountLib**. The project is built from the file **Bank.vb**. This file is identical to the file in the monolithic project, with the single addition of an **Imports** statement. We are now using the **Account** class from a separate assembly. When we created the **Account** project, Visual Studio made a namespace for us, called **AccountLib**. Thus, in a project that uses the **AccountLib** file, we either have to use the fully qualified name for the class **AccountLib.Account** or an **Imports** statement, as shown here:

```
' Bank.vb

Imports System
Imports System.Collections
Imports AccountLib
...
```

BankConsole

The **BankConsole** project, in a directory of the same name, is a console test program for the two components. It consists of the source files **TestBank.vb**, **Atm.vb**, and **InputWrapper.vb**. It has a reference to **AccountLib.dll** and **BankLib.dll**. In our source files, we need **Imports** statements for the associated namespaces:

```
' TestBank.vb

Imports System
Imports System.Collections
Imports BankLib
Imports AccountLib
...

' Atm.vb

Imports System
Imports AccountLib
...
```

Using Components Written in C#

The language used in creating a component is immaterial, as long as the supported interfaces conform to the Common Type System. This means, for example, that we can mix and match assemblies written in VB.NET and C#. As an illustration, the directory **BankMixed** contains subdirectories **AccountLibCs** and **BankLibCs** that have C# versions of our two components. These two projects are taken from our book *Introduction to C# Using .NET*, which uses the same bank case study. We modified the projects slightly to create the same namespaces **AccountLib** and **BankLib** that we are using in our VB.NET assemblies. Other than that, we left the code untouched.

The subdirectory **BankConsole** contains exactly the same VB.NET console test program that we used to test our components written in VB.NET. In the project, we simply set the references to refer to the C# assemblies **Account.dll** and **BankLib.dll**, which we have copied into the source directory. You can then build the test program, and it should work identically to the version that used exclusively VB.NET.

Windows Client Program

The directory **BankGui** contains a graphical user interface for exercising our bank account classes. The project has references to the class libraries **AccountLib.dll** and **BankLib.dll**. (We are using the VB.NET versions, but we would get identical behavior if we had used the C# versions instead.) The graphical user interface is created using Windows Forms classes, as discussed in Chapters 15, 16, and 17. You can examine the code online.

When you start the program, you see the main window, as illustrated in Figure A–1.

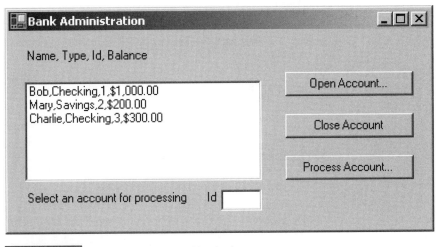

FIGURE A–1   *The main window of bank client program.*

Clicking the "Open Account" button brings up a dialog box for entering information for a new account, as illustrated in Figure A–2. We enter the same test data as we did in our run of the console test program.

Clicking OK accepts the information we just entered and opens a new account. The new account is shown in the list box in the main window. To perform transactions on an account, select an account from the list box. The ID of the selected account is shown, as illustrated in Figure A–3.

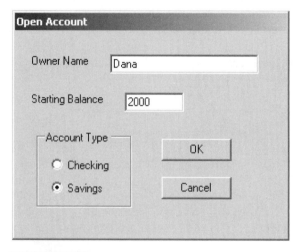

FIGURE A–2   *Dialog box for entering new account information.*

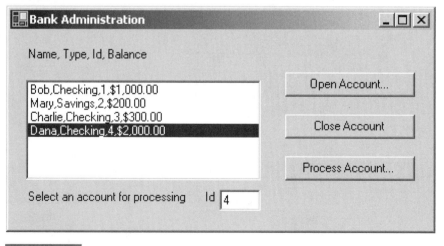

FIGURE A–3   *Selecting an account in the main form.*

You can then click the "Process Account" button. This brings up another dialog box, where you can make deposits and withdrawals, as illustrated in Figure A–4. We are making a deposit of $500 to the account that we just opened.

You can continue making deposits and withdrawals in this dialog. You can also change the owner name, and you can obtain account information. When you are finished, click Close. This brings you back to the main window, where the results of your transactions are shown in the list box.

You can close an account from the main window by selecting an account from the list box and clicking the "Close Account" button.

FIGURE A–4   Dialog box for processing an account.

OBJECT INNOVATIONS' .NET TRAINING PARTNERS

For information about .NET training using OBJECT INNOVATIONS courseware,
please check with our .NET Training Partners.

ANEW TECHNOLOGY CORPORATION   www.Anew.net

Specialized in IT consulting, training, mentoring, and development, Anew Technology has been serving many satisfied clients. Our business mission is threefold: to stay at the forefront of IT technologies, to satisfy client needs by applying these technologies, and to provide the best service in our industry. Anew Technology is a business partner with Object Innovations in operations and courseware development.

COMPUTER HORIZONS EDUCATION DIVISION   www.ComputerHorizons.com/Training

For over seventeen years Computer Horizons Education Division (CHED) has been providing on-site, instructor-led IT training and customized workshops for organizations nationwide. We have developed extensive curriculum offerings in Web Technologies, Relational Databases, Reporting Tools, Process Improvement, UNIX™ and LINUX™, Client/Server, Mainframe & Legacy Systems, Windows® 2000, and much more. CHED will design, develop and deliver a training solution tailored to each client's training requirements.

COMPUWORKS SYSTEMS, INC.   www.CompuWorks.com

CompuWorks Systems, Inc. is an IT solutions company whose aim is to provide our clients with customized training, support and development services. We are committed to building long term partnerships with our clients in an effort to meet their individual needs. Cutting-edge solutions are our specialty.

CUSTOM TRAINING INSTITUTE   www.4CustomTraining.com

Custom Training Institute is a provider of high quality IT training since 1989. Along with our full line of "off-the-shelf" classes, we excel at providing customized solutions - from technical needs assessment through course development and delivery. We specialize in Legacy Skills Transformation (i.e., COBOL to Java), Oracle (DBA, Developer, Discoverer and Applications), UNIX, C++ and Java for computer professionals.

DB BASICS   www.DBBasics.com

DBBasics, founded in 1988 as a Microsoft® solution development company, has developed and delivered Microsoft technology training since its inception. DBBasics specializes in delivering database and developer technology training to corporate customers. Our vast development experience, coupled with the requirement for instructors to consistently provide hands-on consulting to our customers, enables DBBasics to provide best of breed instruction in the classroom as well as customized eLearning solutions and database technology consulting.

DEVCOM   www.dev-cominc.com

Devcom Corporation offers a full line of courses and seminars for software developers and engineers. Currently Devcom provides technical courses and seminars around the country for Hewlett® Packard, Compaq® Computer, Informix® Software, Silicon Graphics®, Quantum/Maxtor® and Gateway® Inc. Our senior .NET/C# instructor is currently working in conjunction with Microsoft to provide .NET training to their internal technical staff.

FOCAL POINT   www.FocalPoint-Inc.com

Focal Point specializes in providing optimum instructor-led Information Technology technical training for our corporate clients on either an onsite basis, or in regional public course events. All of our course curricula is either developed by our staff of "World Class Instructors" or upon careful evaluation and scrutiny is adopted and acquired from our training partners who are similarly focussed. Our course offerings pay special attention to Real World issues. Our classes are targeted toward topical areas that will ensure immediate productivity upon course completion.

I/SRG   www.isrg.com

The I/S RESOURCE GROUP helps organizations to understand, plan for and implement emerging I/S technologies and methodologies. By combining education, training, briefings and consulting, we assist our clients to effectively apply I/S technologies to achieve business benefits. Our eBusiness Application Bootcamp is an integrated set of courses that prepares learners to utilize XML, OOAD, Java™, JSP, EJB, ASP, CORBA and .NET to build eBusiness applications. Our eBusiness Briefings pinpoint emerging technologies and methodologies.

OBJECT INNOVATIONS' .NET TRAINING PARTNERS

*For information about .NET training using OBJECT INNOVATIONS courseware,
please check with our .NET Training Partners.*

RELIABLE SOFTWARE   www.ReliableSoftware.com

Reliable Software, Inc. uses Microsoft technology to quickly develop cost-effective software solutions for the small to mid-size business or business unit. We use state-of-the-art techniques to allow business rules, database models and the user interface to evolve as your business needs evolve. We can provide design and implementation consulting, or training.

SKILLBRIDGE TRAINING   www.SkillBridgeTraining.com

SkillBridge is a leading provider of blended technical training solutions. The company's service offerings are designed to meet a wide variety of client requirements. Offering an integration of instructor-led training, e-learning and mentoring programs, SkillBridge delivers high value solutions in a cost-effective manner. SkillBridge's technology focus includes, among others, programming languages, operating systems, databases, and internet and web technologies.

/TRAINING/ETC INC.   www.trainingetc.com

A training company dedicated to delivering quality technical training, courseware development, and consulting in a variety of subject matter areas, including Programming Languages and Design (including C, C++, OOAD/UML, Perl, and Java), a complete UNIX curriculum (from UNIX Fundamentals to System Administration), the Internet (including HTML/CGI, XML and JavaScript Programming) and RDBMS (including Oracle and Sybase).

WATERMARK LEARNING   www.WatermarkLearning.com

Watermark Learning provides a wide range of IT skill development training and mentoring services to a variety of industries, software / consulting firms and government. We provide flexible options for delivery: onsite, consortium and public classes in three major areas: project management, requirements analysis and software development, including e-Commerce. Our instructors are seasoned, knowledgeable practitioners, who use their industry experience along with our highly-rated courseware to effectively build technical skills relevant to your business need.

DEVELOPER TRAINING

OBJECT INNOVATIONS offers training course materials in fundamental software technologies used in developing applications in modern computing environments. We emphasize object-oriented techniques, with a focus on Microsoft® technologies, XML, Java™, and Linux™. Our courses have been used by businesses, training companies, and universities throughout North America. End clients include IBM®, HP®, Dell®, Compaq®, FedEx®, UPS®, AOL®, U.S. Bank®, Mellon Bank®, and NASA. Our courses are frequently updated to reflect feedback from classroom use. We aggressively track new technologies and endeavor to keep our courseware up-to-date.

Founded in 1993, Object Innovations has a long record of firsts in courseware. Our Visual C++ course was released before Microsoft's, we introduced one of the first courses in JavaServer Pages, and our Linux Internals 2.4 kernel course came out several months before Red Hat's course. Now we are leading the development of comprehensive developer training in Microsoft's .NET technology.

.NET DEVELOPER TRAINING

Object Innovations is writing the premier book series on .NET for Prentice Hall PTR. These authoritative books are the foundation of our curriculum. Each book matches a corresponding course, and the student materials come bundled with the book, so students have comprehensive reference materials after the course. Each core course is five days in length and is very rich in content, containing well over five days worth of material. The courses are modularized, so background information or special topics not needed for a particular class can be cleanly omitted. On the other hand, the courses can be lengthened as required. Thus each course can be easily customized to meet the particular needs and interests of the students. We also have shorter courses.

The first group consists of shorter, overview courses:

    401   Introduction to .NET for Developers (1 day)
    412   .NET Framework Essentials Using C# (3 days)
    422   .NET Framework Essentials Using VB.NET (3 days)
    452   Introduction to ASP.NET (3 days)

The second group constitutes the full-length courses that correspond to the books in The Integrated .NET Series form Object Innovations and Prentice Hall PTR:

    410   Introduction to C# Using .NET (5 days)
    414   Application Development Using C# and .NET (5 days)
    420   Introduction to Visual Basic Using .NET (5 days)
    424   Application Development Using Visual Basic.NET (5 days)
    434   .NET Architecture and Programming Using Visual C++ (5 days)
    440   Programming Perl in the .NET Environment (5 days)
    454   Fundamentals of Web Applications Using .NET and XML (5 days)

See our .NET website for complete course listings: www.objectinnovations.com/dotnet.htm

MICROSOFT DEVELOPER TRAINING

Our Microsoft curriculum is very extensive, with introductory and advanced courses on C++, Visual C++, MFC, COM/DCOM, OLE, COM+, and advanced topics in Visual Basic™. Selected courses include:

123 Programming COM and DCOM Using ATL (5 days)
127 Programming COM and OLE Using MFC (5 days)
149 Distributed COM+ Programming (5 days)
133 Distributed COM+ Programming Using Visual Basic (5 days)
142 Visual C++ Windows Programming for C Programmers (5 days)
145 MFC Windows Programming for C++ Programmers (5 days)
146 Advanced Windows Programming Using Visual C++ (5 days)
157 Advanced C++ Programming (5 days)

XML DEVELOPER TRAINING

Our XML curriculum covers the broad range of XML technology. We offer courses in "pure" XML – all discussion and exercises based entirely in W3C-recommended standards – as well as training in use of XML through today's dominant enterprise platforms, Java and .NET. Selected courses include:

501 XML for the Enterprise (5 days)
504 Powering Websites with XML (4 days)
506 XML Transformations (3 days)
173 XML and Java (5 days)
454 Fundamentals of Web Applications Using .NET and XML

JAVA DEVELOPER TRAINING

Java training courses span the spectrum from beginning to advanced and provide extensive coverage of both client-side and server-side technologies. Selected courses include:

103 Java Programming (5 days)
105 Using and Developing JavaBeans (4 days)
106 Advanced Java Programming (5 days)
107 CORBA Architecture and Programming Using Java (4 days)
109 Java Server Pages (2 days)
110 Java Servlet Programming (2 days)
111 Introduction to Java RMI (1 day)
163 Enterprise JavaBeans (5 days)
172 Java Foundation Classes (5 days)

LINUX COURSES

Linux courses range from fundamentals and system administration to advanced courses in internals, device drivers and networking. Selected courses include:

135 Fundamentals of Linux (4 days)
310 Linux Internals (5 days)
314 Linux Network Drivers Development (3 days)
320 Linux Network Administration (5 days)

See our .NET website for complete course listings: www.objectinnovations.com/dotnet.htm